Intellectual Property Law in China

Max Planck Series on Asian Intellectual Property Law

Volume 11

The Institution

The Max Planck Institute for Innovation and Competition has pioneered intellectual property research and education in Asia since the late 1960s and in 1975 set up a Department for Japan and East Asia. The Institute has not only been involved in fundamental research on Asian intellectual property law, but also in drafting legislation for various Asian countries both on the Institute's own account, and in cooperation with projects funded by the European Union, WIPO, the World Bank, UNDP, the German GTZ and others. In order to foster academic exchange, cooperation agreements were concluded with institutions in Japan, Korea, Taiwan, China and Thailand. The Max Planck Institute regularly receives guest researchers from Asian countries and conducts conferences and workshops on Asian intellectual property law.

Contents/Issues addressed

Spurred by the TRIPS Agreement and an increasing number of bilateral or multilateral free-trade agreements, most Asian countries have completely overhauled their intellectual property systems in the past twenty years. Extension systems for patents, protection of geographical indications or general fair use provisions have been added, enforcement structures have been improved and specialised IP courts been set up in China, Taiwan, Japan, Thailand and Korea.

These developments are reflected in the Max Planck Institute's Asian IP series that includes both country-specific reports and comparative studies on current problems of interest. Particular attention in this respect is given to the non-English speaking countries of Asia where reliable information is often difficult to come by.

Objective & Readership

The Max Planck Series on Asian Intellectual Property Law aims at providing expert coverage of intellectual property rights, their administration and enforcement in Asian jurisdictions for both academic and practicing lawyers. Since the year 2000, more than fifteen volumes have been published.

The titles published in this series are listed in the back of this volume.

Intellectual Property Law in China

Second Edition

By

Peter Ganea

Danny Friedmann

Jyh-An Lee

Douglas Clark

Edited by

Christopher Heath

Max Planck Institute
for Innovation and Competition

Wolters Kluwer

Published by:
Kluwer Law International B.V.
PO Box 316
2400 AH Alphen aan den Rijn
The Netherlands
E-mail: international-sales@wolterskluwer.com
Website: lrus.wolterskluwer.com

Sold and distributed by:
Wolters Kluwer Legal & Regulatory U.S.
7201 McKinney Circle
Frederick, MD 21704
United States of America
Email: customer.service@wolterskluwer.com

ISBN 978-94-035-1952-4

e-Book: ISBN 978-94-035-1981-4
web-PDF: ISBN 978-94-035-1984-5

About the Authors and Editor

Douglas Clark (1967), studied law and Asian studies at the Australian National University and Chinese and Chinese law at Fudan University on a Sino-Australian government scholarship. Doug has practised intellectual property law in China and Hong Kong since 1993. From 2000 to 2010 was based in Shanghai as Managing Partner and Head of China IP with the international law firm Lovells. He practiced as a barrister in Hong Kong from 2011 to 2019 and is now Global Head of Dispute Resolution at Rouse. He is the author of *Patent Litigation in China*, 2nd ed., OUP, 2015 and *Hong Kong Intellectual Property*, LexisNexis, 2019.

He can be reached at doug@douglas-clark.com.

Danny Friedmann is Assistant Professor of Law at the Peking University School of Transitional Law in Shenzhen. Friedmann received his PhD in Laws degree from the Chinese University of Hong Kong, where he was also a research associate and lecturer/tutor. He holds a LL.M degree (*meester in de rechten*) of the University of Amsterdam, the Netherlands (which includes the LL.B). He also studied business at the Nyenrode Business School in Breukelen in the Netherlands (during which he did an exchange programme to McGill University in Montreal, Canada) where he obtained the Bachelor of Business Administration degree.

In 2005 Friedmann started the first English-language blog about IP in China: IP Dragon (http://ipdragon.org). He can be reached at ipdragon@gmail.com.

Peter Ganea (1969) studied Asian studies and Economics at the University of Munich and Hokkaido University. He previously headed the Asia Department of the Max Planck Institute for Patent, Copyright and Competition Law in Munich, where he also wrote his comparative Ph.D. thesis on the neighbouring rights regimes of China, Japan and Germany, and later coordinated an interdisciplinary M.A. programme on modern East Asian Studies at Frankfurt University. He is currently German Co-Director of the Sino-German International Economic Law Institute at Tongji University Shanghai as a long-term lecturer of the German Academic Exchange Service (Deutscher Akademischer Austauschdienst – DAAD) and can be reached by email at ganeap@me.com.

Christopher Heath (1964) studied law at the Universities of Konstanz, Edinburgh and the LSE. He lived and worked in Japan for three years, and between 1992 and 2005 headed the Asian Department of the Max Planck Institute for Patent, Copyright and Competition Law in Munich. Christopher Heath, who wrote his Ph.D. thesis on Japanese unfair competition prevention law, is a judge at the Boards of Appeal of the European Patent Office in Munich.

He can be reached by e-mail at blitzblitzblau@web.de

Jyh-An Lee teaches intellectual property and internet law at the Chinese University of Hong Kong Faculty of Law. He holds a J.S.D. from Stanford Law School and an LL.M from Harvard Law School. Before starting his academic career, he was a practicing lawyer in Taiwan, specializing in technology and business transactions. He is currently the Legal Lead of the Creative Commons Hong Kong Chapter and a domain name dispute resolution panelist appointed by the Asian Domain Name Dispute Resolution Centre (ADNDRC).

He can be reached by email at jalee@cuhk.edu.hk

Table of Contents

Preface

The first edition of this book, published in 2005, was an in-house production of the Max Planck Institute that had systematically started to pour additional resources into its Asian Department: its two co-authors Peter Ganea and Thomas Pattloch and myself were full-time researchers amongst a team of Asian and European IP experts conducting research on Asia.

The twelve volumes of the Max Planck Institute's Asian Series published between 2000 and 2005 were visible results of the Institute's policy and dedication to Asia that started with the foundation of an East Asian department back in 1975 by the Max Planck's directors Eugen Ulmer, Friedrich-Karl Beier and Gerhard Schricker. With a change in directorship and a corresponding change in research preferences thirty years later, the Max Planck Institute's academic focus shifted away from geographical expertise towards a project-based approach.

Yet one should bear in mind that only tenure-based research posts at independent research institutions give a perspective to experts in Asian jurisdictions and guarantee the necessary academic freedom as a prerequisite for research on jurisdictions whose institutions and freedoms are not firmly rooted in democratic traditions.

For the second edition, Peter Ganea, who wrote the chapters on patents and copyrights, is joined by three other experts in Chinese law all based in Hong Kong: Danny Friedman, Jyh-An Lee and Douglas Clark. Needless to say that due to the fundamental changes in Chinese law in the last 15 years, the book had to be completely rewritten.

Christopher Heath

CHAPTER 1

Introduction

Peter Ganea & Danny Friedmann

In recent years in particular, the Chinese intellectual property system, including legislation, institutions and the judicial handling of disputes, has demonstrated its ability to rapidly adapt to new social and economic conditions. Remarkable institutional reforms to the judiciary, first by establishing specialized Intellectual Property Courts, next by establishing an Intellectual Property Division in the Supreme People's Court (SPC) as the second last instance for technically difficult intellectual property cases contributed to streamlining and harmonizing intellectual property adjudication throughout China in light of a dramatically increased intellectual property caseload. Further reforms concerned intellectual property administration, above all the reorganization of the former State Intellectual Property Office (SIPO), which, contrary to its title, has until recently administered only patents (for inventions, utility models and designs) and layout designs of semiconductor topographies, to become the China National Intellectual Property Administration (CNIPA), a super administration in charge of almost all registered intellectual property, including trademarks and geographical indications (GI). Only copyright is still separately administered by the National Copyright Administration of China (NCAC). In recent years, also the legislature has been especially active in adapting the legal framework for the prosecution and enforcement of intellectual property to the ever-changing socio-economic environment, new technologies and an increased domestic importance of effective and robust protection. As will be explained in more detail in the following chapters of this book, legislative reforms, i.e., reforms not only to the main intellectual property laws but also to so-called judicial interpretations issued by the SPC, administrative regulations enacted by the State Council or by lower administrations, including the frequently reformed Patent Examination Guidelines of CNIPA, broadened the scope of protected subject matter, sought to improve the quality of filings, and significantly enhanced enforcement, not only with regard to remedies, e.g., up to quintuple punitive damages for intentional and grave infringement, but also in a procedural respect, for instance, by facilitating the plaintiff's burden of evidence and access to preliminary measures.

The substantial resources devoted to intellectual property prosecution and enforcement do reflect the increased importance of intellectual property for domestic stake holders. According to the Global Innovation Index (GII), China has rapidly risen to a leading innovative economy and is continuing to climb in the rankings, between 2016 and 2019 alone it rose from rank 14 to 22, contributing 24 percent of the world's expenditures in R&D and 44 percent of global patent filings in 2019.[1] Filings and grants of registered intellectual property[2] as well as intellectual property related court disputes[3] grew by double digits each year, whereby the vast majority of patents for inventions (even more so patents for utility models and designs), trademarks and plant variety rights are granted to domestic applicants and the largest part of intellectual property litigation is fought between Chinese parties.

The increased importance of intellectual property for domestic stakeholders is also demonstrated by the intellectual property law reforms of the past decades. The first two amendment waves in the early 1990s and the early 2000s after initial trademark, patent, copyright and unfair competition legislation during the 1980s and the early 1990s (more below) mainly sought to bring the laws in compliance with foreign demands and international treaties that China joined or intended to join, especially to implement the requirements of the TRIPs Agreement after China had become a WTO member in November 2001. This was the legislative framework in the context of which the first edition of this book was written.

The Patent Law reforms of 2008 and 2020, the Trade Mark Law reforms of 2013 and 2019 and the Unfair Competition Law reforms of 2017 and 2019, however, placed more emphasis on domestic needs, in particular on curbing rampant abusive practices by way of bad-faith acquisition of registrable rights and their abusive exercise, and on improving the enforcement of legitimately owned and exercised intellectual property. One exception is the rather minor Copyright Law amendment of 2010, which was necessitated by the outcome of a Sino-US WTO dispute regarding a perceived insufficient Chinese intellectual property enforcement.[4]

In spite of these impressive developments, it should not be overlooked that the concept of intellectual property is alien to Chinese cultural history.[5] As will be shortly discussed in the introduction to this book's part on copyright, this is most likely due to a China-specific perception of law in general rather than a cultural propensity towards copying, as sometimes asserted by Western scholars. Neither Imperial China nor the ensuing, mostly chaotic Republican Era, let alone post-1949 China, provided for the conditions to develop a legal culture in the Western tradition that bound private parties to the declarations of will they made to each other. Written law, if existent at all, such as the Great *Qing* Code of the last Imperial dynasty, was limited to regulating the duties of administrators, the safeguarding of the Imperial

1. Statistics and reports on China, including its GII ranking, can be obtained from https://www.wipo.int/directory/en/details.jsp?country_code=CN.
2. More information in the subsequent parts of this book.
3. Statistical data can be obtained from the SPC's white book on judicial intellectual property protection of 2019, https://www.chinacourt.org/article/detail/2020/04/id/5049570.shtml which are quoted further below.
4. The dispute will be treated in detail in chapter 4, Copyright.
5. William P. Alford, *To Steal a Book Is an Elegant Offense: Intellectual Property Law in Chinese Civilization* (Stanford University Press, Stanford, 1995), *passim*.

rites and specific penal provisions, but remained silent on civil disputes between the Empire's subjects who were expected to settle their quarrels amongst themselves. With regard to intellectual property in particular, occasional privileges granted to innovators and creators during Imperial times and rudimentary intellectual property provisions during the Republican era and the young People's Republic did not provide fertile enough ground to allow the idea of property in technical ideas or artistic creations to flourish. The environment for better protection improved only after the last remnants of the Cultural Revolution finally came to an end in the late 1970s, when Deng Xiaoping heralded the new opening and reform policy, which gave way to entrepreneurial activity and opened up the thus far isolated economy for trade and foreign investment. In order to attract foreign investment, however, China had to guarantee foreigners a minimum of legal certainty, first and foremost in the sensitive area of intangible intellectual property. Mostly motivated by foreign demands to adhere to international protection standards, China's modern intellectual property legislation started in the 1980s with the enactment of the Trade Mark Law on 23 March 1982, followed by the Patent Law of 12 March 1984 and the Copyright Law of 7 September 1990. Finally, the Unfair Competition Law was enacted on 2 September 1993. Even before China enacted its first intellectual property laws, it joined the WIPO on 3 March 1980,[6] committing itself to protect foreign intellectual property in accordance with international standards.

Early intellectual property legislation was therefore largely induced by foreign demands, and soon after the enactment of the first laws, foreign governments, most notably the US, noticed a considerable gap between the laws on the books and their actual enforcement. US allegations that Chinese authorities would tacitly allow mass piracy of US software, films and music, sparked severe trade frictions between both countries during the 1990s, which eased slightly in the run-up of China's accession to the WTO in November 2001 and afterwards, but then culminated again in the above-mentioned Sino-US WTO dispute that in 2009 ended with a tie for both sides. Today, insufficient Chinese protection of IP is still a matter of concern in the US and the EU, but the focus of the frictions has shifted, from rather primitive copyright piracy and trademark counterfeiting to allegedly insufficient protection and enforcement of intellectual property in advanced technology, or even state-guided misappropriation of technical know-how through so-called forced technology transfer, i.e., provisions and administrative practices that render the disclosure of know-how a condition of foreign investment in China. Both the EU and the US initiated WTO consultations with China about insufficient intellectual property protection, with a strong focus on patent-related issues, know-how protection and the mentioned forced technology transfer. In January 2020, the US achieved a first bilateral success, obliging China in a first-phase Economic and Trade Agreement[7] to further improve, *inter alia*, trade secret and patent protection, to substantively dial back the pressure on foreign businesses to disclose their technical secrets when engaging in China and guaranteeing market access for foreign goods that use generic names to counter the November 2019 Sino-EU

6. https://www.wipo.int/treaties/en/ShowResults.jsp?treaty_id = 1&country_id = 38C.
7. https://bit.ly/2tnbXsl.

bilateral agreement on geographical indications.[8] As will be further explained in the subsequent chapter on patents, utility models and designs, the fourth amendment of China's Patent Law of October 2020 has implemented most of the agreement's patent-related requirements.

The above conflicts arose in spite of China's ever-deepening integration in the global intellectual property system over the past decades. After acceding to the WIPO in 1980, China became a member of the Paris Convention for the Protection of Industrial Property on 19 December 1984,[9] of the Madrid Agreement Concerning the International Registration of Marks on 4 July 1989,[10] of the Berne Convention for the Protection of Literary and Artistic Works on 10 July 1992 and of the Universal Copyright Convention on 30 July 1992, which is not administered by WIPO but by UNESCO. Albeit regulating neighbouring rights in its Copyright Law, China did not join the Rome Convention for the Protection of Performers, Producers of Phonograms and Broadcasting Organizations, but in order to appease US concerns about rampant phonogram piracy, it acceded to the Convention for the Protection of Phonogram Producers against Unauthorized Reproduction of their Phonograms on 5 January 1993. By the later part of the 1990s, after accession to the Patent Cooperation Treaty on 1 October 1993, the Nice Agreement Concerning the International Classification of Goods and Services for the Purposes of the Registration of Marks on 5 May 1994,[11] the Budapest Treaty on the International Recognition of the Deposit of Microorganisms for the Purposes of Patent Procedure on 1 April 1995, the Strasbourg Agreement Concerning the International Patent Classification and the Locarno Agreement Establishing an International Classification for Industrial Designs on 17 June 1996, the Madrid Protocol on 1 September 1995[12] and the International Convention for the Protection of New Varieties of Plants on 23 March 1999 (also not administered by WIPO, but by UPOV), China was prepared for the accession to the WTO, which it finally accomplished on 11 December 2001. On 9 March 2007, China became a member

8. EU-China Geographical Indications Agreement, 6 November 2019, available at https://ec.europa.eu/info/sites/info/files/food-farming-fisheries/food_safety_and_quality/documents/infographic-factsheet-eu-china-agreement_en.pdf.
9. China made the reservation that it would not consider itself bound to Article 28(1) Paris Convention, which would make it possible that a dispute that could not be settled by negotiation would be brought by any one of the member countries before the International Court of Justice (ICJ). In practice, this reservation did not matter much, since not once did a member country bring an IP case to the ICJ.
10. Accession to the Stockholm Act (1967) of the Madrid Agreement, on 4 July 1989 and in force on 4 October 1989. Notification No. 145 about Article 14(2)(d) (but withdrawn in 2003); notification no. 41 about Article 3bis. Notifications 91 and 126 refer to the deferred application of the Special Administrative Regions of Hong Kong and Macau, respectively. https://www.wipo.int/treaties/en/ActResults.jsp?act_id = 18.
11. China's accession to the Nice Agreement Concerning the International Classification of Goods and Services for the Purposes of the Registration of Marks, effective on 9 August 1994, Nice Notification No. 80, WIPO 9 May 1994. Available at: https://www.wipo.int/treaties/en/notifications/nice/treaty_nice_80.html.
12. In accordance with Article 5(2)(b) and (c) Madrid Protocol, China has declared that the time limit to notify a refusal of protection shall be 18 months and that, where a refusal of protection results from an opposition to the granting of protection, such refusal may be notified after the expiry of the 18-month time limit.

of the WIPO Copyright Treaty and the WIPO Performances and Phonograms Treaty, committing itself to protect foreign copyright owners, performers and phonogram producers in the digital environment. The last IP treaty China has joined so far is the Beijing Treaty on Audiovisual Performances (ratified on 9 July 2014, entry into force on 28 April 2020).[13] In 1997, China also acceded to the Vienna Convention on the Law of Treaties, which provides rules and procedures for the interpretation of international agreements.

China has furthermore signed, but not joined the Washington Treaty on Intellectual Property in Respect of Integrated Circuits, the Trade Mark Law Treaty,[14] the Singapore Treaty on the Law of Trademarks[15] and the Marrakesh Treaty to Facilitate Access to Published Works for Persons Who Are Blind, Visually Impaired or Otherwise Print Disabled. So far, China did not become a member to the Vienna Agreement Establishing an International Classification of the Figurative Elements of Marks 1973.[16] With the growing number of graphic trademarks, this leads to challenges in graphic trademark search. However, in February 2019, the China Trademark Office (CTMO) launched an intelligent search function in this regard.[17] China further did not accede to any multilateral treaty on indications of source or geographical indications,[18] but instead signed a bilateral GI agreement with the EU in 2019[19] and the mentioned Economic and Trade Agreement with the U.S. in 2020, where GI protection is part of the IP chapter.[20] In November 2020, China signed the Regional Comprehensive Economic Partnership (RCEP)[21] FTA, which includes a chapter on intellectual property

13. A list of WIPO-administered treaties to which China has become a member can be found here https://www.wipo.int/treaties/en/ShowResults.jsp?country_id=38C.
14. China signed the TL Treaty on 28 October 1994, available at: https://wipolex.wipo.int/en/details.jsp?id=12678.
15. STLT 2006, signed on 27 March 2006 and effective on 16 March 2009. China signed the Treaty on 29 January 2007, but did not ratify or accede to it. Available at: https://wipolex.wipo.int/en/treaties/textdetails/12668.
16. Vienna Agreement Establishing an International Classification of the Figurative Elements of Marks 1973, adopted 12 June 1973, effective on 8 August 1973. Available at: https://wipolex.wipo.int/en/treaties/textdetails/13098.
17. Hui Chen and Gang Hu, China: Key Points Of Chinese Graphic Trademarks Searches, MONDAQ, 26 September 2019. Available at: http://www.mondaq.com/article.asp?articleid=848770&email_access=on.
18. Madrid Agreement for the Repression of False or Deceptive Indications of Source on Goods (adopted on 14 July 1967), or the Lisbon System for the International Registration of Appellations of Origin (as amended on 28 September 1979) or Geneva Act of the Lisbon Agreement on Appellations of Origin and Geographical Indications (as adopted on 20 May 2015).
19. See for example: EU-China Geographical Indications – "10 plus 10" project is now complete, European Commission, Press Release, IP/12/1297, 30 November 2012. Available at: http://europa.eu/rapid/press-release_IP-12-1297_en.htm. On 6 November 2019, the EU and China concluded the negotiations on a bilateral agreement to protect 100 European GIs in China and 100 Chinese GIs in the EU against imitations and usurpation (IP/19/6200). Available at: https://ec.europa.eu/commission/presscorner/detail/en/IP_19_6200.
20. *Supra* note 7; Articles 1.15–17, Section F, Chapter 1.
21. The Regional Comprehensive Economic Partnership (RCEP) was signed on 15 November 2020, between the Association of Southeast Asian Nations (ASEAN); Brunei, Cambodia, Indonesia, Laos, Malaysia, Myanmar, Philippines, Singapore, Thailand and Vietnam; plus

but gives priority to TRIPS in the event of any inconsistency between a provision of the chapter and a provision of TRIPS.[22]

According to Article 142 of the General Principles of Civil Law of 1986, treaties automatically become part of Chinese domestic law, except those provisions to which China has declared reservation beforehand. However, the SPC issued judicial interpretations which largely excludes the direct application of IP-related international law within its legal system, an interpretation of 2002 specifically excluding direct application of WTO law and therefore also of TRIPs.[23] Another judicial interpretation of 2012 generally excludes IP treaties that have been transformed or must be transformed into national law.[24] The later revisions of the Civil Law (see below) do not mention anything related to direct applicability of international treaties. Ahl argues that China's domestic legislation seems to have developed a dialectic relation with international agreements: these separate systems infiltrate and complement each other, instead of conflicting with each other. Accordingly, a complex mechanism would control China's domestic application of treaties, enabling state organs to limit the effectiveness of treaty implementation within the legal system.[25]

China's membership in the above treaties does, in general, extend to the former British crown colony Hong Kong, which has been returned to China in 1997 and to the former Portuguese colony of Macao, which has been returned to China in 1999, unless China has deposited a territorial information to the contrary.[26] Both are Special Administrative Regions of China with their own, distinct legal systems under the

---

Australia, China, Japan, New Zealand and South Korea. It will take effect as soon as it has been ratified by at least six ASEAN and three non-ASEAN signatories. Chapter 11 of RCEP is on Intellectual Property.

22. Article 11.3 RCEP, *ibid.*
23. Rule 9 of the Zuigao Renmin Fayuan guanyu shenli guoji maoyi xingzheng anjian ruogan wenti de guiding (Regulations of the SPC on some Questions of the Trial of Administrative Cases relating to International Trade) 27 August 2002, 5 Gazette of the SPC (2002), 165.
24. Rule 4 of the Zuigao Renmin Fayuan guanyu shiyong "Zhonghua Renmin Gonbgheguo Shewai Minshi Guanxi Falv Shiyong Fa" ruogan wenti de jieshi (I) (SPC Interpretation on Some Questions Relating to the Applicsyion of the "Law of the People's Republic of China on the Application of Laws on Foreign-related Civil Relationships" (I)) of 28 December 2012, in English and Chinese accessible on the China International Commercial Court's website: http://cicc.court.gov.cn/html/1/219/199/201/679.html#.
25. Björn Ahl, 'Chinese Law and International Treaties', *HKLJ* (2009), 739; Ahl outlines further four instances in which the direct application of international treaties is likely to be denied: (1) the NPC Standing Committee may choose not to publish the text of the treaty in the Official Gazette which makes it impossible for the treaty to become legally valid according to Article 67(14) of the PRC Constitution; (2) even if the treaty has been published, the courts and administration may be excluded from applying the treaty if no statutory provisions are adopted that refer to the treaty and enable direct application; (3) even in the absence of such a statutory reference provision, the SPC can provide a judicial interpretation that inhibits the direct application (just as the above judicial interpretations are inhibiting the direct application of WTO law and of IP treaties); (4) even without such an interpretation, the effect of the application of a reference norm is questionable due to the fact that reference provisions grant the courts a wide discretionary power.
26. Such territorial notification can accessed on the list of China's membership in WIPO-administered treaties (https://www.wipo.int/treaties/en/ShowResults.jsp?country_id=38C), by clicking on "details" in the respective line.

formula "One Country, Two Systems". In Hong Kong, the legitimacy of the Patent Ordinance[27] is based on Article 139 of the Hong Kong Basic Law,[28] the legitimacy of the Copyright Ordinance[29] on Article 140 Hong Kong Basic Law[30] and the legitimacy of indications of geographical origin,[31] on Article 117 Hong Kong Basic Law.[32] There seems to be no explicit legitimacy provided for the protection of trademarks,[33] unlike in Macao where Article 114 Basic Law[34] provides this legitimization.[35] In Macao, furthermore, patents[36] are legitimized by Article 124 Macao Basic Law,[37] copyright and related rights[38] by Article 125 Macao Basic Law[39] and designations of origin and

---

27. An Ordinance to make provisions in respect of patents and related matters (Cap. 514 Patent Ordinance) 27 June 1997.
28. "The Government of the Hong Kong Special Administrative Region shall, on its own, formulate policies on science and technology and protect by law achievements in scientific and technological research, patents, discoveries and inventions. The Government of the Hong Kong Special Administrative Region shall, on its own, decide on the scientific and technological standards and specifications applicable in Hong Kong."
29. An Ordinance to make provisions in respect of copyright and related rights and for connected purposes (Cap. 528 Copyright Ordinance), 27 June 1997.
30. "The Government of the Hong Kong Special Administrative Region shall, on its own, formulate policies on culture and protect by law the achievements and the lawful rights and interests of authors in their literary and artistic creation."
31. Schedule 3(3), Trade Marks Ordinance, An Ordinance to make new provision in respect of the registration of trade marks and to provide for connected matters, Cap. 559 Trade Marks Ordinance Cap., 4 April 2003.
32. "The Hong Kong Special Administrative Region may issue its own certificates of origin for products in accordance with prevailing rules of origin."
33. The HK IP Department is referring to Articles 139 and 140 to give legitimacy to the government protect IP, so they are interpreting the legitimacy for the protection of patents (Article 139) and protection of copyright (Article 140) broadly. See page 6: https://www.ipd.gov.hk/eng/pub_press/publications/IP_e.pdf.
34. "The Macao Special Administrative Region shall, in accordance with law, protect the free operation of industrial and commercial enterprises and make its own policies on the development of industry and commerce. The Government of the Macao Special Administrative Region shall improve the economic environment and provide legal guarantees for promoting the development of industry and commerce and for encouraging investments, technological progress and development of new industries and new markets."
35. For Chapter IV Trademarks, Part III, Industrial Property Code Decree-Law No. 97/99/M of 13 December 1999.
36. Chapter I – Inventions, Part III, Industrial Property Code Decree-Law No. 97/99/M of 13 December 1999.
37. "The Government of the Macao Special Administrative Region shall, on its own, formulate policies on science and technology and protect by law achievements in scientific and technological research, patents, discoveries and inventions. The Government of the Macao Special Administrative Region shall, on its own, decide on the scientific and technological standards and specifications applicable in Macao."
38. Republication of the Regime of Copyright and Related Rights, approved by Decree-Law no. 43/99/M, of August 16, entered into force on 1 October 1999.
39. "The Government of the Macao Special Administrative Region shall, on its own, formulate policies on culture, including literature, art, broadcasting, film and television programs. The Government of the Macao Special Administrative Region shall protect by law the achievements and the lawful rights and interests of authors in their literary, artistic and

geographical indications[40] by Article 113 Macao Basic Law.[41]

In Mainland China, apart from the mentioned laws on patents, trademarks, copyright and unfair competition, intellectual property legislation consists of a thicket of secondary legislation, which can roughly be divided into two categories. One is the mentioned SPC's "interpretations" of the laws, so as to provide guidance for the lower courts on how to apply them in practice. Article 104 of the Legislation Law endows the SPC with the competency to enact such binding interpretations. On 23 December 2020, the SPC amended 18 intellectual property related interpretations, mostly as part of its endeavours to adapt its own statutes to the newly enacted Civil Code (see below) but also to reflect the recent reforms to the institutions for the prosecution and protection of intellectual property, which will be treated in the following chapters. Another category of secondary law is administrative provisions, the most important ones being enacted by the State Council on administrative procedures and requirements for the prosecution of registrable intellectual property, details on the scope of protection and on so-called administrative enforcement, including procedural matters and sanctions such as confiscation, fines, etc. Administrative enforcement is a specialty of China, a remnant of the beginnings of China's modern intellectual property history, when local administrations in charge of patents, marks and copyright should compensate for what the aborning court system could not yet accomplish. In the meantime, as mentioned above, China's court system has greatly matured but administrative enforcement is still available as a cheaper and quicker alternative to a civil court trial. It will be treated in more detail in the subsequent parts on enforcement and on patents, utility models and designs. Beneath the State Council, various administrations such as CNIPA or the NCAC, do also enact administrative provisions and guidelines.

Important sources of intellectual property are, furthermore, the general laws (and, again, the secondary judicial interpretations and administrative regulations that supplement them), such as the Criminal Code of 14 March 1997 with provisions on criminal liability for copyright, trademark and trade secret infringement (Articles 213–220), the Antimonopoly Law of 30 August 2007, which seeks to draw a dividing line between legitimate exercise and abuses of the market power conveyed by exclusive intellectual property, the Contract Law of 15 March 1999, in particular Part PXVIII on technology contracts, the Tort Liability Law of 26 December 2009 with provisions, *inter alia*, on indirect infringement and on internet service provider liability for tort committed by its clients, the Law on the Application of Law to Foreign-related Civil Relationships of 28 October 2010, which subdues intellectual property related conflict of laws under the *lex loci protectionis* principle or the Civil Procedures Law after its overhaul of 31 August 2012 (last amended on 27 June 2017) with important provisions, *inter alia*, on evidence requirements and on preliminary measures. On 28

other creation. The Government of the Macao Special Administrative Region shall protect by law scenic spots, historical sites and other historical relics as well as the lawful rights and interests of the owners of antiques."

40. Chapter VI – Designation of Origin and Geographical Indications, Part III, Industrial Property Code Decree-Law No. 97/99/M of 13 December 1999.

41. "The Macao Special Administrative Region may issue its own certificates of origin for products in accordance with prevailing rules of origin."

May 2020, the National People's Congress passed China's first Civil Code (entry into force: 1 January 2021), which will henceforth include the above standalone laws on contracts and on tort (but also all the others on family, inheritance, etc.). Some of them were also substantially amended at this occasion, for instance, the mentioned provision on the general tort liability of internet providers, which is now regulated in much more detail in Articles 1195–1197 of the Civil Code.[42]

In recent years, case law has become another significant source of law. In 2019, courts throughout China accepted 399,031 and concluded 394,521 intellectual property cases, increases by 40.79 respectively 44.02 percent over the previous year. 22,272 of the newly accepted cases accounted for patents, utility models and designs, an increase of 2.64 percent over 2018, 65,209 for trademarks, an increase of 25.41 percent over 2018, 293,066 for copyrights, an increase of 49.98 percent over 2018 and 3,135 for technology contracts, an increase of 16.98 percent over 2018. Only the number of unfair competition cases accepted in 2019 (4,128 cases) has slightly decreased by 1.25 percent over the previous year.[43]

The texts of most court decisions can be accessed via online case collections, such as the online version of the SPC's Gazette http://gongbao.court.gov.cn or the IP House database, the bilingual database of Peking University http://en.pkulaw.cn/. Sometimes, however, finding the original text of a decision, also of a newer one, can become difficult, even if a filing number has been indicated in the book or article which quoted it. Quite challenging is also the identification of court decisions of landmark character out of the abundance of case law. Chinese law is different from the Common Law tradition in that the decision of a higher court or even of the SPC does not bind the lower courts (unlike the above-mentioned Interpretations), so that they may decide differently in a similar case.[44] Also, Chinese judges almost never quote precedents in their reasoning. To nevertheless provide at least some orientation as to which decision is worthy of being considered, the SPC regularly publishes its own decisions as well as those of other courts that it considers important in annual collections such as "The 10 Landmark Intellectual Property Cases and the 50 Typical Intellectual Property Cases of 2018".[45]

On 27 July 2020, the SPC issued the Guiding Opinions on Strengthening Searches for Similar Cases to Unify the Application of Law to further encourage lower courts to consider landmark precedents in their decision-making. Rule 4 provides the following hierarchy of cases:[46]

42. More about this in chapter 4, Copyright.
43. Numbers from the SPC's White Book on the Judicial Protection of Intellectual Property, https://www.chinacourt.org/article/detail/2020/04/id/5049570.shtml.
44. Then again, it seems that the increased emphasis on selected cases is to make the decisions more uniform. In this sense, one can argue that China is moving in the direction of a Common Law country, see Danny Friedmann, 'IP in China Closer to Common Law System for the Sake of Uniformity', 12(8) *Journal of Intellectual Property Law and Practice* (OUP 2017), 621–622, Available at: https://ssrn.com/abstract=2988494.
45. http://www.court.gov.cn/zixun-xiangqing-153252.html.
46. Article 4 of Guiding Opinions on Strengthening Searches for Similar Cases to Unify the Application of Law (Provisional) issued on 27 July 2020 by the SPC, China Law Translate, 27 July 2020. Available at: https://www.chinalawtranslate.com/en/case-review/. See also Susan Finder, 'Supreme People's Court's new guidance on similar case search', *Supreme*

(1) Guiding Cases published by the SPC[47] (Stanford Law School provides a bilingual database for these "Guiding cases").[48]
(2) Example cases and cases with effective decisions published by the SPC (in 2019, China's highest court also published a bilingual English-Chinese collection of important recent intellectual property court decisions in collaboration with the WIPO).[49]
(3) Reference Cases and cases with effective decisions published by the High Court of that province (autonomous region, directly-governed municipality);
(4) Cases with effective decisions from the people's court at the level above or of that court.

As far as regulatory material is concerned, the most important laws and regulations are available in English, for instance, in WIPO's WIPOLex law collection[50] or on the English websites of the relevant Chinese authorities, above all the CNIPA and the NCAC.

Secondary material on Chinese intellectual property is abundant. Very instructive is the bilingual Chinese-English journal China Patents & Trademarks published by China Patent Agents, with many articles authored by prominent judges, examiners and other practitioners, and the China IP Magazine.[51] A plethora of academic articles on Chinese intellectual property can, furthermore, be found in various peer-reviewed US and international legal journals. Even more resourceful for those who can read Chinese are, of course, Chinese journals, which can most easily be accessed through a scientific research database, for instance, the China National Knowledge Infrastructure (CNKI). Further information (statistics, news, country reports) is provided by the WIPO and the WTO on their respective websites, as well as on the sites of other non-Chinese institutions, such as EPO, the Sino-EU cooperation programme IPKey or the China IPR SME Helpdesk. Good information on current developments, new landmark cases and the like can also be found in the English-language blogosphere. The most instructive blogs are Danny Friedmann's http://www.ipdragon.org, Mark Cohen's http://www.chinaipr.com, Susan Finder's blog about the Supreme People's Court https://supremepeoplescourtmonitor.com/ and the non-exclusively China-related intellectual property blog IPKat as well as the various Kluwer blogs on patents, copyright, competition law, etc.

Chapter 2 of this book presents the Chinese Patent Law, which actually comprises "patents for inventions" ("patents" in international terminology), utility

---

People's Court Monitor, 27 July 2020. Available at: https://supremepeoplescourtmonitor.com/2020/07/27/supreme-peoples-courts-new-guidance-on-similar-case-search/.

47. In total there are 139 Guiding Cases with 22 cases related to IP: seven trademark cases, one business name case, two unfair competition cases, four invention patent cases, one design patent case, one utility model patent case, three copyright cases and three plant variety right cases.
48. Stanford Law School, China Guiding Cases Project, https://cgc.law.stanford.edu/guiding-cases/.
49. WIPO Collection of Leading Judgments on Intellectual Property Rights – People`s Republic of China (2011–2018), https://www.wipo.int/publications/en/details.jsp?id=4477.
50. Unfortunately, not all secondary law contained therein is up to date.
51. China IP Magazine, http://www.chinaipmagazine.com/en/.

models and designs, its neighbouring provisions and the judicial and administrative practice. This chapter also includes two neighbouring areas of patent law, namely plant varieties and integrated circuit layout designs. Chapter 3 relates to trademarks and related rights, including geographical indications and domain names. Chapter 4 provides an overview of copyright and neighbouring rights. After having presented these three traditional areas of intellectual property, the subsequent parts of the book will focus on adjacent competition law and on the intricacies of intellectual property transactions and enforcement. Chapter 5 outlines the Chinese unfair competition law, including trade secret protection, as well as antitrust law with a special focus on its application to curb abusive exercises of intellectual property. Chapter 6 deals with the vividly debated Chinese technology transfer regulation and practice. The final chapter 7 outlines the emergence and the present state of the Chinese enforcement system, with a strong focus on procedural practice.

CHAPTER 2
Patents, Utility Models and Designs

Peter Ganea

I. OVERVIEW OF CHINA'S PATENT HISTORY

First historical accounts of occasional grants of patent-like exclusive rights for certain industries to use their salt distilling and iron smelting technologies date back to the early Han dynasty (206 B.C.–8 A.D.).[1] Such early rudimentary protection, however, never went beyond the stage of an act of grace by the authorities, to become a statutory patent right. The term "patents" did not appear before the 19th century, at a time when China was a semi-colony of various western powers.[2] It was translated into *zhuanli, i.e.*, "exclusive benefit" or simply "monopoly", a rather negative term that, according to the famous intellectual property scholar Zheng Chengsi, gave rise to misunderstandings in the early days of China's modern patent history.

In 1898, at the end of the last imperial dynasty of the *Qing*, the first patent rules, namely the Regulations on Rewards for the Promotion of Technology, were enacted by the reform-oriented but unsuccessful emperor Guangxu whose efforts were thwarted by the conservative Imperial Court. After the downfall of Imperial China the Republican government and the *Guomindang* regime enacted several patent rules that never became relevant in practice.[3] The first Patent Law for China,

1. See Zheng Chengsi, *Chinese Intellectual Property and Technology Transfer Law* (London, 1987), 51; Flora Wang, 'An Overview of the Development of China's Patent System', Chapter 1, in Mark A. Cohen, A. Elizabeth Bang and Stephanie J. Mitchell (eds.), *Chinese Intellectual Property Law and Practice* (The Hague et al., 1999), 51.
2. For details see the historical overview given by Guo Shoukang, 'Chapter 2. Patents', Suppl.1, in *International Encyclopedia of Laws*, Vol. 1 Intellectual Property, (looseleaf, 1997), 60 et seq.
3. Provisional Regulation of Rewards for Manufactured Products, enacted in 1912 by the new republican government; Provisional Regulation of Rewards for Manufactured Products, enacted in 1923 by the Ministry of Agriculture and Commerce under the northern warlord government; Provisional Regulation of Rewards for Handicrafts, enacted in 1928 by

including Taiwan, was enacted in 1944 by the Guomindang government. This law never entered into force in mainland China, but became the first Patent Law of Taiwan.[4] With subsequent amendments, it is still in force. It protects not only patents, but also utility models and designs.

On 11 August 1950, soon after the proclamation of the People's Republic of China, the new government enacted the Interim Regulations concerning the Grant of Rights over Inventions and Patent Rights.[5] The Regulations contained a dual-track system of inventor's certificates (a right to be remunerated for outstanding technical achievements) and of exclusive patent rights (an immaterial property right) and in general, the type of right that was awarded was left to the inventor, unless the invention resulted from occupational duties at a state-owned organisation or from a commission. In these cases, only an inventor's certificate was available. The Regulations were supplemented by the Interim Regulations Concerning Awards for Inventions with Regard to Products, Technical Improvements and Rationalisation Proposals of 6 May 1954, which contained detailed rules on the remuneration standards for inventors' certificates. The coexistence of inventor certificates and exclusive patent rights was quite similar to the dual-track system practised in the Soviet Union and other former socialist states.[6] In reality, however, the protection rules turned out to be without practical meaning; between 1950 and 1963, only four patents and six inventor certificates were granted.[7]

On 11 December 1963, the Regulations Concerning Awards for Inventions and the Regulations Concerning Awards for Technical Improvement Proposals were enacted. They abolished exclusive patents and replaced them by a system of inventor's rewards and remuneration. Moreover, state-owned enterprises and collective enterprises were expressively permitted to make free use of the results of innovative endeavour but in contrast to the Soviet Union's rewards and remunerations scheme, did not retain a property in the inventions, e.g., under an assumption of assignment, whereby inventions completely fell into public domain.[8]

In the late 1970s, after the Cultural Revolution's aftermaths had cooled off, patent protection re-appeared on the political agenda. After more than a decade of social experiment, political stability was of the utmost importance to the new reform-oriented leadership. One indispensable precondition for this was a sufficiently well-off population. To whip the fallow economy into shape, foreign investment was bitterly needed, and the new leadership recognised that one precondition

---

the Guomindang government and the Provisional Regulation of Rewards for Industrial Technique, enacted in 1932 by the Guomindang government - for details see Henry R. Zheng, 'The Patent System of the People's Republic of China', 23:2/3 *University of San Francisco Law Review* (1987), 345 et seq.; Guo Shoukang, *supra* note 2, 60.

4. See website of the Ministry of Justice, 'Legislative History' at https://law.moj.gov.tw/ENG/LawClass/LawAll.aspx?pcode=J0070007.
5. Zhongyang Renmin Zhengfu faling huibian 1949/1950 (Collection of Law Provisions of the Central People's Government 1949/1950), Renmin chubanshe, 463.
6. Detailed information in Adolf Dietz, 'Das System des gewerblichen Rechtsschutzes in China, Einführung in seinen gegenwärtigen Stand und Ausblick', in Adolf Dietz (ed.), *Die Neuregelung des gewerblichen Rechtsschutzes in China* (Weinheim 1988), 6 et seq.
7. Guo Shoukang, *supra* note 2, 61.
8. Zheng Chengsi, *supra* note 1, 53.

for economic recovery was to abandon autarky and isolation. The creation of an investment-friendly environment was one of the main motives behind the statement in favour of the re-introduction of a legal patent protection in the course of the Reform and Opening Policy that started in 1978.[9] In addition, the establishment of a patent system which required not only the enactment of laws but also substantive investment in infrastructure for patent prosecution, was urged upon China also from abroad, most notably from the United States. In an "Agreement on Trade Relations between The United States of America and the People's Republic of China" signed in Beijing on 7 July 1979, China committed itself to protect US intellectual property, including patents.

Exclusive property in technical ideas was not without controversy in post-Mao China. Many commentators feared that a majority of patents would be owned by foreigners, and there were strong concerns that such foreign monopolies over technical solutions might become obstacles to technological and scientific development.[10] Such concerns were finally refuted, even though they came up again later in the course of the "IP abuse" debate of the mid-2000s.[11] Back in the early 1980s, however, rather the opposite, namely lack of protection of foreign IP, turned out to become an obstacle to industrial development. In the absence of patent and know-how protection, foreign investors either completely refrained from entrusting their technology to Chinese partners, or in anticipation of huge losses from unauthorised use and dissemination of their innovations, charged them prohibitively high license fees.[12]

Due to such apodictic arguments, the debates inevitably gravitated towards a decision in favour of patent protection. The present Patent Law was adopted at the Fourth Session of the Standing Committee of the National People's Congress on 12 March 1984 and entered into force on 1 April 1985.[13] In contrast to the rudimentary patent regulations under the late *Qing* dynasty, the republican era and the early years after 1949, the law of 1984 was the first comprehensive patent system with nationwide patent administration. In addition to the Patent Law, on 19 January 1985 the State Council enacted detailed Implementing Regulations, which became effective

9. Proclaimed by Paramount Leader Deng Xiaoping in the course of the 3rd Plenary Session of the 11th Central Committee, together with the "Four Modernizations" in the areas of agriculture, industry, defence and science and technology.
10. Guo Shoukang, 'Drafting and Promulgation of the Chinese Patent Law', 16 *International Review of Industrial Property and Copyright (IIC)* (1985), 367, 368.
11. See *infra* XIII. 2.
12. Henry R. Zheng, *supra* note 3, 345 (351 et seq.), with examples of both comparably high license fees to anticipate losses from patent infringement and patent grants to US and Japanese companies for inventions made in China, which subsequently prevented Chinese inventors from obtaining their own patents abroad or from entering their domestic markets.
13. The current Patent Law after its third amendment of 2008, as well as the Implementing Regulations and the latest consolidated version of the Examination Guidelines of 2010 can be accessed on CNIPA's website: https://www.cnipa.gov.cn/col/col97/index.html. The Examination Guidelines underwent several amendments since 2010, the latest in 2019 (see *infra*); an English version of the current Patent Law can be obtained from the WIPOLex database: www.wipo.int/edocs/lexdocs/laws/en/cn/cn028en.pdf; WIPO Lex contains further patent-related laws, administrative provisions and Supreme People's Court Interpretations in Chinese and partly in English: https://wipolex.wipo.int/en/legislation/results?countryOrgs = CN&subjectMatters = 1.

on 1 April 1985.[14] The Implementing Regulations further interpret a number of legal provisions, contain detailed procedural instructions directed at the Patent Office, and instructions on law enforcement which are addressed to the local administrative authorities engaged in patent matters. Within the regulatory framework of the Patent Law and the Implementing Regulations, further administrative rules were enacted by the respective administrative authorities engaged in patent matters, e.g. the Patent Examination Guidelines (hereinafter "Examination Guidelines").[15]

Preparation and training of patent administrative staff had started long before the enactment of the Patent Law. On 13 March 1979, a Working Group of Experts on Drafting the Chinese Patent Law was established that comprised experts in the fields of technology and foreign trade.[16] The involvement of foreign trade staff in the preparations demonstrates that patent protection at that time was indeed mainly perceived as an instrument for attracting foreign investment. In 1980, the Chinese Patent Office was established as an administrative organ directly under the State Council. Not long after that, it became a sub-department of the State Intellectual Property Office (SIPO) which, contrary to its title, has only been competent to formulate general patent, utility model and designs policies, to enact administrative rules on patent protection and to participate in patent legislation, but not yet to deal with other kinds of IP. This has changed in 2018, when SIPO was restructured to become the head administration for all kinds of registered industrial property and its English name was changed into China National Intellectual Property Administration/ CNIPA (the Chinese name remained the same).[17] The efforts of the following years concentrated on patent training and education in order to have a staff of patent examiners ready when the new Patent Law entered into force. These initial efforts were substantively supported by international institutions such as the WIPO, to which China acceded in 1980, and by foreign patent administrations.

II. ECONOMIC IMPORTANCE OF THE PATENT SYSTEM

Once introduced to appease foreign demands, the Chinese patent system today caters predominantly to domestic industries. In 2003, domestic invention patent applications[18] outnumbered applications filed by foreigners for the first time, and

---

14. The current version of 2010 can be downloaded in Chinese and in English from the WIPO Lex database http://www.wipo.int/wipolex/en/details.jsp?id = 6504.
15. The latest consolidated version of 2010 can be obtained from CNIPA's website https:// www.cnipa.gov.cn/art/2013/10/23/art_74_27580.html (English translation no longer made available by CNIPA but by several law firms, e.g., at http://www.sptl.com/ newsitem/277586171); CNIPA's explanatory notes on the latest amendments of September 2019 at https://www.cnipa.gov.cn/art/2019/10/30/art_66_11489.html. and of December 2019 at https://www.cnipa.gov.cn/art/2020/1/21/art_66_11475.html.
16. Guo Shoukang, *supra* note 10.
17. More details in Chapter III. 2. *infra*.
18. In Chinese terminology "invention patents" correspond to what would be called "patents" in countries with separate laws on patents, utility models and designs, whereas in China these three types of rights are regulated under one Patent Law and the term "patent" is understood as the grant certificate for each of these rights; more explanations in Chapter III. 1 *infra*.

the year 2006 marked the next turnaround, when for the first time more invention patent grants went to Chinese applicants than to foreigners. Only a minor part of the 1,400,661 invention patent applications filed in 2019, namely 11.2 percent, was filed by foreigners.[19] The number of grants hint at a slightly higher quality of foreign applications, as more than 20 percent of the 452,804 grants in 2019 went to foreign applicants.[20] Interestingly, the invention patent application numbers of 2019 for the first time show a significant decrease in comparison with the previous year in which 1,542,002 applications were filed, which in turn still represented a 19.2 percent increase over 1,246,000 applications in 2017, comparable to the development in previous years. It should also be noted that in the past, annual grants have increased rather moderately in comparison with the annual growth of applications, which implies a growing examination backlog. CNIPA's annual report of 2017 nevertheless alluded to a stable average examination pendency of 22 months. The pendency period may be further alleviated if the recent slump in application numbers hints at least at a more moderate future increase in domestic applications. Along with the continuing boost in Chinese applications abroad (see the following paragraph), this trend may also be interpreted as an increased quality of inventions made in China at the expense of quantity.

In 2019, China for the first time overtook the US as the largest source country of PCT applications (58,990 applications from China v. 57,840 applications from the US), with Huawei as the top PCT applicant of the past years.[21] Simultaneously, CNIPA's attractiveness as a receiving office as well as an ISA is on the rise, whereas the number of requests to conduct an international preliminary examination declined in 2018, following a worldwide trend.[22] In spite of these impressive developments, the numbers of Chinese applications received and examined by the important "IP5" offices, the EPO, the USPTO, the JPO and KIPO, are still low, albeit rapidly increasing. According to the IP5 statistics, Chinese applications in the other four IP offices and grants to Chinese applicants from these offices show a steady and healthy annual growth, whereas the numbers of applications filed with and granted by each of the IP5 offices to applicants from the other four countries are stagnating or even declining.[23]

19. Figures for the year 2019 in comparison with 2018 can be found in CNIPA's English Annual Report http://english.cnipa.gov.cn/col/col2159/index.html ("Appendix I - Statistics") of 2019, which, in contrast to previous annual statistics strictly distinguishes between domestic and foreign applications respectively grants to domestic and to foreign applicants, so that both domestic and foreign-related figures have to added to obtain the total numbers; the CNIPA Annual Report 2017 (English) can be accessed at: http://english.cnipa.gov.cn/col/col1749/index.html.
20. According to the WIPO report "World Intellectual Property Indicators 2019" (p. 211), https://www.wipo.int/edocs/pubdocs/en/wipo_pub_941_2019.pdf, CNIPA has changed its method of compiling application statistics in 2017: since then, only applications for which the necessary fees have been paid are counted, so that analyzing the growth rates between 2016 and 2017 may lead to false conclusions.
21. The data for 2019 are summarized on this WIPO fact sheet: https://www.wipo.int/export/sites/www/ipstats/en/docs/infographic_pct_2019.pdf.
22. https://www.fiveipoffices.org/wcm/connect/fiveipoffices/385f1612-9a4c-4777-ba60-68f2b14588e5/2018IP5SR_chapter5_pct.pdf?MOD=AJPERES&CVID=.
23. Statistics sheets can be downloaded from: https://www.fiveipoffices.org/statistics/statistics_index.

The 7,947 Chinese applications received by the Japanese Patent Office in 2019, for instance, appear rather modest in comparison with 20,394 applications from the EU and 22,867 applications from the US, but they represent a 49.2 percent increase over 2018, whereas among the rest of the IP5 countries, only South Korea could generate double-digit increases in the partner offices, albeit much more moderately than China. The data on grants show a similar picture: while patents granted to Chinese in absolute terms are still comparably few, they show the healthiest growth in comparison with grants to applicants from the US, the EU, Japan and South Korea. The EPO, for instance, granted 6,229 patents to Chinese applicants in 2019, which appears rather low but means an increase of 28.9 percent over the previous year. USPTO grants to Chinese applicants even increased by 33.4 percent over 2018.

EPO statistics of 2019 show that the greatest part of China's patenting activity in Europe is centred on the field of digital telecommunications, with *Huawei*, again, as the top applicant.[24] The growing importance of patents held and enforced by Chinese companies abroad also impacts on litigation practice outside China. A patent battle between the mentioned digital communications giants *Huawei* and *ZTE* in German courts, for instance, substantively contributed to the formation of a German and EU doctrine on standard essential patents and FRAND licensing.[25]

Domestically, having experienced the detrimental effect of foreign-governed patent pools in the entertainment electronics industry on domestic audio-visual equipment manufacturers in the mid-2000s, which even entailed a public outcry and a spectacular move of five law professors to invalidate an essential patent from the pool,[26] patents are increasingly perceived as an instrument of nation building. Through administrative guidance, the patent system shall become a crucial factor in the implementation of China's various national strategies towards technological independence, if not supremacy, such as the "Made in China 2025" strategy or the "Belt and Road" Initiative. The proposals towards a fourth Patent law reform reflect this objective, as a good part of them is dedicated to the creation of a more favourable institutional environment for the commercialization of domestic inventions.[27] Also, government, bureaucracy and local firms increasingly join their forces to create purely Chinese technology bases by the formation of so-called "IP Alliances". IP Alliances are strictly Chinese patent pools in various sectors of technology to increase Chinese bargaining power towards foreign multinationals and to establish national standards to which foreign competitors would then have to adhere. The not immediately revenue-oriented, rather defensive character of these alliances is under criticism,

---

24. EPO Patent Index 2019: http://documents.epo.org/projects/babylon/eponet.nsf/0/BC45C92E5C077B10C1258527004E95C0/$File/Patent_Index_2019_statistics_at_a_glance_en.pdf.
25. ECJ preliminary ruling of 16 July 2015, C170/13.
26. Ying Zhan and Xuezhong Zhu, 'Intellectual property right abuses in the patent licensing of technology standards from developed countries to developing countries: a study of some typical cases from China', 10 *Journal of World Intellectual Property* (2007), 187, https://onlinelibrary.wiley.com/doi/full/10.1111/j.1747-1796.2007.00320.x ; see also Peter Ganea, 'China's amended legal regime on patents for inventions and utility models', 5:9 *Journal of Intellectual Property Law & Practice* (2010), 650, https://academic.oup.com/jiplp/article/5/9/650/880466.
27. See *infra* IV. 2.

especially with regard to their potential to suppress competition.[28] In any case, the perception of patent protection has changed fundamentally, from a bitter pill to be swallowed to satisfy foreign demands, to an instrument of fostering China's ambitious plans to become a world technology leader.

III. SPECIFIC FEATURES OF THE PATENT LAW AND THE PATENT INFRASTRUCTURE

1. Three Types of Protected Subject Matter under One Law

Now, talking about "patent" applications and grants brings us to an already mentioned peculiarity of China's patent system, namely that the Patent Law actually regulates three subject matter of protection: substantively examined "inventions" (which would usually be termed "patents" in most jurisdictions) and only formally examined utility models and designs, the generic term for all three being "invention-creations". Consequently, Chinese legal terminology speaks of "invention patents", "utility model patents" and "design patents", whereby "patent" has the meaning of a grant certificate. This peculiarity can cause confusion, especially when it comes to interpreting statistical data. In 2019, for instance, CNIPA received a total of 4,380,468 patent applications (for the first time in many years a rather moderate increase over the previous year, in which 4,323,112 applications were filed[29]) but this enormous number comprises "only" 1,400,661 invention patent applications, 2,268,190 almost exclusively domestically filed utility model applications and 711,617 design applications.[30]

The Patent Law, in spite of its many common provisions for these three kinds of rights, duly considers the differences between inventions, utility models and designs. Applications for invention patents have to represent a more substantive inventive step than utility models and are available in a broad variety of technical fields, including chemistry and biotechnology and processes, whereas utility model protection is limited to technical solutions pertaining to the shape and structure of a product. A major difference between inventions and the other two subject matter is that only invention applications are substantively examined, whereas utility model and design patents can be obtained after a mere formal examination. Correspondingly low is the reliability of the latter two, so that utility model or design owners who want to enforce their respective right in court or through the administrative route[31] are routinely required to hand in an evaluation report to be elaborated by CNIPA, which provides information about the respective model's or design's compliance with the

28. A good overview of IP Alliances, the regulatory environment for their establishment and the political objectives is given by Oliver Pfaffenzeller, Uwe Schriek and Wen Yu, 'IP Alliances – a cornerstone of Chinese IP strategy', GRUR Int. (2018), 1005.
29. Statistical data for 2018 in CNIPA's Annual Report 2018 at http://english.cnipa.gov.cn/col/col2076/index.html.
30. Statistical data for 2019 in CNIPA's Annual Report 2019 (English), at http://english.cnipa.gov.cn/col/col2159/index.html ("Appendix 1 – Statistics").
31. More information about China's peculiar administrative enforcement in the following section 2.

protection prerequisites. Also, designs have to meet specific protection prerequisites to be patented, namely distinctiveness that separates them from prior designs or the combination of their features and, peculiar to China, "no conflict with prior rights".[32]

After grant, invention patents are protected for a period of 20 years, utility models and designs for a period of 10 years from the application date (Article 42 Patent Law). As will be further outlined below, the fourth Patent Law amendment of 17 October 2020[33] extended the design protection term to 15 years and introduced a patent term extension for pharmaceutical inventions of up to five years. Moreover, it added a new paragraph 2 to Article 42 that entitles invention patent owners to claim a patent term extension in all technical fields as compensation for unreasonable delays in examination caused by CNIPA. Concretely, such compensation shall henceforth be claimable if the patent is granted after four years from the application date and three years from the date of requesting substantive examination have passed.

2. Patent Administration: China's Peculiar Administrative Enforcement and the Expanded Role of CNIPA

Administrative enforcement, which will be treated in greater detail in Chapter 7 of this book, is another peculiarity of China's enforcement not only of patents but also of other kinds of IP. It means that right owners who want to proceed against infringement have the choice between filing a civil suit and requesting a local intellectual property administration under CNIPA's central supervision to proceed against alleged infringers. Right owners who opt for administrative enforcement can expect cheaper and speedier enforcement, as the administrations are bound by strict deadlines, but they cannot claim damages, as administrations are only allowed to mediate in the damage question at request of both parties after infringement has been established, but not to determine them. Another disadvantage is that once the local administration has commenced action, the complainant is largely deprived of opportunities to control further proceedings, e.g., by withdrawing his request upon settlement with the opponent, as in contrast to civil litigation, administrative proceedings are focused on safeguarding the market order against piracy. Administrative enforcement should therefore be most relevant in the areas of copyright and trademarks, in which industrial-scale piracy with immediate adverse effects on the market is rather usual and in which right owners are mostly interested in putting a quick end to the infringement, also because they cannot expect much in terms of damages. In invention patent and utility model litigation, however, plaintiffs often seek to exert pressure on a competitor to achieve something else, e.g., as access to the competitor's own IP portfolio. Such strategies can best be pursued by commencing a civil lawsuit in a People's Court, in any stage of which the litigants have control of the further proceedings and can settle their dispute upon reaching an agreement.

32. More about protection prerequisites for inventions, utility models and designs in section V.

33. Passed by the National People's Congress on 17 October 2020; a comparison table of old and new provisions can be accessed at: https://mp.weixin.qq.com/s/7isXTLQxeV_ZIZYvhmcKjw; the official consolidated version was not yet available when this chapter was completed.

In spite of much criticism from foreign businesses who claim that intellectual property, especially patents, constitute private rights and should therefore be reserved to civil court litigation, the number of patentees who opt for the administrative route is on the rise: in 2018, 33,976 administrative patent infringement disputes were resolved, a remarkable increase over 27,305 cases prosecuted in the previous year.[34] Quite unsurprisingly, however, the majority of administrative cases accounts for comparably "primitive" design piracy, which is not dissimilar from copyright or trademark infringement in that it can be frequently established with the naked eye. In 2018, local IP administrations dealt with 14,159 design cases, followed by 8,550 utility model and 4,596 invention patent cases. Technically sophisticated infringements of utility models and especially of invention patents, which may involve chemical formulae, manufacturing processes, etc. and therefore require a high degree of expertise and familiarity with the intricacies of claim interpretation, are predominantly a matter of court litigation. Of course, also design infringement can pose difficult challenges that should be answered by judges rather than by legally less educated administrators, as will be demonstrated in greater detail below.[35]

The local IP administrations in charge of administrative enforcement are supervised by the CNIPA, which, as mentioned, is also China's patent examination and grant authority. Until 2018, CNIPA had the status of an authority directly under the State Council but according Item 43 of the Plan to Deepen the Reform of Party and State Organs presented by the Central Committee of the Communist Party on 21 March 2018,[36] not only its English name changed but it also became an agency under the State Administration for Market Regulation (SAMR), a new super-ministry that absorbed the former State Administration for Industry and Commerce (SAIC), the General Administration of Quality, Supervision Inspection, and Quarantine (AQSIQ) and the China Food and Drug Administration (CFDA). The SAMR now has, inter alia, jurisdiction over almost all aspects of Antimonopoly Law administration, which has previously been divided between three institutions, among them the powerful Ministry of Commerce (MofCom).

CNIPA's reorganisation came along with an expansion of its duties, as it is no longer solely in charge of patents, utility models, designs and the rather insignificant semiconductor layout designs but has taken over the tasks of the former SAIC's Trademark Office as examination and grant authority. Also, administrative enforcement of trademarks has shifted from the local administrations of industry and commerce to the local IP administrations under CNIPA's supervision. That is, prosecution and enforcement of almost all registered industrial property is now in CNIPA's hands, which may contribute to the unification of the procedural and regulatory framework for the majority of IP rights. Only copyright remained under

34. These figures are quoted from CNIPA's previous web presence, which showed annual administrative enforcement statistics in Chinese and English but it seems that since a recent redesign, only monthly statistics on enforcement in each province are made available, see https://www.cnipa.gov.cn/col/col89/index.html; not included in the above numbers are cases of "passing off a patent" (see XIV. 7. *infra*) but only infringement cases in which the parties had the choice between civil and administrative proceedings.
35. XIV. 6. *infra*.
36. http://www.gov.cn/zhengce/2018-03/21/content_5276191.htm#allContent.

the separate administrative jurisdiction of the National Copyright Administration of China (NCAC). Pursuant to Item 11 of the mentioned Plan, the NCAC has been upgraded from a subdivision of the Agency of Press and Publication to a body directly supervised by the Ministry of Propaganda.[37]

Reorganization also affected the former Patent Re-examination Board, which since 1985 had been in charge of reviewing examination decisions and invalidation requests, and which in March 2019 has become CNIPA's Department for Re-examination and Invalidation (DRI).[38] That the DRI is now officially a mere subdivision of CNIPA becomes also apparent from the terminology used by the reformed Patent Law, which in its provisions on re-examination and invalidation replaced the term "Patent Re-examination Board" by "Patent Administration un-der the State Council", meaning the CNIPA as a whole. The term Patent Re-Examination Board respectively the acronym "PRB" will nevertheless be used throughout this part of the book, as almost all of the quoted re-examination and invalidation decisions were rendered by the pre-vious Re-examination Board.

IV. COMPLETED AND ONGOING REFORMS

The Patent Law of 1984 underwent three overhauls in 1991, 2000 and 2008. Whereas the first two revisions of 1991 and 2000 largely aimed at harmonizing domestic law with international agreements, the focus of the third revision of 2008 has been on aligning patent law with domestic needs. One large part of amendments aimed at enhancing the quality of protected subject matter, for instance, by introducing worldwide novelty, another part at improving the enforcement of what remained worthy of protection, and a third package of amendments was dedicated to countering what was deemed to be "abusive" assertion of patents.[39]

The fourth Patent Law reform, albeit being expected to be completed by 2018, did not come until October 2020. One reason for the delay may have been the ongoing trade tensions between the US and China, which also include intellectual property issues. China may have slowed down the reform process in order not to prematurely forego negotiation assets such as the anticipated patent term extension. On 15 January 2020, however, China finally committed itself to introduce a patent term extension, a patent linkage system and other patent-related improvements in a first-phase *Economic and Trade Agreement Between the United States of America and the People's Republic of China* (hereinafter: "Sino-US ETA"),[40] so that there was no more reason to further delay legislation.

In spite of several remarkable reforms to the scope of protection and to patent enforcement, which will be treated in detail in the following explanations, the

37. More details in chapter 4, Copyright.
38. EPO announcement https://www.epo.org/searching-for-patents/helpful-resources/asian/asia-updates/2019/20190520.html, with references to the DRI's new English and Chinese websites.
39. Third amendment summarized by Peter Ganea, *supra* note 26.
40. Available on the USTR's website: https://ustr.gov/sites/default/files/files/agreements/phase%20one%20agreement/Economic_And_Trade_Agreement_Between_The_United_States_And_China_Text.pdf.

final amendment is much more conservative than earlier amendment proposals. A discussion draft of 2019 already abandoned quite a number of amendments proposed by a much more daring previous draft of 2015[41] and lessened the impact of some others, while proposing even harsher punitive measures against intentional large-scale infringement. The latest discussion draft released by the National People's Congress in June 2020 for gathering opinions from the public remained similarly conservative.

The fourth Patent Law amendment will enter into force on 1 June 2021,[42] so that the currently effective version of the Patent Law, which has been last amended in 2008, will remain in force for quite a while. For this reason, and also because all the quoted cases are based on it and the available secondary law still waits for being adapted to the amendment, the following explanations will also be based on the current version. Of course, whenever reference is made to a current Patent Law provision, any changes to its content entailed by the fourth amendment will be explained, and where a current provision has been moved within the law, its new location will be indicated. The amended Patent Law contains 82 articles, six more than the current version.

While the Patent Law reform has been pending over the past years, numerous neighbouring provisions such as the Patent Examination Guidelines and Supreme People's Court interpretations on the handling of infringement disputes, which are binding for the lower courts and contain detailed instructions on how to tackle certain aspects of patent litigation, have recently been amended or newly enacted.[43]

1. Facilitation of Access to Protection in Certain Technical Fields

An amendment to the Patent Examination Guidelines of 2014 permitted the inclusion of graphic user interfaces (GUI) in design applications, but only as element of the design of a physical product, so that GUI designs alone cannot be protected under the current rules.[44] This may change after the entry into force of the fourth Patent Law amendment, which explicitly extends design protection to "new designs of the shape, pattern or the combination shape and pattern of a product in its entirety or of its parts" (Article 2 (4) of the amended Patent Law). Moreover, since another amendment to the Examination Guidelines of 2019, embryonic stem cells are no longer categorically excluded from patented subject matter.[45] Also, as will be explained in detail below, several previous amendments to administrative provisions on the administration of pharmaceuticals gave rise to a rudimentary patent linkage, and after the fourth amendment's entry into force, a new Article 76 will provide a first legal basis for a full-fledged linkage mechanism.[46]

41. A synopsis of the current Patent Law and the proposal of 2015 as well as explanatory notes of CNIPA have until recently been available on CNIPA's website.
42. A consolidated version is available on CNIPA's website at https://www.cnipa.gov.cn/art/2020/11/23/art_97_155167.html.
43. More *infra* in section XIV.
44. See *infra* V. 2.
45. See *infra* VI. 6.
46. See *infra* XIV. 3.

In recent years, CNIPA has repeatedly amended its Examination Guidelines to facilitate access to patent protection in specific areas, which are deemed to be favourable for domestic industrial development, in particular by lowering the grant prerequisites for inventions in the area of software and biotechnology. An amendment of 2017 facilitated the drafting of software-related claims, but without abandoning the principle that a patentable invention must be a "technical" solution based on the laws of nature.[47] The most recent amendment of 31 December 2019[48] introduced detailed guidance on the patentability of algorithm and business method - implemented inventions, with ten examples of patentable and non-patentable subject matter, in order to adapt the patent system to the challenges posed by artificial intelligence (AI), internet-based inventions, blockchain technologies, etc., also considering that China has become the world's largest source of applications pertaining to AI.[49] However, as will be further outlined below,[50] this amendment only stretches the boundaries of the technicality principle without abandoning it. A complete abandonment would violate the legal definition of an invention in Article 2(2) of the superordinate Patent Law, according to which only "technical" subject matter is patentable. The scope of what will henceforth be regarded as "technical" enough to be patented has nevertheless been remarkably broadened. As will be discussed in more detail with regard to inventorship and patent ownership and with regard to the notion of the person skilled in the art, the recent enhancement of protection stops at improving the accessibility of the patent system for AI-related inventions made by humans. As far as can be seen, there are no concrete plans to further extend patent protection to inventions made by AI. The impact of machine-made inventions is nevertheless vividly discussed in academic circles, with frequent reference to the academic debates abroad.

The mentioned patent term extension of up to five years but not exceeding 14 years of effective protection in Article 42(3) of the amended Patent Law implements Article 1.12.2. b) of the Sino-US ETA.[51] The patent term extension will be further explained below within the broader context of an emerging patent linkage system.[52]

Finally, the amendment extended design protection from presently ten to 15 years (Article 42(2)) to enable China's accession to the Hague Agreement.

2. Fostering the Commercialization of Patented Subject Matter

A large part of the previous Patent Law draft amendment of 2015 had been dedicated to facilitating the commercialization of patents. It proposed, inter alia, an overhaul

47. See *infra* VI. 2.
48. Published by CNIPA on its website: https://www.cnipa.gov.cn/art/2019/12/31/art_527_146034.html; on 21 January 2020, CNIPA published its explanations on the amendment to Part II, Chapter 9 of the Examination Guidelines: https://www.cnipa.gov.cn/art/2020/1/21/art_66_11475.html; more *infra* in section VI. 2.
49. https://www.chinadaily.com.cn/a/201912/19/WS5dfae3d0a310cf3e3557f31d.html; see also https://www.rouse.com/magazine/news/patenting-artificial-intelligence-in-china-and-south-east-asia/; WIPO report "Technology Trends 2019 – Artificial Intelligence", https://www.wipo.int/edocs/pubdocs/en/wipo_pub_1055.pdf.
50. VI. 2.
51. See *supra* IV.
52. See *infra* XIV. 3.

of the provisions on service inventions and new rules on inventions made by public research organizations. Almost all of the employee-invention related draft provisions have been withdrawn by the drafts of 2019 and 2020, and also the final amendment did not readopt them. Furthermore. the amended Patent Law is void of numerous provisions of the 2015 draft on the qualification of patent attorneys, which aimed at a higher, uniform professional knowledge of patent attorneys, patent counsels, etc., probably because the opinion prevailed that these issues should be regulated by separate law.[53] What finally became law, however, is a voluntary uniform license registration system in the newly added Articles 50 – 52 that, according to CNIPA, is modelled after the "license of right" in Article 46 of the 1977 UK Patents Act[54] and also resembles the "Lizenzbereitschaft" (willingness to license) in Secs. 23 and 24 of the German Patent Act. It aims at encouraging licensing by universities and public research organizations, which are quite active in patenting but less so in putting their patents to good use.

3. Institutional and Legislative Reforms to Improve Patent Enforcement

The fourth Patent Law amendment further strengthened the mentioned administrative enforcement, which will henceforth be regulated in Articles 69 and 70 Patent Law, but not to the extent envisaged by the early draft of 2015. Civil litigation still plays a dominant role in IP, especially in patent enforcement. In 2018, 21,699 patent cases were newly tried by courts throughout China, an increase of 35.53 percent over the previous year.[55]

Recent reforms in the area of judicial enforcement included far-reaching institutional rearrangements. To foster the uniformity and quality of IP adjudication especially in technically demanding areas, in particular patent litigation, in 2014 three IP Courts on Intermediate People's Court level were established in those cities which accumulate most of China's IP case load, namely Beijing, Shanghai and Guangzhou.[56] The new Beijing IP Court took over the jurisdiction for first-instance appeals against re-examination, invalidation and other administrative IP decisions from the Beijing Intermediate People's Court No. 1, and all three IP courts have exclusive subject matter jurisdiction to hear civil patent (including utility models and designs), plant variety rights, semiconductor layout design, technical know-how and computer software cases, and to recognize famous trademarks, albeit within the confines of their local jurisdiction. That is, the ordinary Intermediate People's Courts in the municipalities of Shanghai and Beijing and in the province of Guangdong are no longer competent

53. More about the regulation of patent attorneys in section XI.
54. According SIPO explanations previously available on its website sipo.gov.cn; for more details see XII. *infra*.
55. CNIPA report ‚China Intellectual Property Protection Situation 2018', previously available on the SIPO website sipo.gov.cn; see also the Supreme People's Court's report "Judicial Intellectual Property Protection Situation 2018" at http://www.iprdaily.cn/news_21514.html.
56. Based on the SPC Provisions on the Jurisdiction of the Intellectual Property Courts of Beijing, Shanghai and Guangzhou of 27 October 2014, amended on 23 December 2020; original text at http://gongbao.court.gov.cn/Details/b7a6d56264c13d9d6ff2a573d7f88d.html, amendments at http://www.court.gov.cn/fabu-xiangqing-282671.html.

to hear technically challenging types of IP disputes but they still have subject-matter jurisdiction over technically less difficult subject matter, in particular copyright and trademark infringement. Intermediate People's Courts in other localities remain in charge of all kinds of IP disputes, including the technically challenging ones.

The establishment of IP Courts with special regard to technically difficult cases was accompanied by SPC's *Interim Communication on Several Issues regarding the Participation of Technical Investigators in Litigation of the Intellectual Property Courts* of 30 December 2014, which regulate the appearance of court-appointed technical appraisers in court to be questioned by the parties, etc., in accordance with Articles 76–79 of the Law on Civil Procedures on the appointment of experts by court or at request of a party. The SPC itself made first use of these new provisions, which, in spite of being addressed to the IP Courts, also allow other courts to apply them (Rule 10), by relying on the statements made by court-appointed experts in the landmark *Eli Lilly v. Watson* trial.[57]

Moreover, in January 2019 a new Intellectual Property Division has been established within the SPC. According to the SPC Provisions on Several Questions regarding the IP Division of 3 December 2018 (in force since 1 January 2019),[58] the new IP Division became the next higher instance for civil disputes related to patents, utility models (but not designs), plant varieties, integrated circuit layout designs, technical know-how, software and antitrust issues previously tried in one of the IP Courts, in an ordinary Intermediate People's Court or, rarely, in a Higher People's Court in the first instance, as well as for administrative appeals against re-examination or invalidation decisions pertaining to patents (including utility models and designs), plant variety rights and integrated circuit layout designs that are treated by the Beijing IP Court in the first instance. That is, post-Intermediate Court level jurisdiction over technical IP disputes will sooner or later shift from the Higher People's Courts to the new IP Division. This will especially affect the Beijing Higher People's Court, which had to cede not only its role as an important infringement court but also as the second-instance court in administrative appeals against PRB decisions to the IP Division. Its future insignificance in patent litigation should be kept in mind when reference is made to its previous landmark decisions and, especially, to its non-binding Guidelines for the Establishment of Patent Infringement[59] that it amended not long ago, in 2017, obviously without anticipating the above institutional rearrangements.

The Higher People's Courts will, however, continue to perform as second-instance courts in technically less difficult design, copyright and trademark cases, and also the Third Civil Tribunal of the SPC, thus far known as the "IP Tribunal", will remain the final instance for appeals in these "less technical" IP cases. Hearsay has it that the IP Tribunal will perform as the final appeal instance also for decisions rendered by the new IP Division, so that the relationship between these two chambers

57. See XIV. 5. c) *infra*.
58. https://www.chinacourt.org/law/detail/2018/12/id/149825.shtml, based on the Decision of the NPC's Standing Committee on Several Problems pertaining to Court Procedures in Patent and other Intellectual Property Cases of 26 October 2018 http://www.sohu.com/a/271595713_169411.
59. In English available on the site of China Patent Agent (H.K.): http://www.cpahkltd.com/EN/info.aspx?n=20170424155321600369.

within the SPC would be similar to the one between the US Court of Appeals for the Federal Circuit and the US Supreme Court.[60]

On the legislative side, the fourth amendment has strengthened strengthen procedural law, e.g., by facilitating proof of infringement and of damages, and further enhanced damage compensation. It also introduced more detailed stipulations regarding the scope of pre-trial injunctions, which will henceforth be regulated in Article 72, and simultaneously deleted the provisions on the deposit of a guarantee and deadlines, which are regulated in Article 66 of the current Patent Law but have become obsolete since the 2012 overhaul of the Law on Civil Procedures. According to the new Article 72, preliminary injunctions shall encompass property preservation as well as ordering or prohibiting the execution of a specific act, whereas the current Article 66 only regulates the order to cease from infringement.

The earlier Patent Law draft amendment of 2015 also proposed a strengthened administrative patent enforcement by local IP offices but most of these were taken back by the latest draft amendment of 2019, maybe to accommodate the mentioned objections from the US and the EU, which are reserved towards exposing their industries to this unfamiliar type of enforcement.[61] What finally became law after the fourth amendment are several rather undisputed provisions in a new Article 70 Patent Law, namely that upon the patent owner's or an interested parties' request, the central authority CNIPA can assume jurisdiction over cases of significant nation-wide impact, that, again at request of the patent owner or the interested party, the IP administration under the local government can bundle several administrative cases pertaining to the same patent within its regional jurisdiction, and that in case of cross-regional infringements, the IP administration under the People's Government on a higher level can be called upon.

With regard to patent litigation, three "interpretations" of the Supreme People's Court (SPC) will be of relevance for this chapter of the book,[62] namely the Provisions on Several Issues Concerning the Application of Law to Trial of Cases of Patent Disputes of 19 June 2001 (last amended on 23 December 2020; hereinafter "2001 Interpretations"),[63] the Interpretation on Several Issues concerning the Application of

60. Comparison made by Richard Li, Chuanshu Xu and Binxin Li, 'China's SPC Tribunal: Router manufacturer and seller liable for infringement even though patented method performed by a third party', Kluwer Patent Blog http://patentblog.kluweriplaw.com/2020/03/03/chinas-spc-ip-tribunal-router-manufacturer-and-seller-liable-for-infringement-even-though-patented-method-performed-by-a-third-party/.

61. Mark Cohen, David Kappos and Randall Rader, 'Faux Amis: China–U.S. Patent Administrative Enforcement Comparison', 4 *China Patents & Trademarks* (2016), 33 et seq.

62. A few older interpretations such as the SPC interpretation of 2001 on patent-specific pre-trial evidence preservation and provisional measures will not be treated here because they are largely outdated, see Peter Ganea, 'Zur Reform des einstweiligen Rechtsschutzes im geistigen Eigentum der Volksrepublik China' (On the reform of the P.R.C's preliminary measures system), 4 *Zeitschrift für chinesisches Recht* (Journal of Chinese Law) (2017), 288.

63. 2015 version in the SPC's online gazette http://gongbao.court.gov.cn/Details/02326e4b886fd5536a16c0b08db79c.html; 2020 amendment at http://www.court.gov.cn/fabu-xiangqing-282671.html.

Law in the Trial of Patent Infringement Dispute Cases of 28 December 2009[64] (hereinafter "2009 Interpretations") and the Interpretation on Several Issues concerning the Application of Law in the Trial of Patent Infringement Dispute Cases (II) of 25 January 2016 (amended on 23 Dec. 2020) (hereinafter "Interpretations II").[65]

The above interpretations provide guidance on the intricacies of claim interpretation and other subject matter. In parts, they can be regarded as codification of former landmark case law. Rule 28 of the latest Interpretations II, for instance, contains a unique rule that courts shall acknowledge and apply legitimate compensation amounts or damage calculation methods agreed upon by the parties if requested so during trial. The provision is very likely based on the preceding SPC's *Zhongshang Longcheng v. Hubei Tongba* decision of 7 December 2013,[66] which, contrary to the preceding first and second instance decisions, acknowledged the validity of such an agreement reached in a preceding court mediation, according to which the defendant shall pay RMB 1 million in damages if he infringed the plaintiff's patent again. The Interpretations II also contain China's first, albeit rather limited,[67] provision on indirect patent infringement, a concept that the legislature had explicitly refused to adopt in the course of the third amendment to the Patent Act, referring, *inter alia*, to the difficulties that indirect liability could pose to innocent suppliers of means that can be used for patent infringement. The 2015 Patent Law draft amendment contained a similar provision, which, however, has been removed from the two subsequent drafts of 2019 and 2020 and also the final amendment has not reintroduced a corresponding stipulation.

The draft of 2019 still contained a unique "notice and take down" rule initially proposed by the 2015 draft to emphasize the liability of online trading platforms like *Taobao* and *Tianmao* for not taking timely measures against clients who used their platforms for the sale of patent infringing goods after a right owner's notice. The 2019 proposal significantly lessened the provider liability as compared to the proposal of 2015, stating that a provider could only be held jointly liable if it remained passive towards right owner notifications of infringement that are "based on a people's court's judgment, ruling or mediation decision or an injunction decision issued by a patent administration", i.e., if they failed to remove links, etc., in spite of such substantiated request. The preceding draft of 2015 instead allowed establishment of liability merely on the grounds that the provider "knew or should have known" about the infringing use, or that he remained passive in spite of the receipt of a "valid" notification from the patent owner. This version had been criticized for imposing a too harsh duty of care on internet service providers and for facilitating the abusive assertion of patents. The proposed provision was to be understood as a patent-specific interpretation of Article 36 of the Tort Liability Law of 2009 (which,

64. In Chinese: http://gongbao.court.gov.cn/Details/4b8770fa8e9ced993f7a4b2edffeb8.html.
65. 2016 version at http://gongbao.court.gov.cn/Details/409a66a5e85613e92594a31b410220.html; 2020 amendment at http://www.court.gov.cn/fabu-xiangqing-282671.html.
66. 16 *Min To Zi* (2013), summarized in the WIPO Collection of Leading Judgments on Intellectual Property Rights – People's Republic of China (2011–2018), p. 65 et seq. in the English version; both the English and Chinese versions of the collection can be downloaded from: https://www.wipo.int/publications/en/details.jsp?id=4477.
67. Further details in XIV. 4. *infra*.

as has been mentioned in the Introduction and will be further explained in the Part on Copyright, has recently been transferred to the newly enacted Civil Code) that regulates a general joint and several liability of inert web service providers for rights infringements committed by their clients, which has already been applied to the online sale of patent infringing goods.[68] The most recent draft of June 2020, however, removed this rather unusual provision on patent-specific provider liability and also the final amendment did not readopt it.

4. Suppression of Practices Deemed to be Abusive

As already mentioned, a good part of the third amendment of 2008 has been dedicated to suppressing acts perceived as abusive, e.g., by adopting absolute novelty as patentability prerequisite and by strengthening compulsory licensing. The fourth amendment introduced a general rule in a newly drafted Article 20 according to which patent exploitation shall conform to the principle of good faith. This new provision could be applied, for instance, to prevent the bad-faith assertion of patents by so-called non-performing entities or by holders of standard-essential patents (SEP). The amended Article 20 (1), furthermore, prohibits abuses that harm the public interest *or* the legitimate rights and interests of others, or that prevent or restrict competition, just as preceding draft amendment of 2020. The previous draft of 2019 still required harm to both the public interest *and* to the legitimate rights and interests of others as a prerequisite for the establishment of patent abuse, so that the finally amended text rendered it even easier for courts to deny infringement due to the plaintiff's alleged patent abuse. The amendment also added a clarification in Article 20 (2) that prevention or restriction of competition shall be dealt with under the Antimonopoly Law. The more concrete provisions on the abuse of market power derived from SEP proposed by the 2015 draft, however, were removed from the subsequent drafts of 2019 and 2020 and were also not reintroduced by the final amendment. SEPs will be treated summarily below[69] and, in greater detail, in Chapter 5 of this book on Unfair Competition and Antitrust Law.

V. PROTECTION PREREQUISITES

1. Novelty, Inventiveness and Utility of Inventions and Utility Models

Due to their similarity in terms of the above three main protection prerequisites, this section will treat patents and utility models together, whereas the prerequisites for design protection will be separately explained in the following section.

According to Article 22(1) Patent Law, patentable inventions and utility models shall be new, inventive[70] and fit for practical use. Moreover, the legal definitions of

68. *Weihai Jiayi v. Tianmao Mall* decision of Zhejiang Higher People's Court, 186 *Zhe Zhi Zhong Zi* (2015) 17 November 2015, summarized in WIPO Collection of Leading Judgments on Intellectual Property Rights (*supra* note 66), 69 et seq. in the English version.

69. XIII. 3. *infra*.

70. Actually "creative" if directly translated from Chinese, and "creative" is also used in the authoritative English translation on the WIPOLex site: https://www.wipo.int/edocs/

a patentable invention (Article 2(2) Patent Law) and of a utility model (Article 2(3) Patent Law) prescribe that both must be "technical" solutions. Consequently, Article 25(2) Patent Law excludes rules and methods for intellectual activity from patent protection. The fourth Patent Law amendment left all these provisions unchanged. In principle, most business methods should be subsumable under "rules and methods for intellectual activities" but an amendment to the Examination Guidelines of 2017 clarified that business methods that incorporate technical features shall not be automatically excluded from protection just because they are business methods.[71] The legislative aim of this amendment has been to facilitate access to patent protection for enterprises that innovate internet-based technical solutions.[72]

(a) Novelty

(1) Worldwide Novelty

Patentable inventions and utility models require absolute novelty, a feature introduced by the third Patent Law amendment of 2008. Until then, only subject matter *published* worldwide before the application date, e.g. in journals, pamphlets, etc., pertained to prior art and therefore destroyed the novelty of a later filed application, but not subject matter that had been in *public use* outside China. Novelty-destroying prior public use had been limited to uses within China, so that it had been possible to obtain patents for subject matter that had already been in public use abroad, and then to prevent the original inventor from entering the Chinese market. Since the 2008 amendment, also subject matter publicly used abroad pertains to prior art. The introduction of such "absolute novelty" was controversial, but ultimately the interest in enhancing the overall quality of patented subject matter prevailed over concerns that foreign enterprises may henceforth find it easier to challenge patents with reference to prior public use abroad.[73]

(2) Priority

Article 29(1) Patent Law permits an international priority of 12 months for patent and utility model applications, and of six months for design applications. According to Article 29(2), invention and utility model applicants can also claim domestic priority for a period of 12 months. The fourth Patent Law amendment introduced

---

lexdocs/laws/en/cn/cn028en.pdf; the following explanations, however, will stick with conventional patent terminology and use the terms "inventive" and "non-obvious".

71. New Item (2) to Part II, Chapter 1, 4.2, of the Examination Guidelines, pursuant to which "a claim that contains not only business rules and methods but also technical features shall not be excluded from patent protection under Article 25 Patent Law", see also VI. 2. *infra*.
72. Lv Dejun et al., 'Expert Interpretation of Recent Amendments to the Guidelines of Patent Examination', 2 *China Patents & Trademarks* (2017), 19 et seq.
73. A thorough overview of the discussion is given by Bu Yuanshi, 'Prerequisites for Protection', in Stefan Luginbuehl and Peter Ganea (eds.), *Patent Law in Greater China* (Edward Elgar, 2014), 49 et seq.

a domestic priority also for designs[74] and provides more generous deadlines so that applicants for inventions and utility model will henceforth have 16 months instead of three months after the application date to hand in a copy of the original application (Article 30 of the amended Patent Law).

(3) First-to-File and Conflicting Applications

Applications are "conflicting" if they are filed prior to a later application of identical content but published after such later application. True to the first-to-file principle, such earlier conflicting application destroys the novelty of the later application, even if it has been unpublished at the later application's filing date. The basic provision is contained in Article 22(2) Patent Law which, with regard to inventions and utility models, states that novelty is given if the invention-creation does not pertain to prior art, and if any entity or individual has not filed a prior application for the same subject matter, which has been published or announced in the patent application documents after the date of the later application. Important to note is that the term "any entity or individual", unlike the pre-2008 version of the Patent Law which referred to "other entity or individual", may also include the applicant of the later application himself. The previous version enabled applicants to file follow-up applications with amended claims before the publication of the earlier application. Since 2008, such later filed applications that contain subject matter of an earlier application do no longer fulfil the novelty requirement. Applicants who frequently file applications in a specific technical field are therefore well advised to ascertain that their applications do not disclose content that may become subject matter of a later application. Also, they should be cautious with regard to all patent documents, not only the claims, as Article 22(2) clearly refers to the whole "patent documents" that may contain content prejudicial to the novelty of a later application. Part II, Chapter 3, 2.2 of the Examination Guidelines instructs examiners to not limit the search for compromising subject matter to the claims, but to extend it to the description and, where applicable, to the drawings of the earlier application. The Examination Guidelines further clarify that an earlier PCT application that has entered the national phase and is published on or after the date of filing the later application is a conflicting application.

If two or more applicants file applications for the same invention separately, the patent shall be granted to the first applicant (Article 9(2) Patent Law). True to the first-to-file principle, the earliest application will destroy the novelty of the later ones, even if the earliest application is abandoned by the applicant.

Finally, with regard to different applicants filing applications of the same invention on the same date, Rule 41(1) of the current Implementing Regulations, which were last amended on 9 January 2010 and will have to be adapted to the Patent Law revision before its entry into force on 1 June 2021, provides that the applicants, after being notified by CNIPA, shall consult with each other and determine an applicant. Part II, Chapter 3, 6.2.1 of the Examination Guidelines further details that in case in which one applicant does not respond to the notification, his application shall be deemed to have been withdrawn, and if the applicants respond but do not reach

74. More details in V. 2. a) *infra*.

an agreement about the assignment of the application right, all applications shall be rejected.

(4) *Double Application of Invention and Utility Model Patent*

A related, quite controversially discussed question has been resolved by the third amendment to the Patent Act, by a new Article 9(1), which provides an exception to the ban on double patenting set forth in the same provision's first sentence ("*Only one patent can be granted for the same invention*") if certain conditions are met. The amended Article 9(1) permits double applications for invention patent and utility model, which enables applicants to obtain preliminary utility model protection after a quick formal examination for the duration of substantive invention patent application. The need for preliminary utility model protection had been especially pressing until two decades ago, when examination as to substance took several years due to lack of resources. The situation has constantly improved since then, but the legislature nevertheless considered an opportunity to obtain early utility model protection necessary and in 2008 clarified the legal provisions accordingly.[75]

Allowable double applications have to satisfy several prerequisites. Article 9(1) provides a) that at the time of grant of the invention patent, utility model protection must still be in force to avoid the revival of an already expired patent, and b) that after substantive examination, the invention patent will only be granted if the applicant revokes the utility model to avoid the coexistence of two parallel rights for the same subject matter. Moreover, Rule 41(2) et seq. Implementing Regulations require the applicant to declare in each of his two applications that he has simultaneously applied for the other kind of patent and regulate in great detail the procedure of revoking the utility model to be replaced by the invention patent. The amended rules ensure a seamless transformation of one protection right into the other, so that they appear as one right granted for a protection term of no longer than 20 years from the earliest application.

Finally, double application for invention patent and utility model is only permissible by way of simultaneous filing of two domestic applications. Simultaneously filing a PCT invention application and a domestic utility model application or splitting up a PCT application entering the national phase into a domestic invention and a domestic utility model application is not permissible.[76]

(5) *Grace Period*

Pursuant to Article 24 Patent Law, an invention does not lose its novelty if, within six months prior to the application, it has been exhibited for the first time in an international exhibition sponsored or recognized by the Chinese government or disclosed in the course of a specified academic conference. A grace period of six months is, furthermore, available for inventions which have been disclosed by a third

75. More about the history of double patenting in Bu Yuanshi, *supra* note 73, 57 et seq.
76. Toby Mak, 'Utility Models', in Stefan Luginbuehl and Peter Ganea (eds.), *Patent Law in Greater China* (Edward Elgar, 2014), 365 et seq.

party without the applicant's consent. The fourth Patent Law amendment extended the grace period in Article 24 to cases in which the invention is published prior to the application for the sake of the public interest during a national emergency or other exceptional circumstances. This addition has probably been motivated by the Corona pandemic. Rule 30 Implementing Regulations specifies that the above exhibitions and scientific conferences have to be "international exhibitions which are registered with or recognized by the International Exhibitions Bureau as stipulated by the International Exhibitions Convention" or "academic or technological meetings organized by a competent department of the State Council or by a national academic or technological association". They further prescribe that the applicant has to indicate such early disclosure in the application documents. In cases in which the invention has been divulged without the applicant's consent, CNIPA may require further evidentiary documents about the incident. Part II, Chapter 3, Sec. 5 Examination Guidelines explains the specific character of a grace period, which is not to be confused with priority that reserves the applicant a specific date after which others are blocked from filing applications. A grace period merely protects the applicant against a novelty-destroying premature disclosure of his own invention. This means for CNIPA that if another party independently files an application for the same invention during the grace period, the party that had relied on the grace period would be banned from filing a later application, due to the first-to-file principle. However, the even earlier disclosure that triggered the grace period would also destroy the novelty of the interfering application. Reportedly, the grace period does not play a major role in examination practice.[77]

(b) Inventiveness

According to the definition in Article 22(3) Patent Law, inventiveness means that "as compared with the existing technologies, the invention possesses prominent substantive features and indicates remarkable progress, and the utility model possesses substantive features and indicates progress." That is, an invention must possess "prominent" substantive features and represent a "remarkable" technical progress, whereas mere substantive features and a mere technical progress are sufficient for utility model protection.

Examination of inventiveness proceeds in three steps, namely a) by identification of the closest prior art, b) by identifying the distinct features of the invention and of the solution it provides for a technical problem in comparison with such prior art and c) by assessing whether such features are sufficiently non-obvious to a skilled artisan.[78] An amendment to the Examination Guidelines of 23 September 2019 (in

77. Wan Xiaoli, 'The Patent Novelty Grace Period in China in Comparative Perspective', *IIC* (2009), 182.

78. Examination Guidelines, Part II, Chapter 4, 3.2.1.1, see also Bu Yuanshi *supra* note 73; He Huaiwen, 'Assessing Inventiveness in Patent Invalidation Procedure', 4 *China Patents & Trademarks* (2012), 7, downloadable from http://www.cpt.cn/uploadfiles/20121025162216306.Pdf.

force since 1 November 2019)[79] further detailed the second step of identifying the distinct features of the invention and their role in solving the technical problem. The pre-amendment text stated that during this step, the examiner shall determine the distinct features in comparison with the closest prior art and then by determining the technical problem to be solved on the basis of the technical effect achieved by these features. The amendment clarified that such examination shall be limited to effects achieved "within the claimed invention", and not extend to effects identified by comparing prior art with each feature *per se*. Also, the examiner's determination of the technical problem to be solved by the invention may differ from the technical problem indicated in the description, depending on the closest prior art identified by the examiner, which, again, may be different from that indicated in the description. In such case, the closest prior art found by the examiner shall form the base for (re) determining the technical problem. Any technical effect disclosed by the description can be used for such redetermination, as long as it is comprehensible to a skilled artisan.[80] The amendment of 2019 added a sentence to this provision, stressing that where several technical features support each other functionally and are interrelated with regard to their effect, the technical effect these features produce, again, within the claimed invention, shall be comprehensively determined in consideration of their interdependence.[81]

An invention-creation is sufficiently inventive if it is non-obvious to a person skilled in the art. Part II, Chapter 4, 2.4 of the Examination Guidelines contains the only official definition of this person:

> The person skilled in the art refers to a fictional "person", who is presumed to be aware of all the common technical knowledge and have access to all the technologies existing before the filing date or the priority date in the technical field to which the invention pertains, and have capacity to apply all the routine experimental means before that date. However, he is not presumed to have creativity. If the technical problem to be solved impels that person to seek technical means in other technical fields, he should also be presumed to have access to the relevant prior art, common technical knowledge and routine experimental means in the other technical field before the filing date or the priority date.

The international debate[82] whether AI with the ability to invent necessitates a different definition of the person skilled in a specific art towards a multiskilled artisan or even a "multiskilled machine" with the ability to overlook several technical fields is sporadically addressed in academic circles[83] but concrete legislative proposals on this issue are not yet in place.

---

79. https://www.cnipa.gov.cn/art/2019/9/25/art_74_27623.html; CNIPA's explanatory notes (Chinese) at: https://www.cnipa.gov.cn/art/2019/10/30/art_66_11489.html.
80. Examination Guidelines, Part II, Chapter 4, 3.2.1.1 (2).
81. See CNIPA's explanations, *supra* note 79.
82. For instance by the EPO: http://documents.epo.org/projects/babylon/eponet.nsf/0/3918F57B010A3540C125841900280653/$File/AI_inventorship_summary_of_answers_en.pdf.
83. Wu Handong, 'Rengong zhineng shengcheng de faming de zhuanli zhi wen' (Questions of patenting AI-generated inventions), 4 *Dangdai Faxue* (Contemporary Law Review) (2019), 24 et seq.

With regard to inventions, the Examination Guidelines provide further guidance on the extension of the search to such neighbouring fields, which, since their amendment of 2019, not only include "functionally" similar technical fields but also technical fields that are "similar in terms of use".[84] That is, if prior art that performs a similar function or serves a similar use cannot be found in the immediate technical field of the invention but in neighbouring fields, the examiner has to consider prior art in all these fields.

In contrast, the search for prior art prejudicial to the inventiveness of utility models is normally limited to the immediate technical field to which the utility model belongs. As utility models are granted without substantive examination, so that their inventiveness can only be assessed during an invalidation procedure, detailed guidance on how to tell apart the different inventiveness levels for inventions and utility models is given in Part IV of the Examination Guidelines on "Examination of Requests for Re-examination and for Invalidation", Chapter 6, Sec. 4:

> For an invention, the examiner shall consider not only the technical field to which the invention belongs, but also proximate or relevant technical fields, and those other technical fields in which the problem to be solved by the invention would prompt a person skilled in the art to look for technical means.
>
> For a utility model, the examiner will normally focus on the technical field to which the utility model belongs. Where there is a clear technical teaching, for example, where there is an explicit description in the prior art, to prompt a person skilled in the art to look for technical means in a proximate or relevant technical field, the proximate or relevant technical field may be considered.

That is, during the third step of the three-step assessment of inventiveness, the skilled artisan may find the utility model obvious only if it is not sufficiently distinct from prior art found in the immediate technical field to which it belongs, unless the prior art clearly hints at other technical fields to be considered. The immediate field to which the utility model belongs has traditionally been understood as the class of the International Patent Classification for which the utility model has been registered.[85] Reportedly, an SPC decision further facilitated the narrowing down of the relevant prior art, to prior solutions that do not only have to perform the same function but also have to achieve the same effect. That is, a prior technical solution that only functions in the same way as the utility model but does not simultaneously achieve the same effect can be disregarded as prior art.[86]

84. Part II, Chapter 7, 5.3; the amendment also deleted the concrete examples contained in the previous version.
85. Explicitly regulated by the Examination Guidelines, Part II, Chapter 2, 2.2.2 with regard to the examination, but the same standard is applied when determining the relevant prior art in the invalidation procedure, see Oliver Pfaffenzeller, Ming Deng and Xia Pfaffenzeller, 'Die Herausforderung durch chinesische Gebrauchsmuster', *Mitteilungen der deutschen Patentanwälte* (2014), 101 et seq.
86. *Dynamometer* decision, quoted by Oliver Pfaffenzeller, Xia Pfaffenzeller, Ming Deng and Beat Weibel, 'Analysis and Suggestions for Reform of Existing Problems in China's Utility Model System', 2 *China Patents & Trademarks* (2019), 34.

Due to these low requirements as to inventiveness, utility models are very likely to remain unscathed in invalidation procedures and, consequently, to become a dangerous weapon in a parallel infringement litigation.[87] Considering the enormous amount of not substantively examined utility models that are almost exclusively granted to domestic applicants (in 2019, only 8,069 out of 1,574,205 grants went to foreigners[88]), they pose a considerable risk to foreign enterprises doing business in China.

Finally, in a new Section 6 to Part II, Chapter 9, the CNIPA has recently introduced guidance on assessing the inventiveness of inventions that incorporate algorithms or business methods, with concrete examples of which kind is inventive enough to be patented and which not. Most crucial is that inventiveness of an algorithm or a business method can only be established if it is closely connected with the technical features in a functional respect. More detailed information, including the examples, will be given below.[89]

(c) "Practical Use"/Industrial Application

The prerequisite of industrial application or, pursuant to Article 22(4) Patent Law, "practical use", seems to be a rather unproblematic one. It means that the respective invention or utility model can be used for production or otherwise, and that it is capable of producing positive results. Requiring ability to produce "positive results" obviously aims at excluding senseless inventions that do not strive for any improvement, whereas inventions producing harmful results are already excluded under Article 5(1) Patent Law ("Patent rights shall not be granted for invention-creations that violate the law or social ethics, or harm the public interest").[90] Part II, Chapter 5, 3 of the Examination Guidelines regulates in more detail that inventions that are non-reproducible violate the laws of nature, result in products that are in need of unique natural conditions, pertain to surgical methods for non-treatment purposes (surgical methods for treatment purposes are already excluded as non-patentable subject matter[91]) or to methods of measuring physiological parameters of human or animal bodies under extreme conditions (inter alia, due to their non-reproducibility as each body reacts differently to extreme conditions) or produce no effective result, do not meet the requirement of industrial application.

2. Designs: Novelty, Distinctiveness, No Conflict with Prior Rights and Special Provisions on Graphical User Interface (GUI) Designs

Just like utility models, designs are not substantively examined, so that their compliance with the design-specific protection prerequisites in Article 23 Patent Law

87. See Oliver Pfaffenzeller, Ming Deng and Xia Pfaffenzeller, *supra* note 85, with reference to the famous *Schneider v. Chint* case, in which the defendant, after failing to have the plaintiff's utility model in-validated, had to pay a record compensation of RMB 157 million.
88. Annual Report 2019, http://english.cnipa.gov.cn/col/col2159/index.html ("Appendix I – Statistics").
89. VI. 2 *infra*.
90. See also VI. 6 *infra*.
91. VI. 5. *infra*.

(novelty, distinct difference from existing designs or design combinations, no conflict with prior rights) can only be assessed after grant, during an invalidation procedure. In view of 536,251 designs granted in 2018 alone, 517,693 of them to domestic applicants,[92] the danger of being accused of design infringement is relatively high. To counter the abusive assertion of worthless design patents, the 2008 amendment to the Patent Law introduced a new provision in Article 61(2) (Article 66(2) after the fourth amendment's entry into force), stating that People's Courts or IP administrations may instruct the right holder or any interested party (e.g., the holder of an exclusive license with the right to sue in court) to request CNIPA to furnish an evaluation report about the design's conformity with the protection requirements.[93] Before the amendment, such report could only be requested for utility models. According to the former SIPO, 20,000 design evaluation reports were requested in 2016.[94]

According to the Examination Guidelines, CNIPA must finish a design evaluation report within two months.[95] In infringement litigation practice, the court will then normally resort to the report as an important piece of evidence, but it is not bound by its findings. That is, even if the report implies a high likelihood of validity, the court may still suspend litigation to wait for the PRB's decision if the evidence provided by the defendant is sufficiently persuasive. As an alternative to invalidation, defendants may also raise the "prior art defence".[96]

(a) Novelty

Pursuant to Article 23 Patent Law, a design patent can only be granted for designs that do not pertain to an existing design, including subject matter of a previously filed conflicting application, which is published on or after the actual filing date. "Existing" respectively "identical" designs comprise aesthetic solutions that are "substantially identical", and such identity must be determined through a comprehensive comparison of the two designs. Whereas "identity" means total identity of the outer appearance, allowing only differences pertaining to commonly used materials, function, performance but also dimensions of products intended for the same use,[97] "substantial identity" means noticeable but not essential differences, e.g., between identically ornamented cookie jars, one in form of a cube, the other in form of a cuboid,[98] or between multiple-use products that are not used in exactly the same manner, as long as they can also be used in the same manner, as, for instance, two quartz watches with different functions. When examining identity or

92. Statistical data for 2018 on CNIPA's website http://english.cnipa.gov.cn/col/col2076/index.html.
93. More details about the evaluation report for utility models and designs in section IX *infra*.
94. According to news previously published on sipo.gov.cn.
95. Part V, Chapter 10, 4.
96. More in X. 2. g) *infra*.
97. Part IV, Chapter V, 5.1.1 of the Examination Guidelines gives the example of identically designed watches, one mechanical, one quartz. They are still absolutely and not only "substantively" identical because they have the same outer appearance and are intended for the same use.
98. Part IV, Chapter V, 5.1.2 of the Examination Guidelines gives further examples of substantive identity.

substantive identity, the PRB examiner has to compare the designs at issue through a "normal consumer's" naked eye, i.e., without the help of magnifying glasses or comparable equipment.[99]

Part IV, Chapter V, 4 Examination Guidelines defines the normal consumer as a person with a certain knowledge about the variety of designs within a certain product category, i.e., such person must be defined differently with regard to each design category, but not to the extent that he or she is regarded as a professional expert in the respective design field.[100] Thus, the Chinese "normal consumer" can be compared with the "informed consumer" according to EU law. Identity shall be assessed by comparing the noticeable design elements of both solutions, but not to parts which normally do not draw the attention of the normal consumer, which may be hidden parts such as the rotors of an A/C device, or common design elements, i.e., usual elements of design that re-occur in the particular product category and are often dictated by the function of the product. In case of combined products that are disassembled during normal use, e.g., an electric water heater consisting of a kettle and a heater, the comparison shall be limited to the whole product in assembled form, whereas in case of designs pertaining to card or board games, where a fixed assembled form is not given and the normal consumer's observation is rather focused on each single component (e.g. the single card or chess figure), the comparative assessment should also include the single components.[101] In case of products that appear in variable state, only the state(s) when in use shall be considered.[102]

Certain product categories that leave little room for design variations became an issue of contradicting PRB and subsequent administrative court decisions. In the frequently quoted "motorcycle wheel case",[103] the PRB decided to invalidate the design patent for a motorcycle wheel because of substantive similarity with a previous wheel design, the critical design element being the spokes which were shaped in a pattern almost identical to the prior design. The following appeal instances, the Beijing Intermediate People's Court No. 1 and the Beijing Higher People's Court, overturned the PRB's decision, stating that apart from the rim and the hub of the wheel, also the spokes were largely dictated by the product's function, so that the leeway for alternative designs was very limited. The shape of the spokes therefore pertained to "common design elements" that were largely disregarded by the normal consumer, whereas smaller variations would be more noticeable. Upon comparing the wheels, both court instances found such differences, e.g., rod holes in the hub of the design at issue, which were not included in the prior design, and stated that they were of sufficient significance to deny identity between the two designs. The SPC, however,

99. Examination Guidelines, Part IV, Chapter V, 5.2.2.
100. Some commentators actually suggested to confine such fictional person to design experts, see Zhong Hua, 'A Study of Improvement of Design Determination Methods', 3 *China Patents & Trademarks* (2011), 30, online at: http://www.cpt.cn/uploadfiles/20110708083523085.pdf.
101. Examination Guidelines, Part IV, Chapter V, 5.2.5.1.
102. Examination Guidelines, Part IV, Chapter V, 5.2.5.2, without examples, however.
103. See, e.g., Deng Ming, 'Designs', in Stefan Luginbuehl and Peter Ganea (eds), *Patent Law in Greater China* (Edward Elgar, 2014), 373; Zhong Hua, *supra* note 100.

found that room for variation also existed with regard to the shape of the spokes, and found enough similarity to uphold the PRB decision to invalidate the patent.[104]

Article 29(2) of the present Patent Law acknowledges domestic priority of 12 months only for invention and utility model applications, not for design applications. For designs, only foreign priority can be claimed (Article 29(1)). The details of acknowledging foreign design priority are regulated in Section 9 of Part IV, Chapter V of the Examination Guidelines. As mentioned, the fourth Patent Law amendment added to Article 29(2) a domestic priority of six months also for designs. The amendment proposal of 2015, which already proposed an extension of protection to partial designs, justified domestic design priority with the need for more flexibility after the introduction of partial design protection, that domestic applicants shall find it easier to make amendments, to file divisional applications, etc. This justification has lost much of its cogency after the removal of partial design protection from the draft of 2019, but regained it since the latest draft of June 2020 and finally also the fourth amendment readopted it.

(b) Distinctiveness

Distinctiveness, which can be compared with the "individual character" prerequisite under EU law, is required by Article 23(2) Patent Law as follows:

> Designs for which the patent right is to be granted shall be ones which are distinctly different from the existing designs or the combinations of the features of existing designs.

Section 6 of Part IV, Chapter V of the Examination Guidelines contains further guidance on how to establish distinctiveness. Not sufficiently distinct are a) designs that are not significantly different from prior designs from the same or from neighbouring product categories, b) designs that are the result of transformation of a prior design from the same or from a neighbouring category, provided that differences between the two are non-existent or insignificant and the prior design inspired such transformation, and c) designs resulting from a combination of prior designs or design elements from the same or neighbouring product categories, provided that the differences between the design at issue and the prior aesthetic solutions are non-existent or insignificant and that the prior design inspired such combination. When assessing difference according to a), the examiner shall consider the overall visual impact created by the two designs and concentrate on those elements that are clearly visible and do not pertain to commonly known shapes within the respective category, and also disregard shapes that are entirely dictated by the function of the design product. Also, a design of a foldable or extendable product that is hardly distinguishable from a prior design in a specific state of use can still be patentable if it provides distinct views in its other states of use.[105] In case of designs that appear to result from the transformation of a prior design or a combination of prior designs, the examiner shall examine whether

104. 5 *Xing Ti Zi* (2010); see also He Huaiwen, 'Chinese Design Patent: Concept of "Normal Consumer" and Degree of Freedom of Designer', 1 *China Patents & Trademarks* (2012), 38, online at: http://www.cpt.cn/uploadfiles/20120130154602661.Pdf.

105. Deng Ming, *supra* note 103, 373.

the prior design obviously "inspired" such transformation or combination. Pursuant to the Examination Guidelines, inspiration must be assumed if the design has been modelled after the prior design of another product that may belong to another category, but also if the design is modelled after simple geometrical shapes or existing buildings or natural objects or sceneries. A combination of prior designs is inspired by prior designs if it aggregates prior design elements from the same or from a neighbouring product category, if it adopts a prior design and replaces some of its design elements by elements from another prior design or if it combines the shape of a prior design with the pattern and colour of another prior design.

The Examination Guidelines also stress that even if a design has been inspired by prior art, the PRB may exceptionally find it worthy of protection if it is still capable of producing a unique visual effect.

(c) No Conflict with Prior Rights

The "no conflict with legitimately acquired rights" invalidation ground pursuant to Article 23(3) Patent Law is somewhat peculiar because it does not involve a comparison with prior art to assess whether the patented design at issue is not worthy of being protected due to lack of novelty or distinctiveness. Instead, the examiner has to examine whether the design belongs to someone else and has been usurped by the current design patent owner.[106]

Conflict with prior rights is also termed a "relative ground for invalidation" because it is related to the infringement of another parties right, whereas invalidation due to lack of novelty, etc., would form "absolute grounds for invalidation". Conflict with prior rights is also different from the concept of "unlawful misappropriation" under German patent law, which, by the way, gives reason not only to invalidation, but also to revocation of an application and transfer of the unlawfully misappropriated patent to its true owner, in that the usurped subject matter does not necessarily have to be the design of another product but may also be a work, a mark, a name, etc., or the distinctive name, package or decoration of a product (Rule 12 of the 2001 SPC Interpretations as amended in 2020).

Unlike their preceding version that had been in force between 2001 and 2010, the present Implementing Regulations no longer require the requesting party to furnish a previous court decision or administrative judgment confirming the infringement of the prior right. According to Rule 66(3), providing evidence of infringement is sufficient. The PRB then has to assess on its own whether a prior right has been infringed,[107] which can become problematic if a court arrives at the opposite result in a parallel infringement suit. This has indeed occurred in parallel invalidation and infringement proceedings in the *Xinyoushi liquor bottle box* case, in which the SPC on 26 December 2012[108] rejected the defendant's appeal against the Chongqing Higher People's Court's decision that the design at issue violated Article 5(2) of

106. Zhu Li (judge of the SPC's IP Tribunal), 'Relative Grounds for Invalidation and Optimization of Design Patent Invalidation System – Centred on Conflict of Rights', 2 *China Patents & Trademarks* (2018), 10 et seq.
107. Zhu Li, *supra* note 106.
108. 627 *Min Shen Zi* (2012).

the old Unfair Competition Law on the unauthorized use of the name packaging, decoration of well-known goods of another party, whereas the PRB arrived at the conclusion that the design was not sufficiently similar to the plaintiff's trade dress to be invalidated.[109] To avoid such situation, prominent judges opine that in case of a conflict between the invalidation and the infringement decision, priority shall be given to the latter, and that a design may always be invalidated on grounds of an infringement decision that finds conflict with prior rights.[110]

Finally, according to the general provision in Article 45 Patent Law, "any unit or individual" may request invalidation due to conflict with prior rights, whereas Part IV, Chapter 3. 3.2 Examination Guidelines expressly limits the parties entitled to requests to the "owners of a prior right or interested parties". This contradiction between the Patent Law and the lower-ranking Examination Guidelines became apparent in two cases. In the *Showa Ceramics* case, in which the requesting party filed a request for invalidation of a soup cup design, stating that it would infringe upon a tableware maker's copyright, the PRB found that the requesting party failed to prove its eligibility to claim invalidation as a right owner or interested party according to the Examination Guidelines, whereas the Beijing Intermediate People's Court No. 1, back then in charge of accepting appeals against administrative decisions, confirmed the admissibility of the request, as the Patent Law would not limit the parties entitled to file. On 14 November 2013 the same court, after having been confirmed by the appeal decision of Beijing Higher People's Court, submitted a judicial suggestion to the PRB that said provision in subsection 3.2 in Part IV, Chapter 3 of the Examination Guidelines should be cancelled,[111] which the PRB forcefully refuted in a reply. In the later *Staples design* invalidation case of 2016, however, both the Beijing Intermediate People's Court No. 1 and the Beijing Higher People's Court drastically changed their views and found, even in contrast to the preceding PRB decision, that the requesting party was not entitled to request invalidation because it could not provide sufficient proof that it was the holder of the conflicting copyright or at least an interested party.[112]

(d) Prerequisites for GUI Design Protection

In 2014, CNIPA introduced a first set of provisions on applications for graphical user interface (GUI) designs, clarifying that GUIs can also be subject matter of design protection. Non-patentable, however, are displays of images that do not serve human-machine interaction[113] in a manner that a physical machine is manipulated by man through using the graphic interface. GUI protection is therefore not available for video games and other visual subject matter that can be operated independently of a specific device.

In contrast to many other countries, Chinese law does not permit the protection of a GUI design alone, but only in combination with the appearance of a physical

109. PRB decision no. 17185 upheld by the Beijing Intermediate People's Court No. 1 in its administrative decision (2011) Zhong Zhi Xing Chu Zi No. 23 of 20 March 2012.
110. Zhu Li, *supra* note 106.
111. 31 *Si Jian Zi* (2013).
112. 2901 *Jing Xing Zhong* (2016); contradicting cases summarized by Zhu Li, note 106.
113. Examination Guidelines, Part I, Chapter 3, 7.4.

product such as a phone, a tablet or any other device, whereby the GUI must enable the user to operate such device. As mentioned, this bar, which is currently set by Article 2(4) Patent Law, according to which only designs of "products" in the meaning of physical items can be protected, will be lowered by the extension of design protection to partial product views after the fourth amendment's entry into force.

The 2019 amendments to the Examination Guidelines further refined the formal requirements for GUI design application and, for the sake of clarity, moved them in a new Section 4.4 to Part I, Chapter 3.

In its first GUI design invalidation decision in 2017,[114] the PRB found that the GUI at issue, an operating system that enabled the user to scroll down the screen, to browse, etc., actually formed a GUI that enabled interaction with a physical mobile phone and rejected the assertion of the requesting party that it formed a mere ornament detached from the functions of the physical device. That is, the product with which a GUI must be combined is not required to meet the design prerequisites, so that a GUI can also be combined with a common product that pertains to prior art, as long as the design application as a whole pertains to a product and not to a GUI *per se*.[115] This has been clarified by the amendment to the Examination Guidelines of 2019, which introduced detailed guidance on the description and drawings/photographs to be submitted if the GUI is the only design feature for which protection is sought.[116] In an infringement case, the court would then focus on the GUI as the only element of the product that distinguishes it from prior art. The present requirement that a protected GUI must be combined with a physical product is nevertheless a challenging one. Apart from the difficulty of transforming a prior design application first filed abroad for the GUI alone into a Chinese product design application, GUI design owners should find it difficult to proceed against allegedly infringing GUIs that are themselves not part of a device but distributed, for instance, as immaterial software that produces the same visual effect on a screen.[117]

3. Unity and Divisional Application

(a) Unity of Patents and Utility Models

Unity is another requirement that, with regard to invention applications, is examined in the course of substantive examination, but the same standards of unity apply to applications for utility models. Correspondingly, Article 31(1) Patent Law prescribes that an application for invention or utility model shall be limited to one invention creation but that it may contain several invention-creations that belong to a single inventive concept. Rule 34 of the Implementing Regulations further detail that "single inventive concept" means the two or more invention-creations included in one application shall be technically interrelated, and all of these inventions

---

114. PRB Invalidation Decision No. 31958 (2017) – *Cheetah v. Guangzhou Dongjing*.
115. See Jin Yin, 'Tuxing yonghu jiemian (GUI) de waiguan sheji zhuanli baohu – yi GUI diyi an wei li' (Design protection of Graphical User Inferfaces (GUI) – with reference to the first GUI case), 3 *Chuangyi yu sheji* (Originality and Design) (2018), 92.
116. See VIII. 2. b) *infra*.
117. More in XIV. 6. *infra*.

shall contain the same one or several "special technical features" that mark their contribution to prior art. The principles of examining unity in Part II, Chapter 6, 2.2.1 provide further details. Accordingly, not only claims of the same category but also different types of independent claims, for instance, a claim for a manufacturing process and a product claim for the apparatus used for such process, may conform with the unity requirement, as long as both process and apparatus share a technical feature that forms a contribution to prior art. Normally, the question of unity arises only between independent claims but the Guidelines state that also claims that only appear to be dependent but are actually independent because they do not contain all features of the claim listed as independent, may be included in the examination as to unity. This may occur, for instance, if the claim indicated as independent is not new or inventive, but the additional features of the claims indicated as dependent from this claim actually are new and inventive and therefore contribute to prior art. Examination shall then concentrate on the question whether unity between these no longer dependent claims is still existent.[118]

With specific regard to chemical inventions, the Examination Guidelines contain detailed provisions on the unity of claims characterized by Markush-type alternative elements.[119] Accordingly, unity shall be established only if all alternative elements possess a) a common property or activity and b) a common structure distinct from prior art that is essential for the common property and activity.

If the examiner finds lack of unity, the examiner shall notify the applicant to amend the application accordingly. The applicant may then remove the claims lacking unity and file divisional applications for them, replace them by inventions thus far only disclosed in the description or just leave the truncated original application as it is.

Pursuant to Rule 43(1) Implementing Regulations, divisional applications have the application date of the original application and shall not go beyond the originally claimed scope of protection. Therefore, the original application's filing number and date, as well as a copy of its application documents have to be furnished when filing the divisional application. If the divisional application after a notification from the examiner to make corresponding amendments still exceeds the original scope, the application will be rejected due to non-conformity either with the mentioned Rule 43(1) Implementing Regulations and the requirement in Article 33 Patent Law that amendments to the applications shall not broaden the protection scope.

Applicants can also file divisional applications at their own initiative, not only in response to a notification. If the patent is already granted, they can do so within two months after the notification of grant.[120] If the original application is rejected, the applicant is given three months to file a divisional application after receipt of the notification of rejection, irrespective of whether he also filed a request for re-examination, and divisional applications are also admissible during re-examination and subsequent administrative court reviews. In practice, applicants usually divide their application without simultaneously requesting re-examination.[121]

---

118. Examination Guidelines, Part II, Chapter 6, 2.2.2.3.
119. Part II, Chapter 10, 8.1.
120. Rule 42(1) Implementing Regulations, Part I, Chapter 1, 5.1.1 (3) Examination Guidelines.
121. Deng Ming, 'Patent Examination: A General Outline', in Stefan Luginbuehl and Peter Ganea (eds.), *Patent Law in Greater China* (Edward Elgar, 2014), 143 (146 et seq.).

A divisional application can be further divided, but only within the above deadlines, i.e., at latest until the expiration of two months after grant notification or three months after notification of rejection. The Examination Guidelines allow an exception, however, where the subsequent divisional application is filed in reaction to a examiner's notification to rectify the lack of unity of the first divisional application.[122] In such case, the Guidelines until recently provided no clear time limit for the subsequent division, which is reported to have caused uncertainties in examination practice. Therefore, the 2019 amendment to the Examination Guidelines introduced a clarification in Part I, Chapter I, 5.1.1 (3), fourth paragraph, stating that the subsequent divisional application must be filed before the examination of the earlier divisional application is completed.

The amendment furthermore clarified the interplay between divisional application and changes in right ownership, stating that the person who files a divisional application must, at the time of application, be the applicant of the original application, and the one who files the subsequent divisional application must be the applicant of the previous divisional application.[123] Prior to the amendment, the Guidelines only provided that the applicant of the original application and that of the divisional application must be the same, and that where they were not the same, proof about the change in the application right must be provided. According to CNIPA's explanatory notes,[124] the amendment became necessary because examiners normally accepted the mere signed transfer agreement as proof of change in application right, without requiring a "statement of change in bibliographical data" as actually prescribed by Rule 119(2) Implementing Rules in connection with Part I, Chapter 1, 6.7.1.1 Examination Guidelines, so that after a divisional application by the new holder of the application right (or the party claiming to be such new holder), the original applicant was kept in the dark about further fate of the divisional application. The amendment furthermore clarifies that also in case of subsequent divisional applications the indicated inventor(s) of the original application shall remain the same.[125]

(b) Unity of Designs

Article 31(2) Patent Law regulates two instances in which more than one design can be included in one design application, namely a) several similar designs for the same product or b) two or more designs of products of the same class that are sold or used in sets. Rule 35 Implementing Regulations limits the number of similar designs for the same product that can be included in one application to ten variations, and clarifies that the designs of products belonging to the same class and sold or used in sets means that the products belong to the same general class, are usually sold or used in sets, and that their appearance shares a common design concept. Unity of design is subject matter of preliminary examination as to whether the unity requirement is obviously met.

---

122. Chapter 1, 5.1.1 (3) Examination Guidelines.
123. Part I, Chapter 1, 5.1.1 (4) Examination Guidelines.
124. *Supra* note 79.
125. Examination Guidelines, Part I, Chapter 1, 5.1.1 (4).

Products "sold in sets" are products customarily sold as a unit, for instance, bedding ware consisting of bedspread, pillow, sheet, etc., but not a pencil case given away as promotion gift upon purchase of a schoolbag, because both are normally separately sold. "Used in sets" means that the products are commonly perceived as belonging together but not that a single set product cannot be used outside the set in a meaningful manner.[126]

The Examination Guidelines stress that the two instances in which more than one design variation is allowed in on application shall not be cumulated in one application, i.e., one application cannot contain similar variations of a design concept for products sold or used in sets.[127]

VI. SUBJECT MATTER EXCLUDED FROM PATENT PROTECTION

1. Scientific Discoveries

Article 25(1) No. 1 Patent Law excludes scientific discoveries from patent protection. "Scientific discovery" encompasses all kinds of observations of natural phenomena but also scientific theories. The reason for their non-patentability is the lack of human technical intervention to solve a specific problem. To highlight the difference between non-patentable discoveries and patentable inventions, the Examination Guidelines provide the example of the discovery of the photosensitivity of a silver halide if illuminated which would not be patentable, whereas an invention made on grounds of this discovery is, e.g., a photographic film and the process of making it, would form a patentable invention.[128] Just as in many other countries, the idea that something discovered in nature should not be patented is somewhat challenged by the areas of chemical, pharmaceutical and genetic inventions.

According to Examination Guidelines, a chemical substance found in nature in its natural state is a discovery and therefore not patentable. However, if such substance with an hitherto unknown, precisely explained structure, morphology or other chemical or physical parameters is extracted or isolated from nature for the first time and fit for industrial application, such substance as well as the process of obtaining it can be patented.[129] The same applies to genetic inventions, which, pursuant to the Examination Guidelines, do also pertain to the field of chemistry. Accordingly, a gene or DNA fragment with a hitherto unknown base sequence is explained in complete and if it is fit for commercial use, such gene or DNA fragment as well as the process of obtaining it can be patented.[130]

126. Part I, Chapter 3, 9.2.1 and 9.2.2.
127. Part I, Chapter 3, 9.2.4.
128. Part II, Chapter 1, 4.1.
129. Part II, Chapter 10, 2.1.
130. Examination Guidelines, Part II, Chapter 10, 9.1.2.2.

2. Rules and Methods for Mental Activities, and the Special Case of Computer Programs and Business Methods

Article 2 Patent Law requires a patentable invention or utility model to be a *technical* solution, and therefore to be based on the laws of nature, which excludes rules and methods for mental activities from patent protection. Consequently, also software *per se* and business methods *per se* cannot be patented.[131]

Software is, however, not categorically excluded from patent protection, provided that it, again, contributes to solving a *technical* problem, i.e., a solution that must be based on the laws of nature. To facilitate software-related patent applications, an amendment to the Examination Guidelines of February 2017[132] added a few clarifications to the examination of software-implemented inventions, which is regulated in a separate Chapter 9 of Part II. An addition to Sec. 4.2 now expressly states that business method inventions shall not be categorically exempted from patent protection if they contain technical features. According to CNIPA's explanations, the new wording should motivate more companies in the FinTech and insurance sectors to consider patent protection. It may also be relevant for the emerging scientific and commercial activity in the field of artificial intelligence.

The 2017 amendment to the Examination Guidelines further clarified that only computer programs *per se* shall be exempted from patent protection, to emphasize that "medium plus computer program" claims are, in general, patentable. With regard to software-related inventions claimed by way of apparatus claims, the amendment to Part II, Chapter 9, 5.2 of the Guidelines deleted the requirement that an apparatus claim related to software shall "outline in detail which component performs each of the computer program functions, and how these functions are performed", which implied that computer programs could only be expressed as processes or limiting features. Instead, the amendment added a clarification that an apparatus claim may consist of both hardware and software components, so that expressing the computer program as component of the apparatus claim (e.g., "an apparatus comprising a memory and a processor, and a program stored in the memory, which, upon run by the processor, performs...") are now expressly permitted. Correspondingly, also the term "functional module" thus far used throughout Sec. 5.2, which created the impression that software-related claim components could only be expressed as functional features, has been replaced by the term "program module".

The clarifications aim at facilitating the patenting of computer readable medium claims. However, inventions represented by such claims are still required to produce a technical result beyond the mere physical effects arising from the interaction of the program with the hardware on which it is executed.[133]

As mentioned, another amendment of 31 December 2019 added a whole new Section 6 on "Rules on Examining Invention Patents that Include Algorithm Features or Business Rules and Method Features" to Part II, Chapter 9 to the Examination

131. See IV. 2. b) in this book's Part on Copyright on alternative copyright protection.
132. CNIPA explanations in form of a PPT presentation available on CNIPA's website: https://www.cnipa.gov.cn/2017-10/20171031150827538279.pdf.
133. Examination Guidelines, Part II, Chapter 9, 2; See also Yahong Li, 'The Current Dilemma and Future of Software Patenting', *IIC* (2019), 823.

Guidelines to provide more detailed guidance on how to distinguish patentable "technical" software-implemented inventions from non-patentable subject matter. The new Section contains ten examples of patentable and non-patentable algorithm and business method-implemented technical solutions and of the assessment of the inventiveness of such solutions.

As a general rule, when examining an invention that incorporates algorithms or business methods, the algorithm or business method-related features and the technical features of the claim shall not be separately examined but the examiner shall examine the claim in its entirety with regard to technical means, the technical problem it aims to solve and the technical effect.

If the claim consists of a mere abstract calculation method or a business method *per se*, it shall fall under the non-patentable "rules and methods for intellectual activities" pursuant to Article 25(2) Patent Law. Non-patentable under this provisions are, for instance, a purely abstract method of generating mathematical models that increases the number of training samples to enhance the accuracy of the models (Example 1), or a rebate system that aims at enhancing the consumers' willingness to buy. If, however, a claim is not only expressed by features pertaining to calculation methods, etc., but also contains technical features, so that the claim as a whole can no longer be regarded as a "rule or method for intellectual activity", it shall not be excluded from patent protection under Article 25(2).

If the claim is not already excluded from patenting as a "rule of method for intellectual activities" because it also contains technical features, it may still turn out to be non-patentable because it does not conform with the legal definition of an invention in Article 2(2) Patent Law, according to which only a "a new *technical* solution proposed for a product, a process or an improvement thereof" can be patented. A solution is "technical" if it, in its entirety, solves a technical problem by applying technical means. Means are "technical" if they rely on the laws of nature and produce a technical effect, i.e., an effect that can also be explained by the laws of nature. A claim that incorporates a calculation method is technical if a) such method in each and every step of its execution, is intrinsically connected with the technical problem to be solved, b) the data processed by this method pertain to data with an exact technical meaning within the respective technical field, c) the execution of the calculation method directly expresses the application of the laws of nature while solving the technical problem and d) the effect achieved by the invention is of technical nature.

According to Example 2 provided by the amended Guidelines, a calculation method that trains convolutional neural networks (CNN) to recognize images of different dimensions conforms with the technicality requirement because the method is carried out in connection with image processing, aims at overcoming the technical problem that existing CNN can only handle groups of images of the same dimension and produces the technical effect that the trained CNN can now also handle differently sized images. Also sufficiently technical and therefore patentable is a network-based method of facilitating bicycle sharing, by enabling clients to precisely locate free bicycles, to unlock and to ride them, while executed within a controlled technical environment consisting of servers and terminal apparatus. According to the Examination Guidelines, such method would be interconnected with technical features to achieve the technical aim of enabling clients to more precisely locate free bicycles (Example 3). The Examination Guidelines furthermore list a claim that comprises a method and a device to enhance blockchain security by limiting communication with blockchain nodes to those whose access request is accompanied by a CA identifier that can be matched with a pre-configured CA trust list as patentable. According to the Examination Guidelines, such method would employ means that are based on the laws of nature to achieve the technical aim of enhancing data security by preventing data leaks in the course of communication with blockchain nodes (Example 4). No technical solutions within the meaning of Article 2(2) would be the mentioned consumer rebate method that is run as software on a computer and relies on consumer spending data (Example 5) and a method of assessing regional economic prosperity with help of a computer program that processes data on electricity consumption and other economic indicators (Example 6). Both methods would be detached from the laws of nature, in that they employed non-technical means of analysing economic data on consumption, etc., and in that neither the problem to be solved nor the effect achieved involved anything technical.

The amendment, furthermore, introduced guidance on assessing the inventiveness of technical solutions that incorporate algorithms or business rules/methods, which, for the sake of a coherent illustration of the new provisions, is treated here and not in the subsection on inventiveness above.

As a general rule, inventiveness shall only be established if these algorithm or business method-related features intrinsically interact with the technical features of the invention in a manner that they mutually support each other to achieve the desired technical effect. Under this rule, a fuzzy arithmetic algorithm processing sensor information about the movement of humanoid robots, which is distinct from prior art in that it is better capable of foreseeing the probability of falling while the robot is walking, can be inventive if it is functionally connected with the technical features of the invention in a mutually supportive manner and not easily conceivable by a skilled artisan just from reading the prior art documents (Example 7).

Not inventive is the solution described in Example 10, a method of visualizing the development of attitudes on social platforms by a colouring scheme, which appears to be especially instructive to CNIPA because its recently published explanations of the amendment[134] further elaborate on it. The feature that sets this solution apart from prior art is a different rule of classifying the emotions expressed on social platforms, whereby the visualization method by colouring is already covered by the prior art literature. As the same colouring method could be applied to any other classification method, both the technical and the non-technical features of this invention neither supported each other nor had they a causal relationship with each other to contribute an inventive step over prior art. Therefore, the examiner should conclude that the invention, in comparison with prior art, would not solve a technical problem, and therefore deny inventiveness. The CNIPA explanations stress that not the whole claim per se would not aim at solving a technical problem, i.e., it would still form a technical solution according to Article 2(2) Patent Law, but only the feature that sets the claim apart from prior art, namely the new classification method. The claim as a whole would remain "technical" insofar as it contained a technical feature, namely the method of visualizing changes in emotional attitudes by

134. See CNIPA explanations, *supra* note 48.

colours. The explanations subsume such colouring method under technical subject matter that is based on the laws of nature because it would "draw on the natural properties of the human visual sense".

In context with this example, the CNIPA explanations also stress that a mere calculation method incorporated in a claim for which the closest related prior art is found in the same field of application can very well set the claim apart from prior art if it helps to overcome technical difficulties of prior art, for instance, by selecting or adjusting parameters or formulae used in prior technical solutions applied to autonomous driving in a manner that enhances the accuracy of obstacle recognition in comparison with prior art and cannot be easily identified in prior art documents. On the other hand, if the claim is distinct from the closest related prior art in that both the claim and the prior art pertain to different technical fields, the examiner shall consider factors such as the obviousness and the easiness of the application to a different technical field, whether such application actually contributed to overcoming a technical problem, to which extent prior art hinted at such new application and the technical effects it produced. Consequently, a multi robot path planning algorithm that enables robots to take the optimal route, which formed an improvement over the calculation thus far applied to optimal path identification according to the first prior art document, may still not be inventive enough to be patented in spite of its strong interrelatedness with the solution's technical elements if the algorithm has already been described in another prior art document, and if the second prior art document inspires the skilled artisan to consider the first prior art document in a manner that enables him to comprehend the technical solution without inventive labour on his own upon consulting both documents (Example 8).

Another example of a sufficiently inventive business-method implemented technical solution is a method of enabling a more efficient use of an existing logistics distribution system of a courier service consisting of servers, terminal equipment, bar code scanning, etc., by providing mass order arrival notifications to clients in specific areas in a manner not yet described in prior art. Here, the inventiveness requirement would be met due to the functional interaction with the technical features of the solution to generate the, according to CNIPA, technical effect of a more efficient distribution (Example 9).[135]

The new Section 6, furthermore, contains guidance on the draft of claims and description of inventions involving algorithmic and business method-related features. Prerequisite for a correct description is that it contains technical features. It may then, in addition, also contain algorithmic features and business rules and methods, provided that they, as described above, functionally interact with the technical features in a manner that both technical and non-technical features support each other and have a common effect. The description shall detail in how far the technical features and the algorithmic or business method-related features produce such common effect and achieve an effective result by interacting in the above-described manner. Abstract algorithms must be combined with a concrete technical field, in a manner that the definition of at least one entered parameter and the corresponding output must be interrelated with corresponding data from the respective technical field. Business

135. The example also subsumes the enhanced consumer satisfaction due to earlier notice of arrival under the technical effect achieved by the solution.

methods shall be described in very detail throughout the whole process of solving the technical problem to enable the skilled artisan to carry out the invention. The advantages over prior art may not only be described in terms of enhanced quality, precision, efficiency or improvement of the internal operation of a system, but also in terms of an enhanced consumer experience, as, for instance, in Example 9 above. The mentioned CNIPA explanations add that in the latter case the enhancement of the consumer experience must be described in an objectively determinable manner, not in terms of personal happiness and the like. Moreover, the description shall outline how such enhancement is achieved by the functional interaction between the technical features and the features pertaining to the calculation method or the business method and the causal relationship between these technical and non-technical features.

The claims shall be based on the description to clarify the scope of protection in a clear and succinct manner and indicate the technical and non-technical algorithmic or business method-related features.

In sum, especially examples 3, 4 and 9 regarding blockchain security, a bicycle sharing network and an improved logistics scheme demonstrate that the technicality requirement will henceforth be very broadly interpreted, in a manner that almost anything that produces an effect outside the immediate environment, mostly a computer, in which the calculation method or business method is executed, will be regarded as "technical" and therefore pertaining to an invention according to Article 2(2) Patent Law. Also, it seems that the improvement of emotional human well-being *per se*, as long as it can be prescribed in objective terms, e.g., an enhanced consumer experience or maybe even lessened security concerns due to objectively improved identity protection in cryptocurrency transactions, will be regarded as a technical enough advancement over prior art to justify patent protection.[136] This would mean that also non-technical contributions to prior art can give reason to inventiveness as long as they are part of an invention that can be regarded as technical, which is the case if its technical and non-technical components are closely interrelated in the above described manner.

3. Animal and Plant Varieties

According to Article 25(1) No. 4 Patent Law, animal and plant varieties are not patentable, but processes for their production are (Article 25(2) Patent Law), unless also "essentially biological". Not essentially biological and therefore patentable is, for instance, a technical method of enhancing the efficiency of a biological process, e.g., a method of raising high-yield cattle by irradiation.[137] Protection of plant varieties is available under special legislation in compliance with the 1978 version of the International Union for the Protection of New Varieties of Plants (UPOV).[138]

---

136. Different the German Federal Patent Court's judgment of 5 March 2014 (20 W (pat) 18/09, GRUR BeckRS 2014, 9561), with regard to a cryptographic method that, in the court's opinion only contributed in terms of an enhanced feeling of security, which would be nothing "technical".
137. Example given by the Examination Guidelines, Part II, Chapter 1, 4.4.
138. Treated in detail in XV. 1. *infra*.

4. Nuclear Transformation and Substances

Whereas the current Article 25(1) No. 5 Patent Law excludes only the substances obtained by methods of nuclear transformation, the fourth Patent Law amendment extend such exclusion to nuclear transformation methods.

5. Methods for the Diagnosis or for the Treatment of Diseases

Article 25(1) No. 3 Patent Law excludes methods for the diagnosis or for the treatment of diseases. The Examination Guidelines state two reasons for this exclusion. One is the concern that patent monopolies in this field may narrow the physician's freedom to choose the most promising medical treatment in the individual case, the other their lack of industrial application.[139] The exclusion does not extend to the material and equipment used when applying the method.[140]

Only diagnostic methods that are directly applied to the living human body to deal with individual health conditions are non-patentable, but not methods of pathological anatomy, methods that obtain no final ("final" in the sense that they point to a certain medical treatment), but only intermediate data such as physical or physiological parameters and methods of analysing tissue, body fluids, etc., to obtain such intermediate results.[141]

With regard to therapeutic methods, the Examination Guidelines list numerous forms of surgical, pharmaceutical and other forms of treatment (inter alia, electric stimuli, light therapy, acupuncture, fertilization) that pertain to non-patentable therapeutic methods if applied to the living human body. In contrast, methods of making prostheses and of measurements undertaken to adapt them to the human body (the Examination Guidelines give the example of making an individual tooth prosthesis, which consists of measuring the oral cavity of the patient and of the method of making the artificial teeth), non-surgical means of stockbreeding (e.g., an electromagnetic method of improving the quality of lamb), methods of butchering animals and methods of taxidermy, e.g., for the purpose of beautification, are patentable. Also not generally excluded from patent protection are non-invasive cosmetic treatments and methods of making humans and animals feel comfortable, e.g., if they are under special conditions like underwater activity and, finally, methods of removing bacteria, viruses, parasites, etc., from the skin or the hair of a human or an animal body, but not methods of disinfecting wounds, etc.[142] Whether also the fixation of an apparatus in the body of a living animal for the extraction of fluid as an ingredient to a medical substance can be patented is at the very least questionable.[143]

---

139. Examination Guidelines, Part II, Chapter 1, 4.3; see also Part G, 4.2. of the EPO Examination Guidelines.
140. Examination Guidelines, Part II, Chapter 1, 4.3.
141. Examination Guidelines, Part II, Chapter 1, 4.3.1.2.
142. Examples of non-patentable medical treatment and similar acts that are not excluded from patent protection are given by the Examination Guidelines, Part II, Chapter 1, 4.3.2
143. A related case has been disputed before the Chinese Patent Office under the previous patent regime. In this case, the office refused to grant a patent for a method of fixing a drainage tube in the body of an ox for the extraction of bile as an ingredient of a traditional

In practice, applicants frequently seek patent protection for therapeutic methods via Swiss-type medical use claims phrased, for instance, as "use of substance X to manufacture a medicament for the treatment of disease Y", to avoid expressions like "administration of substance X to heal disease Y", which would render the claim non-patentable under Article 25(1) No. 3 Patent Law. Part II, Chapter 10, 4.5.2 of the Examination Guidelines on chemical inventions explicitly permits such Swiss-type claim formats. Item (4) of section 5.4 of the same Chapter 10 on the novelty assessment of chemical use inventions, however, also requires that the new use must be actually represented in manufacturing of the chemical or pharmaceutical product. Otherwise, if the feature that distinguishes the new use from prior art can only be found in the administration of the drug, the invention will be found non-patentable due to lack of novelty. This also pertains to the new *dosage* of a medicament in the course of a known use. In its *Cubist v. Patent Re-examination Board* decision of 19 November 2013,[144] in which the SPC had to decide about the patentability of a claim pertaining to a specific dosage to reduce side effects, China's highest court stated that manufacturing a pharmaceutical referred to the actual making of the product so that technical features pertaining to dosage, etc., would also have to be embodied in the manufacturing. Technical features in form of uses that become relevant during administration only but are not part of the manufacturing process, would not add novelty-conferring features to the claims of an existing technical solution. In other words, even dosages are not categorically excluded from patent protection, provided that the corresponding technical features are formulated as part of the pharmaceutical's manufacturing and do not merely appear as an instruction to the doctor on how to administer it.

6. Inventions Prohibited by Law and *Ordre Public*

Article 5 Patent Law excludes inventions that violate laws (meaning laws in the narrower sense, i.e., only those enacted by the National People's Congress, but no administrative provisions or local regulations),[145] harm social ethics or are detrimental to the public interest.

With regard to inventions that violate laws, Rule 10 of the Implementing Regulations clarifies in conformity with Article 4*quater* of the Paris Convention, that a legal ban on the mere exploitation of the invention-creation is not sufficient for excluding it from patent protection. The Examination Guidelines give the example of product or process inventions pertaining to weapons made for national defence

Chinese medicine because this method constituted a non-patentable surgical method. This view has been by Zhang Xiangling, 'Some Surgical Methods Should be Protected by the Patent Act', 1 *China Patents & Trademarks* (1994), 39. To the author, the method of fixing an apparatus in an animal body to extract a fluid in an effective and safe manner constitutes an industrially applicable and therefore patentable method and rather than a surgical method of healing or preventing diseases.

144. 75 *Zhi Xing Zi* (2012), full text accessible on this non-official site: http://www.fengxiaoqingip.com/ipanli/linianzhishichanquanmingan/zuigaorenminfayuan/zuigaorenminfayuanliniandianxinganli/20141231/9716.html.

145. Examination Guidelines, Part II, Chapter 1, 3.1.1; see also Bu Yuanshi, *supra* note 73.

purposes, which may be patented in spite of the legal ban on the use of the products incorporating such inventions. In contrast, products that are specifically invented for prohibited uses, e.g., gambling machines or devices for drug consumption, are excluded from protection. If only a part of the invention serves illegal uses, e.g., a gaming machine that ejects money, the examiner shall not reject the application but notify the applicant to amend the application respectively to delete the money-ejecting function. The rest of the invention, a gaming machine for mere leisure purposes, would then remain patentable.[146]

Less easy to grasp are inventions that, according to Article 5(1) "harm social ethics" or are "detrimental to the public interest". The Examination Guidelines give the examples of designs depicting violence or obscenity, or inventions pertaining to artificial sexual organs that do not serve medical uses or devices that facilitate sodomy.[147] Also, manipulating the genetic identity of animals is excluded under the "social ethics" reservation if such invention causes unnecessary suffering and does not produce a substantial medical or veterinarian benefit. Non-patentable are, furthermore, inventions that involve the manipulation of the germ line identity of humans or of cloning humans, or of using embryos for industrial and commercial purposes. The mentioned 2019 amendment to the Examination Guidelines significantly lessened the restrictions on patentability in this area, however, by clarifying that the separation of stem cells from embryos grown *ex vivo* within 14 days from fertilization do not fall under subject matter that harms social ethics.[148] The amendment also deleted the categorical exclusion of embryonic stem cells from patent protection and clarified that embryonic stem cells do not pertain to non-patentable "human bodies in all stages of formation and development".[149]

In contrast to inventions that contravene the social morality, inventions that are "detrimental to the public interest" mostly comprise technical solutions that are directly harming if put to use. The Examination Guidelines give the examples of an anti-burglary device that blinds intruders and of inventions that result in substantial waste of resources or cause serious harm to the environment or to the public health. However, applications for subject matter that, in spite of serious negative side effects, is still capable of producing positive results shall not be automatically rejected.[150] The Examination Guidelines further mention applications that contain a politically or religiously offensive text or promote superstition, under the "public interest" exclusion.

Since its amendment of 2008, Article 5(2) Patent Law also excludes inventions "that are accomplished by relying on genetic resources which are obtained or used in violation of the provisions of laws and administrative regulations". According to Rule 26 Implementing Regulations, applicants who seek patent protection for inventions that rely on genetic resources shall indicate this in the request and fill the corresponding forms issued by CNIPA. The Examination Guidelines further outline

146. Examination Guidelines, Part II, Chapter 1, 3.1.4.
147. Examination Guidelines, Part II, Chapter 1, 3.1.2.
148. A new paragraph to Part II, Chapter 1, 3.1.2.
149. By deleting the previous subsection 9.1.1.1 in Part II, Chapter 10 and adding the clarification to the text of the previous subsection 9.1.1.2, which became subsection 9.1.1.1.
150. Examination Guidelines, Part II, Chapter 1, 3.1.3.

that "violating the corresponding laws and administrative regulations" means that, for instance, a genetic resource has been obtained under violation of the "Measures for Examination and Approval in Respect of Entry and Exit of Genetic Resources of Livestock and Poultry and in Respect of Research in Their Utilization in Cooperation with Foreign Entities".[151] The applicant would then be banned from obtaining a patent in China. The Examination Guidelines also clarify that the exclusion under Article 5(2) only applies to violations of Chinese laws and regulations on the utilization of genetic resources, not foreign ones.

7. Subject Matter Specifically Excluded from Design Protection

With reference to the definition of a protected design in Article 2(4) Patent Law, according to which patentable designs are new designs of the shape, pattern or the combination shape and pattern of a product (after the fourth Patent Law amendment's entry into force: "of a product or of parts of it"), or the combination of a colour with such shape and pattern, which are rich in aesthetic appeal and fit for industrial application, Part I, Chapter 3, 7.4 excludes the following from design protection:

- Designs of fixed buildings, which fit into a particular landscape such as bridges, lakeside villas, etc., which implies that, for instance, prefabricated houses or any other standard buildings that do not depend on a particular topography or landscape, can be protected;
- Designs pertaining to shapeless products such as liquids, powders, etc.;
- Designs of components that cannot be separated from the main product and independently marketed and used, but also products that have no independent use, such as the part of a puzzle;
- Designs that can only be perceived with help of instruments, e.g., a pattern that becomes visible under an ultraviolet lamp;
- Designs that do not depict a product in its original shape, e.g., the design depicting a bird folded out of a handkerchief;
- Designs that mainly depict the original shape, pattern or colour of natural objects;
- Works that belong to fine arts, calligraphy or photography, as protection for such works is reserved to copyright
- Mere geometric shapes and patterns that are common to the specific product category
- Pronunciation and meaning of words, numbers, etc.,
- Graphics displayed by gaming interfaces and other display devices that are not related to human-machine interaction, such as screen wallpapers, on-off screen images, and website layouts that are independent of human-machine interaction. The exclusion has been introduced in the course of the 2019 amendment to the Examination Guidelines. It replaces a previous provision that excluded all kinds of images that become visible upon activating an electronic device from design protection. The amendment became necessary

151. Examination Guidelines, Part II, Chapter 1, 3.1.5.

due to the mentioned extension of design protection to the appearance of GUIs that serve human-machine interaction.

VII. INVENTORSHIP, RIGHT OWNERSHIP, EMPLOYEE INVENTIONS

1. Inventor and Creator

(a) *Prerequisites for Inventorship/Creatorship*

According to Rule 13 Implementing Regulations, only a human person ("人" in Chinese) who creatively contributed to the substantive features of the invention-creation can become an "inventor" (the person who completes an invention) or a "creator "(the person who completes a utility model or design). That presently only humans can claim inventorship precludes the patenting of inventions made by AI.

As outlined above, recent amendments to the Examination Guidelines have increased the chances that inventions made by machines be patented, but concrete legislative plans to render the patent system accessible to inventions independently created by intelligent machines are not yet in place. The academic debate gravitates towards a protection of such inventions. With regard to the inventorship question, some propose to treat the organization under the supervision of which an AI has made an invention as quasi-employer and to indicate as inventors the human operators, e.g., the ones who tested the practical application of the AI-made invention in the application document, to meet the requirements even under the present law.[152] Others bring into play the creation of e-persons with legal capacity.[153]

Also according to Rule 13 Implementing Regulations, only a person that made a "creative contribution" to an "essential feature" of the invention, utility model or design can qualify as inventor or creator. According to the Shanghai Higher People's Court,[154] the "essential features" shall be the ones that distinguish the patent from prior art, in the present case a specific claim, and the persons entitled to be the inventors shall be those who contributed such features. Activities of mere auxiliary character such as organisational work or the provision of material facilities are not sufficient. Independent of the application right, the inventor enjoys the right to be named in the patent documents (Article 17 of the current Patent Law, Article 16 after the fourth amendment's entry into force). If a person other than the inventor files the application, the applicant is obliged to indicate the inventor's name as well as other personal data in the request of the application documents. Incorrectly identified

152. Li Zonghui, 'Rengong zhineng shengcheng faming zhuanli shouquan zhi zhengdangxing tanxi' (Analyzing the legitimacy of granting patents in AI-generated inventions), 1 *Dianzi zhishi chanquan* (Electronic Intellectual Property) (2019), 12 et seq., also implying that wrongful indication of the inventor would not be an obstacle to patenting or an invalidation ground according to many patent laws.
153. Wu Handong, *supra* note 83.
154. 30 *Hu Gao Min San (Zhi) Zhong Zi* (2013), text of the decision and comment by judge Tang Zhen, 'Zhumingren xu dui zhuanli de shizhixing tedian zuochu chuangzaoxing gongzuo' (The signee shall be the one who made a creative contribution to the patent's essential features), 10 *Rennim Sifa* (2015), 65 et seq.

inventors may request the applicant or patent owner to amend the bibliographical data.[155]Also, Rule 104(1) No. 4 Implementing Regulations requires that the name of the inventor of subject matter of an international application shall be stated when entering the national phase, even if it has not been stated in the international application.

(b) Misappropriation of an Invention-Creation

The current provisions are at best vague about the question whether the true owner of a patented invention, utility model or design can request the transfer of the application right or the granted patent. As already outlined, usurpation of a design by obtaining a patent for an aesthetic solution that belongs to someone else may give rise to invalidation on grounds of the "no conflict with prior rights" rule,[156] but there are no further provisions regarding the assignment of the application right or the patent right to its true owner.

Rule 85(1) No. 1 of the Implementing Regulations nevertheless lists disputes over applications rights or patent ownership rights under the kind of disputes that can be mediated by the local patent administrations, and Rule 1 No. (1) and (2) of the SPC's Patent Interpretations of 2001 explicitly mentions disputes over the application right and over patent ownership as subject matter of patent litigation to be handled by People's Courts. The patent-specific provisions are silent about the obvious consequence of the plaintiff winning such a dispute, namely that the application rights respectively the already granted patent should be assigned to him. Case law, however, acknowledges a right of the true owner of the invention-creation to claim that the unlawful owner surrenders the patent to him, and based on such court decision the plaintiff can request CNIPA to assign him the patent,[157] i.e., current court practice comes close to the patent vindication claim in other countries, even in absence of clear legal rules. In fact, claiming the assignment of patent ownership to the "true" owner is reported to have become a subject matter of frivolous litigation. Accordingly, some patent owners confronted with an invalidation request would invite third parties as straw men to file suit against them and claim assignment of ownership, because such lawsuit allows them to request the suspension of all kinds of procedures, including invalidation.[158] The PRB would then have to wait for the outcome of the court trial, which would give the patent owner one or two additional years to exploit his most likely worthless patent.

2. Service Invention-Creations

Article 6 Patent Law regulates the legal relationship between the inventor or creator of a service invention-creation and his employer. The use of the term "invention-creation" means that the provisions apply to inventions, utility models and designs alike.

155. Legal Affairs Department of SIPO, *Xin zhuanlifa xiangjie* (Commentary on the new Patent Law) (Beijing, 2001), 111.
156. See V. 2. c) *supra*.
157. Zhu Li, *supra* note 106.
158. Rules 86 and 88 of the Implementing Regulations; Part V, Chapter 7.7 of the Examination Guidelines,

According to Article 6, invention-creations accomplished in the course of performing the duties of an employee, or mainly by using the material and technical conditions of an employer, shall be regarded as service invention-creations. In such case, the employer shall have the right to apply for a patent.

Article 6(1) Patent Law defines a service invention as an invention-creation made in the course of the tasks of the entity to which the inventor or creator belongs or made mainly by using the material facilities provided by that entity. According to Rule 12(1) Implementing Regulations, the term "made in execution of the tasks of the entity to which the inventor or creator belongs" means:

- made in the course of performing the own official duty;
- made in the execution of tasks entrusted to the employee by his entity in addition to his normal duties, or
- made within one year from resignation, retirement or internal rotation to another job, provided that the invention or creation pertains to his duties or other tasks assigned to him by the entity to which he previously belonged.

According to Rule 12(2), the term "entity to which the inventor or creator belongs" shall include entities in which the inventor or creator is only temporarily engaged. The term "material and technical means of the entity" means capital, equipment, spare parts, raw materials of the entity and other technical means which are not publicly available. "Main use" in Article 6(1) Patent Law means that without the material or technical means, the inventor would not have been able to accomplish the invention-creation.[159] Any invention-creation completed by "mainly using" the employer's facilities constitutes a service invention-creation, whether the inventor has accomplished it during the working time or in his spare time.[160]

The draft amendment of 2015 proposed to mitigate the Patent Law's employer-friendliness, by omitting inventions made by "mainly using the material and technical conditions of an employer" from the definition of a service invention-creation. Even under the present Article 6(3), such inventions are treated differently from inventions made in the course of fulfilling occupational duties, stating that employer and inventor-creator may conclude a contract on patent ownership, which would then prevail over the statutory assignment to the employer pursuant to Article 6(1). The 2015 draft also added a clarification to Article 6(3) that in absence of a contract, ownership shall be assigned to the employee. The proposed amendments mainly

159. In its rather old decision of 8 May 1992, the Higher People's Court of Beijing Municipality rejected the plaintiff's claim that the invention at issue constituted a service invention. One decisive argument against a service invention was that the plaintiff's facilities were not used to complete the invention-creation as such, but rather to make the already completed invention-creation fit for entry into the market by testing its conformity with the technical standards prescribed in laws and regulations. The court held that such use had nothing to do with use in the sense of Article 6 Patent Law: 3 *Gazette of the SPC* (1992), 98.

160. This becomes evident from a mediation reached before the Intermediate People's Court of Liaoning City of 24 January 1992 (3 *Gazette of the SPC* (1993), 106). Here, the People's Court concentrated on the fact that plaintiff had mainly made use of the defendant's facilities, without further taking into consideration the plaintiff's argument that he had accomplished the invention-creation in his spare time.

aimed at encouraging employers to draft more sophisticated employment contracts that comprehensively consider the circumstances of a service invention-creation. The fourth amendment, however, refrained from such clarification and left the present provisions largely unchanged, just as the preceding draft of 2020. The 2019 draft contained an addition to Article 6(2), which encouraged employers to share the benefits from employee inventions with their employed inventors and creators via stock shares, options, dividends and the like. The final amendment moved this encouragement to a new paragraph 2 in Article 15 (presently Article 16) on the reward to service inventors, where it indeed appears to be better placed. The only change to Article 6 that found its way into the fourth amendment is a second sentence to its Paragraph 2, clarifying that entities are free to dispose of the patents or application rights in their service inventions and to promote the implementation and application of the respective invention-creations.

On 2 April 2015, CNIPA and the State Council's Legislative Affairs Office (LAO) published a discussion draft on Service Invention Regulations.[161] Their Rule 7(4) further limits the scope of what belongs to inventions accomplished by using the materials and technical means of the employing entity, stipulating that if the inventor returns the capital used for making the invention to the employer or pays him a fee for its use, or if the inventor uses the technical means of the employer for mere experimenting or testing purposes, the invention shall not form a service invention-creation. According to Rule 9 of the draft, however, such allocation of ownership may be overruled by company in-house rules or by a contract with the employee. It is certainly justified to assume that the draft regulations, provided that they become law, will motivate both employers and employees to consider the possibility of a later service invention in advance to entering an employment relationship and to reflect such consideration by drafting proper employment contracts and in-house rules.

With regard to the compensation for service inventions, Article 16 Patent Law (Article 15 after the fourth amendment's entry into force) provides that *the unit that has been granted the patent* shall reward the employed inventor and remunerate him after the patent has been exploited. According to the strict wording of this provision, the reward is only due after the patent grant (and remuneration only after exploitation has started), and reward and remuneration must both be paid by the entity that has been granted the patent, which, however, is not necessarily the immediate employer. This may be the case if the employer is a subsidiary of a parent firm that actually applies for the patent or if the patented invention is the result of R&D outsourced to a company that employs the inventor. The previous Patent Law draft amendment of 2015 proposed to clarify that the immediate employer shall pay reward and remuneration.[162] The later drafts of 2019 and 2020, however, no longer contained such proposal, and also the fourth amendment did not readopt it.

161. Draft and explanations in Chinese can be found on CNIPA's website: http://www.sipo.gov.cn/ztzl/zwfmtlzl/tlcajxyyj/1051318.htm.
162. See Taolue Zhang, Dan Prud'homme and Oliver Lutze, 'China's New Patent Commercialization Strategy', 12:6 *Journal of Intellectual Property Law & Practice* (1 June 2017), 474 et seq., https://academic.oup.com/jiplp/article/12/6/474/3749616; also addressed by Ma Qian and Berrit Roth, 'Employee Inventions', in Stefan Luginbuehl and Peter Ganea (eds.), *Patent Law in Greater China* (Edward Elgar, 2014), 108 et seq.

The present remuneration standards are further detailed in the Implementing Regulations, Rules 76–78. According to Rule 76, the entity to which the service invention shall be granted may incorporate reward and remuneration standards in its in-house rules or employment contracts, which must comply with finance and accounting laws. Rules 77 and 78 contain further provisions on minimum rewards and remunerations. Pursuant to Rule 77, the minimum reward shall be RMB 3,000 for inventions and RMB 1,000 for utility models or designs, to be paid at latest three months after the announcement of the patent grant. Rule 77 also stipulates that if an invention-creation resulted from an employee's proposal, an unspecified reward should be paid, again, *after* the grant of a patent.

Rule 78 further regulates statutory minimum remuneration that has to be paid in absence of corresponding in house-rules or contractual agreements, namely not less than two percent of the revenues gained from the exploitation of an invention or utility model patent, and not less than 0.2 percent of the revenues from exploiting a design patent. Payment in form of an adequate lump sum that corresponds to the above percentages is also permissible, and if the employer licenses the patent to another entity, at least 10 percent of the royalty fee shall be paid to the inventor.

The draft Service Invention Regulations provide significantly higher rewards and remunerations than the present Implementing Regulations. The initial reward, for instance, shall henceforth be not less than the double amount of the average monthly salary of the employing company's employees, and also the other remuneration thresholds are by far more generous to employees than the current minimum standards.

The draft regulations contain numerous further important details on which the present provisions are silent, for instance, an obligation of employees to report any invention creation accomplished in connection with the employer's business to the employer within two months after completion of the invention (Rule 10),[163] a period that some employers may find too long. The submission of such report, which must contain, *inter alia*, the name of the inventor(s), the name of the invention, the reasons why the inventor thinks that the invention does or does not pertain to a service invention and other details (Rule 11). Such notification would then give rise to certain rights and obligations on both sides. If, for instance, the inventor finds that his or her invention is a service invention, the employer has six months from notification to decide whether the invention shall be patented, kept secret or published without any protective measures, and to inform the inventor thereof in writing. Moreover, if the employer has no interest in further pursuing IP protection or if he wants to abandon an already granted patent or other registered IP in the service invention-creation, the inventor shall be the first to be informed thereof and be given the opportunity to become an IP owner by himself (Rule 15), so as to incite the immediate inventors to exploit their inventions or creations if they would otherwise remain unused due to the employer's lack of interest in exploitation.[164] It does not go as far as the explicit right of first refusal of employees in their "employee-developed

163. See Ma Qian and Berrit Roth, *supra* note 162.
164. See Taolue Zhang, Dan Prud'homme and Oliver Lutze, *supra* note 162.

technology" pursuant to Article 326(1) Contract Law of 15 March 1999, however.[165] The provision has recently been transferred to Article 847(1) of the new Civil Code's Book on Contracts (Chapter 20 on Technology Contracts) without major modifications.

That the draft regulations have not yet become law is very likely due to the delay of the Patent Law reform. It can be expected that they will be enacted soon, certainly before the fourth amendment's entry into force on 1 June 2021.

3. Jointly Made Inventions and Inventions Made on Request

The provisions on invention-creations jointly accomplished by two or more entities or individuals or made in execution of a specific request are contained in Article 8 Patent Law, according to which the application right belongs to the person or entity (persons or entities in the case of joint inventions), who has made the invention-creation, unless they have concluded a contract stipulating otherwise.

Further provisions concerning the contract on joint technology development and commissioned technology development are regulated in Part 2 (Technology Development Contract) of Chapter XVIII on Technology Contracts of the Contract Law. With regard to invention–creations accomplished in joint development, Article 340 Contract Law stipulates that in the absence of an agreement, the application right shall be jointly owned by the parties, and that where one party intends to assign the application right, the other parties shall enjoy a preferential right of first refusal. Should one party waive the right to apply for the patent, the other parties are still permitted to apply on their behalf, but once the patent is granted, the waiving party shall be permitted to exploit the patent free of charge. Furthermore, none of the parties to a cooperative development contract shall be permitted to file a patent application if one of the parties disagrees to such filing. The provision has recently been transferred to Article 860 of the new Civil Code, Book 3 on Contracts, Chapter 20 on Technology Contracts, without any major modifications apart from clarifications that the legal provisions shall only apply if the parties haven't agreed otherwise.

Apart from the above contractual provision, the Patent Law itself does not clearly regulate the further fate of an invention shared by two or more individual inventors or entities, for instance, whether one co-owner can file a patent application or subsequent applications against the intention of the others. Article 15(1) Patent Law (Article 14(1) after the fourth amendment's entry into force) regulates in more detail with regard to joint *ownership* (which in most cases belongs to employers, not to the individual inventors) not only of the granted patent but also of the application right that if the co-owners have agreed upon the exercise of the application right or the patent right, such agreement shall prevail, whereas in the absence of an agreement, each co-owner may separately exercise the patent or grant ordinary non-exclusive licences to exploit the patent. In the latter case, the licence revenues shall be distributed among all co-owners.[166] According to Article 15(2) Patent Law

165. 11 *Gazette of the State Council* (1999), 388 (Chapter XVIII on technology contracts, 423–429); English version in 3 *China Patents & Trademarks* (1999), 80 (Chapter XVIII on Technology Contracts, 97–100).

166. More details about patent co-ownership, including case examples, and the difficulty to distinguish it from joint inventorship in China in *Yunling Ren/Yan Hong*, Rights of Joint

(Article 14(2) after the fourth amendment's entry into force), any other exercises of the patent and all exercises of the application right require the consent of all co-owners. Consequently, at least in case of joint non-service inventions where the application right is initially owned by the joint inventors, single co-inventors should be banned from exercising the application right on their own, i.e., they may neither transfer it nor file a first application or subsequent applications on their own without seeking the consent of the other inventors.

With regard to commissioned development of technology, Article 8 Patent Law and Article 339 Contract Law both provide that in absence of an agreement to the contrary, the commissioned party shall have the right to apply for a patent. Article 339 Contract Law further stipulates that in a patent that belongs to the commissioned party, the commissioning party enjoys the right to exploit the invention free of charge. If the commissioned party decides to assign the application right, the principal enjoys a preferential right of first refusal. The present Patent Law draft amendment does not envisage any changes to Article 8. Article 339 of the Contract Law has been transferred to Article 859 of the new Civil Code in largely unamended form, apart from a small modification stipulating that if the patent belongs to the commissioned party, the principal shall be allowed to exploit the patent "according to the law", i.e., no longer necessarily "free of charge."

Finally, in a manner that has obviously been inspired by the US *Bayh-Dole* Act,[167] the Law on Scientific and Technical Progress, originally enacted in 1992 and substantively amended in 2007 regulates that in case of government-commissioned science and technology, the commissioned party, e.g., a university, shall be the owner of the resulting IP but that it is also obliged to actually exploit said IP and to annually report its exploitation activities to the government. In case of failure to exploit, the granting agency or other government agencies are entitled to exercise marching-in rights.

VIII. EXAMINATION AND GRANT

Upon receipt and a first preliminary examination as to whether the documents are complete and accurate, CNIPA awards applications for inventions, utility models and designs a filing date, which is the date of receipt. As China adheres to the first-to-file principle, the filing date is of utmost importance. All identical subject matter filed at a later date by a third party or by the applicant himself is no longer regarded as novel. The first-to-file principle for inventions and utility models is laid down in the definition of novelty in Article 22(2) Patent Law:

> Novelty means that the invention or utility model concerned is not an existing technology; no patent application is filed by any unit or individual for any identical invention or utility model with the Patent Administration Department under the State Council before the date of application for patent right, and no identical invention or utility model is recorded in the patent application

Patent Owners in China, 11 J. Marshall Rev. Intell. Prop. L. 601 (2012), 600 et seq.

167. Taolue Zhang, Dan Prud'homme and Oliver Lutze, *supra* note 162.

documents or the patent documentations which are published or announced after the date of application.

CNIPA only accepts applications filed in Chinese language, with the exception of PCT applications choosing CNIPA as receiving office. They may be filed in English,[168] but later on, when entering the Chinese national phase, they must be translated into Chinese.

1. Invention and Utility Model Application Documents

On 1 January 1994, China joined the Patent Cooperation Treaty (PCT). CNIPA since then has functioned as an international receiving office and has the authority to conduct an international search and international preliminary examination. All these functions are regulated in the Provisions Concerning the Implementation of the Patent Cooperation Treaty in China, promulgated by the Patent Office on 23 November 1993.[169] The PCT application system plays an important role in procedural practice. In 2018, CNIPA received 55,000 international applications, 9.3 percent more than in the previous year and delivered 52,000 international search reports, an increase of 17.6 percent over the previous year, and 451 international preliminary examination reports (330 in 2017). Also in 2017, 93,000 international applications entered the Chinese international phase, an increase of 7.7 percent over the previous year.[170]

Since 2000, Article 20(2) Patent Law expressly allows domestic applicants to file international applications. According to Article 20(3) Patent Law (Article 19(3) after the fourth amendment's entry into force), international applications shall be governed by the relevant international treaty system, the Patent Law and further administrative rules promulgated by the State Council. Subsequently, the State Council added a new Chapter X to the Implementing Regulations of 2001 (Rules 101–117 after the amendment of 2010), which regulates the details of the entry of international applications into the Chinese national phase. It is supplemented by an even more detailed Part III of the Examination Guidelines.[171] The third amendment to the Patent Law of 2008 introduced a mandatory confidentiality examination of inventions made in China for which the applicant seeks patent protection abroad.[172]

The basic requirements with regard to form and content of the application documents are regulated in Article 26 Patent Law for inventions and utility models, and in Article 27 Patent Law for designs.

According to Article 26, the application documents for an invention or a utility model application shall consist of a request, a description and its abstract, and the claims. The request shall contain the basic information about the application,

168. See SIPO sheet of the PCT Applicants Guide, at http://www.wipo.int/pct/guide/en/gdvol1/annexes/annexc/ax_c_cn.pdf.

169. Effective since 1 January 1994; China Patents & Trademarks 1/1994, 93.

170. From the CNIPA annual report 2018, http://english.cnipa.gov.cn/col/col2076/index.html, under "III. Application and Examination" (the figures indicated there are obviously rounded); more about the procedures of entering the Chinese national phase *infra* in VIII. 4.

171. More *infra* in VIII. 4.

172. See *infra* VIII. 8.

namely the title of the invention-creation and name and address not only of the actual applicant, but also of the inventor or creator. The description shall outline the invention in a manner sufficiently clear and complete to enable a person skilled in the art to carry it out; when necessary, drawings shall be added.

The abstract of the description shall outline the main technical points of the invention in brief. The claims must be based on the description and determine the desired scope of patent protection in clear and concise manner. According to the SPC in *Hong Liang v. Patent Reexamination Board* of 11 May 2012,[173] however, this does not mean that every little error renders the application non-patentable, but the person skilled in the art shall be deemed capable of grasping the technical idea in a patent application correctly even if the documents contain obvious errors, i.e., the skilled artisan is expected to be mentally flexible enough not mechanically follow the wording of the patent documents but to identify obvious errors.

Since 2008, Article 26 Patent Law contains an additional requirement with regard to inventions that are based on genetic material, namely that they must indicate the direct and original source of such material.

(a) Request

The request shall contain the basic information about the invention. The title of the invention or utility model that has to be indicated in the request shall be written in a clear and concise manner, which means that it shall contain no more than 25 characters (40 characters may be permitted by the examiner on request) and shall not contain any non-technical or indeterminate expressions.[174]

The request shall indicate not only the applicant, but also the inventor or creator. The Examination Guidelines clarify that only natural persons can be named as inventors, which, as discussed above, excludes AI with the ability to invent from being regarded as inventor. The inventor may also request that his name shall not be published. Foreigners are required to have their names translated/transcribed into Chinese, but they may also indicate their original names.[175] The same applies to individual applicants.[176] Should an international application designating China not indicate the inventor's name, Rule 104(1) No. 4 Implementing Regulations requires that such indication be made in the declaration of entry into the national phase at the latest. Article 4(1) v) PCT allows such treatment of international applications. Once the inventor's name is indicated, CNIPA will not further examine whether the correct person, namely the one who indeed creatively contributed to the invention-creation and did not merely perform organizational assistance or other auxiliary services (Rule 13 Implementing Regulations), is indicated as inventor.[177]

The request must further indicate the name and address of the applicant. Hereby the examiner should in general accept the indications as to whether the invention has been made inside or outside an employment relationship without further scrutiny,

173. SPC's Administrative Judgment (2011) Xing Ti Zi No. 13 of 11 May 2012.
174. Examination Guidelines, Part I, Chapter 1, 4.1.1.
175. Examination Guidelines, Part I, Chapter 1, 4.1.2.
176. Examination Guidelines, Part I, Chapter 1, 4.1.3.2.
177. Examination Guidelines, Part I, Chapter 1, 4.1.2.

unless he has serious doubts that the subject matter of an individual's application could have been accomplished outside an employment relationship. In such case, he can request the applicant to furnish evidence that the invention constitutes a non-service invention. Such evidence must be issued by the employing entity. The same applies to situations in which the status of the applicant of a service invention as employing entity remains doubtful, which may, for instance, occur if a "project group" of a university institute, etc., acts as the applicant of a service invention. In this case, the examiner shall request the applicant to furnish further material that proves its eligibility as applicant.[178]

A foreigner or foreign enterprise may be requested to provide evidence that Chinese applicants enjoy equal treatment in his or its home country (Rule 33(3) Implementing Regulations). In the rare case that such equal treatment cannot be verified, the application will be rejected on the basis of Article 18 Patent Law.

In order to facilitate the communication between CNIPA and the applicant, Rule 15(4) Implementing Regulations provides that in the case of two or more applicants who have not appointed a patent agent, the applicant named first in the request shall represent the others unless the request contains a clear statement that another applicant has been appointed as representative. The representative can deal with all application related subject matter on behalf of the others, except the "formalities directly relating to the joint rights" such as filing the patent application, appointing a patent agency, assigning the right to apply, the priority right or the patent, withdrawal of the patent application or the priority claim or abandoning the granted patent.[179] As will be further outlined below,[180] groups of foreign applicants cannot choose to appoint one of them as a representative, as Article 19(1) of the current Patent Law (Article 18(1) after the fourth amendment's entry into force) obliges foreign parties to handle all patent related matters through a legally established patent agency.

The Examination Guidelines contain further details on the indication of the patent agency and of the various addresses to be indicated in the request.[181] Patent agencies must be legally established and approved by CNIPA.

(b) Description and Drawings

According to Article 26(3) Patent Law, the description must set forth the invention or utility model in a manner sufficiently clear and complete to enable a person skilled in the relevant field of technology to carry it out.

Details about form and content of the description are regulated in Rule 17 Implementing Regulations. Required is the indication of:

The technical field to which the technical solution pertains (Rule 17(1) No. 1):

According to the Examination Guidelines, the technical field to be indicated is the field of technology to which the invention belongs, which in most cases should be consistent with one of the fields of lower rank enumerated in the International

178. Examination Guidelines, Part I, Chapter 1, 4.1.3.1.
179. Examination Guidelines, Part I, Chapter I, 4.1.5.
180. See Chapter XI on Fees and Patent Agencies.
181. Examination Guidelines, Part I, Chapter I, 4.1.6 and 4.1.7.

Patent Classification. Neither the general field to which the technical solution pertains, nor the invention as such shall be indicated as technical field.[182]

The prior art (Rule 17(1) No. 2):

The prior art is defined as that which is necessary for understanding the invention and for search and examination. When possible, the documents reflecting such prior art (patent documents and others), shall be cited. The wording of the provision is largely consistent with Rule 5.1.a) ii) of the PCT Regulations. According to the Examination Guidelines, the prior art may be consistent with the "closest related prior art", which according to Rule 21(1) No. 1 Implementing Regulations shall be indicated in the preamble portion of the independent claim.[183] The Examination Guidelines contain further details on quoting prior patent documents or other reference documents representing prior art, and regulate how documents in foreign languages shall be quoted.

The content of the invention-creation (Rule 17(1) No. 3):

As content of the invention, the technical problem, its technical solution and the advantageous effects of the solution in comparison with the prior art shall be indicated. This wording is largely consistent with the wording of Rule 5.1 a) iii) PCT Regulations. The description of the technical problem detected in prior art shall remain confined to the problems that are actually solved by the invention, or by several inventions contained in a single application, which is admissible as long as they represent a coherent inventive concept. The description of the technical solution should start with the description of the entirety of the indispensable technical features of the independent claim(s), which in case of dependent claims may be followed by the description of the entity of additional technical features to each of the dependent claims. The technical terms in the description shall be consistent with the terms used in the claims.[184] Finally, the advantageous effects that have to be illustrated in the description are of great importance for determining non-obviousness, i.e., whether the invention represents a "notable progress" or whether the utility model represents "progress" over the prior art.[185]

If there are drawings, a description of each drawing (Rule 17(1) No. 4):

In case that the description is accompanied by drawings – in case of utility models, drawings are a compulsory part of the description – the description shall contain a short explanation of each drawing. This provision is consistent with Rule 5.1. a) iv) PCT Regulations.

The precise mode of carrying out the invention (Rule 17(1) No. 5):

The applicant shall outline the best mode of carrying out the invention known to him, preferably with the help of embodiments and with reference to drawings, if any. The explanations have to be sufficiently detailed to enable a person skilled in the relevant field of technology to carry out the invention without any further creative endeavour. To facilitate the examination work, the Examination Guidelines

182. Examination Guidelines, Part II, Chapter 2, 2.2.2.
183. Examination Guidelines, Part II, Chapter 2, 2.2.3.
184. Examination Guidelines, Part II, Chapter 2, 2.2.4 (2).
185. Examination Guidelines, Part II, Chapter 2, 2.2.4 (3).

prescribe that when describing the precise mode of carrying out the invention, all contents indispensable to a full disclosure as required by Article 26(3) Patent Law shall be explained in full, i.e., not by mere reference to other documents or other parts of the description.[186]

With regard to the embodiments, the Examination Guidelines state that their number shall depend on the character of the invention, the field of technology, the existing technology and the scope of protection. As a general rule, the broader the requested scope of protection, the more embodiments are necessary for full disclosure.[187] In case of inventions based on numerical ranges, embodiments shall cover both ends of the numerical range, but if such range is broad, it might be advisable to include another embodiment pertaining to an intermediate value.

Pursuant to Rule 17(1) and (2) Implementing Regulations, the description shall indicate the technical field to which the invention pertains, the background art, the content of the invention (technical problem, its solution and advantageous effect over prior art), the description of figures in the drawings if drawings are attached and the mode of carrying out the invention, preferably in this order unless a different order is more concise and facilitates understanding. The wording of this provision, which has been adopted in 1992, is consistent with Rule 5(b) PCT Regulations.

According to Rule 17(3), the description shall not refer to the claims as "as described in claim...", etc., and shall not contain commercial advertising. Standard terms shall be used and the description shall be written in a clear manner. The requirement of clarity and sufficiency of the description is subject to preliminary examination pursuant to Rule 44(1) with regard to inventions and Rule 44(2) with regard to utility models.

With regard to inventions pertaining to nucleotide or amino acid sequences, Rule 17(4) prescribes that a sequence table in accordance with official standards must be filed as an independent part of the description, such as a copy in machine-readable form. The new provision is largely consistent with Rule 5.2. a) PCT Implementing Regulations. On 1 November 2001, the State Intellectual Property Administration published the Official Standard with Regard to Amino Acid and/or Nucleotide Sequence Protocols and Electronic Sequence Protocol Documents.[188]

Part II of the Examination Guidelines contains a whole Chapter 10 on the peculiarities of examining chemical inventions. Its Sec. 3.4 highlights the importance of embodiments and experimental data for sufficient disclosure, but until recently Para. (2) prohibited examiners from considering embodiments and experimental data furnished after the application date. The 2017 amendment to the Guidelines rendered this practice more liberal by transferring a part of the content of the previous Sec. 3.4(2) in a new Sec. 3.5 and adding that the examiner shall also consider later furnished experimental data to the extent that a skilled artisan can comprehend the technical effect proven by such data from the content disclosed in the patent application.[189] The amendment should largely satisfy the requirement in Article 1.10

---

186. Examination Guidelines, Part II, Chapter 2, 2.2.6.
187. *Ibid.*
188. https://www.cnipa.gov.cn/art/2011/12/24/art_526_145937.html.
189. More details about the practice under the previous Examination Guidelines in Toby Mak, 'Biotechnological, Chemical and Pharmaceutical Inventions II: Support and Experimental

of mentioned Sino-US ETA ("Consideration of Supplemental Data"), which, however, requires that applicants shall be allowed to rely on supplemental data not only during patent examination, but also during patent review and judicial proceedings.

The formalities with regard to the drawings, which must be part of utility model applications because utility model protection is only available for technical solutions pertaining to the *shape or structure of a product* (Article 2(2) Patent Law) but not for methods, chemical or biological compounds, etc., without a drawable shape or structure, are regulated in Rule 18 Implementing Regulations. Accordingly, several drawings must be arranged in numerical order and shall not contain redundant references, neither shall the description refer to non-existing drawings. Also, no text is permitted in the drawings except indispensable terms.

(c) Claims

According to Article 26(4) Patent Law, the claims of an invention or utility model application shall state the requested scope of protection and be supported by the description. Details concerning the content and form of the claims are contained in Rules 19–22 Implementing Regulations, which largely correspond with Rule 6 PCT Regulations, and in Part II on Substantive Examination, Chapter 2, 3.1. Examination Guidelines.

The Implementing Regulations and the Examination Guidelines also regulate the relationship between independent and dependent claims. Whereas according to Rule 20(1) Implementing Regulations, the independent claim shall outline the entirety of the technical solution, the function of the dependent claims according to Rule 20(2) is to further define the independent claim to which it refers, by outlining additional technical features. Therefore, as the Examination Guidelines point out, independent claims shall be characterized by the "essential technical features" of the invention, i.e., those technical features that are indispensable to solve the technical problem, and their aggregation shall form the solution to the technical problem and distinguish the invention or utility model from prior art.

Dependent claims represent, by nature, a narrower protection scope than the independent claim by adding more features to the essential features of the independent claim. The Examination Guidelines stress that in some applications that comprise several inventions pertaining to a single inventive concept, subsequent independent claims may refer to preceding ones in a manner that they are easily confused with dependent claims. For instance, an independent claim pertaining to a product with which the method represented by a previous process claim is carried out, may be drafted in a manner that it appears like a dependent claim. In such cases, the examiner shall not be misguided by different drafting styles, but always consider the essence of the claims.[190]

An independent claim shall, in general, be divided into a preamble portion containing the title of the claimed subject matter and the technical features the solution has in common with the "closest related prior art", and a characterizing

Data', in Stefan Luginbuehl and Peter Ganea (eds.), *Patent Law in Greater China* (Edward Elgar, 2014), 87 et seq.

190. Part II, Chapter 2, 3.1.2.

portion which points out the advantages over such prior art. (Rule 21 Implementing Regulations). Also a dependent claim consists of two parts, namely a reference portion which indicates the claims to which the dependent claim refers, and a characterizing portion which outlines the additional technical features of the invention or utility model (Rule 23). Deviations from this format are permissible in exceptional cases, for instance, if the subject matter of the application pertains to a new field of technology for which no prior art references exist.[191]

The term "closest related prior art" as the prior art from which the technical solution claimed in the independent claim must be distinguishable, was introduced in 2001. The previous use of the mere term "prior art" misled a number of applicants to mention even the most self-evident technical feature instead of restricting their specifications to the technical features that the closest related technical solution of prior art had in common with the actual invention.

According to Rule 22 Implementing Regulations, also dependent claims shall consist of two parts, a reference part that refers to the preceding independent or dependent claim, and a characterizing part that outlines the additional technical feature. Multiple dependent shall cite the preceding claims in alternative form (e.g. "claims 1–3, claim 5 or claim 7") and shall not serve as reference for further multiple dependent claims.

The technical solution for which protection is sought is expected to be sufficiently outlined in the claims, so that in general there is no need to refer to the description and to the drawings, except where absolutely necessary for understanding (Rule 19(3) Implementing Regulations). Reference to corresponding technical features illustrated in the drawings by citing the references in the drawings is permissible, if made in order to facilitate understanding, but such reference shall not be interpreted as limiting the claims. The claims as such may contain chemical or mathematical formulae, but no drawings.

With regard to functional elements ("features of function or effect"), the Examination Guidelines state that they shall be avoided as much as possible to define product claims, unless necessary or more suitable than structural elements. Their function or effect shall be easily comprehensible to a skilled artisan from their application as indicated in the description or from the manner they are customarily applied in the art, or by way of experiments.[192] A functional feature embraces, by definition, several alternative means by which the same inventive aim can be achieved. Therefore, if the examiner finds that only a specific means out of the alternative means is best capable of achieving the inventive aim, he shall not allow the functional feature into the claim.

(d) Abstract

Rule 23 Implementing Regulations on the abstract largely corresponds to Rule 8 PCT Regulations. The abstract shall allow a clear understanding of the technical problem disclosed in the application, the decisive point of its solution and the preferred mode

191. Further exceptions are outlined in the Examination Guidelines, Part II, Chapter 2, 3.3.1.
192. Part II, Chapter 2, 3.2.1, insofar quite similar to the corresponding case law of the EPO Boards of Appeal.

of carrying out the invention. In applications that contain drawings, that drawing that best characterizes the invention shall be included in the abstract. When appropriate, the chemical formula or the drawing that best characterises the invention shall be indicated. The abstract shall not contain commercial advertising and be limited to 300 characters. If the applicant fails to meet these formal requirements, the examiner can instruct the applicant to amend the abstract or make the amendments by himself and notify the applicant thereof.[193]

(e) Deposit of Biological Material

Rule 24 Implementing Regulations regulates the deposit of biological material in case of invention applications related to micro-organisms. Accordingly, such deposit does not have to be made in all cases, but only where it is not publicly available and cannot be sufficiently disclosed by the description alone.

The applicant must deposit a sample of the biological material with a depository institution designated by the CNIPA at the latest on the application date/priority date (Rule 24 No. 1 Implementing Regulations). Part I, Chapter 1, 5.2 of the Examination Guidelines points out that deposit dates between the priority and the application date will not be acknowledged in the course of preliminary examination, and that the examiner shall instruct the applicant to either give up the priority date or the priority claim regarding the subject matter of the deposit, otherwise the deposit will be deemed to not have been made. Furthermore, within four months from the application date, the applicant must submit a receipt of depository and a viability proof issued by the depository institution (Rule 24 No. 1).[194] For international application entering the Chinese national phase, Rule 108(3) Implementing Regulations stipulates that the applicant may submit these certificates within four months from entry.[195]

No later than four months from the application date, the applicant is required to indicate the scientific Latin name of the material, title and address of the depository institution, the date of deposit and number of deposit, both in the request (Rule 24 No. 1). According to the rules on international applications entering the national phase, these formalities are deemed to have been completed if an application that designates China makes reference to the deposited biological material in accordance with Rule 13bis PCT Regulations (Rule 108(1) Implementing Regulations). In such case, the applicant shall indicate the documents noting the particulars of the deposit. If the original international application contains particulars of a deposit of biological material, but no corresponding indication is made in the declaration on entry into the national phase, the applicant may correct his declaration within four months from the completion of formalities for the entry into the national phase (Rule 108(2)).

193. The requirements with regard to the abstract are contained in Part I, Chapter 1, 4.5, of the Examination Guidelines.

194. Only a few WIPO member states, if any, seem to require such proof of viability, see list of requirements regarding deposit of biological material in Annex L of the PCT Applicant's Guide – International Phase: https://www.wipo.int/export/sites/www/pct/guide/en/gdvol1/annexes/annexl/anx_l.pdf.

195. Details concerning the examination of international applications referring to the deposit of biological material are contained in Part III, Chapter 1, 5.4 of the Examination Guidelines.

If the above formalities are not completed within the specific time limits, the deposit is deemed not made. An application for which a deposit is required, but which does not meet the depositing formalities, will be rejected after substantive examination on grounds of non-compliance with the requirement of full disclosure under Article 26(3) Patent Law.

Rule 25 Implementing Regulations provides that after the publication of the application pertaining to deposited biological material, any third party may request CNIPA to allow the experimental use of the biological material. For this, the requesting party must submit statements that it will not make the material available to others and that it will exclusively use it for experimental purposes.

2. Design Application Documents

Design applications consist of a request, drawings or photographs and, since the Patent Law amendment of 2008, a brief explanation (Article 59(2) of the current Patent Law, Article 64(2) after the fourth revision's entry into force).

(a) Request

The request shall contain the name of the design product in conformity with the design as shown in the drawings or photographs as well as with the names of the corresponding subclass of the International Classification of Industrial Designs (Locarno Agreement). Names referring to persons, locations, trademarks, historical epochs, etc., generic terms such as "cooking utensils" or "musical instrument", descriptions of the technical composition or effect such as "oil saving engine", indications of sizes, scale or numbers and unfamiliar foreign language terms shall be avoided. Foreign-language terms that are known in China, for instance, "DVD player" or "LED light" can be used, however. The request shall furthermore contain the details about the creator, applicant, contact person, representative, patent agent and address in the same manner as regulated with regard to invention and utility model applications.[196]

With respect to designs of products incorporating a GUI design element, the newly amended Examination Guidelines emphasize that the product name must specify the kind of GUI (static/dynamic), its main application and the product to which it pertains, e.g., "dynamic GUI of a weather forecast on a cell phone" and that using "GUI" as product name, as in "software GUI" or "control GUI" shall be avoided.[197]

(b) Drawings or Photographs

Properly prepared drawings or photographs are of utmost importance, as according to Article 59(2) Patent Law (Article 64(2) after the fourth revision's entry into force),

196. The details of the request are regulated in Part I, Chapter 3, 4.1 of the Examination Guidelines.
197. Part I, Chapter 3, 4.4.1.

the scope of protection is defined by the appearance of the product as shown in the drawings or pictures, whereas the brief explanation may be used to explain the design as shown in the drawings or pictures. According to practitioners in the field, Chinese examiners are very strict with regard to the requirements set forth in Part I, Chapter 1, 4.2 Examination Guidelines as to views, lines, colours, shades, permitted drawing equipment, etc., in case of drawings and as to perspective, brightness, shadow, reflection, etc. in case of photographs. Design applicants are well advised to painstakingly observe these formalities to avoid the receipt of a *Notification to Make a Correction.*[198]

With special regard to GUI designs, the 2019 amendment to the Examination Guidelines has introduced a new Sec. 4.4.2 to Part I, Chapter 3, stipulating that in cases in which protection is sought for the GUI as the only design element, the application may include one orthographic projection of the GUI display and disregard the views of the product to which the GUI is attached, unless it is necessary to also show size, position and proportion of the GUI design in relation with the final product. Where protection for the design of a dynamic GUI is sought, the applicant shall submit the orthographic illustration of at least one state as the main view whereas the other states can be presented by way of illustrations of key frames, in a manner that embraces the complete animation process. If the illustrations are marked, the marking has to follow the animation process sequence. Finally, if a GUI is used to operate a projection device, at least one view that clearly shows such device must be added to the view(s) of the GUI.

(c) *Brief Explanation*

In 2008, the "brief explanation" has been added to the documents that have to be contained in a design application to enable applicants to describe the scope of protection sought in a more precise manner, especially if it does not become entirely clear by mere reference to the drawings or pictures. The brief explanation shall contain the title of the design product, which must be consistent with the title used in the request, the use of the design product the indication of which shall help to identify the class to which the design pertains, the essential features, i.e., the shape, pattern or their combination or the colour in combination with the shape and/or pattern, that distinguish the design from prior design solutions, and the indication of the drawing or picture, which is best suited to show such essential features. Where necessary, the brief explanation shall also contain specific information, e.g., on the reasons for the omission of views, the indication of a main design in case of similar design applications, the pattern of plane products of non-confined size, materials that generate a special visual effect or the indication of colours where protection for colour in combination with shape or pattern is sought. Applicants who claim a colour in combination with shape or pattern do not have to fear that differently coloured products of the same shape or pattern will be excluded from the protection scope, as the overall visual impression is decisive for its determination. In case of three-dimensional products, the colour normally has a rather negligible effect on the

198. Deng Ming, *supra* note 103, 20.

overall visual impression, but it may have a stronger and therefore limiting effect if applied to a two-dimensional product.[199]

Again, with special regard to GUI, a new Sec. 4.4.3 to Part I, Chapter 3 of the Examination Guidelines provides that the brief explanation shall clearly explain the use of the GUI in conformity with the use indicated in the product name. Where only one view of the GUI has been submitted because it comprises the essential design features, the explanation shall enumerate all products on which it is used, for example as in "this display is used on cell phones and computers". If necessary, also the position of the GUI on the product, the human-machine interaction and the dynamic process shall be explained.

3. Preliminary Examination

After awarding a filing date, the examiner commences the preliminary examination, which, according to Rule 44 Implementing Regulations, includes the following:

(a) Subject Matter of Preliminary Invention and Utility Model Examination[200]

The examiner scrutinizes the application documents as to whether the invention or utility model obviously violates the law or the public interest (Article 5 Patent Law) or obviously belongs to non-patentable subject matter (Article 25), whether the foreign applicant is entitled to apply under a convention, a bilateral treaty or the principle of reciprocity (Article 18; Article 17 after the fourth amendment's entry into force) and whether he has appointed a legally established patent agency as required by Article 19(1), whether the domestic application first filed abroad has undergone the confidentiality examination according to Article 20(1) (Article 19(1) after the fourth amendment's entry into force),[201] whether the request contains all required details (Rule 16 Implementing Regulations), including information about genetic resources in case of biological inventions relying on them (Article 26(5) Patent Law and Rule 26(2) Implementing Regulations), whether the invention-creation obviously does not conform with the definition of an invention (Article 2(2) Patent Law) or of a utility model (Article 2(3) Patent Law) or whether it obviously does not meet the requirements as to unity in Article 31(1) Patent Law, and whether an amendment to the invention-creation has obviously extended the original protection scope (Article 33 Patent Law).

Both invention and utility model applications are, furthermore, examined as to conformity with the formal requirements pertaining to the patent documents (Rules 16–23 Implementing Regulations), but to different extents. Whereas the examination of the description, drawings and claims of invention patent applications concentrates on "obvious" non-conformity with the formal requirements in Rules 17–21 Implementing Regulations, most parts of a utility model application undergo

199. Deng Ming, *supra* note 103.

200. The details of preliminary examination are regulated in detail in Part I, Chapter 1 (inventions) and Chapter 2 (utility models) of the Examination Guidelines.

201. See VIII. 8. *infra*.

a more thorough examination, with the exception of adherence to Rule 20 on the relationship between independent and dependent claims, which, also in case of utility model applications, is only examined as to "obvious" non-conformity. Utility model applications are, furthermore, more thoroughly examined as to compliance with the requirements pertaining to dependent claims (Rule 22) and to the abstract (Rule 23) and, unlike invention application, are subject to examination as to obvious non-compliance with Rule 43(1) Implementing Regulations on divisional applications and Article 9 Patent Law according to which for one invention-creation only one patent shall be granted.[202]

Reportedly, utility model applications are also increasingly scrutinized as to obvious non-conformity with the novelty requirement.[203]

(b) *Subject Matter of Preliminary Design Examination*[204]

Design applications are examined as to whether their subject matter obviously violates the law or the public interest (Article 5 Patent Law) or is obviously non-patentable according to Article 25(1) No. 6 because it is mainly used for marking a print's pattern or colour or their combination, whether the foreign applicant is entitled to file and has appointed a legally established agency (Article 18, 19(1) Patent Law; Articles 17 and 18(1) after the fourth revision's entry into force), whether the requirements as to request (Rule 16 Implementing Regulations), illustrations in case of colour designs (Rule 27) and the description (Rule 28) are met, whether the subject matter of the application obviously contravenes the definition of a protected design (Article 2(4) Patent Law), the novelty requirement in Article 23(1) Patent Law, the clarity requirement with regard to drawings or pictures (Article 27(2) Patent Law), the unity requirements (Article 31(2)), the scope of allowed amendments in Article 33 Patent Law, the requirements regarding divisional applications (Rule 43(1) Implementing Regulations) or the principle that for one invention-creation only one patent shall be granted (Article 9 Patent Law).

(c) *Procedure of Preliminary Examination*

If the examiner detects a deficiency, he must issue a formal *Notification to Make Rectification*, or, in case of substantive effects that cannot be eliminated by rectification, an office action that points out these severe defects and invites the applicant to state his observation, both within a specified time limit. If the applicant does not respond within these time limits, the application shall be "deemed to have been withdrawn", whereas failure to eliminate the defects results in the rejection of the application. Normally, the applicant is given two opportunities to make rectifications, which should not extend the original protection scope because such extension may be another cause for rejection. Pursuant to Rule 51(2) Implementing Regulations,

202. See also Examination Guidelines, Part I, Chapter 2, 13; check as to obvious non-compliance in this case means that the examiner does not examine at his own initiative but only if he knows that another application for an identical invention-creation has been filed.
203. Oliver Pfaffenzeller, Xia Pfaffenzeller, Ming Deng and Beat Weibel, *supra* note 86.
204. Details in Examination Guidelines, Part I, Chapter 3.

design (as well as utility model) applicants may also amend their applications at their own initiative, but only within two months from the application date.

If the application is only "deemed to have been withdrawn" due to failure to meet a deadline for rectification, etc., the applicant may the request restoration of his right to apply pursuant to Rule 6 Implementing Regulations, provided that the delay had been caused by *force majeure* or other justifiable reasons.[205] [206]

If the application does not contain defects or if the defects are limited by rectification or upon an applicant's observation, the examiner shall issue a *Notification of Passing the Preliminary Examination* in case of invention applications,[207] whereas successful utility model and design applicants will receive a *Notification of Patent Grant*.[208]

Finally, with regard to the transfer of the application right (but also of the granted patent) by way of assignment or gift, the 2019 amendment to the provisions on changes to bibliographical data in the Examination Guidelines added a few clarifications, namely that the transfer contract that must be submitted to CNIPA shall be signed and stamped and that the examiner shall, in case of doubt, examine the contract document for irregularities, contradictions, etc.[209]

(d) Further Procedures Regarding Invention Applications during the Publication Period

Pursuant to Article 34 Patent Law and Rule 46 Implementing Regulations, CNIPA shall publish the application at latest upon expiration of 18 full months after the application date, but it may be published earlier at the request of the applicant.[210] Normally, rejected applications, applications deemed to have been withdrawn as well as voluntarily withdrawn applications are not published but in case of voluntary withdrawal, the applicant is well advised to consider that publication can no longer be prevented if the withdrawal is made after the completion of the preparation for publication (Rule 36(3) Implementing Regulations). As there are no provisions on the point of time at which such preparations are deemed to be completed, practitioners suggest that such withdrawal shall be made at latest until the expiration of 15 months after the application date to avoid an undesired publication.[211]

---

205. Restoration will then have to follow the provisions of Part V, Chapter 7, 6 of the Examination Guidelines.
206. The Examination Guidelines provisions on the treatment of defects identified in preliminary examination (Part I, Chapter 1, Sec. 3, Chapter 2, Sec. 3 and Chapter 3, Sec. 3) are basically the same for inventions, utility models and designs.
207. Examination Guidelines, Part I, Chapter 1, 3.1.
208. Article 40 Patent Law; Examination Guidelines, Part I, Chapter 2, 3.1 and Chapter 3, 3.1.
209. The amendment has been introduced in Part I, Chapter 1, 6.7.2.2 (2) on changes in bibliographical information in the course of the preliminary examination of invention patent applications, but according to Part I, Chapter 2, Sec. 4.5 and Chapter 3, Sec. 5.5, the new provisions shall be applied *mutatis mutandis* to utility model and design applications.
210. See also Part I, Chapter 1, 6.5 Examination Guidelines.
211. Deng Ming, *supra* note 121, 143 (148 et eq.).

During publication, patent owners enjoy the right in Article 13 Patent Law to be compensated for unauthorized uses of their invention between publication and grant. Patent owners who rather prefer full-fledged patent protection at the earliest possible date are advised to simultaneously apply for a model patent, which will be granted after a mere preliminary examination.[212]

(e) Substantive Examination of Invention Patent Applications

According to Article 35(1) Patent Law, the request for substantive examination must be made before the expiration of three years after the application date or, where priority is claimed, after the priority date,[213] otherwise the application will be deemed to have been withdrawn. Article 35(2) Patent Law also allows CNIPA to commence substantive examination on its own where deemed necessary, e.g., because the invention may be of great significance for the state or for the public interest.[214]

When requesting substantive examination, the applicant has one opportunity to voluntarily amend the application. Another opportunity arises during three months after the actual receipt of the *Notification that the Application has Entered Substantive Examination* (Rule 51(1) Implementing Regulations). After that, amendments can only be made in response to an examiner's notification (Rule 51(3) Implementing Regulations). For the sake of procedural economy, however, delayed voluntary amendments may be exceptionally considered, namely where the examiner thinks that they have eliminated the defects of an earlier version of the application.[215]

Substantive examination is roughly divided in a phase before and a phase after the First Office action. It includes formal and substantive aspects.[216]

Part II, Chapter 8, 4.2., instructs examiners to first obtain a comprehensive picture of the claimed invention when commencing substantive examination. The amendment of 2019 has introduced more specific instructions, stressing that such initial examination shall, *inter alia*, focus on obtaining a thorough understanding of the entire relevant background art and on identifying the invention's improvements over it.

The Examination Guidelines contain very detailed chapters on the examination of unity and whether priority is correctly claimed.[217] For the sake of procedural economy, however, if the examiner has detected some serious defects that give full reason to a rejection pursuant to Rule 53 Implementing Regulations, the examiner is not obliged to carry on with examination but may issue the First Office Action without having completed a comprehensive examination.[218] Also, the search[219] to identify prior art and to compare it with the invention as to novelty and inventiveness may

212. More about simultaneous invention and utility model application *supra* V. 1. a) (4).
213. Clarified by Part I, Chapter 1, 6.4.1 Examination Guidelines.
214. Deng Ming, *supra* note 121, 149 et seq.
215. Examination Guidelines, Part II, Chapter 8, 4.1.
216. Principle of "comprehensive examination" laid out in Part II, Chapter 8, 4.7 of the Examination Guidelines.
217. Examination Guidelines, Part II, Chapter 8, 4.7.
218. Examination Guidelines, Part II, Chapter 8, 4.8.
219. Detailed in Part II, Chapter 7 of the Examination Guidelines.

be delayed or not commenced before the First Office Action if the examiner identifies defects that are so serious that they have to be clarified through the First Office Action before the examination can be continued. This may occur if the examiner thinks that the subject matter of the application violates the law or the public order (Article 5 Patent Law), pertains to non-patentable subject matter (Article 25), does not form an invention according to the definition of a patentable invention in Article 2(2), lacks practical applicability or is not described in a clear enough manner. The Examination Guidelines stress, however, that a First Office Action without prior search can only be issued if all of these defects are identified. That is, if only a part of these defects is identified, the search must be carried on with regard to the unencumbered parts of the application.[220]

The 2019 amendment to the Examination Guidelines overhauled numerous search-related provisions. Sections 6.2 and 6.3 of Part II, Chapter 7 regarding the mode of carrying out a search are now better structured, detailing that a search is comprised of an initial search, a regular search of the technical field to which the invention belongs and an extended search that also includes neighbouring fields in which technical solutions of similar functionality or use if corresponding prior art cannot be found in the field/class to which the invention belongs. Section 6.3 contains entirely new instructions on the "search strategy", which obviously aims at a more structured course of action by examiners, instructing them to first determine the search systems and databases they want to resort to, to identify the form of documenting the key elements of their search (classification numbers, keywords, etc.), to determine a manner of combining the key elements in a meaningful manner, etc. The search process must also be duly documented in the search report.[221] With regard to this, the amendment modernized Section 2 of Part II, Chapter 7, stating that the documentation shall be comprised of patent literature and non-patent resources. Patent literature shall mainly consist of patent databases searchable with the help of computer search systems (paper, microfiche or CD-ROMs are no longer explicitly mentioned), and the search shall comprise Chinese and foreign patent literature in general and no longer be limited to the materials that CNIPA has stored in electronic and paper form.[222] The focus of the search of non-patent literature is now on computer search systems and material retrievable on the internet, which shall comprise Chinese and worldwide technical literature, periodicals, theses, standards or protocols, indexing tools, manuals, etc.

Further amendments pertain to terminating or not commencing a search. If a search is stopped for the sake of efficiency because its continuation would be unreasonably costly, the examiner must, according to the amendment, at least have searched a specified number of acknowledged Chinese and foreign databases and, in case of certain areas of technology, also a minimum of other databases specific to such areas.[223] Moreover, with regard to the above-mentioned case in which the examiner refrains from a search because he finds the application to be highly deficient, the

220. Examination Guidelines, Part II, Chapter 8, 4.3.
221. Amended Sec. 12 in Part II, Chapter 7 of the Examination Guidelines.
222. Full publications from WIPO, EPO, USPTO and EPO and abstracts from various other countries.
223. Examination Guidelines, Part II, Chapter 7, 8.1.

amended guidelines stipulate that he may still have to take appropriate measures to understand the relevant background art and to evaluate it from the perspective of a skilled artisan, in order to determine whether indeed the entire subject matter of the application cannot be patented.[224]

Pursuant to Rule 48 Implementing Regulations, third party observations are welcome during the publication phase of the invention application and will be taken into account at the latest until the issuance of the *Notification of Patent Grant*. The Examination Guidelines allow[225] but do not oblige examiners to ignore observations filed after this date. Third parties are nevertheless advised to file their observations as early as possible, before the largest part of the examination has been completed, to ascertain that they are given full consideration.[226] The Examination Guidelines further clarify that third-party observations do not have to be communicated to the concerned parties. They can even be filed anonymously. Thus, they do not fall under "other patent-related subject matter" according to Article 19(1) Patent Law (Article 18(1) after the fourth revision's entry into force), which foreign parties would have to handle through a qualified patent agency, but anyone can submit them freely without having to observe formalities.[227] As a matter of course, third-party observations can only be raised against published applications, and therefore not against utility model or design applications, which are granted after a mere formal examination without prior publication.[228]

Third-party observations should have become even less complicated since the 2017 amendment to the Examination Guidelines, which significantly enhanced the content of application documents that can be consulted and photocopied by the general public during the period between publication and grant. Whereas the previous provisions only allowed access to and copying of pre-publication documents, third parties may now also consult notifications to the applicant, search reports and examiner decisions made during substantive examination.[229] Moreover, the inspection of observations submitted by the applicant or interested parties during the examination is no longer limited to their "main text" but may also include accompanying material.[230] After the announcement of grant, third parties are now also permitted to access priority documents and search reports.

Upon completion of the comprehensive or, in case of serious defects, initial examination, the First Office Action should ideally address all identified defects in a substantiated manner, to avoid several subsequent office actions.[231]

The time limit for responding to the First Office Action is four months, whereas in case of other office actions, the examiner shall specify a time limit that duly considers the specific circumstances, e.g., the nature of the observations, the number

---

224. Examination Guidelines, Part II, Chapter 7, 10.
225. Examination Guidelines, Part II, Chapter 8, 4.9.
226. Deng Ming, *supra* note 121, 154 et seq.
227. *Ibid.*
228. With regard to utility models, see Toby Mak, *supra* note 76.
229. Part V, Chapter 4, 5.2 (2).
230. Part V, Chapter 4, 5.2 (3).
231. Form and content of the First Office Action are regulated in the Examination Guidelines, Part II, Chapter 8, 4.10.

of opinions raised by the examiner, their complexity, the workload associated with making the required amendments, and the like.[232]

Applicants may respond to any Office Action by raising observations or objections or by amending the application in accordance with Article 33 Patent Law. Objections and amendments must be substantiated. For instance, an amendment must be accompanied by an explanation of how the amendment has overcome the defects identified by the examiner.[233] When amending their application, applicants are well advised to painstakingly observe the requirement in Article 33 that amendments shall not exceed the scope of the initial patent documents.[234] The interpretation of this requirement especially in re-examination practice has been criticized as overly strict, because only amendments that used the exactly same terminology as the claims and the description of the initial application were accepted. In its *Seiko Epson v. PRB* administrative decision of 2010,[235] which dealt with an invalidation request due to the alleged introduction of new subject matter in the course of an earlier pre-grant amendment by the use of different terminology, the SPC gave reason to hope for a more liberal practice, by overturning the PRB's invalidation decision, holding that the introduction of different terms by amendments made during patent prosecution shall be allowable as long as such terms did not introduce new subject matter into the claims but could be easily inferred from the scope of disclosure of the original application documents by a person skilled in the art. The SPC's *Shimano v. PRB* decision of 27 December 2013,[236] however, upheld a previous PRB's invalidation in a similar case, stating that the broader terms used in the amendment actually broadened the scope of disclosure by introducing new subject matter. This later decision has been interpreted as a return to the rather strict previous examination practice.

The 2019 amendment to the Examination Guidelines rephrased the last paragraph in Part II, Chapter 8 Sec. 4.10.2.2. stating that where the Office Action refers to common knowledge in the respective field of art, it must be conclusively quoted, and where the applicant raises objections against the quoted subject matter, the examiner must be able to provide proof or to explaining his reasons in his response. Also, where the Office Action states that the technical features indicated in the claims as contributions to the solution of a technical problem in fact pertain to common knowledge, such observations must be accompanied by evidence.

The interaction between examiner and applicant may also include interviews, phone conversations and, in rare cases, on-the spot visits to examine, e.g. for a larger apparatus that cannot be moved, the latter only upon approval of the director of the respective examination department.[237] The 2019 amendment to the Guidelines

232. Examination Guidelines, Part II, Chapter 8, 4.10.3.

233. Examination Guidelines, Part II, Chapter 8, 5.1.

234. Part II, Chapter 8, Section 5.2.1.1 of the Examination Guidelines interprets the initial scope of disclosure that an amendment shall not exceed as the contents described in the initial description and the claims as well as the contents that can be directly and unambiguously determined from the contents described in the initial description, drawings and claims; Sections 5.2.2 and 5.2.3 of the Examination Guidelines contain detailed lists of examples of allowable and disallowable additions, changes and deletions.

235. 53-1 *Zhi Xing Zi* (2010); see also Deng Ming, *supra* note 121.

236. 21 *Xing Ti Zi* (2013).

237. Examination Guidelines, Part II, Chapter 8, 4.12–4.14.

facilitated interviews as well as telephone conversations and other forms of distant communication. Interviews can now be held throughout the whole substantive examination, not only after the First Office Action, and a request for an interview shall be accepted by the examiner if he thinks that it may help to clarify problems, resolve differences and help understanding.[238] Also, allowed telephone conversations between examiner and applicant will henceforth not be limited to minor formal issues, but may extend to more complicated issues such as understanding the invention and prior art or problems associated with the application documents.[239]

As mentioned, for the sake of procedural economy, further office actions after the first Office Action shall be avoided as much as possible. Reportedly, adherence to this requirement by most examiners has contributed to an average substantive examination duration of 22 months[240] in spite of double-digit annual increases in patent applications.

After completion of substantive examination, the examiner shall either issue a decision of rejection if the applicant has not deleted the defects pointed out by the examiner or issue a *Notification of Patent Grant*. The decision to reject the patent application must substantiate the grounds for the rejection.[241] Before issuing a *Notification of Patent Grant*, the examiner can correct obvious errors in the documents on his own but must notify the applicant thereof.[242] Upon receipt of the notification, the applicant has two months to go through the administrative work to prepare the grant (Rule 54 Implementing Regulations). After successful completion, CNIPA will issue the patent certificate and announce the patent grant. According to Article 39 Patent Law, the patent right shall be effective from the date of announcement.

4. Special Provisions on International Applications Entering the National Phase

As mentioned, China is fully integrated into the PCT regime in that the Patent Administration serves as receiving office, international search and preliminary examination authority and as a designated or elected office according to the standards set forth in the PCT.

The role of CNIPA as receiving office for international applications such as the mode of conducting international search and preliminary examination are regulated in Chapters II and III of the Provisions Concerning the Implementation of the Patent Cooperation Treaty in China.[243] The same provisions also contain a Chapter V on

238. Part II, Chapter 8, 4.12.
239. Part II, Chapter 8, 4.13.
240. Deng Ming, *supra* note 121, with regard to the SIPO Annual Report of 2012, when the duration was slightly higher, with 22.6 months on the average; according to CNIPA's annual report of 2017 http://english.cnipa.gov.cn/col/col1749/index.html, it could be further reduced to the mentioned 22 months.
241. Details regulated in Part II, Chapter 8. 6.1 of the Examination Guidelines.
242. Details regulated in Part II, Chapter 8, 6.2.2 of the Examination Guidelines.
243. China Patents & Trademarks 1/1994, 93; amended by Order No. 7 of the State Intellectual Property Office (SIPO) amending Provisions Concerning Implementation of Patent Cooperation Treaty in China of 28 May 1995, http://www.wipo.int/wipolex/en/details.jsp?id=7887 (Chinese).

the procedures concerning designation and election of China and the entry of the international applications into the national phase. In the course of the 2001 overhaul of the Implementing Regulations, these rules were further substantiated and accommodated in a new Chapter X Implementing Regulations, which underwent a few modifications when the Implementing Regulations were amended again in 2010. One entirely new provision is contained in Rule 109, which requires that in case of international applications incorporating genetic material, an indication must be made in the written statement on the entry into the national phase, and source and origin of the respective material must be indicated in a form prepared by CNIPA.[244] Fundamental adjustments to the provisions on entry into the national phase in the wake of the fourth Patent Law overhaul are unlikely, as most of its amendments are not related to the examination procedure.

In compliance with the general provision of Article 11(3) PCT, Rule 101 Implementing Regulations prescribes that international applications designating China shall be treated as applications filed with the CNIPA, and that the international application date shall be treated as the filing date pursuant to national provisions. If, however, the international application or the designation of China is withdrawn or deemed to be withdrawn, the effect of the application in China will cease. This provision is in accordance with the PCT, Article 24(1).

With regard to an international preliminary examination conducted by a foreign office, the Examination Guidelines in Part III on the entry of international applications into the national phase clearly state that the standards set forth in the Patent Law and the Implementing Regulations shall be applied, that the international preliminary examination report shall be treated as a non-binding reference document material and not be consulted in a manner that anticipates the examination result. The examiner shall make an independent judgment whether the application meets the patent prerequisites and does not pertain to subject matter excluded from patent protection under national law.[245]

(a) Formalities

The entry of international applications into the national phase necessitates fulfilment of a variety of formalities. According to Rule 103 Implementing Regulations, the applicant must go through the various formalities for entering the national phase within 30 months from the international application date. Before the expiration of this period, CNIPA shall not commence national proceedings. This time limit may be extended to 32 months in case the applicant fails to complete the formalities for entry into the national phase by the deadline, provided that he pays a surcharge for late entry.[246]

---

244. Form 100023 on the Disclosure of Source and Origin of Genetic Material of 2010/100023 遗传资源来源披露登记表2010).

245. Examination Guidelines, Part III, Chapter 2, 5.1.

246. By harmonising the period for applications designating China and for applications electing China, the Implementing Regulations were adapted to the PCT amendment of October 2001 (amendment of 28 December 2002). The amendment to the Implementing Regulations is outlined in detail in IP News of 10 January 2003, 3. Before the amendment,

In accordance with Article 23(2) PCT, Rule 108 stipulates that CNIPA may start with the national processing and examination at an earlier date at the explicit request of the applicant. National processing and examination only means the preparations for examination and preliminary examination, but not examination as to substance. For the latter, Article 35 Patent Law requires a separate request. If an international applicant fully scoops out the longest possible term of 32 months in which the Patent Office is not permitted to commence examination proceedings, only a few months will remain for requesting substantive examination for his invention application. This is because the Examination Guidelines explicitly provide that the three-year term in which the request for substantive examination has to be made shall be counted from the international application date.[247]

For entry into the national phase, Rule 104 Implementing Regulations provides that the following basic formalities must be complied with:

- submission of a written statement of entry in which the international application number, the kind of patent (invention or utility model), the title of the invention, name or title of the applicant and also the name of the inventor shall be indicated. That is, transformation of an international patent application into a utility model is possible in the course of entry into the national phase, but in fact only few applicants make use of this option (1,146 out of 86,753 applications that entered the national phase in 2017).[248]
- payment of the various fees (filing fee, where necessary, additional filing fee and printing fee for publishing). All fees have to be paid when submitting the statement of entry, a period for later payment is not provided for.
- in the case of an international application filed in a foreign language, the submission of a translation into Chinese and of the abstract of the original application; if the application was originally filed in Chinese, the submission of a copy of the internationally published abstract. It is important to note that according to Rule 104(1) Implementing Regulations, the translation must be submitted together with the application, deadlines for delayed submission do not exist.
- if the international application contains drawings, the submission of a copy of the drawings; if the application was originally filed in Chinese, the submission of a copy of the figure contained in the abstract.

Omitting the international patent number in the entry statement and, as mentioned, failing to pay the various fees or to submit a Chinese translation of the claims or the description in time will render the international application without effect in China (Rule 105(1) No. 3). According to Rule 105(2) Implementing Regulations, this means that the application cannot be restored on the basis of Rule 6(2) Implementing

the period in which the arrangements for entry into the national phase was to be made, was 20 months in case of applications designating China and 30 months in case of applications electing China; also, Article 22(3) PCT with regard to designated offices and Article 39(1) b) PCT with regard to elected offices permit national laws to fix such later time limits.

247. Examination Guidelines, Part III, Chapter 1, 5.7.

248. SIPO annual report 2017, http://english.cnipa.gov.cn/col/col1749/index.html.

Regulations which regulates the formalities of the restoration of rights that were lost due to a failure to meet certain time limits for justified reasons. If the other formalities are not accomplished in a timely manner, the applicant will be requested to make the necessary corrections (Rule 104(3)). If the corrections are not made in time, the application will be deemed to have been withdrawn, but not to have ceased in effect, so that the applicant has the opportunity to restore his application pursuant to the above-mentioned Rule 6(2) Implementing Regulations. In accordance with the flexibilities allowed for national requirements pursuant to Article 27 PCT, Rule 104(1) No. 4 requires that the name of the inventor be stated when entering the national phase, even if it has not been stated in the international application. Moreover, according to Rule 107, applicants who claimed a grace period during the international phase do not only have to indicate such statement in the declaration of entry into the national phase but they also have to furnish additional evidence of whether the grace period is justified by one of the events mentioned in Article 24 No. 1 and 2 Patent Law. Otherwise, the grace period will not be considered. Rule 106 provides that translations of corrections made during the international phase, either before the International Bureau (Article 19 PCT) or the International Preliminary Examination Authority (Article 34 PCT) shall be submitted to CNIPA within two months from the date of entry into the national phase, otherwise the amendments will not be taken into consideration.[249] Another national requirement is the mentioned newly added Rule 109, according to which in case of applications pertaining to genetic resources, the statement of entry into the national phase must contain a corresponding indication, and source and origin of such resources must be detailed in a separate form.

Rule 108 furthermore stipulates that indications on the deposit of biological material made during the international phase are deemed to have been made in accordance with the corresponding Rule 24(3) Implementing Regulations but their exact location in the application documents must be indicated in the statement of entry into the national phase, at latest until the expiration of four months after the entry date, otherwise CNIPA will deem the deposit to not have been made.

According to Rule 110(1) Implementing Regulations, one or multiple priorities claimed in the international phase shall be deemed to have been claimed in accordance with the domestic provisions (Article 30 Patent Law), provided that the priority is still valid when entering the national phase. In accordance with Rule 17 PCT Regulations, the applicant himself is not required to furnish a certified copy of the earlier application, i.e. the "priority document" mentioned in Rule 17 PCT Regulations, but the examiner shall request such document from the International Bureau. Only where the examiner is notified by the International Bureau that it has not been submitted in the international phase, he or she may, if deemed necessary, ask the applicant to furnish such copy within a specified time limit, Rule 110(3).[250] Part III, Chapter 1, 5.2.5 of the Examination Guidelines regulates specific circumstances under which the applicant may request restoration of priority if, in the international phase, the priority claim was found not to have been made pursuant to Rule 26bis 2(b) PCT Regulations. The same provision also regulates that priority claims declared

249. See also details in Part II Chapter 1, 4 of the Examination Guidelines.
250. See also Examination Guidelines Part III, Chapter 1, 5.2.2.

invalid due to specific defects can be restored pursuant to Rule 6 Implementing Regulations on prerequisites and procedures for the restoration of rights. It should be noted that China has opted out of the "Incorporation by reference" procedure under Rules 4.18 and 20.6 PCT Regulations, so that "completion" of an international application by way of reference to missing parts contained in an earlier application will not be acknowledged by CNIPA in the national phase.[251]

(b) *Amendments during the National Phase*

For the subject matter of an international application, an invention patent or a utility model patent may be requested when entering the national phase. If utility model protection is sought, the applicant can, at his own initiative, request to amend the application documents within two months from the date of accomplishing the formalities for entry into the national phase according to Rule 112 Implementing Regulations. With regard to voluntary amendments to applications for invention patents, the same provision refers to the Rule 51(1) Implementing Regulations on amendments to invention patent applications in general, stipulating that amendments can be made when filing the request for substantive examination as well as within three months from the receipt of the notification that the application has entered substantive examination. The provisions are compliant with Articles 28 PCT for designated offices and Article 41 PCT for elected offices. It should be noted that the three-years-period after the priority date pursuant to Article 35 Patent Law, in which the applicant must request substantive examination, as otherwise the application will be deemed to have been withdrawn, also applies to PCT applications. That is, if the applicant has fully scooped out the longest possible 32-months-period for entering the national phase as permitted by Rule 103 Implementing Regulations,[252] he has just a short time left for requesting examination, which should therefore best be done right at the date of entering the national phase, but also for filing amendments to the application, which, according to Rule 51(1) Implementing Regulations with regard to amendments in general can be carried out within three months from the request for substantive examination. Practitioners point out that these opportunities to file amendments within a relatively short time should be taken seriously, as later post-grant amendments of the claims in the course of an invalidation procedure are only very limitedly possible.[253]

Moreover, should the international application be filed in a foreign language, Rule 113 allows the applicant to correct translation errors in his invention application before a) the termination of the preparations for national publication or the announcement of the grant of a utility model patent, and b) within three months from the receipt of the notification of entry into substantive examination of the invention patent. Such correction requires adherence to certain formalities, namely a written request and payment of a fee. If these formalities are not carried out within the prescribed time limits, the application will be deemed to have been withdrawn. Finally, if a translation

251. Part III, Chapter 1, 5.3. of the Examination Guidelines.
252. See a) *supra*.
253. Toby Mak, 'PCT Applications', in Stefan Luginbuehl and Peter Ganea (eds.), *Patent Law in Greater China* (Edward Elgar, 2014), 181 et seq.; see also X. 2. c) *infra*.

error remains undetected and later on turns out to broadening the scope of protection beyond the scope of the original application, the claims will be interpreted according to the original scope. If instead the protection scope has narrowed due to such a translation error, the claims will be interpreted according to the limits of the granted patent, i.e., in both scenarios the narrower scope prevails (Rule 117).

(c) Publication Date Relevant to Article 13 Patent Law

As will be further outlined below,[254] Article 13 Patent Law grants the patent owner the right to claim an equitable remuneration for the unauthorized use of his invention during the period in which the application has been published but not yet been granted. In the case of an international application filed in Chinese, this publication period starts with the international application date (Rule 114(2) Implementing Regulations). If instead the international publication has been filed in another language, the date from which remuneration for unauthorized use can be claimed is the date of the national publication of the Chinese translation. This provision is in compliance with Article 29(2) (i) PCT which allows its members to provide that the publication of an international application originally published in another language may become effective in the designated state at the earliest from the date at which a translation into the language of that state has been published.

(d) International Applications and Unity

In case of international applications that comprise more than one invention or utility model, the applicant can, pursuant to Rule 42(1) of the Implementing Regulations, file a divisional application in the course of entry into the national stage, Rule 115(1) Implementing Regulations.

Moreover, the Implementing Regulations provide for a national procedure regarding international applications which have been found to contravene the unity requirement by the International Search Authority or the International Preliminary Examining Authority pursuant to Articles 17(3) b) and 34(3) b) respectively, and where the international search report or the international preliminary examination report is limited to the main invention due to applicant's failure to pay additional fees. Rule 115(2) Implementing Regulations provides the applicant with the opportunity to have these unsearched respectively unexamined parts considered by CNIPA in the national phase upon payment of a "unity restoration fee", provided that the CNIPA concurred with the International Authorities' decision on uniformity.[255] The applicant is then given the opportunity to file divisional applications for those parts not being subject to international search or preliminary examination in accordance with the national provisions. If the fee is not paid in time, those parts of the application which do not belong to the same inventive concept will be deemed withdrawn. In compliance with the above mentioned ground rule that examiners shall decide independently on the adherence of the international application with national patent

254. See XIV. 8. *infra*.

255. Article 17(3) with regard to the International Search; Article 34(3) with regard to International Preliminary Examination.

prerequisites, the Examination Guidelines also stress that where international search or international preliminary examination did not bring to light lack of unity but later on substantive examination in the national phase does, further procedures shall be carried out according to the standards for national applications in the Guidelines' Part II, Chapter 6 ("Unity of Invention and Divisional Applications").[256]

(e) Review of Erroneous Decisions Made by International Authorities

If, in the international phase, the relevant authority has refused to accord an international application day or declared the international application (or the designation of China) to be considered withdrawn or if the International Bureau has declared the international application withdrawn due to failure to submit a "record copy" according to Article 12(3) PCT, the applicant may request the International Bureau to submit the application documents to the designated offices for review. If the designated office finds the decision of the international authority untenable, it shall treat the international application as if the erroneous decision has not been made (Article 25 PCT). With regard to entry into the Chinese national phase, Rule 116 Implementing Regulations provides applicants with the opportunity to request the International Bureau to submit the relevant documents to CNIPA within two months from the notification that the international application has not been accorded or the application has been considered to withdrawn, and to request CNIPA to review whether such decision has been correct.

5. Procedural Peculiarities Regarding Hong Kong and Macau

As a former British crown colony, Hong Kong had no patent regime under which independent patents could be obtained, but a registration system under which patents filed with the UK Patent Office were extended to the territory of Hong Kong. True to the motto "One Country, Two Systems" under which Hong Kong was returned to China as a Special Administrative Region (SAR), the Legislative Council of Hong Kong enacted an independent patent regulation, the Patent Ordinance of 28 May 1997.[257] According to the Ordinance, the so-called re-registration of "standard patents" in the sense of invention patents, which have undergone an examination by SIPO/CNIPA, the UK Patent Office or the EPO (provided that the European Patent was granted for the UK), and of non-examined "short-term patents" of lower economic value[258] may be filed with the Hong Kong Intellectual Property Department (IPD).[259] European applications do not have to be translated into Chinese and, apart from title

256. See also Part III, Chapter 2, 5.5 of the Examination Guidelines.
257. Ordinance No. 52 of 1997.
258. But different from the Chinese "utility model" in that it also protects non-three-dimensional subject matter such as inventions on the field of biology or chemistry.
259. An in-depth overview of Hong Kong's patent system before the amendment of 2016 is given by Douglas Clark, 'Introduction to the Patent System in Hong Kong SAR', in Stefan Luginbuehl and Peter Ganea (eds.), *Patent Law in Greater China* (Edward Elgar, 2014), 423; see also Michael Pendleton, Peter Garland and Jared Margolis, 'The Law of Intellectual and Industrial Property in Hong Kong' (looseleaf), V. Patents and Registered

and abstract, not even into English if first filed in one of the other official languages (German or French) when registering them in Hong Kong.[260]

On 10 June 2016, the Ordinance underwent an overhaul, which entered into force together with new Patent (General) (Amendment) Rules on 19 December 2019. Most importantly, independent standard patent applications undergoing substantive examination can now be filed directly with the SAR's Patent Registry ("original grant patent system" – OGP) as an alternative to the re-registration system, and short-term patent owners as well third parties with an interest in the validity of the patent can now request a post-grant substantive examination of the short-term patent.[261]

Direct designation of Hong Kong for PCT applications is not possible, as Hong Kong as a SAR of China is not a member of any WIPO-administered treaty. The same applies to the former Portuguese colony of Macau, which was returned to mainland China as an SAR in 1999.[262] For both SARs, China has submitted notifications to the General Director of the WIPO that the present WIPO status of Hong Kong and Macau as colonies has terminated simultaneously with the return to China, and that the Paris Convention shall be extended to both on the basis of the Convention membership of the People's Republic.[263] As far as the application of the PCT is concerned, an additional notification has been made to the Director General of WIPO that the designation of China in any international application filed from 1 July 1997 shall cover the territory of Hong Kong, and that further special rules on the procedures for entering the national phase will be published.[264] International applications designating China are not extended to the territory of the SAR Macau, though.[265]

The procedure of extending international applications to Hong Kong is regulated in Announcement No. 57 of the former Chinese Patent Office of 29 December 1997.[266] Accordingly, such applications shall be received by the CNIPA or, alternatively, by the International Bureau. With regard to international applications for which standard

---

Designs; Patent Office under the State Intellectual Property Administration (ed.), *Zhuanli shenqing xuzhi* (Basic Knowledge on Patent Applications) (Beijing, 2001), 101 et seq.

260. https://www.epo.org/law-practice/legal-texts/official-journal/2016/etc/se4/p580.html

261. More information, including the amended provisions in English on the website of Hong Kong's Intellectual Property Department, https://www.ipd.gov.hk/eng/intellectual_property/patents/New_Patent_System.htm.

262. See Zhu Xuezhong, 'Priority and Patents for Foreign Applicants in China Under "One Country, Two Systems"', 33 *IIC* (2002), 6.

263. The notification with regard to Hong Kong was issued on 6 June 1997 and is in force since 1 July 1997: *Industrial Property and Copyright* (July/August 1997), 233; the notification concerning Macau was delivered to the Director General of WIPO on 30 November 1999 and has been in force since 20 November 1999: *Industrial Property Laws and Treaties* (formerly "*Industrial Property and Copyright*") (December 1999), 138; the legal bases for these notifications are Article 153 of the Basic Law of Hong Kong and Article 138 of the Basic Law of Macau, which provide the Chinese central government with the authority to decide whether international agreements the People's Republic has already joined or will join shall be applied to the respective SAR.

264. *Industrial Property and Copyright* (July/August 1997), 237.

265. Wen Xikai, 'The Patent System of Hong Kong After Its Reversion to China and the Application of International Treaties', 2 *China Patents & Trademarks* (1998), 45 et seq.

266. 2 *China Patents & Trademarks* (1998), 94 et seq.; in Chinese: https://www.cnipa.gov.cn/art/2001/9/17/art_74_27888.html.

patent protection is sought, the registration formalities before the Hong Kong Intellectual Property Department shall be initiated within six months from the national publication of the application in China or within six months from the attribution of a national application number if the application has been internationally published in Chinese. Within another term of six months from the date of announcing the patent grant in China, the grant and registration of the patent can be requested with the Hong Kong Intellectual Property Department. For an international application seeking utility model protection in China, only a short-term patent can be obtained in Hong Kong. The grant and registration of such a short-term patent can be requested within six months from the issue of a Chinese national application number.

6. Patent Prosecution Highways and Other Forms of Expedited Examination

Expedited examination is possible under international Patent Prosecution Highway (PPH) cooperation as well as under recent national provisions with regard to specific types of inventions. Since its first bilateral PPH agreement with the Japanese JPO, CNIPA has concluded a variety of PPH agreements with foreign patent offices. It would go beyond the scope of this contribution, however, to describe them in detail.

Apart from accelerated examination through reliance on the search and examination results of a foreign partner office, CNIPA since August 2012 also offers detailed rules on the application for preferential examination by CNIPA. The corresponding provisions have been replaced by the "Administration Method on Preferential Patent Application" of 27 June 2017 (Ordinance No. 76/2017).[267] Moreover, since their amendment of 2019, the Patent Examination Guidelines also contain more specific provisions on preferential examination in Part V on "Processing Patent Applications and Procedural Matters", Chapter 7, which has been renamed from "Time Limit, Restoration of Right and Suspension" into "Time Limit, Restoration of Right, Suspension and Order of Examination", with a new Section 8 on "Order of Examination".[268]

Subsection 8.2 provides that preferential examination can be requested for inventions made by industries that are recommended by the national government or regional governments, inventions of importance for the national or public interest and inventions for which a certain market demand exists. The Examination Guidelines stress that in general, preferential examination shall not be approved where simultaneous invention and utility model applications have been filed, obviously out of the consideration that the earlier full protection upon the grant of the utility model renders expedited procedures unnecessary.

Rule 3 of the mentioned Administration Method further details the subject matter for which preferential examination (but also re-examination) can be requested, namely for applications pertaining to reduced energy consumption and environmental protection, new-generation information technology, high-end equipment manufacturing, new energies, new materials, new vehicle fuels, etc., for applications pertaining to

267. In Chinese: https://www.cnipa.gov.cn/art/2017/6/28/art_74_27621.html.
268. Actually, the "Order of Examination" has been previously regulated in Part II, Chapter 8, 3.4 of the Examination Guidelines. The 2019 amendment extended it and transferred it to Part V, Chapter 7.

rapidly changing technologies such as internet, Big Data or cloud computing and for inventions in branches promoted by local governments. Preferential examination is furthermore possible in cases of urgency, where the applicant has made the necessary preparation to implement his invention or has already started the implementation or where he can prove that another party has started such implementation, in case of abroad applications, provided that the first application has been filed in China, and in other cases in which expedited procedures appear necessary to safeguard the national interest or the public welfare. Accelerated procedures can also be requested for invalidation cases, either by the requesting party or by the patentee, namely where the patent is simultaneously subject to an administrative or judicial infringement procedure or a dispute resolution procedure or where obtaining clarity about validity is in the national interest or serves public welfare (Rule 4). Local patent administrations, courts or dispute resolution authorities may also request accelerated examination on their own (Rule 5(2)). Moreover, if CNIPA decides to commence examination on its own pursuant to Article 35(2) Patent Law, it may do so according to the procedure for preferential examination.[269]

A request for expedited examination must be accompanied by evidence, *inter alia*, on prior art and a recommending opinion that the subject matter of the application indeed belongs to one of the above-mentioned prioritized technological fields, which must be issued by the relevant department under the State Council or by a provincial intellectual property department, depending on the nature of the request. If the CNIPA accepts a request, it must adhere to the following deadlines (Rule 10):

1. invention applications: first Office Action opinion to be furnished within 45 days, the whole examination and grant procedure to be closed within one year;
2. utility model and design applications: closure of all procedures within six months;
3. re-examination requests for all kinds of patents: closure within seven months;
4. invention patent and utility model invalidation: closure within five months;
5. design invalidation: closure within four months

Not only CNIPA but also the requesting parties have to adhere to strict deadlines, which are regulated in Rule 11 of the Method, otherwise CNIPA may, according to Rule 12 No. 2 of the Method, terminate the expedited treatment and return to regular procedures. Rules 12 and 13 contain further grounds for the termination of preferential examination.

Expedited procedure should be available for both domestic and foreign applicants, provided, however, that they do not already enjoy preferential treatment under one of the PPH agreements that China has concluded with foreign patent offices (Rule 2).

---

269. Examination Guidelines, Part V, Chapter 7, 8.4.

7. New Provisions on Deferred Examination

The amended Chapter 7 in Part V of the Examination Guidelines also contains a subsection 8.3 on "Deferred Examination", stating that invention and design patent applicants (not utility model applicants) can request delayed commencement of examination. The period of delay may be one, two or three years. In case of invention patents, the delay can only be requested with regard to substantive examination and the request must be filed with the request for substantive examination, whereas in case of designs, the request must be filed together with the design application. The delay then starts with the date of filing the request. The new provision aims at providing applicants with more flexibility to consider whether they really want to carry on with patent prosecution. With regard to invention patents it should be noted, however, that the delay has no effect on the publication of the application, i.e., only substantive examination will be delayed, but not the publication of the application after 18 months from the application date. CNIPA may also, if it deems necessary, commence the examination on its own during the delay period, which will simultaneously be terminated.

8. Confidentiality Examination

The Patent Law amendment of 2008 introduced a new provision in Article 20(1) Patent Law (Article 19(1) after the fourth amendment's entry into force), according to which inventions and utility models made in China have to undergo a confidentiality examination before being allowed to be filed abroad, to prevent subject matter of greater national interest from being patented and exploited outside China. The preceding provision according to which Chinese entities or individuals had to file an application in China before they could apply abroad, had, according to official statements, turned out to be too weak to control the outflow of potentially sensitive technology, also because it was not applicable to inventions made by foreigners in China, Sino-foreign joint ventures and the like. The new regime does no longer distinguish between Chinese and foreign parties but the only factor giving reason to confidentiality examination is that the invention has been made in China or, more precisely, that the invention's "essential part" has been accomplished on Chinese territory (Rule 8(1) Implementing Regulations). The consequence of filing abroad without requesting confidentiality examination is the loss of the opportunity to obtain a patent in China or to lose an already granted patent if an application has been first filed in China and later on abroad without going through confidentiality examination, because failure to undergo such examination is listed as one invalidation ground in Rule 65(2) Implementing Regulations.

The above provisions leave much room for interpretation of what actually constitutes an invention made in China. In general, if an application is filed without requesting confidentiality examination, and the examiner thinks that there is evidence that the invention has been made in China, the burden of proof that confidentiality examination should have been requested lies with CNIPA or with the party requesting invalidation due to non-compliance with the current Article 20(1) Patent Law. In practice, it seems that the mere indication of a Chinese individual as inventor or co-inventor may be sufficient to cast doubt about the origin of the invention, so that the burden of proof that the invention has not been made in China will be shifted to the applicant.[270]

Rule 9 Implementing Regulations further clarifies the procedure and the aim of the confidentiality examination. Accordingly, inventions that turn out to be relevant for national security or the vital interests of the state may fall under confidentiality and be banned from being patented abroad. A definition of what would come into question as relevant for "security" or "vital interests of the state" is absent, however. Inventions that are relevant for national security should encompass a broader range of subject matter than defence-related inventions, because the latter are already separately regulated in Rule 7 of the Implementing Regulations, which stipulates, inter alia, that CNIPA shall forward applications of potentially defence-related inventions to the National Defence Patent Institution for separate examination.

Examined as to confidentiality is subject matter intended for direct patent application abroad, subject matter for which already a domestic patent application has been filed and subject matter of international applications for which CNIPA has been chosen as receiving office. According to Part V, Chapter 5, 6.1.1 of the Examination Guidelines, the request for examination of an application to be directly filed abroad shall contain a description of the invention, which must conform with the requirements regarding patent application documents (Part V, Chapter 1), so that in practice, the request for confidentiality examination and the accompanying documents correspond to a full patent application.[271] If a domestic application has been filed, the request for confidentiality examination may be filed together with the domestic application or afterwards, whereby the subject matter to be applied for abroad must correspond to the subject matter of the domestic application (Part V, Chapter 5, 6.2). In case of international applications filed with CNIPA, no action on the side of the applicant is required, but the request will be deemed to have been made and the confidentiality examination will be carried out automatically.[272]

If, according to Rule 9 Implementing Regulation, the applicant/requesting party does not hear from CNIPA within four months from filing the request, or within six months after receiving a notice that confidentiality examination is carried out, he is free to file abroad. If CNIPA decides that the application must be kept secret, the provisions in Part V, Chapter 5, 4 of the Examination Guidelines apply, i.e., the application and, later on, the granted patent will not be published, and applicant/patent owner is obviously banned from working his invention. In case of international applications that turned out to be of vital interest to the state, etc., CNIPA will terminate the international phase and inform the applicant and the International Bureau thereof.[273]

The applicant/patent owner who thinks that his application or patent does no longer have to be kept secret may request declassification, or CNIPA will declassify

270. Stefan Luginbuehl, 'Confidentiality Examination', in Stefan Luginbuehl and Peter Ganea (eds.), *Patent Law in Greater China* (Edward Elgar, 2014), 188 (190).
271. *Ibid.*
272. Examination Guidelines, Part V, Chapter 5, 6.3.
273. Examination Guidelines, Part V, Chapter 5, 6.3.2

it upon re-examination whether secrecy is still necessary, which must take place in two-year intervals.[274]

Filing an application abroad without going through the confidentiality examination does not only result in the loss of the opportunity to obtain a patent in China but may be administratively prosecuted or even punished under criminal law if it resulted in the divulgation of state secrets (Article 71 Patent Law, which will become Article 78 after the fourth amendment's entry into force). The meaning of "state secrets" presumably includes subject matter that would have been classified as state secret if confidentiality examination had been carried out.

After the third Patent Law amendment, the new provisions on confidentiality examination raised considerable commotion among foreign business circles, not least due to the legal uncertainty caused by nondescript terms like "vital interest of the state" or "essential part of which was made in China". After more than ten years, however, the confidentiality examination appears to be rather another administrative burden to go through. Reportedly, only very few of tens of thousands of requests result in classification as confidential,[275] and the impressive annual increases in international filings originating from China[276] also demonstrate that the confidentiality examination is obviously not a major burden. Undoubtedly, however, the examination has helped the CNIPA and China's policy makers to document what subject matter invented in China is deemed worthy of being patented abroad.[277]

IX. UTILITY MODEL AND DESIGN EVALUATION REPORT

Article 61(2) of the current Patent Law stipulates that in case of utility model or design disputes, the court or local IP administration may request the patent owner or the interested party, i.e., the licensee with authorization to sue,[278] to furnish an evaluation report which must be drafted by CNIPA and provide information about the compliance of the respective patent right with the protection prerequisites. Moreover, an evaluation report is also required for customs registration of utility models and designs. The fourth Patent Law amendment of 2020 added a sentence to this provision, which will become Article 66(2) after the amendment's entry into force, according to which a patentee, an alleged infringer or any other interested party may henceforth also request evaluation reports at its own initiative, without having been ordered to do so by the court or by a local enforcement agency.

According to Rule 57 Implementing Regulations, evaluation reports must be drafted within two months after being requested. Part V, Chapter 10 of the Examination Guidelines regulates form and content of the request and of the evaluation report, including procedures for the rectification of errors or erroneous assessments in the report, either at the request of the petitioner or at the CNIPA's own initiative. Before requesting a report, patent owners should consider that anyone, also a competitor

274. Examination Guidelines Part V, Chapter 5, 5
275. Stefan Luginbuehl, *supra* note 270.
276. See II. *supra*
277. Stefan Luginbuehl, *supra* note 270.
278. Examination Guidelines, Part V, Chapter 10, 2.2.

who may want to assess the risk of infringement, is allowed to view the report and to copy it after completion.

An evaluation report is a mere opinion, not an administrative act as, for instance, a decision to invalidate a patent. Infringement courts therefore consider them as a persuasive source of information but they are not bound by their result. In practice, this means that if the report confirms the validity of the right at issue, judges will in most cases not suspend infringement litigation in spite of an invalidation request, but they may change their mind if the defendant manages to provide further convincing proof of invalidity that is not addressed by the report.[279]

Prior to the amendment of 2008, the Patent Law regulated a "search report" only with regard to utility models. According to a CNIPA (then SIPO) communication of 2010, utility models and designs applied for after the entry into force of the third amendment to the Patent Law in 2009 should be treated according to the new provisions, whereas older utility models and designs shall be governed by the Patent Law's previous version, depriving the owners of older design patents of the opportunity to also request an evaluation report. Similarly, Rule 4 of the 2001 Interpretations prescribes that plaintiffs whose utility model have been applied before 1 October 2009 may issue a search report whereas owners of utility models and design patents of later application dates may furnish an evaluation report. Some commentators criticized the choice of the application date instead of the date of infringement as unfair to holders of older design rights who would be banned from averting a trial suspension due to invalidation proceedings by furnishing a convincing evaluation report, but the reforms of 2020 did not entail any changes to the previous regime.[280]

X. RE-EXAMINATION AND INVALIDATION

Administrative decisions made by the CNIPA are reviewed by the Patent-Reexamination Board, which, as mentioned, has been restructured and renamed into Department for Re-examination and Invalidation (DRI) but these rearrangements have not impacted on the re-examination and invalidation procedures, which are detailed in Part IV of the Examination Guidelines. As all re-examination and invalidation decisions quoted in this chapter have been made by the old PRB, the explanations hereinafter will continue to use the old name "PRB" instead of "DRI" to avoid confusion, even if, as explained, the amended Patent Law does not even use the term "DRI" but made the former PRB disappear completely and will henceforth only refer to its superordinate authority, the "Patent Administration under the State Council", aka CNIPA.

According to the general principles of re-examination and invalidation in Part IV, Chapter 1 of the Examination Guidelines, the PRB is composed of technical and legal experts. A panel normally consists of three, in technically complicated cases, cases of national importance and cases of great economic value of five members, whereas very simple cases may be dealt with by one examiner. Where a case has

279. Zhang Guangliang, 'Reflection on Patent Evaluation Report System in China', 3 *China Patents & Trademarks* (2010), 84 et seq., downloadable from: http://www.cpt.cn/uploadfiles/20100712170304183.Pdf
280. Zhang Guangliang, *supra* note 279.

to be reassessed because a court has overturned a previous PRB decision, a new panel shall be formed.

In 2018, CNIPA received 38,000 re-examination requests (75.8 percent invention patent related, 23.1 percent utility model related and only 1.2 percent design related),[281] a double-digit increase by 11 percent over the previous year, which appears rather moderate in comparison with the thus far unique increase by 160 percent in 2017[282] but still substantial in comparison with the annual increases before 2017. CNIPA nevertheless alluded to a continuously improving social satisfaction with its work. In 2018, the average re-examination duration was 11.1 months.[283]

Requests for invalidation grew by 15 percent over 2017 (5,235 requests received in 2018, the vast majority, namely 41.4 percent, accounting for utility models, 32.1 percent for designs and 26.5 percent for inventions). The average pendency of invalidation procedures was 5.1 months.[284]

Unfortunately, the CNIPA figures are silent about the success rate of re-examination and invalidation requests but a study covering the period between 2008 and 2018 at least revealed some interesting data about the outcome of invalidation requests.[285] Accordingly, among the total of invalidation proceedings held between 2008 and 2018, 50.38 percent resulted in complete invalidation and 10.04 percent in partial invalidation, whereas the patent could be maintained in 0.53 percent of cases after amending it and in 39.05 percent of cases in the originally granted version. Also, within the observed period, the ratio between completely invalidated, partly invalidated and upheld patents remained rather stable, with the exception of the last fully observed year 2017, when the total of patents that survived invalidation for the first time exceeded the total of fully or partially invalidated patents. It is unclear, however, whether this represents a stable future trend. The study also brought to light that the vast majority of invalidation requests between 2008 and 2018 has been raised against unexamined utility model and design patents (13,682 and 10,705 respectively, as opposed to 5,791 requests to invalidate invention patents), but that at least the success rate of design-related requests (ca. 57 percent of requests resulted in full or partial invalidation) did not significantly exceed the rate of successful requests to invalidate invention patents (ca. 53 percent). Utility model invalidation requests showed a significantly higher success rate of ca. 64 percent, however.

281. CNIPA Annual Report 2018, Chapter III on 'Application and Examination', 52 et seq., http://english.cnipa.gov.cn/col/col1749/index.html.

282. CNIPA Annual Report 2017, Chapter IV on 'Patent Application and Examination', 51, http://english.cnipa.gov.cn/art/2018/6/29/art_1749_143827.html, all parts of the annual report available at http://english.cnipa.gov.cn/col/col1749/index.html.

283. According to CNIPA, this period was shorter than in the previous years; the annual report lists several measures such as organizational rearrangements and digitization as means of further optimizing re-examination (and invalidation) procedures.

284. CNIPA Annual Report 2018, *supra* note 281.

285. Zheng Haiyang, '2008–2019 niandu zhongguo zhuanli wuxiao anjian tongji fenxi baogao' (Report on the analysis of statistics on Chinese patent invalidation cases between 2008 and 2018), 3 *Zhongguo Zhishichanquan* (China Intellectual Property) (2019), available on this site in Chinese only: https://www.sohu.com/a/293164554_656884.

Since the second Patent Law amendment of 2000, all PRB decisions are open to judicial review. Before that, Article 43(2), (3) and Article 49(2), (3) of the old Patent Law permitted only a judicial review of re-examination and invalidation decisions regarding invention patents, whereas in the case of utility models and designs, the decision of the PRB had been final.[286]

Until recently, the Intermediate People's Court of the City of Beijing No. 1 had exclusive subject matter jurisdiction to review of PRB decisions in the first instance, with the Beijing Higher People's Court as the second instance, but this has changed in recent years. Since 2014, the newly established Beijing IP Court is in charge of dealing with PRB decisions in the first instance, and in 2019, second instance jurisdiction shifted from the Higher People's Court to the SPC's new IP Division.[287]

1. The Re-examination Procedure

According to Article 41 Patent Law, applicants who are not satisfied with the examiner's decision to reject their application may request a review before the PRB within three months from the date of receipt of notification. Together with the request, the applicant may furnish further amendments to his application, which, however, shall not go beyond the points that led to the rejection decision. The request shall also conform to certain formal requirements which are regulated in detail in the Examination Guidelines,[288] state the reasons for the objection and present the necessary evidence.

According to Rule 62 Implementing Regulations, the PRB shall forward the request to the examination department that has made the original decision, which has to respond within one month.[289] If the original department agrees to the petitioner's objections or finds that the corrections of the application documents have eliminated the defects, the PRB will decide accordingly without further re-examination on its own. If the original examination department upholds the rejection, the justification must be confined to the original reasons for rejection and the amendments or counterarguments brought up by the petitioner, and it shall not introduce new reasons for rejection, unless they are solely of clarifying nature (e.g., they pertain to commonly known subject matter that a skilled artisan may find conclusive upon resorting to a technical textbooks, etc.).[290] The PRB will then commence re-examination. Rule 61(1) of the Implementing Regulations also permits the applicant to furnish further amendments when responding to the re-examination notification, which, according to the Examination Guidelines, includes the permission to make corrections during

286. See on this topic Yu Xiang, 'The Second Amendment of the Chinese Patent Act and the Comparison between the New Patent Act and TRIPS', *Journal of World Intellectual Property* (2001), 137, 148.
287. See IV. 3. *supra*.
288. Amongst other things, the request as such is examined as to whether it was made in time and whether the person requesting re-examination is the actual applicant or the patent agency authorised by the applicant to make such request: Examination Guidelines, Part IV, Chapter 2, 4.1.
289. Examination Guidelines, Part IV, Chapter 2, 3.1.
290. Examination Guidelines, Part IV, Chapter 2, 3.3.

oral hearings.[291] If the PRB finally decides to overturn the rejection, the examination department will be notified to resume examination (Rule 62(2) Implementing Regulations). A second rejection for the same reasons is not permitted.[292]

2. The Invalidation Procedure: Inventions, Utility Model and Designs

(a) *History*

The procedure of objecting to a patent has undergone two reforms. The 1984 law provided for a pre-grant opposition, according to which within three months from the announcement of grant any person could request the Chinese Patent Office to reject the application. The pre-grant opposition was meant to enhance the examination efficiency by public participation. Soon, however, lawmakers recognised that the public did not participate sufficiently so as to outweigh the disadvantage of a delay in grant. In 1992, the pre-grant opposition was therefore replaced by a post-grant revocation procedure. Within six months from the patent grant, any person could file a revocation request with the Patent Office. In contrast to the previous regime, which did not limit the reasons for which an opposition could be filed, a revocation request could only be filed on grounds of lacking novelty, inventiveness or practical applicability in the case of inventions and utility models, and on grounds of identity with or similarity to a prior aesthetic solution in case of designs.[293] The introduction of the revocation procedure in 1992 can be regarded as another attempt to enhance the quality of the examination by enabling the Patent Office to reconsider its former decision. In contrast to the previous regulation on the pre-grant opposition, however, Article 43(1) Patent Law 1992 allowed the requesting party to proceed before the PRB if the Patent Office decided to uphold the patent right. After the expiration of the six-month term for revocation, any party could request the PRB to invalidate the patent for a variety of reasons, provided, however, that in the meantime no other party had initiated a revocation procedure. For this case, Rule 66(3) of the amended Implementing Regulations 1992 stipulated that as long as a revocation procedure was pending, no invalidation procedure could start. This turned out to be particularly disadvantageous to the defendant in an infringement case, because the pending revocation procedure initiated by a third person blocked him from making a timely request for invalidation of the plaintiff's patent.[294] If the defendant was finally found liable for patent infringement and the patent was afterwards revoked, there was hardly any possibility of repairing the damage, as the Patent Law back then already stipulated that the invalidation should have no retroactive effect on previous judicial or administrative decisions.[295]

291. Part IV, Chapter 2, 4.2 of the Examination Guidelines.
292. Examination Guidelines, Part IV, Chapter 2, 9.
293. This limitation has become necessary because the variety of reasons for which a pre-grant-opposition could be initiated according to Rule 55 Implementing Regulations of 1985 overstrained the capacities of the Patent Office.
294. Commentary on the new Patent Law, *supra* note 155, 272.
295. See X. 2. e) *infra*; see also Feng Xiaoqing and Liu Jiaqi, 'A Review of Recent Developments in Patent Act in the People's Republic of China', 4:6 *Journal of World Intellectual Property*

Due to such disadvantages and also due to the fact that there was hardly any procedural difference between the revocation and the invalidation procedure (in both cases, it was the PRB that made the final administrative decision, and the reasons for which a revocation could be requested were the same reasons for which an invalidation could be requested) the legislature decided to abolish the revocation system. Since the amendment of 2000, only one way of preventing a patent grant remains, namely requesting invalidation pursuant to Article 45 Patent Law.

(b) General Principles of Patent Invalidation

An invalidation procedure can only be initiated at request, which may be filed by anyone, not only by parties with a vested interest in the fate of the patent at issue (Article 45 Patent Law). Also, considering the civil importance of a PRB decision to invalidate or to uphold a patent, Article 46(2) Patent Law allows the respective opposing party in the invalidation hearing, either the patent owner whose patent has been upheld or the party who has succeeded with its invalidation request, to participate in the subsequent administrative court trial as third party.

In general, the PRB may not go beyond the arguments and evidence asserted by the parties when examining the validity of the patent,[296] with little room for *ex officio* examination.[297] The petitioner may even renounce part or all of his request, and in such case, the PRB shall no longer examine the renounced subject matter. Also, if the parties demonstrate their willingness to reach an agreement, the PRB shall defer the final decision to enable the parties to find a mutually acceptable solution.[298]

The 2015 draft amendment aimed at providing the PRB with a higher degree of *ex officio* examination authority, by allowing it to investigate further reasons for invalidation not contained in the request to facilitate the elimination of worthless patents and to avoid repeated invalidation procedures pertaining to the same patent but for different reasons. However, neither the subsequent drafts of 2019 and 2020 nor the final fourth amendment contain such a provision, maybe because the drafters gave in to criticism from industry circles that it would too severely interfere with the *inter partes* character of the invalidation procedure.

Even under the present rules, the PRB is entitled to examine *ex officio* further grounds for invalidation not contained in the request for invalidation in certain well-defined cases,[299] namely where the petitioner has chosen the wrong invalidation ground for his request e.g. by confusing Article 9 Patent Law on the first-to-file-principle with the novelty requirement in Article 22 Patent Law,[300] where an obvious defect resulting in invalidity has not been indicated in the request, where a defect not indicated in the request, e.g., lack of clarity, renders further examination along the request impossible or where the request points to the defect of only one claim,

(2001), 827 (846).

296. Examination Guidelines, Part IV, Chapter 3, 4.1.

297. More about the circumstances under which the PRB may carry on investigation at its own initiative *infra*.

298. Examination Guidelines, Part IV, Chapter 3, 2.2.

299. Detailed in the Examination Guidelines, Part IV, Chapter 3, 4.1.

300. In this case, the PRB may also instruct the petitioner to amend the request.

which, however, gives rise to the suspicion that other interrelated claims have the same defect. The PRB may, furthermore, without being requested to do so, retrieve and use the original application documents as evidence in case of requests alleging that a divisional application exceeds the original protection scope or identify technical means pertaining to common knowledge with help of technical dictionaries, manuals and textbooks.

According to Rule 65(2) Implementing Regulations, invalidation can be requested on grounds of the following provisions:

- Article 2 Patent Law: non-conformity with the definition of an invention, utility model or design;
- Article 5 Patent Law: the invention violates public morality or relies on unlawfully acquired genetic material;
- Article 9 Patent Law: the applicant is not entitled to the patent due to the first-to-file rule, because he has not abandoned the simultaneously filed utility model or because he has not been the first who filed an application for the same subject matter;
- Article 25 Patent Law: the invention-creation pertains to non-patentable subject matter;
- Article 20(1) Patent Law (henceforth: Article 19(1)): an invention or utility model application for an invention made in China has been filed abroad without having been examined as to confidentiality;
- Article 22 Patent Law: the invention or utility model is not novel, non-obvious or industrially applicable;
- Article 23 Patent Law: the design is not novel, not significantly different from prior designs or conflicts with a prior right;
- Article 26(3) and (4): Patent Law: description and claims are not clear and concise enough to determine the scope of protection;
- Article 27(2) Patent Law: the design is not clearly shown in the drawings or pictures;
- Article 33 Patent Law: an amendment to the application extended the original scope of protection;
- Rule 20(2) Implementing Regulations: the independent claim does not outline the technical solution or does not include the necessary technical features;
- Rule 43(1) Implementing Regulations: a divisional application exceeded the scope of the original application;
- The unlawful usurpation of another parties' invention is not a ground for invalidation but, as already explained, at least the usurpation of a design may fall under the invalidation ground of "no conflict with prior rights".[301]

Rule 65(1) Implementing Regulations specifies that an invalidation request must contain the necessary evidence and that the indicated grounds for invalidation must be based on such evidence. The Examination Guidelines regulate in more detail that for requests based on lack of inventiveness the petitioner shall furnish supporting reference documents and indicate which ones it deems most important. If several reference documents, e.g., of prior art, are furnished, the requesting party

301. See VII. 1. b) *supra*.

shall indicate which one is closest prior art and explain its relationship with the patented invention. Where the references are to be read in combination and several combinations are possible, the petitioner shall clarify which combination he had in mind as the closest prior art and explain its relationship with the invention.[302] Since the 2019 amendment to the Examination Guidelines, petitioners who furnish several combinations of prior art documents are well advised to clearly indicate which combination they deem most important, because otherwise the examiner will assume that the first listed shall be the most important one.

Rule 66(2) Implementing Regulations prohibits the PRB from accepting any further requests for invalidation that are based on the same grounds as a previous one on which the PRB has already decided.[303] Also, for reasons of procedural economy, several invalidation requests concerning one and the same patent should be treated together if possible.[304]

The parties may request the PRB to conduct an oral hearing or the PRB may initiate a hearing at its own initiative (Rule 70 Implementing Regulations). If the petitioner does not respond to the corresponding notification or does not appear at the hearing, the invalidation request will be deemed withdrawn. If the opposing party does not appear, the hearing will be conducted in its absence. The Examination Guidelines further specify the procedure of an oral hearing.[305] According to Rule 67 Implementing Regulations, a petitioner can add more reasons for invalidation or evidence within one month from filing the request. Additional reasons for invalidation after one month are only permissible under certain circumstances, for instance, in reaction to a patentee's amendment by limiting claims or by correcting obvious errors.[306] If the petitioner wants to furnish new evidence after the expiration of one month, he may do so only in response to counter-evidence submitted by the patentee or, before the closure of the oral hearing, if his own evidence pertains to commonly known subject matter as described in technical dictionaries, manuals or textbooks, or to complementary material such as notary statements or original documents to complete the originally furnished evidence for the sake of compliance with legal requirements.[307] An extension of the deadline for translating evidence in foreign languages into Chinese is not admissible.[308]

Under the same circumstances, the patentee may extend the time limit set by the PRB for providing counter-evidence until the end of the oral hearing, namely where such counter-evidence pertains to commonly known subject matter described in technical dictionaries, manuals or textbooks or serves as complementary material that must be furnished to adhere to formal requirements, such as notarial recordings

---

302. Examination Guidelines, Part IV, Chapter 3, 3.3 (5).
303. Further detailed in Part IV, Chapter 3, 2.1 of the Examination Guidelines.
304. Examination Guidelines, Part IV, Chapter 3, 4.5.
305. Examination Guidelines, Part IV, Chapter 4.
306. Examination Guidelines, Part IV, Chapter 3, 4.2 after the amendment of 2017; summary of the 2017 amendments to the Examination Guidelines 'SIPO revises the Guidelines for Patent Examination', at http://www.cpahkltd.com/UploadFiles/20170309184413307.pdf.
307. Examination Guidelines, Part IV, Chapter 3, 4.3.1.
308. *Ibid.*

or original documents. The need to translate foreign-language evidence into Chinese does not give reason to a further extension of the deadlines.[309]

(c) Amendments during Invalidation

When confronted with an invalidation request, the patentee is given another opportunity to amend the claims. The 2017 amendment to the Examination Guidelines slightly relaxed the limited scope of permissible amendments. Permitted are now the deletion of a claim, the deletion of a technical solution from a claim, the further limitation of a claim and the correction of obvious errors,[310] whereas the previous version permitted only the deletion of a claim or of a technical solution of a claim and the "combination of claims". Amendment in the form of "combination of claims", namely of dependent claims depending on the same independent claim, is no longer listed, and "further limitation of a claim" is now defined as incorporating limiting technical features from other claims to narrow down the protection scope. In its *Xiansheng v Patent Re-examination Board* decision of 8 October 2011,[311] the SPC broadened the notion of "deleting a technical solution from a claim" to also include the narrowing down of a numerical range to a specific numerical value, whereas the PRB held that only deletions in form of separating a technical solution from parallel other technical solutions shall be allowed. The amended Examination Guidelines list three events in which post-grant amendments "other than by deletion", i.e. by further limitation of a claim or by correcting obvious errors, are possible, namely in response to an invalidation request, in response to additional invalidation grounds or evidence furnished by the requesting party and in response to invalidation grounds identified by the PRB.[312]

With special regard to Markush-type claims, i.e., claims expressed by a variety of alternative structural elements which are typical for chemical inventions, the SPC's *Beijing Winsunny v. Daiichi Sankyo*[313] has largely affirmed the PRB's long-standing

309. Examination Guidelines, Part IV, Chapter 3, 4.3.2.
310. Part IV, Chapter 3. 4.6.2.
311. 17 *Zhi Xing Zi* (2011); http://www.pkulaw.cn/case_es/payz_1970324838148682.html?match=Exact (Chinese); see also He Huaiwen, 'Amendment to Claims of Granted Patent Under Chinese Patent Law', *Journal of Intellectual Property Rights* (Jan. 2013), 67 et seq.
312. Part IV, Chapter 3. 4.6.3.
313. 41 *Zui Gao Fa Xing Zai* (2016), summarized in WIPO Collection of Leading Judgments on Intellectual Property Rights (*supra* note 66), 58 et seq. in the English version; more about the diverging views of the PRB and the lower-instance courts in this matter in IP Tribunal of the Beijing Higher People's Court, 'Latest Developments in Adjudication of IP Cases by Beijing Higher People's Court in 2013', 3 *China Patents & Trademarks* (2014), 9, available at http://www.cpt.cn/uploadfiles/20140929161529196.Pdf; see also the very instructive article by Wang Jingchao, 'Probe into Amendments to Markush Formula Compound Claims by Deletion and Protection Thereof', 3 *China Patents & Trademarks* (2016), 86 et seq., available at http://www.cpt.cn/uploadfiles/20161013110141903.pdf; see also *Chen Wenping/Mao Jin/Zhang Zhanjiang*, Wuxiao chengxu zhong Makushi quanli yaoqiu de xiugai (Amendments to Markush-type claims in the invalidation procedure), China Invention & Patent,2/2019, 91 et seq.

practice not to permit amendments in an invalidation procedure. It regarded Markush-type claims as integrated technical solutions rather than an aggregation of parallel inventions from which one could be easily deleted without impact on the scope and essence of the remaining ones, as the Beijing Higher People's Court had opined in its previous instance decision. According to commentators, the SPC's findings are similar to that of the EPO's Boards of Appeal's T 0948/02 decision.[314]

(d) Design Invalidation

Rule 69(2) Implementing Regulations prohibits amendments to the drawings, photographs or explanation during design invalidation procedures. Design owners are therefore deprived of any opportunity to avert a complete invalidation by partially abandoning their design.[315] The ban on amendments has existed since the 2000 Patent Law amendment. Back then, some commentators expressed concerns that it may be especially harmful to owners of product set designs, which henceforth would be in danger to be completely invalidated if only one of their constituents turned out to be non-protectable.[316] On the other hand, the Examination Guidelines explicitly allow the partial invalidation of a design incorporated in several products of independent use.[317]

(e) No Retroactivity of the Decision to Invalidate the Patent

According to Article 47(1) Patent Law, an invalidated patent is deemed to be non-existent from the beginning. In 1992, a new subsection 2 was added to this provision, according to which the invalidation of a patent shall have no retroactive effect on any prior judicial judgment or mediation of patent infringement which has been made and enforced by a People's Court, on any prior (administrative) decision concerning the handling of a dispute over patent infringement which has been complied with or compulsorily executed or on any prior performance of a license or transfer agreement. Any damages another party suffered due to bad faith on part of the patent owner, however, for example by assigning an unexamined utility model patent while being fully aware that it does not meet the protection prerequisites, shall be compensated. Moreover, even in absence of bad faith, previous defendants, licensees or assignees may claim partial or full reimbursement of previous compensation or fees if otherwise the fairness principle would be clearly violated (Article 47(3) Patent Law).

---

314. Hui Zhang, Yi Wei and Jiao Yuxin, 'China: Supreme People's Court Provides Guidance on Amendment and Inventiveness Evaluation for Markush Claims', http://patentblog.kluweriplaw.com/2018/08/15/supreme-peoples-court-provides-guidance-amendment-inventiveness-evaluation-markush-claims/.
315. See Zhao Jiaxiang and Zhang Yueping, 'Invalidation and "Partial" Invalidation of Patent Right for Design Colliding with Other's Prior Right', 2 *China Patents & Trademarks* (2001), 44.
316. Xue Jilin, 'Recommended Revision of the Provisions of Patent Laws Relating to Designs of Products in Set', 2 *China Patents & Trademarks* (2004), 30.
317. Examination Guidelines Part IV, Chapter 3, 5.

(f) The Interdependence of Invalidation and Infringement Procedures

As already indicated with regard to the hard-to-invalidate utility models, a majority of invalidation requests are made in response to an infringement suit. Hereby, China, just like Germany, separates infringement and invalidation suits. An infringement court cannot determine the validity of the patent at issue but, if in doubt about its further fate, must stay the infringement proceedings until the PRB or, in the following court instances, the Beijing IP Court and the new IP Division of the SPC have decided about the fate of the patent.

The SPC Interpretations of 2001 (last amended 2020) contain further guidance on the interplay between infringement and invalidation proceedings. As a general rule, Rule 7 prescribes that in case of substantively examined invention patents or utility model or design patents that have already sustained a previous invalidation procedure, the infringement court shall in general not stay the proceedings to await the result of the invalidation case. With special regard to utility model and designs (meant are obviously the previously uncontested ones that do not fall under Rule 7), Rule 4 (2) prescribes that courts shall stay proceedings upon a defendant's request if this request as well as the invalidation request is made within the defence period that starts with the submission of the plaintiff´s arguments to the defendant, which is 15 days if the defendant is Chinese and 30 days if the defendant is a foreign party. Otherwise, the court shall continue with infringement proceedings, unless special circumstances prompt it to suspend the trial (Rule 6). According to Rule 5, however, the court may also continue infringement proceedings if the request for invalidation has been filed without delay, namely a) if the evaluation report that has to be furnished by the plaintiff in utility model infringement litigation has not brought to light any prior art that would result in the loss of novelty or inventiveness of the respective utility model, b) if the evidence presented by the defendant is sufficient proof that his or its solution is commonly known, c) if the evidence or grounds for invalidity presented by the defendant are clearly insufficient, d) if there are other circumstances that prompt the court to continue infringement proceedings. Pursuant to Rule 8, the judge who has accepted a request to stay the proceedings may, at the request of the plaintiff, issue a preliminary injunction to order the defendant to cease from further alleged infringement or from other acts that would increase the damage to the plaintiff during the period of suspension, provided that the plaintiff deposits a security.

In judicial practice, more than 90 percent of patent disputes are continued without waiting for the outcome of a parallel invalidation case.[318] What infringement courts are reported to frequently do, however, is to adapt the trial schedule to the invalidation proceedings, which are governed by strict albeit not always kept deadlines. If the PRB upholds the patent, the infringement court normally relies on this judgment and does not further adapt the schedule to wait for the result of the defendant's subsequent appeal to the Beijing IP Court. However, if the PRB has

318. Liu Ming, 'Guanzhu! Zhuanlifa xiugai shijiaoxia de zhuanli wuxiao chengxu redian wenti' (Notice! Hot issues related to the invalidation procedure, viewed from the perspective of the Patent Act amendment), http://ip.people.com.cn/n1/2019/0515/c179663-31085545.html (extracted from Zhishi chanquan bao).

invalidated the patent and the plaintiff appeals against this decision, infringement courts are reported to be more willing stay the proceedings and to wait for a final result. The successful invalidation of a patent for the same subject matter in another country can at best serve as another piece of evidence to convince the court to stay infringement proceedings.[319]

In parallel proceedings, both plaintiff and defendant tend to present different claim interpretations. In infringement litigation, the plaintiff wants to have the claims interpreted as broad as possible to cover the defendant's solution, in invalidation proceedings as narrow as possible to avoid conflict with prior art, whereas the defendant who has requested invalidation strives for the contrary in both proceedings. Ideally, both the infringement court and the PRB (and later on the appeal courts) should interpret the same technical solution in the same way, through the eyes of the same fictional skilled artisan. In practice, this has not always been the case.[320]

The separation between infringement and invalidation is sometimes described as an obstacle to timely infringement decisions, and some commentators support the introduction of a new invalidity defence in infringement litigation. Accordingly, courts should at least be competent to decide about the validity of designs, as the assessment of compliance with the novelty, distinctiveness and "no conflict with prior rights" requirements would not require special technical expertise. Considering the hundreds of thousands of design applications and grants per year, allowing the defence of invalidity in infringement proceedings would significantly lessen the PRB's heavy workload.[321] CNIPA and PRB representatives, however, are opposed to such a fundamental piercing through the bifurcation between infringement and invalidation. They refer to statistics showing that the vast majority of invalidation requests do not entail a suspension of infringement litigation and to the very low rate of court-remanded PRB invalidation decisions that are repeatedly appealed in court after the PRB has made a new decision (about 0.2 percent).[322] Moreover, the example of Japan, where the invalidity defence can be raised since the Supreme Court's famous *Kilby* decision of 11 April 2000,[323] demonstrated that such rearrangement could entail new difficulties, such as diverging court and PRB opinions on the validity of a patent.[324] The latter view seems to have prevailed, as none of the

319. Details regarding the practice of parallel infringement and invalidation proceedings in Nils Heide, 'The Interplay between Infringement and Invalidity Proceedings', in Stefan Luginbuehl and Peter Ganea (eds.), *Patent Law in Greater China* (Edward Elgar, 2014), 257 et seq.

320. *Ibid.*

321. Zhu Li, *supra* note 106, with reference to Article 81 d) of the Design Regulation, which grants Community Design Courts jurisdiction over counterclaims regarding invalidity in connection with an infringement suit.

322. Liu Ming, *supra* note 318.

323. English translation in IIC 2004, 91, with comment by Christopher Heath and Mineko Mohri; see also Christopher Heath, 'Case No. 50', in Christopher Heath and Atsuhiro Furuta (eds.), *Japanese Patent Law – Cases and Comments* (Wolters Kluwer, 2019), 537 et seq.

324. Summary of a CNIPA workshop on "challenges encountered in cases related to the maintenance of patents and possible solutions", https://mp.weixin.qq.com/s/Ky0-r4cIM4lpJCoMXE3E_A

hitherto published draft amendments to the Patent Law suggested the introduction of the invalidity defence, and also the final amendment did not entail any changes to the present system.

Rules 2 and 3 of the SPC Interpretations II aims at further lessening the burden arising from parallel infringement and invalidation proceedings, also taking into account that judicial review of invalidation decisions rarely contradict the findings of the PRB.[325] Rule 2 states that where a claim is found to be invalid by the PRB during the infringement procedure, courts may *dismiss* the plaintiff's claims pertaining to these claims, without having to wait for the final outcome of the subsequent administrative court appeals. According to Rule 2(2), mere "dismissal" instead of "rejection" means that the plaintiff who can prove that he succeeded in the subsequent administrative court trial against the PRB invalidation decision can file another lawsuit without any *res iudicata* objection. The two-year limitation for filing a subsequent lawsuit according to Article 68(1) of the current Patent Law, which will be extended to three years after the fourth amendment's entry into force (then Article 74(1)), shall then be counted anew from the date of delivery of the decision that confirmed validity. Commentators from the SPC also point out that in such a subsequent trial, the findings of the instance that preceded the previous decision to "dismiss" the plaintiff's arguments pertaining to the PRB-invalidated but finally upheld claims shall not have lost their value, especially the undisputed content of the records of the court hearings.[326]

Rule 3 of the Interpretations II further alleviates the complexities arising from parallel proceedings, providing that if the patent at issue is clearly non-compliant with the clarity requirements in Article 26(3) and (4) Patent Law in that the description cannot be used to interpret the claims, and if an invalidation request is filed on this ground, the court shall, in general, suspend the infringement proceedings to await the result of the invalidity proceedings, yet where the defendant fails to file an invalidation request in due time, the court shall interpret the scope of protection according to the contents of the claims. Rule 4 exempts from this scenario cases where wording, grammar, punctuation etc., in claims, description and drawings are ambiguous but still allow the skilled artisan to comprehend the scope of protection in a specific manner after reading the claims, the description and the drawings. This specific understanding shall then also be applied by the court to determine the scope of protection.

325. Li Jian, 'Comments on Interpretation of the Supreme People's Court on Several Issues Concerning the Application of Law in the Trial of Patent Infringement Dispute Cases (II)', 2 *China Patents & Trademarks* (2016), 7 et seq.

326. See Song Xiaoming, Wang Chuang and Li Jian, '"Guanyu shenli qinfan zhuanliquan jiufen anjian yingyong falv ruogan wenti de jieshi (II)" de lijie he shiyong' (Understanding and applying the "Interpretation on the Application of Law to Patent Infringement Disputes (II)"), 10 *Renmin Sifa Yingyong* (2016), 28, accessible at https://wenku.baidu.com/view/54653cd60722192e4436f661.html.

(g) *The Prior Art Defence as an Alternative to Invalidation*

Instead of going through a lengthy and burdensome invalidation procedure, the defendant may also raise the "prior art defence" during the infringement trial, claiming that the technical solution he uses already pertained to prior art at the application date. This is different from questioning the validity of the patent but is similar to the German "Formstein" defence (although the latter can only be invoked where infringement by equivalents is alleged, see below). The prior art defence has long been admitted by courts until the Patent Law amendment of 2008 elevated it to a statutory provision in Article 62 Patent Law (which will become Article 67 after the fourth amendment's entry into force):

> In a patent infringement dispute, if the accused infringer has evidence to prove that the technology or design exploited is an existing technology or design, the exploitation shall not constitute a patent right infringement

Rule 14 of the SPC Patent Interpretations 2009 clarifies that only those technical features of the defendant's solution which are alleged of falling within the protection scope must pertain to prior art to give reason for a valid prior art defence, not the defendant's whole technical solution, as implied by the strict wording of the current Article 62 Patent Law:[327]

> Where all the technical features alleged to fall within the scope of protection of the patent right are identical to or of no substantial difference from the corresponding technical features of a single existing technical solution, the courts shall determine the technical solution implemented by the accused infringer as a prior art as prescribed in Article 62 of the Patent Law.
>
> Where a design alleged for infringement is identical to or of no substantial difference from a prior design, the courts shall determine the design implemented by the accused infringer as a prior design prescribed in Article 62 of the Patent Law.[328]

With regard to inventions and utility models, the Chinese prior art defence resembles the German "Formstein defence" (as above) but goes a significant step farther in that it is applied not only to equivalent infringement but also to literal infringement. However, even if the defendant succeeds with a prior art defence in a literal infringement case, the court's finding of non-infringement is not tantamount to declaring the patent invalid. As mentioned, a patent can only be invalidated in a separate invalidation procedure, and this will most likely not change in future. Among the various defences available in China, the prior art defence seems to be rather frequently applied, albeit rarely with success.[329] In a dispute listed among China's landmark IP cases, the SPC found that manuals describing the allegedly

327. Contradiction between both provisions debated by Deng Ming, *supra* note 105, (395 et seq.), with regard to the prior art defence in design cases.
328. English translation of the Interpretations available from the website of China Patent Agent (H.K.) http://www.cpahkltd.com/UploadFiles/20100317113813391.pdf.
329. Christopher Bailey and Lucy Wang, 'Exceptions and Limitations', in Stefan Luginbuehl and Peter Ganea (eds.), *Patent Law in Greater China* (Edward Elgar, 2014), 123 et seq.

infringing technical solution and having been handed out to customers without any confidentiality obligations prior to the application date formed prior publications that gave reason to a valid prior art defence.[330]

The prior art defence is especially popular among defendants accused of infringement of unexamined design patents, which are often of dubious quality. In another landmark judgment of 1 March 2011, the SPC clarified that in case of a prior design defence, not only the defendant's aesthetic solution but also the patented design shall be included in the comparison with prior art. Accordingly, the patented design shall first be compared with the prior design to identify those features that created its distinct overall visual impact. The prior art defence shall be then be denied if the same features also distinguish the allegedly infringing design from prior art.[331] The decision was still based on the previous judge-made prior art defence before its statutory introduction in Article 62 of the current Patent Law, which, as mentioned will become Article 67 after the fourth amendment's entry into force.

Finally, with regard to the scope of prior art to be considered, Rule 22 of the SPC Interpretations II clarifies that courts shall adhere to the principle of non-retroactivity,[332] by applying the scope regulated by those provisions that had been in force at the application date of the respective patent. That is, holders of patents applied for before the third amendment became effective should find it easier to refute a prior art defence because they can rely on the previous "relative novelty" regime, under which technical solutions publicly used abroad did not pertain to novelty-destroying prior art.[333]

XI. FEES AND PATENT AGENCIES

The various fees to be paid for administrative services related to the acquisition, maintenance and invalidation of patents, as well as for obtaining a compulsory licence,[334] are regulated in CNIPA's official fee schedule of 22 November 2019.[335] The amounts listed therein are not extraordinarily cheap but still moderate in international comparison, especially in light of the huge and increasingly wealthy market for which the respective patent is sought. The initial filing fee, for instance, is RMB 900 for invention patent applications and RMB 500 for utility and design applications (EPO: EUR 95–260 for patent applications respectively "invention patent applications" in Chinese terminology, depending on whether they are filed online in character-coded format or conventionally), a substantive examination fee of RMB 2,500 (EPO:

330. 179 *Zui Gao Fa Min Zai* (2016), summarized in WIPO Collection of Leading Judgments on Intellectual Property Rights (*supra* note 66), 62 et seq. in the English version
331. 189 *Min Ti Zi* (2010), http://www.pkulaw.cn/Case/payz_119228306.html?match=Exact; see also *Deng Ming*, *supra* note 103.
332. See Song Xiaoming, Wang Chuang and Li Jian, *supra* note 326.
333. See V. 1. a) (1) *supra*.
334. The various standard forms can be downloaded from this site: https://www.cnipa.gov.cn/col/col192/index.html.
335. The current fee scheduled can be downloaded from https://www.cnipa.gov.cn/col/col1518/index.html.

EUR 1,700 to 1,900) and annual renewal fees that increase from RMB 900 to 8,000 over the full 20-year patent term (EPO: EUR 490 to 1,640).[336]

As far as patent agencies are concerned, Article 19(1) Patent Law (Article 18(1) after the fourth amendment's entry into force) prescribes that foreign parties who want to apply for a patent in China or handle other patent-related matters, for instance, file an invalidation request, have to resort to a legally established patent agency. Chinese nationals instead can choose whether they want to appoint a patent agency or handle their patent matters on their own (Article 19(2) of the current Patent Law; Article 18(2) after the fourth amendment's entry into force).

Article 19(3) Patent Law (Article 18(3) after the fourth amendment's entry into force) prescribes in general terms that patent agencies shall abide by the laws, handle patent-related matters in accordance with the entrustment by their clients and keep the contents of the inventions of their clients confidential until the publication or announcement of the patent application. The provision, furthermore, entrusts the State Council with regulating patent agencies in detail. On 4 March 1991, the State Council enacted the "Regulations on Patent Agencies", which have been amended on 6 September 2018.[337] The Regulations are supplemented by the "Method on the Administration of Patent Agencies" enacted by the new super administration SAMR on 4 April 2019,[338] which, according to Rule 58 replace the Method on the Administration of Patent Agencies of 30 April 2015 and the Method on the Patent Agent-related Punishments of 12 December 2002, both enacted by the former SIPO.

The Regulations detail the prerequisites and formalities for establishing a patent agency, which can be, for instance, a partnership or a limited liability firm, and for individuals acting as patent agents. They furthermore delineate the scope of subject matter that can be entrusted to patent agencies, ranging from patent application, patent invalidation, contractual issues pertaining to licensing or the assignment of patent or application rights to consulting services, and regulate quite in detail administrative sanctions for various misconduct, ranging from fines, orders to not accept new cases for a period of six to twelve months, to revocation of business licenses.

Actually, a great deal of the 2018 amendments to the Regulations on Patent Agencies account for the responsibility of patent agents for misconduct and unlawful behaviour, to curb aberrations and excesses that the previous Regulations of 1991 had not anticipated. A new Rule 16, for instance, obliges patent agents to only engage for the patent agencies that employ them and to be personally responsible for the businesses that they have taken over with their signature. Also, pursuant to Rules 21 and 22, patent agent associations shall develop mechanisms to sanction misconduct, and the local patent administrations shall, inter alia, by way of random checks, control the patent agencies within their jurisdiction. One especially rampant problem of the past decades has been "black agents", i.e., individuals or organizations posing as patent agents with fake certificates, etc., and providing poor advice to credulous

336. Current EPO fee schedule: https://www.epo.org/law-practice/legal-texts/official-journal/2020/etc/se3/p1.html.

337. Amended text in Chinese at http://www.gov.cn/zhengce/content/2018-11/19/content_5341736.htm.

338. In Chinese at https://www.cnipa.gov.cn/art/2020/1/10/art_526_145919.html?xxgkhide=1.

clients. The newly introduced provision in Rule 27 of the Regulations obliges the local authorities to stop their unlawful business, to confiscate the illegal gains and to impose a fine of one to five times the illegal revenue. The 2015 Patent Law draft amendment contained similar provisions on the prosecution of "black agents" and on patent agent associations being in charge of internal sanctioning of misconduct by members. The later drafts of 2019 and of 2020, however, no longer contained such provisions and also the subsequently amended Patent Law is void of them, obviously because the legislature now believes that these rules are better accommodated in the more specific Regulations. Further amendments to the Regulations lowered bureaucratic obstacles and streamlined the administration of patent agencies.[339]

According to Rule 10 of the Regulations, only Chinese nationals with a university background in science and engineering[340] can register for the nation-wide patent agent examination. CNIPA operates a separate website on patent agent-related matters, containing information and guidelines on the examination, regulatory notices, annual reports, information about blacklisted agencies, etc.[341] According to a CNIPA notice on the entry into force of the 2018 amendment to the Regulations on 1 March 2019,[342] 42,569 individuals were holding a patent agent qualification and 18,463 individuals were actively engaged in the patent agent business in 2,126 approved patent agencies by end of October 2018.

Finally, with regard to the costs of using the services of a patent agency, the All-China Patent Agents Association has published a fee standard quite long ago, on 1 August 2005.[343] The fees proposed therein appear to be rather moderate. The standard fee for a conventional invention patent application, for instance, is RMB 4,500, for a PCT application RMB 5,000 and for a request to invalidate a patent RMB 5,800. The fees for services associated with utility models and designs are correspondingly lower. In practice, however, individual fee arrangements that supersede this rather old fee schedule are common.

XII. THE NEW "OPEN LICENCE" REGIME

All the above-mentioned incentives may have encouraged public research institutes and universities to file more patent applications, but not yet to put their inventions to profitable use. The fourth Patent Law amendment therefore introduced an "open licence" regime, which should foster the commercialization of inventions

339. A synopsis of the old Regulations of 1991 and the amended ones is available here: https://www.sohu.com/a/277288215_465968; an outline of the amendments and a transcript of a press meeting with CNIPA officials can be obtained at https://www.sohu.com/a/275182661_99927285.

340. Exceptionally also students with a background in economics or business can apply if their transcripts evidence that they have specialized in a relevant discipline, see CNIPA's detailed FAQ on the 2020 Patent Agents Examination, downloadable at: https://www.cnipa.gov.cn/art/2020/7/17/art_2421_154266.html, p.1, Questions 2–4.

341. http://dlgl.cnipa.gov.cn.

342. https://www.cnipa.gov.cn/art/2018/11/14/art_53_117753.html.

343. An official pdf document issued by the All-China Patent Agents Association in the author's possession, which is consistent with the fee schedule issued by the law firm Liu Shen & Associates at http://www.liu-shen.com/docs/SFBEN.pdf.

by allowing patentees to register with CNIPA a declaration of their willingness to grant a license to anyone under predetermined conditions, which will then be publicly announced. The newly introduced Articles 50–52 on open licenses do not specifically refer to universities and research institutes, but CNIPA's references to a survey of 2014 in its explanation of the previous 2015 draft amendment, where this special type of license was first proposed, according to which only 14 percent of patents held by universities and 39.7 percent of the patents held by public research institutes were actually exploited, leave no doubt that the proposed provisions are targeted at them.[344]

The CNIPA explanations also referred to similar provisions in foreign laws, such as Article 23 of the German Patent Act on the "Lizenzbereitschaft" (willingness to license). Some commentators recommended also to adopt the German law's additional incentive of a halved annual fee for those who declare such willingness,[345] and unlike the preceding drafts, the fourth amendment finally considered this recommendation to a certain extent, stipulating that during the execution of the open licence, the annual fees shall be reduced or suspended (Article 51(2)). The concrete prerequisites for such reduction or suspension will then very likely be detailed by the soon to be revised Implementing Regulations and further CNIPA provisions.

With regard to putting open licences into effect, Article 50(1) of the amended Patent Law provides that where a patentee declares to CNIPA in writing his willingness to license his patent to anyone and indicates the licence fee payment method and standard, CNIPA shall announce and execute the open licence. Open licenses can also be declared with regard to not substantively examined utility model and design patents, but such declaration must be accompanied by an evaluation report.[346] According to Art.50(2), open licences can also be withdrawn by a written declaration to CNIPA, which shall announce such withdrawal, Such withdrawal shall not affect the previous validity of the open licence, however.

With regard to the interaction between patentee and licensee, a new Article 51(1) Patent Law provides that anyone who wishes to exploit the patent shall be allowed to do so upon notifying the patentee thereof and paying the announced license fee. During the open license period, the patent owner may negotiate with the licensee about the fees, but not about the type of licence, as he is only allowed to grant a general license, not a sole or an exclusive license (Article 51(3)). In case of a dispute, licensor and licensee are expected to negotiate. If they are unwilling to to so or if their negotiations have failed, they may request CNIPA to mediate or file suit in court (Article 52).

344. https://www.cnipa.gov.cn/art/2015/4/1/art_317_134082.html.
345. Li Huihui, 'Introduction to the Fourth Revision of Chinese Patent Law', 3 *China Patents & Trademarks* (2015), 59 (60).
346. See IX. *supra*.

XIII. NON-VOLUNTARY LICENSING

1. Earlier Forms of Non-voluntary Licensing "with Chinese Characteristics"

The initial version of the Patent Law was characterized by an excessive scope for non-voluntary licensing. There were two forms of compulsory exploitation of patents, one conventional compulsory licensing as regulated by many national laws and permitted by international treaties, the other "licenses according to the state plan", a product of the duality of the Chinese economy in these early years of economic reform. Such duality consisted in the coexistence of a state-owned sector and private players in one and the same market. A special kind of enterprises, namely those "owned by the whole people" were different from other kinds of enterprises (e.g. cooperatives in the hands of certain local communities) in that their main entrepreneurial task was the fulfilment of the state plan. Such enterprises were mere "holders" and not "owners" of their production resources, because full property would have implied a right to exclude the people from what originally belonged to it. Consequently, Article 6(1) Patent Law as of 1984 stipulated that enterprises owned by the whole people were "holders" but not "owners" of their patents According to Article 14(1) Patent Law, a competent authority under the State Council or a local People's Government at provincial level had the authority to instruct such patent holders to assign their patents to another entity if deemed necessary to fulfil the state plan. Such special compulsory exploitation was called "license according to the state plan". In the course of economic transformation during the 1980s and 1990s, however, new private enterprises emerged and the separation between ownership and holdership became increasingly obsolete,[347] not least because not a single license according to the state plan had been granted over the years.[348] Both "holdership" and "license according to the state plan" were consequently abolished in the course of the second Patent Law amendment of 2000. What remained in Article 14(1) and (2) of the current Patent Law, however, is the obligation of state-owned enterprises (Para.1) as well as collective enterprises and Chinese individuals (Para.2) to make their inventions available to certain designated entities for a "widened" exploitation within certain limits and after payment of a prescribed license fee, in case of inventions made by collective enterprises and Chinese individuals with the proviso that the invention had to be of "great significance" to the interest of the state or the public. Only inventions, but not "invention-creations", which would also include utility models of lower technical importance and even designs, could become subject to such special non-voluntary licensing.

The third amendment of 2008 further lessened the impact of Article 14, clarifying that henceforth only state-owned enterprises could be confronted with such special state-ordered licenses, provided that their inventions were of great significance to the interest of the state or of the public. The fourth Patent Law amendment left this provision unchanged but moved it to Article 49 in Chapter VI Patent Law, presently

347. See Wen Xikai, 'Thoughts on Second Revision of the Chinese Patent Law', 1 *China Patents & Trademarks* (1999), 19.

348. Commentary on the New Patent Law, *supra* note 155, 103

on "Compulsory Licenses", henceforth on "Special Licenses" which will not only comprise the various non-voluntary licences but also the above-mentioned new "open licence" regime.

2. Conventional Compulsory Licensing

Apart from the very special provision in Article 14 (Article 49 after the fourth amendment's entry into force), the current Patent Law provides for a full Chapter VI (Arts. 48–58) on "genuine" compulsory licenses, i.e., permissions to use that are also regulated in other national laws and permitted by international treaties. The current Chapter VI on "Compulsory Licences" (on "Special Licenses" after the fourth amendment's entry into force, comprising Articles 48-63 and therefore also the mentioned three new Articles 50-52 on non-compulsory open licenses and the provision on special licenses imposed on state-owned enterprises, which has been moved to Article 49) has undergone significant amendments since 1984. The very first version of the Patent Law of 1984 still obliged patent owners to exploit their patents by producing the patented product or making use of the patented process in China. In case the patent was not exercised in China within three years from grant, it could become subject to a compulsory license. Such a provision, which would be typical for developing countries with a strong interest in having the patented technology domestically exploited, is now prohibited by Article 27.1 TRIPS Agreement. The Chinese legislature abolished it in the course of the first amendment to the Patent Law (1992), obviously due to its self-commitments in an IP Memory of Understanding concluded with the United States on 16 January 1992,[349] but also in anticipation of China's accession to the WTO (which actually took place in 2001). After that amendment, compulsory licenses could only be requested a) if the requesting party was unsuccessful in obtaining a regular license at reasonable conditions, b) if a national emergency or public needs required so and c) if a patent or a utility model represented technical progress over a prior invention-creation but depended on its exploitation. Moreover, the 1992 amendment to the Implementing Regulations further limited the scope of these three kinds of compulsory licenses, by clarifying that a compulsory license could only be requested after the expiration of three years from the grant of the patent, that compulsory licenses aimed at overcoming a national emergency were only permissible for non-profit purposes, that the authority in charge of granting a compulsory license, i.e., CNIPA, has to limit scope and duration of the license and that the patent owner can request the abolishment of the license if the reasons for its grant are no longer existent.

The amendment of 2000 transplanted these provisions from the Implementing Regulations to the Patent Law and introduced another restriction to align the Chinese Patent Law with Article 31 l (i) of the TRIPS Agreement, namely that a compulsory license for exploiting a patent that depended on a prior technical solution shall only

349. See Qiao Dexi, 'A Survey of Intellectual Property Issues in China–U.S. Trade Negotiations under the Special 301 Provisions', 2:2 *Pacific Rim LaW & Policy Journal* (1993), 259 et seq., also available online https://digital.lib.washington.edu/dspace-law/bitstream/handle/1773.1/652/2PacRimLPolyJ259.pdf;sequence=1.

be permissible if the later invention "involved an important technical advance of considerable economic significance" over the prior solution.

Retrospectively, the compulsory licensing regime in the years after 2000 can be regarded as the most right owner friendly one in China's modern patent history, but under the impression of the Doha Declaration on TRIPS and Public Health of 2001 and the growing domestic debate about "abuse" of patents, the third Patent Law amendment of 2008 reassumed a much tougher stance towards licensing-averse patentees.

First, the 2008 amendment adopted said Doha Declaration by adding a new Article 50 (Article 55 after the fourth amendment's entry into force) to the Patent Law which permits compulsory licenses for manufacturing and exporting patented drugs to "countries which conform to the provisions of international treaties that China joined", i.e., the "eligible countries" according to the coming new Article 31bis (1) TRIPS and Para.2 of the Annex. Rule 73(2) Implementing Rules clarifies that also drugs which are directly obtained from a patented process, as well as the diagnostic equipment needed for the use of the pharmaceutical product shall fall under this compulsory license. The debate about high drug prices has recently been sparked by the true-story inspired movie *Dying to Survive,* China's version of *Dallas Buyers Club*, portraying a pharmacist who illegally imports generic versions of a patented anti-Leukemia drug from India to make it available to the poor. Reportedly, the movie motivated Prime Minister *Li Keqiang* to voice his concerns over too costly anti-cancer drugs and to promise countermeasures.[350]

Furthermore, two more reasons for the grant of a compulsory license were introduced in 2008. According to Article 48(1) Patent Law (Article 53(1) after the fourth amendment's entry into force), a compulsory license can be requested if the patent owner does not or not sufficiently exploit his patent without due reason for three years since grant and four years since application, a wording that slightly deviates from the stipulation in, Article 5 A (4) Paris Convention, which also regulates these two periods but clarifies that the competent authority shall opt for the one which ends last.

The other new reason for compulsory licensing has been introduced in Article 48(2) Patent Law (Article 53(2) after the fourth amendment's entry into force), according to which a compulsory license can be requested if the exercise of the patent at issue has been legally confirmed to be anticompetitive. Statutory grounds for such confirmation can be found in the Antimonopoly Law (Article 55), which declares itself applicable to the abuse of intellectual property to exclude or to obstruct competition and, more recently and more precisely, in the SAIC's Provisions on Prohibiting the Abuse of Intellectual Property to Abolish or to Restrict Competition of 7 April 2015.[351] As mentioned, the SAIC has been absorbed by the new super ministry SAMR but its provisions on IP abuse are still frequently quoted and therefore seem to be of unabated relevance. They deal with a variety of issues regarding anticompetitive IP exercises. Rule 7, for instance, prescribes three factors to be considered when assessing the abusive character of a patent exercise by a *dominant* enterprise, namely that

350. http://cpc.people.com.cn/n1/2018/0718/c64094-30155172.html.
351. Available in Chinese on the WIPOLex site: https://wipolex.wipo.int/en/legislation/details/15668.

a) whether license seeking enterprise can take part in the relevant (downstream) market without access to the patented technology, b) whether the refusal to license jeopardizes competition and innovation on the relevant market and therefore has a negative impact on public welfare and c) whether licensing does not unduly harm the IP owner. Rule 7 is related to all kinds of IP, but their main field of application would be the patent area. Another provision, Rule 13, even contains patent-specific provisions on SEP abuse, which will be treated in the following subsection. The Provisions provide administrative injunctions and fines as sanctions, and their imposition should be sufficient proof of a "legally confirmed anticompetitive conduct" to justify the issuance of a compulsory license according to Article 48(2) Patent Law (Article 53(2) after the fourth amendment's entry into force).

All in all, the importance attached to compulsory licensing in academia belies their low relevance in practice. Thus far, CNIPA has not issued a single compulsory license. That does not mean, however, that their availability is entirely meaningless. In 2005, the mere threat of imposing one prompted the pharmaceutical company *Roche* to give in and to permit local industries to produce its patent protected *Tamiflu* drug under a different name and for exclusive procurement by the government to satisfy domestic demand.[352]

Finally, it should be noted that the occasional denial of an injunction against clearly established patent infringement as in the famous *Wuhan Jingyuan v. Fuji Water* decision of 21 November 2009[353] to safeguard the public interest, e.g., in cases in which stopping an ongoing infringing act could result in an undersupply with essential goods or services, can have a similar effect as a compulsory license.

3. The Special Case of Non-voluntary Licensing and Standard-Essential Patents

Rule 13 of the above SAIC Provisions also prohibits anticompetitive behaviour of the, again, *dominant* owner of a standard essential patent (SEP) in the course of formation and implementation of a standard, by not disclosing it as standard-essential to the respective standard organization, by expressly waiving his patent just to assert it against implementers after its inclusion in the standard and by refusal to license at FRAND terms, i.e., by imposing tie-in conditions or other unreasonable conditions to exclude or to restrict competition. The exclusion of non-dominant SEP owners from the application of said Rule 13 is also criticized, because at the time of joining a standard, the patent owner may not yet have a dominant status, but this may change later on, just because of his strong, non-bypassable SEP.[354] The provisions, moreover, do not sufficiently clarify the consequences of such anticompetitive behaviour especially for those affected by it, whether, e.g., standard implementers

352. Chen Wei, 'Jiaxing H1N1 liugan yiqing yu yaopin zuanli qiangzhi xuke' (The Type H1N1 Influenza Epidemic and Compulsory Licenses for Pharmaceutical Patents), 10 *China Invention & Patent* (2009), 8 et seq.
353. See the SPC's debated *Wuhan Jingyuan v. Fuji Water* decision, 8 Min San Zhong Zi (2008).
354. See Bu Yuanshi, 'Anti-Monopoly Provisions in the Field of Intellectual Property Rights in China: Disputes and Solutions', 1 *China Patents & Trademarks* (2016), 73 (75 et seq.), pointing to similar problems in the European approach towards SEPs.

who were unaware of the standard-essential patent or who could not obtain a license at FRAND terms, could escape infringement liability.

In its preliminary ruling of 8 July 2008 in *Ji Qiang and Liu Hui v. Chaoyang Xing Nuo Construction Company*[355] in response to the Liaoning Higher People's Court, the SPC formulated a rather harsh consequence for patent owners joining a standard, namely an implied permission to use:

> Considering that the standardization system of our country does not yet provide for a public disclosure and use system, the participation of a patent owner in a standard or the incorporation of the patent with his consent in a national, industry or local standard, shall be deemed as the patent owner's permission to use the patent when using the standard, so that such use shall not form patent infringement according to Article 11 of the Patent Law. The patent owner can demand a license fee from the implementer, but its amount shall be significantly lower than that of an ordinary license fee; if the patent owner has declared to waive the license fee, such declaration shall prevail.

In its later *Zhang Yinting v. Hengshui Ziyahe* decision of 2 January 2014,[356] however, the SPC obviously modified its previously strict stance, finding that the defendant who, without seeking a license, implemented the plaintiff's non-disclosed SEP and, after being notified, continued to refuse payment of license fees, committed patent infringement, so that the plaintiff was entitled to injunctive relief and damages.

Rule 24 of the SPC's Interpretations II of 2016 clearly builds on this latter view, prescribing that where a recommended national, industry or regional standard clearly indicates information about the SEP at issue, the court shall in general not support the allegedly infringing standard implementer's argument that he would simply implement such standard and therefore not infringe the patent. On the other hand, where the SEP is properly disclosed but where failure to conclude a license contract is due to the SEP owner's unwillingness to adhere to FRAND terms and where there is no obvious fault on the side of the license-seeking party, the courts shall, in general, not support the SEP owner's demand for an injunction. Finally, courts shall be open to requests from parties to determine the licensing conditions for them if they are unable to reach an agreement by themselves. Principles on how to solve cases in which the SEP is not disclosed shall, according to a renowned SPC judge,[357] be developed by courts in future judicial practice.

Rules 149–153 of the Beijing Higher People's Court's Guidelines for Patent Infringement Determination of April 2017[358] and, in even greater detail, the Guangdong Higher People's Court's (Tentative) Working Guidelines on SEP-Related Disputes of 26 April 2018,[359] provide such further guidance on how to deal with SEPs. As mentioned, interpretations or guidelines issued by a mere Higher People's Court are, unlike the SPC interpretations, not legally binding but at least for now they nevertheless serve

355. 4 *Min San Ta Zi* (2008) Da Fu Han.
356. 125 *Min Ti Zi* (2012), in Chinese at http://pkulaw.cn/case/payz_a25051f3312b07f3a01de4f0fcee04aa4e17058376d7ed52bdfb.html?match = Exact.
357. Li Jian, *supra* note 325.
358. English version at http://bjgy.chinacourt.org/article/detail/2017/04/id/2825592.shtml.
359. Full text in Chinese: http://www.gaohangip.com/article/3187.html; with explanations under each provision: http://www.chinaiprlaw.cn/index.php?id = 5546.

as important additional reference material for other, less experienced courts. It should be kept in mind, however, that their importance is likely to fade because the Higher People's Courts, as mentioned, should have lost much of their authority as appeal courts in technically complicated IP cases.

With regard to the SEP owner's failure to adhere to FRAND commitments made when joining the standard, the Beijing Higher People's Court's Guidelines clarify that in addition to non-compliance with "national, industry and regional standard as according to in Rule 24 of the SPC Interpretations II, also non-compliance with FRAND commitments made to international and other (foreign) standard setting organizations (SSO) shall result in the denial of an injunction against the implementer. To avoid this, adherence to the disclosure policy of the respective SSO shall be sufficient but there is no clear rule on how explicit such disclosure must be.[360] Since December 2013, the Interim Provisions on the National Standards involving Patents[361] enacted by the National Standardization Committee and CNIPA at least provide Chinese SSO with guidance on how to formulate a disclosure policy, which may contribute to alleviating a too great variety of disclosure requirements. The Beijing Higher People's Court's Guidelines, furthermore, provide several criteria to assess whether the SEP holder fulfilled its FRAND commitments, and under which circumstances the implementer is at fault in negotiations, so as to decide whether an injunction is justified in a given case. The mentioned Guangdong Higher People's Court's Working Guidelines are also focused on the behaviour of the parties in license negotiations, but with 32 provisions altogether in a much more detailed manner than the Beijing Higher People's Court's Guidelines.

Provisions on an implied consent to license by an SEP holder who failed to disclose his patent as standard-essential were, furthermore, contained in the 2015 Patent Law draft amendment but were deleted from the the later drafts of 2019 and 2020, and also the subsequently amended Patent Law silent on this issue. Abusive assertion of SEPs may in the future fall under the newly proposed Article 20 of the 2020 draft, according to which patent rights shall not be abused to damage the public interest or the legitimate rights and interests of others or to prevent or to restrict competition, whereby exclusion or restriction of competition shall be specifically dealt with under the Antimonopoly Law.

Also the more recent SEP-related litigation places most emphasis on the behaviour of the parties during license negotiations. In its *Huawei v. IDC* decision of 21 October 2013,[362] the Guangdong Higher People's Court (which subsequently formulated the above tentative guidelines) found that *IDC* abused its dominant position as holder of mobile communication-related SEPs in multiple ways, inter alia by charging excessive licencing fees in comparison with the fees charged from other licensees, by tying SEPs with non-SEPs and by forcing Huawei to license back patents from its portfolio, which violated several provisions in Article 17 Anti-Monopoly

360. Yang Boyong and Jiao Yan, 'Interpretation of Amendments to Guidelines for Patent Infringement Determination (2017) issued by Beijing High People's Court', 3 *China Patents & Trademarks* (2017), 25.

361. http://www.wipo.int/wipolex/en/text.jsp?file_id=337261, in English at http://www.cpahkltd.com/EN/info.aspx?n=20130108104438093806.

362. 306 *Yue Gao Fa Min San Zhong Zi* (2013).

Law. The court determined drastically lower license fees,[363] and ordered *IDC* to compensate *Huawei* for losses suffered due to the abusive SEP assertion. The more recent Beijing Higher People's Court's *Iwncomm v. Sony* decision of 28 March 2017[364] stressed that SEP owners do not have to tolerate the exploitation of their patent if the license-seeker negotiated in an unfair manner, upholding the previous instance decision which found standard implementer *Sony* liable for the infringing use of *Iwncomm*'s SEP-protected WAPI method and ordered it to cease from infringing use and to pay triple damages. Hereby, the court resorted to damage calculation in licence analogy pursuant to Article 65 Patent Law (Article 71 after the fourth amendment's entry into force), by determining a "reasonably multiplied amount of royalties".[365] The court justified the high damage amount with the defendant's bad-faith obstruction of license negotiations by requiring the plaintiff to submit detailed claim charts while refusing to sign a confidentiality agreement. Apart from issues related to SEP negotiations, the court also rendered interesting opinions with regard to indirect infringement[366] and the question whether a method patent can be subject to exhaustion.[367]

More explanations about law and practice regarding SEPs are contained in Chapter 5 of this book on Unfair Competition and Antitrust Law.

XIV. SCOPE OF PROTECTION AND PATENT-SPECIFIC ASPECTS OF ENFORCEMENT

The following explanations will be focused on the scope of granted patents, in particular claim construction, product-by-process protection, patent-specific limitations and estoppels, and the like. Aspects of general enforcement, for instance, civil procedures including provisional measures and damage calculation,[368] specific rules for IP protection in the course of exhibitions, China-specific administrative enforcement or border protection will be treated in Chapter 7 of this book on Enforcement.

As a general rule, Article 11(1) Patent Law provides that invention or utility model patent owners are entitled to prohibit the making, use, offer for sale, sale and import of the patented product, and the owner of a process invention patent is protected against the use of the patented process and the use, offer for sale, sale and import of the products that directly resulted from such patented process. According to Article 11(2), design patent owners are entitled to prevent the unauthorized production, offer for sale, sale and import of products incorporating their designs. Someone who entrusts another party with the processing and making of a patented product by providing such party with a sample of it is also regarded as infringer.[369]

363. Yuanshi Bu, 'Die kartellrechtlichen Einschränkungen des Immaterialgüterrechts in China' (Antitrust limitations to intellectual property in China), *GRUR Int.* (2015), 1097.
364. 454 *Jing Min Zhong* (2017); English translation by Li Jingtian in *GRUR Int.* (2019), 913.
365. More details in XIV. 9. *infra*.
366. See XIV. 4. *infra*.
367. See XIV. 2 a) *infra*.
368. Except the patent-specific details of damage calculation in XIV. 9. *infra*.
369. SPC decision *Chen Shundi v. Zhejiang Lexue'er Homeware* of 25 Dec. 2013 (2013) Min Ti Zi No. 225; http://gongbao.court.gov.cn/Details/040c1d7ee266f6167ff995907d4fe5.html?

The statute of limitation in patent cases is currently two years, counted from the date the patent owner knew or should have known about the infringement (Article 68 Patent Law). The patentee does not necessarily have to file suit within these two years but the chances that a court will accept the case even after their expiration are good if he has not remained totally passive during this period but proceeded by other means, e.g., by seeking an out-of-court settlement or by filing an administrative complaint.[370] As mentioned, the fourth Patent Law amendment extended the limitation to three years, henceforth counted from the date on which the patentee knows or ought to know about both the infringement *and* the infringer (Article 74 of the amended Patent Law). That the limitation period shall be counted from the date on which also the infringer is known has been first proposed by the Patent law draft amendment of 2020, It obviously aims at avoiding the situation that a patentee who is only aware of the infringement has to fear that the time for settlement negotiations, etc., will run out while he is trying to identify the actual infringer.

1. Invention and Utility Model Claim Interpretation

(a) General

Ideally, the whole patent shall be comprehensible on its own terms or, as it is sometimes put, "act as its own dictionary".[371] The general relationship between claims and description is laid down in Article 59(1) Patent Law (Article 64(1) after the fourth amendment's entry into force):

> For the patent right of an invention or a utility model, the scope of protection shall be confined to what is claimed, and the written description and the pictures attached may be used to explain what is claimed.

Under certain circumstances, which will be further outlined below, the information contained in the description, embodiments and drawings may be read in a manner that limits the protection scope.

During infringement litigation, the judge is required to assess through the eyes of a person skilled in the art whether the allegedly infringing technical solution extends into the claimed scope of protection. Such skilled artisan is not defined by the Patent Law or by any of the SPC's judicial interpretations. The only official definition is the already mentioned one in Part II, Chapter 4, 2.4 of the Examination Guidelines. Another, non-official definition is provided by Rule 11 of the Beijing High Court guidelines:

> A person with ordinary skills in the art is a hypothetical "person" who is presumed to be aware of all the common technical knowledge and have access to all the technologies existing in the art prior to the filing date, and have capacity to apply all the routine experimental means prior to the filing date.

---

sw=%e6%8d%90%e7%8c%ae%e5%8e%9f%e5%88%99.

370. Christopher Bailey and Lucy Wang, note 329, with reference to corresponding case law.

371. Thomas Pattloch, 'Patent Enforcement in China', in Christopher Heath (ed.), *Patent Enforcement Worldwide* (3rd ed., Hart Publishing, 2015), 315.

> A person with ordinary skills in the art does not specifically refer to one person or one type of person, and cannot be labelled by reference to such specific standards like education background, professional title and rank. Where there is any disagreement arising from the party over whether a person with ordinary skills in the art is aware of some common technical knowledge and has the capacity to apply certain routine experimental means, evidence shall be provided.

(b) Equivalence

Infringement is not only established if the allegedly infringing solution contains a literal counterpart for each and every element of the patent, but the judge shall also consider equivalents. The Patent Law and the Implementing Regulations are silent on the doctrine of equivalence, but it is applied at least since the enactment of the SPC Interpretations 2001 (last amended 2020). Rule 13 of the Interpretations reads as follows:

> "The extent of protection of the right for invention or utility model shall be determined by the content of the claims. The description and the appended drawings may be used to interpret the claims" in Article 59(1) Patent Law means that the scope of protection of patent right should be determined by all technical features stated in the claims, including the scope as determined by the features equivalent to the necessary technical features.
>
> The equivalent features refer to the features which use essentially the same means, perform essentially the same function and produce essentially the same result as the stated technical features, and which can be contemplated by an ordinarily skilled artisan at the date when the infringement occurred without inventive labour.

Rule 13 (before 2020: Rule 17) has undergone two amendments in the past. One replaced "necessary" by "all", so that now "all" technical features of the claims shall be included in the comparison with the defendant's technical solution, not only the necessary ones, obviously to remind courts to strictly adhere to the all elements rule and to refrain from the generous practice to exclude "unnecessary" features of the claims from the comparison.[372]

Moreover, the amended provision clarifies that the knowledge of the skilled artisan at the *infringement* date shall be decisive for establishing equivalence. That is, also equivalent technical features that were unknown at the *priority* date but later on became part of the standard knowledge in the course of technical progress shall be considered by courts, whereas the previous version of the Interpretations remained silent on this important aspect. In effect, this broadens the scope for equivalent infringement and is consistent with the practice in the US, but not in Europe.

The hardly intelligible Rule 60 of the non-authoritative Beijing Higher People's Court's Guidelines somewhat modifies this rule by exempting from the application of the equivalence doctrine to *invention* patents non-inventive technical features or features introduced through an amendment that had been known or foreseeable to

372. See XIV. 1. c) *infra*.

the patent owner at the application date. With regard to *utility models*, the exclusion from equivalence is even more rigid, encompassing known or foreseeable features introduced through amendment and all technical features known or foreseeable at the application date, not only the non-inventive ones. Judges from the Beijing Higher People's Court justify the discrimination of utility models with the necessity to protect competitors from an overly broad scope of these non-examined, easily obtainable rights.[373]

Rule 13 of the 2001 Interpretations furthermore regulates two sets of prerequisites for establishing equivalence, namely "three times essentially the same" (essentially same means, essentially same function, essentially same result) and "identification by the skilled artisan without inventive labour". In its *Xinjiang Yongchang Inc. v. Shanxi Jingye Inc.* decision of 2010,[374] the SPC clarified that these two sets shall be cumulatively applied. For instance, not all variations that easily come into the skilled artisan's mind upon reading the patent documents are automatically equivalent, but some may still be so different from the patented solution that they cannot be regarded as "using substantially the same means, performing substantially the same function and producing substantially the same result".

(1) Equivalence and Functional Elements

According to Rule 4 of the SPC's 2009 Interpretations, courts shall resort to the embodiments of the description to identify the scope of claims defined by functional elements:

> The People's Courts shall, with regard to technical features in the claims which are expressed by function or effect, determine the content of such features by way of combination with the concrete mode of performing such function or result as laid down in the description and the drawings, or equivalent modes of performing.

That is, in case of functional elements, not all conceivable alternative means that perform the same function and have the same effect fall within the protection scope, but only those identical with or equivalent to the concrete means as outlined in the description and in the drawings.

In its *Tesa v. Qinghai Measuring and Cutting Tools* decision of 27 December 2016,[375] the SPC denied infringement due to lack of identity or equivalence with the functional element, here a leakage preventing function, which was achieved by a specific manner of sealing according to the description, whereas the defendant's solution achieved leakage prevention in a manner not mentioned in the description.

The SPC Interpretations II added further clarifications with regard to functional elements. Rule 8(1) describes them as "elements that limit the function or the effects achieved by structure, composition, steps, conditions or their relationship and the

373. Yang Boyong and Jiao Yan, *supra* note 360.
374. 181 *Min Shen Zi* (2010).
375. 176 *Zui Gao Fa Min Zai* (2016). https://www.tianyancha.com/lawsuit/4862013070744ecea8443c9dcb547b35 ; English summary at https://www.lexology.com/library/detail.aspx?g=69e006a2-0591-43ce-b979-cbe584b58480.

like within the invention-creation, except working modes that the skilled artisan, merely upon reading the claims, can clearly determine as achieving the same function or effect." In its decision of 27 March 2019,[376] the SPC interpreted this provision as excluding technical features that limited the structure, composition, steps, conditions, etc., and at the same time also the function that they achieved, from the definition of a "functional element" and the application of the above provision, and found that in the present case the limiting statements with regard to structure, etc., in the technical features sufficed to enable the skilled artisan to comprehend the limits to function and effect. This can be interpreted in a manner that technical elements or features limiting the structure, etc., of an invention cannot simultaneously perform the role of functional elements. Rule 18 of the Beijing Higher People's Court's Guidelines also states that elements which, while being expressed in functional terms, are simultaneously expressed by way of structure, composition, material, steps, etc., shall not be regarded as functional elements. They furthermore exclude elements described in terms that have become standard technical terms in the respective field from the definition of functional elements.

Rule 8(2) of the SPC Interpretations II prescribes that the corresponding element from the defendant's technical solution shall be regarded as identical with or equivalent to a functional element only if it applies *essentially the same* means to perform the *same* function and to achieve the *same* effect (i.e., not "essentially" but exactly the same function and the same effect), which must be easily comprehensible to a person skilled in the art at the time of infringement. SPC judges justify the restriction, again, with the need to avoid overprotection especially for unexamined utility models. It would be sufficient to limit equivalence to the means applied, and not necessary also to include equivalent functions and effects achieved by these means into the protection scope.[377] Rule 56 of the subsequently enacted Beijing Higher People's Court's Guidelines contains a similar provision.

(2) "Dedication to the Public"

Chinese (but also foreign, e.g., German[378]) courts are reluctant to apply the equivalence doctrine to equivalents mentioned in the description but not referred to in the claims. Such described but not claimed equivalents are usually regarded as having been abandoned, in Chinese terminology as "dedicated to the public".[379] Rule 58 of the Beijing Higher People's Court's Guidelines explicitly state that a technical solution

376. 2 *Zui Gao Fa Zhi Min Zhong* (2019); https://mp.weixin.qq.com/s/aZyPElLDxMqDE8didFgTHA.

377. Song Xiaoming, Wang Chuang and Li Jian, *supra* note 326.

378. The German Federal Court decisions Pemetrexed (14 June 2016) and V-shaped guide formation (23 August 2016) has somewhat softened but not abandoned this strict stance towards the equivalence doctrine; a good comparative overview of the converging case law on the equivalence doctrine in Germany and UK is given by Wolfgang Kellenter, 'Das Comeback der Äquivalenz – Anmerkungen zur neueren Rechtsprechung zur Äquivalenz in Deutschland und im Vereinigten Königreich', *GRUR* (2018), 247 et seq.

379. Therefore called non-infringement under the "dedication rule" in Chinese terminology – see Li Jian, 'Chinese Characteristics of Claim Interpretation by Courts', in Stefan Luginbuehl and Peter Ganea (eds.), *Patent Law in Greater China* (Edward Elgar, 2014), 288 et seq.

mentioned in the description and the drawings but not included in the claims shall be deemed to have been abandoned by the patentee.

(3) Prosecution History Estoppel

Quite in contrast to German and European practice but similar to US-style claim interpretation, Rule 6 of the Interpretations II explicitly permits Chinese courts to consider the prosecution history and limiting statements therein to deny equivalence. Courts[380] and academia in China unanimously agree that the prosecution history shall be considered, but the question whether it should be applied only to subject matter abandoned at the applicant/patent owner's initiative or to all limitations of the protection scope, e.g., undertaken at the request of the examiner in order to save the application, is under debate.[381] The SPC's *Zhongyu v. Jiuying* decision of 12 April 2012[382] favours the former opinion, clarifying that only voluntary abandonments shall be considered, not abandonments resulting from a partial invalidation.[383]

(c) All Elements Rule

The SPC Interpretation 2009 put an end to a generous practice of some courts to disregarded technical features of the patent that were not necessary to achieve the inventive aim, and to rule in favour of the plaintiff if the defendant's solution lacked these features.[384] Rule 7 now obliges courts to give priority to the protection scope expressly sought by the patentee himself, stating that all technical features of a claim shall be assessed and compared with the allegedly infringing solution, and if the latter lacks a technical feature mentioned in the claims, the court shall establish non-infringement irrespective of how necessary such feature is deemed to realize the inventive aim. The mentioned amendment to Rule 13 of the 2001 Interpretations points in the same direction.[385] Patent applicants are therefore well advised to ascertain that each technical feature of a claim performs a single, independent function, and to avoid combining several units that perform different technical functions into one feature, otherwise the defendant's technical solution may be found non-infringing because one of its technical features lacks one of these functions.[386]

380. See, e.g., the SPC's *Hubei Wushi Pharmaceutical Industries v. Aonuo Pharmaceuticals* decision of 23 March 2010, (2009) Min Ti Zi No. 20, http://gongbao.court.gov.cn/Details/fe0b7bdfdf9ea9d35127e5ca0dba8a.html?sw=%e8%91%a1%e8%90%84%e7%b3%96.
381. See Yuan Xiuting and Wang Cuiping, 'Dengtong yuanze de sifa shijian: yuanze, xianzhi he anli' (Judicial practice of the equivalence doctrine: principles, limits and a case), 8 *Zhishi Chanquan* (2013), 96 et seq.
382. 306 *Min Ti Zi* (2011); 10 *Gazette of the SPC* (2012), http://gongbao.court.gov.cn/details/f798428cce796682f537a8363438ef.html.
383. Rules 61–64 of the Beijing Higher People's Court's Guidelines provide further guidance on how to apply the prosecution history estoppel.
384. Li Jian, *supra* notes 378, 287 et seq.
385. See XIV. 1. b) *supra*.
386. SPC decision of 30 December 2019, (2019) Zui Gao Fa Min Zai No. 348; https://mp.weixin.qq.com/s/OOy8yKVdk5ilPRJrtL60gg.

(d) Closed Claims

If instead the defendant's solution does not only incorporate all elements of the patent but comprises additional elements, infringement is normally established, unless the patented solution is expressed by way of closed combination claims, which are most common in the chemical and pharmaceutical field.[387] Rule 7(1) of the SPC Interpretations II provides that if the allegedly infringing solution adds an element to a close-ended combination claim that goes beyond the normal impurities, such solution shall not fall into the protection scope. The wording of the provision seems to be based on the preceding SPC's *Hu Xiaoquan v. Shaanxi Zhendong Taisheng Pharmaceuticals* of 20 December 2012[388] decision. Rule 41 of the Beijing Higher People's Court's Guidelines contains a similar provision. Previous drafts of the SPC Interpretation II still contained a limitation to this rule, instructing courts to exclude the allegedly infringing solution from the protection scope only if its additional feature produced a substantial effect, but for the sake of clarity of the protection scope chosen by the patentee himself it was finally omitted. Rule 7(2) of the Interpretations II exempts combination claims in the field of Traditional Chinese Medicine (TCM) from the definition of closed combination claims in the preceding paragraph. According to commentators from the SPC, this means that in case of TCM-related inventions represented by way of closed claims, the judge has to consider whether the additional feature of the allegedly infringing solution produces an essential effect, and only when it does, it shall not be included in the protection scope.[389] The more generous protection of TCM aims at inciting innovation in this area.

(e) Claims Limited by Numerical Ranges

Rule 12 of the SPC Interpretations II states that if a claim contains language that limits the protection scope by numerical ranges, e.g., terms like "at least" or "not exceeding", thereby leaving the skilled artisan with the expression that patentee explicitly wanted to limit the scope of protection, courts shall refrain from including technical solutions expressed by different ranges in such scope.[390] Rule 57 of the Beijing Higher People's Court's Guidelines further stipulate that in general, courts shall not include different numerical ranges in the protection scope of claims that contain numerical ranges, unless the different numerical range came into existence after the application date. Only where the claims use language like "at least" or "not exceeding" in a manner that points to a clear intention of the applicant to limit his

387. The drafting of open-ended and closed-ended claims in case of chemical inventions is further regulated by the Examination Guidelines, Part II, Chapter 10, 4.2.1.
388. 10 *Min Ti Zi* (2012), http://pkulaw.cn/case/payz_a25051f3312b07f3905b738a2b085014e8e1b722e4d5adc5bdfb.html?match=Exact; see also case comment by Li Mingde, 'Fengbishi quanli yaoqiu de baohu fanwei' (Protection scope of closed claims), 11 *Zhongguo faming yu zhuanli* (China Invention and Patent) (2018), 92 et seq.
389. Song Xiaoming, Wang Chuang and Li Jian, *supra* note 326.
390. Based on the SPC's *Renda Building Materials v. Xinyi Inc.* decision of 22 August 2005, 1 *Mi San Ti Zi* (2005), http://gongbao.court.gov.cn/Details/480d63c4c22c3d460e6412e5086811.html?sw=%e5%a4%a7%e8%bf%9e%e4%bb%81%e8%be%be.

claim in numerical respect, solutions that comprise alternative numerical ranges should categorically be excluded from the protection scope, even if they came into existence after the application date. With special regard to utility models, Rule 57(3) states that a corresponding numerical feature (i.e., any numerical indication, not only a numerical range) in the defendant's solution shall in any case (i.e., not only "in general" as in case of invention patents) not be a ground for establishing equivalence, unless it forms a different numerical feature pertaining to technical subject matter that came into existence after the application date. The full meaning of this provision is hard to grasp. According to judges from the Higher People's Court, it aims at factually excluding numerical features in utility model claims from protection under the doctrine of equivalence, as a properly drafted claim of a utility model, pursuant to Article 2 Patent Law a technical solution that pertained to "product shapes, structures or their combinations", would not be in need of numerical indications at all.[391]

(f) Elements Limiting the Field of Application

Rule 24 of the Beijing Higher People's Court's Guidelines is the only provision that expressly mentions the limitation of the claim by elements that delineate the invention's field of application. Accordingly, if the plaintiff's invention is limited by a feature that determines the field of application, the defendant's technical solution shall still be regarded as providing the same feature if it *can* be applied within this field, irrespective of whether it actually *is* applied within such field, unless the patent documents clearly state that the invention can only be applied to this specific field. If, in the latter case, it can be proven that the defendant's technical solution can be applied to other fields, it does not fall within the patent's protection scope. The same shall apply to cases in which the defendant's solution cannot be applied to the field of application delineated by the technical feature. Rule 24 also clarifies that a technical feature that limits the field of application shall not be equated with the title of the claimed subject-matter that must be indicated in the claim's preamble portion (Rule 21 Implementing Regulations). It can only be a technical feature in the claim that describes the background of or the conditions for the application of the invention and which is connected or combined with the technical solution. An SPC decision of 27 March 2019[392] added that in general, technical features that limit the field of application shall in general be understood as prescribing that the invention may be used within said field, but not that it can only be applied within this field, unless the skilled artisan upon reading the patent documents arrives at the conclusion that the application of the invention is strictly limited to said field. Largely in compliance with Rule 24 of the lower court's Guidelines, the SPC further states that only in cases in which the defendant's technical solution cannot be used within the field of the invention's application as delineated by the technical feature, the defendant's solution shall not fall within the protection scope, but not in cases which the defendant's solution can be applied to such field, irrespective of whether it can also be applied to other fields.

---

391. Yang Boyong and Jiao Yan, *supra* note 360, 25.
392. 2 *Zui Gao Fa Zhi Min Zhong* (2019), http://gongbao.court.gov.cn/Details/3105e8a1662bed-59f46fd39b4478bb.html.

2. Limitations/Non-infringing Uses

Article 69 Patent Law (Article 75 after the fourth amendment's entry into force) regulates five uses that do not infringe the patent, namely exhaustion, prior use, use of patented inventions incorporated in transportation means transiting China, use for scientific research and experiments, and use of the patented solution to obtain regulatory approval ("Bolar exemption").

(a) Exhaustion

The Patent Law is the only intellectual property law that contains a clear provision on the exhaustion of rights. The corresponding Article 69 No. 1 (Article 75 No. 1 after the fourth amendment's entry into force) stipulates that after a patented product or a product directly obtained by using the patented method is sold by the patentee or sold by any unit or individual with the permission of the patentee, its use, offer for sale, sale or import by any other person shall not be deemed to be infringing. That is, the present law exempts from the patent right not only the use, offer for sale or sale of patented products or products directly obtained from a patented process which have been first sold within China, but also the parallel import of such products first sold abroad with the consent of the patent owner.

With regard to the question whether the patent right also exhausts in case of collecting, recycling and reselling legally sold products, as far as can be seen, only one old decision of the Shandong Higher People's Court in 2000[393] is available, rendered at a time when exhaustion was not yet even regulated by the Patent Law. Accordingly, the collecting and refilling of design protected wine bottles was not considered infringing, as the design right in them would be exhausted upon their first sale. Also, Rule 131 No. 3 of the Beijing Higher People's Guidelines (the preceding Guidelines of 2001 and 2013 provided similar provisions)[394] exempts "use, offer for sale or sale of specific parts of a patented product by the patent owner or his licensee, or the assembly of such parts to manufacture the patented product" from infringement.

Rule 131 No. 4 of the same Guidelines furthermore exempt the use of legally sold equipment specifically intended for carrying out the patented process from infringement, irrespective of whether such apparatus itself is also covered by the same patent or not.[395] This provision, however, is obviously understood as an implied license to the purchaser to implement the process by using the equipment in the

393. 339 *Lu Min Zhong Zi* (2000); commentators also refer to a settlement in the Heilongjiang Higher People's Court in 2007 in another liquor bottle related design exhaustion dispute, 3 *Hei Zhi Zhong Zi* (2007).

394. See Peter Ganea, 'Predominantly Process-Patent Related Aspects of Infringement', in Stefan Luginbuehl and Peter Ganea (eds.), *Patent Law in Greater China* (Edward Elgar, 2014), 295 et seq.

395. Under German case law, the sale of apparatus that is not or separately patented with the patentee's consent does not result in the exhaustion of the rights in the process patent. However, the court would normally assume that the patent owner has given his tacit consent in the intended use of the apparatus, i.e., to implement the process, see German Federal Court decisions *Fullplastverfahren* of 24 September 1979 (*GRUR* (1980), 38) and *Handhabungsgerät* of 16 September 1997 (*GRUR* (1998), 130)

intended manner, not as an extension of the exhaustion doctrine to processes. In the mentioned *Iwncomm v. Sony* decision of 2018,[396] the very same Beijing Higher People's Court rejected the defendant's argument that the plaintiff's method patent was exhausted (or there was an implied licence to use) because the defendant implemented it with help of equipment sold by patentee. The court opined that the exhaustion doctrine would be irrelevant in this case because the current Article 69(1) Patent Law (henceforth: Article 75(1)) clearly limited its application to products, either patented products or products directly obtained by a process.[397]

(b) Prior Use

The prior art defence as an alternative to an invalidation trial has been treated in detail above. Loosely related is the prior use exemption, which, however, does not require the defendant's technical solution to belong to the publicly known prior art, but only proof of the defendant's legal use of the patented technical solution before the application date. Article 69(2) Patent Law (Article 75(2) after the fourth amendment's entry into force) provides that if a party has already manufactured identical products, used an identical method or has made necessary preparations for the manufacture or use and continues to manufacture the products or use the method within the original scope, such act will not be deemed to be infringing. Rule 15 of the SPC Interpretations of 2009 further clarifies that the defendant must have obtained the patented subject matter legally to be released from infringement liability. Rule 15 also defines the term "necessary preparations", as either the finalization of the main technical drawings or documents for later manufacture, use, etc. or the production or purchase of the necessary main facilities or raw materials. "Original scope" means the scope of ongoing production at the application date or the scope achievable from operating the existing manufacturing facilities or from the preparations made at the date of filing. Finally, the Interpretations clarify that manufacture and use within the original scope but carried out by another entity upon transfer of the manufacturing process shall not be covered by the prior use exemption, unless such transfer is made as part of transferring or bequeathing the whole entity.

In practice, case law in which defendants invoked the prior use exception is abundant, which, according to commentators, can be explained by the high amount of bad faith applications of subject matter invented by someone else, mostly by the prior user himself. Yet, proving evidence of ongoing manufacturing or completion of the necessary preparations is reported to be burdensome, and in the majority of cases, the defence would be rejected. Commentators therefore suggest that wherever evidence can be provided that the technical solution at issue also pertains to prior art, the defendant should rather resort to the prior art defence, which would require a lower burden of proof.[398]

---

396. *Supra* note 364.
397. On the understanding of Item 131 No. 4 as implied license see Hui Zhang, Mengling Liu and James Yang, 'Beijing High Court upholds China's first-ever SEP injunction in Iwncomm v. Sony', http://patentblog.kluweriplaw.com/2018/05/29/beijing-high-court-upholds-chinas-first-ever-sep-injunction-iwncomm-v-sony/.
398. See Christopher Bailey and Lucy Wang, *supra* note 329, quoting related case law.

(c) *Use in Foreign Transportation Means*

In conformity with Article 5*ter* Paris Convention, the current Article 69(3) Patent Law (henceforth: Article 75(3)) provides that the use of patents in foreign transportation means temporarily passing the aerial, water of land territory of China shall not be infringing, provided that such use occurs within the devices and installations of the transportation means for their own needs. That is, transportation devices, etc., that are themselves transported are excluded from this exemption. Also, the exemption does not extend to spare devices stored in Chinese territory for repair purposes.[399] As will be further explained in subsection 3 on indirect infringement below, at least the Beijing Higher People's Court's Guidelines stipulate that providing means for the use of a patented invention in a foreign transportation device does not fall under the exception, so that the provider may be prosecutable as indirect infringer.

(d) *Scientific Research and Experimental Use*

Article 69(4) of the current Patent Law (Article 75(4) after the fourth amendment's entry into force) provides that uses "specifically" for research and experimentation purposes shall be exempted from infringement liability. The provision leaves much room for interpretation, in particular as to what kind of uses are "specific" enough to fall under the exception. A hint at how courts may identify permissible uses under the current Article 69(4) is contained in Rule 115 of the Beijing Higher People's Court's Guidelines, which states that "making, using, importing or using the patented process as a tool to carry out experiments related to other technology or test the business prospects of a patented technical solution, whereas the results are not directly related to the patented technology" are infringing, which can be summarized as "experiments and research *on* a patented solution are permitted, but not experiments and research *with* a patented solution".[400] That is, experiments immediately focused on the patented technology shall be permitted, for instance, to test or to improve it, but not the experimental etc. use of a patented invention to achieve something in a different field. Permissible seem to be experimental uses with the purpose of developing a more advanced technical solution that will, if later on marketed, enter into direct competition with the patented invention. Court cases that could help to further confine the scope of allowable experimental use are rare, even the most recent academic articles refer to case law from the early 1990s.[401] The majority of academic

399. *Ibid.*, 133.
400. So characterized in *ibid.*
401. See, e.g., Ding Wenjie, 'Zhuanli qinquan kangbian zhong "kexue yanjiu he shiyan" de shiyong yuanze – Lu Zhenming su Shanghai Gongcheng Chengtao zonggongsi, Wuxi-shi Huangjing Weisheng Gongcheng Shiyan Guang zhuanli qinquan shangsu'an' (Rules for applying "scientific research and experimental use" – the *Lu Zhengming v. Shanghai Engineering Equipment Co., Ltd. and Wuxi Environmental Sanitation Engineering Experimental Factory* patent infringement appeal case), *China Invention & Patent* (Jan. 2019), 112, referring to a case decided by the Shanghai Higher People's Court in 1992 or 1993 (exact date not indicated), available in English and Chinese at http://en.pkulaw.cn/display.aspx?cgid = 1970324837041332&lib = case.

commentators suggest a generous application of the experimental use exemption to promote technological progress.[402]

As will be further explained in subsection 3 below on indirect infringement, the Beijing Higher People's Court's Guidelines do not apply this exemption to parties who provide means to enable permissible experimental use.

(e) Bolar *Exemption*

Since 2008, Article 69(5) Patent Law (Article 75(5) after the fourth amendment's entry into force) regulates the so-called *Bolar* Exemption allowing the production, use or import (but not the sale or offer for sale) of patented drugs or patented medical apparatus for the purpose of providing information required for administrative examination and approval, as well as the production or import of the medicines respectively apparatus for the party which applies with the regulatory authority.

Reportedly, the requirement in Article 11 Patent Law pursuant to which only uses "for production or business purposes" are infringing formed a relatively safe harbour for generics producers even before the amendment, as courts usually denied the commercial character of uses aimed at obtaining regulatory approval.[403]

Until recently, the *Bolar* Exemption has not been supplemented by a noteworthy patent linkage mechanism, but this is about to change rapidly, as will be explained in the following chapter 3.

3. The Emergence of a Patent Linkage Mechanism

The fourth amendment of 2020 added a new Article 76 to the Patent Law, which for the first time elevates patent linkage to higher levels in the law hierarchy. The Drug Administration Law (DAL), even after its recent amendment of 26 August 2019,[404] does not contain any provisions on patent linkage. Thus far it has been up to lower-ranking administrative provisions, the State Council's Implementing Regulations to the Drug Administration Law, which have been amended on 6 February 2016,[405] to regulate a first rudimentary linkage regime. According to their Rule 34(1), self-obtained and undisclosed test data and other data submitted by the manufacturer or seller of a pharmaceutical approved for production and sale that contains a new chemical compound shall be protected against the unfair commercial use of such data. The provision obviously aims at accommodating the test data exclusivity requirement in Article 39.3 TRIPS. Rule 34(2) of the DAL Implementing Regulations translates this widely interpretable international provision into an obligation of the National Medical Products Authority (NMPA) to prohibit follow-up applicants from using such test data without the permission of the original applicant for a period of six years from the receipt of the license for production and sale. Also, pursuant to Para 3, the

402. See, e.g,, Sun Ying, Wang Xiaohui and Xu Mingyue, 'Shiyan liwai de kuodaxing jieshi' (Extended interpretation of the experimental use exemption), 2 *Fazhi Bolan* (Legality Vision) (2019), 88.
403. References in Christopher Bailey and Lucy Wang, *supra* note 329.
404. http://www.npc.gov.cn/npc/c30834/201908/26a6b28dd83546d79d17f90c62e59461.shtml.
405. https://www.nmpa.gov.cn/xxgk/fgwj/flxzhfg/20160601100401621.html.

Authority is banned from disclosing the test data, except where necessary in the public interest or where precautions have been taken to ascertain that the data will not be used for commercial purposes in an unfair manner. Only test data pertaining to drugs that contain a new chemical compound fall under this protection, and the unclear extent of this "novelty" requirement is another cause of dissent between the US and China. The US prefer "new" in the meaning of "new in China", whereas present Chinese rules seem to understand "new" in the sense of worldwide novelty, which would exclude drugs already marketed outside China from test data exclusivity.[406]

Rules 18 and 19 of the administrative "Method for the Registration of Pharmaceuticals" of 2002 (last amended 2007)[407] regulate further rudimentary patent linkage, stating that applicants for registration have to make a declaration that they do not infringe upon another person's patent and that the authorities have to publish such declaration on their website. Also, the earliest possible date for the registration of a drug in which another party holds a patent is two years before the expiration of the patent, and the authority shall then issue the necessary permissions and certificates after the expiration of the patent term.

In their joint Opinion on Deepening the Reform of the Evaluation and Approval System to Promote Innovation with regard to Pharmaceuticals and Medical Apparatus of 8 October 2017,[408] the CPC's Central Office and the State Council urged the relevant authorities, inter alia, to further deepen the linkage between drug administration and patent protection. One of the proposals has already been realized, namely to publish a list of admitted entirely new medicines and new medicines that are improvements of existing ones, as well as generic medicines which have undergone bioequivalence testing, including indication of active ingredients, mode of delivery, holder of the marketing license, patent information, duration of data exclusivity, etc. (Item 15).[409]

In Item 16, the Opinion proposed the exploration of a more substantial patent linkage to reduce the likelihood of infringement disputes between patent holders and applicants for generic versions. For this, applicants for the registration of a new drug shall henceforth indicate and explain in their application the related patents and their ownership status and inform the owners of the related patents within a specified time limit. It remains unclear, however, whether such indication shall be made with reference to the above list, i.e., whether the list should play a similar role as the Orange Book in the US.[410] That China's final linkage mechanism will ultimately rely on such an Orange Book-like list is relatively certain, as a new draft Method formulated by CNIPA and NMPA on patent linkage, which will be explained in detail a few paragraphs below, refers to a "platform" on which patent information about marketed drugs shall henceforth be recorded. Should a dispute arise in spite of such precautions, the Opinion further suggest that NMPA shall be

---

406. So the USTR's 2018 Special 301 Report, https://ustr.gov/sites/default/files/files/Press/Reports/2018%20Special%20301.pdf, p.43
407. http://samr.cfda.gov.cn/WS01/CL1031/24529.html.
408. http://www.gov.cn/zhengce/2017-10/08/content_5230105.htm; comparatively analysed by Liang Zhiwen, 'Patent Linkage System Centered on Information Disclosure', 1 *China Patents & Trademarks* (2018), 11.
409. The list is available in Chinese http://202.96.26.102/.
410. Rather not, according to the explanations of Liang Zhiwen, *supra* note 408.

involved insofar as it continues the evaluation of the drug during the dispute but aligns its marketing approval decision with the outcome of the patent dispute. If the infringement proceedings exceed a fixed period of time, the NMPA may approve the drug without waiting for a final outcome. Also these suggestions have been incorporated in the mentioned draft Method, as will be further explained below. The Opinion, finally, suggested the improvement and implementation of the already available data exclusivity (see above) especially for self-obtained and undisclosed data submitted to obtain approval for innovative drugs, drugs for the treatment of rare diseases, drugs for children, innovative drugs relying on biological material, and drugs that are successfully challenging a patent.

As mentioned, a further huge step towards a full-fledged patent linkage regime was the introduction of a new Article 76 to the Patent Law, which will become effective on 1 June 2021. The new provision implements the requirements in Article 1.11 of the above-mentioned Sino-US ETA ("Effective Mechanism for the Early Resolution of Patent Disputes"), which urges China to further refine its regulatory environment for the resolution of disputes between the party who first submitted drug safety and efficacy information for marketing approval and the party who wants to rely on such data to obtain a marketing approval on its own. Such system shall include a system of notification to the original applicant (holder of a patent, a license or a marketing approval) that another person is seeking approval, adequate time and opportunity for the original applicant to proceed against possible infringement by the other party and adequate remedies *per se*, in particular provisional measures. To accommodate the peculiar Chinese enforcement infrastructure, Article 1.11 stresses that disputes of this kind may also be resolved through administrative proceedings.

Article 76(1) of the amended Patent Law now provides that where a patent dispute arises over a new medicine waiting for examination and approval between the applicant for approval and the patentee or other interested party (licensee), both parties, i.e., either the applicant or the patentee/interested party may sue in court so as to obtain a decision whether the technical solution incorporated in the pharmaceutical waiting for approval falls into the patent's protection scope. The Administration for Drug Supervision under the State Council (i.e., the NMPA) shall then, based on the court's effective judgment, decide whether or not to suspend the approval. That is, the fourth amendment established a first legal basis for obtaining a court or administrative decision merely on whether a new pharmaceutical up for marketing approval falls into the protection scope of an existing patent, something that could not really be subsumed under the thus far available provisions on patent infringement. According to Article 76(2), the parties may also request CNIPA to render an administrative decision on the patent dispute. A final paragraph 3 to Article 76 obliges CNIPA and NMPA to jointly formulate linkage measures for the settlement of disputes over patent rights at the stage of the application for marketing approval. It should be noted that the preceding Patent Law draft amendment of 2020 proposed much more detailed provisions on patent linkage with regard to time limits, procedures and the like, The finally amended Patent Law is void of such specifics but delegates the formulation of detailed rules to CNIPA and NMPA.

As mentioned, both administrations have already released a draft of such rules, the draft "Method of a Mechanism for the Early Resolution of Disputes Pertaining to

Pharmaceutical Patents".[411] The draft, which was published on 11 September 2020 and therefore even prior to the fourth Patent Law amendment, appears to be in parts modelled after the US Abbreviated New Drug Application (ANDA) procedure under the Hatch-Waxman Act. In Rule 2 of the draft Method, both administrations commit themselves to establish and to operate a platform for patent information about marketed drugs (hereinafter: the platform), which probably corresponds to the above-mentioned, already existing list. The Method would then only be applicable to drugs recorded therein (Rule 2). Applicants and their agents who publish false statements on that platform, including "irrelevant patents", will be administratively punished and applicants banned from applying for the registration of the same type of drug for one year (Rule 15). The draft Method covers patents for chemical drugs, which may be registered as active ingredient compound patents, pharmaceutical composition patents containing active ingredients and pharmaceutical use patents on the one hand (Rule 5) and patents for biological drugs, which can only be registered on the platform as patents claiming sequence structures, as well as patents for TCM (registrable as patents claiming compositions, extracts and medical uses) on the other hand (Rules 12 and 13). As will be further outlined below, patents in biological drugs and TCM are treated less favourably than patents in chemical drugs but they are not completely excluded from the linkage mechanism as implied by the latest Patent Law draft amendment of 2020, which seemingly limited such mechanism to "chemical drugs" only. The US-based Intellectual Property Owner's Association (IPO) nevertheless criticizes such different treatment in its comments on the draft Method submitted to both administrations on 25 October 2020,[412] referring, inter alia, to Article 1.11 of the Sino-US ETA, which would not make such difference. With regard to all three kinds of pharmaceuticals, Rule 6 of the draft Method, very similar to the ANDA certification requirements, requires applicants for marketing approval of a generic drug to reflect their drug against the patent information on the platform and to submit a statement, which will be published on the platform and has to belong to one of four categories: (1) no patent information obtainable from the platform; (2) the corresponding patent has expired or been invalidated; (3) there is a valid patent for an original drug recorded but the applicant states that he will not market his drug before the patent's expiration; (4) the applicant states that the recorded patent should be invalidated or that his generic drug does not fall into the patent's protection scope. According to Rule 8 of the draft Method, the patentee or interested party then has 45 days from the publication of the application including the statement to sue in court or to request administrative action with CNIPA to determine whether the subject matter of the application falls into the protection scope and, after the acceptance of the lawsuit/request for administrative judgment, 10 days to provide NMPA with the notification of such acceptance. The IPO comments suggest, also with reference to Article 1.11 of the Sino-US ETA, that the Method should regulate

411. The text of the draft and explanatory notes can be downloaded from the NMPA's website: https://www.nmpa.gov.cn/xxgk/ggtg/qtggtg/20200911175627186.html?type=pc&m=.; note that the site may be taken down when a new draft is presented or when the final Method is enacted.

412. https://chinaipr2.files.wordpress.com/2020/10/ipo-comment-patent-linkage.pdf, made available on Mark A. Cohen's very resourceful blog China IPR (https://chinaipr.com).

an obligation to notify the patentee, licensee or holder of the marketing approval at least in case of statements pertaining to categories (2) to (4), and that the 45 days period should then be counted either from the publication on the platform or from the receipt of such notification, whichever is later. The mentioned Item 16 of the CPC's and State Council's earlier Opinions actually supports this proposal, as it also suggest that the applicant shall directly notify the patent owner. Rule 7 of the draft Method further provides that if the patentee, etc., fails to initiate judicial or administrative proceedings, the NMPA may, upon consideration of the technical evaluation and the applicant's statement, decide at its own discretion whether or not to grant a marketing approval.

If a lawsuit or administrative proceeding are initiated in time, the NMPA shall, if a chemical drug is at issue, suspend the approval for nine months from the acceptance of the case by the court or by CNIPA, which appears to be a bit short, unless the SPC plans to enact another interpretation on expedited litigation specifically with regard to patent linkage. The IPO proposes to extend this period to 24 months. The NMPA shall be allowed to continue the technical examination during the nine-months suspension. Depending on the judicial or administrative judgment and on whether it is delivered before or after the expiration of the nine-month period, the NMPA then has different options to decide on the marketing approval, which are regulated in Rules 9 and 10 of the draft Method. If the applicant's patent statement belonged to the first or the second category, the decision of the NMPA whether to grant a marketing approval shall solely depend on the technical examination. If the statement belonged to the third category, the NMPA shall grant the approval under the condition that marketing can only be commenced after the expiration of the patent term (Rule 9). Only if the patent statement belonged to the fourth category and the patentee, etc., filed suit or initiated administrative proceedings within the mentioned deadline of 45 days, the patentee or other interested party shall submit the judicial or administrative decision to the NMPA within 10 days from receipt. If the decision confirms that the generic drug falls into the protection scope and reaches NMPA before the expiration of the nine-months-period, the NMPA shall decide that the approval should not commence before 20 working days prior to the patent's expiration. If such confirmation reaches NMPA after the nine-months period but still during the approval phase, it shall suspend the approval and resume it 20 working days before the patent's expiration. If no judicial or administrative decision or settlement reaches the NMPA, it shall proceed with examination and approval. The same shall apply if the court or the administration decides within nine months that the generic drug does not fall into the protection scope or that the patented drug should be invalidated (i.e., the applicant would be entitled to the invalidity defence; more about this a few paragraphs below). The court or CNIPA may also order the NMPA to halt the approval procedure, and if the next higher judicial instance, which should in most cases be the SPC's IP Division, overturns this judgment, the NMPA shall resume the procedure at the applicant's request and base its decision on whether to grant a marketing approval on the outcome of its technical examination and on the final court decision (Rule 10).

The draft Method does not apply the nine-months-suspension to disputes related to biological drugs or TCM. If in such case the patent owner, etc., files suit in court or requests administrative proceedings within 45 days from the NMPA's publication of the application for marketing approval and the court or CNIPA still manages to timely decide that the biosimilar drug or generic TCM falls into the respective patent's protection scope before the NMPA grants the marketing approval, the final approval must be accompanied by a clarification that the drug may only be marketed after the expiration of the patent term (Rule 13). That foreign right owners are concerned about this less favourable treatment of innovative biological drugs has been mentioned, but that the draft Method also proposes to exclude mostly domestic innovators of TCM from the nine-months suspension is remarkable.

Rule 14 of the draft Method clarifies that patent infringement proceedings shall be possible after the grant of a marketing approval, but that their outcome shall not result in the marketing approval's revocation or otherwise affect its validity. Rule 11, finally, proposes an "encouragement policy" for those applicants who first succeeded in challenging a patent and also first obtained a marketing approval, stating that they shall be rewarded with a market exclusivity of 12 months from the date of approval, which, however, shall not exceed the term of the challenged patent. Important to note is that the draft provision limits this market exclusivity to applicants for the marketing approval of generic chemical drugs, i.e., those who for the first time successfully challenge a patent in a biological drug or TCM shall not enjoy it.

Shortly after the fourth Patent Law amendment, on 29 October 2020, the SPC published its own draft provisions, the draft "Rules on Several Questions of the Application of Law Pertaining to Civil Patent Disputes Related to Drug Marketing Examination and Approval" for soliciting opinions from the public.[413] According to Rule 1 of the draft Rules, the Beijing Intellectual Property Court shall have exclusive first instance jurisdiction over linkage-related lawsuits. When filing suit, the parties, i.e., either the patentee, licensee or holder of the marketing approval or the applicant for marketing approval who seeks confirmation that his generic drug does not fall into the patent scope, shall submit the patent information as indicated on the mentioned platform, the relevant information about the drug waiting for approval, including the applicant's statement that his solution does not fall into the patent scope, and initial evidence that supports the suing party's view (Rule 3). The applicant is furthermore required to furnish a copy of those technical data submitted to NMPA, which are relevant for determining whether his drug falls into the patent scope. Pursuant to Rule 4, the court shall not accept cases in which the rights asserted by the patentee or other interested party are not related to the types of patents allowed on the platform or dismiss the case afterwards it if was erroneously accepted. If this applies to only a part of the rights claimed, the court may decide to not accept such part or, if it has already accepted all claims, to ignore such part during the trial. The court may, furthermore, bundle several disputes pertaining to the same patent and the same drug waiting for marketing approval, and it may allow the patentee or other interested party to join the case as third party in compliance with the relevant provisions of the Law on Civil Procedures (Rule 5).

Quite importantly, Rule 6 of the draft SPC Rules stipulates that the court shall disregard requests to not commence a linkage trial or to suspend an ongoing one if

413. Presently available at: http://www.court.gov.cn/zixun-xiangqing-267401.html.; this site may be taken down after the deadline for the submission of opinions on 14 December 2020.

they are based on the argument that CNIPA has already accepted a parallel request for administrative proceedings under Article 76 Patent Law. Moreover, according to Rule 7, the court shall, in general, disregard requests to suspend the trial because of an ongoing invalidation procedure in CNIPA. This would pertain to normal procedural practice in ordinary infringement litigation, as has been explained above in context with the interplay between infringement and invalidation proceedings. Where CNIPA has declared the patent invalid or such invalidation has been upheld in a subsequent administrative court decision, the court may, depending on who has filed suit, either dismiss the claims of the patentee or the interested party or, upon the applicant's request, declare that the generic drug does not fall into the patent scope (Rule 9). According to Rule 9(1), the same shall apply to cases in which the applicant successfully invokes the prior art defence or non-infringing use. Very interestingly, Rule 9(2) of the draft SPC Rules proposes to introduce the invalidity defence in addition to the prior art defence, albeit exclusively with regard to patent linkage related trials. As explained above, a successful prior art defence already comes close to factually declaring the patent invalid, as it can be raised not only in case of equivalence but also in case of identity.[414] According to Rule 9(2), the court shall now also dismiss the patentee's or interested parties' claims or declare that the applicant's drug does not fall into the patent scope if the applicant convincingly asserts that the patent shall "obviously" be declared invalid. This is very similar to the gist of the mentioned *Kilby* decision of the Japanese Supreme Court,[415] which, unlike the even more defendant-friendly subsequent introduction of the invalidity defence into the Japanese Patent Law, also limited the application of this defence to cases of "obvious" invalidity. It remains to be seen whether Rule 9(2), provided that it finally becomes law, will be a starting point for extending the invalidity defence to ordinary infringement suits. However, there is also good reason to assume that it will remain limited to patent linkage cases, a distinct type of litigation to be regulated by specific administrative decree according to Article 76(3) of the amended Patent Law. As mentioned, the first draft version of such a decree issued by CNIPA and NMPA, the US-inspired Method, proposes to permit the invalidity defence in patent linkage cases.

According to Rule 10 draft SPC Rules, patentees or other interested parties may request preliminary injunctions in a linkage trial only to prevent the exploitation of the patent during the patent term, not to prevent applications for marketing approval or the subsequent examination and approval. Also, requests for preliminary injunctions are only accepted upon the deposit of a security. Rule 11 obliges the parties in a patent linkage trial to keep each other's trade secrets confidential. If the applicant submits to the court information about his drug which is clearly not consistent with the information submitted to the NMPA and this negatively affects the trial, the court may subject the applicant to coercive measures according to Article 111 of the Law on Civil Procedures (Rule 13).

Just as the NMPA's and CNIPA's draft Method, Rule 15 of the draft SPC Rules also clarifies that the patentee, etc., may file an ordinary patent infringement suit if the linkage-specific decision that the applicant's drug actually falls into the patent

---

414. X. 2. g) *supra.*
415. X. 2. f) *supra.*

scope becomes effective after the grant of the marketing approval. Rule 16 furthermore obliges courts to accept the request from a party in a later infringement or declaration of non-infringement trial to consider an earlier effective linkage-specific judgement that confirms or denies that the former applicant's solution falls into the patent protection scope, unless there is evidence that the pharmaceutical solution alleged of infringement is not consistent with the drug that has been subject matter of the previous application for marketing approval or new relevant facts have come to light. Finally, Rule 17 clarifies that patentees, etc., who litigate abusively, for instance, by filing suit and then withdrawing it without justified reason, shall be obliged to compensate the applicant for the economic damage caused by the delayed approval and for the reasonable expenses incurred.

Both the draft Method and the draft SPC Rules would, once they have become law, regulate a quite comprehensive patent linkage mechanism under the new Article 76 Patent Law. There is still room for adjustments between both sets of provisions, for instance in that NMPA and CNIPA could also address the situation in which the applicant seeks confirmation that his drug does not fall into the patent scope.

As mentioned, the fourth Patent Law amendment also introduced a patent term extension of up to five years for innovative pharmaceutical products but not in excess of an effective protection term of 14 years for innovative drugs intended for marketing in China and abroad (Article 42(3)). The two periods, namely "up to five years" and "not exceeding 14 years", are also regulated in Article 1.12 2.b) of the mentioned Sino-US ETA, but according to the ETA they shall not only be applied to "patents pertaining to new pharmaceuticals" as regulated by the amended Patent Law, but also to methods of making and using pharmaceutical products. Maybe the term "patents pertaining to" is to be understood as covering more types of inventions than just pharmaceutical product inventions,

Finally, according to Article 1.12 2.a) of the ETA, a patent term extension shall also be available in all technical fields to compensate for unreasonable delays in the grant of a patent of more than four years from the filing date or more than three years from the request for substantive examination, whichever is later, provided that the delay has not been caused by the patent owner himself. As mentioned, Article 42(2) of the amended Patent Law implements this requirement.

4. Indirect Infringement

As mentioned, the drafters of the third Patent Law amendment of 2008 abstained from a clear regulation on indirect infringement out of concern that afterwards innocent providers of materials and means that themselves do not have to be patented may be harmed.[416] In recent years, however, the judiciary and, at least for a while, the legislature, seem to have become less reserved towards liability for indirect infringement. The 2015 Patent Law draft amendment still proposed its introduction, but the later drafts of 2019 and 2020 as well as the subsequently amended Patent Law amendment are silent on this point.

416. SIPO statement quoted by Peter Ganea, *supra* note 394, 305.

In 2016, however, maybe under the impression of the 2015 draft, the SPC accelerated the legislative process and included a provision on indirect infringement in Rule 21 of its Interpretations II, which, after their 2020 amendment, read as follows:

> Where a person, for manufacturing and business purposes, supplies another party with products for the infringing implementation of a patent without the authorization of the patent owner, whereby such person is well aware of the fact that such products form material, equipment, spare parts, intermediary products or the like specifically used for the implementation of the patent, the People's Courts shall support the patent owner's claim that such supplier's act constitutes "assisting another person to commit an infringing act" under Article 1169 Civil Code.
>
> Where a person who is well aware that a certain product or a certain method is protected by a patent gives, without the authorization of the patent owner and for manufacturing or business purposes, active guidance to another person to commit patent infringement, the People's Courts shall support the patent owner's claim that such person's act forms an abetment according to Article 1169 Civil Code.

Even though a Patent Law provision on indirect infringement is not in sight, SPC judges claimed that the above Rule 21 of the Interpretations II would already be based on a solid legal foundation, namely Article 9 of the previous Tort Liability Law on abetting and aiding ("*One who abets or assists another person in committing a tort shall be liable jointly and severally with the tortfeasor*"),[417] Para. 1 of Rule 21 dealing with patent-specific "aiding" and Para.2 with patent-specific "abetting". On 1 January 2021, the former Tort Liability Law has become the new Civil Code's Seventh Book on Tort Liability, its former Article 9 having been moved to Article 1169 of the Civil Code. Some commentators regard a patent-specific provision on "abetting" as unnecessary, as all thinkable acts of abetting patent infringement could be dealt with directly under general tort law. Others criticize that "aiding" according to general tort law required a too strict linkage between the direct and the indirect infringing act, in that a) the indirect infringer must have knowingly collaborated with a specific direct infringer, and b) liability for indirect infringement presupposes that the direct infringement has already been committed. Accordingly, providers of means who merely knew or had reason to know that the means can be used for infringing purposes without having actually collaborated with the direct infringer, as well as those who actively contributed to a not yet commenced infringement would remain non-prosecutable. With regard to the latter, SPC judges clarified that the liability of the supplier of means can already be established when there is yet no court decision confirming direct infringement.[418] Without at least an imminent concrete direct infringement in sight, however, indirect infringement cannot be established.

417. See Li Jian, *supra* note 325.

418. Clarified by Yuanshi Bu, 'Die mittelbare Patentverletzung im chinesischen Recht', *GRUR Int.* (2019), 1 et seq.; Li Jian, *supra* note 324; Song Xiaoming, Wang Chuang and Li Jian, *supra* note 326.

As already indicated above, Rule 119 of the Beijing Higher People's Court's Guidelines expand initial indirect infringement liability to parties who enabled non-commercial personal and private uses of a patented invention or contribute to certain non-infringing uses pursuant to Article 69 Patent Law (Article 75 after the fourth amendment's entry into force). These uses are a) use of patent in a foreign transportation device that temporarily passes Chinese territory, b) general experimental use and c) pharma-specific experimental use under the Chinese *Bolar* Exemption in the current Article 69(5) Patent Law to obtain approval from a medical regulatory authority.

In the mentioned *Sony v. Iwncomm* decision of 28 March 2018,[419] the Beijing Higher People's Court grasped the opportunity to further substantiate the above provision, stating that in certain cases, acts that resulted in a non-infringing use could nevertheless be regarded as indirect infringement, because otherwise patent protection may be insufficient to foster innovation in specific areas. Such indirect infringement required, however, that a) the indirect infringer clearly knows (which obviously excludes cases in which the infringer "should have known") that he, without the patent owner's consent, provided means that enabled the direct use of the invention, b) the means provided are not only indispensable but also play a substantial role in realizing the direct act, c) said means have no noteworthy alternative uses, whereby the burden of proof that this is not the case lies with the party accused of indirect infringement, and d) there is proof of a party that uses the invention for said non-infringing purposes. In the present case, the Beijing Higher People's Court found no indirect infringement due to the lack of an identifiable direct infringer, as required by prerequisite d).

Meanwhile, on 6 December 2019, the newly established SPC's IP Division rendered another landmark decision,[420] which may impact on the further fate of the *Iwncomm v. Sony* dispute that is presently appealed in the SPC's IP Tribunal. In this latest *Tengda v. Dunjun* decision, the IP Division held that manufacturing and selling a product, here a router, that enables end users to carry out the plaintiff's patented process, here a method of accessing websites via a virtual web server, by merely operating such product, qualifies as *direct* infringement. That is, the degree to which the party that sold the equipment committed aiding and abetting is no longer relevant. There are two prerequisites for establishing such direct infringement, however, namely that the defendant's device fully embodies the patented process so that end users do not have to add further equipment to execute it, and that it is indispensable for executing the process, meaning that it cannot be executed with help of alternative equipment. The IP Division's reasoning leaves room for speculation whether these principles can be applied to all kinds of processes, e.g., conventional manufacturing processes, or only to processes related to network technology, as it stressed the high degree to which network solutions depended on software-based processes and that the physical equipment like browsers that embodied such software

419. *Supra* note 364; see also comments with regard to the part of the decision that is related to indirect infringement by Xuting Huang, 'Mittelbare Patentverletzung in China' (Indirect patent infringement in China), *GRUR Int.* (2019), 908.

420. 147 *Zui Gao Fa Zhi Min Zhong* (2019), summarized and commented by Richard Li, Chuanshu Xu and Binxin Li, *supra* note 60.

would be not more than fixations of the process and directly result in its recurrent execution by the end users, which would justify the qualification of manufacturing and selling such equipment as direct infringement.

5. Specific Aspects of Process Claims

(a) *Process Claim Interpretation*

In its famous *OBE v. Kanghua* decision of 29 August 2009,[421] the SPC held that even where the claims of a process patent were silent about a preferred order/sequence of process steps but a skilled artisan upon reading the claims and the description in a holistic manner arrived at the conclusion that the inventive aim could only be achieved by this order, the court shall limit the claim scope to such specific order.[422] Or, in other words, the SPC added a limiting feature, namely a specific order of process steps, to the invention. Meanwhile, the Interpretations II have incorporated this interpretation method in Rule 11, which states that if the claims are unclear about the order of process steps but a specific order becomes obvious to a skilled artisan upon reading the claims, the description and the drawings, such order shall have a limiting effect on the protection scope. Rule 20 of the Beijing High Court's Guidelines contains a similar provision.

(b) *"Products Directly Obtained from a Patented Process"*

Article 11 Patent Law extends process patent protection to the use, offer for sale, sale or import of the products that are directly obtained from the patented process. Rule 13 2nd Sentence of the SPC Interpretations 2009 clarifies that also products resulting from further processing or treating the initial products that originated from the patented process shall be treated as "directly obtained" products. Rule 20 of the subsequent Interpretations II of 2016 put a clear limit to this extension of protection, stating that the results of further processing or treatment of these follow-up products shall be exempted from the application of Article 11 Patent Law.[423] The SPC's reasoning in its *Zhangxitian v. Ouyi* decision of 9 September 2010,[424] which limited product-by-process protection to the pharmaceutical substance immediately generated by the process, without extending it to the pharmaceutical products resulting from further treatment, seems to be even narrower.

---

421. 980 *Min Shen Zi* (2008), http://gongbao.court.gov.cn/Details/89119ed16a5b57f00ec4e8c737de32.html.
422. Case outlined by Li Jian, *supra* note 379 (290 et seq.); previous instance decision of the Beijing Higher People's Court critically commented by Nils Heide, 'Harmonisierungsaufgaben im internationalen Technologietransfer – Zum Schutz von Herstellungstechnologien in der Volksrepublik China', *GRUR Int.* (2008), 12.
423. A similar provision is contained in Item 111(2) of the Beijing Higher People's Court's Guidelines.
424. 84 *Min Ti Zi* (2009), text available from the online *Gazette of the SPC*: http://gongbao.court.gov.cn/details/67d2edb3e6de2aecdb672fe643c40d.html.

(c) Reversal of Burden of Proof

Another process patent-specific issue is the reversal of burden of proof in cases in which the products obtained from the defendant's process give rise to the allegation that he uses the patented process, but where it is impossible for the plaintiff to prove that they have actually been obtained from the same process. According to Article 34.1 TRIPS Agreement, member states shall ascertain that the burden of proof that the products did not result from the patented process shall be on the defendant if a) the product obtained by the process is "new" or if b) there is substantial likelihood of infringement but the plaintiff failed to identify the defendant's process in spite of substantial efforts, Both prerequisites a) and b) may be applied alternatively.

Article 61(1) Patent Law (Article 66(1) after the fourth amendment's entry into force) has opted for the "novelty" prerequisite but is silent on the question how "new" the product must actually be to give reason to the reversal of burden of proof: new in the "novelty" sense, meaning not publicly known at the application date, or new at the date of putting the product on the market. The SPC in its 2009 Interpretations opted for novelty at the application date, stating that a technical solution pertaining to a product or a manufacturing process publicly known in China and abroad at the patent application date shall not pertain to "new products" pursuant to the current Article 61(1) Patent Law. This solution favours owners of older process patents because the defendant can be forced to prove that his process is not infringing even after considerable time has passed since the application date, in which alternative processes to make the same product may have come into existence. Rule 112 of the Beijing Higher People's Court's Guidelines adds further clarifications that "novelty" at the application date means "obvious differences in product component, structure, or quality, performance and function" in comparison with already existing products of the same class, and that plaintiffs who can provide initial evidence of this have met their obligation to prove "novelty". In its *Eli Lilly v. Watson* decision of 31 May 2016, the SPC found that the documents the defendant filed with the former State Food and Drug Administration/SFDA (now: National Medical Products Administration/ NMPA) to obtain a drug manufacturing approval sufficiently evidenced that it used a different, non-infringing process.[425]

Article 61(1) of the current Patent Law (Article 66(1) after the amendment's entry into force) lists novelty as the sole ground for reversal of burden of proof, but Rule 15 of another set of judge-made provisions, the SPC's Opinion on Several Issues Related to Sufficient Utilization of Intellectual Property Adjudication to Foster the Development and Prosperity of Social Culture and to Promote Autonomous and Coordinated Economic Development of 16 December 2011,[426] adds another ground, stating that courts shall also require the defendant to prove that he uses a different process for an identical product if the plaintiff has been unable to prove infringement in spite of reasonable efforts and if the court, upon consideration of all relevant

425. Decision 1 *Min San Zhong Zi* (2015) (overruling the Jiangsu Higher People's Court's decision of 14 October 2014, 0002 *Su Min Chu Zi* (2013)), summarized in WIPO Collection of Leading Judgments on Intellectual Property Rights (*supra* note 66), 45 et seq. in the English version.

426. Available at http://www.law-lib.com/law/law_view.asp?id = 370632.

circumstances, sees a very high likelihood of infringement. That is, the SPC basically orders courts to apply prerequisite b) of Article 34.1 TRIPS. In a dispute between the holder of a patent for a method of colouring the ceilings of historical buildings and therefore a method that did not generate any products at all, and the Chinese Academy of Cultural Heritage, the Beijing Higher People's Court seemingly applied this rule by contending itself with the plaintiff's initial evidence of infringement after the defendant failed to prove that it used an alternative non-infringing method.[427]

To obtain evidence from the defendant, the SPC's Opinion even allows courts to order evidence preservation measures but simultaneously alerts them to keep a due balance between the patentee's interest in protection and defendant's interest in maintaining the secrecy of his possibly non-infringing process.

6. Protection Scope of Designs

According to Article 59(2) Patent Law (Article 64(2) after the fourth amendment's entry into force), the scope of a design patent shall be limited to the content illustrated in the drawings or pictures of the application, whereas the brief description may be used to explain the design as shown by said illustrations. Pursuant to Rule 8 and 9 of the 2009 SPC Interpretations, infringement shall be established if a product of the same category has an identical or similar design.

Pursuant to Rule 10 of said Interpretations, the reference person through the eyes of which the court shall determine identity or similarity is, again, a "normal consumer", but one different from the "normal consumer" defined in Section 4 of Part IV, Chapter V of the Examination Guidelines to whom the PRB resorts when assessing identity or similarity with prior designs. The level of knowledge of the "normal consumer" in infringement cases has been debated, and it was up to the SPC Interpretations II of 2016 to add some clarifications. According to their Rule 14, the level of knowledge and awareness of the normal consumer shall depend on the leeway for design variations within the respective product category at the time of infringement. If such leeway is relatively broad, courts shall assume that the normal consumer pays little attention to rather small differences between the two designs, but where there is little room for variety, the normal consumer shall be assumed to notice also slight differences.[428] The Beijing Higher People's Court's Guidelines specify further criteria for determining the leeway for alternative designs, namely how much room the function of the product or its parts leave for alternative designs, the strength of common features that all products from the respective product category have to possess due to their specific nature, the variety of existing designs, and other elements such as economic factors, e.g., the capital intensity of design development.

427. 402 *Jing Min Zhong* (2017), summarized as Case No. 2 of the "10 innovative IP cases of 2017" on the Beijing IP Court's website http://bjzcfy.chinacourt.gov.cn/article/detail/2018/04/id/3277627.shtml.

428. With reference to Rule 14, the Shanghai Higher People's Court's decision of 17 February 2020 (495 *Hu Min Zhong* (2019)) found the differences between the plaintiff's and the defendant's design to be insignificant, due to a broad leeway for alternative designs within the respective product category, https://mp.weixin.qq.com/s/Lea7TQHM74HbKV-IBw_vVQ.

SPC judges stress that the "leeway for alternative designs" shall not be applied in a generalized manner, but that such concept should rather help to more accurately determine the consumer's knowledge and awareness where appropriate. And indeed, the "leeway for design variety" criterion alone would have helped little to define the normal consumer, for instance, in the "street lamp" decision of the Higher People's Court of Jiangsu Province of 19 June 2007,[429] which found infringement because it qualified the pedestrian as the "normal consumer" who looked at such lamps from a longer distance below and therefore noticed fewer differences between the patented and the allegedly infringing lamp than a purchaser of street lamps as "normal consumer" would have.[430] Also pursuant to Rule 80(2) No. 1 of the Beijing Higher People's Court Guidelines, the court's evaluation of the overall visual effect of the compared designs shall give special consideration to those parts of the product that are visible in the course of normal use.

Design infringement shall, furthermore, only be established if the defendant's design product comprises all characteristic features that distinguish the patented design from prior art, as the SPC pointed out in its *Grohe v. Jianlong* decision of 11 August 2015,[431] in which the court considered the design product, a shower head, in its entirety, from all visible sides, and found that apart from a similar runway-shaped water outlet, the outer appearance of the whole product of the defendant was substantively different from the plaintiff's design.

The Interpretations II contain further guidance with regard to product sets and products that consist of components. In case of products sets, it is sufficient that the allegedly infringing design is identical with or similar to the design of only one of the items of which the set is composed to determine infringement (Rule 15). In case of products that can be separated into components, Rule 16 stipulates that if such components can be assembled in only one possible form, only identity or similarity with such assembled product falls into the scope of protection, whereas in case of products consisting of components that cannot be assembled or can be assembled in various ways, establishment of infringement requires identity or similarity with each and every of these components. Where the allegedly infringing design lacks such components or where for one or more of its components an identical or similar counterpart in the components of the patented design cannot be identified, courts shall establish non-infringement. Rule 94 of the Beijing Higher People's Court's Guidelines mitigates the latter provision, stating that where the differences between single components do not notably impact on the similarity of the overall visual appearances of the compared designs, the defendant's design may still fall into the protection scope.

With regard to products that can appear in a variety of states of use, in particular dynamic GUIs, Rule 17 of the SPC Interpretations II states that infringement shall be established if the compared design is identical with or similar to each of these states as highlighted in the illustration of variations. Rule 87 of the Beijing Higher

429. 0061 *Su Min San Zhong Zi* (2007), http://www.cnipr.net/article_show.asp?article_id=11658.
430. See also Deng Ming, *supra* note 103.
431. 23 *Min Ti Zi* (2015), summarized in WIPO Collection of Leading Judgments on Intellectual Property Rights (*supra* note 66), 55 et seq. in the English version.

People's Court's Guidelines stresses that dynamic GUIs can only be protected in connection with the product to which it is attached, stating that GUI's position, dimension, etc. in relation with the product shall be considered when comparing it with the allegedly infringing design.[432] This may change after the fourth Patent Law amendment, according to which henceforth also designs of partial product views shall be protected (Article 2(4) of the amended Patent Law). The Guidelines further stipulate that if the allegedly infringing GUI lacks some states of the protected GUI design, infringement shall be denied unless a unique dynamic process that is consistent with that of the patented design can still be identified. Decisive is the overall visual effect on the consumer.

As far as can be seen, so far there has been only one court ruling regarding GUI design infringement, albeit an important one that highlights the problems arising from the requirement that GUI designs can only be protected in connection with a product. In its *Qihoo v. Jiangmin* decision of 25 December 2017,[433] the Beijing Intellectual Property Court rejected plaintiff's argument that its design for a "computer bearing a GUI" has been infringed by the defendant, as the latter distributed the GUI alleged of infringement as mere software, and it would be impossible to establish identity or similarity between a computer bearing a GUI design and a mere software displaying such GUI.[434]

7. Passing off as Patented

Articles 63 and 64 of the Patent Law deal with "passing off as patented" as a particular category of infringement or, rather, offences against the Patent Law because this particular form of unlawful behaviour does not necessarily infringe another party's rights. Rule 84 Implementing Regulations defines passing off in a non-exhaustive catalogue of possible offences. It basically means to either indicate a non-patented product or no longer patented product as patented or to pass the existing patent of another person off as one's own. Apart from this, also acts of counterfeiting or altering existing patent certificates and other patent-related documents can be subsumed under passing off.

From Articles 63 and 64 Patent Law (Articles 68 and 69 after the fourth amendment's entry into force) it becomes clear that passing off is mainly understood as an offence against the public interest, as prosecution thereof is in the hands of the local IP administrations. The current Article 63 stipulates that if another party's patent is passed off, civil liability may be established but in general it shall be the task of local administrations to order rectification, inform the public about the passing off, confiscate unlawful gains and impose a fine of up to four times the unlawful gains or, in absence of unlawful gains, of up to RMB 200,000. The fourth Patent Law amendment increase the fines to five times the illegal revenue or to RMB 250,000

432. The same applies even more to GUIs in general according to Rule 73 of the Guidelines, i.e., infringement shall only be established if, e.g., the defendant's integration of the interface in a corresponding product does not leave the consumer with a different visual impression.
433. 276 *Jing 73 Min Chu* (2016).
434. Critically discussed by Jin Yin, *supra* note 115.

if there were no illegal revenues or where the illegal revenue was less than RMB 50,000 (Article 68 of the amended Patent Law). Cases of criminal magnitude shall be submitted to the criminal authorities. Article 216 of the Criminal Code contains a corresponding provision, which, however, only qualifies the passing off of "another person's patent" as a criminal act if the circumstances are serious. The infringer may then be sentenced to imprisonment or criminal detention of up to three years and/or a fine. According to the SPC Report on the State of Intellectual Property Protection of 2016,[435] five passing off cases were prosecuted in criminal court and one person had been convicted.

To enable the authorities to effectively prosecute "passing off" in general, also in form of indicating a non-patent product as being patented, the current Article 64(1) Patent Law endows the authorities with the competencies to inquire the parties concerned, to carry out investigations, *inter alia*, by way of on-the-spot inspection, accessing and copying contracts, invoices, account books and other relevant material, checking suspect products and sealing or detaining identified illegal products. According to Article 64(2), the involved parties have the legal obligation to cooperate in the investigation. When the fourth Patent Law amendment enters into force, the administrative competencies in passing off proceedings will be listed in in greater detail in a new Article 69. Acts of passing off seem to be a popular means of sales promotion. In 2018, local patent authorities prosecuted 42,679 cases, a significant increase over the 38,492 cases prosecuted in 2017.[436]

According to the 2001 SPC Interpretations before their 2020 amendment, courts could also establish civil liability in the special case of passing off another person´s patent as one`s own. In cases in which the offender had not yet been punished by an administrative authority, Rule 19 allowed courts to impose a special civil-law fine according to Article 134 (3) of the old General Principles of Civil Law of 1986 and to apply the current Article 63 Patent Law to determine its amount (i.e., up to four times the illegal income or up to RMB 200,000 if no illegal income has been gained; up to five times the illegal income or up to RMB 250,000 if no or less than RMB 50,000 of illegal income was earned according to Article 68 after the fourth amendment's entry into force), but this provision has been deleted in 2020.

8. Unauthorized Use Prior to Grant

According to Article 13 Patent Law, patentees can claim an exploitation fee from parties who exploit their patent application between publication and grant. Even though not explicitly stipulated, it is deemed to be a matter of course that such request can only be made after the grant of the patent. As mentioned, according to the current Article 68(1) Patent Law, the general limitation for patent infringement is two years from the date at which the infringed party knew or should have known about the infringement. The same applies according to the current Article 68(2)

435. https://www.chinacourt.org/article/detail/2017/04/id/2825053.shtml; more recent data could not be found.
436. These annual statistics are quoted from CNIPA's previous web presence, which contained annual statistics on administrative enforcement but since a recent redesign seems to provide only monthly numbers (see *supra* note 34).

Patent Law to the special case in which the patentee wants to claim compensation for unauthorized uses during the publication period. However, if the patentee obtained such knowledge prior to the grant, the two years shall be counted from the date of grant, to avoid situations in which the infringed party obtained knowledge more than two years prior to patent grant. After the fourth Patent Law amendment's entry into force, the current Article 68 will be moved to Article 74, and the limitation will be extended to three years, also with regard to claiming compensation for unauthorized use during the publication period. The SPC's *Chen Shundi v. Zhejiang Lexue'er Homeware* of 25 Dec. 2013[437] clarified that unauthorized use during the publication period is different from patent infringement by way of exploiting a patent without the patentee's permission, and that fees for unauthorized use can only be claimed under Article 13 Patent Law, not as compensation for damages suffered from infringement.

9. Patent Specific Aspects of Damage Calculation[438]

According to the current Article 65(1) Patent Law (which has been substantially amended and will become Article 71 after the fourth amendment's entry into force), compensation for damages shall first be calculated according to the actual damage suffered by the patentee. According to Rule 14(1) of the 2001 Interpretations, the actual losses shall be calculated by the plaintiff's reduction in sale of patented items due to the infringement, multiplied by a reasonable profit per item. If the reduction in sales cannot be determined, the number of items sold by the infringer shall be multiplied by such reasonable profit. In a decision of 7 August 2019,[439] the Shanghai Intellectual Property Court adjusted this calculation method to accommodate situations in which not the whole profit per sold item could be attributed to the technical advantages entailed by the patented solution. In such cases, so the court, the contribution of the patent to the profit margin shall be estimated as a percentage of the profit, whereby factors such as the strength of the patent shall be considered.

If the plaintiff's actual loss cannot be determined, the damage may be calculated according to the infringer's reasonable profit, i.e., the number of sold infringing items multiplied by a reasonable profit per item, which is normally the infringer's operating profit but may also be the sales profit if the infringer's business solely depended on the infringement (Rule 14(2) of the 2001 Interpretations).

The fourth Patent Law amendment entailed important changes to the damage determination mechanism. According to the new Article 71(1), the plaintiff can henceforth choose between calculation according to actual losses and calculation according to the infringer's profits, whereas the strict wording of the present Article 65 implies that calculation of the infringer's profits can only be applied if calculation of the actual loss is not possible.

If calculation by the above two methods is impossible, both the current and the amended Patent Law allow for a third method, namely calculation by way of licence analogy (verbatim "reasonable determination of a multiple of the license fees",

437. 225 *Min Ti Zi* (2013), http://gongbao.court.gov.cn/Details/040c1d7ee266f6167ff995907d4fe5.html?sw=%e6%8d%90%e7%8c%ae%e5%8e%9f%e5%88%99.
438. See also the corresponding passages in chapter 7, Enforcement.
439. 615 *Hu 73 Min Chu* (2017), https://mp.weixin.qq.com/s/zfI53taYY6iAMk1ib0l_Rw.

which can be read as allowing multiple punitive damages). Finally, if calculation by all three methods is impossible, courts may finally resort to so-called "statutory damages", i.e., a damage amount to be determined by court, presently within a range of RMB 10,000 to 1 million (Article 65(2) of the current Patent Law), under consideration of the type of patent, gravity of infringement, etc. The fourth Patent Law amendment has significantly increased the highest possible statutory damage, as will be explained below.

Even though originally intended as the very last resort, statutory damages, which are presently capped at a rather low RMB 1 million, have become the most frequently applied determination method,[440] resulting in notoriously low compensation amounts over the past decades. In addition to that, the stipulation in the last sentence of the current Article 65(1) Patent Law (which has become paragraph 3 of Article 71 of the amended Patent Law) that calculation shall include the "reasonable" (i.e., not the actually incurred) expenses of the patentee to put an end to infringement regularly barred patentees from recovering the real costs of investigating and prosecuting infringement. The prospect that there is not much to expect in damages may even have prompted a significant number of patent owners to take the alternative route of administrative enforcement.

The situation is about to change, however. Rule 27 of the SPC's Interpretations II was the first provision which significantly alleviated the plaintiff's burden of proof in case of damage calculation according to the infringer's profit, the second calculation method. Accordingly, if the plaintiff finds it impossible to prove his compensation claim because the infringer refuses to hand out the corresponding account books and other material under his control without justified reason, the court shall rely on the arguments and initial evidence provided by the plaintiff to determine the amount of compensation. This rule has recently been applied by the SPC's IP Division in the mentioned *Tengda v. Dunjun*[441] decision. The fourth Patent Law amendment has elevated this reversal of burden of proof to a statute and expanded it. According to Article 71(4), it shall apply whenever the damage is otherwise difficult to determine, irrespective of the calculation method, whereas the Interpretations II specifically applies it to cases in which it is difficult to calculate the damage by the infringer's profit. The new Article 71(4) concretely stipulates that if the damage cannot be determined in spite of the plaintiff's best efforts because the necessary account books and other materials are mainly under the control of the defendant, the court shall order the defendant to furnish these materials. If the defendant does not furnish them or provides false account books, etc., the court shall determine the damage according to the plaintiff's claims and the evidence he managed to provided.

Recent case law demonstrates that courts have, in general, become more willing to impose higher damages, see the cases Beijing Higher People's Court's *Iwncomm vs Sony* or the Beijing IP Court's *Watchdata v. Hengbao* decision of 9 December

440. Oliver Pfaffenzeller, 'Patent Infringement Procedures and Remedies', in Stefan Luginbuehl and Peter Ganea (eds.), *Patent Law in Greater China* (Edward Elgar, 2014), 209 (228 et seq.).
441. 147 *Zui Gao Fa Zhi Min Zhong* (2019), summarized and commented by Richard Li, Chuanshu Xu and Binxin Li, *supra* note 60.

2016,[442] which for the first time included the plaintiff's actual costs of investigating and prosecuting as "reasonable expenses" in the amount to be paid as compensation. The fourth Patent Law amendment has not made any changes to the wording of the stipulation that the "reasonable" expenses shall be considered, but only transferred it to a new paragraph 3 of Article 71, so that the recent, more generous inclusion of actual costs in the damage calculation is purely judge-made.

Moreover, as mentioned, also the last resort of damage calculation if determination of the actual damage is still not possible in spite of the above facilitation of proof, namely "statutory damages", will become more generous in future. Article 71(2) of the amended Patent Law stipulates that their amount shall henceforth range between RMB 30.000 and RMB 5 million, a significant increase over the range between RMB 10.000 and RMB 1 million according to Article 65(2) of the current Patent Law.

Finally, Article 71(1) of the amended Patent Law regulates punitive damages of up to five times the determined damage amount in case of wilful infringement of serious gravity. Punitive damages are already regulated by other intellectual property laws and also Article 1185 of the new Civil Code stipulates them specifically for intentional, serious intellectual property infringements.

XV. SUBJECT MATTER REGULATED OUTSIDE THE PATENT LAW: NEW VARIETIES OF PLANTS AND INTEGRATED CIRCUIT LAYOUT DESIGNS

1. New Varieties of Plants

Plant varieties obtained through conventional breeding are protected by *sui generis* provisions outside the Patent Law, the Regulations of the People's Republic of China on the Protection of New Plant Varieties enacted by the State Council on 20 March 1997.[443] On 29 August 1998, China became a member of UPOV (1978).[444] Since its 2015 amendment, the Seeds Law of 2000 incorporates a new Chapter 4 on "Protection of New Varieties of Plants" (Articles 25–30), which basically reiterates the provisions of said Regulations on protection prerequisites, first-to-file principle, allowable denominations, exclusive rights and exceptions for scientific purposes and farmer's use, Article 73 on administrative and judicial enforcement, Article 74 on disputes about the application right and Article 92 on legal definitions, *inter alia*, of "novelty", "distinctiveness", "homogeneity" and "stability". That is, the introduction of a new

442. 441 *Jing Zhi Min Chu Zi* (2015).

443. 12 *Gazette of the State Council* (1997), 550; amended on 31 January 2013 by Order No. 635 of the State Council http://www.gov.cn/zhengce/content/2013-02/08/content_2716.htm to improve administrative protection and, a rather minor amendment, on 29 July 2014 by Order No. 635 of the State Council https://wipolex.wipo.int/en/text/341986 to adapt the wording of Rule 26 to clarify that the "organs in charge of examination and approval" with which Chinese nationals intending to apply for plant variety rights abroad for varieties generated in China shall register, the administrations for agriculture and for forestry on provincial level and above; current version available in Chinese at http://ip.people.com.cn/n1/2019/0704/c192427-31214434.html

444. Decision on the accession in 4 *Gazette of the Standing Committee of the National People's Congress* (1998), 426.

chapter on plant varieties to the Seeds Law aimed at elevating existing administrative provisions to a legal statute[445] but the Plant Variety Regulations, which have last been amended on 29 July 2014,[446] are still in force and should be of greater practical relevance because they contain more detailed rules on prosecution and enforcement.

Since the enactment of the Regulations, protection has been granted for relatively short 20 years for varieties pertaining to vines, forest trees, fruit trees or ornamental trees, and 15 years for other kinds of varieties (Rule 34). The protection terms conform to the minimum requirements of UPOV 1978. Also in accordance with UPOV, Rule 23 stipulates that residents of countries which are member to a relevant international convention, partner to a bilateral agreement with China or which have a reciprocal relationship with China, enjoy a priority right of 12 months.

Rule 3 of the Regulations prescribes that for the examination and grant of rights, the Ministry of Agriculture and the Ministry of Forestry shall operate an examination authority. Both ministries have enacted their own Detailed Regulations on the Protection of New Plant Varieties,[447] which have undergone several amendments in the past two decades. The provisions issued by the Ministry of Forestry were last amended on 1 August 2014,[448] the provisions of the Ministry for Agriculture (now: "Ministry for Agriculture and Rural Affairs") on 25 April 2014.[449] The shared administrative competence of these two ministries for plant varieties seems to have remained unaffected by the mentioned institutional reorganization, which put, *inter alia*, protection of trademarks and GIs under the auspices of CNIPA. Also the renaming of the former Ministry of Forestry into "Ministry of Forestry and Grasslands" (Item 42 of the above mentioned "Plan") and the expansion of its competencies to the administration of grasslands, marshes, natural landscapes, etc., does not seem to have impacted on its tasks in the area of plant variety protection.

According to Rule 27 of the Regulations, an application for a variety protection right is preliminarily examined as to whether its subject matter is listed in one of the official lists on protectable varieties,[450] whether the foreign applicant is entitled to apply, whether the subject matter of the variety complies with the novelty requirement

445. Gao Jinghe, 'Xin Zhongzifa shiye xia de xin pinzhong sifa baohu de ruogan wenti' (Several problems associated with the judicial protection of new varieties of plants, viewed from the new Seeds Law), 4 *Henan Keji Zhishichanquan* (2016), 51 et seq.
446. A Chinese version can be found here: http://www.gov.cn/gongbao/content/2016/content_5139623.htm; the previous version of 2013 is available in English on the WIPOlex site; https://wipolex.wipo.int/en/legislation/details/15503.
447. The first rules of the Ministry for Forestry were published in 4 *Gazette of the State Council* (2000), 39 et seq.; the rules of the Ministry for Agriculture on its Chinese website, www.agri.gov.cn (the original version is no longer available).
448. https://wipolex.wipo.int/en/text/344296.
449. Available in Chinese on the website of the Ministry of Agriculture: http://jiuban.moa.gov.cn/zwllm/zcfg/nybgz/201405/t20140516_3906803.htm.
450. E.g. the second list of 17 tree species published by the Forestry Ministry on 2 February 2000 in 20 *Gazette of the State Council* (2000), 46; the first list was issued on 22 April 1999; another list of agricultural plant varieties was published by the Agriculture Ministry on 16 June 1999; both lists are contained in Zhang Xiaodu, 'Biotech Inventions as Subject-Matter of Protection under Chinese Patent Act', 1 *China Patents & Trademarks* (2003), 31. Initial comments on these lists voiced doubts about the conformity of the restriction of protectable varieties to a list of genera or species with international rules:

in Rule 14 according to which a variety is new if the breeding material concerned has not been sold before the application date or has not been sold domestically for longer than a year or abroad for longer than four years (six years if the variety relates to a vine or forest, fruit or ornamental tree) with the consent of the breeder, and whether the variety is appropriately designated.

The preliminary examination shall be concluded within six months. Applications which have passed the stage of preliminary examination will be published (Rule 28). After that, according to Rule 29, the application will be substantively examined with regard to the other three protection prerequisites, namely:

- distinctiveness (Rule 15) – whether the variety can be clearly distinguished from varieties known at the date of filing the application;
- homogeneity (Rule 16) – whether the result of propagation has corresponding elements or features in common;
- stability (Rule 17) – whether the common elements or features of the variety remain unchanged even after repeated propagation or reproduction or, should a certain cycle of reproduction or multiplication be defined, at the end of each cycle.

Unauthorized use in the period between publication and grant of the protection right entitles the right owner to a claim for compensation (Rule 33). After grant, the right owner has the exclusive right to authorize the commercial production and sale of his propagating material and the repeated use of the propagating material for the commercial production of another variety (Rule 6). Further rights, such as a right to import and a right to offer for sale, are not included in the catalogue of exclusive rights. Some criticize the catalogue of rights as too limited to create incentives in the area of plant breeding.[451] Breeder's rights are further limited by two kinds of permitted uses, namely a) use for purely scientific purposes and b) a rather generous farmer's privilege that categorically permits the use of the variety by the farmer himself and its propagation by himself, without further limiting provisions, e.g., that only "small" farmers shall enjoy such privilege. The exchange of protected material with other farmers does not seem to be covered by that privilege, however.

The exclusivity of the plant variety right may, furthermore, be limited due to food-related security concerns. In its two *Tianjin Tianlong v. Jiangsu Xunong* decisions of 29 December 2013,[452] the Jiangsu Higher People's Court refused injunctions against two plant breeding enterprises accusing each other of infringement by using each other's plant variety, one male, one female, for the production of one and the same hybrid rice variety, which, in the court's opinion, was too valuable to be withheld from food supply because of an intellectual property dispute. Instead, the

---

see John Mo, 'Protection of Plant Varieties in China', 4:6 *Journal of World Intellectual Property* (2001), 871 (897 et seq.).

451. Chen Hong, 'Jiaqiang woguo zhiwu xinpinzhong quan xhingzheng zhifa de jianyi' (Suggestions to invigorate administrative enforcement of the right in new plant varieties in China), 7 *Zhongguo Zhongye* (China Seeds Business) (2017), 6 et seq.

452. 0194 *Su Zhi Min Zhong Zi* (2011), 0055 *Su Zhi Min Zhong Zi* (2012), summarized in WIPO Collection of Leading Judgments on Intellectual Property Rights (*supra* note 66), 145 et seq. in the English version.

court decided that the less innovative of the two litigants shall pay RMB 500,000 to the breeder who had spent more efforts to overcome obstacles to planting the hybrid variety, but that otherwise both parties were allowed to continue the production of the rice variety without having to pay royalties to each other.

After the grant of the variety right, any person can file a request with the respective Re-examination Board established either by the Ministry of Agriculture and Rural Affairs or by the Ministry of Forestry and Grasslands to invalidate the right on grounds of nonconformity with the requirements of novelty, distinctiveness, homogeneity and stability. The Re-examination Board may also invalidate *ex officio*. Invalidation decisions can be challenged in administrative court within three months from the date of being notified about the invalidation (Rule 37).

Rule 3 of the SPC's *Interpretation of Several Questions Related to New Plant Variety Right Litigation* of 25 December 2000 (amended on 23 December 2020)[453] prescribes that the Beijing Intellectual Property Court shall be competent to review invalidations and other administrative matter in the first instance, that the Intellectual Property Courts respectively intermediate-level courts or SPC-appointed courts in the other provinces shall deal with other types of litigation, and that the SPC (respectively its IP Division) shall be the next higher instance in administrative cases.

The provision in Rule 38 Regulations on the effect of invalidity, namely that the respective variety right shall be deemed to be non-existent from the beginning and that invalidity shall not have a retroactive effect on previous administrative and judicial court decisions as well as on license and assignment contracts performed prior to the invalidation, is very similar to the corresponding patent provisions.[454]

Also the enforcement of plant variety rights is not different from that of other IP in that the right owner can choose between administrative and judicial proceedings. Competent for administrative proceedings are, according to Rules 39 et seq., the administrations for agriculture and for forestry on provincial level and above. The 2013 amendment to the Regulation broadened the catalogue of sanctions against infringers, providing that in case of unauthorized production and sale or repeated use of the propagating material, the respective authority shall be entitled to confiscate illegal gains and the propagating material and to impose a fine of up to five times the value of the found material if it exceeds RMB 50,000, or a fine of up to RMB 250,000 if such value is less than RMB 50,000 or cannot be determined (Rule 39(3)). The previous version only sanctioned infringement that had already resulted in illegal gains, by confiscation of the illegal gains and a fine of up to five times the gains. Moreover, since 2013, the "counterfeiting" of a plant variety right results in the confiscation of illegal income and in fines of up to five times the illegal income or, if the illegal income is less than RMB 50,000 or cannot be determined, a fine of up to RMB 250,000. Serious cases of counterfeiting shall be handed over to the criminal authorities.

The term "counterfeiting" is defined in Rule 57 of the Detailed Regulations on the Protection of New Varieties of Plants issued by the Ministry of Agriculture and Rural Affairs, namely as printing or using a) faked certificates, numbers,

453. Original text at https://wipolex.wipo.int/en/text/342805; 2020 amendment at http://www.court.gov.cn/fabu-xiangqing-282671.html.

454. See X. 2. e) *supra*.

etc. indicating a variety applied for protection or a protected variety right; b) the application number, etc., of a rejected application or an application deemed to be withdrawn; c) indications of an invalidated or otherwise terminated protection right as still being valid; d) manufacturing or sale of varieties labelled in the above three manners, e) manufacturing and sale of a variety with a false indication that an application is pending or a variety right granted; f) any other act misleading thirds to believe that a variety right is applied for or has already been granted. Some commentators support the introduction of a further, separate act of "counterfeiting", namely marking a non-protected variety with the name, application number, variety right number, etc., of another variety that is in the process of application or already protected. Protection against such counterfeiting should then ideally be regulated as a private right of the plant breeder to proceed against violations of his business reputation, whereas the other forms of counterfeiting presently listed in said Rule 57 would rather endanger the public interest and should thus remain a domain of administrative enforcement.[455]

More details of judicial litigation regarding plant variety rights are contained in the SPC's *Interpretation of Several Matters Concerning the Application of Law to Litigation Involving Disputes over Infringement Upon the Rights in New Plant Varieties* of 25 December 2006 (amended on 23 December 2020).[456] They regulate, *inter alia*, that infringement shall also be found if differences between the protected variety and the produced/sold variety can be identified, provided that these differences do not result from genetic manipulation, and if repeated use involves use of the protected variety as parents for propagation with other parent material. Further provisions detail the role of appraisers either at request of the parties or at the court`s request and the option to convert the detected infringing material into money to reduce the compensation amount to be paid to the infringed party. They also stipulate that individuals and rural households that propagated infringing material received from thirds in good faith shall be exempted from infringement liability, provided that they hand out information about their supplier.

The 2020 amendment of the Interpretations also adapted the damage calculation regime to the corresponding Seeds Law provisions. Pursuant to Article 73 of the Seeds Law, damage calculation is not different from the calculation in patent and other IP infringement cases, in that the right owner can opt for the infringer's profit as calculation method if assessment of the actual damage is not possible, and calculation of license analogy as a third alternative if also the infringer's profit cannot be determined. As a last resort, if the damage cannot be determined by these three methods, court can impose a statutory damage of up to RMB 3 million, which is three times higher than the present upper limit of statutory damages that can be imposed under the Patent Law. Also, unlike the present Patent Law, the Seeds Law

455. See Gao Jinghe (*supra* note 445); see also the discussion of the related Corn Hybrid Seed case in first instance litigated in the Zhengzhou Intermediate People's Court in 2006 (exact decision date not available) by Wang Fuqiang and Ma Jing, 'Zhiwu xinpinzhong jiamao qinquan xingwei fenxi' (Analysis of infringement by counterfeiting new plant varieties), 22 *Renmin Sifa* (2008), 107 et seq.

456. Original text at https://wipolex.wipo.int/en/ legislation/details/8747; 2020 amendment at http://www.court.gov.cn/fabu-xiangqing-282671.html.

already stipulates punitive damages of up to three times the actual damage in serious cases of wilful infringement.[457]

Plant variety-related litigation is rare. According to practitioners, most breeders prefer administrative proceedings over civil litigation because disputes normally occur within confined business circles of breeders, and infringed parties would rather avoid highly antagonistic standoffs in court with a former or a potential future cooperation partner.[458]

2. Integrated Circuit Layout Designs

Since 28 March 2001, the protection of integrated circuit layout designs is governed by the State Council Regulation on the Protection of the Layout Design of Integrated Circuits,[459] which are supplemented by two CNIPA provisions, the Implementing Rules to the Regulations on the Protection of the Layout Design enacted on 1 October 2001[460] and the Method on Administrative Enforcement of Layout Designs of Integrated Circuits of 28 November 2001.[461] All these provisions have remained unchanged since their enactment. The various fees for obtaining and maintaining a layout design right and for obtaining a compulsory licence are regulated by CNIPA's comprehensive fee schedule that also lists the fees for all kinds of patent related services.[462]

Just like in many other countries, Chinese integrated circuit layout design protection lived a rather shadowy existence for the past decades but CNIPA statistics show that at latest since 2015, applications for and grants of protection certificates show a stable double-digit growth, albeit on a rather low level in comparison with other registrable subject matter in terms of absolute figures. In 2019, CNIPA received 8,319 applications and granted 6,614 certificates, which almost doubled the numbers of 2018 (4,431 applications and 3,815 grants).[463]

The wording of the Regulation is closely modelled after the Treaty on Intellectual Property in Respect of Integrated Circuits (IPIC Treaty), which China has not joined, however. Protected subject matter according to Rule 2(2) of the Regulation is the three-dimensional disposition of the elements, at least one of which is an active element, and of some or all of the interconnections of an integrated circuit, or such a three-dimensional disposition prepared for an integrated circuit intended for manufacture. This wording is largely consistent with the corresponding IPIC provision (Article 2 (ii)). The same applies to the protection prerequisite. Similar to Article 3(2) IPIC, Rule 4 of the Regulations prescribes that a layout design must

457. See XIV. 9. *supra* with regard to damages for patent infringement.

458. Chen Hong, *supra* note 451.

459. 17 *Gazette of the State Council* (2001), 5; English translation in 3 *China Patents & Trademarks* (2001), 104; in English and Chinese available on the WIPOlex site: https://wipolex.wipo.int/en/legislation/details/842.

460. In English and Chinese available on the WIPOLex site: https://wipolex.wipo.int/en/legislation/details/843.

461. In Chinese available on the WIPOLex site: https://wipolex.wipo.int/en/legislation/details/6605.

462. https://www.cnipa.gov.cn/col/col1518/index.html.

463. See 2019 Annual Report (English), downloadable at http://english.cnipa.gov.cn/col/col2159/index.html, "Appendix I – Statistics" (p. 132).

possess originality, that is, it must be the result of the creator's own intellectual effort and not commonplace to those engaged in the creation and the manufacture of integrated circuits at the date of creation.[464] Layout designs consisting of an original combination of commonplace elements and interconnections can also be protected (Rule 4 of the Regulations; Article 3(2) IPIC).

Rule 8 stipulates that only registered layout designs are protected. The protection term of ten years starts either from the date of application for registration or from the date of commencing commercial exploitation anywhere in the world, whatever the earlier date, provided that from the date of creation not more than 15 years have elapsed (Rule 12). No protection is available to designs the first commercial exploitation of which dates back more than two years. The competent registration authority is CNIPA, which conducts a preliminary examination on the basis of an application form, a copy or a drawing of the layout design, a sample of the integrated circuit if it is already marketed and other documents which have to be filed at special administrative request (Rule 16 of the Regulation). Neither the Regulation nor the Implementing Rules, the latter being confined to formalities (Rules 12–17), do further clarify how the protection scope will be defined on grounds of these furnished documents, samples, etc., and the uncertainty arising from lack of clarity would, according to commentators, form a major reason for the low popularity of the integrated circuit layout design protection system.[465] In the case of rejection, the applicant can request a re-examination with CNIPA's Re-examination and Invalidation Department (the former PRB). The re-examination authority is also competent to revoke a right which has already been granted. If an applicant or layout design right owner is not satisfied with an administrative decision, he can initiate judicial proceedings. Problematic for competitors who want to get rid of a registered layout design is that according to Rule 20 of the Regulation and Rules 29–30 of the Implementing Rules, only the PRB/RID can initiate a revocation procedure, i.e., third parties are banned from requesting such revocation.[466]

Layout design protection comprises the rights to exclusively reproduce the original layout design partly or completely and to commercially exploit the layout design, i.e., to import to sell or to offer by other means the integrated circuit incorporating the layout design such as articles incorporating the integrated circuit.

Rule 2(4) Regulation defines reproduction as the "act to repeatedly produce a layout design or integrated circuit incorporating the layout design". Rule 23 No. 1 and 2 contains far-reaching limitations to the reproduction right, stipulating that reproduction for private purposes, for purposes of evaluation and analysis, and the creation of another original layout design on the basis of such evaluation and analysis

464. Which, according to the Shanghai Higher People's Court's *Shanghai Hitrend Technology v. Renergy Mictrotechnologies Shenzhen and Shanghai Yachuang Electronics* decision of 23 September 2013, does not mean that the right owner shall exhaust all thinkable conventional layout designs to prove that his own design is not conventional (12 *Hu Gao Min San (Zhi) Zhong Zi* (2014)); the case was adopted to the SPC's list of the ten most important IP disputes of 2014 and found its way into the WIPO Collection of leading IP judgments (*supra* note 65), p.151 et seq. in the English version.

465. Dan Prud'homme and Zhang Taolue, *China's Intellectual Property Regime for Innovation: Risks to Business and National Development* (Springer, 2019), 37 et seq.

466. *Ibid.*

are permission-free. Also, according to No. 3 of the same provision, anyone who independently creates a layout design that is identical with a protected layout design can reproduce and exploit it commercially without having to ask the right owner for permission or to remunerate him. Rule 2 No. 5 defines commercial exploitation as the import, sale or other distribution for commercial purposes.

There is no explicit provision about reverse engineering, but the mentioned decision of the Shanghai Higher People's Court clarified that at least direct copies of layout designs made with help of reverse engineering, i.e., where the defendant's acts are not limited to photographing the layout or analysing the circuit's mechanism, infringes the reproduction right.[467]

Rule 24 contains an exhaustion rule, stating that integrated circuits which incorporate a protected layout design or products which incorporate such integrated circuit that have been put on into market circulation by the right holder himself or with his authorization can be commercially exploited by third parties without having to ask the right owner for permission or to remunerate him. The provision obviously extends the exhaustion rule to the permissibility of parallel imports, as according to the legal definition in Rule 2 No. 5, "commercial exploitation" includes the import of integrated circuits bearing the protected layout design or products incorporating the integrated circuits.

In conformity with the requirements of Article 31(c) TRIPS, the compulsory licensing of layout design rights is quite restricted. Accordingly, compulsory licensing is only permissible in the case of a national emergency or extraordinary state affairs, for enabling public non-commercial use or for remedying anti-competitive practices established in a previous judicial or administrative procedure (Rule 26). A corresponding provision on layout designs for which patent protection is sought had been contained in Rule 72(4) of the amended Patent Law Implementing Regulations of 2002 but is no longer contained in the present text that after the amendment of 2010.

Further provisions deal with the revocation of a compulsory license when the reasons for its grant have ceased to exist, the ban on sublicensing subject matter under a compulsory license and the reasonable fee for a compulsory license.

Just like other IP, semiconductor layout design rights can be enforced via the administrative or civil litigation route. In case of administrative proceedings, CNIPA[468] is competent to order the infringer to desist from further infringement and to confiscate and destroy the infringing products (Rule 31). With regard to damages, it can only mediate at the request of the parties but it cannot determine the compensation amount.

With regard to court proceedings, Rule 32 of the Regulation contains a layout design-specific provision on preliminary measures but in present practice the corresponding provisions of the Law on Civil Procedures should be more relevant. In accordance with Article 37(1) TRIPS, Rule 33 of the Regulations provides that

467. *Supra* note 464.

468. The provision indeed only refers to the central patent administration department under the State Council as competent enforcement authority, not to the local IP administrations; Rule 2 of the above mentioned "Method" provides that CNIPA shall establish a Committee for the Administrative Enforcement of Integrated Circuit Layout Designs and that the local intellectual property administrations shall assist CNIPA in its enforcement related work.

a party which unknowingly circulates products incorporating an infringing layout design shall not bear liability for infringement, but can continue the commercial exploitation of the products kept in stock or already ordered, provided that the right owner is adequately remunerated.

CHAPTER 3

Trade Marks and Related Rights

Danny Friedmann

I. CURRENT LAW IN FORCE

The current trade mark law in force is the Fourth Amendment of the Trade Mark Law (TML) as of 1 November 2019[1] which will subsequently be discussed.[2] For China's entry into international agreements and its corresponding obligations thereunder, see Chapter 1, Introduction, in this book.

II. HISTORY

A history of the Chinese trade mark law until 1 November 2005 was covered in the previous edition of this book. A major revision was made with the Third Amendment of the TML in 2013. This revision brought about the following changes:

- Multi-class registration of a single trade mark in one application;[3]
- Introduction of the good faith principle;[4]

1. Trade Mark Law of the PRC, amended for the fourth time in accordance with the Decision to Amend Eight Laws Including the Construction Law of the PRC adopted at the 10th Session of the Standing Committee of the Thirteenth National People's Congress of the PRC on 23 April 2019, which came into force on 1 November 2019.
2. Peter Ganea and Thomas Pattloch, in Christopher Heath (ed.), *Intellectual Property Law in China* (Kluwer Law International, The Hague, 2005), 81.
3. Troy Rice, 'Benefits and Drawbacks of Using Madrid in China', SIPS, 23 March 2017. Available at: https://sips.asia/knowledge/trademark-registration/using-madrid-china-benefits-drawbacks/.
4. In a draft of the Third Amendment of June 2009, a provision was included which stated that trade mark applications should be made in honesty and with credibility. A State Council revision in September 2011, however, deleted this reference to the good faith principle. Instead, it included a more restrictive provision that addressed bad faith only

- Introduction of a genuine intention to use the trade mark in commerce;
- Invalidation of marks registered in bad faith beyond the five-year limit. Article 18(4) Beijing High People's Court (BHPC) Guidelines 2019[5] now provides factors that could be taken into account to assess whether there was a bad faith registration under Article 45(1) TML 2013;
- Enhanced protection of prior, unregistered trade marks in respect of a subsequent registration of identical or similar goods by a third party;
- Enhanced good faith requirements for trade mark agencies who without authorization apply for a trade mark under their own name or accept registration of a mark knowing that this would infringe a prior right;
- Rules for solving the conflict between an earlier unregistered mark with a certain recognition ("influence") and a mark subsequently registered for the same goods or services;
- Adding rules against misleading indications of unregistered marks as registered ones, and against advertising marks as "well-known marks";
- Possibility of the China Trade Mark Office (CTMO) to invalidate a registered trade mark *ex officio* if it violated either absolute grounds for refusal of registration or was acquired by fraud or any other unfair means. Any organization or individual might request the TRAB to declare such a registered trade mark invalid.

Under the TML 2013, especially after 2017, courts were more willing to grant higher damage awards.[6] In bad faith cases and where the circumstances were serious, for example in case of a repeat infringer, punitive damages could be imposed: according to Article 63(1) TML 2013, the amount of damages should be more than one time but less than three times the amount assessed by referring to the above calculation. The amount of damages should also include the reasonable expenses of the rights holder incurred for stopping the infringing act. The TML 2013 raised the amount of statutory damages from a cap of RMB 500,000 to a cap of RMB 3,000,000, according to the circumstances of the act.

The TML 2013 started promoting genuine use and tried to prevent the hoarding of trade marks. Article 64(1) TML 2013 clarified that there could be "no compensation

---

in terms of an existing relationship between two parties. Freshfields Bruckhaus Deringer, Draft amendments to PRC Trade Mark Law published: two steps forward and one step back, February 2013. Available at: https://bit.ly/36g1VI4.

5. BHPC Guidelines for the Trial of Trade Mark Right Granting and Verification Cases, 24 April 2019. Available at: https://file.chinacourt.org/f.php?id=37014&class=file. Despite the publication one day after the TML 2019, the guidelines refer to the TML 2013. Hui Huang and Paul Ranjard, 'Beijing High Court guidelines on administrative trademark cases come with surprises', International Law Office, 26 August 2019. Available at: https://www.internationallawoffice.com/Newsletters/Intellectual-Property/China/Wanhuida-Peksung-IP-Group/Beijing-High-Court-guidelines-on-administrative-trademark-cases-come-with-surprises.
6. On 17 August 2017, the Suzhou Intermediate People's Court awarded RMB 10 million damages to New Balance for the trade mark infringement of its stylized "N" and "N15" mark on sport shoes, by four defendants. Anna Mae Koo and Fandy Ip, 'Learning from recent significant Chinese court cases: New Balance, Under Armour and Michael Jordan', 19 *Vivien Chan & Co., Newsletter* (2017). Available at: http://www.vcclawservices.com/sources/publications/2017issue19.pdf.

for damages incurred for the infringement of an unused registered trade mark".[7] However, even without using its trade mark in commerce in China, the trade mark proprietor's reputation could be adversely affected in the future by an infringer who had not acquired a commercial reputation of the registered trade mark,[8] but was trying to block the proprietor from accessing the market.[9]

III. COMPETENT ADMINISTRATION

The plan to deepen the reform of Party and State institutions was introduced in March 2018.[10] Before this watershed moment, the State Administration of Industry and Commerce (SAIC), which was directly under the State Council, was administering and supervising the Chinese Trade Mark Office (CTMO), the Trade Mark Review and Adjudication Board (TRAB), and the General Administration of Quality, Supervision, Inspection and Quarantine (AQSIQ), which was also directly under the State Council in charge of administering and supervising geographical indications (GIs).[11]

Article 2 TML 2019 does not yet fully reflect this institutional reform and obliges the SAIC to establish a Trade Mark Appeal Board to be responsible for handling trade mark disputes. Moreover, the SAIC should further develop details regarding the registration and administration of collective and certification trade marks.

The CTMO should keep a Trade Mark Register recording registered trade marks and relevant registration items.[12] The CTMO shall issue the Trade Mark Gazette to publish trade mark registrations and other relevant items.[13] The Trade Mark Gazette is published in electronic format or on paper. The content of the publication shall be considered as already known or ought to be known by the public as of the date of the publication.[14] The fees that shall be paid for trade mark registration or for other trade mark matters shall be stipulated by the finance department and competent pricing department of the State Council.

After approval, the CTMO should issue a Trade Mark Registration Certificate to the applicant as proof it has a right to enjoy the exclusive right to use a registered trade mark. The registration items recorded in the Trade Mark Registration Certificate

7. Xiaoqing Feng, 'Internationalization and Local Elements: Research on Recent Amendments to the Trademark Law of China', 7 *Akron Intell. Prop. J.* (2015), 101–178, 128.
8. Feng, *supra* note 7, 129.
9. Feng, *supra* note 7, 129.
10. Bai Gang, Regulations Clarify Role of New Agencies Following China's IP Institutional Reform, 73(19) *INTA Bulletin* (1 November 2018), 15–17. Available at: https://www.inta.org/INTABulletin/PublishingImages/Vol73/No19/INTA%20Bulletin%20Homepage%20Nov%201-FINAL.pdf.
11. The Ministry of Agriculture also registers GIs. These are exclusively domestic.
12. Article 94 IRTL 2014. Implementing Regulation of the Trade Mark Law, No. 651 promulgated by the State Council on 29 April 2014, went into effect on 1 May 2014. Available at: http://sbj.cnipa.gov.cn/zcfg/sbflfg/201405/t20140522_232849.html.
13. Article 96 IRTL 2014, *supra* note 12.
14. The Trade Mark Gazette is published on the 6th, 13th, 20th and 27th of each month. Troy Rice and Joe Simone, 'Bad Faith Trademark Filings in China', SIPS Asia, 24 April 2104. Available at: https://sips.asia/knowledge/trademark-enforcement/bad-faith-trademark-filings-in-china/.

shall be in conformity with those in the Trade Mark Register; where any discrepancy occurs, the Trade Mark Register shall prevail, unless there is clear evidence proving that the information recorded in the Trade Mark Register is in error.

IV. THE PURPOSE OF THE TML, TRADE MARKS AND SUBSEQUENT OBLIGATIONS CONNECTED TO TRADE MARKS

1. Purpose of the TML

The purpose of the TML is to strengthen trade mark administration, to protect the right to exclusive use of a trade mark, to urge producers and dealers to guarantee the quality of goods and services, maintain the reputation of trade marks, protect the interests of consumers, producers and dealers, and promote the development of the socialist market economy.[15] Where the TML 1993 protected in particular the interests of consumers, the TML 2001, 2013 and 2019, extended the protection to the interests of consumers, producers and dealers.

2. Trade Mark Functions

Article 1 TML 2019 states that the TML should protect the right of exclusive use of trade marks. This purpose can be performed by three overlapping functions, each reinforcing the other two: the more distinctive a trade mark is, the better symbol it is to guarantee quality, and therefore the better vehicle it is for investment and advertisement.

(a) Origin

The essential function of the trade mark is to distinguish the source of the goods or services of one undertaking from those of other undertakings.[16] Adequate distinction can avoid a likelihood of confusion by the relevant public. According to Article 9(1) TML 2019, trade marks that are submitted for registration shall be readily distinguishable, as this will reduce the search costs for consumers in case they want to make a repeat purchase or avoid a good or service from a certain source or origin. Since the TML 2001, there is a right (instead of an obligation, as before) to use the words "registered trade mark" or a sign standing for registration.[17]

15. Article 1 TML 2001, 2013 and 2019. Trade Mark Law 2019, adopted by the Standing Committee of the NPC on 23 April 2019, effective on 1 November 2019. Available at: http://sbj.cnipa.gov.cn/zcfg/sbflfg/201911/t20191122_308740.html.
16. Article 19(11) BHPC Guidelines 2019, *supra* note 5: If the goods using a trade mark of another person are affixed with the litigious trade mark, and it is difficult for the relevant public to identify such goods from the registrant of the litigious trade mark, then this may not be determined as use of the litigious trade mark.
17. Article 9(2) TML 2001, 2013, 2019, *supra* note 15.

(b) Quality

Article 1 TML 2019 explicitly mentions the quality function: "to urge producers and dealers to guarantee the quality of their goods and services and preserve the reputation of trade marks, so as to protect the interests of consumers, producers" and the economy at large.

(c) Investment and Advertising Function

A trade mark can be seen as a property appurtenant to commercial goodwill.[18] The investments made in the quality and promotion of the goods or services will add to the goodwill of the brand, and therefore to the value of the trade mark. However, some commentators argue that the concept of goodwill derived from trade mark use does not exist in China: trade marks are bought and sold in a way that would be considered "naked assignments" in other jurisdictions.[19]

V. PROTECTABLE SIGNS AND SUBJECT MATTER

Signs can be registered as trade marks for goods and services,[20] collective marks and certification marks.[21] For some categories of goods such as medicines and tobacco,[22] as required by laws or administrative regulations,[23] the signs need to be approved and registered as trade marks, otherwise they cannot be offered for sale.[24] The holder of an unregistered mark has the right to use a trade mark, no matter whether it is registered, except for the signs that need to be registered under Article 6 TML 2019.[25] A merely descriptive mark can acquire distinctiveness by domestic use after entering the Chinese market. Actual use of the mark can be proven by providing evidence of advertisements and promotion, as well as the possibility of identifying the source

18. Adam Mossoff, in Adam Mossoff (ed.), *Intellectual Property and Property Rights* (2013), ix.
19. 'Non-Use Cancellations in China – Offensive and Defensive Applications', SIPS Asia, 19 March 2018. Available at: https://sips.asia/knowledge/trademark-registration/non-use-cancellation-actions-in-china/.
20. Article 4(2) TML clarifies that provisions for trade marks for goods in the TML shall apply to service marks (service trade marks). Service marks were introduced in Article 4(3) TML 1993. See also Articles 3(1) TML 2001 and Article 4(2) TML 2013. Trade Mark Law 2013, adopted by the Standing Committee of the NPC on 30 August 2013, effective on 1 May 2014. Available at: http://govt.chinadaily.com.cn/s/201812/31/WS5c19b048498ee2f0291e4089/trademark-law-of-the-peoples-republic-of-china-2013.html.
21. Article 3(1) TML 2001, 2013 and 2019, *supra* note 15.
22. In the "Seven Wolves" trade mark dispute case, the Beijing Higher People's Court held that the use of unregistered trade marks on cigarettes violated Article 20(1) Tobacco Monopoly Law of the PRC. Therefore, the prior use of cigarettes by Longyan Cigarette Factory could not create prior rights protected by law. BHPC 463 *Gao Xing Zhong Zi* (2004).
23. Notice of the State Administration for Industry and Commerce on Promulgating Products that Must Use Registered Trade Marks, 14 January 1998.
24. Article 6 TML 2001, 2013 and 2019, *supra* note 15.
25. Article 6 TML 2019 (Article 5 TML 1993 and Article 6 TML 2001 and 2013), *supra* note 15.

of the goods of the trade mark,[26] which will make it eligible for registration.[27] The CTMO examines the degree of distinctiveness at the moment of application or re-application. Trying to achieve distinctiveness for an unregistered (and from the outset unregistrable) mark is a risky strategy, since one needs to massively use an unprotected trade mark, which is then vulnerable to be exploited by counterfeiters.

As will be pointed out below, there are categories of signs that cannot be registered as trade marks because of the inherent characteristics of the signs, and signs that cannot be registered because they interfere with a prior right. In China, like in other civil law jurisdictions with a first-to-file system in place, prior use of the trade mark is not a prerequisite for registration.[28]

1. Expansion of Subject Matter

The current law provides the following definition of the eligible elements for application and registration of trade marks: "Any sign, capable of distinguishing the goods or services of one natural person, legal person or any other organization from those of other persons, including words, devices, letters, numerals, three-dimensional signs, combination of colours, sounds, as well as the combination of such signs, shall be eligible for application for registration as a trade mark."[29] The methods of how a sound mark can be applied for and what the examination criteria are, have been clarified.

2. Available Types of Trade Marks

(a) *Trade Marks, Service Marks*

Provisions that concern trade marks for goods also apply to service marks and are dealt with in this section. Differences for collective marks and certification marks are explained as below.

(b) *Collective Marks and Certification Marks and Geographical Indications*

Collective marks are signs registered in the name of a group, association or other organization for use by the members of such an organization in the course of trade to indicate the users' membership of the organization.[30]

Certification marks are signs controlled by an organization capable of monitoring certain goods or services for use by organizations or persons other than such an

26. Zhidao anli 114 hao: Kelisidi ang di'ao er xiangliao gongsi su guojia gongshang hang zheng guangli zongju shangbiao pingshen weiyuanhui shangbiao shengqing bohui hui fu xingzheng jiufen an (Guiding Case No. 114: *Christian Dior Perfumery Company v. TRAB SAIC* trade mark application refusal review administrative dispute), Judicial Committee of the SPC, 14 January 2020, summary. Available at: http://www.court.gov.cn/fabu-xiangqing-216761.html.
27. Article 11(3) TML 2019 (Article 11(2) TML 2001, 2013), *supra* note 15.
28. Pattloch, *supra* note 2, 86.
29. Article 8 TML 2013 and 2019, *supra* note 15.
30. Article 3(2) TML 2013 and 2019, *supra* note 15.

organization on their goods or services to certify the geographical origin, material, mode of manufacture, quality or other specific characteristics of the goods or services.

The TML 2001 for the first time mentioned collective and certification marks and clarified that they could also be used to certify the geographical origin of products.

Geographical indications (GIs) can be registered and protected via collective and certification marks,[31] or via one of two *sui generis* systems. For details, see section XII. 1. on Geographical Indications.

(c) *Defensive Marks*

The TML 2019 no longer provides for the registration of defensive trade marks in classes where the trade mark will not be used in the course of trade. An example is Starbucks, which registered in all 45 classes of goods and services.[32] The TML 2001 repealed Article 10(2) Implementing Regulation of Trade Mark Law (IRTL) 1993 which had specifically provided that the goods in respect of which a trade mark could be registered should not exceed the registered scope of the applicant's business. Defensive trade mark registrations were tolerated in the past,[33] but they may now be vulnerable to cancellation on the ground of non-use.[34] In addition, Article 3(6) China National Intellectual Property Administration (CNIPA) Provisions 2019 draft, qualifies applications for trade mark registration where there is no intention to use as "abnormal" registrations.[35] A serious drawback of using defensive marks is that the more extensive protection as a well-known mark would not be concurrently available, see below.

(d) *Word, Picture (Device) Marks and Combined Signs, Chinese Character Marks*

As Article 8 TML 2019 clarifies, signs such as words, graphs, letters, numbers, etc., or any combination thereof can be registered as a trade mark. Signs whose components

31. Article 4(1) IRTL 2014, *supra* note 12.
32. Matthew Dresden, 'China Trademarks: Register in More Classes, Take Down More Counterfeit Goods', China Law Blog, 11 January 2017. Available at: https://www.chinalawblog.com/2017/01/china-trademarks-register-in-more-classes-take-down-more-counterfeit-goods.html.
33. Walt Disney was able to register the trade mark "MICKEY MOUSE" as a defensive mark in China. Zheng Chengsi, *Intellectual Property Enforcement In China* (Butterworths, Hong Kong, 1999), 105.
34. Article 49(2) TML 2013 states that if a registered trade mark which has not been put to use for three consecutive years without a justifiable reason, any entity or individual may apply to the trade mark office for revocation of the registered trade mark, and the trade mark office shall make a decision within nine months upon the receipt of the application, *supra* note 20.
35. Several Provisions on Regulating the Registration of Trade Marks (CNIPA Provisions) (Consultation Draft), CNIPA, 12 February 2019. Members of the public had until 14 March to give comments and suggestions. Available at: http://www.cnipa.gov.cn/gztz/1135919.htm or https://mp.weixin.qq.com/s/ufqEwyew-47DPy4IGUrz9A.

suggest the features of the goods in respect of which the trade mark is used, but which do not affect its identifying function, shall be distinctive and eligible for registration.[36]

The CTMO registers both simplified characters and traditional characters.[37] To be safe, a company should register its trade mark in both simplified and traditional Chinese characters.[38] Japanese company Muji found out to its cost that registering a traditional Chinese character trade mark in China is not sufficient. See this case below under Scope and Right of Infringement.

Until 2001,[39] alphabetical letters and numbers were often considered merely descriptive and thus lacked inherent distinctiveness.

Chinese characters can be Romanized using the *pinyin* or *Wade-Giles* system.[40] "QIAODAN" is for example the *pinyin*-version of "JORDAN". *Pinyin* versions of well-known marks are frequently registered as domain names by cyber squatters (see Domain names).

Combinations of Chinese characters and alphabetical letters are also possible. China applies the foreign equivalents doctrine unevenly; it takes the translation of foreign words into account in case of absolute grounds of refusal, but not so much for relative grounds of refusal. If a cited trade mark is in a foreign language, the CTMO takes the knowledge of that particular language by the relevant public into account. If the relevant public is not familiar with such a language, a Chinese translation of the trade mark should be considered.[41]

With regard to absolute grounds of refusal, an example is the CTMO, TRAB, the Beijing Higher People's Court (BHPC) and the Beijing IP Court all rejecting the registration of the trade mark "CLASH OF CLANS" for Finnish mobile game development company Supercell Company, because it could also be translated as "Clash of Tribes", which could have an adverse effect on socialist ethics, one of the absolute grounds of refusal,[42] and of harmony between China's 56 ethnicities.[43] With regard to the relative grounds of refusal, transliterated well-known marks are often not recognized as such (see *Michael Jordan v. Qiaodan* below).

The Chinese-language version of a trade mark is obviously the most important in China, even though a growing contingent of Chinese consumers start to recognize and purchase goods with foreign language trade marks. Even before a trade mark is launched in China, Chinese consumers are often able to buy foreign trade

36. Article 11 SPC Provisions 2016, *infra* note 112.
37. Simplified characters are used in Mainland China, Singapore and Malaysia; traditional characters are used in Hong Kong, Macau and Taiwan.
38. The case *Jun Country Distillery v. Wendeng County Distillery* demonstrates that the registration of both versions of Chinese characters is advisable. ZHENG, *supra* note 33, 124.
39. China acceded to the WTO Agreement in 2001 and thus needed to be compliant with TRIPS, including Article 15(1) TRIPS. Trade-Related Aspects of Intellectual Property Rights (TRIPS), available at: https://www.wto.org/english/docs_e/legal_e/27-trips_01_e.htm.
40. The difference between *pinyin* and *Wade-Giles* is in the spelling. 真功夫 (real Kungfu), which is a fast food chain in China is "Zhen Gongfu" in *pinyin* and "Chen Kungfu" in *Wade-Giles*.
41. See *Daikin Industry Co., Ltd. v. TRAB infra*.
42. Article 10(8) TML 2001, 2013, 2019, *supra* note 15.
43. *Supercell Co., Ltd. v. TRAB* 2016, *infra* note 117.

marked goods via platforms such as Taobao.com, JD.com etc. Consequently, it is recommended that foreign companies devise and register Chinese-language trade marks even before they become active in China or even if they have no plans to become active in China. If not, consumers or distributors in the best case scenario, and trade mark squatters in the worst, could proactively devise a Chinese-language version of their trade mark. The trade mark squatter would then sell the goods using this Chinese-language version of the trade mark to consumers.[44] *Shanyin v. Zhongjun* demonstrates an example of a trade mark squatter that focused on Chinese character trade marks. Beijing Shanyin Qiyi Technology Co. Ltd. started using the sign "闪银", which means "lightning-fast cash" for its payment services in November 2013. A month later, Wuhan Zhongjun Co. Ltd. filed a trade mark application for the same "闪银" mark. Shanyin's own trade mark application, filed some months later, was blocked by Zhongjun's earlier application. In 2015, after the squatted mark was granted registration to Zhongjun, Shanyin filed an invalidation procedure against it. The Supreme People's Court (SPC) accepted the retrial procedure after it fully maintained all the previous decisions, suggesting that this case was selected to set the record straight on invalidations on the catch-all basis of "illicit means" of Article 44 TML, and confirmed at the highest level that hoarding and registering trade marks without the intention to put them to genuine commercial use may lead to the invalidation of such hoarded marks.[45]

(e) Foreign Marks and Issues of Transliteration

When selecting Chinese characters for a trade mark one should check whether a Chinese version already exists in the relevant markets (PRC, Hong Kong, Macau, Taiwan, Singapore and Malaysia).[46]

Foreign brands can opt for a translation of the trade mark into Chinese. Although the name does not sound similar, this option will maintain the meaning of the name. For example, Apple chose this option: "苹果" (Píngguǒ); Microsoft: "微软" (Wēiruǎn), or Shell: "壳牌" (Képái). One can argue that in such translation cases, the right of priority under the Paris Convention is applicable. Although Article 4 D(3) Paris Convention instructs Union members not to require any authentication of the application, they may require applications to be accompanied by a certificate from the relevant authority showing the date of filing, and importantly "by a translation".

44. Daniel Chee King Chow, 'Trademark Squatting and the Limits of the Famous Marks Doctrine in China', 47(1) *George Washington International Law Review* (1 January 2015). Available at: https://ssrn.com/abstract=2443923.
45. Grace Guo and Stefaan Meuwissen, 'China's highest court slams trademark squatter, confirming that hoarding trademarks is unlawful', Hogan Lovells, 28 November 2018. Available at: https://www.engage.hoganlovells.com/knowledgeservices/news/chinas-highest-court-slams-trademark-squatter-confirming-that-hoarding-trademarks-is-unlawful.
46. 'A Guide to Creating Chinese-Language Trademarks', SIPS Asia, 30 April 2014. Available at: https://sips.asia/knowledge/trademark-registration/guide-to-creating-chinese-language-trademarks/.

Foreign countries can also opt for a non-Chinese trade mark. *Daikin Industry Co., Ltd. v. TRAB* demonstrates that the degree of the relevant public's understanding of a foreign language trade mark plays an important role.

Daikin Co., Ltd, a Japanese company, had registered the trade marks "大金", and "DAIKIN" and "DAIKIN and device" in China in 1997 and 1992, respectively. Both trade marks were designated for air-conditioning equipment. In Japan, Daikin Industries is not written in characters, but in Katakana: ダイキン工業株式会社.

On 1 July 2002, Huo Yiping filed an application for the trade mark "イダイキンさガイジ" ("idaikin sa gaiji") in Katakana/Hiragana, which are Japanese syllabaries,[47] for amplifiers, radios, computers, telephones, electric vending machines, integrated circuits, batteries, etc.

Daikin Co., Ltd filed an opposition. On 24 March 2008, the CTMO rejected the opposition and approved the registration. Daikin Co., Ltd filed an opposition review application at the TRAB on 17 April 2009. On 29 December 2011, the TRAB issued its ruling: since the opposed trade mark is a combination of Katakana, and Japanese is a minor language in China, generally Japanese is not easily identified by the relevant Chinese public. According to the Japanese-Chinese dictionary, the syllable "ダイ" ("dai") corresponds to the Chinese characters 大, 台, 第 or 题; while "キン" ("kin") corresponds to 斤, 近, 金, 菌, 琴. The Japanese pronunciation of the character 大 can be "ダイ" ("dai") or "タイ" ("tai") (when used in composition, onyomi), or "おお" ("ō") or "おおきい"(ōkī") (when used as a standalone character – kunyomi); while the Japanese pronunciation of 金 can be "コン" ("kin") (onyomi), "かね" ("kane") or "かな" ("kana") (kunyomi), which are all different pronunciations. This means that the relationship between "DAIKIN" and "大金" is not the only one possible.[48] In addition, the opposed trade mark has one katakana before "ダイキン" and four hiragana/katakana after it. Thus, according to the TRAB, there is a clear difference between the opposed trade mark and the cited trade marks.

Daikin Co., Ltd filed a lawsuit at the BFIC. This Court held "DAIKIN" to be a well-known mark in China and revoked the TRAB's opposition review ruling.[49]

TRAB appealed to the BHPC. In addition to its previous arguments, TRAB argued that the popularity of "大金" and "DAIKIN" was not extended to "ダイキン". The BHPC held that although the opposed trade mark was composed of a combination of katakana, its meaning and pronunciation did not form a unique correspondence with "大金" and "DAIKIN".[50] For a native speaker of Japanese, "イダイキンさガイジ"

47. Read more about the intricacies of the Japanese language in relation to trade mark similarity, in Christopher Heath, 'Similarity in appearance, concept or pronunciation alone does not automatically lead to similarity of marks in Japan', in Kung-Chung Liu (ed.), *Annotated Leading Trademark Cases in Major Asian Jurisdictions* (Routledge, 2019).

48. The character combination "大金" in Japanese would ordinarily be pronounced as "taikin" rather than "daikin", and as a Japanese surname "大金" – "ōgane". In the reverse, Kenkyusha's New Japanese-English dictionary lists as character combinations for "daikin" only:"代金" and not "大金".

49. BFPC Administrative Judgment, 2122 *Yizhong Zhixing Chuzi* (2012).

50. BHPC Administrative Judgment, 9 June, 939 *Gao Xing Zhong Zi* (2013). See also a similar anonymous case where a Japanese company's trade mark application in Hiragana was refused by the CTMO, TRAB, first and second instance courts, but was accepted by the SPC. 'The judgment of the similarity of the trade marks in foreign languages should be

has hardly meaning even though it includes the Katakana word "ダイキン", which may be read the same as "大金" or "DAIKIN".

It seems BFIC focused more on the protection against dilution, while TRAB and BHPC focused more on the protection against a likelihood of confusion.

Conversely, a transliteration sounds similar to a name, but could lose the meaning of a name in Roman text. Names such as Adidas "阿迪达斯" (ādídásī),[51] where the meaning is less important, are suitable for transliterations. It is of course preferable to use relevant or positive characters to create a transliteration. Carrefour, which means cross-roads in French, selected the following characters for its transliteration: 家乐福 (Jiālèfú), which means "Family happy and lucky". BMW got it right: it uses the name "宝马" (Bǎomǎ), which literally means "precious horse" for automobiles in China.

The German beer brand Warsteiner got it wrong: it transliterated its trade mark as "沃斯乐" (Wòsīlè), which, even though different tones are used, sounds similar to "我死了" (Wǒ sǐle), which means "I am dead".[52] Before the Coca-Cola Company came up with a successful Chinese equivalent name, some shopkeepers used variations of transliterations that sounded similar to Coca-Cola but that were neither relevant nor positive, including the transliteration which literally means "female horse fastened with wax".[53] Coca-Cola was able to turn the tide and register "可口可乐" (Kěkǒukělè). These characters mean "Drinkable, tasty and happy".

Because Chinese characters have many homophones,[54] a transliterated name bears the risk that it has to compete with a name that is pronounced the same but has one or more different characters. French fashion-house Hermès International SCA, which used the trade mark "爱马仕" (Àimǎshì) tried to stop Shunde Dafeng Garment

based on the recognition of the relevant public in China', Beijing Wei Chixue Law Firm, 10 April 2020. Available at: http://www.law-wei.com/en/case/our_case/20200410/307.html.

51. Adidas is composed of the nickname of its founder Adolf Dassler, "Adi" and the first syllable of his last name.

52. Yang Zhang and Xiaolin Dang, 'Translate and protect – Chinese versions of foreign brands', Beijing Sanyou IP Agency, Ltd., 3 December 2014. Available at: https://www.lexology.com/library/detail.aspx?g=44a82bda-8b76-42ac-af58-e650375f8806.

53. 'Prosecuting Trademarks in China: An Insider's Guide for Foreign Brand Owners in 2019 (Part I)', SIPS 31 March 2019. Available at: https://sips.asia/knowledge/trademark-registration/prosecuting-trademarks-in-china-an-insiders-guide-for-foreign-brand-owners-in-2019-part-1/.

54. To give an indication of the different homonyms brandholders can choose from, Paul Jones provided the alternatives for the transliteration of MCDONALD'S as an example: 麦当劳 (Maidanglao) Mai: cover up, bury – 埋; buy, purchase – 买; step, stride, advanced in years – 迈; wheat, a surname – 麦; sell – 卖; arteries and veins – 脉; Dang: equal, ought to, just at, work as, deserve, manage, sound of a gong – 当; keep off, block, a fender, gear of a car – 挡; political party, the Party (Communist) – 党; earring, eunuch – 珰; crotch – 裆; proper, match, treat as think, that very day, to pawn – 挡; manure pit – 凼; loose in morals, a marsh – 荡; delay – 宕; outspoken – 谠; Lao: scoop up from a liquid, get by improper means – 捞; enclosure for animals, jail – 牢; work, reward – 劳; old, tough, dark – 老; waterlogged – 涝; bake in a pan – 烙; – kind of farm tool – 耢; fruit jelly – 酪. Paul Jones, 'Intellectual Property Protection in China: Best Practices', 7 May 2009. Available at: http://www.jonesco-law.ca/89/files/pdfs/PIP%20-%20China%20Best%20Practices-%20HKCBA%202009-05-07.pdf.

Factory's registration of the trade mark "爱玛仕" which is pronounced identically (same sounds in the same tones) to Hermès' transliteration, and appealed the TRAB's decision in 1997 and again in 2009. The Beijing First Intermediary People's Court (BFIPC) held that the names are sufficiently different because Dafeng does not use the character for horse "马", but the character "玛" used for the word for agate.[55]

Hybrids are also possible. Between 2011 and 2013, New Balance Athletic Shoe Inc. marketed and sold its sneakers under the name "新百伦" (Xīnbǎilún) which consists of 新 (Xīn) which means new, and 百伦 (Bǎilún) which is the transliteration of "Balance". Unfortunately for New Balance, this hybrid trade mark was previously registered by Zhou Lelun, a local merchandiser. New Balance argued that "新百伦" is the Chinese equivalent of New Balance. However, in June 2015 the Guangdong Higher People's Court held that 新百伦 was neither a translation nor a transliteration, but a combination. It ordered New Balance to pay RMB 98 million to Mr Zhou for trade mark infringement,[56] and reduced the damages award to RMB 5 million in August 2015.[57] Another example of a hybrid is Starbucks, which combined the translation of "Star": 星 (Xīng) and the transliteration of "bucks": 巴克 (Bākè).[58]

Some brands choose a new mark that is positive. Blu Spa uses "富丽花" (Fùlì Huā), which literally means "Rich beautiful flower", but that is unconnected to the meaning or pronunciation of Blu Spa.

Zhejiang Higher People's Court ruled that Castel Frères SAS had to pay RMB 33 million to distributor Panati Wine (Shanghai) Co. for using the transliteration " 卡斯特" (Kǎsītè) without authorization from Panati that had registered the 卡斯特 trade mark first. Castel appealed all the way to the SPC, which reduced the damages to RMB 500,000 and agreed to retry the case. In January 2015, the SPC upheld the lower court's ruling.[59]

Another cautionary tale for companies that do not create user-friendly equivalent Chinese character names for their Roman text trade marks is the Sony Ericsson case. The joint-venture of Sony and Ericsson manufacturing mobile phones used a combination of the transliteration of the names of Sony and Ericsson: "索尼爱立信" (Suǒní Àilìxìn). However, these five Chinese characters were hard to remember.

55. 玛 agate is a kind of stone. It has the pronunciation of "horse" 马"Mǎ" and the radical of "king" 王 (there are 214 radicals, and these radicals are a way to classify Chinese characters).

    Melanie Lee, 'France's Hermes loses China trademark fight: report', Reuters, 27 February 2012. Available at: https://www.reuters.com/article/us-hermes-china/frances-hermes-loses-china-trademark-fight-report-idUSTRE81Q05420120227.

56. Scott Cendrowski, 'How New Balance Ran Into a Wall in China', Fortune, 28 May 2016. Available at: https://fortune.com/longform/new-balance-chinese-trademark/.

57. Deanna Wong, 'A sigh of relief: Guangdong Higher People's Court reduces record trademark damages award in its New Balance appeal judgment', Hogan Lovells, August 2016. Available at: https://www.hoganlovells.com/~/media/files/a_sigh_of_relief_guangdong_higher_peoples_court_reduces_record_trademark_damages_award.pdf?la=en.

58. Danny Friedmann, 'Xingbake wakes up and smells the coffee', IP Dragon, 2 January 2006. Available at: https://www.ipdragon.org/2006/01/02/xingbake-wakes-up-and-smells-the-coffee/.

59. Cassie Lam, '"Things are Different in China", Alleged Trademark Squatter Claims After Court Win', *World Trademark Review*, 25 March 2016. Available at: https://www.worldtrademarkreview.com/enforcement-and-litigation/things-are-different-china-alleged-trademark-squatter-claims-after.

Therefore, the relevant public and media started to abbreviate the brand: "索爱" (Suǒ'ài), which is a combination of the first Chinese character of Sony and that of Ericsson. Sony Ericsson itself did not adopt this abbreviation of its name. However, these two characters were applied for in March 2003 by Liu Jianjia for Class 9 with regard to MP3, mobile phone, etc., and were granted in 2004. Sony Ericsson filed for an invalidation application in June 2005, which was rejected by TRAB in November 2007.[60] Sony Ericsson appealed to the BFIPC, which overturned the TRAB decision in August 2008.[61] Liu appealed to the BHPC which reverted the judgment in 2010,[62] because Sony Ericcson had no evidence of prior use of "索爱" as its Chinese character mark. Until October 2007, the vice president and executive had even repeatedly declared that the use of the abbreviation to represent its brand was unacceptable. Sony Ericsson applied for a retrial at the SPC which was rejected.[63]

Some numbers are considered auspicious, and can be successfully used for a trade mark. The British brand of cigarette "STATE EXPRESS 555" became very popular in China with its trade mark "555".[64] In contrast, a trade mark "444" is not commendable in China, since the number 4, 四 in Chinese, is pronounced "sì" which is similar to 死 "sǐ", meaning death.

The message from the above examples is that foreign trade mark owners wanting to do business in the Chinese market[65] should pour considerable resources into market research and public perception prior to registering their mark, and should attentively monitor the market afterwards to understand how the general public and the media react to the trade mark. The examples are also evidence that companies do well in seeking the advice of cultural intermediaries so as to avoid market entry becoming an expensive disaster area.

Shorter Chinese transliterations have also caused considerable problems for trade mark proprietors.[66] In December 2000, the Beijing Second Intermediary People's Court (BSIPC) held that the transliteration the pharmaceutical giant Pfizer

60. TRAB Ruling 2007 No. 11295.
61. BFIPC Administrative Judgment, 196 *Yizhong Zhixing Chuzi* (2008).
62. BHPC Administrative Judgment, 717 Gao Xing Zhong Zi (2008).
63. SPC Retrial Rejection Notice, 48 *Zhi Xing Zi* (2010).
64. According to his physician, 555 cigarettes was the favourite brand of Mao Zedong. The Chinese character for number 5 is 五 sounds similar to 无 (wú), which means "not" or "without" which could be viewed as bad luck. However, the number is also associated with positivity because many Chinese traditional philosophical concepts revolve around the number 5, such as the five elements 五行 (wǔ xíng), which is used in traditional Chinese medicine, *feng shui*, martial arts, and music.
65. If a company wants to be active in an area within the Chinese market where they predominantly speak a certain dialect next to Mandarin, it should take into account what the pronunciation of the trade mark is in that dominant dialect and whether it is compatible with that particular culture. In Canton province, the dominant dialect is Cantonese, which has a different pronunciation from Mandarin and is spoken by approximately 60 million people in Canton Province, by almost 7.5 million people in Hong Kong, 700,000 people in Macau and by around 12 million Overseas Chinese.
66. See for example the case study on DIESEL. Lin Jiuchu and Zhang Jiaqi, 'Case Study of Invalidation against "迪赛" (Di sai in *pinyin*): Application and Protection of Transliteration Trademarks in China', KWM, 23 March 2020. Available at: https://www.chinalawinsight.com/2020/03/articles/intellectual-property/case-study-of-invalidation-against-%e8%

had chosen for its world famous brand Viagra "万艾可" (Wàn ài kě),[67] was neither used outside China, nor well-known in China. However, Pfizer's competitor in China, Guangzhou Viamen Pharmaceutical Company was able to register "伟哥" (Wěigē) which became the most popular brand for erectile dysfunction medicine in China due to its meaning: "Great Older Brother".[68]

Also in *Harley-Davidson v. Beijing Harley Trading Center*, the defendant was more adept in selecting a more meaningful transliteration of the trade mark than the plaintiff. Before this case, Harley-Davidson used the transliterations "哈利-戴维森" (Hālì-Dàiwéisēn)[69] and "哈利" (Hālì) as trade marks. In 2008, after the BSIPC had decided that Harley-Davidson prevailed (see below for more about this case),[70] Harley-Davidson started to use the "雷" character in its transliterations, which means thunder (suitable for a motorcycle company that prides itself on manufacturing motors that produce a thunderous roar) instead of the "利", which means benefit.[71]

By contrast, Starbucks was acknowledged as a well-known mark in its case against Shanghai Xingbake,[72] even though it had registered "星巴克" (Xīng bākè) after Shanghai Xingbake had pre-registered the trade name[73] and used the name as a trade mark on its menus and sign boards to mislead consumers, according to the Shanghai Intermediate People's Court.[74] This Court held that Starbucks' marks were well-known not just internationally, but particularly in China due "to their widespread use, publicity and reputation", because the company had massively invested in promoting and using its marks worldwide, including "星巴克" in Chinese-speaking regions.[75]

---

bf%aa%e8%b5%9b-disai-in-pinyin-application-and-protection-of-transliteration-trademarks-in-china/.

67. The three characters used for the transliteration of Viagra "万艾可", lack effective marketing value: "万" means 10,000; 艾 is used for the sound "ai"; 可 means can.
68. SPC 24 June, 313 *Minshen Zi* (2009). Daniel Chee King Chow, 'Lessons from Pfizer's Disputes Over its Viagra Trademark in China', 27 *Md. J. Int'l L.* 82 (2012), *passim*. Available at: http://digitalcommons.law.umaryland.edu/mjil/vol27/iss1/9.
69. The transliteration of "Davidson" 戴维森, does not have any significant meaning other than the name.
70. Zhang Zaiping (translation Wang Hongjun), 'Analytical comments on legal protection of Chinese equivalents of unregistered trademarks and judicial practice', *China Intellectual Property*, 25 February 2011. Available at: https://ipr.chinadaily.com.cn/2011-02/25/content_12080585.htm.
71. Harley-Davidson also changed the transliteration of its full name from "哈利-戴维森" (Hālì-Dàiwéisēn) to "哈雷-戴维森"(Hāléi-Dàiwéisēn), and "哈利" (Hālì) into "哈雷" (Hāléi).
72. Shanghai Higher People's Court made its ruling on 20 December 2006.
73. Mary K. Alexander, 'The Starbucks Decision of the Shanghai No. 2 Intermediate People's Court: A Victory Limited to Lattes', 58 *Case W. Res. L. Rev.* (2008), 881, 907. Available at: https://scholarlycommons.law.case.edu/caselrev/vol58/iss3/14.
74. Shanghai Intermediate Court, IP Tribunal, 2004 No. 1, 1 *Hu Er Zhong Min Wu (Zhi) Chu Zi* (2004).
75. Jing Li and Shaobin Zu, 'Starbucks Corporation Wins in a Trademark Infringement and Unfair Competition Case in Shanghai, China', 14 *C.A.S.R.I.P. Newsl.* (Spring 2007) 2. Available at: http://www.law.washington.edu/Casrip/NewsletterVoll14/newsvl4i2LiandZhu.

In short: to select a Chinese trade mark wisely, one needs to combine knowledge of marketing, trade mark law and the Chinese language.

(f) Sound Marks

Since the Third Amendment to the TML, sound marks can be registered as trade marks.[76]

If an application is filed for registration of a sound mark, this shall be made explicit by a statement in the application. A qualified sound sample[77] and a description of the sound for registration as the trade mark shall be submitted, and the method of use of the trade mark shall be indicated.[78] Sound marks cannot be registered if they are part of an absolute ground for refusal of Article 10 TML 2019, including sounds that are identical or similar to the melody of the national or military anthem of the PRC or any foreign country or to the *Internationale* in melody. However, the first registration of a sound mark in China by the State broadcaster China Radio International (CRI) on 14 May 2016,[79] used a musical adaptation of the beginning of China's national anthem as a jingle played first on vibraphone, then on a trumpet, followed by a woman broadcaster saying 中国国际广播电台 (Zhōngguó guójì guǎngbò diàntái) China Radio International (CRI)),[80] to introduce the radio programmes of the eponymous State broadcaster.

Sounds which directly represent the content, consumer or quality function of the designated goods or services,[81] which lack inherent distinctive features,[82] or which are generic,[83] cannot be registered as a trade mark. For example, the sound of children's laughter cannot be registered as a trade mark for "infant formula" or the barking or meowing sounds cannot be registered as a trade mark for cat food. Then again, these inherently non-distinctive sounds can acquire distinctiveness, according to Article 11(2) TML 2019. An example is technology company Tencent, which prevailed in registering the sound mark "Di Di Di Di Di Di" as a notification

76. Article 8 TML 2013 and 2019, *supra* note 15.
77. The applicant shall submit sound samples which shall be stored on an audio file. If the application is submitted via paper, the audio file shall be stored on a CD-ROM. If the application is submitted by data message, the sound samples shall be uploaded correctly in accordance with relevant requirements. The format of the audio file of the sound samples shall be WAV or MP3 audio file format, and the audio file shall be less than 5MB, and clear and easy for identification. Standards for Trade Mark Examination and Trial 2016, *infra* note 88, 112.
78. Article 13 IRTL 2014, *supra* note 12.
79. 'China Approves Signature Tune of China Radio International as its First Sound Mark', China Patent Agent Hong Kong Ltd., undated. Available: http://www.cpahkltd.com/EN/info.aspx?n=20160825163613370610.
80. CRI's sound mark can be listened to on the site of CRI. Available at: http://mod.cri.cn/eng/news/reports/2015/4/0416cri.mp3.
81. Article 11(1)(2) TML 2019, *supra* note 15.
82. Article 11(1)(3) TML 2019, *supra* note 15.
83. Article 11(1)(1) TML 2019, *supra* note 15.

for its QQ Messenger software in final appeal at the BHPC on 27 September 2018.[84] The Court held that although the sound was a common and simple repetition and lacked any distinctive feature, it had been used on QQ software for such a long time that it had established a stable relationship with QQ messaging software, and thus had acquired distinctiveness.[85]

(g) *Olfactory Marks*

Scent or smell marks are not included in the list of Article 8 TML 2019 and at the moment cannot be registered in China as a trade mark. However, since the TML 2013 introduced sound marks, and the law does not explicitly provide a graphical representation requirement, it might open the door for scent marks too.[86]

(h) *Colour Combination Marks*

In contrast to filing a trade mark in black and white, which will protect in relation to all potential colour combinations, filing colour combinations will exclusively protect these colour combinations. Since the TML 2013, isolated colour combinations of two or more colours are eligible for trade mark registration[87] if they are capable of distinguishing the source of the goods or services of one party from those of others. According to the Standards for Trade Mark Examination and Trial 2016, a colour combination trade mark would generally only acquire distinctiveness after long-term use.[88] The CTMO may issue Examination Opinions to require the applicant to submit use evidence and give an explanation of the trade mark's acquisition of distinctive features through use.[89]

Applicants must clearly state in the application that they are applying for colour combination marks and provide the colour specimens,[90] naming the colours using the Pantone numbers system.[91] Evidence of secondary meaning is required for

84. Kaifang Wang, 'First Sound Trademark Case IN China: Registrable but only on THE Product Actually Using the Mark', CCPIT Patent & Trademark Law Office via MONDAQ, 29 January 2019. Available at: http://www.mondaq.com/china/x/775644/Trademark/First+Sound+Trademark+Case+In+China+Registrable+But+Only+On+The+Product+Actually+Using+The+Mark.
85. Wang, *supra* note 84.
86. Danny Friedmann, 'EU Opens Door for Sound Marks: Will Scent Marks Follow?', 10(12) *Journal of Intellectual Property Law & Practice* (2015), 931–939. Available at: https://ssrn.com/abstract=2717940.
87. Article 8 TML 2013 and 2019, *supra* note 15.
88. The Standards for Trade Mark Examination and Trial uses power plugs, containers, shaver heads, loudspeakers, life buoys and climbing sticks as examples. Standards for Trade Mark Examination and Trial, CTMO and TRAB, 2016, 110. Available at: https://ipkey.eu/sites/default/files/legacy-ipkey-docs/standards-for-trademark-examination-and-trial.pdf.
89. Standards for Trade Mark Examination and Trial, *supra* note 88, 110.
90. Article 13(1) IRTL 2014, *supra* note 12.
91. The lack of graphical representation of the combination colours will lead to the rejection of the trade mark application. *Roxtec Corporation v. TRAB* Lao Ke Sai Ke gongsi su Shangbiao pingshen weiyuanhui yanse zuhe shangbiao shenqing bohui fushen xingzheng an; yishen

registration. Functionality of a colour combination mark can prevent registration, for example in the case of the dosage of medicines that is symbolized by using colours.

Single colours in combination with other elements that are eligible subject matter of Article 8 TML 2019, may also be registered. If one extrapolates the continuing extension of trade mark subject matter, and one takes the developments in other jurisdictions into account, single colours might be eligible for protection in the future.

Article 49(1) TML 2019 stipulates that in the process of using a registered trade mark, trade mark registrants may not change the registered trade marks themselves, also in case of colour combinations. If they do so, the local Administration of Industry and Commerce (AIC)/Administration of Market Regulation (AMR) will order them to correct the registered trade mark within a time limit. If they fail to pass the corrections, the CTMO can cancel the registered trade mark.[92] Deere & Company successfully asserted its colour combination mark and sued JOTEC at the BSIPC in June 2013 for using the green and yellow colour on their tractors and other agricultural equipment and in their promotional material.[93]

(i) Three-Dimensional Marks

Since the TML 2001, three-dimensional marks can be registered in China. However, despite Article 8 TML 2019, which lists three-dimensional symbols as one of the enumerated signs capable of distinguishing the source of the goods of one undertaking from those of other undertakings, in practice CTMO, TRAB and the courts often apply a higher standard for three-dimensional marks. Their rationale is that "under most circumstances, the relevant public is not likely to take such a sign as a source identifier of the goods to which it is attached".[94] This position can also be observed by the Court of Justice of the European Union.[95] In case of foreign trade marks, three-dimensional marks can *a fortiori* be more easily recognized and recalled than words written in a non-Chinese script. The Swiss chocolate bar Toblerone is a case in point: not many Chinese consumers remember its Roman script trade mark name,

an hao: Beijing IP Court, 1638 *Jing zhixing chu zi* (2015); ershen an hao: BHPC, 55 *Jing xing zhong* (2016), China IP Magazine, 1 June 2018. Available at: http://www.chinaipmagazine.com/Topics/InfoShow.asp?47-2093.html.

92. Article 49(1) TML 2013 and 2019, *supra* note 15.

93. *Deere & Company v. JOTEC International Heavy Industry (Qingdao) Co Ltd. and JOTEC International Heavy Industry (Beijing) Co Ltd.* at the BSIPC in June 2013. The Chinese court, in an unpublished decision, found for Deere & Company and issued an injunction and compensatory damages, confirming that combination colour marks are protected in China, in this case the colour combination of "green body of a tractor and yellow wheels". The CTMO approved Deere's registration of its colour combination mark (upper portion in green, lower portion in yellow) in the international classes 7 and 12 in respect of the goods "tractors, harvesting machines, lawnmowers, agriculture machines, etc." already on 21 March 2009. The Court ordered the two defendants to stop infringement and pay RMB 450,000 for Deere's damages and other reasonable fees. This was the first Chinese court ruling on an infringement of a registered colour combination mark.

94. Article 9 SPC Provisions 2016, *infra* note 112.

95. Danny Friedmann, 'The Bottle Is the Message: only the distinctive survive as 3-D community mark', *GRUR Int.* (2014), 1195.

but most do know and remember its three-dimensional mark, and the public has even given it a Chinese name based on its shape: "三角巧克力" (Sānjiǎo qiǎokèlì), which means Triangular chocolate. The shape of Toblerone[96] chocolate[97] and its packaging[98] were registered as three-dimensional marks by Toblerone.

Three-dimensional marks, even though considered a distinctive identifier of source, may nonetheless be refused registration for reasons of public policy, see below under absolute grounds of refusal.

(j) Advertising Slogans

Slogans, important for advertising purposes, can be protected both under the TML and (when original), by copyright law. Of course, the absolute and relative grounds for refusal of trade mark registration also apply to slogans. Thus, slogans should not indicate the characteristics of the products as such. In addition, slogan trade marks should be distinctive and not be commonly used, which sets a higher threshold for distinctiveness. The slogan "你值得拥有!" ("You're worth it!") was applied for trade mark registration by L'Oréal, but rejected as not sufficiently distinctive. In contrast, the slogan "钻石恒久远·一颗永流传" (paraphrased as "Diamonds are forever") was successfully registered by diamond company De Beers Group.

Arbitrary and fancy words are most distinctive. However, one can argue that the public familiarizes itself most easily with a slogan composed in the vernacular, which is not necessarily distinctive. Therefore, a slogan that comprises distinctive and less distinctive words is most effective. A slogan that is not inherently distinctive can acquire distinctiveness through use under Article 11(2) TML 2019, so that it can be registered as a trade mark. In that case, evidence needs to be provided to the CTMO that the slogan is associated with the trade mark applicant by the relevant public and that the slogan has been used on the designated goods or services.[99]

In *Red Bull AG v. TRAB*, the BFIPC upheld by the BHPC,[100] confirmed that the slogan "Red Bull 给你一对翅膀" ("Red Bull gives you wings") was a combination of a Roman script and Chinese characters phrase with originality, and there was no evidence indicating that it was commonly used in advertising. Therefore, the slogan did not lack distinctiveness.

---

96. Toblerone is a play on the words "Tobler" and "torrone". "Tobler" is the family name of the original chocolate manufacturer, "torrone" is Italian word for nougat.
97. Toblerone Swiss chocolate, see Mondelez Europe GmbH, China Trade Mark Registration No. G615994, in Nice Class 30, as an extension of its international registration under the Madrid system in 1994.
98. Packaging of Toblerone, see Mondelez Europe GmbH, China Trade Mark Registration No. G615992, in Nice Class 30, as an extension under the international registration under the Madrid system in 1994.
99. Jiang Ling, 'Just Do It!? Protecting Advertising Slogans in China Part I', King and Wood, 23 February 2010. Available at: https://www.chinalawinsight.com/2010/02/articles/intellectual-property/just-do-it-protecting-advertising-slogans-in-china-part-i/.
100. BHPC Administrative Judgment, 1170 *Gao Xing Zhong Zi* (2009). Crystal J. Chen, 'Red Bull Wins the Fight Against Fly Bull', Lexology, 3 November 2015. Available at: http://www.lexology.com/library/detail.aspx?g=9b3c09ad-7aa7-4cf0-8aa6-744403536201.

3. Absolute Grounds of Refusal

(a) Signs Prohibited per se: Signs that are Misleading or Against Good Morals

To implement Article 6*ter* Paris Convention, which prescribes the prohibition of the trade mark registration and use of State Emblems, Official Hallmarks, and Emblems of Intergovernmental Organizations, China has enlisted signs that shall not be used as a trade mark. Article 10(1)(1) TML 2019 prohibits the use of those signs that are identical with or similar to the state name, national flag, national emblem, national anthem, military flag, military emblem, military anthem, medals or the like of the PRC, as well as those identical to the names or emblems of central government agencies, the names of the specific sites where central government agencies are located, or the names or designs of landmark buildings.[101]

An example: Jing Brand filed a trade mark application for "China Jing Wine", which consisted of two characters for China "中国", one for Jing "劲" (which is not only a name but also means vigour) and one for wine "酒".[102] The characters for China and wine were within a square stamp, while the character for Jing was much larger and also outside the stamp and in a so called *Xing*-style font. The CTMO and TRAB both rejected the application, and held that the mark violated Article 10(1)(1) TML, since it included the characters for China. Jing Brand argued that the China characters were there to demonstrate the source country of the wine, and pointed to the Standards for Examination of Trade Marks which stated that the applied mark which included China should not be prohibited for registration if the mark as a whole had sufficient distinctiveness. The BHPC revoked TRAB's decision, which was affirmed by the SPC, but the latter held that the BHPC erred in its reasoning: TRAB should re-examine whether the applied mark violated other relevant provisions of the TML.[103]

101. The "state name" mentioned in this Article includes full name, abbreviation and acronym. In Chinese, the full state name of China is "华人民共和国", and the abbreviation is "中国" and "中华". In English: "THE PEOPLE'S REPUBLIC OF CHINA", and the abbreviation or acronym is "CHN", "P.R.C.", "CHINA", "P.R. CHINA", "PR OF CHINA".

    The "national emblem" of China comprises the design of Tian'anmen in its centre under the lights of five stars and encircled by ears of grain and a cogwheel. The "national anthem" is the March of the Volunteers. The "military flag" and "military emblem" have the Chinese characters for "Eight" and "One" in common, which refer to August 1st. The "medals" are badges of honour awarded to persons or organizations which have made contribution to the country or the society by relevant national authority, for example, the Eight One Medal. The names of the specific sites where central government agencies are located, or the names or designs of landmark buildings include "National People's Congress", "State Council", "Zhongnanhai", "Diaoyutai", "Tian'anmen", "Xinhuamen", "Ziguangge", "Huairen Hall" and "Great Hall of the People", etc.

102. Jing Brand filed a trade mark application for China Jing Wine, No. 4953206, in Class 33 of alcoholic beverages except beers to the CTMO on 20 October 2005.

103. *Jing Brand v. TRAB*, SPC, 4 *Zui Gao Xin Ti Zi* (2010). Robert Merges and Seagull Haiyan Song, *Transnational Intellectual Property Law* (Edward Elgar, Cheltenham, 2018), 518–521.

The Administrative Regulations for the Management of Special Signs[104] were promulgated by the State Council in 1996, and are expected to be revised in 2020/2021. Special signs are not directly reflecting the source of the goods or the provider of the service, and instead indicate that the goods or services carrying them are related to national and international cultural, physical, scientific research and other public-interest activities sanctioned by the State Council. Generally, they are composed of names and abbreviations with characters, figures, emblems and mascots that can be used on goods and services with permission. In accordance with these Regulations, the Information Office of the State Council devised several special signs. These include the signs related to the Olympic Games,[105] and to the 70th anniversary of the Founding of the PRC.[106]

According to Article 10(1)(5) TML 2019, in case of those signs identical or similar to the symbol or name of the Red Cross or Red Crescent,[107] or, according to Article 10(1)(6) TML 2019, those being discriminatory against any nationality, the prohibition to register these as trade marks is absolute.

The following categories are less absolute: Article 10(1)(2) TML 2019 clarifies that signs identical with or similar to the state name, national flag, etc., of a foreign country, can be registered with the consent of the government of that country. In that case, the trade mark registrant needs to demonstrate that it has received explicit permission from the particular country. Despite this, in the case of SWISSGEAR, trade mark registration in the country of origin was not sufficient, see below.

Article 10(1)(3) TML 2019 makes it clear that in the case of signs identical with or similar to the name, flag or emblem of an Intergovernmental Organization (IGO), there are two exceptions to the prohibition: with the consent of the IGO or where it is unlikely to mislead the public.[108] In one of its "model" enforcement cases in 2016,

104. Administrative Regulations for Special Signs, State Council order No. 202, promulgated by the State Council on 13 July 1996 and effective on the same date. Available at: http://www.law-lib.com/law/law_view.asp?id=289.

105. Regulations on the Protection of the Olympic Symbols, Decree of the State Council of the PRC, No. 699, promulgated 28 June 2018 and effective 31 July 2018. Available at: http://www.gov.cn/zhengce/content/2018-06/30/content_5302468.htm.

106. CNIPA announced an application of the logo for events in celebration of the 70th anniversary of the founding of the PRC filed by the State Council Information Office for special signs registration was approved, certified to be used on all 45 categories of the International Classification of Goods and Services for the Purposes of the Registration of Marks from 27 August 2019 to 27 August 2023. http://www.gov.cn/xinwen/2019-09/05/content_5427660.htm. Wang Guohao, 'The 70th Anniversary of the Founding of the People's Republic of China', China IPR Net, 20 September 2019. Available at: http://www.cnipr.com/sj/zx/201909/t20190920_235312.html.

107. A third, more neutral, protocol emblem "the Red Crystal" with equal status to the Red Cross and Red Crescent was adopted during an extended International Conference of the Red Cross conference organized by the Swiss government on 7 December 2005. 29th International Conference of the Red Cross and Red Crescent – Resolution 1, ICRC, 22 June 2006. Available at: https://www.icrc.org/en/doc/resources/documents/misc/international-conference-resolution-220606.htm.

108. IGOs, mentioned in this Article, refer to those organizations with certain bylaws that are established by governments of several countries and regions for a particular purpose via a treaty or agreement. For example: the UN, EU, ASEAN, the Organization of African

the Shanghai Municipal AIC discovered that since February 2016, Shanghai Youxiang Culture Development Co., Ltd. had used the name UNITED NATIONS in English and Chinese and the UN emblem on their official website, WeChat and Weibo public accounts, and other promotional materials, registration agreements, etc. without the authorization of the UN organization. In the name of the UN World Youth Summit, they recruited personnel to attend the US conference and received income from illegal activities such as participation fees of more than RMB 6 million. The Shanghai Municipal AIC forced the company to immediately stop using the unauthorized sign and imposed a fine of RMB 400,000 for the violation of Article 10(1)(3) TML.[109]

Article 10(1)(4) TML 2019 states that signs identical with or similar to an official mark or inspection stamp that indicates control and guarantee cannot be registered as a trade mark, except when authorized by the organization that provides these official marks or inspection stamps.

One can argue that the signs prohibited from registration in Article 10(1)(1)-(6) TML 2019 are all deceptive and likely to mislead the public in terms of the quality, place of production or other characteristics of the goods. Article 10(1)(7) TML[110] prohibits these signs explicitly. Article 4 SPC Provisions 2016 clarified that the above types of misleading marks are comprised in the old wording of the TML 2001: "signs that constitute exaggerated and deceitful advertising." In 2016, the Weihai AIC prosecuted a local company for using "高纯盐藻" (high pure *Dunaliella salina*), a type of micro algae, as an unregistered mark on the packaging of beta carotene supplements. The CTMO had rejected the trade mark application because the mark was held to be descriptive of the raw materials of the product. However, after investigating the ingredients, the Weihai AIC found that the product lacked any micro algae. Therefore, it ruled that the use of the unregistered trade mark was deceptive and in violation of Article 10(1)(7) TML.[111] According to the SPC Provisions 2016, findings by the TRAB that signs used in advertising goods which exaggerate or are fraudulent, as proscribed in Article 10(1)(7) TML 2001, shall be upheld.[112]

Article 10(1)(8) TML 2019 prohibits signs that are detrimental to socialist ethics or customs, or have other unwholesome influences. Signs that contain the state name of China, but are not identical with or similar to it as a whole and thus fall outside of the scope of Article 10(1)(1) TML 2019, if deemed to be detrimental to the national sovereignty, dignity and image, can be excluded from registration

Unity, the WTO, WIPO, and the Asia-Pacific Economic Cooperation, etc. The name of an international organization includes its full name, abbreviation or acronym. For example: the abbreviation of European Union is "欧洲联盟", EU is "欧盟".

109. In 2016, the industrial and commercial and market supervision departments investigated and handled typical cases of trademark infringement, *China Market Regulation News*, 25 April 2017. Available at: http://www.cicn.com.cn/zggsb/2017-04/25/cms96746article.shtml.
110. Article 10(1)(7) TML 2013 and 2019, *supra* note 15.
111. Article 10(1)(7) TML 2013 and 2019, *supra* note 15.
112. Provisions of the SPC on Several Issues Concerning the Trial of Administrative Cases Concerning Trade Mark Authorization and Confirmation, promulgated on 12 December 2016, effective on 10 January 2017. Available at: http://www.court.gov.cn/zixun-xiangqing-34732.html.

based on Article 10(1)(8) TML.[113] China's emphasis on harmony between its 56 ethnic groups is reflected in this provision: if the name[114] or image of a public figure in the political, economic, cultural, religious,[115] folk belief,[116] ethnic or other field is filed to be registered as a trade mark, this should be interpreted as "other unhealthy influences".[117]

Also trade marks composed of numbers, for example "8 1" (八一) can have political significance.[118]

(b) Signs that Lack Distinctiveness

Only signs that are inherently distinctive or that have acquired distinctiveness[119] can be registered.[120] The Trade Mark Examination and Trial Standard jointly issued by the CTMO and TRAB in December 2016 sets out when marks will be considered to lack distinctiveness, namely if too simple or too complex; one or two letters represented in a common way - CTMO, TRAB, BFIPC all held that Audi's model numbers, such as A4, A6, A8, etc., lacked distinctiveness;[121] ordinary forms of Arabic numerals used on merchandise that normally have model numbers or item numbers expressed in numbers; commonly used packages; a monochromatic colour scheme; descriptive phrases or sentences; business location names, generic trade terminology or logos that

113. Article 3(2) SPC Provisions 2016, *supra* note 112.
114. "Name" includes the name used in the household registration, alias, pseudonym, stage name, nickname, etc. Standards for Trade Mark Examination and Trial 2016, *supra* note 88, 37.
115. The exception is where, pursuant to the Regulations on Religious Affairs (published by the Order No. 426 of the State Council in 2004 and came into force from 1 March 2005) under which social and public benefits undertaking may be legally established at the site of religious groups and activities, and without prejudice to the interests of other sites of religious activities, a religious group and the religious enterprise it authorizes applies for registration of a trade mark based on the name exclusive to the site of its religious activities. Standards for Trade Mark Examination and Trial 2016, *supra* note 88, 42.
116. The folk belief used in this standard mainly refers to Mazu, which is a Chinese sea goddess, and other folk beliefs. Standards for Trade Mark Examination and Trial 2016, *supra* note 88, 41.
117. Article 5 SPC Provisions 2016, *supra* note 112. *Supercell Co., Ltd. v. TRAB*, BHPC Administrative Judgment, 29 March, 2226 *Jing Xingchu* (2016). Available at: https://bit.ly/2MQerGu.
118. Which refers to the 1 August Declaration made by the CPC under the Seventh World Congress of the Comintern, to organize a National United Front against Japan, on 1 August 1935. 'Reporting to All the Compatriots for the Fight Against Japan', CPC. Available at: http://cpc.people.com.cn/BIG5/33837/2534283.html.
119. Article 11(2) TML 2001, 2013 and 2019, *supra* note 15.
120. China is a member of WIPO, which uses the non-binding Abercrombie & Fitch spectrum, without giving attribution to this case, in its 1993 training manual. *Introduction to Trademark Law and Practice, The Basic Concepts, A WIPO Training Manual* (1993). Available at: https://www.wipo.int/edocs/pubdocs/en/wipo_pub_653.pdf.
121. Luo Yanjie, 'Why did the Trademark Office Reject Audi's "A4" Trademark Application?', China IP Lawyer, 30 October 2013. Available at: http://www.chinaiplawyer.com/trademark-office-reject-audis-a4-trademark-application/.

are commonly used in the industry or in related industries; the form of organization of the enterprise, the industry name or its abbreviation; only comprising of elements such as telephone numbers, addresses, house numbers; and commonly used slang and greetings.[122]

As pointed out in Article 11(1)(3) TML 2019,[123] marks that otherwise lack distinctive features refer to marks which, *per se* or when being used on designated goods as a trade mark, do not represent the source of the goods and would thus be considered descriptive (see below). However, the above-mentioned marks could become distinctive in combination with other elements.[124]

According to the relevant SPC Provisions 2016, the courts should make their decision on the distinctiveness of a trade mark based on the common perception of the relevant public of the goods on which such mark is designated to be used, taking the trade mark into consideration as a whole.[125] If the descriptive component of a sign does not affect its distinctiveness as a whole, or a descriptive sign is displayed in a specific manner so as to serve as a source identifier of the goods to which it is attached by the relevant public, the court shall find such sign distinctive. The court shall base its distinctiveness finding over a trade mark in a foreign language on the common perception of the relevant public within the Chinese territory.

If an application is filed to register the shape or partial shape of a product as a three-dimensional mark, the SPC holds that under most circumstances the relevant public is not likely to take such a sign as a source identifier of the goods to which it is attached, and should not be held distinctive by the courts. The fact that a three-dimensional sign has been originally created or first used by the applicant shall not necessarily be admitted as proof of distinctiveness of such a sign. One can argue that this provision promotes the diffusion of innovation rather than its creation. Instead of rewarding innovators, this facilitates copying (see also below).

If an inherently non-distinctive sign through long-term or extensive use has become a source identifier of the goods to which it is attached by the relevant public, the court may recognize such a sign as distinctive.

(c) Descriptive Marks

If a trade mark only indicates the quality, principal raw materials, function, use, weight, quantity or other features of the goods, it does not indicate the source of the goods. In that case the mark is merely descriptive and cannot be registered.[126] A descriptive name is the statutory or customary name of the goods to which they are attached. The common perception of the relevant public in China shall be considered in this regard. It is an indication of descriptive character if a name has been classified as a name of certain goods by professional reference books, dictionaries, etc. The court shall base its finding of descriptive character on the *de facto* status at the time of the application of the trade mark, and irrespective of whether the status changes

122. Trade Mark Examination and Trial Standard, *supra* note 88, 56.
123. Article 11(1)(3) TML 2001, 2013 and 2019, *supra* note 15.
124. Standards of Trade Mark Examination and Trial, *supra* note 88, 57–58.
125. Article 7 SPC Provisions 2016, *supra* note 112.
126. Article 11(1)(2) TML 2001, 2013 and 2019, *supra* note 15.

later in the process. Those signs or the signs whose components insinuate the features of the goods in respect of which the trade mark is used, but do not affect their identifying functions, could be registered as trade marks. The distinctiveness of a litigious trade mark shall be assessed on the common perception of the relevant public of the goods on which such a mark is designated, by taking said trade mark into consideration as a whole. If the translation of the trade mark would be confusingly similar to an existing trade mark, it should be excluded from registration due to a conflict with prior rights, see below. However, if the translation of the trade mark provides a descriptive mark, and the relevant public of the goods is aware of the language in which the trade mark has been made, the trade mark should be excluded from registration if it has not acquired distinctiveness. If, as the SPC Provisions 2016 make clear, the relevant public within the Chinese territory "is hardly aware" of the inherent meaning of the foreign trade mark name, it does not matter if the inherent meaning is descriptive or not, since it can be perceived as distinctive in the eyes of the relevant public within the Chinese territory.[127]

Article 11(2) TML 2019[128] clarifies that a merely descriptive trade mark, such as "Best Buy" can acquire distinctiveness as to the source of the goods or services.[129] In that case it can be registered as a trade mark. The examination of trade marks that have acquired distinctive features through use, shall consider the awareness of the relevant public about these features on such trade marks as a source indicator. An example is "酸酸乳" (Suān suān rǔ), which means Sour Sour Milk, which is merely descriptive of the dairy product sold by Mengniu and lacked distinctiveness.[130] However, the trade mark acquired distinctiveness after massive advertisement campaigns.[131]

(d) Geographical Names as an Absolute Ground for Refusal

Article 10(2) TML 2019 states that no geographical names of administrative divisions at or above county level or foreign geographical names known to the public may be used as trade marks, except where geographical names have acquired secondary meaning or are part of a collective or certification mark. If a trade mark is composed of or contains a geographical name whose applicant is not from such a place, use on the designated goods will likely mislead the public with regard to the place of origin and the application will be rejected.

Eligible for registration are signs that are the combination of a geographical name of administrative divisions at or above the county level or a foreign geographical name well-known to the public in combination with other elements, if the whole

127.
128. Article 11(2) TML 2001, 2013 and 2019, *supra* note 15.
129. *BestBuy v. TRAB*, SPC, 9 *Xing Ti Zi* (2011).
130. Article 11(1)(2) TML 2001, 2013 and 2019, *supra* note 15.
131. Huang Hui, '(Chimeng shangbiao) wei zhuce shangbiao yi ke goucheng chiming shangbiao ("suan suan ru" shangbiao qinquan ji bu zhengdang jingzheng an)' ((Famous trade marks) unregistered trade marks may also constitute well-known trade marks ("acid sour milk" trade mark infringement and unfair competition case)) Wanhuida, 24 March 2017. Available at: http://www.wanhuida.com/content/details_7_1143.html. Higher People's Court of the Inner Mongolia Autonomous Region, 16 October, 7 *Nei Min San Zhong Zi* (2006).

has a meaning that can distinguish it from the geographical name,[132] or of which the designated goods have no particular association with the place or territory it indicates, and therefore will not mislead the public with regard to the place of origin of goods.

The prohibition of Article 10(2) TML 2019[133] applies where the Chinese character composition of a trade mark is different from the geographical name of an administrative division at or above the county level or well-known foreign geographical name, but the form or pronunciation thereof is similar thereto and sufficient to cause the public to mistake it as that geographical name, which therefore causes misunderstanding of the place of origin of the relevant goods.[134]

In 2013, in *Zurich Insurance Co., Ltd. v. TRAB*, the insurance company was dissatisfied by the decision of the TRAB to reject its trade mark application for ZURICH HELPPOINT designated for Class 16 in respect of insurance stationery, and Class 36 for insurance and financial services, based on Article 10(2) TML. The BFPC held that Article 10(2) TML was only applicable to names that consist of geographical names of administrative divisions above the county level[135] or foreign geographical names known to the public and that therefore the trade mark registration should be granted. The TRAB appealed and the BHPC held that the trade mark should indeed be accepted, but that the reasoning of the court of first instance was too absolute. According to the BHPC, Article 10(2) TML was not only applicable to trade marks "consisting" of only geographical names of administrative divisions above the county level or foreign geographical names known to the public, but also to trade marks "containing" geographical names of administrative divisions above the county level or publicly known trade marks of foreign geographical names.[136]

The ZURICH HELPPOINT case also makes it clear that geographical names that are not known to the Chinese public, for example "Chiemsee",[137] are eligible for trade mark registration.

In 2015, Wenger filed the SWISSGEAR trade mark registration for Class 8 products of manual tools etc. in China. A competitor opposed the registration. The CTMO, TRAB and the Beijing IP Court rejected the registration based on Article 10(2) TML.[138] Wenger appealed at the BHPC, but the Court held in its final ruling

132. Article 6 SPC Provisions 2016, *supra* note 112.
133. Article 10(2) TML 2001, 2013 and 2019, *supra* note 15.
134. Standards for Trade Mark Examination and Trial 2016, *supra* note 88, 34.
135. There are five levels of local government in the PRC: the provincial (Province, Autonomous Region, Municipality, and Special Administrative Region), Prefecture, County, Township and Village. See more administrative divisions in John Donaldson, 'China's administrative hierarchy: The balance of power and winners and losers within China's levels of government', in *Assessing the Balance of Power in Central-Local Relations in China* (2017), 105–137. Available at: https://ink.library.smu.edu.sg/soss_research/2031.
136. "Shangbiao fa" di shi tiao di er kuan shiyong yi "jin" you diming goucheng de shangbiao he "hanyou" diming de shangbiao liang zhong qingkuang (The second paragraph of Article 10 TML applies to trade marks that "only" consist of geographical names and trade marks that "contain" geographical names) BHPC, 26 December 2013. Available at: http://www.bjcourt.gov.cn/article/newsDetail.htm?NId=25000076&channel=100015003.
137. Compare the Joined Cases C-108/97 and C-109/97, *Windsurfing Chiemsee*, Judgment of the ECJ, 4 May 1999. ECLI:EU:C:1999:230.
138. Victorinox acquired Wenger in 2005 and filed for the registration of the trade mark SWISSGEAR in 2007. 'SWISSGEAR Trademark Dispute Concluded', CNIPA, 14 October

that, even though SWISSGEAR was registered in Switzerland, this was insufficient evidence to prove the permission of the Swiss government.[139] Local AMRs in the context of the "Purification Action Plan" will prioritize tackling violations involving state and geographical names and misleading signs likely to cause significantly adverse effect in the market. The Ningbo AMR previously prosecuted a local train components manufacturer for violation of Article 10(2) TML by marking "北仑" (Běilún), a county level geographical name in China, on their products. A fine of around USD 7,500 was imposed.[140]

TRAB v. Yantai Médoc Châteaux Wine Ltd. clarified that the geographical name either needs to fulfil the definition of a GI according to Article 16(2) TML[141] or it should have been known as a source indicator in China.[142]

In contrast to their ongoing global battle to use the geographical name BUDWEISER,[143] the Czech beer manufacturer Budějovický Budvar and its American rival Anheuser-Bush each chose a Chinese character trade mark that does not directly refer to the geographical name "Budweis" or even the word white, although the pronunciation of white in Chinese 白 is "Bái". Budějovický chose a transliteration of the first part of Budějovický "百爺" (Bǎi Yé), which literally means "hundred grandfather", focusing on the Czech beer's long tradition. Anheuser-Bush selected "

2015. Available at: http://english.cnipa.gov.cn/news/iprspecial/920236.htm.

139. Wang Guohao, '"SWISSGEAR" Zai hua shenqing shangbiao zhong bei bohui' ('SWISSGEAR' Trademark Rejected by Beijing Court in Final Decision), *China Intellectual Property News*, 7 December 2018. Available at: http://english.cnipa.gov.cn/docs/2018-12/20181207091841530223.pdf.

140. Dora Si, 'China's new powerful market regulator tackles the use of deceptive trademarks', Deacons, 8 September 2018. Available at: https://bit.ly/2ppPCrY.

141. Article 16(2) TML 2013 and 2019, *supra* note 15.

142. *TRAB v. Yantai Médoc Châteaux Wine Ltd.*, Beijing IP Court 23 June, 130 *Jing 73 Xingchu* (2016).

26 June 2016, the Beijing IP Court upheld the decision by the TRAB to invalidate "玛歌 鹰贵" (Mage Yinggui) in Class 33 for wine etc., which included the transliteration of the French GI "Margaux", which was not registered and had not attained a distinctive meaning other than that of its geographical name in China. The French organization *Institut national de l'origine et de la qualité* (INOA) invoked Article 10(2) TML, which prohibits foreign geographical names known to the public to be registered as trade marks and Article 16(2) TML, which provides a definition of a GI. INOA failed to adduce sufficient evidence to prove that Margaux fulfilled the substantial requirements of a GI according to Article 16(2) TML and Article 10(2) TML was not accepted. However, its invocation of Article 10(1)(8) TML, that such registration had an unwholesome influence, was accepted, since the use of the litigious mark in respect of wine was likely to mislead the relevant public to misconstrue that the wine came from the French place called "Margaux".

'Guojia gongshang hang zheng guanli zongju shangbiao pingshen weiyuanhui, yantai mei duo ke zhuangyuan putaojiu youxian gongsi yu faguo guojia yuan chandi mingcheng ju wuxiao xuangao (shangbiao) yishen xingzheng panjueshu' (Administrative judgment of the first instance of invalidation (trade mark) by the TRAB of the SAIC, Yantai Medoc Estate Wine Co., Ltd. and the French National Institute of Appellations of Origin), IP House, undated. Available at: https://v1.iphouse.cn/cases/detail/305863.html.

143. Christopher Heath, 'The Budweiser Cases: A Brewing Conflict', in Christopher Heath and Anselm Kamperman Sanders (eds.), Landmark Intellectual Property Cases and Their Legacy (Kluwer Law International, Alphen aan de Rijn, 2011), 181–244.

百威" (Bǎi Wēi) which is a transliteration of Budweiser and literally means "hundred power", yet could figuratively mean "awesome". Importantly, these trade marks seem to sufficiently differ from each other so that litigation between these rivals might be averted.

Trade marks that contain any enterprise name that is substantially different in respect of the administrative division or territory from the name of the applicant also fall under the scope of Article 10(2) TML 2019 (see section XII. 2. on Enterprise and Trade Names).

(e) Restrictions on the Registrability of Three-Dimensional Marks

A three-dimensional mark for the shape of an element or packaging of a good can be renewed indefinitely. In contrast, the protection of a shape via design patents[144] or copyright[145] is temporally limited. Therefore, Article 12 TML 2019[146] provides three non-functional requirements to prevent three-dimensional marks from blocking legitimate use by other traders. Registration is not possible where the three-dimensional mark: (1) arises from the natural shape of the product itself; (2) is exclusively necessitated by its technical features; or (3) has aesthetic features giving substantial value to the goods. An unusual shape that has nothing to do with the product but everything with the source of the product is eligible for protection of a three-dimensional mark. An example is car fresheners that could be designed in any shape, but where the company chose to use the shapes of "little trees" and refer exclusively to the corresponding source of the goods: CAR-FRESHNER Corp.[147]

In *Kaiping Weishida Seasoning v. Nestlé*, the BHPC rejected the Maggi square-shaped bottle with designated colours for seasoning products, not because it was considered aesthetically functional, but because "consumers usually make purchase decisions of seasoning products based on factors such as the quality or manufacturers of such products",[148] which presumably means that the shape was not considered to confer a commercial origin.

---

144. Ten years from the application date. Patent Law 2008.

145. Fifty years after the death of the author. Article 21 Copyright Law 2010, Second Amendment) in accordance with a decision of the Standing Committee of the NPC on 26 February 2010. Available at: http://english.www.gov.cn/archive/laws_regulations/2014/08/23/content_281474982987430.htm.

146. Article 12 TML 2001, 2013 and 2019, *supra* note 15.

147. Xiangrong Wu, 'TRAB rules that unusual product shape is eligible for 3D trademark registration', ILO, 18 December 2017. Available at: https://www.internationallawoffice.com/Newsletters/Intellectual-Property/China/Wanhuida-Peksung/TRAB-rules-that-unusual-product-shape-is-eligible-for-3D-trademark-registration.

148. *Kaiping Weishida Seasoning v. Nestlé*, BHPC, 1750 *Gao Xing Zhong Zi* (2012). In this case Nestlé's application for the three-dimensional trade mark for the Maggi bottle was rejected based on a lack of distinctiveness according to Article 11 TML. Before Nestlé applied, there were already identical and similarly shaped bottles being used on the Chinese market. Nestlé could not provide sufficient evidence to prove the reputation of the disputed mark in China even though the bottle was created by Julius Maggi in 1886. Merges and Song, *supra* note 103, 552–557.

The absolute ground of refusal of Article 12 TML 2019 cannot be overcome. However, a functional three-dimensional mark could be protected in combination with other elements, according to Article 8 TML 2019.[149]

4. Relative Grounds of Refusal

Relative objections to registration and infringement are based on seniority of entitlements, whether prior marks or other prior rights.

Applications that conflict with prior registered marks, unregistered marks,[150] copyrights, design patents, portrait rights,[151] rights to a name,[152] etc., are excluded from trade mark registration.[153]

According to Article 31 TML 2019, where two or more applicants apply to register an identical or similar trade mark for identical or similar goods or services, the CTMO shall examine, approve and announce the trade mark that was applied earliest.

In respect of prior registered marks, the first-to-file principle applies. Since 2001, foreigners have been able to avail themselves to the rights of priority under the Paris Convention: to file a trade mark application within six months in one of the countries in the Paris Union based on the trade mark application in another country of the Paris Union or the exhibition of a good with the trade mark during an international exhibition. In both the foreign trade mark registration and international exhibition case, the applicant shall state in writing that it claims priority at the time when it files the application for trade mark registration and shall, within three months, submit a copy of the original application documents, or submit the name of the exhibition, and evidence supporting the use of the trade mark on the goods displayed, documents

149. Xiaomeng Dong and Jianjun Fu, China: 'Judgment of Distinctiveness of Trademarks Combining 3D Marks and Other Elements', Mondaq, 9 December 2016. Available at: http://www.mondaq.com/china/x/551480/Trademark/Judgment+Of+Distinctiveness+Of+Trademarks+Combining+3D+Marks+And.
150. Article 32 TML 2013 and 2019, *supra* note 15. Article 16(1) BHPC Guidelines 2019, *supra* note 5: "If a party concerned claims its legitimate prior rights and interests pursuant to Article 6 Anti-unfair Competition Law, then Article 32 TML may apply when hearing this case. The law providing the prior rights shall be generally taken as the basis for determining whether the application for registration of the trade mark in dispute violates the prior rights of others."
151. *Michael Jeffrey Jordan v. TRAB and Qiaodan Sports Co., Ltd.*, SPC, 27 *Xing Zai* (2016). 'Zhidao anli 113 hao: Maike'er · Jie fu li · Qiaodan yu guojia gongshang hang zheng guanli zongju shangbiao pingshen weiyuanhui, qiaodan ti yu gufen youxian gongsi "Qiadan" shangbiao zhengy xingzheng jiufen an' (Guiding Case No. 113: Michael Jeffrey Jordan and the TRAB of the SAIC, Jordan Sports Co., Ltd. "Jordan" trade mark dispute administrative dispute) Judicial Committee of the SPC, 14 January 2020. Available at: http://www.court.gov.cn/fabu-xiangqing-216751.html.
152. Article 32 TML also protects the prior right of a person's name, such as in the case of Dr. Li Wenliang, who sounded the alarm on COVID-19. The two companies who had filed his name as a trade mark withdrew their trade mark applications and apologized. Sun Yang, The intolerable misuse of trademark registration, CGTN, 2 March 2020.
153. Article 9(1) TML 2001, 2013 and 2019, *supra* note 15.

proving the date of the exhibition, etc. Failure to do so before the expiration of the time limit shall be regarded as not claiming priority.[154]

The proprietor of an unregistered well-known mark can oppose the registration of a trade mark that is an imitation or translation of its unregistered trade mark for identical or similar goods or services, or request invalidation of such a registered trade mark, where confusion in the market can be proven.[155]

(a) Identity, Similarity and Confusion

Likelihood of confusion is a criterion that is broader than trade mark similarity. Similarity is examined between the senior and junior trade mark and between the goods or services designated for the senior trade mark and those designated for the junior trade mark. But similarity does not necessarily lead to confusion.

Confusion can be presumed without factual proof that consumers assume there is an association between the cited trade mark and a consistent commercial source, in which case the most distinctive part of the trade mark is used by the contested trade mark.[156]

The registered trade mark rather than the trade mark actually used by the trade mark registrant shall be used for a comparison with the contested trade mark.

The level of attention consumers pay when buying a product is proportional to the value of the purchased product. The greater the value of the product, the more likely it is that more attention will be paid by consumers, and *vice versa*. Time also plays a factor. Generally speaking, consumers' cognitive ability tends to change with time. As knowledge grows, their ability to identify a certain mark with a consistent commercial source will become stronger and stronger.

(b) Similarity of Trade Marks

While Article 30 TML 2019 states that the CTMO shall reject an application of a trade mark that is identical or similar to a registered prior[157] trade mark and to its goods, according to the SPC during the presentation of the SPC Provisions 2016,[158]

154. Articles 25(2) and 26(6) TML 2019, *supra* note 15.
155. Article 13(2) TML 2001, 2013 and 2019, *supra* note 15.
156. 'Zai hou jingying zhe dui zai xian quanli de birang yiwu – jian ping zhongliang gongsi su jiayu gongsi "Changcheng" shangbiao qinquan yi an' (Late Operator's Obligation to Avoid Prior Rights – A Brief Comment on the Case of COFCO Sued Jiayu Company for "Great Wall" Trade Mark Infringement), 17 *China IP Magazine* (April 2007). Available at: http://www.chinaipmagazine.com/journal-show.asp?712.html.
157. If two or more applicants apply respectively on the same day for the registration of an identical or similar trade mark in respect of the same or similar goods, both or all of the applicants shall, within 30 days from the date of receipt of the notification of the CTMO, submit evidence of prior use of such trade mark before the application is filed.
158. Paul Ranjard, 'Likelihood Of Confusion And Dilution Clarified By The Supreme People's Court In Its Recent Interpretation Of The Revised Trademark Law', Wan Hui Da – Peksung IP Group, 23 June 2017. Available at: http://www.mondaq.com/china/x/604806/Trademark/Likelihood+Of+Confusion+And+Dilution+Clarified+By+The+Supreme+Peoples+Court+In+Its+Recent+Interpretation+Of+The+Revised+Trademark+Law.

the factors for determining a likelihood of confusion (Article 12 SPC Provisions 2016) should be taken into account. A "trade mark identical to" means that the later trade mark is compared with the earlier registered trade mark and the two trade marks are essentially without visual difference.[159] The font, pronunciation or meaning of the words or the composition or colouring of the device are similar, or the overall structure of its combined main elements is similar, or its three-dimensional shape and combination of colours are similar, thereby easily leading the relevant public to mistake the source of the products or to believe that their source has a certain connection to products using the plaintiff's registered trade mark.[160]

In short: the similarity of appearance, pronunciation or meaning between the cited and contested marks are elements of trade mark similarity, but they need to meet the threshold of "being sufficient to cause confusion or misconception amongst the relevant public", which is the necessary condition for constituting a conflicting trade mark similarity.[161]

The Chinese language has many homophones: Chinese words that are identical in sound and in the same tone, or similar when they are pronounced with the same consonants and vowels in another tone and are written using different characters. Examples of identical pronunciation are: yóuyú which can be written由于, which means "because of; due to" and 鱿鱼, which means "squid"; jìyì: 记忆, which means "remember" and 技艺, "skill; art".

Examples of similar pronunciations and different meaning are shī 尸 (corpse); shí 食 (food); shǐ使 (unusable); and shì 市 (market).

Then there are some characters that are similar but their pronunciation and meaning is different. For example: 日 is pronounced rì and means "sun" and 曰 is pronounced yuē and means "to say".

The BHPC states another category of similar word marks: "A meaningless trade mark composed of foreign letters, some letters and the arrangement order is the same as the cited mark, or although the arrangement order is different but the pronunciation and font are similar."[162]

In 2012, in *Audi AG v. TRAB*,[163] the BHPC made it clear that the protection of a stylized word mark comprising two identical letters lies in its unique appearance rather than the letters *per se*.[164]

On 29 March 2006, Audi AG filed for the international trade mark "TT" for various goods including "apparatus for locomotion by land, air or water" in Class 12. This trade mark was further extended to China on 12 October 2006 under the

159. Article 9(1) SPC Interpretation 2002, *infra* note 400.
160. Article 9(2) SPC Interpretation 2002, *infra* note 400.
161. Answer 11 of the BHPC to Several Questions in the Trial of Trade Mark Civil Dispute Cases, 18 February, Jinggao Fafa [2004] No. 48. Available at: https://v1.iphouse.cn/lawinfo/121.html?keyword=.
162. Answer 14(5) of the BHPC to Several Questions in the Trial of Trade Mark Civil Dispute Cases, 18 February, Jinggao Fafa [2004] No. 48. Available at: https://v1.iphouse.cn/lawinfo/121.html?keyword=.
163. BHPC, Administrative Judgment, 12 December, 1678 *Gao Xing Zhongzi* (2012).
164. Hu Gang, 'Beijing Court Issues Breakthrough Ruling on Similarity', *World Trademark Review*, June/July 2013, 88–89. Available at: https://www.worldtrademarkreview.com/article/5205265CFC76B6B0F646A33D62C3AD8648CEDC16/download.

Madrid Agreement. The CTMO refused the registration, citing an earlier Chinese trade mark "TT" which was filed on 23 December 2004 for other goods in Class 12. The similarity of goods analysis of this case will be dealt below under "Similarity of Goods and Services".

Audi AG filed for a review by the TRAB. In July 2010, the TRAB upheld the decision to refuse the registration. Audi AG filed an appeal with the BFIPC. The defendant and TRAB held that the opposed trade mark differed from the cited trade mark only in colour, which did not constitute a substantial difference according to the relevant provisions of the TML, especially Article 28 TML 2001.

Audi AG held that any comparison between the two marks should be based only on a correct perception of them in order to arrive at an objective and fair conclusion. Both the TRAB and Audi AG agreed that its applied for mark was formed of two identical figurative letters, which were capitalised, italicised and hollow. In contrast, the cited trade mark were two T's in black where the arms of both T's ran into each other so that consumers can perceive this as a device mark: a balance beam or a bridge with two pillars under it. Audi AG argued that the cited mark should be granted protection only for its special design, instead of the two letters *per se*, as to not monopolise these common letters.

The BFIPC accepted Audi AG's arguments and issued its judgment on 20 September 2011: the TRAB's review decision was not based on established facts and a proper application of law, and should thus be cancelled. The BHPC confirmed that, compared as a whole, the applied for mark was not similar to the cited mark.[165]

Graphic trade marks are compared in a similar manner as word marks: although there might be differences between the cited trade mark and the contested trade mark, if the overall impression given to the relevant public is the same, there is trade mark similarity; likewise if the two graphics are small and the composition and design are difficult to identify by the relevant public without close scrunity, as long as the overall appearance of the two graphics is similar. If the composition and design of the two graphics are similar, even if the colours or elements are different, they should be recognized as similar trade marks. However, if the two graphics reflect the same thing but the composition and design are different, they should not be recognized as similar trade marks.[166]

In case of marks that are combinations of text and graphics, there is trade mark similarity according to the BHPC if (1) the trade mark provides a similar overall impression; (2) the trade mark text is identical or similar; (3) the graphics are identical or similar; (4) other circumstances that can be determined as similar for combined trade marks.[167] with the last-mentioned, the BHPC might refer to situations where the colour schemes are identical.

165. BHPC, Administrative Judgment, 12 December, 1678 *Gao Xing Zhongzi* (2012).

166. Answer 15 of the BHPC to Several Questions in the Trial of Trade Mark Civil Dispute Cases, 18 February, Jinggao Fafa [2004] No. 48. Available at: https://v1.iphouse.cn/lawinfo/121.html?keyword=.

167. Answer 16 of the BHPC to Several Questions in the Trial of Trade Mark Civil Dispute Cases, 18 February, Jinggao Fafa [2004] No. 48. Available at: https://v1.iphouse.cn/lawinfo/121.html?keyword=.

The *Gao Wenxin v. De Beers Centenary AG*[168] case illustrates trade mark similarity based on the identical meaning of the marks which lead to confusion. If the Chinese characters "永恒印记", which mean Forevermark are used on a Chinese trade mark to translate the meaning of the foreign trade mark "FOREVERMARK", there is similarity. Since the cited and contested marks were both used for diamonds, this led to a likelihood of confusion.

Article 10 SPC Interpretation 2002 adds the following principles to determine identity or similarity:[169]

(1) Taking into account the general attention of the relevant public as the standard - the BHPC interprets this standard as based on the degree of ordinary attention given by the relevant public with general knowledge and experience of the relevant goods when purchasing goods.[170]

(2) Both the overall comparison of the trade mark and the comparison of the main elements of the trade mark must be carried out, in other words the comparison should be carried out both as a whole and separately for the individual elements - the question is whether the main part of a trade mark affects the overall impression of the relevant public on the trade mark.

If there is a part of the registered trade mark where the exclusive right was waived (disclaimer), the entire registered trade mark including the part where the exclusive right was waived should still be used for comparison.[171]

Disclaimer statements by the applicants can help examiners distinguish between the main elements and the decorative or descriptive elements in a trade mark, especially when the disclaimed elements are not in a prominent position.[172]

However, the disclaimed portion of the trade mark application should not be excluded from consideration during the trade mark examination and could conflict with the prior rights of others. This insight was developed in the following case law:

An administrative lawsuit was filed against the rejection of the trade mark application of "MATERIA" over the cited trade mark "GNMaterials and device", by the Beijing IP Court in 2015. The trade mark holder of the cited trade mark "GNMaterials" had disclaimed the exclusive right to use "Materials". The Beijing IP Court decided that it is feasible to only compare the non-disclaimed portion: to compare the words "GN" and the device part of the cited trade mark with "MATERIA" in the trade mark application, when determining whether the two marks constitute similar trade marks. [173]

168. SPC, 49 *Zhai Xingzi* (2014).
169. SPC Interpretation 2002, *infra* note 400.
170. Answer 9 of the BHPC to Several Questions in the Trial of Trade Mark Civil Dispute Cases, 18 February, Jinggao Fafa [2004] No. 48. Available at: https://v1.iphouse.cn/lawinfo/121.html?keyword=.
171. Answer 13 of the BHPC to Several Questions in the Trial of Trade Mark Civil Dispute Cases, 18 February, Jinggao Fafa [2004] No. 48. Available at: https://v1.iphouse.cn/lawinfo/121.html?keyword=.
172. 'China: How Do Trademark Disclaimers Affect Similarity Examination', AFD China, 20 May 2020. Available at: https://www.mondaq.com/china/trademark/936428/how-do-trademark-disclaimers-affect-similarity-examination.
173. Beijing IP Court, 2610 *Jing Zhixing Chuzi* (2015).

The TRAB appealed the BHPC judgment and pointed out that although the owner of the cited trade mark had disclaimed the exclusive right to that particular portion of its trade mark, it did not have an effect on consumers. The BHPC ruled that the disclaimed portion of the trade mark should be considered as an indivisible part of the trade mark and should thus be included in the overall comparison.[174]

(3) In judging whether trade marks are similar, the distinctiveness and popularity of the registered trade marks requested for protection shall be considered[175] – there is sufficient trade mark similarity to cause confusion and misunderstanding in the relevant public if the relevant public mistakenly believes that the goods marked by the contested trade mark and the cited trade mark are from the same commercial source, or even though they believe that the goods marked by the two are from different commercial sources, they mistakenly believe that there is an operational, organizational or legal connection between the two commercial sources.[176]

In the "FOREVERMARK" case, the SPC decided that the level of awareness of the meaning of the English mark "FOREVERMARK" was high amongst the relevant public; that there was correlation and congruity of the meaning of the cited and contested marks. These similar marks were both used in the sales of diamonds and were thus considered confusing.[177]

In the "FOREVERMARK" case, the SPC also made it clear that the same standards for assessing similarity apply whether in examination or infringement action.[178] The SPC confirmed this in a presentation of the SPC Provisions 2016, in that the factors of Article 12 SPC Provisions 2016 which were drafted for administrative disputes should also be taken into account for Article 57(2) TML, even though this provision is for civil disputes.[179] Thus, both determining similarity of marks and similarity of services is judged by the same criteria in administrative proceedings and civil litigation.

In September 2004, wine producer China Great Wall Wine Co., Ltd., a subsidiary of the COFCO Group, sued Beijing Jiayu Oriental Wine Co., Ltd. (Jiayu Company) for infringement of its "GREAT WALL" trade mark at the BHPC and requested the Court to order Jiayu Company to cease its infringing activities and pay RMB 100 million in economic compensation. China Great Wall Wine Co., Ltd uses the English words "great" and "wall" as one word, the Chinese characters "长城葡萄酒" which mean Great Wall Grape Wine, and a depiction of the Great Wall on the wine label. In short, it used three different expressions of the same concept "Great Wall". Although there

174. BHPC, 32999 *Gaoxing Zhongzi* (2015).
175. See also: Chen Jiamin, 'Shangbiao xiangsi xing de rending' (Identification of trade mark similarity), 16 *China IP Magazine* (February 2007). Available at: http://www.chinaipmagazine.com/journal-show.asp?181.html.
176. Answer 12 of the BHPC to Several Questions in the Trial of Trade Mark Civil Dispute Cases, 18 February, Jinggao Fafa [2004] No. 48. Available at: https://v1.iphouse.cn/lawinfo/121.html?keyword=.
177. Cindy Kang, 'Judging Similarity Between Chinees and English Language Marks', *Rouse Magazine Editor*, 7 Jul 2015. Available at: https://www.rouse.com/magazine/news/judging-similarity-between-chinese-and-english-language-marks/.
178. Kang, *supra* note 177.
179. Ranjard, *supra* note 158.

were some differences in the overall composition, Jiayu also used "Great Wall" in words and device.

In April 2005, the BHPC found Jiayu Company had infringed China Great Wall Wine Co., Ltd.'s trade mark and ordered the production and sales of "Jiayu Great Wall" wine to be immediately stopped upon the effective date of the judgment. In addition, Jiayu Company should pay RMB 15,527,479 in compensation within ten days. Jiayu Company appealed to the SPC. On 10 August 2006, the SPC held that Jiayu Company used similar marks on similar products without the permission of China Great Wall Wine Co., Ltd., which constituted a violation of the exclusive right to use a registered trade mark, and Jiayu should immediately cease using the production and sale of "JIAYU GREAT WALL" marks and graphical representation of the Great Wall, and compensate RMB 10,614,090 for economic losses within ten days from the effective date of the judgment.[180] The registered trade mark "GREAT WALL" had been on the register for a long time, enjoyed a good market reputation and was recognized as a well-known mark by the SAIC. The "GREAT WALL" trade mark is distinctive as a source indicator to China Great Wall Wine Co., Ltd. and acquired popularity among the relevant public, and Jiayu Company was destroying its referential function that was already formed. Because of the similar constituting elements and the distinctiveness and popularity of the "GREAT WALL" trade mark, the possibility of consumer confusion in the market was considered extremely high.

Zhang Hui argued that if the distinctive part of a trade mark is A + B, any trade mark used by others that contains A, B or A + B constitutes similarity, regardless of whether prefixes or suffixes[181] or other modifications with different shapes, sounds and meaning are added.

Cashbox Partyworld Co., Ltd v. Long You Jin Qian Gui Entertainment Co., Ltd. and Long You Hao Le Di Fitness Co., Ltd, provides an example that a prefix cannot prevent trade mark similarity. In this case the cited mark was "钱柜" and the contested mark 金钱柜.[182]

However, in *Daikin Industry Co., Ltd. v. TRAB*, see above, the prefix and suffix were used as a factor to distinguish between the opposed trade mark "イダイキンさガイジ" and the translation "ダイキン" of the cited trade mark "大金" and "DAIKIN".

Local standards are applied in respect of trade marks in the English language. For example, if an English trade mark might be spelt the same as a Chinese trade mark in *pinyin* (see more about Chinese characters above), this would make it identical or similar.[183]

The CTMO and TRAB have acknowledged that a junior two-dimensional mark that is identical with or similar to the graphical representation of a senior

180. SPC 10 August 2006, 5 *Min San Zhong Zi* (2005).
181. As could also be seen in the DAIKIN case. *Infra* note 182.
182. 225 *Zhe Qu Zhi Chu Zi* (2015).
183. 'Shangbiao jinsi huo xiangtong, shangbiao ju de panduan yiju shi shenme?' (If the trade marks are similar or identical, what is the basis of the Trade Mark Office's judgment?), Yixiu Intellectual Property, 12 August 2019. Available at: https://zhuanlan.zhihu.com/p/77727112.

three-dimensional mark is likely to confuse the relevant public with regard to the source of the goods or services, and vice versa[184]

(c) *Similarity of Goods or Services*

The term "similar goods" means goods that have identical functions, uses, production entities, sales channels, target consumers, etc., or goods that the relevant public would normally consider to have a certain connection and thus easily cause confusion.[185] "Similar services" means services whose purpose, content, method of provision, target users, etc., are identical or services that the relevant public would normally consider to have a certain connection and thus easily cause confusion.[186] "Similar goods and services" means that a certain connection exists between the goods and services that could easily cause the relevant public to be confused.[187]

The "relevant public" are consumers related to the type of product or service branded with the trade mark or business operators that have a close connection to the marketing of the aforementioned product or service.[188] Their observation of the trade mark's distinctiveness, notoriety and proximity of the designated goods and service is the standard to determine their identity or similarity.

(d) *Market Conditions when Assessing Similarity of Goods*

In *Audi AG v. TRAB*, the BHPC also made it clear that due attention should be given by official guidance such as the Similar Goods and Services Classification Book, but that market conditions should also be taken into account.[189]

On 29 March 2006, Audi AG filed for the international trade mark "TT" for various goods including "apparatus for locomotion by land air or water" in Class 12. This trade mark was further extended to China on 12 October 2006 under the Madrid Agreement. After substantial examination, the CTMO refused the registration, citing an earlier Chinese trade mark "TT" which was filed on 23 December 2004 for "clutches for land vehicle; engines for land vehicle; brakes for land vehicle; pumps (auto parts); vehicle chassis; turbine for land vehicle; shock absorbers for land vehicle; transmission boxes for land vehicle; vehicle axles; power setting for land vehicle" in Class 12.

The BFIPC held that the goods designated by the compared marks were not similar due to their different functions, usages, commercial channels and targeted consumers. Therefore, the TRAB's review decision was cancelled and it was ordered to issue a new review decision to approve the registration in respect of "apparatus for locomotion by land".

184. Standards for Trade Mark Examination and Trial 2016, *supra* note 88, 102.
185. Article 11(1) SPC Interpretation 2002, *infra* note 400.
186. Article 11(2) SPC Interpretation 2002, *infra* note 400.
187. Article 11(3) SPC Interpretation 2002, *infra* note 400.
188. Article 8 SPC Interpretation 2002, *infra* note 400.
189. Hu Gang, 'Beijing Court Issues Breakthrough Ruling on Similarity', *World Trademark Review*, June/July 2013, 88–89. Available at: https://www.worldtrademarkreview.com/article/5205265CFC76B6B0F646A33D62C3AD8648CEDC16/download.

The goods covered by the subject mark applied for (i.e., "apparatus for locomotion by land") were closely related to those covered by the cited mark (i.e., "clutches for land vehicles"). Further, according to the Classification of Similar Goods and Services Book, the goods classed as "apparatus for locomotion by land" and the auto parts covered by "clutches for land vehicles" both fall into Sub-class 1202.

Audi AG argued that the automobile industry embodies a country's machinery manufacturing industry where a finished car is made up of thousands of parts and accessories, and results from the coordination and cooperation of many relevant upstream and downstream companies.

The TRAB held that the goods designated "apparatus for locomotion by land" by the applied for mark were similar to the parts and accessories of vehicles covered by the cited trade mark. The only basis for such a judgment is the Classification of Similar Goods and Services Book.

Audi AG held that those goods are different in function and purpose: goods that fall under the sub-class "apparatus for locomotion by land" are used to transform mechanical energy into kinetic energy in the process of freight transportation, so as to speed up logistics operations; while a part or accessory can only be combined with other parts of a vehicle to form the transmission system, the driving system, the steering system or other systems in order to realize a specific function."[190] Audi AG argued that goods within the sub-class "apparatus for locomotion by land" are directed at drivers of vehicles, but parts and accessories of vehicles are directed at manufacturers or maintainers of vehicles. These categories of consumers might overlap, but end users usually buy a car from a showroom of a particular brand, and purchase parts from the relevant accessories dealer. In short: the goods under comparison have different sales and distribution markets and channels. Because of the difference in function, purpose, manufacturer, consumers and sales channels, consumers with common sense familiar with the market would be unlikely to be confused by the goods designated by the two marks. This was confirmed by the BHPC.[191] Therefore, the TRAB's review decision was cancelled and it was ordered to issue a new review decision to approve the registration in respect of "apparatus for locomotion by land".

Article 18 Opinions of the SPC on Several Issues Concerning the Utilization of the Judicial Function of IPRs to Promote the Development and Prosperity of Socialist Culture and Economy[192] states:

> Discretionary legal standards, regarding similarity of trade marks, similarity of goods, prior use of trade marks that are already of certain influence, obtainment of trade mark registration by fraud or other unjustifiable means, etc., shall be appropriately applied in light of the popularity, distinctiveness, etc. of the trade marks. Whether trade mark registration applicants or registrants have a real intention to use the trade marks shall be well identified, and the subjective malice shall be determined in consideration of imitation of famous brands in

190. Hu Gang, *supra* note 189.
191. BHPC, Administrative Judgment, 12 December, 1678 *Gao Xing Zhongzi* (2012).
192. Opinions of the SPC on Several Issues Concerning the Utilization of the Judicial Function of IPRs to Promote the Development and Prosperity of Socialist Culture and Economy Fafa [2011] No. 18

> the process of trade mark use. The relevant provisions of the TL shall be applied sufficiently and correctly to strengthen containment of malicious pre-emptive registration, imitation of famous brands, and other improper acts and fully embody the orientation of law for the protection of trade mark rights.

In accordance with these Opinions, the TRAB held the following elements to be grounds to derogate from the Similar Goods and Services Classification Book: the prior mark has significant distinctiveness; the prior mark has obtained a certain reputation; the contested trade mark is confusingly similar to the prior mark; the goods or services on which the contested trade mark was designated have strong relevance to the goods or services approved for use of the prior mark; the bad faith of the owner of contested trade mark is obvious; the registration or use of the contested trade mark is likely to cause confusion and misunderstanding among the relevant public.

In the same vein, CNIPA decided that the disputed trade mark "地素佳人" (Di Su Jia Ren) designated on "shower caps" and the citations "地素" (Di Su) designated on "clothing; shoes; hats; hosiery; gloves (clothing); scarves; belts (clothing); down garments" goods, as similar trade marks on similar goods, would cause a likelihood of consumer confusion. The contested trade mark was designated for "shower caps" which is considered dissimilar to one of the citations according to the Similar Goods and Services Classification Book. However, CNIPA considered the "intention of confusion" to be a strong argument to derogate from the Similar Goods and Services Classification Book and affirm similarity in accordance with Article 30 TML. The goods that have been refused at the stage of examination can be used to deduce that the applicant of the contested trade mark was in bad faith with the "intention of confusion".[193]

(e) *Presumption of Confusion in Case of Double Identity*

For the first time, Article 57(2) TML 2013 explicitly mentioned a presumed likelihood of confusion in case of identical or similar marks for identical or similar goods. Similarity in trade marks and products alone does not necessarily lead to confusion. Feng observed that similar trade marks on identical or similar goods could belong to different owners who could still enjoy separate reputational benefits with consumers that are able to distinguish between these trade marks in a specific market.[194]

According to the principle confirmed by the SPC in its *Jia Yu Chang Cheng v. Chang Cheng Pai* judgment, likelihood of confusion can be established through presumption without the burden of proof of actual confusion, as long as a later mark contains the distinctive element of an existing registered trade mark which may easily

193. Cissy Zhou and Cai Chongshan, 'New Approach for Similarity Judgment of Cross-class Goods', King & Wood Mallesons, 7 August 2020. Available at: https://www.chinalawinsight.com/2020/08/articles/intellectual-property/new-approach-for-similarity-judgment-of-cross-class-goods/.

194. Feng, *supra* note 7, 131.

cause consumers to believe there is some special connection between such other trade marks and the existing registered trade mark.[195]

Applications Made by the Trade Mark Agent Without the Principal's Approval

Article 15(1) TML 2019 states that where an agent or a representative applies for registration of a trade mark of the principal or the represented party in the agent's or the representative's own name without authorization, the trade mark shall not be registered and shall be prohibited from use upon opposition from the principal or the represented party. Article 15 SPC Provisions 2016 already made it clear that the CTMO was prohibited from approving applications for trade marks identical or similar to that of the party on the same or similar goods being represented by trade mark agents or representatives who do not have the proper authorization.[196]

According to Article 15(2) TML 2019, beside the trade mark agency-client relationship, there are representatives that are clearly aware of the existence of an unregistered mark used by another party, due to a contractual, commercial or other relationship with the latter. Such other relationship includes if the trade mark applicant is kin to the prior user; has labour relations with the prior user; or is in the proximity of the prior user's business location; or if the trade mark applicant and the prior user have negotiated for the conclusion of an agency or representative relationship, but such relation has not been concluded.[197]

5. Ownership of Natural and Legal Persons, Joint Ownership

Since 2001, natural persons, next to legal persons and other organizations, can apply for trade marks if they have the intention to acquire the exclusive right to use a trade mark for goods produced, manufactured, processed, selected or marketed by them.[198]

Two or more natural persons, legal persons, or other organizations can jointly apply to the CTMO for the registration of the same trade mark, and jointly own and exercise the right to exclusively use the registered trade mark.[199] If one holds that trade marks are a species of property, then the General Principles of Civil Law 1986

195. Harry Yang and Liu Ying, 'The Determination of Trademark Proximity in the Case Study of "长城" Trademark Infringement', 16 *China IP Magazine* (February 2007). Available at: http://www.chinaipmagazine.com/en/journal-show.asp?id=356.
196. Article 15 SPC Provisions 2016, *supra* note 112.
197. Article 16 SPC Provisions 2016, *supra* note 112.
198. Article 4(1) TML 2001, 2013 and 2019, *supra* note 15. Compare this with Article 96 General Principles of Civil Law 1986: "The rights to exclusive use of trade marks obtained by legal persons, individual businesses and individual partnerships shall be protected by law." General Principles of Civil Law, adopted at the Fourth Session of the Sixth National People's Congress on 12 April 1986 and promulgated by Order No. 37 of the President on 12 April 1986, effective as of 1 January 1987. Available at: http://english.mofcom.gov.cn/article/lawsdata/chineselaw/200211/20021100049916.shtml.
199. Article 5 TML 2001, 2013 and 2019, *supra* note 15.

already allowed joint ownership.[200] The General Rules of the Civil Law 2017 define property rights as the exclusive rights to directly dominate a specific object, including ownership and the right to use,[201] and states that civil subjects enjoy the exclusive trade mark rights of the persons,[202] and thus that the exclusive trade mark right can be, at least, analogized as a property right.[203] Some commentators have argued that IP Laws, including the TML, need to be incorporated into the planned Special Rules of the Civil Law.[204]

6. Registration Procedures

(a) *Classes of Goods and Services*

Since 1994, China has adopted the Nice Classification system. The CTMO formulated and promulgated the Classification of Goods and Services for the registration of trade marks.[205] The CTMO follows WIPO's International Classification of Goods and Services for the Purpose of Registration of Trade Marks to a certain extent. The 2019 version of the eleventh edition of the Nice Classification (NCL) came into force on 1 January 2019.[206] It uses the 45 classes; 34 classes for goods and 11 classes for services, as the basis to make the Similar Goods and Services Classification Table.[207] This Table includes the goods and services not listed in WIPO's international classification, and provides the subclasses within each of the 45 classes designed according to the similarity of the goods or services, and categorized into identities of basic numbers of six digits.[208] An uncertainty is caused by goods and services that may be related even if they fall within different subclasses, or goods and services that may be unrelated even within the same class. However, in most cases, the goods or the services falling in different subclasses are not regarded as similar by the CTMO. This means that similar or identical marks can be registered within the same class because their specifications fall in different subclasses.

200. Article 78 General Principles of Civil Law 1986 distinguishes between co-ownership by shares and common ownership, *supra* note 198.
201. Article 114 General Rules of the Civil Law 2017, *infra* note 420.
202. Article 123(3) General Rules of the Civil Law 2017, *infra* note 420.
203. Adam Mossoff, 'Trademark as a Property Right', George Mason Law & Economics Research Paper No. 17-15 (25 March 2017). Available at: https://ssrn.com/abstract=2941763. See also, Brian Frye, 'Metaphors on Trademark: A Response to Adam Mossoff, "Trademark as a Property Right" (9 September 2018)', 107 *Ky. L.J. Online* (2019), 1. Available at: https://ssrn.com/abstract=3246704.
204. Chun Liu Chun and Kung-Chung Liu, 'On the Necessity of Incorporating IP Laws into the Civil Law of China and How', in Kung-Chung Liu and Uday S. Racherla (eds.), *Innovation, Economic Development, and Intellectual Property in India and China* (ARCIALA Series on Intellectual Assets and Law in Asia, Springer, Singapore 2019).
205. Article 93(1) IRTL 2014, *supra* note 12.
206. NCL (11-2019). Available at: https://www.wipo.int/classifications/nice/en/ITsupport/Version20190101/index.html.
207. Article 13 IRTL 2014, *supra* note 12.
208. An overview is provided by ChinaTM.hk. Available at: https://www.chinatm.hk/en/nice-classification/class-1/index.html.

If an applicant is filing in a subclass not in the exact wording of the Similar Goods and Services Classification Table, the CTMO will send a notice to amend the application. The advantage of filing a national application instead of an international registration is that idiosyncratic Chinese subclasses can be applied for.[209] The disadvantage of filing a national application in different classes is that when there is an office action or opposition against one class of goods or service, it can hold up the application for all classes. Multiple single-class applications could avoid this hold-up.[210]

If an applicant who runs a shopping mall, a supermarket or otherwise, can prove that it cooperates with the sellers in its offer of the site or other means, and sufficiently confirms that it provides advice, planning, publicity, consultation and other services for selling the goods, then the trade mark may be determined to be used on the services of "sales promotion for others".[211]

(b) Domestic Applications

One can apply for registration directly with the CTMO. After a formal examination and a substantial examination, the trade mark is preliminarily approved for registration and published in the Trade Mark Gazette (see below).

As of 20 May 2020, both standard and non-standard specifications of acceptable goods and services can be applied for online. Before that date, only standard specifications could be applied for online, and the non-standard specifications on paper.[212] Non-standard specifications are acceptable as long as the descriptions are specific, accurate, standardized, and consistent with the classification principle.

In the first half of 2019, the number of pending trade mark applications was 3.438 million, a decrease of 4.1% compared to the first half of 2018. The number of actually registered trade marks stood at 3.515 million, an increase of 67.8% compared to the first half of 2018. As of the end of June 2019, the number of valid trade mark registrations was 22.743 million, a year-on-year increase of 35.3%.[213] To accommodate for the massive numbers, many new examiners were hired, which puts pressure on the quality of the examinations. In order to streamline the process, the CTMO has launched an e-filing system on 1 September 2018. Instead of the one to two months it takes in the case of paper filings, applicants now receive a filing number within 24 hours.[214]

---

209. Rice, *supra* note 3.
210. Rice, *supra* note 3.
211. Article 19(14) BHPC Guidelines 2019, *supra* note 5.
212. Hins Li and Jady Yuchan Xu, 'China: Trademark Filings Now Completely Electronic', INTA 29 July 2020. Available at: https://www.inta.org/perspectives/china-trademark-filings-now-completely-electronic/.
213. 'Guojia zhishi chanquan ju fabu 2019 nian shang bannian shuju: Zhuyao zhibiao fuhe yuqi zonghe shili wenbu tisheng' (CNIPA released data for the first half of 2019: The main indicators are in line with expectations, and the overall strength has been steadily improved), CNIPA, 9 July 2019. Available at: http://sbj.cnipa.gov.cn/gzdt/201907/t20190709_303293.html.
214. 'Prosecuting Trademarks in China: An Insider's Guide for Foreign Brand Owners in 2019 (Part I)', SIPS, 31 March 2019. Available at: https://sips.asia/knowledge/

In the domestic application process, there might be some variation within the classes of goods and services in respect of the duration of the application process. For example, Class 25 for clothing and footwear, has many applications, thus the process might take a bit longer. The duration of a domestic application is typically six months, while the time frame for an international publication is nine months.

In the process of trade mark registration, if a party files a claim under Article 13 TML 2019, the CTMO may determine whether the trade mark is a well-known mark if it is necessary for examination or handling the case. See section XI on Scope of Protection of Well-known Marks for further details.

(c) International Applications

The Madrid Agreement made it possible for Contracting Parties to extend the registration to their own jurisdiction and obtain a bundle of national trade marks whereby each Contracting Party would examine the application separately. China is party to both the Madrid Agreement 1979[215] and Madrid Protocol 1989,[216] to which it acceded in 1989 and 1995, respectively. The two agreements operate independently and in parallel, and together are called the Madrid System. Their common implementation rules are dealt with by the Common Regulations under the Madrid Agreement Concerning the International Registration of Marks and the Protocol Relating to that Agreement, as in force on 1 February 2019.[217]

Since China was a party to the Paris Convention, it could become a member of the Special Union for the International Registration Marks.[218] Nationals of any of the contracting countries may, in all the other countries party to this Agreement, secure protection for their marks applicable to goods or services, registered in the country of origin, by filing the said marks at the International Bureau, through the intermediary of the Office of the said country of origin.[219] Thus, after registering a trade mark at the CTMO in Chinese,[220] extension to other parties to the Madrid

trademark-registration/prosecuting-trademarks-in-china-an-insiders-guide-for-foreign-brand-owners-in-2019-part-1/.

215. Madrid Agreement Concerning the International Registration of Marks, adopted on 28 September 1979, entered into force on 23 October 1983. Available at: https://wipolex.wipo.int/en/treaties/textdetails/12599.

216. Protocol Relating to the Madrid Agreement Concerning the International Registration of Marks, adopted on 27 June 1989, entered into force on 1 December 1995. Available at: https://wipolex.wipo.int/en/treaties/textdetails/12911.

217. Common Regulations under the Madrid Agreement Concerning the International Registration of Marks and the Protocol Relating to that Agreement, WIPO, adopted and as in force on 1 February 2019. Available at: https://wipolex.wipo.int/en/text/509449.

218. Article 14(2)(a) Madrid Agreement 1979, *supra* note 215.

219. Article 1(2) Madrid Agreement 1979, *supra* note 215.

220. Article 3 SAIC IR Measures 2003: "Whoever applies for international registration of a trade mark with China as the country of origin shall have a genuine and effective industrial and commercial business place in China, or have its domicile in China, or have the nationality of China." SAIC Measures for the Implementation of International Registration of Marks under the Madrid Agreement of 2003. Available at: http://www.cta.org.cn/english/LawsRegulations/201608/t20160811_41892.html. Article 47 IRTL 2014, *supra* note 12.

Agreement can be requested by completing an international registration which must be submitted in French to the International Bureau. Or, after registering a trade mark at the trade mark office of a party to the Madrid Agreement, international registration can be extended to China. These international registrations will be accepted by the International Bureau if they satisfy the formal requirements and will then be sent to the national offices of the countries the applicant has designated. In the national phase, the national offices will do a substantive examination of the application and have 12 months to reject the trade mark. If the national offices approve the trade mark, it will be valid for 20 years[221] and renewable for additional 20-year periods.[222] For the first five years after the date of priority, registrations by the national offices are dependent on the registration in the country of origin. The registrations are all lost if the registration in the country of origin is declared invalid or cancelled during the first five years after the date of priority. This is called a "central attack".

The Madrid Protocol was conceived to solve some of the problems that trade mark applicants met under the Madrid Agreement. In case of a "central attack", the applicant can transform its international registration to one or more individual national or regional registrations in the countries or regions in which the mark was protected,[223] and can still benefit from the date of priority of the cancelled international registration. The CTMO makes a stringent examination of an application for substitution of an international registration for a domestic application.[224]

The international registration of the Madrid Protocol can be based not only on the registration but also the application of a trade mark at the Office of origin.[225] National offices have 12 months or 18 months to refuse a trade mark.[226] If the trade mark is accepted, the registration is valid for ten years and renewable for further ten-year periods.

Where the Madrid Agreement required the applicant to submit its international registration in French, the Madrid Protocol has extended the possible submission languages with English and Spanish.[227] As well as countries, the Madrid Protocol allows territories and intergovernmental organizations (IGOs) to become party to the Protocol.[228]

China's Implementation of the Madrid System

Since 2013, the TML stipulates that the international registration of trade marks shall comply with the rules established by the relevant international treaties concluded or

221. Article 6(1) Madrid Agreement 1979, *supra* note 215.
222. Article 7(1) Madrid Agreement 1979, *supra* note 215.
223. Article 9*quinquies* Madrid Protocol 1989, *supra* note 216.
224. The CTMO requires that the sample photographs of the international registration be exactly identical with that of the domestic trade mark, the goods or services designated by the international registration fully cover all the goods or services of the domestic registration. Any small variation in the form or words or inconsistence in the goods or services designated is likely to result in the refusal of the application.
225. Article 3(1) Madrid Protocol 1989, *supra* note 216.
226. Article 5(2)(a) and (b) Madrid Protocol 1989, *supra* note 216.
227. Article 16(1)(a) Madrid Protocol 1989, *supra* note 216.
228. Article 2(4) Madrid Protocol 1989, *supra* note 216.

acceded by China, referring to the Madrid System.[229] It adds that the State Council shall develop specific measures.[230]

As pointed out above, the CTMO does not accept certain non-standard coverage for a national registration, because it is not identical to the wording of the Nice Classification. However, as long as WIPO accepts the identities of the goods or services, they will almost always be accepted in China and merely translated into Chinese and placed in relevant similarity subgroups.[231] Rice pointed to the main exception: identities that run against current CTMO policy, such as for "retail services" in Class 35 (even though WIPO would accept it, that exact identifier is not yet accepted in China).[232] According to Rice, extending an international regulation to China usually leaves significant subgroup coverage gaps in each class, giving free rein to trade mark squatters.[233]

Once entering into the national phase, the CTMO may deny extension of protection based on national law and will notify the International Bureau. Proprietors may apply to the TRAB for a review of such decisions. International trade mark registrants who need to deal with the CTMO, TRAB or the courts, relating to international registration of trade marks, should appoint a qualified trade mark agency recognized by the PRC in relation to the relevant matters.

If the mark of international registration is a three-dimensional, colour combination, sound, collective or certification mark, the applicant for the territory extension of an international registration designating China should submit, under the relevant provisions, proof of qualification for use of such a mark and the regulations for managing the use of the mark to the CTMO through a trade mark agency within three months from the date of registration of the mark in the International Register of the International Bureau of WIPO.[234] If the proof and regulations or any other certifying documents are not submitted within this time limit, the CTMO will refuse the application filed for territory extension of said marks. Any applicant designating China to protect the international registration of trade marks may, as of the date when the time limit for rejection of its trade mark has expired, entrust a trade mark agency to apply to the CTMO for issuing the certificate proving that its trade mark has been protected in China.[235] At the expiry of the time limit, an international registration is automatically protected in China whether the examination was finalized or not.

In the Guiding Case 114, the SPC held that applicants for international registration of trade marks should be given a reasonable chance to submit supplements and make corrections to the application documents. In its international registration, Christian Dior made it clear that it applied for a three-dimensional trade mark for the "J'adore" perfume bottle, but did not submit the three photos as required. Because of this omission, the TRAB examined the trade mark as a common trade mark and

229. Article 21 TML 2013 and 2019, *supra* note 15.
230. Article 21 TML 2013 and 2019, *supra* note 15.
231. Rice, *supra* note 3.
232. Rice, *supra* note 3.
233. Rice, *supra* note 3.
234. Article 43 IRTL 2014, *supra* note 12.
235. Article 20 SAIC IR Measures 2003, *supra* note 220.

held it not distinctive. Neither the Beijing IP Court,[236] nor the BHPC[237] corrected this mistake. The SPC held that "[w]hen the information applied for the international registration of a trade mark lacks only partial views and other formal requirements stipulated in the Implementing Regulations of the Trade Mark Law, the trade mark administrative agency shall uphold the spirit of actively fulfilling the obligations of the international conventions and give the applicant reasonable opportunities for corrections."[238]

(d) Form of Application and Additional Documents Required

The format of the documents for applying for trade mark registration or for other trade mark matters have been formulated and promulgated by the CTMO and the TRAB.[239]

China's regulators are pursuing a policy of real-name registration both for online platforms[240] and for business licences and trade mark registrations.[241]

The filing date of an application for trade mark registration shall be the date on which the application documents are received by the CTMO.[242] In applying for

236. Beijing IP Court, Administrative Judgment, 29 September, 3047 *Jing 73 Xingchu* (2016).
237. BHPC, Administrative Judgment, 23 May, 744 *Jing Xing Zhong* (2017), Administrative Judgment.
238. 'Zhidao anli 114 hao: Kelisidi ang di'ao er xiangliao gongsi su guojia gongshang hang zheng guangli zongju shangbiao pingshen weiyuanhui shangbiao shengqing bohui hui fu xingzheng jiufen an' (Guiding Case No. 114: *Christian Dior Perfumery Company v. TRAB SAIC* trade mark application refusal review administrative dispute), Judicial Committee of the SPC, 14 January 2020, para 2. Available at: http://www.court.gov.cn/fabu-xiangqing-216761.html.

    See also: *Christian Dior Perfumes LLC v. TRAB*, SPC, 26 *Zui Gao Fa Xing Zai* (2018). WIPO, *WIPO Collection of Leading Judgments on Intellectual Property Rights People's Republic of China (2011–2018)*. Available at: https://www.wipo.int/edocs/pubdocs/en/wipo_pub_1065.pdf.
239. Article 93(2) IRTL 2014, *supra* note 12.
240. Chow makes it clear that even though each business licence contains a unique 18-digit number known as the "unified social credit code" (Administrative Measures for Online Trading, promulgated by the SAIC, Order No. 60, 26 January 2014, effective 15 March 2014), which includes the name and address of the business entity, the name of the legal representative, e-commerce platforms often do not require the online traders that make use of their site to register this information with them. Daniel Chee King Chow, 'Why China's Crackdown on Commercial Bribery Threatens Multinational Companies in China', 31 *Ariz. J. Int'l and Comp. L.* (2014), 23–25. Available at SSRN: https://ssrn.com/abstract=2443926.
241. Article 14 IRTL 2014, *supra* note 12. If an application is filed for registration, modification, assignment, renewal, opposition or cancellation of a trade mark, the applicant shall submit documents certifying its identity.

    Examples are a copy of the applicant's certificate of incorporation or good standing, or in the case of individual applicants, a copy of their passport. How to Register Trademarks in China, SIPS Asia, 1 June 2016. Available at: https://sips.asia/knowledge/trademark-registration/how-to-register-trademarks-in-china/.
242. Article 18(1) IRTL 2014, *supra* note 12. Article 18(2) IRTL 2014, *supra* note 12. If the application formalities for trade mark registration are completed, the application documents are filled in as required, and the fees are paid, the CTMO shall accept the application

registration of a trade mark, an application shall be prepared and submitted based on the published Similar Goods and Services Classification Table.[243] If the actually used or approved goods are not the same as the titles of standard goods or services provided in the Similar Goods and Services Classification Table, the determination of the category of the specific goods shall comprehensively take into account those goods' functions, use, production department, consumption channels and consumer groups as well as the effects of the market factors (including consumption habits, production patterns, industry management needs) on the nature or title of the goods.[244] For each application for trade mark registration, one copy of the Application for Trade Mark Registration and one copy of the reproduction of the trade mark[245] shall be submitted to the CTMO.[246] Here, too, it shall be explicitly stated in the application whether the trade mark is a three-dimensional mark, a colour combination, a sound mark or a collective or certification mark.

In the application, three views of a three-dimensional mark need to be submitted. In the application form, it shall be declared that the sound mark meets the requirements.[247] If an application is filed for registration of a collective or a certification mark, documents certifying the qualifications of the applicants and the rules on the administration of use of the trade mark shall be submitted.[248] If a trade mark is in a foreign language, or consists of foreign words, the meaning shall be explained in Chinese.[249] Since 2013, the TML makes it clear that trade mark registration applications and other relevant documents can be filed electronically or in writing.[250]

---

and notify the applicant in writing. If not, the CTMO shall not accept the application and shall notify the applicant in writing and give the reasons. If supplements or amendments need to be made, they need to be sent back to the CTMO within 30 days from the date of receipt of the notification. If the supplements or amendments are made and sent back to the CTMO within the specified time limit, the filing date shall be reserved; where no supplements or amendments are made at the expiration of the specified time limit, or the supplements or amendments are not made as required, the CTMO shall not accept such application and shall notify the applicant in writing. The provisions on these requirements for acceptance apply to all other trade mark matters.

243. Article 13(1) IRTL 2014, *supra* note 12.
244. Article 19(7) BHPC Guidelines 2019, *supra* note 5.
245. The reproduction of a trade mark shall be clear, easy to paste, and printed on smooth and durable paper or be replaced by photographs. The length and width of the reproduction shall be not more than ten centimetres and not less than five centimetres respectively, Article 13(2) IRTL 2014, *supra* note 12.
246. Article 13(1) IRTL 2014, *supra* note 12. If an application is filed for registration, a statement shall be made in the application, and the method of use of the trade mark shall be indicated. If the trade mark is a combination of colours or coloured pattern, one copy of the coloured reproduction of the trade mark and one in black and white shall be submitted. If the trade mark has no colour, a reproduction of the trade mark in black and white shall be submitted.
247. Article 13(3) IRTL 2014, *supra* note 12. For the description of the sound mark, the sound applied for use as a trade mark shall be described by musical notes or staves, and a caption shall be attached. If this is not possible, a description in words that is consistent with the sample of the sound need to be submitted.
248. Article 13(6) IRTL 2014, *supra* note 12.
249. Article 13(7) IRTL 2014, *supra* note 12.
250. Article 22(3) TML 2013 and 2019, *supra* note 15.

Applications filed directly with the CTMO must also be accompanied by a copy of a Power of Attorney (PoA) in favour of a local trade mark agent or law firm, and a Chinese-language version of the applicant's name and address.[251]

(e) Corrections

If the trade mark applicant or registrant discovered that there is an evident error in the trade mark application or registration documents,[252] excluding any substantive content,[253] it may apply for a correction at the CTMO. If the application satisfies the conditions as required, the CTMO shall approve the application and correct the corresponding content. A publication of the correction, after the preliminary publication or publication of the registration, shall be made.

(f) Communications

Before 2001, examiners could issue examination opinions that informed applicants why the CTMO did not approve a registration. However, the TML 2001 discontinued with this practice in order to avoid unwanted business practices such as trade mark agencies establishing *guanxi* through corruption.[254] Since TML 2013, a new method has been chosen: CTMO examiners can communicate with applicants while at the same time an attempt is made to mitigate unwanted consequences. Under the TML 2019, examiners may request applicants to provide explanations and make corrections to their trade mark applications within 15 days from the date of the notification by the CTMO. The law also explicitly provides that an examiner's final decision shall not be affected by whether the applicant responded to a correction request.

If the CTMO refuses an application on certain designated goods, the applicant may divide the application and continue with the part of the application for which the preliminary approval has been granted into another application.[255] For the divided application, the filing date of the original application shall be preserved. If an applicant applies to divide an application, it shall file an application for division to the CTMO within 15 days from the date of receipt of the Notification of Partial Refusal to an Application for Trade Mark Registration issued by the CTMO. Upon receipt of the application for division, the CTMO shall divide the original application into two separate applications, give a new application number to the divided application for which preliminary approval has been granted and announce it in a publication.[256]

251. SIPS Asia, *supra* note 241.
252. Article 38(1) TML 2019, *supra* note 15.
253. Article 38(2) TML 2019, *supra* note 15.
254. More generally, Chow noticed that *guanxi* or influence peddling is deeply rooted in China's culture and as long as there is no tangible *quid pro quo*, such as property or money, it is not considered illegal. Chow, *supra* note 240, 27.
255. Article 22 IRTL 2014, *supra* note 12.
256. Article 22 IRTL 2014, *supra* note 12.

(g) *Time Limits of the CTMO*

The TML 2013 for the first time provided guidelines for the maximum period of time that the CTMO and TRAB would be able to spend on specific types of procedures.

The CTMO should send the applicant an Issuance of Official Filing Receipts for a new application within 15 days after the application.[257] The CTMO will carry out a formalities review and issue objections within one-and-a-half to two months.[258]

The CTMO needed to complete the substantive examination within nine months from the receipt of the filing, decreased to six months in 2018, further decreased to five months by the end of 2019,[259] and to four months by 2020.[260] If one extrapolates this trend, one wonders how fast substantive examination can become in the future. It is clear that artificial intelligence will play a big role. In January 2019, the CTMO announced that it was implementing artificial intelligence solutions developed by CNIPA together with Beijing Huazhi Jingwei Company, Shanghai Yitu Company and Tencent, to increase productivity and limit the similarity comparisons of trade mark applications that need to be checked further from tens of thousands to around 5,000 applications.[261]

The CTMO will make a preliminary publication for opposition purposes in six to seven months.

The CTMO needs to allow or refuse an opposition within 12 months from the expiration of the preliminary publication, extendable by six months.[262]

In case of a non-use cancellation procedure, the CTMO issues a decision within eight to nine months. The CTMO deals with the applications to change name or address within three months, with the change of trade mark agent within two months, renewals of the trade mark in one to two months, assignments in six to seven months, and withdrawal of applications or registrations within two months.

The CTMO will issue certified copies of registration certificates within two months.

(h) *Fees*

The CTMO has reduced its trade mark prosecution fees and that of the TRAB in accordance with the Notice of the National Development and Reform Commission and the Ministry of Finance on Reducing Some Administrative Fees, effective from

---

257. Recent Developments in IP Protection in China, SIPS Asia, 29 April 2019. Available at: https://sips.asia/knowledge/trademark-enforcement/recent-ip-developments-in-china/.
258. *Supra* note 257.
259. 'China to Introduce More Measures on IPR Protection', *China IP News*, 24 July 2019. Available at: http://english.cnipa.gov.cn/docs/2019-07/20190724151735589312.pdf.
260. Amanda Yang, 'A Call for Public Comment on Further Amendments to the Chinese Trade Mark Law', Rouse, 7 June 2018. Available at: https://www.rouse.com/magazine/news/a-call-for-public-comment-on-further-amendments-to-the-chinese-trademark-law/.
261. 'Jie li rengong zhineng kaiqi zhihui shencha – shangbiao tuxing zhineng jiansuo gongneng zhengshi shangxian' (Leveraging artificial intelligence to open smart review – the smart search function of trade mark graphics is officially launched), CNIPA, 31 January 2019. Available at: http://sbj.cnipa.gov.cn/gzdt/201901/t20190131_281363.html.
262. Article 35 TML 2013 and 2019, *supra* note 15.

1 July 2019.[263] The CTMO provides a cost incentive to file trade mark prosecution applications online.

Table 1.

Charge item	*Paper application*	*Online application*
Trade mark registration	RMB 300 (limited to 10 items) Additional items cost RMB 30.	RMB 270 (limited to ten items) Additional items cost RMB 27.
Reissue trade mark registration certificate	RMB 500	RMB 450
Assignment application	RMB 500	RMB 450
Renewal application	RMB 500	RMB 450
Grace period late filing	RMB 250	RMB 225
Charge item	*Paper application*	*Online application*
Appeals to CTMO, e.g. registration application refusals, opposition, non-use cancellation) Invalidations	RMB 750	RMB 675 (this will be possible soon)
Change of agent, applicant/ registrant name, applicant/ registrant address	RMB 150	Free
Issue a trade mark certification	RMB 50	RMB 45
Collective mark registration	RMB 1,500	RMB 1,350
Certification mark registration	RMB 1,500	RMB 1,350
Opposition	RMB 500	RMB 450 (this will be possible soon)
Non-use cancellation	RMB 500	RMB 450 (this will be possible soon)
Trade mark licence contract filing fee	RMB 150	RMB 135

(i) ***Trade Mark Search***

Conducting trade mark searches can ultimately save costs, and also help to accelerate the registration process by allowing an early opportunity to eliminate potentially conflicting marks, for example by cancelling them for non-use, purchasing them or

263. Announcement on Adjusting the Fees for Registration of Trademarks, CTMO (No. 914), 19 June 2019. Available at: http://sbj.cnipa.gov.cn/gzdt/201906/t20190619_302481.html.

obtaining consent from their owners.[264] There is no longer a central search service available from the CTMO. However, applicants can conduct searches themselves by using the CTMO's database of published and pending applications before filing applications.[265] The CTMO has six different search engines, but they do not provide real-time updates and are without legal effect:

- Similar Identical Search Trade Mark: for similar or identical trade marks on the basis of figures and characters;
- Search for General Trade Mark Information: trade mark information can be searched based on trade mark number, trade mark content, and name of applicant, etc.;
- Search of Trade Mark Application Status: provides information about the status of a trade mark based on an application number or registration number;
- Search of Trade Mark Gazette: provides the announcements in and information of the Trade Mark Gazette.

In addition, there is a search engine for goods and services, and one where users can report inaccurate information to the CTMO for correction.

(j) Joint Applications

If an application is jointly filed for registration of a trade mark, or when proceeding to other matters concerning a jointly owned trade mark, a representative shall be designated in the application; where no representative is designated, the person named first in the application shall be taken as the representative.[266]

(k) Representation: Trade Mark Agencies

A Chinese applicant may apply for trade mark registration and handle other trade mark-related matters by itself, or through a legally formed trade mark agency authorized by it.[267]

Non-Chinese companies who want to be active in China should not underestimate the complexities in selecting an appropriate name for their Chinese character brands and trade marks. For this process, they are well-advised get expertise from specialized marketing agencies or consultancies who can work together with trade mark agencies. Sometimes, trade mark agencies also have such expertise in-house. One needs to know the target consumers and the socio-cultural and linguistic aspects of a trade mark.[268]

264. One can pay for access to private commercial databases, or outsource it via professions or use those free databases operated by the CTMO to facilitate trade mark registration inquiries by the public.
265. CTMO Search. Available at: http://wsjs.saic.gov.cn.
266. Article 16 IRTL 2014, *supra* note 12.
267. Article 18 TML 2019, 15.
268. Feifei Xu, 'Chinese Brand Naming: Four Mistakes to Avoid', Prophet, 23 January 2019. Available at: https://www.prophet.com/2019/01/chinese-brand-naming-four-mistakes-to-avoid/.

A foreign national or a foreign enterprise without a permanent residence or business office in China[269] shall authorize a legally formed trade mark agency to do this.[270] If a party entrusts a trade mark agency to apply for trade mark registration or handle other trade mark-related matters, it shall submit to the trade mark agency a PoA that shall specify the contents and authority of the agency, and if the PoA is of a foreigner or foreign enterprise, also the nationality of the principal. In case of foreigners or foreign enterprises, the PoA needs to be notarized and certified, which is cumbersome and time-consuming.

Article 19(1) TML 2019 explicitly clarifies that trade mark agencies shall follow the principle of good faith, abide by laws and administrative regulations, handle trade mark registration applications and other trade mark-related matters as authorized by clients, and maintain confidential clients' trade secrets known by acting for clients. They also should make it clear to the applicant when a trade mark application has been refused.[271]

If a trade mark agency knows or should have known that a client's trade mark registration application would lead to a bad faith application, pre-emptive registration or to the infringement of prior rights, it may not accept the client's authorization.[272] Trade mark agencies may also not apply for the registration of trade marks other than those applied for on behalf of their clients.[273]

The Trade Mark Agency Association shall enforce disciplinary action against the violation of self-regulatory rules. The Trade Mark Agency Association shall disclose information about new members and the disciplinary actions taken against its members to the public in a timely manner.[274] In addition, Article 68(1) TML 2019 provides more severe sanctions for trade mark agencies imposed by the AIC: corrections, warnings and fines of between RMB 10,000 and RMB 100,000. The directly liable person and other personnel in charge of the trade mark agency can be fined between RMB 5,000 and RMB 50,000.[275] If one of the following crimes is committed, criminal liability shall be investigated: forging documents; acquiring business by defaming other trade mark agencies or disturbing the trade mark agency market order by other illicit means; and bad faith applications, according to Article 4 TML 2019 and Article 19(3) or (4) TML 2019.[276] For a bad faith case, the court shall impose a punishment according to the law.[277]

The AIC shall record such crimes into its social credit file; and if the circumstances are serious, the CTMO and the TRAB may also decide to stop accepting its trade mark agency business, and publicize this.[278] A trade mark agency which infringes

269. Article 5(4) IRTL 2014, *supra* note 12.
270. Article 18 TML 2019, *supra* note 15.
271. Article 19(1) TML 2019, *supra* note 15.
272. Article 19(2) TML 2019, *supra* note 15.
273. Article 19(3) TML 2019, *supra* note 15.
274. Article 20 TML 2019, *supra* note 15.
275. Article 68(1) TML 2019, *supra* note 15.
276. Article 68(1) TML 2019, *supra* note 15.
277. Article 68(2) TML 2019, *supra* note 15.
278. Article 68(3) TML 2019, *supra* note 15.

upon the lawful rights and interests of clients must also assume civil responsibility in accordance with the law.[279]

The staff members of the CTMO and TRAB must enforce laws impartially, have integrity and self-discipline, be devoted to their duties, provide services properly, and may not engage in trade mark agency work, production of goods and trading activities.[280] To remain impartial and have integrity, staff members of the CTMO and TRAB should recuse themselves in the following circumstances: (1) being the party or a close relative of the party or agent; (2) have other relationships with parties and agents that may affect impartiality; (3) have a stake in applying for trade mark registration or handling other trade mark matters.[281]

7. Trade Mark Review and Adjudication Board/Trade Mark Appeal Board

The Trade Mark Review and Adjudication Board (TRAB) Rules were promulgated in 1995,[282] revised in 2002,[283] in 2005,[284] and in 2014.[285] They were issued to standardize the procedure of trade mark review and adjudication.[286] On 14 February 2019, the CNIPA announced that the TRAB, CTMO and the Trade Mark Examination Cooperation Centre (TECC) would be reorganized as the new Chinese Trade Mark Office (CTMO) under the CNIPA.[287] This new Trade Mark Office will be responsible for all duties formerly performed by the TRAB, CTMO and TECC under the name of the CNIPA as of 1 April 2019. The successor of TRAB is the Trade Mark Appeal Board (TAB).

TAB is responsible for:

- Reviewing and adjudicating the CTMO's decisions on refusal of registration, normally due to prior conflicting marks on the registry, according to Article 34 TML;
- Pre-grant opposition, according to Articles 33 and 35 TML. If the opposition is rejected, the opposing party is not allowed to appeal the CTMO's adverse decision;
- Post-grant opposition, according to Articles 44 and 45 TML;
- Non-use cancellation according to Article 54 TML.

279. Article 68(4) TML 2019, *supra* note 15.
280. Article 68(4) and Article 69 TML 2019, *supra* note 15.
281. Article 7 IRTL 2014, *supra* note 12.
282. TRAB Rules 1995 promulgated by the Order No. 37 of the SAIC, 2 November 1995.
283. TRAB Rules 2002 by the Order No. 3 of the SAIC, 17 September 2002. Available at: http://home.saic.gov.cn/sbj/sbjEnglish/LawsRegulations/201506/t20150625_264735.html; http://www.lehmanlaw.com/resource-centre/laws-and-regulations/intellectual-property/rules-for-trademark-review-and-adjudication-2002.html.
284. TRAB Rules 2005 by the Order No. 20 of the SAIC, 26 September 2005. Available at: https://www.wipo.int/edocs/lexdocs/laws/en/cn/cn046en.pdf.
285. TRAB Rules 2014 by the Order No. 65 of the SAIC, promulgated on 28 May 2014, and effective on 1 June 2014. Available at: https://wipolex.wipo.int/en/text/337809; http://www.lindapatent.com/en/law_trademark/676.html.
286. Rule 1 TRAB Rules 2014, *supra* note 285.
287. 'Announcement on changes to business chapters and related forms (No. 295)', CNIPA, 18 February 2019. Available at: http://www.cnipa.gov.cn/zfgg/1135993.htm.

If the TAB must determine prior rights based on the results of another case being tried by a People's Court or handled by an administrative agency, it may suspend the review. After the cause of suspension is eliminated, the review process shall be resumed.

(a) Review of TRAB/TAB

The review rules of the TRAB have been formulated and promulgated by the SAIC of the State Council.[288] Until 2001, a decision of the TRAB was final.[289] However, since that time, an appeal can be brought against all TRAB/TAB decisions [290] before the Beijing IP Court, then the BHPC, and finally the SPC.

Appeals of these CTMO decisions must be lodged with the TAB within 15 days of issuance of the decision. However, the CNIPA recently implemented an electronic filing system for trade mark applications, where the deadline for appeals of rejected marks is extended to 30 days when the initial trade mark filing was completed electronically. A period of 30 days is also allowed when the refusal relates to an International Registration.

The administrative cases involving the granting and affirmation of trade mark rights referred to in the SPC Provisions 2016 is litigation brought before the courts by the administrative counterparts or interested parties against the decisions rendered by the TRAB in respect of cases of review on trade mark refusal, review on disapproval of trade mark registration, review on trade mark revocation, trade mark invalidation declaration, review on trade mark invalidation declaration, etc.[291]

The court does not have to remain passive if it concludes that the TRAB's findings were obviously inappropriate.[292] The TRAB violates legal procedure as provided in Article 70(3) Administrative Procedure Law if it misses a substantial argument, should have recused itself, fails to inform a competent party to join procedure, or other circumstances that violate the statutory procedure.[293]

If during the court's hearing it becomes clear that the cause on which the TRAB based its decision no longer exists, the court might revoke the TRAB's decision on the basis of new facts and order the TRAB to review its decision anew according to the changed facts.[294] If evidence is discovered after the previous administrative act, or is based on evidence that due to objective causes was either unattainable during the previous administrative proceeding or impossible to be produced during the

288. Article 93(3) IRTL 2014, *supra* note 12.
289. Article 21 TML 1993. Trade Mark Law 1993 adopted by the Standing Committee of the NPC on 23 August 1982, amended according to the Decision of the 30th Meeting of the Standing Committee of the NPC on 22 February 1993. Available at: https://www.jus.uio.no/lm/china.trade.mark.law.1993/portrait.pdf.
290. Articles 36 TML and 55 2019, *supra* note 15. If the applicant fails to apply for a review at the TAB, or fails to bring a lawsuit to the Court against the decision of review made by the TAB, the TAB decision shall become effective.
291. Article 1 SPC Provisions 2016, *supra* note 112.
292. Article 2 SPC Provisions 2016, *supra* note 112.
293. Article 27 SPC Provisions 2016, *supra* note 112.
294. Article 28 SPC Provisions 2016, *supra* note 112.

prescribed time limit, or where such party files its application based on new legal grounds, filing another application for review and adjudication *de novo* is allowed.[295]

(b) TRAB Hearings

Another important change was the implementation of the Measures of TRAB Hearings in Trade Mark Review Cases 2017.[296] These rules allowed hearings before the TRAB, thereby improving the quality of TRAB decisions.[297] TRAB hearings will be heard by a collegial panel of at least three examiners, always being an odd number.[298]

Under the Measures for TRAB Hearings, parties can apply for a hearing if the taking of evidence is necessary. The TRAB has the discretion to approve this request and can also initiate a hearing *ex officio* if necessary.[299] At hearings, parties can adduce evidence and cross-examine the other party's evidence.[300]

It is often impossible for parties to submit original versions of their evidence. A hearing could be used to prove the authenticity of evidence by bringing the original documents to the hearing. With the consent of the TRAB, witnesses may be invited to give evidence at the oral hearing. Witnesses are not allowed to attend oral proceedings.[301]

The Measures for TRAB Hearings make it clear that during the hearing, parties can settle their dispute.[302] If an applicant requests an oral hearing, it shall so request within 30 days from the date of submission of the application for review or at the latest from the date of receipt of the copy of the respondent's reply.[303] The respondent may request an oral hearing with the statement of defence to the TRAB.[304]

An applicant may, before the TRAB makes a decision or ruling, request the withdrawal of its application whereupon proceedings shall be terminated.[305]

After withdrawal, the applicant shall not file an application for review of the trade mark again on the basis of the same facts and grounds. If the TRAB has made a ruling or decision on an application for trade mark review and adjudication, no one may apply for review and adjudication again based on the same facts and grounds.

On 15 December 2017, the SAIC announced that as of 28 December 2017, all trade mark review decisions of the TRAB would be published in the Review Decisions

295. Article 29(1) SPC Provisions 2016, *supra* note 112.
296. Measures for TRAB Hearings in Trade Mark Review Cases, SAIC No. 65 promulgated and effective on 4 May 2017. Available at: http://www.gov.cn/xinwen/2017-05/10/content_5192163.htm. TRAB Hearings in Trade Mark Review Cases, promulgated by the SAIC, effective on 4 May 2017.
297. Deanna Wong, Zhen Feng and Eugene Low, 'A step in the right direction: China's TRAB launches new trademark review hearing system', Hogan Lovells, July 2017, 2. Available at: https://bit.ly/2pXToZI.
298. Article 9 Measures for TRAB Hearings 2017, *supra* note 296.
299. Articles 2 and 5 Measures for TRAB Hearings 2017, *supra* note 296.
300. Article 3 Measures for TRAB Hearings 2017, *supra* note 296.
301. Article 14 Measures for TRAB Hearings 2017, *supra* note 296.
302. Article 17(2) Measures for TRAB Hearings 2017, *supra* note 296.
303. Article 4 Measures for TRAB Hearings 2017, *supra* note 296.
304. Article 4 Measures for TRAB Hearings 2017, *supra* note 296.
305. Article 61 IRTL 2014, *supra* note 12.

section of its website within 20 business days after delivery, except where public disclosure was prohibited under relevant laws and regulations.

VI. RENEWAL

The period of validity of a registered trade mark is ten years, counted from the day the registration is approved,[306] and can be renewed indefinitely. If the trade mark registrant intends to continue using its trade mark, it must file a renewal request within 12 months prior to the expiry date in accordance with relevant provisions.[307] If the registrant fails to do so during said time limit, an extension of six months may be granted by the CTMO.[308] The CTMO shall issue corresponding certification and publish the renewal.[309] If no application for renewal was filed upon expiry of the extension period, the registered trade mark will be cancelled.[310]

Within one year from the time that a registered trade mark is cancelled or declared invalid, or is not renewed upon the expiry of its validity period, the CTMO shall not approve any application for registration of a trade mark identical with or similar to the aforesaid trade mark.[311] In case of an expired trade mark, this provision becomes relevant, since the time period from application to registration is being significantly reduced, and should generally be much shorter than one year.[312]

1. Post-Grant Issues

(a) Subsequent Obligations Connected to Trade Mark Registration

Until the TML 1993, guaranteeing the quality of goods and maintaining the reputation of trade marks so as to protect the interests of consumers was an explicit function of the TML. The protection of reputation was replaced in the TML 2001, 2013 and 2019 by "encouraging producers and dealers to guarantee the quality of their goods and services and preserve the credibility of trade marks, so as to protect the interests of consumers, producers and dealers."[313]

(b) Requirements of Use

When a trade mark holder puts its registered trade marks to use, words such as "registered trade mark" or a registration logo may be indicated on the goods, packages,

306. Article 39 TML 2013 and 2019, *supra* note 15.
307. Article 40(1) TML 2013 and 2019, *supra* note 15. Article 33 IRTL 2014, *supra* note 12.Under the TML 1982, 1993 and 2001, the trade mark registrant had to file a renewal request within six months of the expiry of the trade mark, with a grace period of six months. See Article 23 TML 1982; Article 24 TML 1993; Article 38 TML 2001.
308. Article 33 IRTL 2014, *supra* note 12.
309. Article 40(2) TML 2013 and 2019, *supra* note 15. Article 33 IRTL 2014, *supra* note 12.
310. Article 40(1) TML 2013 and 2019, *supra* note 15.
311. Article 50 TML 2019, *supra* note 15.
312. Article 50 TML 2019, *supra* note 15.
313. Article 1 TML 2001, 2013 and 2019, *supra* note 15.

manuals or other attachments. The registration logos include "注" (Zhù) which is the abbreviation of "注册" (Zhùcè), which means "registered", and ®, which shall be indicated on the upper or lower right-hand corner of the trade mark when used.[314]

If a Trade Mark Registration Certificate is lost or damaged, the trade mark holder needs to apply for reissuance of the certificate with the CTMO.[315] If the trade mark holder needs the reissuance of a certification on modification, assignment or renewal of a trade mark, or the issuance of a certification on the registration of a trade mark, or where a trade mark applicant needs the issuance of documents verifying a right of priority by the CTMO, it shall file a corresponding application with the CTMO.[316] Those forging or altering a Trade Mark Registration Certificate or other trade mark related certifications shall be investigated and prosecuted for criminal liability in accordance with the provisions of the Criminal Law[317] on the crime of forging or altering certificates of state organs or on other crimes.[318]

VII. OPPOSITION PROCEDURE

The TML provides both the possibility of a pre-grant[319] and post-grant opposition.[320] The pre-grant opposition can be filed against a trade mark which has been preliminarily approved and published.

1. Grounds of Opposition

An opposition can either be based on absolute or relative grounds of refusal.

Oppositions based on absolute grounds can be filed by any party that is of the opinion that there is a violation of Articles 10 (prohibited signs), 11 (lack of distinctiveness) or 12 (restrictions on three-dimensional marks) TML 2019.

In contrast, oppositions based on relative grounds can only be filed by the holder of prior rights and interested parties. These must be done within three months from the date of the preliminary review announcement.[321] Articles 33 (pre-grant opposition) and 45 (post-grant opposition) TML 2019 refer specifically to violations of: Articles 13(2) and (3) (unregistered and registered well-known marks); 15 (pre-emptive registration of a trade mark agency); 16(1) (misleading GIs); 30 (earlier double-identity trade mark); and 32 TML 2019 (no prejudicing or pre-empting of rights). In addition to a pre-grant opposition, the CTMO started to allow brand owners to submit interference letters for examiners' review. This could offer relief in case

314. Article 63 IRTL 2014, *supra* note 12.
315. Article 64(1) IRTL 2014, *supra* note 12.
316. Article 64(2) IRTL 2014, *supra* note 12.
317. Article 280 Criminal Law adopted in 1979; revised at the Fifth Session of the Eighth National People's Congress on 14 March 1997, promulgated by Order No. 83 of the President of the PRC on 14 March 1997, and entered into force on 1 October 1997. Available at: http://www.fdi.gov.cn/1800000121_39_2925_0_7.html.
318. Article 63(3) IRTL 2014, *supra* note 12.
319. Article 33 TML 2019, *supra* note 15.
320. Article 45 TML 2019, *supra* note 15.
321. Article 33 TML 2019, *supra* note 15.

a brand owner has identified a bad faith application before it is gazetted instead of waiting for three months until the end of the examination period. Then again, the CTMO is not obliged to review the interference letter.[322]

(a) Opposition to International Marks

For an international application, the opposition period is not three months like the national registration, but three months from the first day following the month after the WIPO Gazette of International Marks is published.[323] Anyone may file an opposition to the CTMO regarding the application for territorial extension designating China.

The opposition against an international application is filed before the substantive examination of trade marks. One opposition application may involve one or more classes of goods or services.[324] If the opponent withdraws its application for opposition, the CTMO shall terminate the opposition procedure, and notify the party concerned in writing.[325] If an opposition is filed and the CTMO rejects it and grants the trade mark, the decision is final; if the CTMO agrees with the opposition, the applicant can appeal and request a review from the TRAB. The decision from the TRAB can take up to 12 months and is extendable by three months. If the applicant is unsuccessful at the TRAB, it can appeal at China's Intellectual Property Courts and then the High People's Court. Each appeal takes about six to 12 months.

(b) Prior Rights

Prior rights include legitimately acquired senior trade mark rights, unregistered and registered. Only the latter is called a prior mark. However, Article 1(2) SPC provides that a prior mark in conflict with a registered mark that is operating within its scope first has to go through a compulsory settlement procedure before a court handles the case.[326]

Article 32 TML states:

> No application for trade mark registration may infringe upon the existing prior rights of others, and bad-faith registration by illicit means of a trade mark with a certain reputation already used by another party shall be prohibited.

---

322. Dan Plane and Doug Berman, 'Prosecuting Trademarks in China: An Insider's Guide for Foreign Brand Owners in 2019 (Part I)', SIPS Asia, 31 March 2019. Available at: https://sips.asia/knowledge/trademark-registration/prosecuting-trademarks-in-china-an-insiders-guide-for-foreign-brand-owners-in-2019-part-1/.
323. Article 14(1) SAIC IR Measures 2003, *supra* note 220, Article 45 IRTL 2014, *supra* note 12.
324. Article 14(2) SAIC IR Measures 2003, *supra* note 220.
325. Article 14(2) SAIC IR Measures 2003, *supra* note 220.
326. Article 1(2) SPC Interpretation 2008 explains that in case of a conflict between a senior and junior registered trade marks that is used within its scope, courts did not accept such a case, instead the administrative authorities would insist on a settlement effort.

This demonstrates the threshold in the legal protection of unregistered trade marks, where protection is limited to trade marks which have been previously used extensively and obtained a certain degree of fame.

If a defendant used the Chinese equivalent of its trade mark and that Chinese equivalent had become the denomination of the plaintiff in the eyes of the relevant public and media, even though the plaintiff never registered that equivalent, the plaintiff is protected against its use. Returning to the *Harley-Davidson v. Beijing Harley Trading Center* case, even though Harley-Davidson did not register the Chinese equivalent of Harley, 哈雷 (Hāléi), which was registered by the defendant, these Chinese characters had become a denomination of the plaintiff and its related products among the relevant public.[327]

The same threshold of a certain degree of fame is also applicable to labels identical or similar to name, packaging or decoration (Article 6(1) Unfair Competition 2019, see Chapter 5 on Unfair Competition and Antitrust Law). According to Xue and Zheng, prior rights also include "copyright, the right of trade name, the right of portrait and the right of using the characteristic designation, packing or decoration of a well-known product."[328] Li added design patents and GIs as prior rights.[329] Point 3 Trade Mark Trial Standard (Trial Standard 2009), promulgated jointly by CTMO and TRAB in 2009, referred to five specific rights as prior rights: "[the] right[s] in a trade name, copyright, design patent, name right, and portrait right."[330]

In 2016, in the *Michael Jeffrey Jordan v. TRAB* case,[331] the SPC decided that a right in a personal name can constitute an "existing prior right", as protected under the TML, as long as three conditions are met:

(a) the specific name, the transliteration of Jordan "乔丹", shall have a certain level of popularity in China and must be a name known to the relevant public;
(b) the relevant public shall use the specific name, "乔丹", to refer to the natural person, Michael Jordan claiming the protection; and
(c) a stable connection shall have become established between the natural person and the specific name, which was the case.[332]

327. Zhang Zaiping (transl. Wang Hongjun), 'Analytical comments on legal protection of Chinese equivalents of unregistered trademarks and judicial practice', *China Intellectual Property*, 25 February 2011. Available at: https://ipr.chinadaily.com.cn/2011-02/25/content_12080585.htm.

328. Xue and Zheng, *Chinese Intellectual Property Law in the 21st Century* (2002), 258. See also Duan Xiao-mei, 'Conflict between Trademark Right and Prior Copyright, Case and Academic Research on Solutions to this Conflict in the Chinese and Japanese Legal Systems', JPO Study-Cum-Research Fellowship Program, 1 April – 30 September 2019. Available at: https://bit.ly/2NFDn2X.

329. Zuming Li, 'Trademarks', in Rohan Kariyawasam (ed.), *Chinese Intellectual Property and Technology Laws* (2011), 46 at 53.

330. Trade Mark Trial Standard, promulgated by CTMO and TRAB on 18 June 2009. Available at: http://spw.sbj.cnipa.gov.cn/zcfg/200906/t20090618_226598.html.

331. *Michael Jeffrey Jordan v. TRAB and Qiaodan Sports Co., Ltd.*, SPC, 27 *Zui Gao Fa Xing Zai* (2016).

332. WIPO, *WIPO Collection of Leading Judgments on Intellectual Property Rights People's Republic of China (2011–2018)*, 11–18. Available at: https://www.wipo.int/edocs/pubdocs/

Trade names and enterprise names can also conflict with trade marks as prior rights.

In March 2013, the BHPC already held that Ningbo Wubian Rubber and Plastic's application to register the trade mark "FREUDENBERG" for Class 17 associated with Freudenberg, a German manufacturer, was done in bad faith.[333] Although Freudenberg had been active in China under this trade name even before 1992, the name "FREUDENBERG" had never been registered or used as a trade mark for the goods in Class 17 in China. The Beijing First Intermediary People's Court (BFIPC) put it clearly: "A trade name [Freudenberg] which is included as a part of the enterprise name and is famous on the market to some extent and known to the relevant public is a prior right within the meaning of Article 31 TML 2001 [identical to Article 32 TML 2019]."[334]

In the 2013 case *Luxin Venture Capital Group Co., Ltd v. Qingdao Sisa (Group) Abrasives Co., Ltd.*,[335] an enterprise named Sisha Group Abrasives Co., Ltd (Sisha Group), used its trade name "四砂" (Sìshā) for abrasive instruments. In 2004, Sisa, a close relation of the Sisha Group, applied for the trade mark registration of "四砂". In 2005, Sisha Group changed its enterprise name into Luxin Venture Capital Group Co., Ltd. (Luxin). In 2007, the trade mark application was preliminarily published. Luxin opposed the trade mark registration, but this was rejected by the CTMO. Luxin applied for an administrative review by the TRAB. The TRAB held that Luxin had continued to use the unregistered mark "四砂", which made it popular among the relevant public. Sisa and Luxin were both located in Shandong province, and thus Sisa should have known the "四砂" mark, and there was recognition that the two enterprises had cooperated before. Sisa used the mark for abrading instruments, just like Luxin, violating Article 32 TML. Sisa filed a lawsuit before the BFIPC, which held that Luxin had changed its enterprise name and could therefore not invoke any prior rights based on its prior enterprise name. In addition, no one could have registered the same enterprise name within one year from the enterprise name change in order to avoid confusion in the market. Luxin appealed to the BHPC.[336] This Court held that at the moment of the trade mark application, Luxin had not yet changed its enterprise name and could thus invoke Article 32 TL. The existence of a business cooperation between the two companies made a good faith trade mark application unlikely.[337]

---

en/wipo_pub_1065.pdf.

333. *Ningbo Wubian Rubber and Plastic Co., Ltd.* (first known as Ninghai County Wubian Rubber and Plastics Co. Ltd) *v. TRAB*, BHPC, Administrative Judgment, 1658 *Gao Xing Zhong Zi* [2012], decision on 6 March 2013. Liu Guangming and Richard Yao, 'In Good Faith', *The Trademark Lawyer*, August/September 2014, 14. Available at: http://fujaelaw.com/wp-content/uploads/2017/02/In-Good-Faith-The-Trademark-Law-PDF.pdf.

334. *Ningobo Wubian Rubber and Plastic Co., Ltd. v. TRAB*, BFIPC, Administrative Judgment, 2298 *Yi Zhong Zhi Xing Chu Zi* [2011], decision 5 September 2012). Guangming and Yao, supra note 333.

335. *Luxin Venture Capital Group Co., Ltd v. Qingdao SISA (GROUP) Abrasives Co., Ltd.*, BHPC, 354 *Gao Xing Zhong Zi* (2013).

336. Wang Ting and Yunting You, 'Are Enterprise Entitled to the Rights for Its Prior Enterprise Name?', *Bridge IP Law Commentary*, 14 November 2014. Available at: http://www.chinaiplawyer.com/enterprises-entitled-rights-prior-enterprise-name/.

337. Ting and You, *supra* note 336.

In addition, one can think of geographical names and domain names.[338]

Since China has been a member of the Berne Convention since 1992,[339] and copyright does not require any formality to be protected, a company could possibly claim copyright over logos and stylized word marks as prior rights. The prerequisites are that the logos are works eligible for copyright,[340] the company is the copyright proprietor (and needs to prove that),[341] and the litigious trade mark is infringing the company's copyright.[342] If a party claims that registration of a trade mark shall not be approved or be declared invalid on the ground of damage to a prior copyright, the categories of the goods or services designated by the litigious trade mark shall not be considered.[343]

According to the Trade Mark Trial Standard 2009, the prior right in Article 31 TML 2001 (and since its material identity also Article 32 TML 2013) did not include prior trade marks, since these were explicitly protected in the later part of the same Article: "nor may he, by illegitimate means, rush to register a trade mark that is already in use by another person and has a certain degree of influence."[344] According to Rule 17 SPC Opinions Regarding Administrative Cases of Trade Mark Rights Granting and Determination issued in 2010 (SPC Opinions 2010): "the court shall protect prior rights which are specifically enumerated in the TML pursuant to the specific provisions thereof. If the TML is silent, the legitimate rights [are] to be protected pursuant to the General Principles of Civil Law[345] and other laws and regulations." The opponent of a trade mark needs to submit documents to prove it was the proprietor of a prior right or an interested party.[346]

Lee and Mehaffy argue that a standard similar to the requirements for passing off under British law should be considered in China:[347] protectable goodwill or reputation in the country; relevant misrepresentation; and likelihood of damage. This would be in conformity to Article 5(2) Law Against Unfair Competition 1993 which prohibits: "using, without authorization, the name, packaging or decoration peculiar to well-known goods or using a name, packaging or decoration similar to that of well-known

338. Pattloch, *supra* note 2, 105.
339. China acceded to the Berne Convention for the Protection of Literary and Artistic Works on 15 July 1992. Berne Notification No. 140. Available at: https://www.wipo.int/treaties/en/notifications/berne/treaty_berne_140.html.
340. Original works that are created independently and reflect the creativity of the author are eligible for copyright protection.
341. Article 19(2) SPC Provisions 2016, *supra* note 112. Examples that can prove copyright include, "the design manuscript, original copy, contract vouchering the acquisition of rights, copyright registration certification prior to the application date of the litigious trade mark."
342. Article 19(1) SPC Provisions 2016, *supra* note 112.
343. Article 16(11) BHPC Guidelines 2019, *supra* note 5.
344. Point 4 Trade Mark Trial Standard 2009.
345. General Principles of Civil Law 1986, *supra* note 198.
346. Article 24 IRTL 2014, *supra* note 12.
347. Jyh-An Lee and Thomas Mehaffy, 'Prior Rights in the Chinese Trademark Law', 37:10 *EIPR* (11 September 2015), 677. Available: https://ssrn.com/abstract=2659404.

goods, so that its goods are confused with the well-known goods of another person, causing buyers to mistake them for the well-known goods of another."[348]

(c) Trade Mark Squatting

Bad faith registrations and bad faith use of trade marks have been some of the most challenging issues related to China's first-to-file system. Provisions in the TML 2013 made a start with upgrading the "good and bad faith" principle to the level of law, broadening the exception to the first-to-file principle. The TML 2019 furthers this goal and provides guidance about how to provide evidence of bad faith registration and use in case of administrative and civil litigation. The second clause of Article 32 TML 2019 states that unfair means may not be used to pre-emptively register a third party's hitherto unregistered trade mark that is already in use and has a certain degree of reputation.

According to Article 23 SPC Provisions 2016,[349] pre-emptive registration by unfair means is presumed when the applicant definitely knew or should have known of the earlier trade mark which has a certain reputation, and nevertheless applied to register the same trade mark for the same or similar goods or services. For a trade mark applicant, especially if it is operating in the same industry as the holder of the earlier trade mark with a certain degree of reputation, it is hard to refute an attempt to exploit the goodwill of the prior trade mark in bad faith.

A certain degree of reputation must be adduced by the holder of the prior trade mark to prove that the mark has been continuously used for a certain period of time, or has certain geographical coverage, sales volume or advertisement. An earlier unregistered mark is considered "already in use" if a party identifies the sources of goods through commercial advertising, production and management activities, and the relevant publicity has established a connection between the "unregistered trade mark" and the party.[350] A "certain recognition" can be determined if a party can prove that the popularity, including duration of use, region, sales or advertising, of its prior unregistered trade mark is sufficient to enable the applicant of the litigious trade mark to know or should have known the existence of the prior unregistered trade mark.[351]

The BHPC defines malicious intent where the cited trade mark enjoys distinctiveness and popularity; the business place of the applicant of the contested trade mark is adjacent to that of the proprietor of the cited trade mark; the applicant of the contested trade mark and the proprietor of the cited trade mark belong to the same industry; and the contested trade mark is substantially identical with that of the cited trade mark and the applicant of the contested trade mark does not give reasonable explanations for the choice of mark to be registered.

348. Law Against Unfair Competition, adopted at the Third Session of the Standing Committee of the Eighth NPC, and promulgated by Order No. 10 on 2 September 1993. Available at: https://www.wipo.int/edocs/lexdocs/laws/en/cn/cn011en.pdf.
349. SPC Provisions 2016, *supra* note 112.
350. Article 16(24) BHPC Guidelines 2019, *supra* note 5.
351. Article 16(25) BHPC Guidelines 2019, *supra* note 5.

According to the BHPC, to determine whether the applicant of the contested trade mark knows or should have known the unregistered trade mark of another person, the following factors may be considered: (1) the applicant of the contested trade mark and the prior trade mark user were in contact with each other with respect to the trade mark licence, transfer and otherwise; (2) whether this actual or constructive knowledge of the applicant is determined by the relevant organ, CTMO, TAB or courts; (3) the applicant of the contested trade mark and the prior trade mark user belong to the same industry; and (4) the contested trade mark is highly similar to the prior trade mark with higher distinctiveness.[352]

The draft of the CNIPA Provisions 2019[353] articulates which applications/registrations are considered to be filed in bad faith: pre-emptive applications of unregistered marks with a certain degree of recognition; identical and similar registered trade marks the applicant knows or should have known of another's prior rights; repeated applications for an obviously improper purpose; applications in large numbers within a short period of time; and applications without intention to use the trade mark for relevant goods or services. Indeed, selling a trade mark to a prior user of an identical or similar mark is not considered trade mark use, but trade mark squatting. Aiding or abetting such applications is considered improper.

In 2009, Nike applied for the trade mark registration of JORDAN for Class 25 for sports bags, clothing and footwear in China. This was opposed by Qiaodan Sports Company, Ltd., which already in 1997 had registered "乔丹" (Qiáodān), the transliteration of JORDAN. In 2012, Michael Jordan filed to invalidate about 80 trade mark registrations held by Qiaodan Sports. In December 2015, the SPC issued decisions rejecting Michael Jordan's claims that the CTMO, TRAB, BFIPC and BHPC had erred rejecting his invalidation actions against Qiaodan Sports.[354] In its decision on the Class 25 registration for QIAODAN in *pinyin*, the SPC stated that the BHPC did not err in its decision. The BHPC stated that Qiaodan Sports' registration of QIAODAN was recognized as a famous Chinese trade mark, and that the company's nearly 200 registrations for related marks were connected to its business and did not count as trade mark squatting.[355] The BHPC listed the evidence of the company's investment in the trade marks, and concluded that there was no violation of law or procedure in the lower courts or TRAB rulings. Michael Jordan's evidence dated mostly after 2010, including a consumer survey conducted on 10 April 2015. Michael Jordan's fame in 2010 and later was not relevant to prove fame in 1999, when the registration was issued.[356] It was further held that QIAODAN is a translation of part of Michael Jordan's name, but not his full name, and so registration of QIAODAN did not qualify as a fraudulent registration according to Article 10(8)(7) TML: "those having the nature of fraud, being liable to mislead the public about the characteristics of the

352. Article 16(23) BHPC Guidelines 2019, *supra* note 5.
353. CNIPA Provisions 2019 draft, *supra* note 35.
354. SPC, 17 March 2016, 312 *Zhi Xing Zi*(2015).
355. BHPC, IP Tribunal, 1053 *Gao Xing (Zhi) Zhong Zi* (2015).
356. Laura Wen-yu Young, 'Understanding Michael Jordan v. Qiaodan: Historical Anomaly or Systemic Failure to Protect Chinese Consumers?', 106 *TMR* (2016), 883, 893. Available at: https://www.inta.org/TMR/Documents/Volume%20106/vol106_no5_a2.pdf.

goods such as the quality or the place of origin."[357] The BHPC specifically stated that it is not proper to try to apply the "immoral trade mark category" of Article 10(8)(8) TML to Qiaodan Sports' registration, since the trade mark is not inherently immoral, and that use of a transliteration of a foreign name trade mark causing consumer confusion does not make a trade mark immoral, or qualify it as obtained by fraud or other improper means, for which reason the registration could not be invalidated.[358]

In 2005, Nike applied for trade mark registration of the transliteration of the full name of basketball player LeBron James: "勒布朗.詹姆斯" (Lēi bùlǎng Zhānmǔsī), but a trade mark squatter had already registered it without ever using it in commerce. Nike litigated all the way to the SPC and managed to invalidate the blocking trade mark ten years later.[359]

(d) Post-Registration Evidence of Bad Faith

(1) Plaintiff and Defendant in the Same Geographical Region

In the JINZHU and device case 2012, the BFIPC took the following circumstances into account to determine bad faith registration: (1) the registrant and the unregistered well-known mark proprietor were located in the same geographical region, and the registrant was supposed to be aware of the mark (*ex ante* evidence); and (2) the registrant had conducted various infringements and unfair competition practices after registration (*ex post* evidence).[360]

(2) Plaintiff and Defendant in the Same Industry

In 2016, the SPC in the Weishida Yulan case acknowledged that the conduct after registration of a trade mark can be evidence of "bad-faith registration".[361] The plaintiff Proctor & Gamble Company (P&G) and defendant Santou Weishida Cosmetics Co., Ltd. (Weishida) were both in the cosmetics industry. The plaintiff's trade marks, " 玉兰" (Yulan) and "玉兰油" (Yulanyou) were well-known to the public before the defendant applied for "威仕达玉兰" (Weishida Yulan), the existence of which the defendant ought to have been aware at the time of application. Further, the defendant's conduct when using the trade mark manifested its intention to take advantage of

357. Young, *supra* note 356, 893.

358. The SPC did not discuss that Qiaodan Sports registered number 23, "杰弗里乔丹" (Jie Fu Li Qiao Dan) and "马库斯乔丹" (Ma Ku Si Qiao Dan), which are the transliterations of Jeffrey Jordan and Marcus Jordan, the names of Michael Jordan's sons, nor the characteristic silhouette. These registrations take away any doubt that the Qiaodan Sports associated itself with and traded on the reputation and goodwill of Michael Jordan.

359. China Trade Mark Reg. No. 4903847 for LEBRON JAMES in Chinese. SPC July, 7 *Xing Ti Zi* (2015).

360. *Shen Zhen Bao Song Li Industrial Ltd and the TRAB v. Si Chuan Mian Zhu Jian Nan Chun Jiu Chang Ltd.*, BFIPC, 3359 *Yi Zhong Zhi Xing Chu Zi* (2012).

361. *P&G Ltd. and TRAB v. Santou Weishida Cosmetic Ltd.*, SPC, 13 *Zui Gao Fa Xing Zai* (2016). Weishida Yulan case (well-known trade mark protection on similar goods, bad faith), Wan Hui Da via NiuYie, 8 October 2017. https://niuyie.com/weishida-yulan-case-well-known-trademark-protection-on-similar-goods-bad-faith/.

the business reputation of the plaintiff, which supported the conclusion that the registration had been made in bad faith. The evidence showed that the defendant had used the cited trade mark together with the Chinese characters "玉兰" and a device mark that was similar to the plaintiff's (P&G) Yulanyou products. Meanwhile, the defendant had also imitated P&G's product packaging. Taken together, such acts demonstrated the defendant's bad faith.

(e) Registered or Applied-for Mark, but Recently Cancelled, Invalidated or not Renewed

Prior registrants and prior applicants can oppose trade mark applications that are identical or similar for identical or similar goods.

Those losing their trade mark have a grace period of one year from the cancellation, declaration of invalidity, or non-renewal upon the expiry of the validity period of their trade mark. During this year, the CTMO will not approve any application for registration of a trade mark that is identical with or similar to the trade mark.[362]

(f) Procedure

In case of an opposition, the applicant shall submit documents certifying its identity[363] and furnish an original copy and a duplicate of: an Application for Trade Mark Opposition; documents that certify the identity of the opponent; and documents certifying that the opponent is a holder of the prior right or an interested party where the opposition is filed on the grounds of violation of Articles 13(2) and (3), 15, 16(1), 30, 31, or 32 TML 2019. An Application for Trade Mark Opposition shall indicate explicit requests and a factual basis, with the relevant evidence attached.

The CTMO shall not accept the application: if it is not filed within the statutory time limit; if the qualification of the applicant or the grounds of the opposition are not in compliance with Article 33 TML (for example if an opposition applicant who is claiming relative grounds of refusal is not a holder of prior rights or an interested party); if the grounds, facts and legal basis of the opposition are not made explicit; or if the application for opposition is filed by the same opponent against the same trade mark on the same grounds, facts and legal basis.

If the conditions for acceptance are satisfied, the CTMO will accept the application for opposition and issue a Notification of Acceptance to the applicant.

The CTMO shall promptly send the duplicate copy of the opposition materials to the opposed party which shall be required to respond within 30 days from the date of receipt of the duplicate copy of the opposition materials. If the opposed party fails to make a response, the making of a decision by the CTMO shall not be affected, although some commentators have argued that if the applicant fails to respond in the opposition procedure, there should be a default judgment in favour of the opponent.[364]

362. Article 50 TML 2019, *supra* note 15.
363. Article 14 IRTL 2014, *supra* note 12.
364. Yang, *supra* note 260. AIPLA argued that there should be a default judgment not only in case of oppositions but also invalidations, when the trade mark registrant is not

A party may supplement related evidence within three months from the date on which the application is filed or a response is made. If evidence accrued after the expiration of the time limit or a party failed to submit the evidence within the time limit for other justifiable reasons, and when such evidence is submitted after the expiration of the time limit, the CTMO shall send the evidence to the other party and may accept it after cross-examination.

Depending on the outcome of the opposition, the trade mark shall either be republished after the entry into force of the decision to approve its registration, or the publication be revoked.

If the CTMO rejects the opposition, either party within 15 days can pursue an opposition before the TRAB that is responsible for a second review. If the TRAB also approves the registration, then that decision is final for the opponent, while the trade mark applicant can apply for a third review by the Court (BFIPC) and in second instance by the BHPC. However, the owner of a prior right can apply for an invalidation at the TRAB.

2. Post-Registration Grounds of Cancellation

(a) Genericide

If a registered trade mark becomes a common name of goods on which it is approved to be used, any entity or individual may apply to the CTMO for cancellation of the registered trade mark.[365]

Article 10 SPC Provisions 2016 made it clear that one can distinguish between statutory and customary generic names. Statutory generic names were always deemed generic in accordance with laws, regulations, national or industry standards. Customary generic names could have become the victim of their own success in that the proprietor did not sufficiently protect its trade mark against becoming generic by asserting the exclusive right to use the trade mark. If a name has been classified in professional reference books, such as dictionaries, as a class of goods, this supports that the mark has become generic. To determine whether a name has become generic, the common perception of the relevant public nationwide should be taken into account. If the owner knows or should know that the name of its trade mark has become generic for goods in some areas, the People's Court should determine the name as being generic. The determination of whether a name is *de facto* generic or not should be made at the moment of application, or if the status of the name has changed, at the moment of registration.

In case the mark has become generic or has not been used as prescribed in Article 49(2) TML 2019, the following circumstances are considered to be justifiable reasons: *force majeure*; restrictions imposed by government policy; bankruptcy liquidation; and other justifiable reasons not attributable to the trade mark registrant.[366]

---

defending himself. 'AIPLA'S Comments on the Revision of the Trademark Law of the People's Republic of China', 30 July 2018. Available at: https://bit.ly/342KCZc.

365. Article 49(2) TML 2013 and 2019, *supra* note 15.

366. Article 67 IRTL 2014, *supra* note 12.

(b) Non-use Cancellation

If a trade mark has not been used for three consecutive years without a justifiable reason, anyone may apply to the CTMO for cancellation.[367] Upon acceptance of the application for cancellation in case of a generic mark, the CTMO shall notify the trade mark registrant, requiring a response within two months from the date of receipt of the notification. If no response is made at the expiration of the time limit, the making of a decision by the CTMO shall not be affected.[368] If the trade mark proprietor has a real intention to use its trade mark and has made the necessary preparation for such use, but has not put such registered trade mark into actual use due to objective causes, the court may determine that the owner has a just cause.[369]

The trade mark owner can refute a claim of non-use by providing evidence of use: "through manufacture, promotion, distribution, sales, provision of services, or the licensing of third parties to engage in such actions where the registered mark is used."[370] After a non-use cancellation petition, the registrant has the burden of proof to demonstrate use. Use includes: "use on product packaging, invoices, labels, brochures, and catalogues."[371] Use by the trade mark proprietor or licensee is considered trade mark use under Article 49(2) TML.[372] Subtle differences with the registered trade mark without changing its distinctiveness are also considered trade mark use as long as the distinctive features of the trade mark are not altered.[373] If the trade mark has not been actually used, a mere assignment is not sufficient to constitute trade mark use.[374] To be on the safe side, some brand owners engage in small scale production or advertisement of the relevant products.[375]

If the grounds for cancellation or declaration of invalidation involve only certain designated goods, the CTMO or the TRAB shall cancel or declare invalid the registration of the trade mark used only on certain designated goods.[376]

When a trade mark squatter is blocking the registration of the original brand holder's trade mark, because it is similar to its trade mark, this can be challenging for the brand holder. If a brand holder wants to apply for a trade mark in China, it would be well advised to first do a search for identity or similar marks, and if such a mark was found to directly file for a non-use cancellation of that mark. This way, the brand holder does not have to first react to the opposition of the trade mark

367. Article 49(2) TML 2013 and 2019, *supra* note 15.
368. Articles 65 and 66 IRTL 2014, *supra* note 12.
369. Article 26(4) SPC Provisions 2016, *supra* note 112.
370. SIPS Asia, *supra* note 19.
371. SIPS Asia, *supra* note 19.
372. Article 26(1) SPC Provisions 2016, *supra* note 112.
373. Article 26(2) SPC Provisions 2016, *supra* note 112.
374. Article 26(3) SPC Provisions 2016, *supra* note 112.
375. Jude Chen, 'Defensive Mark Registration under China's Current Trademark Law', Rouse, 2013. Available at: https://www.rouse.com/media/299713/clp-defensive-mark-under-the-current-trademark-law-of-the-prc-marandapr-2013.pdf.
376. Article 68 IRTL 2014, *supra* note 12.

squatter by filing a review of the rejection with the TRAB, because this cannot be suspended after the date the brand holder has applied for trade mark registration.[377]

Thus, trade mark applicants are advised to search for possible blocking marks, and proactively move to cancel them before filing their trade mark application, instead of waiting for the application to be rejected by the CTMO and only then filing the non-use cancellation simultaneously with the rejection appeal.[378]

In 2014, Sunpower Corporation filed a partial non-use cancellation against the trade mark registration "MAXON" by a local company designated for "batteries, battery chargers and chargers". The registrant submitted evidence of use only for "cell phones" and no evidence for batteries or chargers. The TRAB accepted the non-use cancellation. The registrant brought the case to the Beijing IP Court, which held that "cell phones" and "batteries" are "similar" goods, therefore, the use of the trade mark on "cell phones" can be regarded as use on "batteries".

Sunpower Corporation appealed to the BHPC and argued that (1) "cell phones" and "batteries" are not similar goods according to the Nice Classification and the Similar Goods and Services Classification Book as adopted by the CTMO; (2) "cell phones" and "batteries" are not similar goods in terms of functions, usage, target consumers and marketing channels; therefore, the use of the trade mark on "cell phones" could not maintain the registration of the trade mark on "batteries". The BHPC held that the Nice Classification and the Similar Goods and Services Classification Book needs to be followed. The local company filed an application of re-examination to the SPC. The SPC held that even though batteries and chargers are necessary parts of a cell phone, they are independent commodities which have independent functions. The use of the trade mark on cell phones cannot be extended to "batteries, chargers".[379]

On 8 April 2003, Consolidated Artists B.V. filed a non-use cancellation application against the MANGO trade mark in Class 25 regarding clothes, underwear and hats, registered by H. Daya International Co., Ltd. (Daya) in 1992. CTMO decided to cancel the trade mark for non-use. Daya filed an appeal claiming that in the preceding three years, its licensee (Sonnetti International S.A.) and sub-licensee (Shaoxing Kailiya International Supplies Co., Ltd.) had been manufacturing in Mainland China products labelled with the MANGO trade mark and exported the same to Panama. Daya also submitted the licensing agreement which granted Sonneti International S.A. the permission to use the trade mark, and other related agreements between it and Shaoxing Kailiya International Supplies Co., Ltd. The TRAB sustained registration of the MANGO trade mark for the designated goods.

Consolidated Artists appealed this decision to the BFIPC, which overturned the TRAB's decision. This first instance judgment was further upheld by the BHPC. After a retrial, the TRAB cancelled the MANGO trade mark.

The BHPC's reasoning was that a company in China, licensed by a foreign brand that has no trade mark in China, should be able to manufacture goods for that foreign

377. 'Non-Use Cancellations in China – Offensive and Defensive Applications', SIPS Asia, 19 March 2018. Available at: https://sips.asia/knowledge/trademark-registration/non-use-cancellation-actions-in-china/.

378. SIPS Asia, *supra* note 19.

379. SPC, 8597 *Zui Gao Fa Xing Shen* (2017).

brand with the trade mark it uses outside China, if these goods are exclusively for export. In this sense, the BHPC held that the trade mark on the goods were neither used as a source indicator in China nor put in market circulation in China.[380] This is called the Original Equipment Manufacturer (OEM) exception.

However, on 20 December 2018, the SPC in *Montfort Services Sdn. Bhd. & USA Pro IP Ltd v. TRAB*,[381] made it clear that OEM use can constitute trade mark use by the foreign brand that licensed the OEM to manufacture products with its brand. In the SPC's opinion, the domestic OEM only physically attaches the marks at issue to the relevant products in China and exports said products from China.[382] See section IX on Scope of Right and Infringement for a further discussion on this issue.

(c) Surrender

If a trade mark registrant applies for the surrender of its registered trade mark, or of its trade mark registration on certain designated goods, it shall file an Application for the Surrender of the Trade Mark to the CTMO, and return the original Trade Mark Registration Certificate.[383] If a trade mark registrant applies for the surrender of its registered trade mark, or of its trade mark registration on certain designated goods, and where the surrender is approved by the CTMO, the exclusive right to use the registered trade mark or the effect of the exclusive right to use the registered trade mark on the designated goods shall be terminated from the date on which the CTMO receives the application for surrender.[384]

(d) Other

If the trade mark registrant dies or ceases to exist, and if at the expiration of one year from this date no procedures have been taken to transfer the mark, any person is entitled to apply to the CTMO for removal of the mark from the register. The applicant must furnish proof of the death of the trade mark proprietor or the cessation of the enterprise of the trade mark proprietor.

---

380. Ma Qiang, 'China – Is Trademark Use In OEM Products Valid to Maintain Registration? A Brief Comment On The Appeal On Non-Use Cancellation Against Trademark "MANGO"', Conventus Law, 26 March 2019. Available at: http://www.conventuslaw.com/report/china-is-trademark-use-in-oem-products-valid-to/.
381. *Montfort Services Sdn. Bhd. & USA Pro IP Ltd v. TRAB*, 8135 *Zui Gao Fa Xing Shen* (2018).
382. Jiaohongbin and Liu Yuxin, 'Trademark Use or Not? Trademark Infringement or Not? –The Supreme People's Court of the P.R.C. Made its Latest Voice in an OEM Related Trademark Infringement Case', KWM, 25 October 2019. Available at: https://www.chinalawinsight.com/2019/10/articles/intellectual-property/trademark-use-or-not-trademark-infringement-or-not-the-supreme-peoples-court-of-the-p-r-c-made-its-latest-voice-in-an-oem-related-trademark-infringement-case/.
383. Article 73(1) IRTL 2014, *supra* note 12.
384. Article 73(2) IRTL 2014, *supra* note 12.

(e) Unilateral Change of the Registered Trade Mark or Registered Matter

A trade mark registrant may not change the registered trade mark, the name or address of the registrant, or any other registered matter without approval.[385] If it does so, the AIC shall order the registrant to make the corrections within a prescribed time limit, and if the registrant fails to do so within the time limit, the CTMO shall cancel the registered trade mark.[386] This leads to tensions for trade mark registrants who in the operation of their business often have to adjust a font or composition of the graphic of a trade mark, even though this would not have any substantial influence on the distinctiveness in the eyes of the relevant public.[387] By contrast, infringers often can take advantage of the changes of a trade mark with regard to different pronunciations, shapes or meanings concerning text or graphics that do not affect the distinctiveness of the trade mark. This can force trade mark registrants to protect all kinds of variations of their trade mark.

VIII. TRANSFER AND LICENSING

1. Transfer

The Provisions on Issues Related to the Transfer of Trade Mark Applications were promulgated in August 2009.[388]

If a registered trade mark is assigned, the assignor and the assignee shall enter into an assignment agreement, and jointly file an application with the CTMO.[389]

If an applicant transfers its application for trade mark registration, it shall go through the formalities of the CTMO.[390] If the CTMO approves the transfer of a registered trade mark application, it shall issue the corresponding certificate to the transferee and publish it in the Trade Mark Gazette. The assignee shall have the right to exclusively use the registered trade mark from the date of publication. The assignee shall guarantee the quality of the goods on which the registered trade mark is used.

If a registered trade mark is transferred and the trade mark registrant fails to transfer the same or similar trade mark registered on the same or similar good, the CTMO shall notify the trade mark registrant to make corrections within a specified time limit. If no corrections are made at the expiration of the time limit, the application for assignment of the registered trade mark shall be considered abandoned, and the CTMO shall notify the applicants for assignment in writing.[391] This ensures that trade

385. Article 49(1) TML 2019, *supra* note 15.
386. Article 49(1) TML 2019, *supra* note 15.
387. Zhang Hui, 'Comparison Principles to Determine Trademark Proximity', 16 *China IP Magazine* (February 2007). Available at: http://www.chinaipmagazine.com/en/journal-show.asp?id = 357.
388. Provisions on Issues Related to The Transfer of the Trademark application, promulgated on 10 August 2009 and effective as of the same day. Available at: http://sbj.cnipa.gov.cn/sbjg/200908/t20090811_199369.html.
389. Article 42(1) TML 2019, *supra* note 15. Article 31(1) IRTL, *supra* note 12.
390. Article 17(2) IRTL 2014, *supra* note 12.
391. Article 31(2) IRTL 2014, *supra* note 12.

mark owners cannot transfer one trade mark, receive the royalties from the transfer, but then continue to operate under other registered trade marks that would compete with the transferred mark.

If an assignment may easily cause confusion or have any other adverse effect, the CTMO shall disapprove it and notify the applicant of disapproval in written form with an explanation of the reasons.[392]

Under the Measures for the Registration and Administration of Collective Marks and Certification Marks 2003,[393] it is allowed to transfer a collective or certification mark if the assignee has the right qualifications and complies with the TML and the IRTL.[394]

If in the trade mark review process, the trade mark in dispute has been transferred and the transferee participates in the forthcoming review process, the transferor shall generally no longer be a party. In the event that the transferor files an administrative lawsuit, such lawsuit may be rejected. The litigation actions completed by the transferor are binding on the transferee.[395]

2. Transfer by Other Means

If the exclusive right to use a registered trade mark is transferred due to reasons other than assignment, the party accepting the exclusive right to use the registered trade mark shall go through the formalities for the transfer of the exclusive right to use the registered trade mark with the relevant certification documents or legal documents.[396] If the exclusive right to use a registered trade mark is transferred, the same or similar trade mark registered by the exclusive rights holder of the registered trade mark on the same or similar commodity shall be transferred together; if it is not transferred together, the CTMO shall request correction within a time limit; if the application is not corrected, the transfer cannot be completed and the CTMO shall notify the applicant in writing.[397] If the application for trade mark transfer is approved, this shall be published. The parties accepting the transfer of the exclusive right to use the registered trade mark shall enjoy the exclusive right to use the trade mark from the date of the announcement.[398]

392. Article 42(3) TML 2019, *supra* note 15.
393. Measures for the Registration and Administration of Collective marks and Certification Marks 2003, SAIC promulgated it on 17 April 2003 and effective on 1 June 2003. Available at: https://www.ccpit-patent.com.cn/node/1177/1178 and http://sbj.saic.gov.cn/english/show.asp?id = 60&bm = flfg.
394. Article 16(2) SAIC Measures Collective and Certification Marks 2003, *supra* note 393.
395. Article 1(6) BHPC Guidelines 2019, *supra* note 5.
396. Article 32(1) IRTL 2014, *supra* note 12.
397. Article 32(2) IRTL 2014, *supra* note 12.
398. Article 32(3) IRTL 2014, *supra* note 12.

3. Licences

A trade mark registrant may, by entering into a trade mark licensing contract, allow another party to use its registered trade mark.[399] This can considerably extend the business opportunities for trade mark proprietors.

When the exclusive right to use a registered trade mark is infringed, the exclusive licensee can bring a suit in the People's Court.[400] Sole licensees can do so only together with the trade mark proprietor or by themselves in the case that the trade mark proprietor fails to bring a suit.[401] Non-exclusive licensees can bring a suit provided that they have been given clear authorization to do so by the trade mark proprietor.[402]

(a) Types of Licences

The SPC Interpretation 2002[403] distinguished between exclusive, sole, and non-exclusive licences.[404] An exclusive licence no longer allows the trade mark owner to use to mark. Thus, the licensor's reputation is completely dependent upon the licensee's quality of the goods or service that were used in combination with the trade mark. If the licensee lets the quality deteriorate, this could mean that the licensor could eventually lose the goodwill of its trade mark and therefore the prospect of using the trade mark again in the future.[405] In case of a sole licence, the licensor agrees that beside itself, only one licensee can use the trade mark, and if the licensee does not guarantee the quality of the goods or service associated with the trade mark, the reputational damage could have a direct effect on the economic interests of the licensor.[406] In case of a non-exclusive licence, the licensor can allow many licensees to use the trade mark. If one licensee does not guarantee the trade mark, the reputational damage can adversely affect not only the licensor, but the other licensees as well.[407] Then, not only the licensor, but also the licensees have an incentive to supervise and guarantee the quality of the goods or service associated with the trade mark.

399. Article 43(1) TML 2019, *supra* note 15.
400. Article 4(2) SPC Interpretation 2002. Several Questions on the Application of Law in Trial of Trade Mark Civil Dispute Cases Interpretation 2002, promulgated by the SPC on 12 October 2002 and effective as of 16 October 2002. Available at: https://www.wipo.int/edocs/lexdocs/laws/en/cn/cn149en.pdf. Amended on 23 December 2020, No. 3. Available at: https://bit.ly/2LBY3eE.
401. Article 4(2) SPC Interpretation 2002, *supra* note 400.
402. Article 4(2) SPC Interpretation 2002, *supra* note 400.
403. SPC Interpretation 2002, *supra* note 400.
404. Article 3(1)-(3) SPC Interpretation 2002, *supra* note 400.
405. Article 3(1) SPC Interpretation 2002, *supra* note 400.
406. Article 3(2) SPC Interpretation 2002, *supra* note 400.
407. Article 3(3) SPC Interpretation 2002, *supra* note 400.

(b) Registration Requirements

If another party is licensed to use a registered trade mark, the licensor shall report the licence to the CTMO for registration, which is subsequently published. An unrecorded licence may not be invoked as a defence against a third party in good faith.[408]

While no longer compulsory since 2013, registration is still advisable if a licensor wishes to repatriate royalties generated by licences of registered trade marks, according to the guidelines of the State Administration of Foreign Exchange (SAFE). SAFE eliminated this recording requirement in 2013, but these rules change frequently.[409] Registration is also necessary if the licensor wants the licensees to be able to enforce the trade mark against infringements, according to SPC Interpretation on Interim Injunction of Trade Marks.[410]

The Trade Mark Licence Contract Registration Measures[411] require that foreign documents should be accompanied by a Chinese translation, a separate application for recordation need to be submitted for each registered mark licensed under the contract. The approval process usually takes eight to 18 months.[412]

(c) Compulsory Indications

The name of a licensee and the origin of the goods must be indicated on the goods on which the registered trade mark is used.[413] In the case of service marks, the indication should be used for example on the tools of service[414] and commercial documents delivered to the customer.[415]

408. Article 43(3) TML 2019, *supra* note 15.
409. Joe Simone and Troy Rice, 'Should You Record Trademark License Contracts?', SIPS Asia, 31 October 2014. Available at: https://sips.asia/knowledge/technology-and-commercial-ip/should-you-record-trademark-license-contracts/.
410. Article 4 Interpretation of the Law on the cessation of the exclusive right to infringe registered trade marks and the application of the law for the preservation of evidence before the prosecution, SPC promulgated it on 9 January 2002. Available at: https://bit.ly/36ajIAB. See also Duan Lihong, '"Zuigao renmin fayuan guanyu su qian tingzhi qinfan zhuce shangbiao zhuanyong quan he baoquan zhengju shiyong falu wenti de jieshi" de lijie yu shiyong' (Understanding and Application of the Interpretation of the Supreme People's Court on Stopping the Infringement of the Exclusive Right to Use Registered Trademarks and the Legal Issues Concerning the Protection of Evidence), SPC, 21 December 2008. Available at: http://www.npc.gov.cn/zgrdw/huiyi/lfzt/qqzrfca/2008-12/21/content_1462867.htm.
411. Trade Mark Licence Contract Recordation Measures, SAIC promulgated No. 39, 1 August 1997. Available at: https://sips.asia/knowledge/technology-and-commercial-ip/should-you-record-trademark-license-contracts/.
412. Simone and Rice, *supra* note 409.
413. Article 43(2) TML 2019, *supra* note 15.
414. Article 7(1)(3) Opinions on Several Issues Concerning Service Mark Protection, adopted by the SAIC, and entered into force on 30 March 1999. Available at: https://wipolex.wipo.int/en/text/475171.
415. Article 7(1)(6) Opinions on Several Issues Concerning Service Mark Protection, *supra* note 414.

(d) Obligation for Quality Control and Administrative Control

The licensor shall supervise and the licensee shall guarantee the quality of the goods on which the licensee uses the licensor's registered trade mark.[416] A licensee of the registered trade mark needs to indicate on the goods its name and the origin of the goods.

The user of a trade mark shall be responsible for the quality of the goods on which the trade mark is used. The AICs at all levels shall, through trade mark administration, prevent consumer fraud.[417] It is expected that these activities will be carried out by the AMRs (Administrations for Market Regulation) in the future.

Of course, if the licensee violates the quality assurance clause of the licence contract and causes damage to others, the licensor might subsequently recover compensation from the licensee if the licence agreement was notified to the CTMO for record and publication.[418]

The TML and its supplementing IRTL remain silent about who is liable in case of insufficient product quality. Article 122 General Principles of the Civil Law 1986[419] stipulates: "If the product quality is insufficient and causes damage to others' property or personal injury, the manufacturer or seller of the product shall bear civil liability according to law." In other words: the licensor should bear joint and several liability.[420] Article 179 General Provisions of the Civil Law 2017 provides the main ways and means to bear civil liability that could be used in case of substandard quality.[421] Both provisions are now reflected in the Civil Code 2020 whose Chapter 4 relates to product liability.[422]

In *Jing Kelian, Zhang Xinrong, etc. v. U.S. GM Corp.*, the SPC gave an official reply as to whether the aggrieved party could bring a civil lawsuit against the licensor of the trade mark:[423] "[W]e believe that any company or individual that displays its name, trade mark or other identifiable logo on the product and indicates that it is the manufacturer of the product, falls under Article 122 General Principles of the Civil Law 1986. In other words, the trade mark links the proprietor-manufacturer

416. Article 43(1) TML 2019, *supra* note 15.
417. Article 7(2) TML 2019, *supra* note 15.
418. Article 43(3) TML 2013 and 2019, *supra* note 15.
419. General Principles of Civil Law 1986, *supra* note 198.
420. Article 178 General Rules of the Civil Law of the PRC, promulgated by the NPC on 15 March 2017, effective on 1 November 2017. Available at: https://www.dimt.it/images/pdf/GeneralRules.pdf.
421. General Provisions of the Civil Law 2017. Available at: http://www.npc.gov.cn/englishnpc/lawsoftheprc/202001/c983fc8d3782438fa775a9d67d6e82d8.shtml#: ~ :text = Article%20 3%20The%20personal%20rights,equal%20status%20in%20civil%20activities.
422. Articles 1202–1207 Civil Code 2020. Civil Code/Title 7 Tort Liability, adopted by NPC on 28 May 2020, effective as of 1 January 2021.
423. 'Zuigao renmin fayuan guanyu chanpin qinquan anjian de shouhai ren neng fou yi chanpin de shangbiao suoyou renwei beigao tiqi minshi susong de pifu [xianxing youxiao]' (Official Reply on Whether the Aggrieved Party in A Product Infringement Case May Bring A Civil Lawsuit Against the Product Trade Mark Owner [effective]), adopted at the 1229th meeting of the members of the Judicial Committee of the SPC on 4 July 2002, Legal Interpretation [2002] No. 22, promulgated on 11 July 2002 and in effect as of 28 July 2002. Available at: http://pkulaw.cn/fulltext_form.aspx?Gid = 40780&Db = chl.

to the consumer." Article 122 General Principles of the Civil Law 1986 stated: "If a substandard product causes property damage or physical injury to others, the manufacturer or seller shall bear civil liability according to law. If the transporter or storekeeper is responsible for the matter, the manufacturer or seller shall have the right to demand compensation for its losses." A "producer" was specified in Article 22 Product Quality Law 2000.[424] The SPC in this case identified the U.S. GM Corp. as the trade mark holder of the vehicle with a defective axle that caused an accident and held the company liable for the product quality damage. Therefore, it held the BHPC qualification of the GM Corp., GM Overseas Corp., and GM Brazil as defendants as "not inappropriate."[425]

IX. SCOPE OF RIGHT AND INFRINGEMENT

1. Legal Definition of Infringement

The requirements of trade mark infringement that damage the rights and interests of others' registered trade marks are the same requirements that constitute tort: the conduct should violate the law; when the perpetrator committed an illegal act, it had intentional or negligent fault; and there is causality between the damaging fact and the illegal act.

The TML defines seven categories of infringement of the exclusive right to use a registered trade mark, and CNIPA's Standard to Determine Trade Mark Infringement (Trade Mark Infringement Standard)[426] further interprets these categories for administrative enforcement actions by the Administrations of Market Regulation (AMRs).

Article 57 TML 2019 lists the following categories of infringing conduct.

(a) Unauthorized Use in a Double-Identity Case

This is the typical case of selling counterfeit goods, the purpose of which is to confuse consumers of the origin of the goods, mislead consumers, and harm the legitimate

424. Product Quality Law (Amended) Order of the President No. 33, Decisions of the Standing Committee of the NPC on Amending the Product Quality Law adopted at the 16th meeting of the Standing Committee of the NPC on 8 July 2000, are hereby promulgated and shall come into force as of 1 September 2000.

425. Reply on Whether a Victim of a Product Infringement Case Can File a Civil Lawsuit with the Trade Mark Owner of the Product as the Defendant, SPC Interpretation 2002, *supra* note 400.

'Zuigao renmin fayuan guanyu chanpin qinquan anjian de shouhai ren neng fou yi chanpin de shangbiao suoyou renwei beigao tiqi minshi susong de pifu [xianxing youxiao]' (Official Reply on Whether the Aggrieved Party in A Product Infringement Case May Bring A Civil Lawsuit Against the Product Trade Mark Owner [effective]) adopted at the 1229th meeting of the members of the Judicial Committee of the SPC on 4 July 2002, Legal Interpretation [2002] No. 22, promulgated on 11 July 2002 and in effect as of 28 July 2002. Available at: http://pkulaw.cn/fulltext_form.aspx?Gid = 40780&Db = chl.

426. Notice of the CNIPA on the Trade Mark Infringement Determination Standards, 23 *Guozhifabaozi* (2020), 15 June 2020. Available at: http://www.gov.cn/zhengce/zhengceku/2020-07/07/content_5524771.htm.

rights and interests of trade mark registrants and consumers. However, one needs to realize that this category also applies to the situation where vendors clearly display counterfeit goods and consumers are not confused.

The sale of goods first marketed by the trade mark owner or with its consent is normally not deemed infringing due to a lack of confusion, yet see below for the Chinese approach to exhaustion and parallel imports.

If a trade name in an enterprise name is used prominently on identical goods or services, which is identical with a registered trade mark, it also constitutes trade mark infringement under Article 57(1) TML.[427]

The AMRs in Shandong and Henan provinces asked CNIPA whether recycling beer bottles, with an original trade mark embossed in the glass that could not be removed, in this case "青岛啤酒" (QINGDAO Beer), which is distinctive trade mark with a reputation, constituted trade mark infringement. On 20 November 2019, CNIPA replied that when a trade mark embossed on a bottle cannot be removed, the recycler should ensure that it covers the embossed trade mark with another label. Affixing another label bearing another trade mark on a bottle, leaving the original embossed trade mark visible, is insufficient to avoid confusion. Consumers could believe that the owner of the label has a relationship with the original trade mark owner.[428]

In August 2016, the plaintiff New Balance Trading (China) Co., Ltd. brought a lawsuit against five defendants for a claim of trade mark infringement and unfair competition by false promotion before the Suzhou Intermediate People's Court and applied for preliminary injunction. In September 2016, the Suzhou Intermediate People's Court made an order that the five defendants should immediately stop their manufacture and sale of footwear with the same stylized uppercase "N" letters on both sides of the shoes as those on New Balance shoes. However, the defendants refused to comply with the order until 11 April 2017. Therefore, on 24 April 2017, the Suzhou Intermediate People's Court made a decision for the imposition of a total fine of RMB 1.7 million against the defendants for refusal to comply with the order and served the decision on the defendants.[429]

(b) Where the Mark that is Used Without Consent is Identical or Similar to the Registered Mark, and is Used on Identical or Similar Goods Without There Being a Double Identity

This defines the scope of protection under China's TML. Reference is made to the explanations on determining similarity of marks and similarity of goods, as above. In general, to determine whether the cited and contested trade marks are similar, the Trade Mark Registration Certificate of the rights holder should be compared

427. Article 23(1) Trade Mark Infringement Standard, *supra* note 426.

428. Paul Ranjard, Hui Huang and Binbin Du, 'Use of recycled beer bottle without original embossed trademark deemed illegal', Wan Hui Da, 2 March 2020. Available at: https://www.international-lawoffice.com/Newsletters/Intellectual-Property/China/Wanhuida-Intellectual-Property/Use-of-recycled-beer-bottle-without-original-embossed-trademark-deemed-illegal.

429. 2017 Chronicle of China's IP Industry (I), China IP Today, 3 April 2019. Available at: http://www.chinaiptoday.com/post.html?id=138.

with the contested trade mark, and the actual use of the rights holder's trade mark is irrelevant.[430]

If marks are used on identical or similar goods, there is a likelihood of consumer confusion and a higher risk that it would be considered infringing.

Note however that Article 57(2) TML 2019 not only needs to take the factors of identity or similarity of trade marks and proximity of goods into account, but also factors of an actual or likelihood of confusion due to specific market circumstances. In other words, in addition to proving identity/similarity of the mark and identity/similarity of the goods, the trade mark owner needs to prove circumstances that point to actual or potential consumer confusion.

Whether it is easy for the relevant consumers to be confused is therefore the issue to be determined, and the conditions that contribute to actual confusion need to be determined as well.

The *Chateau Lafite Rothschild v. Golden Hope Company* "拉菲庄园" (Lā Fēi Zhuāng Yuán) case[431] concerned the Golden Hope Company starting to use "拉菲", which is the transliteration of "LAFITE" as part of its trade mark. However, this transliteration of LAFITE as "拉菲", was already used in various Chinese media in reference to Chateau Lafite Rothschild wine. Some media commended "拉菲" as a wine with a high reputation even before the French vintner Chateau Lafite Rothschild registered the transliteration as its trade mark. The SPC held that after many years of commercial operations, Chateau Lafite Rothschild had established a stable objective connection between "拉菲" and "LAFITE", and the relevant public in China often referred to "拉菲" as a transliteration of "Lafite".[432] Golden Hope Company failed to prove that it had carved out a specific market with a distinct relevant public for its products as a result of its use of the contested trade mark. News reports demonstrated that the relevant public had indeed confused the contested trade mark with the cited trade mark.

CNIPA clarifies that by changing a registered trade mark's use the registrant can move within the scope of another's registered mark with regard to similar goods, or that combining someone else's registered trade marks without authorization on similar goods or services of that registered trade mark can constitute trade mark infringement according to Article 57(2) TML.[433] If a trade name in an enterprise name is used prominently for goods or services which are similar to someone else's registered trade mark and easily cause confusion, such act constitutes trade mark infringement stipulated in Article 57(2) TML.[434]

The following cases are examples of use of a similar trade mark for identical/similar goods or services:

---

430. Answer 19 of the BHPC to Several Questions in the Trial of Trade Mark Civil Dispute Cases, 18 February, Jinggao Fafa [2004] No. 48. Available at: https://v1.iphouse.cn/lawinfo/121.html?keyword=.
431. *Chateau Lafite Rothschild v. TRAB and Nanjing Gold Hope Wine Industry*, SPC Administrative Judgment, 23 December, 34 *Zui Gao Fa Xing Zai* (2016).
432. WIPO and SPC, *WIPO Collection of Leading Judgments on Intellectual Property Rights People's Republic of China (2011–2018)* (2019), 28–30. Available at: https://www.wipo.int/edocs/pubdocs/en/wipo_pub_1065.pdf.
433. Article 22(2) Trade Mark Infringement Standard, *supra* note 426.
434. Article 23(2) Trade Mark Infringement Standard, *supra* note 426.

Beijing iYuba Tech Company (iYuba) used the logo of the BBC for applications to learn English without authorization in its WeChat official account and the Android version of the mobile phone software, with a slightly changed colour and font, and with the addition of certain words such as "English". The British Broadcasting Company (BBC), which has a relatively high reputation in China, sued iYuba for trade mark infringement. The Beijing Haidian District People's Court ordered iYuba to immediately cease using the logo and compensate the BBC for economic losses and reasonable expenses for an amount of RMB 1 million.[435]

In 2016, in *3M v. 3N*, the Zhejiang Higher People's Court held that one different letter is within the scope of similarity of marks if the goods were also similar: retro-reflective marking products for "3M" and luminescent sheet and paving for "3N".[436]

In 2018, in *Dunhill v. Danhuoli*, the Foshan Intermediate People's Court held Danhuoli liable for trade mark infringement of the Dunhill trade mark logo. The "DUNHILL" trade mark was designated for clothing and Danhuoli had also registered its trade mark "DANHUOLI" in Roman script for clothing in a plain font, but then started to imitate Dunhill's elongated "D", "h" and "ll" by using an elongated "D", "h" and "li".[437]

In *New Balance v. New Barlun (China) Co. Ltd.*, New Balance sued New Barlun over a mark with close similarity but not identity designated for identical goods. On 16 April 2020, the Shanghai Pudong People's Court held Zhao Chengpeng of New Barlun guilty of unfair competition in using the stylized uppercase letter "N" trade mark logo of the US footwear producer, New Balance. Since New Barlun's "N" was only slightly different from that of New Balance's "N", with two diagonal stripes on the second leg of the "N", consumers were confused. New Barlun was ordered to pay damages in the amount of RMB 10.8 million to New Balance: RMB 10 million for economic losses and RMB 800,000 for reasonable expenses for the protection of New Balance's trade mark.[438] New Barlun's act arguably caused both trade mark infringement and unfair competition and New Balance could have chosen either or both claims. Perhaps because New Barlun's "N" was registered as a trade mark as

435. 'China court rules in favor of BBC in trademark infringement case', Xinhua, https://www.chinadailyhk.com/articles/239/109/82/1578378062887.html. He Lu, '"BBC" shangbiao bei lanyong, yingguo guangbo gongsi su pei bai wan bai wan huo quan e zhichi' (Unauthorized use of the "BBC" trade mark, the British Broadcasting Corporation's lawsuit for compensation of one million received full support), 6 January 2020. Available at: http://bjhdfy.chinacourt.gov.cn/article/detail/2020/01/id/4758153.shtml

436. Aileen Wu and Sisi Liang, '3M wins trademark infringement case against 3N', Wan Hui Da, 7 March 2016. Available at: https://www.internationallawoffice.com/Newsletters/Intellectual-Property/China/Wan-Hui-Da-Law-Firm-Intellectual-Property-Agency/3M-wins-trademark-infringement-case-against-3N.

437. Niall Fraser, 'Alfred Dunhill awarded 10 million yuan in "groundbreaking" trademark infringement case against Chinese clothing firm Danhuoli', SCMP, 11 October 2018: https://www.scmp.com/news/hong-kong/hong-kong-economy/article/2167986/alfred-dunhill-awarded-10-million-yuan.

438. '"N" zimu yundong xie zhi zheng hu shang luochui "New Balance" yishen huo pei 1080 wan yuan' ("N" letter sports shoes dispute "New Balance" received a compensation of 10.8 million yuan in the first instance), China News Network, 17 April 2020. Available at: https://news.sina.com.cn/o/2020-04-16/doc-iircuyvh8160629.shtml.

well and acted under the cover of legal channels, New Balance chose for an action of unfair competition.

In April 2016, Fujian Ting Fei Long Sporting Goods Co. introduced its "Uncle Martian" brand of athletic footwear at a fashion show including shoes that were virtually identical to those offered by US brand "Under Armour", using the "Uncle Martian" logo which is similar to Under Armour's logo. In June 2016, Under Armour started a legal action before the Fujian Higher People's Court seeking preliminary and permanent injunctions, monetary damages against Uncle Martian's trade mark infringement and unfair competition. On 2 November 2016, in *Under Armour, Inc. v. Fujian Ting Fei Long Sporting Goods Co.*, the Court issued a preliminary injunction prohibiting Uncle Martian from manufacturing, selling, and advertising shoes bearing the infringing Uncle Martian marks. A year later, the Court issued a permanent injunction to stop using the contested trade marks, destroy all infringing products, pay RMB 2 million in damages, and publish a statement to "eliminate the adverse effect of Uncle Martian's infringement." The Fujian Higher People's Court recognized the reputation of Under Armour's mark backed by evidentiary submissions demonstrating Under Armour's extensive commercial and advertising activities in China. In view of the strength of Under Armour's mark, and the similarities of the parties' marks and products, consumers were likely to be confused, according to the Court.[439] The ruling was confirmed by the SPC on 17 July 2020.[440]

In the following case, the SPC decided that the use of simplified Chinese characters was sufficiently dissimilar as not to constitute infringement of the traditional Chinese character trade mark. The Japanese retail company Ryohin Keikaku Co. Ltd. (Muji) had been using the MUJI trade mark since 1980 and outside Japan since 1990. In 1999, Muji filed trade marks for the "MUJI" trade mark in traditional Chinese characters "無印良品"[441] (Wúyìn Liángpǐn) (which literally means "brandless quality goods") in China, designating Classes 16, 20, 21, 35 and 41. Hainan Nanhua filed the MUJI trade mark in simplified Chinese "无印良品" (Wúyìn Liángpǐn) in Class 24 regarding fabric products, towels, sheets, pillow cases, bed covers, etc., on 6 April 2000 and then transferred the trade mark to Beijing Cottonfield Textile Corp. Muji's opposition to the use of the "无印良品" trade mark was rejected by the CTMO, TRAB and the courts of first and second instance. On 29 June 2012, the SPC ruled against Muji and dismissed its appeal based on the trade mark opposition it filed in 2001. Muji could only prove the use and reputation of "无印良品" on towels etc. before 6 April 2000 in Japan and Hong Kong, but not in Mainland China.[442]

---

439. Danny Awdeh and Yinfei Wu, 'IP Rights in Shining Armour', Lexology 25 January 2018. Available at: https://www.lexology.com/library/detail.aspx?g=73d926e2-e9e3-4bc4-ad5d-ad920540e967.

440. SPC, 851 *Zui Gao Fa Min Zhong* (2017). Available at: http://wenshu.court.gov.cn/website/wenshu/181107ANFZ0BXSK4/index.html?docId=e7d854fec01448199110abfa01171373.

441. The choice by Muji, a Japanese company, of traditional Chinese characters was perhaps prompted by its familiarity with Kanji, which are Chinese characters used in the Japanese language that are often identical to traditional Chinese characters (the Japanese have also altered some Chinese characters and invented some of their own Kanji, and the Japanese government has simplified some Kanji).

442. 'MUJI CASE: the dilemma of Chinese trademark filings', Lexology 3 March 2020. Available at: https://www.lexology.com/library/detail.aspx?g=7e3c3579-6651-42e3-

In 2015, Hainan Nanhua and Beijing Cottonfield initiated proceedings against Muji before the Beijing IP Court for disputes over trade mark infringement, alleging that Muji, without Beijing Cottonfield's authorization, used the trade mark in simplified characters on bed covers, towels and several other related goods, thereby infringing Beijing Cottonfield's trade mark rights. The Beijing IP Court ruled in favour of Beijing Cottonfield. The Court confirmed that Muji infringed Beijing Cottonfield's trade mark and ordered that Muji should stop the alleged infringing acts, pay Beijing Cottonfield damages of RMB 626,000 and make a statement in Muji's online and retail stores in China to eliminate the negative impact that Muji caused by its trade mark infringing acts. Muji appealed to the BHPC on 4 November 2019. The BHPC held that Muji did not file the trade mark "无印良品" in Class 24 in China until 2001, and that Hainan Nanhua was the first to do so. The BHPC confirmed the decision by the Beijing IP Court. This case once more highlights the importance of filing strategies for foreign applicants, and of getting professional advice in respect of linguistics and culture prior to registering and developing brands in China.

An example of a service mark infringement of a slogan is the "If You Are The One" case. The plaintiff, Jin Ahuan is the holder of the "If You Are the One" trade mark designated for the Class 45 "dating service and dating agency". Jiangsu TV used an identical registered trade mark name for its programme. Due to the high popularity of Jiangsu TV as well as the substantial promotion of such a programme, the relevant public may be misled into assuming a connection between the use of the dating agency's registered trade mark and the TV programme, which may cause reverse confusion.[443]

(c) Other Types of Infringing Acts

The BHPC considers free give-aways as a form of sales and the distribution of free gifts (e.g. as a bonus) infringing if within the range of similarity of marks/goods. The person distributing the gifts is thus responsible for the infringement.[444]

If a licensee sells goods with a trade mark manufactured after the set term of the licence contract, this constitutes trade mark infringement.[445]

(d) Forging, Manufacturing or Selling Forged Trade Mark Labels[446]

Manufacturing and selling forged labels is considered trade mark infringement even though they are not yet put onto goods. Of course, forged labels are inextricably linked

94df-ffc2e158dd24.

443. 'Enterprises' Trademark Cases', 72 *China IP Magazine* (April 2016). Available at: http://www.chinaipmagazine.com/en/journal-show.asp?id=1287

444. Answer 22 of the BHPC to Several Questions in the Trial of Trade Mark Civil Dispute Cases, 18 February, Jinggao Fafa [2004] No. 48. Available at: https://v1.iphouse.cn/lawinfo/121.html?keyword=.

445. Answer 23 of the BHPC to Several Questions in the Trial of Trade Mark Civil Dispute Cases, 18 February, Jinggao Fafa [2004] No. 48. Available at: https://v1.iphouse.cn/lawinfo/121.html?keyword=.

446. A form of passing off.

to counterfeiting when this happens. Unauthorized manufacturing of the isolated labels usually occurs during contracting activities, that is, when the contractor is contracting to produce the registered trade mark logo for another person, without the consent of the other, and the trade mark logo is privately printed in addition to the number of prints stipulated in the trade mark printing contract.[447]

(e) Replacing the Registered Trade Mark with Another Trade Mark[448]

Without the consent of the trade mark registrant, the act of exchanging a registered trade mark and putting the goods with the changed trade mark on the market qualifies as infringement. Since the trade mark was removed, the trade mark can no longer be used and there can also be no consumer confusion. Nevertheless, the TML deals with this category as if it were trade mark infringement.

(f) Aiding and Abetting Infringement[449]

This mainly refers to the intentional act of assisting infringement by storage, transportation, mailing, concealment, etc., so as to help others to infringe the exclusive right of trade mark.

CNIPA clarifies that if fair and exhibition organizers, landlords, e-commerce platform operators, etc., fail to perform their management duties, and know or should have known that their tenants or vendors are selling infringing goods in their bricks-and-mortar or virtual facilities, this may lead to liability unless upon notification by the relevant trade mark enforcement department or by the trade mark holder with an effective administrative or judicial document, necessary measures to stop the trade mark infringement are implemented, according to Article 57(6) TML.[450]

In *Dazhong Banchang v. Baidu*, the plaintiff found that the trade mark "DAZHONG BANCHANG" was used as a keyword in the Baidu.com search engine for websites that advertise and sell counterfeit goods and provide information related to the plaintiff. The Shanghai Second Intermediate People's Court held that the websites that paid Baidu for the keywords were infringing the trade mark of the plaintiff, and that Baidu should have scrutinized the keywords and its clients' qualification to use such keywords. Failure to do so led to contributory liability for trade mark infringement.[451]

---

447. The phenomenon of making an extra batch of unauthorized products is called the "third shift"; and refers to a shift in addition to the two ordinary shifts in Chinese factories.
448. A form of reverse passing off.
449. Article 75 IRTL 2014, *supra* note 12, provides some examples of such behaviour: storage, transport, mailing, printing, concealing, using business premises, or an online goods trading platform for infringing upon another person's exclusive right to use a registered trade mark.
450. Article 30 Trade Mark Infringement Standard, *supra* note 426.
451. *Dazhong Transportation Ltd., Shanghai Dazhong Bachang Logistics Ltd v. Beijing Baidu Wangxun Technology Ltd, Baidu Online Network Technology Ltd (Beijing), Shanghai Software Technology Branch of Baidu Online Network Technology Ltd (Beijing)* Shanghai Second Intermediate People's Court, Civil Judgment (2007) Huerzhong Minwu (Zhi) Chuzi No. 147. Mingde Li,' Intellectual Property Law Revision in China: Transplantation

Beijing Xiushui Street Apparel Market, Ltd. v. Chanel S.A.S. provides an example of contributory liability of trade mark infringement of Chanel by the Beijing Xiushui Street Apparel Market. In April 2006, the BHPC affirmed the Beijing Second Intermediate People's Court's decision that the shopping mall, where several shops sold counterfeit goods with the "CHANEL" trade mark, had the contractual power to determine the mall hours of operation, type of merchandise, scope, etc., depending on the needs of the market, and oversee the sales activities and the contractual obligation to maintain discipline, prohibit illegal activities, and report to the relevant executive authorities.[452]

(g) "Otherwise Causing Damage" to the Right to Exclusive Use of a Registered Trade Mark of Others[453]

According to Article 1 SPC Interpretation 2002,[454] the following acts are deemed to be "otherwise causing damage" to the exclusive rights of others to register trade marks:

(1) Words that are identical or similar to the registered trade marks of others are used prominently on the same or similar goods as the company's trade name, which is likely to cause misunderstanding by the relevant public;
(2) Copying, imitating, or translating a well-known trade mark registered by another person or its main part for use as a trade mark on different or dissimilar goods, thereby misleading the public and causing the interests of the registrant of the well-known trade mark to be harmed;
(3) Registering words that are identical or similar to the registered trade mark of another as a domain name, and conducting e-commerce related commodity transactions through the domain may easily mislead the relevant public.

CNIPA points out that act (3) qualifies as trade mark infringement under Article 57(7) TML.[455]

The Guiding Case 58 clarifies that if an individual or company with no historical relationship with a time-honoured brand registered an identical or a similar brand as a trade mark for the same goods, this will be considered false propaganda and constitute trade mark infringement and unfair competition if the time-honoured brand is used for publicity, which falls under Article 57(7) TML. Chengdu Tongdefu Company used the "同德福" (Tongdefu) name as part of its trade mark for peach slices even though it had no historical relationship with "同德福斋铺" (Tongdefuzhaipu)

and Transformation', in Nari Lee, Niklas Bruun and Mingde Li (eds.), *Governance of Intellectual Property Rights in China and Europe* (Edward Elgar Publishing, Cheltenham, 2016), 156–157.

452. Timothy Lau, Kyle Niemi and Lanna Wu, 'Protecting Trademark Rights in China through Litigation', 47 *Stan. J. Int'l L.* (2011), 441, 448–450.

453. If the infringed trade mark is well-known, this rest category can be compared to trade mark dilution by blurring or tarnishment.

454. Interpretation of the SPC on Several Issues Concerning the Application of Law in Trial of Civil Dispute Cases of Trademarks of 12 October 2002. Available at: http://sbj.cnipa.gov.cn/zcfg/sbsfjs/200210/t20021012_232857.html.

455. Article 31 Trade Mark Infringement Standard, *supra* note 426.

of 1898, which became well-known for its peach slices. In contrast, the plainfiff Yu Xiaohua was the fourth-generation successor of this time-honoured brand and thus could rightfully use Chongqing Tongdefu Company as a trade mark for peach slices.[456] In other words: registration and subsequent use of a trade mark is as such no defence against the infringement of a prior mark.

2. Infringement of Unregistered Marks

In addition to the protection of registered trade marks against infringement, unregistered marks that have gained a certain reputation are also protected under Article 32 TML 2019 against being registered by others (see above).

The Anti-Unfair Competition Law 2019 provides protection against confusing or misleading conduct, which also protects unregistered marks having obtained a reputation. For details, see Chapter 5, section I. 4. (a) (1).

X. DEFENCES AGAINST TRADE MARK INFRINGEMENT

(1) From a doctrinal point of view, a trade mark does not give a right to use and for this reason, relying on an own registered mark cannot be a defence against the infringement of another's mark. However, in a constellation where the owner of a younger mark raises the defence that it uses its mark as registered both for the mark as such, and the goods concerned, the owner of a senior mark cannot directly raise an infringement action in court. Rather, according to Article 1(2) SPC Interpretation 2008, in such a case the administrative authorities insist on a settlement effort.[457] If non-litigation efforts have been to no avail, parties are advised to go through invalidation or non-use cancellation. After the foundation of a party's case is weakened by invalidation or revocation of the registered trade mark, a subsequent civil infringement lawsuit can be filed in court. In other words, relying on an own registered mark and using it within the scope as registered provides a *de facto* defence against infringement. Yet in case of a dispute between a normal senior registered trade mark and a similar junior registered trade mark that is used *outside* its scope, Article 1 SPC Interpretation 2008 provides protection to the senior mark without the above-mentioned necessity to go through administrative mediation efforts.[458]

---

456. 'Zhidao anli 58 hao: Chengdu Tongdefu hechuan tao pian youxian gongsi su Chongqing shi hechuan qu Tongdefu tao pian youxian gongsi, yuxiaohua qinhai shangbiao quan ji bu zhengdang jingzheng jiufen an' (Guiding Case No. 58: *Chengdu Tongdefu Hechuan Peach Slice Co., Ltd. v. Chongqing Hechuan District Tongdefu Peach Slice Co., Ltd. and Yu Xiaohua* in a dispute over trade mark infringement and unfair competition), Judicial Committee of the SPC, 20 May 2016. Available at: http://www.court.gov.cn/fabu-xiangqing-27511.html.

457. Provisions on Several Issues Concerning the Trial of Civil Disputes in Conflict of Registered Trademarks, Business Names and Prior Rights, Judicial Interpretation [2008] No. 3, promulgated by the Judicial Committee of the SPC on 18 February 2008 and effective on 1 March 2008. Available at: https://bit.ly/2WvRR9t. Amended on 23 December 2020, No. 5. Available at: https://bit.ly/2LBY3eE.

458. SPC Interpretation 2008, *supra* note 457.

(2) Comparative advertising, provided that consumers are not misled regarding the source or origin of the products or services and that, when used in comparative advertising, the comparison made, is, in all circumstances, fair.[459]

Article 3 Advertising Law 2018 states: "Advertisements should be true and legal, express the contents of advertisements in a healthy form, and meet the requirements of the construction of a socialist spiritual civilization and the promotion of the excellent traditional culture of the Chinese nation."[460] In addition, advertisements must not contain false or misleading content, deceive or mislead consumers,[461] or belittle the goods or services of other producers and operators.[462] Comparative advertisement between drugs and medical devices with regard to their efficacy and safety, or a comparison between medical institutions is not allowed.[463] Health food advertisements shall not make a comparison with medicines and other health foods.[464]

Keyword advertising is an important area which involves comparative advertising. In *Taishan Gangyi Co. Ltd v. Beijing Guxiang Information Technology Co.*, the plaintiff's registered trade mark "NEDFON" was sold by Google as a keyword to the Third Electrical Appliance Factory, which was a competitor from Gangyi. When "NEDFON" was entered into the Google search engine, the homepage www.gzmeihao.com of the Third Electrical Appliance Factory, who purchased it through Google's AdWords service, appeared at the top of the sponsored search results, while Gangyi appeared at the top of the organic search results. The Guangzhou Intermediate People's Court held the Third Electrical Appliance Factory as the direct infringer liable, and Google jointly and severally liable for trade mark infringement.[465]

In 2012, in the case of "汤姆叔叔" (Tāngmǔ shūshu) which means "Uncle Tom" designated for shoe repair, this trade mark was used in the headline of the promotional link: "Uncle Tom's shoe repair chain organization, click on the link", which led to the website of the defendant who was a competitor of Uncle Tom and bought the keyword from the search engine provider. The Chongqing Higher People's Court held that there was trade mark infringement.[466]

(3) If a mark is not used as a source indicator of the goods or services, for example as a decoration, one can argue that the use is non-infringing. Article 48 TML makes it clear that "use of a trade mark" means using a trade mark on goods, on the packages or containers of goods, in the trade documents of goods, or for advertisements, exhibitions, and other commercial activities for the purpose of identifying the origin of goods.

An example of this is "慧鱼" (Huìyú) (2013), where the BHPC ruled that linking the keyword to an unrelated website does not constitute trade mark use. According

459. Article 5 Advertisement Law 2018.
460. Article 3 Advertisement Law 2018.
461. Article 4 Advertisement Law 2018.
462. Article 13 Advertisement Law 2018.
463. Article 16(3) Advertisement Law 2018.
464. Article 18(4) Advertisement Law 2018.
465. *Taishan Gangyi Co. v. Beijing Guxiang Info. Tech. Co.*, Guangzhou Intermediate People's Court, 27 November 2009, 119 *Hui Zhong Fa Min San Zhong Zi* (2008).
466. Chongqing First Intermediate People's Court, Civil Judgment, 00430 *Yuyi Zhongfa Minchuzi* (2012).

to the Court, the keyword was not clearly presented to internet users and only used for the operation of the internal system.[467]

Chanel Co., Ltd. lost a trade mark infringement case regarding its "double C" trade mark logo in China. The Guangzhou IP Court defined the primary issue as whether Chanel's exclusive trade mark rights had been infringed by the defendant Ye Mengzong, which in essence "involved the question of whether the shape of the [allegedly infringing] jewellery products alone could be deemed as infringing" or merely a decoration. The "double C" logo was not used as a trade mark: the products in question were sold with labels of "ZHOUBAIFU", under the roof of a Zhoubaifu franchise store. Chanel failed to submit sufficient evidence to prove the unlawful use of Chanel's trade marks in the store, such as soliciting customers or promoting products, which took advantage of the similarities between the products and Chanel's trade mark registration. In addition, there was no confusion with the relevant consumers. Therefore, the Guangzhou IP Court overturned the findings of the Guangzhou Haizhu District People's Court.[468]

(4) Descriptive fair use is the use of a term in good faith to describe a product rather than to identify its source, according to Article 59(1) TML. Courts generally examine three factors in evaluating a fair use defence:

(1) whether the term at issue is a common name or descriptive term instead of a fanciful name;
(2) whether the party adopted the term only to describe the product and not to identify its source; and
(3) whether or not there is a likelihood of consumer confusion.

The following cases are illustrative of this defence.

The Guiding Case No. 46 involves a common name that had been registered as a trade mark.[469] Shandong Lu Jin Industrial Co., Ltd. sued Juancheng County Lu Jin Arts & Crafts Co., Ltd. and Jining Lizhibang Home Textile Co., Ltd. for infringement of its registered trade mark Lu Jin. The Intermediate People's Court of Jining Municipality,

467. *Taicang Fei xi er chang youxian zeren liang he gongsi v. Beijing Jianzhu mao shuan youxian gongsi yu mei jian li*, BHPC Civil Judgment, 918 *Gao Min Zhong Zi* (2012). See also Fandy Ip, 'Competitors and keyword advertising: how to protect your mark', IAM, 23 January 2019. Available at: https://www.lexology.com/library/detail.aspx?g=dffa03ce-6c27-453e-8b65-717f079a3836.

468. 'Chanel China's road to rights protection is not smooth and loses', Xinhua, 8 July 2019. Available at: http://www.xinhuanet.com/fashion/2019-07/08/c_1124722194.htm.

Tian Lu, 'Chanel's "Double C" trade mark loss in China – an unacceptable conclusion?', IP Kat, 13 July 2019. Available at: http://ipkitten.blogspot.com/2019/07/chanels-double-c-trade-mark-loss-in.html.

469. 'Zhidao anli 46 hao: Shadong lu jin shiye youxian gongsi su juan cheng xian lu jin gongyipin youxian zeren gongsi, jining li zhi bang jiafang youxian gongsi qinhai shangbiao quan ji bu zhengdang jingzheng jiufen an' (Guiding Case No. 46: *Shandong Lu Jin Industrial Co., Ltd. v. Juancheng County Lu Jin Arts & Crafts Co., Ltd. and Jining Lizhibang Home Textile Co., Ltd.* for trade mark infringement and unfair competition disputes), Judicial Committee of the SPC, 23 April 2015. Available at: http://www.court.gov.cn/fabu-xiangqing-14244.html.

Shandong Province,[470] held that Juancheng Lu Jin Company should immediately cease the use of "LU JIN" for goods in Class 25 it manufactured and sold, pay RMB 250,000 to the plaintiff and change its enterprise name; and Lizhibang Company should immediately cease the sale of the allegedly infringing commodities produced by Juancheng Lu Jin Company and pay RMB 10,000 to the plaintiff. Juancheng Lu Jin Company and Lizhibang Company appealed to the Higher People's Court of Shandong province.[471] This Court overturned the decision by the court of first instance: before Shandong Lu Jin Company registered "LU JIN" as a trade mark in 1999, it had already become a generic name for cotton handmade folk textile products in Shandong; "Lu Brocade Weaving Techniques" was an intangible cultural heritage. The acts of Juancheng Lu Jin Company and Jining Lizhibang Company did not constitute trade mark infringement, nor did they amount to unfair competition.

However, henceforth Juancheng Lu Jin Company should clearly use the words "Lu Jin" to indicate the nature of the fabric of its products and should use its own trade mark ("JING YI FANG") in a prominent fashion on the packaging of its products so as to "significantly distinguish the source of its products and facilitate consumer identification".[472]

In December 2003 in *Inner Mongolia Hangjinghouqi Jinsui Food Industrial Co., Ltd v. Beijing Jinyumi Grain & Oil Co., Ltd.*, the BFIPC held that "snowflake flour" was a common name of flour that meets certain standards, and that the use of the term "snowflake" on flour packaging using the plaintiff's trade mark was fair use.

In December 2010, in *Softstar Entertainment Inc. v. Shanghai Shanda Games Ltd.*, the Shanghai First Intermediate People's Court decided that Shanda's use of "盛大富翁", which literally means "tycoon" is descriptive use of the characters which include "大富翁" (Dàfùwēng), which was registered by Softstar, a Taiwanese game developer that was well-known on the mainland. "大富翁" is also the name for the American board game "Monopoly" published by Parker Brothers.

The Shanghai First Intermediate People's Court reasoned as follows: (1) the term "大富翁" can be legitimately used to describe the game of Monopoly's rules, goals, content and features; (2) Shanda's mark "盛大富翁" enjoyed a high public recognition so that free-riding was unlikely; and (3) the online game could be accessed only from the home page of Shanda's website and therefore was less likely to cause consumer confusion with Softstar as to the source of an online gaming service.[473]

---

470. Intermediate People's Court of Jining Municipality, Shandong Province, Civil Judgment, 25 August 2008, 6 *Ji Min Wu Chu Zi* (2007).
471. Higher People's Court of Shandong Province, Civil Judgment 5 August, 34 *Lu Min San Zhong Zi* (2009).
472. 'Zhidao anli 46 hao: Shadong lu jin shiye youxian gongsi su juan cheng xian lu jin gongyipin youxian zeren gongsi, jining li zhi bang jiafang youxian gongsi qinhai shangbiao quan ji bu zhengdang jingzheng jiufen an' (Guiding Case No. 46: *Shandong Lu Jin Industrial Co., Ltd. v. Juancheng County Lu Jin Arts & Crafts Co., Ltd. and Jining Lizhibang Home Textile Co., Ltd.* for trade mark infringement and unfair competition disputes), Judicial Committee of the SPC, 23 April 2015, last sentence. Available at: http://www.court.gov.cn/fabu-xiangqing-14244.html.
473. *Softstar Entertainment Inc. v. Shanda Games Ltd.*, 24 December, 2010 (Shanghai First Intermediate People's Court). This case was transferred from the BFIPC. See also *Softstar Entertainment Inc. v. Shanda Games Ltd.*, September 2006 (BFIPC). 12(182)

In *Guinness World Records Ltd v. Chery Automobile Co. Ltd. and Anhui Chery Automobile Sales Co.* (Chery), the defendant Chery unsuccessfully invoked the generic trade mark defence after it was sued for trade mark infringement for using trade marks owned by Guinness, such as the transliteration/translation of Guinness World Records "吉尼斯世界纪录" and "GUINNESS WORLD RECORDS" designated for the services of Classes 35 and 41.[474] Since 10 April 2014, Chery had organized a series of events entitled "Chery Arrizo Challenging Guinness China Tours" in several cities across China. The word mark "吉尼斯" and "GUINNESS" were used extensively used during these events. Chery also falsely claimed to have achieved several "Guinness World Records" on its official website. The defendant argued that "Guinness World Records" has become synonymous for "being superlative in the world" and "world records" and that it used these terms generically. The Foshan Intermediate People's Court analysed (1) whether "吉尼斯" and "GUINNESS" have inherent meanings such as "being superlative in the world" or "world records"; (2) whether these word marks have been given such meanings in the course of their usage; (3) the cognizance of the relevant public; and (4) actual situations of the authentication of relevant world records. In August 2017, the Court held that this was not the case and ordered Chery to cease infringing use of Guinness' trade marks and to pay it RMB 2.12 million.[475]

(5) Nominative fair use is the use of another party's trade mark to refer to genuine goods or services associated with that mark. Already in 1995, the SAIC issued the Notice Regarding the Prohibition Against the Unauthorized Use of Registered Trade Marks by Automobile Spare Parts Dealers and Auto Repair Shops. This notice was amended by the Notice Regarding the Prohibition Against the Use of Registered Trade Marks as Trade Names or as Signboards on Boutique Shops in 1996.

However, according to the BHPC, even though the name of goods had been approved by the relevant industry competent authority, if the use of words that are identical or similar to previously registered trade marks of others on identical or similar goods, it constitutes trade mark infringement.[476] Although the product name has been approved by the competent authority of the industry, if the name is used as a trade mark and is sufficient to cause confusion and misunderstanding by the relevant public, it constitutes a trade mark infringement.[477]

The following cases are illustrative of this defence.

SPC Gazette (2011). Available at: http://gongbao.court.gov.cn/Details/fad96d1e44d-c148a603519f7f11d75.html?sw = %e5%a4%a7%e5%ae%87%e8%b5%84%e8%ae%af.

474. Tracy Shen and Nancy Qu, 'The generic name defence in trademark infringement cases', *China Business Law Journal*, 2 April 2018. Available at: https://www.vantageasia.com/the-generic-name-defence-in-trademark-infringement-cases/.

475. 'Guinness World Records Wins the Trademark Infringement Case Against Chery in the First Instance Court', Press release, Guinness, September 2017. Available at: https://www.guinnessworldrecords.com/news/press-release/2018/1/guinness-world-records-wins-the-trademark-infringement-case-against-chery-in-the-508616.

476. Answer 24 of the BHPC to Several Questions in the Trial of Trade Mark Civil Dispute Cases, 18 February, Jinggao Fafa [2004] No. 48. Available at: https://v1.iphouse.cn/lawinfo/121.html?keyword = .

477. Answer 24 of the BHPC to Several Questions in the Trial of Trade Mark Civil Dispute Cases, *supra* note 474.

In 2015, in *ASUS Computer (Shanghai) Co., Ltd. v. Sichuan New World Technology Co., Ltd.*, the Chengdu Intermediate People's Court held that the New World retail store can use its store name on the signboard and the "ASUS" trade mark on the counters while selling ASUS computers.[478]

In April 2007, in *Caterpillar, Inc. v. Rui'an Changshen*, the Shanghai Pudong New District People's Court held that Rui'an Changshen, a manufacturer of automobile filters, was not liable for trade mark infringement and could use "C" and "For Caterpillar" on its filters to clarify that the filters are for Caterpillar models.[479]

In September 2003, in *U.S. Educational Testing Service v. Beijing Haidian New Oriental Private School*, the BFIPC held New Oriental liable for trade mark infringement for using "TOEFL" on its published English test review materials without permission. New Oriental appealed and in December 2004, the BHPC denied infringement and held that that New Oriental used "TOEFL" merely to show that its materials were designed to allow the user to prepare for the Educational Testing Service's TOEFL examination.[480]

However, just as in descriptive fair use, nominative fair use should not be disproportional and may not mislead people into believing that the user's operations are commercially linked to the trade mark registrant.

In 2015, in *Hefei Yunfan Digital Technology Co., Ltd. and Lenovo (Beijing) Co., Ltd.*, the Anhui Higher People's Court decided that the use of the "LENOVO" trade mark by Yunfan on its signboard and store decorations exceeded the need for a nominative use and could mislead consumers into believing that the Yunfan operation was linked to Lenovo other than Yunfan being a reseller of Lenovo products. Therefore, the nominative fair use defence failed, and trade mark infringement was determined.[481]

In 2013, in *YKK Co., Ltd. v. Xiyang Company*, the Zhejiang Higher People's Court held that Xiyang exceeded the need of nominative use of the "YKK" trade mark for fastening products when it printed this trade mark on the business cards of its employees, thereby misleading the relevant public into believing that Xiyang was an official sales agent.[482]

(6) Utilitarian fair use: As discussed above, Article 59(2) TML 2019 provides that a three dimensional registered trade mark which contains any shape derived from the goods themselves, product shape required to obtain the technical effect, or shape

478. Chengdu Intermediate People's Court of Sichuan Province, 9 September, 78 *Chengzhi Minchu Zi* (2015).

479. *Caterpillar, Inc. v. Rui'an Changshen*, April 2007 (Shanghai Pudong New District Court). Available at: http://www.wptn.com/wptn-in/Mailing/May_2007_5/details/trademarks/china.html.

480. *U.S. Educational Testing Service v. Beijing Haidian New Oriental Private School*, BHPC, 24 December 2004, 1393 *Gao Min Zhong Zi* (2003). Available at: http://pkulaw.cn/case_es/payz_a25051f3312b07f322a62c4427a8722e203cc1fad8d684b5bdfb.html?match=Exact.

481. Anhui Higher People's Court 12 June, 00061 *Wanmin San Zhongzi* (2015).

482. Zhejiang Higher People's Court (2013) Zhejiang Zhizhongzi No. 407. Chen Yu,' Zhe zhi xi fa | zhengpin zhuan shou guocheng zhong shiyong shangye biaozhi xingwei de hefa xing jieding' (Zhejiang Knowledge Analysis Method | Definition of the Legality of the Use of Commercial Marks in the Resale of Genuine Products), Zhi Chan Li, 22 March 2019. Available at: http://www.zhichanli.com/article/8083.html.

that gives a substantive value to the goods does not give the holder of the exclusive trade mark right the right to prohibit others from duly using it.[483]

(7) Honest concurrent use is normally not a defence against infringement in China, and the TML does not stipulate the validity of trade mark coexistence agreements in the judgment of trade mark similarity. However, the SPC decided in the NEXUS case between Google and Shimano[484] that trade mark coexistence agreements can be used as a factor in considering trade mark similarity judgments if they comply with some formal prerequisites.[485]

As a reaction to the economic crisis in 2009, the SPC issued the Opinions on Several Issues Concerning Giving Full Play to the Role of IP Judgments in Promoting the Great Development and Prosperity of Socialist Culture and Promoting Independent and Coordinated Economic Development in 2009, 2010 and 2011.[486] In paragraph 19, the SPC stated:

"When the relevant trade marks are well-known, or the coexistence of relevant trade marks is formed under special circumstances, the identification of similar trade marks should also be based on the actual use of the two, the use history, the cognitive state of the relevant public, and the subjective state of the user. Courts should pay attention in their comprehensive judgment to respect the market structure that has been objectively formed, prevent simply equating trade mark constituent elements with similar trade marks, and achieve inclusive development among operators."[487]

Despite this opinion, which promotes the coexistence of similar trade marks under certain conditions, it was not frequently applied by courts.[488] For example in the

483. George Fu and Cathy Wu, 'The Balancing of Fair Use and Exclusivity – Trademark Rights under the Chinese Trademark Law: A Third Amendment Perspective', 104 *TMR* (2014), 1241, 1251.

484. On 23 December 2016, the SPC accepted the trade mark coexistence agreement between Google and Shimano, the registrant of the cited trade mark submitted by Google in the "NEXUS" trade mark refusal review case, and judged the use of it in handheld computers and portable computer products. The "NEXUS" trade mark and the "NEXUS" trade mark used on bicycle computer products did not constitute similar trade marks. Edward Chatterton and Horace Lam, 'China's Supreme People's Court Switches Approach on Trademark Co-Existence Agreements for Google's "Nexus" Marks', DLA Piper, 11 May 2017. Available at: https://www.lexology.com/library/detail.aspx?g=5fbfa129-7824-43d3-96a6-7b93d823db4b.

485. 'Guojia zhishi chanquan ju shangbiao pingshen weiyuanhui fawu tongxun zong di 72 qi (2018 nian 6 yue)' (CNIPA Trade Mark Review and Adjudication Committee Legal Newsletter, Issue 72 (June 2018)), CNIPA, 19 June 2018, para 3. Available at: http://spw.sbj.cnipa.gov.cn/fwtx/201806/t20180619_274666.html.

486. Ni Zhuliang, 'Sifa zhong shangbiao gongcun de kunjing yu chulu '(The Predicament and Way Forward of the Coexistence of Trademarks in the Judicature), 12 *IP Journal* (2014). Available at: https://ip.pkulaw.cn/ipjournal/1510149407.html.

487. SPC, Opinions on Promoting the Great Development and Prosperity of Socialist Culture and Promoting Independent and Coordinated Economic Development (Fafa [2011] No. 18) 16 December 2011. Available at: http://gongbao.court.gov.cn/Details/90857967e518c766c368851b1b705a.html.

488. The SPC applied the inclusive development theory in the Alligator case. SPC, Civil Judgment, 3 *Min San Zhong* (2009).

3M v. 3N dispute, it was not applied, even though 3N satisfied the abovementioned conditions.[489] One can safely argue that this doctrine is not of major relevancy.

(8) Prior use of an unregistered mark can be a defence against infringement if the unregistered mark has achieved a certain reputation. Article 59(3) TML 2019 stipulates that the trade mark proprietor has no right to preclude such other party from continuing to use the trade mark within its original scope, but may require such other party to add a distinction to the mark.

In 2018, in *Lin Mingkai v. Fuyun,*[490] the SPC provided an analysis of the preconditions required for a prior use defence. Lin Mingkai sued Chengdu Fuyun Furniture Store for the infringement of two trade marks which had been applied for with regard to furniture in Class 20 on 19 November 2002 and 25 September 2009. Chengdu Fuyun Furniture Store claimed that it had been authorized to use the trade marks by Fuyun Company, which had been using the contested trade marks since 2001, and invoked the prior use defence.

The first instance court ruled in favour of the plaintiff. It found that although Fuyun Company's use of the disputed trade marks had led them to acquire a certain influence before the registration of the plaintiff's trade marks, the evidence failed to show that Chengdu Fuyun Furniture Store had used the contested trade marks itself before the application date. In addition, the authorization that Chengdu Fuyun Furniture Store claimed to have received from Fuyun Company concerned another trade mark, registered by Fuyun Company in 2010 in a different class.

The second instance court ruled in favour of the defendant and supported the prior use defence. It also affirmed that Chengdu Fuyun Furniture Store was authorized to use such trade marks from Fuyun Company. In addition, the appeal court held that the contested trade marks were not identical and Chengdu Fuyun Furniture Store had not copied the plaintiff's registered trade marks in bad faith.

The SPC reversed the appeal court's judgment. It found that the evidence proved only that Fuyun Company's prior use of the trade marks had caused them to acquire a certain influence before 2009, but not before 2002.[491]

The SPC clarified the conditions required for invoking the prior use defence:[492]

489. Aileen Wu and Sisi Liang, '3M wins trademark infringement case against 3N', Wan Hui Da, 7 March 2016. Available at: https://www.internationallawoffice.com/Newsletters/Intellectual-Property/China/Wan-Hui-Da-Law-Firm-Intellectual-Property-Agency/3M-wins-trademark-infringement-case-against-3N.

490. *Lin Mingkai v. Fuyun*, SPC 3 September 2019, 43 *Zui Gao Fa Min Zai* (2018). 'Shangbiao fa 59.3 Gun zuigao yuan mingque zai xian shiyong kangbian zhongyuan you fanwei ying kaolü diyu yinsu (lixiang kongjian an)' (Trade Mark Law 59.3 The Supreme People's Court clarified that the original scope of the prior use defense should take into account regional factors (ideal space case)), Wan Hui Da, 15 December 2019. Available at: http://www.wanhuida.com/content/details_7_2190.html.

491. Paul Ranjard, Hui Huang and Binbin Du, 'SPC clarifies requirements for citing prior use defence in trademark infringement cases', Wan Hui Da, 17 February 2020. Available at: https://www.internationallawoffice.com/Newsletters/Intellectual-Property/China/Wanhuida-Intellectual-Property/SPC-clarifies-requirements-for-citing-prior-use-defence-in-trademark-infringement-cases

492. Ranjard, Huang and Du, *supra* note 491.

- The prior use should predate not only the application for registration of the claimed trade mark, but also the trade mark holder's use of the registered trade mark (note that this differs from the viewpoint of the Beijing IP Court in *Zhongchuang v. Beijing Qihang* in 2015,[493] which was even selected as number 5 of the "Top 10 IP Cases in Chinese Courts in 2015");[494]
- The prior use should concern a mark identical or similar to the registered trade mark;
- The prior use should concern goods or services identical or similar to those designated by the registered trade mark;
- The prior use should have led the mark to acquire a certain recognition before the application for registration and the trade mark owner's use of the registered trade mark;
- The prior use defence cannot be raised by a person other than the prior user, so whether someone is authorized by the prior user to use the mark is irrelevant (note that this is in contrast to *Jiang Yuyou v. Fuzi Temple Catering Company*);[495]
- The prior use should be maintained within the original scope, which should be decided according to the scope defined by the reputation created by the prior use, including geographical scope. Production capacity and operation scale should be taken into account when interpreting "exceeding the original scope".[496]

(9) Guiding Case No. 82 provides an example of abuse of rights.[497] Wang Suiyong sued Shenzhen Ellassay Clothing Co., Ltd. for trade mark infringement, even though this party had registered the trade marks "歌力思", "ELLASSAY" and the enterprise name of Shenzhen Ellassay Clothing Co., Ltd. According to the facts, Wang Suiyong had applied for the trade mark registration "歌力思" in bad faith and was not granted this trade mark and used Shenzhen Ellassay Clothing Co., Ltd's trade mark "ELLASSAY" and enterprise name without authorization. The maxim "the offence is the best defence" did not work for Wang Suiyong.[498]

---

493. *Beijing Zhongchuang Oriental Education Technology Co., Ltd. v. Beijing Haidian District Qihang Examination and Training School, Beijing Qihang Century Technology Development Co., Ltd.*, Beijing IP Court, 31 December, 588 *Jing Zhi Min Zhong Zi* (2015).
494. '2015 nian zhongguo fayuan shi da zhishi chanquan anjian' (Top Ten IP Cases in Chinese Courts in 2015), SPC, 22 April 2016.
495. *Jiang Yuyou v. Fuzi Temple Catering Company*, Jiangsu Higher People's Court, 37 *Su Zhimin Zhongzi* (2013).
496. Ranjard, Huang and Du, *supra* note 491.
497. Danny Friedmann, 'Protection Against Abuse of Trademark Law in Greater China: A Brief Analysis of the People's Republic of China, Hong Kong, Macau, and Taiwan', 47(2) *California Western International Law Journal* (2017), 157–192.
498. 'Zhidao anli 82 hao: Wang Suiyong su Shenzhen Ge Li Si fushi gufen youxian gongsi, hangzhou yintai shiji baihuo youxian gongsi qinhai shangbiao quan jiufen an' (Guiding Case No. 82: *Wang Suiyong v. Shenzhen Gelisi Clothing Co., Ltd. and Hangzhou Yintai Century Department Store Co., Ltd.* for trade mark infringement disputes), Judicial Committee of the SPC 6 March 2017. Available at: http://www.court.gov.cn/fabu-xiang-qing-37652.html.

Guiding Case No. 30 makes it clear that if a business operator has carried out an act that exceeds its legal business scope and violates administrative licensing laws and regulations, this cannot be used as a defence against trade mark infringement and unfair competition.[499]

(10) The "exhaustion" of the right, also known as the first sale doctrine, applies to TML, meaning that once a proprietor of the right to exclusive use of a registered trade mark or its licensee sells goods to which the trade mark is attached, that right to exercise the trade mark in respect of such goods is exhausted and other persons can commercially distribute the goods without the proprietor's consent. Unlike patents, however, the construct of exhaustion is not needed, because commercially selling goods marketed by the trade mark owner or with its consent does not lead to any confusion in trade unless these goods are altered. There is no provision that would deal with cases of parallel imports, i.e. the third-party importation of goods marketed abroad by the trade mark owner or with its consent. Also here, there cannot be a case of origin confusion, but the Chinese courts have raised concerns about consumer misconceptions in respect of differences in quality or safety between domestic and imported goods, or between goods intended for the domestic market and the market abroad.

In May 2016, the BHPC issued Several Legal Matters to Note in Current Intellectual Property Trials which dealt with the question of whether parallel import constitutes trade mark infringement: if the suspect goods are sourced from the rights holder or the authorized dealer, the rights holder would have fully realized the commercial value of the trade mark from the first sale of such goods, and thus could no longer prevent others from carrying out secondary sales or reasonable commercial marketing of these goods.[500]

It seems the Chinese government has been stimulating parallel import programmes in particular for automobiles via Free Trade Zones since 2013, and in Shanghai since 2015 so as to "promote the structural reform of the supply of automobiles, accelerate the innovation and development of the automobile circulation system, and stimulate the vitality of the automobile market."[501]

499. 'Zhidao anli 30 hao: Lan Jianjun, Hangzhou Xiaomuzhi qiche weixiu keji gufen youxian gongsi su Tianjin Shi Xiaomuzhi qiche weixiu fuwu youxian gongsi deng qinhai shangbiao quan ji bu zhengdang jingzheng jiufen an' (Guiding Case No. 30: *Lan Jianjun, Hangzhou Little Thumb Auto Maintenance Technology Co., Ltd. v. Tianjin Little Finger Auto Maintenance Service Co., Ltd.*, trade mark infringement and unfair competition dispute case), Judicial Committee of the SPC, 5 July 2014. Available at: http://www.court.gov.cn/fabu-xiangqing-13347.html.

500. BHPC, Several Legal Matters to Note in Current Intellectual Property Trials, 7 May 2016. He Fang, 'Does parallel import infringe trademark rights?', King & Wood Mallesons, 19 June 2016. Available at: https://www.kwm.com/zh/cn/knowledge/insights/does-parallel-imports-infringe-the-trademark-rights-20160919.

501. Seon Shin, 'A critical analysis of innovative approaches to parallel import in China, South Korea and the USA', 15:6 *JIPLP* (June 2020), 470–480. Notice of the Shenzhen Municipal Bureau of Commerce on the issuance of the "Operational Regulations for the Support Plan for Parallel Imported Automobiles under the Special Fund of the Shenzhen Municipal Bureau of Commerce for Industry Development" Shenzhen Municipal Commission Office, release and implementation date 16 April 2019. Shanghai Municipal Commission

A number of cases relate to parallel imports.

In 2009, in *Michelin Group v. Tan Guoqiang and Ou Can*, the Changsha Intermediate People's Court decided that the import and sale in China of tyres originally intended for the Brazilian market without permission from the Michelin Group and without obtaining a Chinese Compulsory Product Certification was detrimental to the interests and rights of the trade mark owner and thus an act that infringed the Michelin trade mark.[502] If the defendants had applied for the 3C Certification before selling the imported tyres, the tyres would not have been of questionable quality or of doubtful safety and thus not damaging to the reputation of the Michelin Group. Infringement was thus based on an injury to the trade mark owner's reputation.[503]

In 2013, in *Victoria's Secret Stores Brand Management, Inc. v. Shanghai Jintian Clothing Ltd.*, the plaintiff discovered that the defendant, without authorization, sold genuine products that were imported from Victoria's Secret's parent firm through authorized channels and acted as a distributor of the parent firm by utilizing the labels, hangers, and packages of Victoria's Secret.[504] The defendant further declared that it was the plaintiff's general distributor, carried out business activities in the form of direct sales or franchises in China, and used the plaintiff's "VICTORIA'S SECRET" and "VICTORIA'S" in shop interior decoration and on sign boards, shop furniture (e.g., cashiers' desks and counters). The plaintiff argued that the defendant's actions infringed the plaintiff's right to exclusive use of its registered trade marks and constituted unfair competition in the unauthorized use of other people's business names and false advertising. The Shanghai Intermediate People's Court held that selling genuine goods was "unlikely to produce confusion" among the relevant consumers and thus constituted no trade mark infringement.

However, Victoria's Secret appealed to the Shanghai Higher People's Court, which held in 2014 that the defendant's use of the above trade marks in shop interior decoration etc. constituted trade mark infringement.[505]

---

of Commerce, China (Shanghai) Pilot Free Trade Zone Administrative Committee Free Trade Zone Administration on the declaration of parallel imports of steam from China (Shanghai) Pilot Free Trade Zone, Shanghai Municipal Commission Office, 13 September 2018.

502. *Michelin Group v. Tan Guoqiang and Ou Can*, Changsha Intermediate People's Court, 24 April 2009. See Fu Haiying, 'Trademark Infringement in Parallel Importation', King & Wood IP Bulletin, (Sept. 2010). Available at: https://bit.ly/2JAuS7Q.

503. Shin, *supra* note 501.

504. *Victoria's Secret Stores Brand Management, Inc. v. Shanghai Jintian Clothing Ltd.*, Shanghai Second Intermediate People's Court (2012) Hu Er Zhong Min Wu (Zhi) Chu Zi No. 86. The SPC described this case as a model case: 41(206) *SPC Gazette* (2013). See also: You Yunting, 'Why VICTORIA'S SECRET could not Prevent Selling a Parallel Imported Genuine Product Online in China?', China IP Lawyer, 24 January 2014. Available at: http://www.chinaiplawyer.com/victorias-secret-prevent-selling-parallel-imported-genuine-product-on-line-china/.

505. Shanghai Higher People's Court, Civil Judgment, 104 *Hu Gao Min San (Zhi) Zhong Zi* (2014).

This case was selected to be number 12 of 50 Typical IP Cases in Chinese Courts in 2015. '2015 Nian Zhongguo fayuan shenli de 50 jian dianxing zhishi chanquan anjian' (50 typical intellectual property cases in Chinese courts in 2015), SPC, 22 April 2016. Available at: http://www.court.gov.cn/fabu-xiangqing-19852.html.

Finally, the TML in China does not take into account humour or criticism as a defence against trade mark infringement: it does not recognize parody or satire just as there is no such exception in the Copyright Law.

1. Remedies and Legal Consequences of Infringement – Specific Trade Mark Issues

While the system of remedies against IP infringement in general is further explained in Chapter 7, Enforcement, of this book, some remarks on trade mark infringement in particular may be in order.

(a) Interim Injunctions

The TML 2019 gives the trade mark registrant or an interested party the possibility of immediately[506] applying to the court for cessation of infringement and property preservation prior to instituting a main action. When a court adopts any preservation measure, it may order the applicant to provide a security. If the party refuses to provide such security, the court shall reject the application.[507] The applicant must initiate a lawsuit within 30 days after the injunctive order, otherwise the court will revoke the order.

Courts are often reluctant to grant preliminary injunctions in trade mark infringement cases, because it is difficult to monitor the defendant's business activities. In the case *Under Armour v. Tingfeilong Sporting Goods (Uncle Martian)*, the plaintiff Under Armour applied for a preliminary injunction on 27 June 2016, but had to wait until 2 November 2016 before it was actually granted by the Fujian Higher People's Court. The final ruling which included a permanent injunction was issued on 19 June 2019.[508]

(b) Damages

The amount of damages shall include reasonable expenses of the rights holder for stopping the infringement.[509] If it is difficult to determine the actual losses suffered by the proprietor from the infringement, the profits acquired by the infringer from the infringement, or the royalties of the registered trade mark, a court may award

---

See also Cindy Zhen and Jack Su, 'Trademark use on signboards by unauthorised retailers', Wan Hui Da, 4 May 2020. Available at: https://www.internationallawoffice.com/Newsletters/Intellectual-Property/China/Wanhuida-Intellectual-Property/Trademark-use-on-signboards-by-unauthorised-retailers.

506. Article 100(3) Civil Procedure Law 2017: "When a people's court receives an application for preservation in an emergency, it shall decide within 48 hours after the receipt of the application; if the court accepts the application, such measures shall come into force immediately."
507. Article 100(2) Civil Procedure Law 2017.
508. 'Finnegan Client Under Armour Wins High-Profile Trademark Infringement Decisions in China', Finnegan, 3 August 2017. Available at: https://bit.ly/2MUfCEP.
509. Article 63(1) TML 2019, *supra* note 15.

statutory damages of not more than RMB 5 million according to the circumstances of the infringement.[510]

In August 2017, New Balance was awarded the highest amount of damages in a trade mark infringement case in China: RMB 10 million,[511] and in November 2018 Dunhill was awarded the same amount.[512] Because of the possibility of punitive damages, according to Article 63 TML 2019, this amount was topped in May 2020, when the Guangdong Provincial Higher People's Court ordered Guangdong Zhimei Electric Co., Ltd. to pay the award of RMB 50 million for economic losses and RMB 450,000 for reasonable legal costs to Guangzhou Redsun Gas Appliances Co., Ltd. for malicious trade mark infringement. The four provincial distributors were held jointly and severally liable with the Zhimei Company.[513]

Goods on which a registered trade mark is falsely used may not enter commercial channels even if the registered trade mark so used is removed.[514] The court that tries a trade mark dispute case shall, at the request of the proprietor: order destruction of goods on which a registered trade mark is falsely used, except under special circumstances; order destruction of materials and tools primarily used for the manufacture of such goods without compensation; or under special circumstances, order prohibition of the said materials and tools from entering commercial channels without compensation.[515]

In the case of trade mark infringement of a rights holder that has never used or authorized others to use its registered trade mark, the amount of damages can be reduced based on the duration of the rights holder's non-use of the registered trade mark. The rights holder's reasonable expenses to stop the infringement, the nature, circumstances, and scope of the infringement form the remaining factors of such a case.[516]

510. Article 63(3) TML 2019, *supra* note 15.
511. Steve Brachmann, 'New Balance wins largest verdict ever for foreign plaintiff in Chinese trademark suit', IP Watchdog, 27 August 2017. Available at: https://www.ipwatchdog.com/2017/08/27/new-balance-largest-verdict-foreign-plaintiff-chinese-trademark/id=87201/.
512. Niall Fraser, 'Alfred Dunhill awarded 10 million yuan in "groundbreaking" trademark infringement case against Chinese clothing firm Danhuoli', SCMP, 11 October 2018. Available at: https://www.scmp.com/news/hong-kong/hong-kong-economy/article/2167986/alfred-dunhill-awarded-10-million-yuan.
513. 'Guangzhou Redsun Company Awarded CNY 50 Million (approx. US$ 7,000,000) in Trademark Infringement and Unfair Competition Case against ex-employee', Rouse, 28 June 2020. Available at: https://www.lexology.com/library/detail.aspx?g=e78ffea1-003b-44c6-b5fc-8630ea9aae75.
514. Article 63(5) TML 2019, *supra* note 15.
515. Article 63(4) TML 2019, *supra* note 15.
516. Answer 31 of the BHPC to Several Questions in the Trial of Trade Mark Civil Dispute Cases, 18 February, Jinggao Fafa [2004] No. 48. Available at: https://v1.iphouse.cn/lawinfo/121.html?keyword=.

(c) Declaration of Non-infringement

Longbao, a patent holder, alleged that Langlifu, a competitor of Longbao had infringed its patent and sent warning letters to Langbao distributors, but did not actually file any infringement action. The case, *Suzhou Longbao Bioengineering Industrial Company v. Suzhou Langlifu Health Products Co., Ltd.*, reached the Jiangsu Higher People's Court, which asked the SPC for a written opinion. In 2002, the SPC issued a reply: declarations of non-infringement of patent rights could be used as a cause of action in the case.[517] With the Peter Rabbit case the declaration of non-infringement doctrine leapt from patent law to the field of trade marks. In 2003, the British publishing company Frederick Warne, owner of eleven Chinese trade marks related to Peter Rabbit, the character in Beatrix Potter's books, successfully brought an action before a local AIC in Beijing against China Social Science Press (CSSP) for trade mark infringement.[518] CSSP appealed and asked the BFIPC to file a declaration of non-infringement.[519] According to the Court's guidelines, declaratory judgment in case of non-infringement should be given if a letter proposes a licence, notifies the IPR, makes an inquiry, but does not promptly bring an action, as this is likely to harm the rights and interests of the accused infringer.[520]

In a trade mark non-infringement declaration litigation, it is possible that a plaintiff initiates the non-infringement declaration litigation after the trade mark registrant (defendant) files a complaint with a competent administrative authority, but before the administrative authority makes any decision. In that case, the Court held that the administrative complaint could prove an existing conflict caused by trade mark use and sufficiently uncertain status of legal rights.[521]

A customs seizure is another warning that leads to a sufficient uncertain status of an alleged infringer's legal rights. If an alleged infringer receives a Notification of Detention of Suspected Infringing Goods, issued by customs, it has an influence on the alleged infringer's business activities. Before customs makes a determination on whether there really was an infringement, the alleged infringer has the right to initiate non-infringement declaration litigation against the party who filed the application for detention of the goods with customs.[522]

Just like IP infringement cases according to Article 28 Civil Procedure Law 2012 and 2017, the jurisdiction for non-infringement declaration litigation is determined by the court of the *locus delicti commissi* or where the defendant has its domicile.[523]

517. SPC, Civil Judgment, 12 July 2002 (2001) Min San Ta Zi No. 4.
518. 'Peter Rabbit trademark protection tested by case', China Daily, 1 July 2004. Available at: http://www.chinadaily.com.cn/english/doc/2004-07/01/content_344528.htm.
519. 'Declaratory Judgment of Non-Infringement In China, China Sinda Intellectual Property Ltd', Mondaq, 24 July 2014. Available at: http://www.mondaq.com/china/x/329546/Trademark/Declaratory+Judgment+of+NonInfringement+in+China.
520. *Supra* note 519.
521. Bin Zhang and Lei Fu, 'Declarations of non-infringement require particular strategy and procedure', 43 *CCPIT Patent and Trademark Office Newsletter* (April 2019), 18. Available at: https://www.ccpit-patent.com.cn/sites/default/files/publication/Newslette%20No.43%2C%20Apr.2019.pdf.
522. Bin Zhang and Lei Fu, *supra* note 521, 18.
523. Article 28 Civil Procedure Law 2017.

Article 24 SPC Interpretation Civil Procedure Law interprets the *locus delicti commissi* of Article 28 Civil Procedure Law, as the place where the tort (infringement) or offence was committed and the place where results of such tort (infringement) or offence occurred.[524]

In addition to a declaration of non-infringement, a claim for compensation can be filed. Article 13 SPC Interpretation 2001,[525] states that

> where the applicant does not institute legal proceedings or the erroneous application causes injury to the respondent, the respondent may institute legal proceedings in the Court having the jurisdiction, requesting the applicant to make compensation, or requesting for compensation of damages in the proceedings instituted by the trade mark registrant or interested party against infringement of the exclusive right to use a trade mark. The Court may simultaneously handle the matter.[526]

(d) Criminal Sanctions

Since IP criminal offences are crimes undermining the order of China's socialist market economy, China has passed laws and established policy to also criminally enforce IPRs.[527]

A party shall be subject to criminal liability in counterfeit cases: where without being licensed by the trade mark registrant, a party uses a trade mark identical with the registered trade mark on identical goods;[528] where a party forges or manufactures without authorization the labels of a registered trade mark of another party or sells the labels of a registered trade mark forged or manufactured without authorization;[529] where a party knowingly sells goods on which a registered trade mark is falsely used.[530]

The Interpretation by the SPC and Supreme People's Procuratorate (SPP) of Several Issues Concerning the Specific Application of Law in Handling Criminal Cases Involving Infringement of IPR 2004[531] provides the following thresholds: in serious cases of double-identity (identical trade mark, identical goods), the threshold of the

524. Interpretations of the SPC on Applicability of the Civil Procedure Law, adopted by the Judicial Committee of the SPC on 18 December 2014. Available at: https://bit.ly/2NovheP.
525. *Infra* note 526.
526. Interpretation by the SPC of the Issues Relating to Application of Law to Pre-trial Suspension of Acts of Infringement of Exclusive Right to Use Trademarks and to Evidence Preservation, adopted at the Judicial Committee of the SPC on 25 December 2001, and entered into force on 22 January 2002. Available at: https://www.wipo.int/edocs/lexdocs/laws/en/cn/cn058en.pdf.
527. Haiyan Liu, 'The Policy and Targets of Criminal Enforcement of intellectual Property Rights in China and the United States', 24 *Wash. Int'l L.J.* (2015), 137, 172.
528. Article 67(1) TML 2019, *supra* note 15.
529. Article 67(2) TML 2019, *supra* note 15.
530. Article 67(3) TML 2019, *supra* note 15.
531. Interpretation of the SPC and SPP on Several Issues Concerning the Specific Application of Laws in Handling Criminal Cases of Infringement of IPR 2004, Judicial Interpretation No. 19, promulgated by the SPC and SPP on 11 November 2004 and effective on 22 December 2004. Available at: https://bit.ly/31WtbYE.

illegal business revenue is more than RMB 50,000 or for illegal profit of more than RMB 30,000;[532] and counterfeiting of two or more registered trade marks, where the threshold of illegal business revenue is more than RMB 30,000 or for illegal profit more than RMB 20,000.[533] In particularly serious cases of double-identity, the thresholds for illegal business revenue is more than RMB 250,000 or for illegal profit of more than RMB 150,000;[534] and counterfeiting two or more registered trade marks, where the illegal business revenue is more than RMB 150,000 or the illegal profit of more than RMB 100,000.[535]

In the case of a seller of counterfeit goods using a registered trade mark, the large amount of the sales is more than RMB 50,000.[536] The amount of sales is huge if the sales amount is more than RMB 250,000.[537]

In serious cases of forging, unauthorized manufacture or selling falsified or unauthorized, registered trade mark labels, the number of registered labels forged, manufactured without authorization or sold for falsification or unauthorized manufacture is more than 20,000, or the illegal business revenues are more than RMB 50,000, or the illegal profit is more than RMB 30,000;[538] in case of forging, arbitrarily manufacturing or selling counterfeit unauthorized manufacture of more than 10,000 registered trade mark labels, or illegal business revenues of more than RMB 30,000, or illegal profit of more than RMB 20,000.[539] In particular serious cases, the number of registered trade mark labels forged, manufactured without authorization or sold for falsification or without authorization, is more than 100,000, or the illegal business revenue is more than RMB 250,000, or the illegal profit is more than RMB 150,000;[540] forging, arbitrarily manufacturing or selling counterfeit unauthorized manufacture of more than 50,000 registered trade mark labels, or illegal business revenues of more than RMB 150,000, or illegal profits of more than RMB 100,000.[541]

In the Guiding Case No. 87, the Intermediate People's Court of Suqian City, Jiangsu Province, issued a criminal judgment,[542] convicting three defendants for the particularly serious crime of counterfeiting registered trade marks of Samsung (China) Investment Co., Ltd. via a counterfeit "Samsung Digital Counter" online store on Taobao to promote "genuine licensed products", generating illegal income

532. Article 1(1)(1) Interpretation of the SPC and SPP on Several Issues Concerning the Specific Application of Laws in Handling Criminal Cases of Infringement of IPR 2004, *supra* note 531.
533. Article 1(1)(2) SPC and SPP Interpretation 2004, *supra* note 531.
534. Article 1(2)(1) SPC and SPP Interpretation 2004, *supra* note 531.
535. Article 1(2)(2) SPC and SPP Interpretation 2004, *supra* note 531.
536. Article 2(1) SPC and SPP Interpretation 2004, *supra* note 531.
537. Article 2(2) SPC and SPP Interpretation 2004, *supra* note 531.
538. Article 3(1)(1) SPC and SPP Interpretation 2004, *supra* note 531.
539. Article 3(1)(2) SPC and SPP Interpretation 2004, *supra* note 531.
540. Article 3(2)(1) SPC and SPP Interpretation 2004, *supra* note 531.
541. Article 3(2)(2) SPC and SPP Interpretation 2004, *supra* note 531.
542. Intermediate People's Court of Suqian City, Jiangsu Province 8 September, Criminal Judgment, 8 September (2015) Suzhong Zhi Xing Chu Zi No. 0004. Zhidao anli 87 hao: Guumingsheng, guomingfeng, sunshubiao jiamao zhuce shangbiao an (Guiding Case No. 87: Guo Mingsheng, Guo Mingfeng, Sun Shubiao Counterfeit Registered Trade Mark Case), Judicial Committee of the SPC, 16 March 2017. Available at: http://www.court.gov.cn/fabu-xiangqing-37702.html.

of more than RMB 20 million and an illegal profit of more than RMB 2 million. Guo Mingsheng was sentenced to five years' imprisonment and a fine of RMB 1.6 million; the defendant Sun Shubiao committed the crime of counterfeiting a registered trade mark and was sentenced to three years in prison, five years of probation and fined RMB 200,000. Defendant Guo Mingfeng committed the crime of counterfeiting registered trade marks and was sentenced to three years in prison, four years of probation, and a fine of RMB 200,000.

According to the BHPC, trade mark infringers should not be ordered to issue an apology since the exclusive right to use a registered trade mark is a right with property value.[543] However, the SPC affirmed the decision by the SPC IP Tribunal that the Japanese company MUJI was ordered to pay USD 89,000 and issue an apology.[544]

On 2 September 2020, in the case of *Lego v. Le Pin*, the Shanghai Third Intermediate People's Court, announced that Li Nan and eight other defendants were guilty of counterfeiting the trade mark LEGO. Between 2015 and 2019, without the permission of Lego, they used "乐拼" and its transliteration "LE PIN" (Lèpīn), which means "happy puzzle" as the brand to sell toys that were imitations of "LEGO" whose transliteration is "乐高" (Lègāo), which means "very happy". The group bought the Lego series of toys, disassembled them, copied them, commissioned others to make moulds, set up a toy factory, copied 47 series of the Lego brand, a total of 663 products, and sold a total of 4 million boxes of infringing products. Li Nan was sentenced to six years in prison and fined RMB 90 million; the remaining eight defendants were sentenced to three to four-and-a-half years in prison and also fined.[545]

XI. SCOPE OF PROTECTION OF WELL-KNOWN MARKS

1. Legislation and Legal Practice

In China, one needs to make a distinction between internationally well-known marks also recognized in China[546] and locally famous marks[547] (so called "national

543. Answer 32 of the BHPC to Several Questions in the Trial of Trade Mark Civil Dispute Cases, 18 February, Jinggao Fafa [2004] No. 48. Available at: https://v1.iphouse.cn/lawinfo/121.html?keyword = .
544. Phoebe Zhang, Muji ordered to pay Chinese firm US$89,000 and apologise after losing trademark appeal, SCMP 11 December 2019. Available at: https://www.scmp.com/news/china/society/article/3041684/muji-ordered-pay-chinese-firm-us89000-and-apologise-after-losing.
545. Fangzhi Legao jiu ren pan qiu fa yu shi yi, Oriental Daily, 3 September 2020. Available at: https://orientaldaily.on.cc/cnt/china_world/20200903/mobile/cdn-20200903-0903_00178_005.html.
546. Well-known mark: 中国驰名商标.
547. Local famous mark: 本地著名商标. In 2009, the SAIC issued the Working Instructions for the Determination of Famous Marks (Working Instructions 2009). The rationale behind the famous mark can be found in Article 3 Working Instructions 2009: to guide enterprises in implementing trade mark strategies, "enrich ... the meanings of trade marks, attach ... importance to the innovation and protection of trade marks as IP", create superior enterprises that own independent IPRs, promote well-known brands with stronger international competitiveness, develop enterprises, the "economy and society, and boost the building of an innovative country." Notice of the State Administration for Industry

champions"). The first category protects primarily foreign marks that may or may not be registered in China. The latter category lacks any extra-territorial dimension. Enhanced protection of well-known marks in China is particularly relevant against bad faith registration and bad faith use, as will be pointed out below.

Proprietors of foreign well-known marks often suffer from insufficient comprehension of China's linguistic intricacies (see the explanations in section V. 4. (a) on Identity, Similarity and Confusion). In addition, foreign brand owners at times seem to underestimate the fact that recognition in certain jurisdictions or economic regions may not necessarily correlate with recognition in China, a market where a large part of the population is unfamiliar with English or the Latin alphabet.

(a) Definition of Well-known Marks

China implemented its obligations to protect well-known marks under the Paris Convention and TRIPS.[548] A "well-known mark" was defined in Article 1 SPC Interpretation 2009, as "a trade mark that is widely known to the relevant public within the territory of China".[549] According to this judicial interpretation, a Court needs to determine whether a trade mark is well-known in one of the following cases:

(1) Where a trade mark infringement action is based Article 13 TML directed against a third party trade mark registration that is allegedly a duplication, imitation, or translation of either a trade mark not registered in China and "likely to cause confusion"[550] or of a well-known, China-registered trade mark where the new mark "misleads the public and is likely to create prejudice to the interests of the well-known mark registrant";[551]
(2) Where a trade mark infringement or unfair competition action is based on the ground that an enterprise name is identical with or similar to a well-known mark;
(3) Where an infringement action is defended on the ground that the plaintiff's trade mark has been reproduced, imitated, or translated from a prior unregistered well-known trade mark.[552]

---

and Commerce on Issuing the Working Instructions of the SAIC for the Determination of Famous Trademarks (2009) (promulgated by the SAIC, 21 April 2009, effective 21 April 2009).

548. Article 6*bis* Paris Convention protects unregistered well-known marks of the identical goods and services, while Article 16(2) TRIPS is broadening the scope of protection to well-known services and Article 16(3) TRIPS to registered well-known marks for dissimilar goods and services. *Supra* note 39.

549. Interpretation on Several Issues Concerning the Application of Law in the Trial of Cases of Civil Disputes Concerning the Protection of Well-Known Marks, Judicial Interpretation [2009] No. 3, promulgated by the Judicial Committee of the SPC on 22 April 2009 and effective on 1 May 2009. Available at: https://bit.ly/2WnR1vx. Amended on 23 December 2020, No. 6. Available at: https://bit.ly/2LBY3eE.

550. Article 13(1) TML 2001; Article 13(2) TML 2013 and 2019, *supra* note 15.

551. Article 13(2) TML 2001; Article 13(3) TML 2013 and 2019, *supra* note 15.

552. Article 2 SPC Interpretation 2009, *supra* note 549.

The competent authorities cannot recognize or cite a well-known mark[553] at the request of the interested party.[554] The recognition of a mark as well-known is exclusively intended to solve legal disputes and is not to be used by manufacturers and business operators in advertising, exhibition or other commercial activities.[555] Still, a proprietor can advertise the recognition of its well-known mark status as an event on its company websites, WeChat accounts, etc.[556]

(b) Competent Authority

In the 1990s, only the CTMO could recognize well-known marks.[557] Then in 2002, the TRAB also received this competency.[558] In addition to administrative recognition of well-known marks, China allowed judicial recognition after it became a member of the WTO in 2001.[559]

If a party files a claim under Article 13 TML 2019 via the administrative channels before the AIC, the CTMO may determine whether the trade mark is a well-known mark if it is necessary for examination purposes.[560] The TRAB[561] and the courts may also determine whether the trade mark is well-known if it is necessary for handling a given case.[562] If a party requests protection in respect of a trade mark that has been previously determined as a well-known mark by the AIC, CTMO, TRAB or a court, the other party can dispute this and the court shall carry out an examination.[563]

553. Article 4 SAIC Interim Provisions 1996, allowed CTMO to *ex officio* determine well-known marks, "according to the needs of trade mark registration and management."
554. Article 5 IRTL 2002, only permits CTMO and TRAB to determine well-known marks at the request of the party. IRTL 2002, promulgated by Decree No. 358 of the State Council on 3 August 2002, and effective as of 15 September 2002. Available at: http://www.wipo.int/edocs/lexdocs/laws/en/cn/cn018en.pdf or http://www.china.org.cn/business/laws_regulations/2007-06/22/content_1214797.htm.
555. Article 14(5) TML 2019, *supra* note 15.
556. Hongxia Wu, 'Protection of Well-Known Trademarks in China', CCPIT, Patent and Trademark Law Office, 23 September 2019, available at: http://www.mondaq.com/china/x/846830/Trademark/Protection+of+wellknown+trademarks+in+China.
557. Article 3 SAIC Interim Provisions 1996. Interim Provisions on the Recognition and Management of Well-known Marks 1996, SAIC Order No. 56, promulgated by the SAIC on 14 August 1996 and effective on the same date. Available at: http://www.law-lib.com/law/law_view.asp?id=63160.
558. Article 5 IRTL 2002, *supra* note 554.
559. An example is the IKEA case. *Inter IKEA System BV v. Beijing Information System Co. Ltd* (CINET), Beijing Second Intermediate People's Court, 76 *Gao Zhi Zhong Zi* (2000). See also, Connie Carnabuci and Minny Siu, 'China takes new path with Ikea landmark', *World Trademark Review*, 5 June 2001. Available at: https://www.worldtrademarkreview.com/online/china-takes-new-path-ikea-landmark.
560. Article 14(2) TML 2019, *supra* note 15.
561. Article 14(3) TML 2019, *supra* note 15. Article 22(3) SPC Interpretation 2002, *supra* note 400.
562. Article 14(4) TML 2019, *supra* note 15. Article 22(1) SPC Interpretation 2002, *supra* note 400.
563. Article 22(3) SPC Interpretation 2002, *supra* note 400.

(c) *Determining Recognition*

Article 14 TML 2019 uses similar factors as Article 5(1) SPC Interpretation 2009[564] to constitute evidence for a well-known mark:

(1) The degree of recognition of the trade mark among the relevant public;
(2) The duration in which the trade mark has been in use;
(3) The duration, extent and geographical scope of all publicity operations carried out using the trade mark;
(4) The history of protection of the trade mark as a well-known trade mark;
(5) Other factors making the trade mark well-known.

Transferring these factors from judicial interpretation to law was conducive to the applicability of these norms by the AIC, CTMO, TRAB and the courts.

In the SAIC Interim Provisions 1996, well-known status is granted for up to three years.[565] This has led to criticism,[566] since well-known marks are dynamic in time and place, should be revisable and not give consumers the wrong impression that it is a government endorsed badge of quality. Therefore, SPC Interpretation 2009 provides that a determination as well-known can be merely regarded as fact-specific in an individual case.[567] Article 14 TML 2019 confirms the determination of the well-known mark "as a fact". The logical consequence is a case-by-case doctrine: if a mark had been granted well-known status in one case, this does not bind the competent authorities to grant well-known protection in another case. Then again, where a mark had been granted well-known protection before, it is a strong reference for future cases.

Case Law

The Beijing IP Court held that "Xinhua Dictionary" was an unregistered well-known mark.[568] "Xinhua Dictionary" had both a specific historical origin and an identifiable evolution. It has been a long-term unique provider of information and occupies an objectively successful position of over 50 per cent market share in China. "Xinhua

564. Article 5(1) SPC Interpretation 2009, *supra* note 549: market share, sales territory, and profit and tax of goods bearing the trade mark; the continuous use of the trade mark; the methods, duration, extent, capital investment, and regional scope of the marketing and promotion of the trade mark; records indicating that the trade mark received protection as a well-known mark; the trade mark's reputation in the market; and other facts proving the trade mark to be well-known.
565. Article 4 SAIC Interim Provisions 1996.
566. Xiao Mu, *The Evolution of Well-Known Trademark Protection in China* (PhD thesis, University of Hong Kong 2016), 78–79.
567. Article 13 SPC Interpretations 2009, *supra* note 549.
568. *Commercial Press Co., Ltd. v. Sinolingua Co., Ltd.* Beijing IP Court, 77 *Jing 73 Min Chu* (2016). The SPC selected this case as one of the Top 10 IP cases of 2017. 'Zuigao renmin fayuan fabu 2017 nian zhongguo fayuan 10 da zhishi chanquan anjian' (The Supreme People's Court released the top 10 intellectual property cases in Chinese courts in 2017), SPC, 23 April 2018, No. 5. Available at: http://bjzcfy.chinacourt.gov.cn/article/detail/2018/04/id/3277569.shtml.

Dictionary" maintains the mixed attributes of product and brand, and it has a stable recognition among relevant consumers. The Court decision was based on the length of time for which Commercial Press has been using the name "Xinhua Dictionary", the sales volumes it achieves and the extremely extensive reach of those sales, 567 million copies of its Xinhua Dictionary have been sold across the whole country in the past 60 years.[569]

Determining the Status as a Well-Known Mark Must be Necessary

An important prerequisite of recognition of a well-known mark is that such recognition must be necessary, e.g. when protection outside the scope of similarity of goods is requested, as Article 2 SPC Interpretation on Several Issues Relating to the Application of Law to the Trial of Cases of Civil Disputes Involving Well-known Marks 2009 has established.[570] This Interpretation does not provide the factors to be considered when applying this principle. However, in 2014, in *Exxon Mobil Corp. v. Beijing Beinongguoxin Kejifazhan Co., Ltd*,[571] the Beijing IP Court held that if an ordinary registered trade mark receives protection equivalent to that granted to a well-known mark against use for identical or similar goods, the recognition of well-known trade mark will not be considered necessary. Exxon Mobil had registered the trade marks "MOBIL" and "美孚" designated for Classes 1 and 4 (pesticides and fertilizer chemicals) and 5 (lubricating oil products), but had never used these trade marks for pesticides or fertilizer chemicals. Defendant Beinongguoxin used the Exxon Mobil trade marks for pesticides and fertilizer chemicals.

The Beijing IP Court held that in the following cases, recognition of the trade mark as well-known might be necessary:

- cross-class protection;
- claiming protection against registered trade marks;
- request for declaration of invalidity of another's mark made beyond the time limit for doing so;
- anti-trade mark dilution;
- bypassing the similarity test;
- sufficient compensation for damages.[572]

569. WIPO and SPC, *WIPO Collection of Leading Judgments on Intellectual Property Rights People's Republic of China (2011–2018)* (2019), 38–43. Available at: https://www.wipo.int/edocs/pubdocs/en/wipo_pub_1065.pdf.
570. SPC Interpretations 2009, *supra* note 549.
571. In this case, the legal representative of Beijing Beinong Guoxin Technology Development Co Ltd, Zhang Zhimin and his daughter, Zhang Dandan, were sued as co-defendants. Gang Hu, 'China: Piercing The Corporate Veil In Chinese Trademark Infringement Cases', CCPIT, 3 April 2019. Available at: https://www.mondaq.com/china/trademark/794334/piercing-the-corporate-veil-in-chinese-trademark-infringement-cases.
572. Beijing IP Court, 143 *Jing Zhi Min Chu Zi* (2014).

Exxon Mobil could not provide evidence for using its trade marks for pesticide or fertilizer chemicals products in order to claim damages, but it succeeded in proving that its trade marks in lubricating oil product had become well-known and the defendant's act had caused trade mark dilution and confusion. The Court held that confusion was necessary in order to be eligible for damages and since "confusion" was considered broader than "misleading", which is the standard of Article 13(3) TML, this standard was also met. The plaintiff was awarded RMB 3.3 million.[573]

In 2019, in *Volkswagen Company v. Shanghai Xizhong Auto Parts Co., Ltd*, the BHPC clarified that there is a difference in degree between the determination of "reproduction, imitation, or translation" relating to well-known trade marks and the similarity test for ordinary registered trade marks. Volkswagen wanted to protect its mark "大众" (Dàzhòng) by invalidating Xhizhong's trade mark "大夊" (Dàzhōng) that was registered for Class 7 goods, such as engine spark plugs, water pumps, shock absorbers, all for automobiles. The Court held that given the high popularity and distinctive character of well-known trade marks, they should receive stronger protection compared to ordinary trade marks. Although Chinese characters should be considered as the most distinctive part of the trade mark, the pronunciation between these marks was almost the same. The Court also held that there was some convergence in the trade marks' functions, sales channels and the targeted consumers. Therefore, the contested trade mark constituted an imitation of a well-known trade mark which was misleading the relevant public. The Court held that it was necessary to apply the "reproduction, imitation, or translation" standard for protecting well-known marks since the "similarity test" for ordinary trade marks would fail.[574]

(d) Scope of Protection

When a trade mark is recognized as well-known in China, it enjoys protection even against marks registered for more than five years but acquired in bad faith. One has to distinguish between an unregistered and registered well-known mark. See Table 2 below.

573. Feynman Liang, 'Exxon Mobil Was Awarded CNY 4.5 million as Damages in Trademark Infringement Case due to the Recognition of Well-known Trademark', Jiaquan IP Law, 22 December 2016. Available at: https://www.jiaquanip.com/news.asp?ArticleID = 131&ClassID = 40.

574. 'Beijing High awarded Volkswagen well-known trademark, denies local company's registration in other class', China IP News, 16 January 2020. Available at: http://www.yfiplaw.com/info.php?cid = 30&id = 364.

Table 2.

Unregistered well-known mark (Article 13(2) TML 2019	Protection against copy, imitation or translation for identical or similar goods or services
Registered well-known mark (Article 13(3) TML 2019	Protection against copy, imitation or translation for identical/similar and dissimilar goods or services, however case law has suggested that the goods or services cannot be too dissimilar.

Although Article 13(3) TML 2019 only refers to dissimilar goods,[575] one can argue *a maiore ad minus*: if a registered well-known mark is protected against third party applications of the mark for dissimilar goods, it should *a fortiori* be protected against applications for identical or similar goods, since the passing-off character of using such marks is even stronger.

Article 14 SPC Provisions 2016 provides a solution for this situation: if the proprietor of a registered well-known trade mark has filed an opposition or invalidation application against a conflicting trade mark for identical or similar goods, and the TRAB has ruled in favour of the registered trade mark proprietor (but citing Article 30 TML 2019), the court may apply Article 30 TML 2019 if the case is within the five-year period after the registration of the contested trade mark, or Article 13(3) TML 2019 if the contested trade mark has been registered for more than five years. Ranjard expounds that a plaintiff who can only prove a likelihood of association and dilution could also rely on Article 13(3) TML 2019 and have the well-known status of the registered trade mark recognized within the five years.[576] This was the case in *P&G v. TRAB* and Weishida (19 May 2016).[577]

Where the registered trade mark is well-known, and a suspected infringer is in the same industry as the registered well-known trade mark owner or in an industry but where goods or services are different to the goods or services of the suspected infringer, and where there is no legitimate reason to use the same or similar signs as the registered trade mark, the suspected infringer should be deemed having the intention of free riding,[578] which qualifies as trade mark infringement under Article 57(2) TML.

The scope of protection for registered well-known marks, which in most jurisdictions extend cross-class, is sometimes applied in a more limited manner in China. The scope of protection does not necessarily refer to all the specifications in the 45 classes of the Nice Classification. For example, if a mark for specialized goods

575. In 2008, in *Guangdong Haotai Environmental Technology Co., Ltd. v. Zhongshan Haotaitai Electric Co., Ltd.*, the SPC held that the well-known mark "Good Wife" of Haotai for drying rack products could be granted protection across categories, including gas stoves for which Zhongshan used the name Good Wife. SPC, 17 July 2009, 1465 *Minshen Zi* (2008). Available at: http://blog.sina.com.cn/s/blog_62fa69390100gqrc.html.

576. Ranjard, *supra* note 158.

577. Paul Ranjard, 'What To Expect From The SPC's New Trademark Judicial Interpretation?', Wan Hui Da – Peksung IP Group, 25 January 2017. Available at: https://bit.ly/2BNJEns.

578. Article 24(2) Trade Mark Infringement Standard, *supra* note 426.

is well-known within but not beyond a segment, the scope of the well-known mark's protection could be more limited.[579] The courts take the following factors into account:

(1) The degree of distinctiveness and recognition of the well-known mark;
(2) Whether the litigious and cited marks are sufficiently similar;
(3) The conditions of their designated goods/services;
(4) The degree of overlap and attention of the relevant public;
(5) The situation in which the mark similar to the well-known mark is legally used by other entities in the market or other relevant factors.[580]

Unlike the dispute between two ordinary marks with different application dates where the owner of the senior mark cannot directly attack the junior mark in court, Article 11 SPC Interpretation 2009 provides protection of a prior unregistered well-known mark or prior registered well-known mark in case of a junior registered trade mark that is used within its scope.[581]

Article 11 SPC Interpretation 2009 also protects senior unregistered and registered well-known marks in case of a junior registered mark that is used outside of its scope.[582]

In case of a dispute between a normal senior registered trade mark and junior unregistered mark on identical or similar goods, Article 57(1) and (2) TML 2019 gives protection to the senior mark. Article 2 SPC Interpretation 2002 provides protection to a senior unregistered and registered well-known mark against a junior unregistered mark on identical or similar goods.[583]

In case of a dispute between a normal senior registered trade mark or an unregistered well-known mark and a junior unregistered mark on dissimilar goods, there is no protection. However, in case of a dispute between a senior registered well-known mark and a junior unregistered mark on dissimilar goods, Article 1 SPC Interpretation 2002 provides protection.[584]

In 2014, the Italian luxury brand Bvlgari extended its luxury goods business by entering the entering the market of luxury hotels and residential property development in China. It came to Bvlgari's attention that Hunan Taskin Investment Co. (Taskin), Ltd. had been using "宝格丽" (Bǎogélì) as a transliteration of Bvlgari and "宝格丽公寓" (Bvlgari Residential Building) and sued Taskin asserting its well-known mark with regard to accessories and jewellery. In December 2017, the Shenzhen Intermediate People's Court made the ruling that Taskin should cease infringement activities and compensate Bvlgari with RMB 1,000,000. According to the first instance procedure, Bvlgari had registered four trade marks in respect of Class 36 services regarding the"sales of commercial residential buildings; real estate services" in China. According

579. Hongxia Wu, 'How to Recognize a Well-known Trademark in China?', CCPIT, Patent and Trade Mark Office, 2 August 2019. Available at: https://www.ccpit-patent.com.cn/node/11086.
580. Article 11(3) BHPC Guidelines 2019, *supra* note 5. Available at: https://file.chinacourt.org/f.php?id=37014&class=file.
581. SPC Interpretation 2009, *supra* note 549.
582. SPC Interpretation 2009, *supra* note 549.
583. SPC Interpretation 2002, *supra* note 400.
584. SPC Interpretation 2002, *supra* note 400.

to the Shenzhen Intermediate People's Court, there was no need to decide whether "宝格丽" constituted a well-known mark. Both parties appealed.

In December 2019, the Guangdong People's Higher Court ruled that the "宝格丽" trade mark for "accessories (jewellery); watches" was a well-known mark, and that the defendant had used "宝格丽" and "宝格丽公寓" (Bvlgari Residential Building) in a prominent manner on promotional materials and commercial properties it developed, which constituted trade mark infringement and unfair competition. The compensation that Taskin had to pay was raised to RMB 3,100,000.[585]

Courts are often reluctant to qualify a trade mark as a well-known mark. BMW uses the name 宝马 (Bǎomǎ), which literally means "precious horse" for automobiles in China. Guangdong Tianma Fruit Drinking Company in June 2007 filed for the registration in Class 30 products including chocolate and sweets using the same characters, "宝马". The mark was registered in January 2010. In April 2014, BMW filed for revocation of the trade mark, alleging that Tianma had copied BMW's trade mark in bad faith and diluted its famous "宝马" and BMW trade marks it used on automobiles.

The TRAB made a decision in April 2015, claiming that the trade mark in dispute was not similar to the cited trade mark when used on the same or similar products. The trade mark in dispute did not copy, imitate and translate the trade mark of BMW and thus did not impair the right of the well-known mark status or damage the prior trade name of BMW. The TRAB thus upheld the registration of the trade mark in dispute. BMW then brought the case to Beijing IP Court. The Beijing IP Court held that the trade mark in dispute was similar to the cited trade mark when used on the same or similar products, and it was not necessary to invoke the well-known marks provision. The Court thus revoked the TRAB's decision. The TRAB then brought the case to BHPC which held that the BMW trade mark "宝马" enjoyed a reputation among the relevant public, so if both trade marks appeared in the market, this could cause confusion or at least confusion by association amongst the public in respect of the origin of products when used on the same or similar products. According to the Court, there was no need to invoke the provision on protection of well-known mark. In this connection, the Court affirmed the judgment.[586] To compensate its reluctance to recognize "宝马" as a well-known mark for cars, the BHPC extended the protection against confusion by association for dissimilar goods.

However, even though the principle is that registered well-known marks protect against the use of an identical or similar mark for competing and non-competing goods and services, sometimes the courts will take the relationship between the goods of the well-known mark and the disputed mark into account. An example is the 2016 Hermès case. The BHPC held the unauthorized use of the combination of "

585. 'KWM assisted Italian luxury brand Bvlgari to win trademark infringement & unfair competition suit with well-known trademark recognition', King & Wood Mallesons 23 March 2020. Available at: shttps://www.chinalawinsight.com/2020/03/articles/intellectual-property/kwm-assisted-italian-luxury-brand-bvlgari-to-win-trademark-infringement-unfair-competition-suit-with-well-known-trademark-recognition/.

586. Wang Guohao, 'BMW Knocks Local Candy Maker Off Free-ride of Trademark', China IP News, 10 April 2019. Available at: http://www.cn12330.cn/cipnews/news_content.aspx?newsId = 115108. dcfb71764ae8.

好美思", "HERMES" and a logo by a wine marketeer and vendor to be non-infringing, even though the trade mark "Hermès" was considered well-known for clothing and luggage,[587] because clothing and luggage were considered too far distanced from wine. In other words: registered well-known marks protect only against dissimilar goods within a certain bandwidth.

(e) Criminal Protection of Well-Known Marks

Under Article 123 Criminal Law,[588] the use of a trade mark that is identical to another's prior registered trade mark in respect of identical goods is a criminal offence if the circumstances are serious. No distinction is made between a normal registered trade mark and a well-known mark. The protection of a well-known mark by invoking this provision is explicitly mentioned in the official letter from CNIPA dated 12 July 2019.[589] It is expected that the well-known mark will be better protected in terms of criminal punishment.

2. Trade Mark Infringement and the OEM Exception

This specifically Chinese issue under trade mark law is relevant for two reasons.

1. Original equipment manufacturers (OEM), that is, manufacturers that outsource the production of parts or equipment labelled with a registered mark and exporting the same outside China, are very common in China, and original equipment manufacturing is an important industry.
2. It has been as unfortunate as common that Chinese companies have registered foreign trade marks in China so that they can try to hold the foreign trade mark proprietor without a trade mark in China or its local manufacturer

---

587. Even though Hermès is pronounced with a silent "H", the French company also tried to stop the transliteration "好美思" (Hǎo měi sī), which literally means "What a beautiful thought" in combination with the Roman script "HERMES" and a logo used by Anhui Haomeisi Wine Marketing Co., Ltd. for Class 33 in regard of distilled alcohol beverages, bitters, etc., also to no avail. In 2014, the BFIPC held that the prior rights were not impaired. Beijing First Intermediate People's Court, 5948 *Yizhongxing (Zhi) Chuzi* (2014).

   In 2016, the BHPC held that the combination of transliteration, Roman script and logo provided an overall visual effect that is obviously different from Hermès. BHPC, 2504 *Jing Xing Zhong* (2016).

   The use of HERMES alone was not sufficient to determine that the trade mark constitutes an imitation of the trade mark. Even if the evidence in the case submitted by Hermès International SCA proved that its trade mark was registered in 2000 and recognized as a well-known trade mark used on clothing and luggage products before the Haomeisi trade mark application for registration, this will not lead to the misunderstanding of the relevant public and does not harm the interests of the Hermès trade mark. 'Hao mei si "HERMES" shangbiao huozhun zhuce' (The trade mark "HERMES" was approved for registration), *People's Daily*, 23 September 2016. Available at: http://ip.people.com.cn/n1/2016/0923/c136655-28735490.html.
588. *Supra* note 317.
589. Letter from CNIPA to the Reply No. 4133 of the Second Session of the 13th NPC. Available at: http://114.247.84.107:8080/ogic/view/govinfo!detail.jhtml?id=4543.

of parts or equipment to ransom by holding them liable for trade mark infringement.[590]

To counter the threat by such trade mark squatters, courts and Customs (but not the AICs) have created an "OEM exception" whereby the mere export of trade marked goods on behalf of a foreign trade mark owner is not deemed an infringement of a domestically registered mark. The BHPC explicitly provides an OEM exception in its 2019 Guidelines.[591]

In 2015, the SPC decided in *Pujiang Yahuan Locks Co., Ltd. v. Focker Security Products International Limited*[592] that an OEM's use of the trade mark PRETUL on padlocks made solely for export is not an act of infringement. The SPC defined three requirements for such exception to apply:

- the OEM is authorized to make the goods by a foreign trade mark proprietor that has a valid, prior trade mark rights in the country of destination;
- the OEM has done a due diligence search in verifying the trade mark rights of its foreign client;
- the OEM makes goods that are exclusively for export.

In 2018, in *Shanghai Diesel Engine Co., Ltd* (Diesel) *v. Jiangsu Changjia Jinfeng Dynamic Machinery Co., Ltd.* (Changjia), the SPC confirmed its earlier stance on the OEM exception to trade mark infringement. It overturned the Jiangsu Higher People's Court's ruling that Changjia, which performed OEM activities for PTADIPER-KASABUANA, an Indonesian company with an effective Indonesian trade mark registration certificate, was infringing the well-known mark DONG FENG for diesel engines. According to the SPC, the OEM used the trade mark in a way that it was not perceived as a badge of origin and would not result in trade mark infringement. The OEM had verified the trade mark rights of the foreign consignor. All products were exported to Indonesia, would not circulate on the Chinese market and thus not cause confusion to consumers in China.[593] If the goods using a contested trade mark are directly exported without being circulated in China, Diesel, the registrant of the trade mark in China can claim to maintain the registration of such a trade mark. This depends on genuine "trade mark use".[594]

---

590. BHPC, 2504 *Jing Xing Zhong* (2016).
591. Article 16(26) BHPC Guidelines 2019, *supra* note 5: "If goods using the prior unregistered trade mark that are directly exported without being circulated in China, and a party concerned claims that the application for registration of the trade mark relied upon should fall under the circumstances of 'use of improper means to forestall registration of a trade mark which is already in use by another person or have a certain influence' provided in Article 32 TML, this claim shall not be supported."
592. *Pujiang Yahuan Locks Co., Ltd. v. Focker Security Products International Limited*, SPC 2015 (No. 7 of the 50 Model Cases concerning Intellectual Property Rights Adjudicated by China's Courts in 2015, issued by the SPC. Available at: http://en.pkulaw.cn/display.aspx?cgid=a25051f3312b07f3c1ff58710cd39741f4379428fb541b5fbdfb&lib=case.
593. Yu Du and Matthew Murphy, 'PRC Supreme Court Revisits OEM Manufacturing Defense to Trademark Infringement', HG.org, 8 April 2018. Available at: https://www.hg.org/legal-articles/prc-supreme-court-revisits-oem-manufacturing-defense-to-trademark-infringement-47438.
594. Article 19(6) BHPC Guidelines 2019, *supra* note 5.

It is possible that bad faith proprietors abusively record their trade mark with Customs in China so that when the OEM products with the same trade marks are about to get shipped for export, they could be seized and detained by Customs.[595] In that case, the bad faith trade mark proprietor can demand a ransom from the good faith proprietor in return for release of the goods.[596] The good faith trade mark proprietor can present Customs with a notarized and legalized version of the trade mark in its country of destination of the goods to try to invoke the OEM exception. Interim injunctions are likely to be rejected by the courts, which means that the good faith trade mark proprietor has to wait for at least nine months for a decision on the merits.[597]

However, on 14 October 2019, the SPC seems to have qualified the OEM exception in *Honda Motor Co., Ltd. v. Chongqing Hengsheng Xintai Trading Co., Ltd. et Chongqing Hengsheng Group Co., Ltd.*[598] According to the SPC, the trade mark HONDAKIT on motorcycle parts should be deemed trade mark use if the trade mark was used as a source indicator. A likelihood of confusion amongst the relevant public should be determined broadly, not only including consumers but also business operators. The SPC did not agree with the appellant court's judgment that OEM products could not cause confusion since they were destined for export; with the advent of the internet and e-commerce, the probability has increased that exported products might later return to China and Chinese consumers.[599]

The OEM exception was created as a solution for a situation whereby foreign genuine trade mark holders that failed to register their trade marks in China could still make use of the manufacturing strength of Chinese factories for their trade marked products, even though the identical trade mark was registered by a Chinese company as well. Now that the TML has provisions against bad faith registrations and courts have seriously begun tackling this issue, the OEM exception seems unsustainable. Especially since the OEM exception neither takes the exclusive right of the Chinese trade mark seriously (because the goods can find their way back into the Chinese market) nor the possibility that the OEM products will infringe a trade mark in the country of the consignor and beyond. In other words: paradoxically, the OEM exception neither respects the territoriality nor extra-territoriality of trade marks.

595. Joe Simone and Dan Plane, 'OEM Exception to Trademark Infringement', SIPS Asia, 15 July 2015. Available at: https://sips.asia/knowledge/trademark-enforcement/oem-exception-to-trademark-infringement/.
596. Simone and Plane, *supra* note 595.
597. Simone and Plane, *supra* note 595.
598. SPC, 14 October (2019) Min Gao Fa Zai No. 138.
599. Tom Zhang and Linda Zhao, 'China Trademark: SPC Reverses Its Precedent on Original Equipment Manufacturing', *Managing Intellectual Property*, 22 November 2019. Available at: https://bit.ly/2DkVsyj.

XII. RELATED RIGHTS – OTHER BUSINESS IDENTIFIERS

1. Geographical Indications

The poster child for China's GI system is the Fuling pickled mustard tuber of Chongqing with its "inimitable piquant flavour" derived from the *terroir* of soil and weather conditions in the District, as well as the traditional techniques used in its preservation. Fuling pickled mustard tuber was granted GI registration in 2000. This prevented producers from outside the region pre-emptively registering an eponymous trade mark. Between 2000 and 2004, it raised the income of mustard tuber growers in Fuling District by 194 per cent.[600]

(a) Definitions and Applicable Laws

(1) Appellation of Origin and other GIs, Treaties

China's membership of the Paris Convention became effective in 1985. Since that time, China has the obligation to protect appellations of origin, which is a special type of GI. The difference between a GI and appellation of origin is that for the latter the link with the place of origin should be stronger. The quality or characteristics of a product protected as an appellation of origin must result exclusively or essentially from its geographical origin. China is neither a member of the Lisbon Agreement for the Protection of Appellations and Their International Registration of 1958, and last amended in 1979, nor a member of Geneva Act of the Lisbon Agreement on Appellations of Origin and Geographical Indications of 2015.

When China ascended to the WTO in 2001, it also had to comply with the TRIPS protection of GIs. Article 16 TML 2019 provides a definition of a GI: "The geographic indication as mentioned ... means a sign that indicates the region where the goods originate and the natural or human dimensions which primarily determine the specific quality, reputation, or other features of the goods." This protects a broader category of signs than Article 22(1) TRIPS, since the specific quality, reputation or other features of the goods need to be essentially attributable to its geographical origin, but could also be due to the natural or human factors or a combination thereof.

TRIPS prescribes the standard of protection for GIs, but not the method, which could be by way of unfair competition prevention, certification and collective trade marks, and *sui generis* GIs.[601]

600. Xin Xin and Ai Jie, 'Chinese Farmers Cash in on Intellectual Property Rights', 17th National Congress of the CPC. Available at: http://www.chinatoday.com.cn/17ct/17e/1013/el01.htm.

601. Standing Committee on the Law of Trademarks, Industrial Designs and Geographical Indications, Eighth Session Geneva, 27 to 31 May 2002, Document SCT/6/3 REV. on Geographical Indications: Historical Background, Nature of Rights, Existing Systems for Protection and Obtaining Protection in Other Countries, C. Available at: https://www.wipo.int/edocs/mdocs/sct/en/sct_8/sct_8_4.pdf.

China had chosen to implement a GI system via its trade mark system and introduce two *sui generis* systems. This choice was criticized,[602] but can also be seen as a way to experiment and retain the best system.

(2) *Nature of the Right*

GIs are not private rights, since no private or legal person exclusively owns the right to use them.[603] GIs are used to stimulate rural development and add value to brand names that help small scale agricultural enterprises without owning them individually.[604] As Blakeney pointed out, GIs are unlikely to be considered more than descriptive.[605] It is not possible to protect a descriptive, and thus inherently non-distinctive sign as a normal trade mark. The exception is where the GI has acquired distinctiveness through use.

(b) Protection of GIs in China

In 1987, the SAIC first intervened to protect the "Danish Butter Cookies", trade mark[606] and again in 1989 when it banned the appellation of the origin "Champagne" in both Roman script and Chinese characters.[607]

In 1989, China joined the Madrid Agreement Concerning the International Registration of Marks,[608] and the SAIC began to accommodate collective and certification marks designated for China and registered under the Madrid system.

The practice before 1993 to allow GIs to be registered as normal trade marks has led to conflicts between registered trade marks, which after five years cannot be

---

602. Bradley M. Bashaw, 'Geographical Indications in China: Why Protect GIS with Both Trademark Law and AOC-Type Legislation', 17 *Pac. Rim L. & Pol'y J.* (2008), 73, 74, 75 and 100.
   Zhang Haizheng and Hu Didi and Li Yanhui, 'Protection of Geographical Indications Under China's Intellectual Property Legal Framework', 17(2) *Australian Journal of Asian Law* (2016), Article 10; 1,23. Available at: https://ssrn.com/abstract=2938181.
   Haiyan Zheng, 'A Unique Type of Cocktail: Protection of Geographical Indications in China', in Irene Calboli and Wee Loon Ng-Loy (eds.), *Geographical Indications at the Crossroads of Trade, Development, and Culture: Focus on Asia-Pacific* (Cambridge University Press, Cambridge, 2017), 396.
603. Pattloch, *supra* note 2, 144.
604. Xin Xin and Ai Jie, *supra* note 600.
605. Michael Blakeney, 'Geographical Indications and TRIPS', in Michael Blakeney, Thierry Coulet, Getachew Mengistie, Marcelin Tonye Mahop (eds.), *Extending the Protection of Geographical Indications – Case Studies in the Protection of Agricultural Products in Africa* (Earthscan, London, 202), 7–34. Available at: https://ssrn.com/abstract=2177435.
606. Xin Xin and Ai Jie, *supra* note 600.
607. SAIC Notice of Stopping the Use of the Word 'Champagne' on Goods Classified as Alcoholic Drinks, CTMO, 26 October 1989. Zhonghua renmin gongheguo guojia gongshang hang zheng guanli ju "guanyu tingzhi zai jiu lei shangpin shang shiyong xiangbin huo Champagne ziyang de tongzhi" (gong shangbiao zi (1989)) No. 296.
608. China acceded to the Madrid Agreement 1979, *supra* note 215.

cancelled and thus become exclusive rights for the proprietor, and GIs, which may be used by third parties other than the proprietor.[609]

In 1993, China commenced its GI protection via collective and certification marks. Article 6 Implementation of the TML 1993[610] introduced the protection of collective and certification marks according to Article 3 TML 1993 via the CTMO.

In 1994, the SAIC promulgated the Procedures for the Registration and Administration of Collective Marks and Certification Marks,[611] which provided that certification marks could be used to certify the place of origin, raw materials, method of production, quality, accuracy, or other characteristics of the said goods or services,[612] and that collective marks refer to members of an industrial or commercial group, association or other collective organization for the purpose of indicating that the dealers in the goods belong to the same organization.

In 2001, China elevated its GI protection to the level of law by introducing it into Article 16 TML 2001. Article 3(3) TML 2001 states that a certification mark is a sign controlled by an organization capable of monitoring certain goods for use by organizations or persons other than such an organization on their goods to certify the geographical origin, material, mode of manufacture, quality or other specific characteristics. Article 3(2) TML 2001 provides that a collective mark is a sign registered in the name of a group, association or other organization for use by the members of such an organization in the course of trade to indicate the users' membership of the organization.

The SAIC Collective and Certification Marks Measures 2003 stipulates parties applying for GI registration as a collective or certification mark shall also furnish the approval documents issued by the government, which has jurisdiction, or the competent authority of the industry. Article 6(2) SAIC Collective and Certification Marks Measures 2003 states that for GI registration as a collective or certification foreign persons or enterprises shall furnish documents certifying the qualification of the subject and submit the detailed information of the professionals and special testing equipment of their own or of any other organization authorized by them to show their capability of supervising the particular quality of the GI goods as well as certifying that the GI is under legal protection in the country of origin.

If a GI is registered as a certification mark, any natural person, legal person or other organization whose goods satisfy the conditions under which the GI is used may request the use of the certification mark, and the organization in control of such certification mark shall permit the use. If a GI is registered as a collective mark, any natural person, legal person or other organization whose goods satisfy the conditions under which the geographical indication is used may request membership of the society, association or any other organization that has the GI registered as a

609. Pattloch, *supra* note 2, 88.

610. IRTL 1993 (Second Revision) promulgated by the State Council on 15 July 1993. Available at: https://www.wipo.int/edocs/lexdocs/laws/en/cn/cn010en.pdf.

611. Procedures for the Registration and Administration of Collective Marks and Certification Marks, promulgated by the SAIC on 31 December 1994. Available at: http://www.lehmanlaw.com/resource-centre/laws-and-regulations/intellectual-property/procedures-for-the-registration-and-administration-of-collective-marks-and-certification-marks-1994.html.

612. Article 2(2) SAIC Procedures 1994, *supra* note 611.

collective mark, and the society, association or any other organization shall accept the membership in accordance with its articles of association. However, those who do not request membership of the society, association or any other organization that has the geographical indication registered as a collective mark may legitimately use the GI, and the society, association or any other organization is not entitled to prohibit such use.

If an application for registration of the original trade mark is followed by a collective or certification mark containing a GI, then factors such as the objective existence of this GI or its popularity, distinctiveness and the perception of the relevant public may be comprehensively considered by the court to judge whether the relevant public might well confuse the sources of the goods or services.[613]

If an application for a collective or certification mark registration containing a GI is followed by a normal trade mark, one can assume, from the perspective of improperly adhering to the popularity of this GI, that the relevant public might well confuse the sources of the goods or services.

If a collective or certification mark containing a GI is well-known, Article 13(3) TML may apply for the purposes of protecting this trade mark. If such an application for registration of the collective or certification mark containing the GI filed by a party concerned pursuant to Article 13(3) TML is not approved or is declared invalid, then factors such as the objective existence of this GI or its popularity, distinctiveness and the perception of the relevant public may be comprehensively considered to determine whether the registration of the collective or certification mark containing the GI misleads the public and would harm the interests of the registrant of the ordinary trade mark. If a litigious trade mark applicant or registrant applies for registration of the whole of a GI or its main identification part as a normal trade mark, Articles 16(1) (misleading registration of goods which do not originate from the region indicated on the goods), 10(2) (restricted special signs) or 11(1) TML (generic nature) may apply when hearing the case. Also, if the geographical scope indicated by the applicant of a collective or certification mark containing the GI in the application document is inconsistent with the actual place of origin, Article 16(1) TML can be invoked. If a party claims that another person's application for registration of a certification or collective mark containing a GI violates the provisions of Article 16(2) TML and therefore this trade mark should not be approved or be declared invalid, the contents ("the trade mark for registration does not comply with the relevant provisions of this Law") of Article 30 TML shall apply when hearing this case.

The registration and administration of GIs as collective and certification marks have been effected by CTMO of CNIPA under the State Administration for Market Regulation (SAMR) since 2018.

According to May 2019 statistics, 4,996 domestic GIs have been registered as collective or certification marks: the top five provinces are Shandong (680 GIs), Fujian (459 GIs), Hubei (426 GIs), Sichuan (343 GIs) and Jiangsu (305 GIs). There have been 183 foreign GIs registered in particular from France (125 GIs), Italy (23 GIs) and US (14 GIs).[614] Examples of foreign GIs registered as collective marks include: Champagne,

613. Article 13(5) BHPC Guidelines 2019, *supra* note 5.

614. Bae based her article on the presentation of Guizeng (Wayne) Liu, at the 141st INTA Annual Meeting in Boston, USA, 18–22 May 2019. Kate Bae, Update of Geographical

Scotch Whisky, Solingen, Chianti Classico and Prosciutto di Parma.[615] Examples of foreign GIs registered as certification marks include: Parmigiano Reggiano, Amarone della Valpolicella, Grapes from California, and Idaho potatoes. [616]

(1) *Case Law*

On 10 January 2010, Fujian Longwang Trading Ltd applied for the registration of the trade mark name "罗曼尼 • 康帝", which is the transliteration of "Romanée-Conti", for goods in Class 33 (i.e., wine) with the CTMO. Seven years later, Fujian Longwang Trading Ltd assigned the trade mark to Wu Liping.[617]

On 21 January 2017, the *Institut national de l'origine et de la qualité* (INAO) filed a request to invalidate the "罗曼尼·康帝" trade mark with the TRAB. The INAO argued that "Romanée-Conti" is an appellation of origin in France. However, the TRAB held that "Romanée-Conti" had not been registered as a GI in China. Moreover, the TRAB held that the INAO did not provide sufficient evidence to prove an association between "Romanée-Conti" and "罗曼尼 • 康帝" that would mislead the public, so that the trade mark could not have violated Article 16(1) TML 2001.[618] The INAO brought the case before the Beijing IP Court, which overturned the TRAB decision[619] and held that the region indicated by "Romanée-Conti" featured distinctive natural and human factors, that the name had been recognized by France as an appellation of origin since 1936;[620] and that there was a stable corresponding relationship between "Romanée-Conti" and "罗曼尼 • 康帝".[621]

The TRAB and Wu Liping appealed to the Beijing High People's Court which, however, upheld the first instance court's decision on 10 June 2019.[622] The court for the second instance held that there is no prerequisite for registration of a GI in

---

Indications Protection in China, Your IP Insider, 12 September 2019. Available at: http://www.youripinsider.eu/update-geographical-indications-protection-china/. See also Wang Yu, Woguo dili biaozhi zhengming shangbiao zhuce qingkuang fenxi (Analysis on the Registration Status of Geographical Indication Certification Marks in China), IPRDaily, June 2019. Available at: http://www.iprdaily.cn/news_22138.html.

615. Jane Chen, 'Worldwide: Geographical Indications in China', Kangxin, 11 February 2020. Available at: https://www.mondaq.com/china/trademark/892392/geographical-indications-in-china.
616. Chen, *supra* note 615.
617. Ming Xingnan, 'Shangbiao Ran Li · zhiding shiyong shangpin yu biaozhi diqu bufu di dili biaozhi bu yu zhuce' (Trade Mark Burning Quinoa · Geographical indications that do not match the designated goods and the marked area will not be registered), IP House, 19 June 2019, available at https://mp.weixin.qq.com/s/hAWfiLVMrxGyQbxNZMaq1A.
618. Ming, *supra* note 617.
619. (2018) Beijing IP Court 73 administrative case first instance No. 397. Ming, *supra* note 617.
620. INAO submitted the Official Gazette of the French Republic No. 2009-1175 of 2 October 2009 on the origin of Romanée-Conti to demonstrate that France had recognized Romanée-Conti as an appellation d'origine contrôlée by a decree dated 11 September 1936. Ming, *supra* note 617.
621. Ming, *supra* note 617.
622. (2019) Beijing High People's Court administrative case second instance No. 1343, 10 June 2019.

China to be protected: since China's accession to the WTO, China has an obligation under TRIPS to protect GIs.[623]

(2) GI Protection via Sui Generis Systems

There are over 2,400 agricultural product GIs registered by the Ministry of Agriculture (MoA), and over 6,800 types of agricultural products are included in the List of Agricultural Products of Regional and Local Characteristics in China.[624]

In the 1990s, the former State Administration of Quality and Technical Supervision, a precursor to General Administration of Quality Supervision, Inspection and Quarantine (AQSIQ), set up a *sui generis* protection system for GIs, by drawing lessons from the appellation of origin system in France.

In 1999, the Regulation of the Protection of Designated Origin Products[625] was promulgated in accordance with the Law of Product Quality,[626] and the Law of Standardization.[627]

In 2001, to accommodate WTO accession and comply with TRIPS, the former State Administration of Entry-Exit Inspection and Quarantine promulgated the Notice on Issuing the Regulations on the Administration of Appellations of Origin and the Measures for the Implementation of the Regulations on the Administration of Appellations of Origin.[628]

AQSIQ was established in April 2001, with the technical assistance of France.[629] On the basis of the previous regulations, AQSIQ was entrusted with further developing the *sui generis* system with Chinese characteristics.

In 2005, the Regulation of the Protection of GIs was promulgated[630] to effectively protect GI products, regulate the use of GI product names and special signs that can

623. Ming, *supra* note 617.
624. Bae, *supra* note 614.
625. Regulations on the Protection of Products of Origin was approved by the State Council for Quality and Technical Supervision on 30 July 1999 and was promulgated and effective on 17 August 1999. Available at: http://www.aqsiq.gov.cn/xxgk_13386/xxgkztfl/zcfg/201210/t20121017_265767.htm.
626. Product Quality Law, Order No. 71, promulgated by the President of the PRC on 22 February 1993, effective on 1 September 1993. Available at: http://english.mofcom.gov.cn/article/policyrelease/Businessregulations/201303/20130300046024.shtml.
627. Standarization Law 1988, Order No. 11, promulgated by the President of the PRC on 29 December 1988, and effective on April 1, 1989. Available at: https://bit.ly/2Pzn6yV. The revision of the Standarization Law was promulgated on 11 April 2017 and became effective on 1 January 2018. Available at: http://en.pkulaw.cn/display.aspx?cgid = 304266&lib = law.
628. Notice on Issuing the Regulations on the Administration of Appellations of Origin and the Measures for the Implementation of the Regulations on the Administration of Appellations of Origin, No. 51 [2001], promulgated by the State Administration of Entry-Exit Inspection and Quarantine on 5 March 2001 and effective on 1 April 2001. Available at: http://www.fdi.gov.cn/1800000121_23_67973_0_7.html.
629. Min-Chiuan Wang, The Asian Consciousness and Interests in Geographical Indications, 96 TRADEMARK REP. 906 (2006), 914, 922. Available at: https://www.inta.org/TMR/Documents/Volume%2096/vol96_no4_03.pdf.
630. Regulations on the Protection of Geographical Indications, No. 78, reviewed and approved by AQSIQ on 16 May 2005, promulgated on 7 June 2005 and effective on 15 July 2005.

only be used for the GI products if the quality and characteristics of the GI products can be guaranteed.[631] As of 2005, China has used the term GI instead of appellation of origin.

Applications for the protection of GI products shall be submitted by the institution, association or enterprise that applies for protection of GI products, designated at the local or above level People's Government, and recognized by the People's Government, and shall seek the opinions of the relevant departments.[632]

According to Article 10 Regulation of the Protection of GIs, the applicant shall submit the following information:

(1) Suggestions on the delineation of the geographical origin of GI products by local governments. In contrast to Article 8(2) SAIC Measures Collective and Certification Marks 2003, it is not possible for the name of the GI to not be fully consistent with the name or boundary of the region;[633]
(2) Documents concerning the establishment of an applicant institution by a local government or the identification of an association or enterprise as an applicant;
(3) Evidence material for the GI product, which includes:
   - application for the protection of the GI product;
   - description of the product name, category, origin and geographical characteristics;
   - description of the physical and chemical characteristics of the product, its sensory characteristics, and its relationship with the natural and human factors of the place of origin;
   - technical specifications (such as product processing technology, safety and hygiene requirements, technical requirements of processing equipment);
   - visibility of the product, the description of the production, sales and historical origin of the product;
(4) Technical standards for the GI product.

AQSIQ shall establish a corresponding expert review committee in accordance with the characteristics of the GI products to be responsible for the technical review of the application for the protection of GI products. AQSIQ arranges for the committee to conduct a technical review of an application that has no objection or had an objection but which has been rejected. If the examination is successful, the AQSIQ shall issue an announcement to approve the product to obtain protection of the GI product. If the examination fails, the applicant shall be notified in writing. Relevant units and individuals that disagree with the application may oppose and provide their submission to AQSIQ within two months after the announcement.

Until 2018, producers of products within the scope of production of the GI needed to apply to the local quality and technical supervision bureau or the Entry-Exit Inspection and Quarantine Bureau. They would be reviewed by the Provincial

Available at: http://www.cnipa.gov.cn/ztzl/dlbzzl/dlbzzcfg/1141010.htm.

631. Article 1 Regulations on the Protection of GIs 2005, *supra* note 630.

632. Article 8 Regulations on the Protection of GIs 2005, *supra* note 630.

633. Article 8(2) SAIC Measures Collective and Certification Marks 2003, *supra* note 393.

Quality and Technical Supervision Bureau or directly by the Entry-Exit Inspection and Quarantine Bureau, and after the examination and approval of AQSIQ, the announcement shall be made, and the producer may use the special mark of the GI product on its product.

The registered products range from wines, spirits, Chinese liquors, teas, fruits, flowers to herbal medicines, condiments, and marine products, as well as other foodstuffs.[634]

Just like the objective of protecting GIs via collective or certification trade marks, the two administrative *sui generis* regulations protect consumers and producers. Provisions for the Protection of Products of GI, promulgated by AQSIQ in 2005,[635] and Measures for the Administration of GIs of Agricultural Products, promulgated by the former MoA[636] in 2007,[637] both protected quality and characteristics of products with GIs. Before the institutional reforms of 2018, GIs could be accepted, registered and protected by three government institutions: by the end of 2014, 43.79 per cent of the GIs were protected by the SAIC[638] via TML;[639] 25.66 per cent by MoA via the Measures for Administration of GIs of Agricultural Products,[640] and 21.16 per cent by AQSIQ via the Provisions on the Protection of GIs.[641] Although the Measures for the Administration of GIs of Agricultural Products are exclusively for domestic agricultural products, the objectives of the three methods for protecting GIs had a significant overlap in the scope of subject matter: 4.82 per cent of GIs are protected

634. Basic Situation of Special Protection of Geographical Indication Products in China, AQSIQ, May 2012, Part I: available at: http://www.aqsiq.gov.cn/zxfw/ptxfz/dlbzcp/201205/P020121018306652546223.jpg; Part II: available at: http://www.aqsiq.gov.cn/zxfw/ptxfz/dlbzcp/201205/P020121018306651372961.jpg; Part III: available at: http://www.aqsiq.gov.cn/zxfw/ptxfz/dlbzcp/201205/P020121018306650148078.jpg.

635. Article 1 Provisions for the Protection of Products of GI Promulgated by the General Administration of Quality Supervision, Inspection and Quarantine, promulgated on 16 May 2005, entered in effect on 15 July 2005. www.wipo.int/edocs/lexdocs/laws/en/cn/cn041en.pdf.

636. MoA is now called the Ministry of Agriculture and Rural Affairs (MARA) (农业农村部).

637. Article 1 Measures for the Administration of GIs of Agricultural Products, promulgated by the Ministry of Agriculture, Order of the Ministry of Agriculture, No. 11, on 25 December 2007 and entered into force on 1 February 2008. http://jiuban.moa.gov.cn/zwllm/nybz/200808/t20080825_1168527.htm.

638. Zhu Yuanhua, Song Wei and Ghulam Nabi, 'The Legal Protection of China's Geographical Indications in the Context of TRIPS Agreement' (2016) 7(2) *International Journal of Business and Social Science* 102. Available at: https://ijbssnet.com/journals/Vol_7_No_2_February_2016/9.pdf.

639. TML 1982 adopted by the NPC Standing Committee on 23 August 1982, amended in 1993, 2001, and on 30 August 2013 by the NPC Standing Committee. Available at: http://www.wipo.int/wipolex/en/text.jsp?file_id=341321.

640. Measures for the Administration of GIs of Agricultural Products, promulgated by the Ministry of Agriculture, Order of the Ministry of Agriculture, No 11, on 25 December 2007 and entered into force on 1 February 2008. Available at: http://jiuban.moa.gov.cn/zwllm/nybz/200808/t20080825_1168527.htm.

641. Provisions for the Protection of Products of GI Promulgated by the General Administration of Quality Supervision, Inspection and Quarantine, promulgated on 16 May 2005, entered in effect on 15 July 2005. Available at: www.wipo.int/edocs/lexdocs/laws/en/cn/cn041en.pdf.

by both SAIC and AQSIQ; 3.79 per cent by SAIC and MoA; 0.52 per cent by MoA and AQSIQ; and 0.27 per cent by SAIC, MoA and AQSIQ.[642] These three parallel GI systems could lead to conflicts if three applicants registered the same GI via the three different GI protection systems.[643]

As to the protection of foreign GIs, AQSIQ 2016 Provisions for the Protection of GI Products[644] clarified that AQSIQ only recognized foreign GIs on the basis of reciprocity. However, on 27 November 2019, Announcement 338 stated that CNIPA would administer the protection of foreign GI products in China[645] and clarified that CNIPA not only recognized foreign GIs on the basis of reciprocity, but also under an agreement concluded between the country of origin and China, or an international treaty acceded to by China and the country of origin.[646]

Those foreigners who were the original applicants whose GIs were protected by the country of origin or region could apply to CNIPA as recommended by the competent authority of the country of origin.[647] To this end, CNIPA shall make a formality examination within 30 days. It may either accept the application, order the applicant to make supplements or amendments, or reject the application.[648] Once accepted, the application is published on the CNIPA website. Any organization or individual can file an opposition during a period of 60 days after the publication date. If the opposition is deemed justified, the administration notifies the applicant. CNIPA may arrange to resolve the dispute; if the negotiation is not regular, CNIPA shall organize the GI Committee to deliberate and decide.

In case the opposition is rejected, the opponent may apply for review with CNIPA within 30 days from the date of receipt of the notice. CNIPA shall make a decision within 60 days from the date of receipt of the application and notify both parties in writing that the review decision is final.

If there is no opposition, or the opposition period expired or the opposition was invalid, CNIPA organizes experts to conduct a technical review. This substantial examination is held only after any opposition, which is in line with the objective of judicial economy. The substantial examination consists of a technical review which includes an examination meeting and the necessary verification of the place of origin. The technical review panel consists of five to seven people. The applicant

642. Zhu, Song and Nabi, *supra* note 638.

643. Wang Xiaobing and Irina Kireeva, 'GI protection in China: new measures for administration of geographical indications of agricultural products', 5(11) *JIPLP* (2010), 790.

644. Notice on the Measures for the Protection of Foreign Geographical Indication Products, AQSIQ, 28 March 2016. Available at: http://kjs.aqsiq.gov.cn/dlbzcpbhwz/zcfg/zx-zcxx/201604/t20160413_464279.htm (Chinese) and https://www.origin-gi.com/images/stories/PDFs/English/oriGIn_Alert/measures-on-protection-of-foreign-gis-under-aqsiq-1.pdf (bilingual).

645. Announcement No. 338 of CNIPA on Amending the Measures for the Protection of Foreign Geographical Indication Products, 27 November 2019. Available at: http://en.pkulaw.cn/display.aspx?cgid = fae90a4aedb8ab36bdfb&lib = law.

646. Article 3 Announcement 338, *supra* note 645.

647. Article 7 Measures for the Protection of Foreign GI Products 2016, *supra* note 644, *juncto* Article 4 Announcement 338, *supra* note 645.

648. Article 11(1) Measures for the Protection of Foreign GI Products 2016, *supra* note 644, *juncto* Article 4 Announcement 338, *supra* note 645.

shall invite professional and technical personnel and translators who are familiar with the product to participate. The conclusion of the technical review is that CNIPA either approves, modifies or rejects the application.

CNIPA has become responsible for the registration and administration of GIs using both the *sui generis* and trade mark system. Alternatively, domestic agricultural products can still be protected via the Ministry of Agriculture and Rural Affair's GI register.

(3) *EU-China Bilateral GI Agreements and the US-China Economic and Trade Agreement*

In 2012, the EU and the PRC agreed that each jurisdiction would protect ten of each other's GIs.[649] In 2019 both jurisdictions concluded another agreement to protect 100 EU GIs in the PRC and 100 Chinese GIs in the EU against imitations and usurpation.[650] EU GIs include Cava, Champagne, Port, Scotch Whisky and Parmigiano Reggiano.[651] Chinese GIs include Anji Bai Cha (Anji White Tea), Panjin Da Mi (Panjin rice) and Anqiu Da Jiang (Anqiu Ginger).[652] Four years after its entry into force, the list of protected IGOs will be expanded to cover an additional 175 GIs from both sides.

The "first phase" of the US-China Economic and Trade Agreement was signed on 15 January 2020.[653] In reaction to the concerns of the US about continued market access of its goods using generic names, China's perception of what constitutes generic names, and the possibility that China would interpret multi-component terms according to the *pars pro toto* strategy, China provided concessions.[654]

649. EU-China Geographical Indications – 10 plus 10 project, 30 November 2012, available at https://ec.europa.eu/commission/presscorner/detail/en/IP_12_1297.
650. EU-China Geographical Indications Agreement, 6 November 2019, available at https://ec.europa.eu/info/sites/info/files/food-farming-fisheries/food_safety_and_quality/documents/infographic-factsheet-eu-china-agreement_en.pdf.
651. List of EU GIs protected in China. Available at: https://ec.europa.eu/info/sites/info/files/food-farming-fisheries/food_safety_and_quality/documents/eu-100-list-of-gis-eu-china-agreement_en.pdf.
652. List of Chinese GIs protected in the EU. Available at: https://ec.europa.eu/info/sites/info/files/food-farming-fisheries/food_safety_and_quality/documents/china-100-named-products-eu-china-agreement_en.pdf.
653. Economic and Trade Agreement Between the Government of the U.S. and the Government of the PRC, USTR, 15 January 2020. Available at https://ustr.gov/sites/default/files/files/agreements/phase%20one%20agreement/Economic_And_Trade_Agreement_Between_The_United_States_And_China_Text.pdf.
654. Article 1.17(1) U.S.-China Economic and Trade Agreement (Phase 1): "Each Party shall ensure that an individual component of a multi-component term that is protected as a geographical indication in the territory of a Party shall not be protected in that Party if that individual component is generic."

    Danny Friedmann, 'Grafting the Old and New World: Towards a Universal Trademark Register that Cancels Generic IGO Terms', in Julien Chaisse, Fernando Dias Simões and Danny Friedmann (eds.), *Wine Law and Policy: From National Terroirs to a Global Market* (Brill Publishers, Boston, 2020). Available at SSRN: https://ssrn.com/abstract=3585557.

(4) GI Protection via Anti-Unfair Competition

The Anti-Unfair Competition Law 1993[655] had two provisions applicable to GIs. Article 5 Anti-Unfair Competition Law 1993 explicitly prohibited an "operator" from engaging in unfair means of competition, such as forging or falsifying the origin of the goods, for the purpose of causing damages to its competitors. Article 9 Anti-Unfair Competition Law 1993 provided that an operator "may not use advertisements or other means to give false, misleading publicity as to the origin [...] of the [...] goods." Acts of falsifying the origin of the goods or making false representations are subject to the sanctions provided by the Product Quality Law.

The amended Anti-Unfair Competition Law 2017 removed the words "origin of the goods", but can still be useful to protect against confusion and deception under Article 6 Anti-Unfair Competition Law 2017. Article 8 Anti-Unfair Competition Law 2017 states that a business operator may not make false or misleading publicity about product performance, function, quality, sales, user comments and prizes. The operator is not allowed to assist other operators in making false or misleading publicity by organizing false transactions.[656]

2. Enterprise and Trade Names

(a) Introduction

In August 1982, the State Council promulgated the first "Regulations on the Administration of the Registration of Industrial and Commercial Enterprises".

The Interim Provisions on the Registration of Industrial and Commercial Enterprises Names, promulgated by the SAIC in 1985[657] were replaced by the Provisions on the Administration of Enterprise Name Registration issued by the SAIC in 1991 which were revised in 2012.[658]

Under the Enterprise Name Registration Provisions 1991, applicants of enterprise name registrations are required to provide two or three name proposals to be reviewed by SAIC. The problem was that they did not have any official channel to make sure

655. Anti-Unfair Competition Law, Order No. 10, promulgated by the Standing Committee on 2 September 1993 and effective on 1 December 1993. Available at: https://www.wipo.int/edocs/lexdocs/laws/en/cn/cn011en.pdf.

656. Amendment to the Anti-Unfair Competition, promulgated by the Standing Committee of the NPC on 4 November 2017, and effective on 1 January 2018. Available at: https://www.lehmanbrown.com/wp-content/uploads/2017/12/the-amended-Anti-Unfair-Competitive-Law-of-Peoples-Republic-of-China-Amended-AUCL2.pdf.

657. Interim Provisions on the Registration of Industrial and Commercial Enterprises Names, approved by the State Council on 23 May 1985 and promulgated by the SAIC on 15 June 1985.

658. Provisions on the Administration of Enterprise Name Registration, approved by the State Council on 6 May 1991, and promulgated by Order No. 7 of the SAIC on 22 July 1991, and effective on 1 September 1991, revised in accordance with the Decision of the State Council on Amending and Abolishing Some Administrative Regulations, promulgated on 9 November 2012, effective on 1 January 2013. Available at: http://gkml.samr.gov.cn/nsjg/fgs/201908/t20190820_306155.html.

in advance whether the names they intended to use might wholly or partially conflict with any existing registered enterprise names in a certain administrative division. This problem has been overcome by an online search engine and comparison system of SAMR,[659] where applicants can type in enterprise names and where the database will display comparable existing enterprise names for their reference.

The Implementation Measures for the Registration of Enterprise Names came into effect in July of 2004.[660] The establishment of a company needed to apply to the AIC for pre-approval of the enterprise name: the name of the enterprise, domicile, registered capital, business scope, names of the investors, investment amount signed by all investors. The AIC will decide whether it will issue a Notice of Pre-approval of Enterprise Name or Notice of Rejection of Enterprise Name to the enterprise. If the establishment of an enterprise name involves laws and administrative regulations that must be submitted for approval, and these approval documents are not submitted, the registration authority may decide not to pre-approve the enterprise name. The validity of the pre-approval is six months, during which period the enterprise name must be fully approved for registration.

Due to "mass entrepreneurship and innovation by all", enterprise names have become scarce.[661] In 2016, the State Council's "Thirteenth Five-Year Plan for Market Supervision" proposed to reform the enterprise name approval system, giving enterprises the right to choose their own names. To implement this reform goal, the experience of some pilots was summarized, starting with opening the enterprise name database and establishing a query comparison system.[662] In addition a "five certificates in one", system was implemented across China by the end of October 2017, and full electronic registration in China as of 30 June 2018.

The pre-approval system of Provisions 1991 will be abolished and replaced by a pre-approval registration system for which the SAIC or its local counterparts are responsible, with a declaration system in combination with a post-event supervision mechanism and with a social credit system as the core to strengthen the self-restraint function of enterprises.[663]

659. SAMR's Administrative Division Excluding Company Name Inquiry System. Available at: http://wsdj.saic.gov.cn/saicmccx/.

660. Implementation Measures for Enterprise Name Registration Management of 8 December 1999, Decesion No. 93 SAIC, revision of 14 June 2004, Order No. 10 SAIC, has been revised by the General Affairs Meeting of the SAIC and was promulgated on 14 June 2004 and came into force on 1 July 2004. Available at: http://www.samr.gov.cn/djzcj/zcfg/gz/200406/t20040614_281796.html

661. Service Reform and Opening-up Enterprise Registration Reform Goes Forward, SAMR 29 August 2018. Available at: http://www.samr.gov.cn/djzcj/gzdt/201808/t20180829_282609.html.

662. Opinions of the State Administration for Industry and Commerce on Improving Registration Efficiency and Actively Promoting the Reform of Enterprise Name Registration Management, SAIC, 19 April 2017. Available at: http://www.samr.gov.cn/djzcj/zyfb/zjfb/201704/t20170419_282210.html.

663. Drafting Instructions for the Regulations on the Administration of Enterprise Name Registration (Draft for Review), 9 November 2018. Available at: http://www.moj.gov.cn/news/content/2018-11/09/zlk_42358.html.

A draft for public comment of a revision of the Regulations on the Administration of Enterprise Name Registration was announced by SAMR on 9 July 2018.[664] In order to implement this, SAMR issued a draft for public comment of the Implementation Measures for the Administration of Enterprise Name Registration.[665] The public could provide feedback until 29 May 2020.

Under the proposed law,[666] the requirements of protection are as follows:

The name of an enterprise shall use Chinese characters that conform to the national norms, and shall not use foreign languages, letters or Arabic numerals.

The name of an enterprise shall be composed of administrative divisions, trade name, industry and organization. The administrative division in the name of the enterprise is the name or place name of the administrative division at or above the county level where the enterprise is located. The name of the municipal district cannot be used solely as an administrative division in the name of the business. The trade name in the name of an enterprise shall consist of more than two Chinese characters that conform to the national norms. Administrative divisions, industries, and organizational forms shall not be used as the trade name.

An enterprise shall indicate its industry or business characteristics in the name of the enterprise according to its main business and the categories classified according to the national industry classification standards. Where national laws, regulations, and decisions of the State Council have special requirements for industries in the name of the enterprise, they shall be indicated in the name of the enterprise. Industries that are prohibited from operating under the laws, regulations, and decisions of the State Council may not be marked in the name of the company.

An enterprise shall, in accordance with its organizational structure or form of responsibility, indicate in its name the organizational form that conforms to the provisions of national laws, regulations, and decisions of the State Council, and may not use organizational forms that are inconsistent with its organizational structure or form of responsibility.

The name of an enterprise shall not be similar to the name of an enterprise in the same industry that has been registered or approved by the same enterprise registration authority, except for investment relations.

The name of a legal person of an enterprise shall not contain the name of other non-profit legal persons, except for an investment relationship or authorization by the legal person, nor the use of the legal person's abbreviation or specific title. The abbreviation of the legal person or the specific title has other meanings or points of uncertainty and may be unauthorized.

664. Regulations on the Administration of Enterprise Name Registration, General Administration of Market Supervision, 9 July 2018. The public could comment until 8 August 2018. Available: http://www.samr.gov.cn/djzcj/zyfb/zjfb/201807/t20180711_282238.html.
665. Notice of the General Administration of Market Supervision on Public Consultation on the "Implementation Measures for the Administration of Enterprise Name Registration (Draft for Comment)", SAMR 28 April 2020. Available at: http://www.samr.gov.cn/hd/zjdc/202004/t20200428_314807.html.
666. Regulations on the Administration of Enterprise Name Registration, General Administration of Market Supervision, 9 July 2018. The public could comment until 8 August 2018. Available: http://www.samr.gov.cn/djzcj/zyfb/zjfb/201807/t20180711_282238.html.

The name of an enterprise shall not contain another name of an enterprise, except for an investment relationship or authorization by the enterprise, nor the use of the abbreviation or specific title of the enterprise. The short name or specific title of an enterprise that has other meanings or leads to uncertainty, may be unauthorized.

The name of an enterprise shall not be expressly or implied as a non-profit organization or beyond the purpose of establishment of the enterprise, except if the name has another (secondary) meaning or exclusions by laws, regulations and decisions of the State Council.

Except for enterprises established with the approval of the State Council, the names of enterprises shall not be marked with the words "中国"(China) "中华"(China) "中央"(central) "全国"(whole country) "国家"(national) "国际" (international). If the words "中国" (China) "中华" (China) "全国" (whole country) "国家" (nation) are used in the middle of the name, the word should be the qualifier of the industry. Foreign-invested enterprises that use overseas investors' names and foreign-invested enterprises controlled by foreign parties may use the word "China" in the middle of the name.

Article 20 Enterprise Name Prohibition Rules[667] states that the enterprise name shall use the name of the administrative division of the province (including the autonomous region or municipality) or the city (including the state, the land, the alliance) or the county (including the municipal district, autonomous county, and the flag).

The trade name of an enterprise name shall consist of characters, words or a combination thereof. Statements, sentence groups and paragraphs shall not be used, except for short sentences with significant recognition or other meanings.

The name of the enterprise name shall not contain misleading content or words such as "国家级" (national level) "最高级" (top level) "最佳"(best), except for other meanings or partial use, and the trade name has other meanings as a whole.

The enterprise name shall not use as trade name the jurisdiction, the city name and its abbreviation or the specific title of the foreign country (region), except for other meanings or partial use, and the trade name has other meanings as a whole. Administrative divisions may not be used as the trade name, except where the geographical names of administrative divisions above the county have other meanings.

The name of an enterprise shall not consist of occupation, position, degree, title, rank, police rank, etc., and its abbreviation or specific title, except for other meanings or partial use, and the trade name size as a whole has other meanings.

An enterprise shall not use the standardized Chinese characters that the Industrial and Commercial Administration has given to the protection of well-known marks as the name of the enterprise name in the same industry, except when it has obtained the authorization of the holder of the well-known mark.

---

667. Notice of the SAIC on Issuing the Rules for the Prohibited and Restricted Use of Enterprise Names and the Rules for Identifying Identical and Similar Enterprise Names, promulgated and effective on 31 July 2017. Available at: http://wsdj.samr.gov.cn/saicfile/mcdj/material/doc_3.pdf.

(1) Registration Procedure

The two drafts use the following registration procedure:

1. If an applied-for name of an enterprise violates the prohibition rules or is the same as the name of another company's enterprise, the basis for violating the prohibition rules or the listing of the same enterprise name shall be indicated, indicating that the application cannot be passed;
2. If an applied-for name involves the restriction rules, the applicant will be reminded of the restricted content in the name, and the applicant will be reminded that the use of the name needs to provide corresponding certification or authorization documents;
3. If the applied-for name is similar to the name of another company, a list of similar company names will be listed to remind the applicant that there is a possibility that the review will not be approved. In case of similarity, even though there is approval, an infringement dispute might make the name unsuitable and a risk warning is provided.[668]

The name of an enterprise shall be registered at the time of registration of the enterprise, except as otherwise provided by laws, administrative regulations, decisions of the State Council and these Regulations.

The name of the enterprise as stipulated in Article 14 Regulations 2018 draft may be used if it is authorized by the market supervision and administration department of the State Council or the local market supervision and administration authority.

The name of the enterprise applying for registration shall comply with the provisions of these Regulations 2018 draft.

When applying for business registration, the applicant may submit the name of the enterprise to be registered in the following manner:

(1) Submit the name of the enterprise to be registered through the enterprise name declaration system;
(2) Submit the name of the enterprise to be registered directly to the enterprise registration authority when handling the enterprise registration.

If the law, administrative regulations or the State Council stipulates that the establishment of an enterprise must be approved, or the business scope of the enterprise is subject to laws, administrative regulations or decisions of the State Council that require approval before registration, the applicant applies to the enterprise registration authority for pre-registration of the enterprise name. If it is confirmed by the enterprise registration authority to retain it, it may be directly registered when the applicant applies for business registration.

The applicant shall be responsible for the authenticity of the application materials and submit an undertaking that bearing similar names may constitute a similar legal responsibility and correct as required by the registration authority.

668. Opinions of the State Administration for Industry and Commerce on Improving Registration Efficiency and Actively Promoting the Reform of Enterprise Name Registration Management, SAIC, 19 April 2017. Available at: http://www.samr.gov.cn/djzcj/zyfb/zjfb/201704/t20170419_282210.html.

The retention period of the enterprise name submitted through the enterprise name declaration system shall be 30 days. If the enterprise registration has not been completed at the expiration of the retention period, the applicant may apply for a retention period of one duration before the expiration of the period, with a term of 30 days. If the enterprise registration is not completed after the expiration of the retention period and no application for extension is made, the name of the enterprise will not be retained.

According to of Article 21 (4) Enterprise Name Registration Regulations, the name of the enterprise to be retained shall be confirmed and the retention period shall be six months. If the enterprise registration is not completed after the expiration of the retention period, the applicant may apply for a retention period of one duration before the expiration of the term, with a term of six months. The same investor shall not have more than three enterprise names during the retention period. The name of the enterprise shall not be used for business activities during the retention period and may not be transferred.

If two or more applicants apply to the enterprise registration authority for registration of the same enterprise name, the enterprise registration authority shall register in accordance with the principle of "first come, first served".

Real-Name Registration

As of 24 June 2019, the enterprise name system has been updated with the real-name authentication function. When handling the user registration and enterprise name registration, both the agent and the investor need to register the user's real name through the "Registration and Authentication" app and agree to apply for the enterprise registration and validity period before proceeding. This system accepts the enterprise name application business that should be approved by the SAMR.[669]

(2) *Scope of Protection*

Enterprise names can be protected by themselves; they can be part of a trade mark or they can make up a trade mark as a whole.

Enterprise names enjoy local protection in the administrative district where they are registered. This means that there can be two or more identical enterprise names registered in the same district, but for different types of business. However, foreign trade and enterprise names need not be registered to enjoy protection and are not limited in their scope of protection to some specific administrative region, but are protected nationwide in accordance with Article 8 Paris Convention. The result is that foreign trade and enterprise name holders are better treated than Chinese enterprise name holders, which Pattloch calls a case of national discrimination.[670]

In situations where an entity uses a registered trade mark or an unregistered well-known trade mark of others as a trade name in its enterprise name to mislead

669. Announcement on the Real-name Verification of the Trial Ownership of the Enterprise Registration Online Registration Application Business System. Available at: http://wsdj.samr.gov.cn/saicfile/static/realName/realNameAnnouncement.pdf.

670. Pattloch, *supra* note 2, 135–136.

the public, it is considered an act of unfair competition according to Article 58 TML 2019, which shall be handled in accordance with the Anti-Unfair Competition Law.

The use of the enterprise name shall follow the principle of good faith and shall not abuse the right to name the enterprise to damage the national interest, the public interest or the legitimate rights and interests of others.

Transfer

The name of an enterprise may be transferred with the enterprise. The name of the company can only be transferred to another company. The transferor of the enterprise name and the transferee shall sign a written contract and disclose the enterprise name transfer information to the public through the national enterprise credit information publicity system. After the transfer of the business name, the transferor may not continue to use the transferred business name.

An enterprise may authorize other enterprises to use the company's trade name, but may not damage the prior legitimate rights and interests of other enterprises.

(b) Conflict of Rights

Trade names are one category of prior rights that can be invoked against the registration of an identical or similar trade mark according to Article 32 TL (see the previous discussion on what can be invoked as prior rights).

In the opposite situation (earlier trade mark, subsequent trade name), Article 1 SPC Interpretation 2002 provides protection within the ambit of similarity, yet no protection for the prior registered trade mark if the enterprise name is for dissimilar goods.

The enterprise registration authority has the right to correct the name of the enterprise that does not comply with the provisions of these Regulations. The registration authority of the higher-level enterprise has the right to request the registration authority of the lower-level enterprise to correct the enterprise name that does not comply with the provisions of these Regulations.

If the enterprise name is suspected of unfair competition, the market supervision and administration department shall deal with it according to the Anti-Unfair Competition Law and other legal provisions.

If the court or administrative authority finds that a company should stop using the enterprise name, the enterprise shall receive a legal decision after which the enterprise must apply within 30 days for a name change; before the name change, the enterprise registration authority replaces the name with a unified social credit code.

3. Domain Names

(a) Introduction

Just like trade mark registrations, domain name registrations are based on a first-to-file system. After registration the domain name is accessible from anywhere in the world.[671] A domain name registration excludes any subsequent registration of the identical domain name. In contrast to territorially bound trade marks, the challenge for domain names, active in seemingly boundless cyberspace, is how to protect and enforce them. Domain names have their universal uniqueness in common with well-known marks. But where at least some registered well-known marks are protected for all classes of goods and services, it is not feasible for trade mark proprietors to register their domain names for all top-level domains.

The domain name system, which is largely privately managed, can conflict with the publicly administered IPR systems because of domain name squatters and their bad faith registrations and use.[672] Domain name administrators do not have to do a prior right (trade mark and trade name) clearance before registration. The domain name registrants are supposed to be self-compliant and will be liable for any dispute that arises out of registration. This provides the opportunity for domain name squatters.

(b) General Framework

In 1987, the first email was sent from China. China then became intermittently connected to the internet and as of 20 April 1994 on a permanent basis.[673] The registry for domain names under the country-code top-level domain (ccTLD) ".cn" and ".中国", and the other Chinese domain names ".公司" or ".网络", is governed by the China Internet Network Information Center (CNNIC), which was founded in 1997.

CNNIC is an administrative authority responsible for domain name registration and domain name administration, supervised by the Ministry of Industry and Information Technology (MIIT).[674] However, there are special rules for the application for registration of the third-level domains under ".edu.cn"; ".mil.cn" and ".政务.cn" or ".公益.cn". These shall be separately formulated, respectively, by China Education and Research Network Information Center (CERNIC),[675] China Great Wall Network Information Center, and the China Organizational Name Administration Center. In case of applying for a third-level domain name under ".gov.cn", the applicant shall be a legal person of administrative body or institution and submit the domain name application bearing the official seal and material that can prove the applicant's identity.

671. 'WIPO Internet Domain Name Process, The Management of Internet Names and Addresses: Intellectual Property Issues', Final Report of the WIPO Internet Domain Name Process, 30 April 1999. Available at: https://www.wipo.int/amc/en/processes/process1/report/finalreport.html.
672. Mo Zhang, 'Governance of Internet Domain Names Against Cybersquatters in China: A Framework and Legal Perspective', 26 *Hastings International and Comparative Law Review* (2002), 62. Available at SSRN: https://ssrn.com/abstract=989982.
673. Evolution of Internet in China, China Education and Research Network, 1 January 2001. https://web.archive.org/web/20120527120608/http://www.edu.cn/introduction_1378/20060323/t20060323_4285.shtml.
674. Until 2008, MIIT was called Ministry of Information Industry.
675. Article 21 CNNIC Implementing Rules of Domain Name Registration 2012, 30 August 2012. Available at: https://cnnic.com.cn/PublicS/fwzxxgzcfg/201208/t20120830_35735.htm.

On 22 August 2002, the former Ministry of Information Industry promulgated the China Internet Domain Name Regulations,[676] which were revised in 2004.[677] Subsequently, the MIIT promulgated the second revision on 24 August 2017.[678] On 1 September 2017, MIIT provided an interpretation of the China Internet Domain Name Regulations.[679]

Any registrars holding the "Letter of Intent" signed with CNNIC (that is authorized by MIIT for domain name registration), shall sign relevant agreements with CNNIC.[680] There are 64 registrars in China,[681] and 32 registrars outside China,[682] that are accredited by CNNIC and are able to undertake the registration of ".cn" domain names.

Those intending to provide services of registration of the ".cn" domain name and the Chinese domain names as ".中国", ".公司" or ".网络" are required to obtain the licence for value-added telecom service of internet information service according to the law; to set up a domain name registration service system within China with technical and customer service staff specializing in domain name services; to have the credibility or capability of providing clients with long-term services; to develop business development plans and related technical schemes; to take effective network and information security safeguard measures; to establish a sound domain name registration exit mechanism; and to comply with other relevant national rules and regulations.[683]

The first CNNIC Implementing Rules of Domain Name Registration came into effect on 1 December 2002.[684] A first revision of the Implementing Rules came into effect on 5 June 2009 and a second revision on 29 May 2012.[685]

676. The first China Internet Domain Name Regulations promulgated by the former Ministry of Information Industry on 22 August 2002.
677. The first revision of China Internet Domain Name Regulations promulgated by the former Ministry of Information Industry, 5 November 2004 (Decree No. 30 of the former Ministry of Information Industry). Available at: https://wipolex.wipo.int/en/text/475215.
678. China Internet Domain Name Regulations (Second Revision) No. 43, promulgated by the Ministry of Industry and Information Technology, on 24 August 2017, became effective on 1 November 2017. Available at: http://www.miit.gov.cn/n1146285/n1146352/n3054355/n3057254/n3057264/c5778555/content.html.
679. Opinions of MIIT on The Measures for the Administration of Internet Domain Names of China, 2017, 1 September 2017. Available at: http://www.miit.gov.cn/newweb/n1146295/n1652858/n1653018/c5778697/content.html.
680. Article 7 CNNIC Implementing Rules of Domain Name Registration, *supra* note 675.
681. There are 66 ".cn" accredited domestic registrars, according to CNNIC. Available at: https://cnnic.com.cn/IS/CNym/CNymzcfwjgsq/201305/t20130509_39446.htm.
682. There are 40 ".cn" accredited overseas registrars, according to CNNIC, *supra* note 681.
683. Article 6 CNNIC Implementing Rules of Domain Name Registration 2012, *supra* note 675.
684. CNNIC Implementing Rules of Domain Name Registration went into effect on 1 December 2002. Available at: http://www.chinaipmagazine.com/en/law-show.asp?id = 12.
685. Second revision of CNNIC Implementing Rules of Domain Name Registration 2012, *supra* note 675.

In 2008, China became the country with the largest population connected to the internet,[686] and has remained so ever since.[687] As of December 2017, the number of ".cn" domain names reached more than 38 million (including combinations with generic second-level domains (2LD), such as ".com", ".中国", ".net", ".info", ".org", ".biz", etc.).[688] The number of websites in China was 5.33 million, among which 3.15 million used only the ".cn" domain name.[689] This relatively small number, compared to the massive number of internet users in China, could be explained by companies that sell their goods via e-commerce sites such as those of Alibaba (Taobao and Tmall) or Jingdong, or are not online yet.[690]

(c) Definition of a Domain Name

A domain name is a string of numbers that corresponds to an Internet Protocol (IP) address. These IP addresses are hard to remember; therefore, the Domain Name System (DNS) makes it easier by allowing a familiar string of letters (the domain name) to be typed by the internet users instead. DNS names have a hierarchical structure. This is reflected in the anatomy of the domain name, which can go up to 128 levels.[691]

(1) Top-Level and Second-Level Domain Names

".cn" and ".中国" are China's national TLDs.[692] China's second-level domain names are divided into category domain names and administrative division domain names. There are six category domain names. ".ac.cn" for scientific research institutions; "com.cn" for enterprises in the fields of industry, commerce, finance, etc.; ".edu.cn" for educational institutions: ".gov" for government agencies; ".net" for information centres (NICs) and operation centres (NOCs) of interconnecting and accessing networks; and ".org" for all kinds of non-profit organizations.[693] Then there are 34

686. Nick Mackfie, 'China becomes world's largest Internet population', Reuters, 24 April 2008. Available at: https://www.reuters.com/article/us-china-internet/china-becomes-worlds-largest-internet-population-idUSPEK34240620080424.
687. On 31 March 2019, China had 829 million internet users. 'Internet Top 20 Countries', Internet World Stats, 31 March 2019. Available at: https://www.internetworldstats.com/top20.htm.
688. Statistical Report on Internet Development in China, CNNIC, January 2018, 15–16. Available at: http://cnnic.com.cn/IDR/ReportDownloads/201807/P020180711391069195909.pdf.
689. Statistical Report on Internet Development in China, CNNIC, January 2018, supra note 688, 21.
690. Kassey Lee, 'Is .Com still king in China?', Domain Name Wire, 24 April 2018. Available at: https://domainnamewire.com/2018/04/24/is-com-still-king-in-china/.
691. About Domain Names, ICANN, 30 August 2018. Available at: https://www.icann.org/resources/pages/about-domain-names-2018-08-30-en.
692. Article 6 Internet Domain Name Regulations 2017.
693. Article 8 Provisional Administrative Rules for Registration of Domain Names on China's Internet. Available at: https://docplayer.net/89467957-Provisional-administrative-rules-for-registration-of-domain-names-on-china-s-internet.html.

administrative division domain names assigned for China's provinces, autonomous regions and municipalities directly under the central government.[694] Examples are ".gd.cn" (Guangdong Province); "gx.cn" (Guangxi Zhuang Autonomous Region); ".bj.cn" (Beijing Municipality).

(2) Chinese Language Top-Level Domain

Since 2000, it has been possible to register the Internationalized Domain Name Country Code Top Level Domain Name (IDN ccTLD) in Chinese: ".中国".[695] At first ".中国" IDN ccTLD could only be used within China or by computers using Chinese Domain Name Systems (DNS) servers.

On 16 July 2008, CNNIC launched "From China to the World – China Domain Name Global Upgrade Action".[696] During the ICANN 36th Annual Meeting from 25–30 October 2009, the ICANN Board decided that the implementation of ".中国" and other Internationalized Domain Name suffixes (IDN ccTLD) would be fast-tracked. On 22 March 2010, China completed this process.[697] On 10 July 2010, ICANN authorized IANA (Internet Assigned Numbers Authority) to officially enter ".中国" into the global DNS root zone. This made it possible for internet users to directly enter the registered ".中国" domain name in the browser address bar to visit the associated site.[698] From 29 October 2012, the ".cn" and ".中国" domain name was registered and serviced separately.[699] The implication is that the ".中国" domain name operates independently and that registrants of a ".中国" domain name no longer automatically get the associated ".cn" domain name.

China has promoted these Chinese domain names, since they provide access to part of its population that is less familiar with typing Latin script, especially *pinyin*. However, most Chinese are very familiar with using alphanumerical characters to type domain names. It seems that keywords typed into search engines are the way most internet users find the websites that they are looking for.

According to 43rd CNNIC Statistical Report on Internet Development,[700] by December 2018 the number of ".cn" domain names reached 21.24 million, increasing

694. Article 8 Provisional Administrative Rules for Registration of Domain Names on China's Internet, *supra* note 693.
695. China applied for the non-Latin word for "China" in simplified Chinese characters ".中国", and ".中國", in traditional Chinese characters.
696. 'CNNIC Launches "China Domain Name Global Upgrade Action"', 16 July 2008. Available at: http://www.cnnic.net.cn/gywm/xwzx/rdxw/2008nrd/201207/t20120710_31592.htm.
697. 'CN/China Completed Fast Track String Evaluation, Proceeding to Synchronized IDN ccTLD Evaluation Process', ICANN, 22 March 2010. Available at: https://www.icann.org/news/announcement-2-2010-03-22-en.
698. GAC Plenary, 'IDN ccTLD Fast Track and PDP', 25 October 2009, ICANN Meeting Seoul, Korea, Transcripts. Available at: https://archive.icann.org/en/meetings/seoul2009/bitcache/Transcript_%20GAC%20Plenary%20-%20IDN%20ccTLD%20Fast%20Track%20and%20PDP-vid=7449&disposition=attachment&op=download.txt.
699. .中国, ICANNWiki. Available at: https://icannwiki.org/.%E4%B8%AD%E5%9B%BD#cite_note-7.
700. 43rd China Statistical Report on Internet Development, CNNIC, February 2019. http://www.cnnic.cn/hlwfzyj/hlwxzbg/hlwtjbg/201902/P020190318523029756345.pdf.

by 1.9% on a year-on-year basis and accounting for 56% of all domain names in China; there were 12.78 million ".com" domain names, accounting for 33.7% of the total; and 1.72 million ".中国" domain names, accounting for 4.5% of the total.

(d) Persons Eligible to Register

Any natural person or organization that can independently bear its own civil responsibilities has the right to apply for the domain registration under the TLD but exclude the conditions defined by the implementing rules.[701] Before the third version of the Implementing Rules of Domain Name Registration of 2012, only businesses registered in China could buy a ".cn" domain name. Now, anybody intending to provide domain name registration services in China shall obtain approval from MIIT and sign agreements with CNNIC.[702]

(e) Registration Proceedings

The domain name registration follows the principle of "first come, first served".[703] Although the registration of domain names that correspond to third-party well-known marks are prohibited, there is no prior-use examination.

The applicant shall submit the following identification materials to a registrar when applying for the domain name:

- ID material of applicant (for a company outside China: company's registration certificate, a copy of an identity card from the company's representative (national ID, passport, driver's licence, and so on); for a company in China: a copy of a Chinese business licence, a copy of the Certificate of Organization Code, a copy of a Chinese Citizen National ID of the company's representative);
- ID material of the contact of domain name registration; other materials required by CNNIC.

Registrars shall verify the authenticity, accuracy and integrity of the materials stated as above and submit the materials to CNNIC within one working day after the valid verification result. Then the applicant shall submit the following information to registrars:

the domain name applied for; the host names and IP addresses of the primary domain name server and the secondary domain name server; a natural person shall submit the name, mailing address, telephone, email; an organizational applicant shall submit the organizational name, organization code certificate, mailing address, email and telephone and so on; names, mailing addresses, e-mails, and telephone numbers of the applicant's domain name technical contact, management contact, payment contact and the principal undertaker.

701. Article 14 CNNIC Implementing Rules of Domain Name Registration, *supra* note 685.
702. Article 5 CNNIC Implementing Rules of Domain Name Registration, *supra* note 685.
703. Article 24 China Internet Domain Name Regulations 30 August 2012. Available at: https://cnnic.com.cn/PublicS/fwzxxgzcfg/201208/t20120830_35734.htm.

Registrars shall submit the registration information as stated above to CNNIC within one working day after receiving the application. The application date shall be the date when CNNIC receives the first valid registration application. CNNIC and the registrars shall inform the applicants of the application dates.

All applicants shall commit in the domain name registration agreement to comply with laws and regulations related to the internet networks; CNNIC Implementing Rules of Domain Name Registration and other regulations, such as the domain name dispute resolution policy; to ensure the authenticity, accuracy and integrity of the registration information submitted.

Registrars shall strengthen the review of domain name registration to ensure the domain name does not breach the China Internet Domain Name Regulations.

Article 27 China Internet Domain Name Regulations 2012[704] makes it clear that any of the following shall not be included in any domain name registration nor used by any organization or individual:

- content that is against the basic principles prescribed in the Constitution or that might
  - jeopardize national security, leak state secrets, intend to overturn the government, or disrupt state integrity;
  - harm national honour and national interests;
  - instigate hostility or discrimination between different nationalities, or disrupt the national solidarity;
  - violate the state religion policies or propagate cult and feudal superstition;
  - spread rumours, disturb public order or disrupt social stability;
  - spread pornography, obscenity, gambling, violence, homicide, terror or instigate crimes;
  - insult, libel against others and infringe other people's legal rights and interests; or
- other content prohibited in laws, rules and administrative regulations.

CNNIC will review the registered domain name[705] and notify the registrars to cancel the domain name for a violation of Article 27 China Internet Domain Name Regulations and inauthentic, inaccurate and incomplete domain name registration information.

(f) Alternative Dispute Resolution

In 2000, CNNIC promulgated a trial implementation of procedures for solving domain name disputes of exclusively Chinese characters.[706] The CNNIC Domain Name Dispute Resolution Policy (CNDRP), was adopted on 20 September 2002 and became effective

704. Article 27 China Internet Domain Name Regulations 30 August 2012. Available at: https://cnnic.com.cn/PublicS/fwzxxgzcfg/201208/t20120830_35734.htm.
705. Article 19 CNNIC Implementing Rules of Domain Name Registration, *supra* note 685.
706. Article 1 Chinese Domain Names Dispute Resolution Policy (Trial Implementation). CNNIC promulgated it on 1 November 2000 and effective 1 December 2000. Available at: http://unpan1.un.org/intradoc/groups/public/documents/APCITY/UNPAN002939.pdf.

on 30 September 2002.[707] This CNDRP was revised in 2006,[708] 2012,[709] 2014,[710] and 2019.[711] The CNDPR is supplemented with the Rules of CNDRP.

The CNDRP is applicable to disputes that result from the registration or usage of domain names of ".cn" and ".中国" that are under the administration of CNNIC. Domain name dispute cases shall be accepted and heard by CNNIC accredited Dispute Resolution Service Providers. These Dispute Resolution Service Providers shall develop supplementary rules following the Policy and Rules of CNNIC ccTLD Dispute Resolution Policy. The Dispute Resolution Service Providers of Chinese domain names, China International Economic and Trade Arbitration Commission (CIETAC) and Hong Kong International Arbitration Centre (HKIAC) carry out the actual dispute resolution via expert teams that are composed of one or three professionals, who master the knowledge of the internet and relevant legal affairs, possess high professional ethics and the ability to judge disputes independently and neutrally. The Dispute Resolution Service Providers list the names of the experts for plaintiffs and defendants to choose from. Since 1 August 2019, CNNIC has designated WIPO to also provide dispute resolution services under the China ccTLD Dispute Resolution Policy.[712]

According to Article 19 CNDRP, CNNIC can amend its Policy, and according to Article 21 CNDRP, it should also interpret its Policy.[713] If a domain name holder does not agree to be bound by the policy or its amended version thereof, it shall notify the registrar in a timely manner. The registrar will continue the domain name services for the domain name holder for 30 calendar days after the receipt of such notification and cancel the relevant domain name registration after the passage of the 30 calendar days.[714]

(1) Comparison Between CNDRP and UDRP

CNDRP and the supplemental rules are largely modelled after the provisions of the Uniform Domain Name Dispute Resolution Policy (UDRP) and UDRP Rules. However, different from the UDRP system, Dispute Resolution Service Providers of Chinese domain names appear not to accept a complaint regarding domain names

707. CNDRP, implemented on 30 September 2002. Available at: https://www.ccpit-patent.com.cn/node/1231/1232.
708. CNDRP, implemented on 17 March 2006. Available at: https://www.wipo.int/edocs/lexdocs/laws/en/cn/cn109en.pdf.
709. CNDRP, implemented on 28 June 2012. Available at: https://wipolex.wipo.int/en/text/339796.
710. CNDRP, implemented on 21 November 2014. Available at: https://cnnic.com.cn/PublicS/fwzxxgzcfg/201208/t20120830_35737.htm.
711. CNDRP, implemented on 18 June 2019. Available at: http://dndrc.cietac.org/web/domainDispute.action?mz07.infoType = 1&mz07.textType = 2&mz07.CNEN = 1.
712. WIPO ADR Highlights, 1 August 2019. Available at: https://mailchi.mp/wipo/wipo-adr-highlights-second-quarter-2019.
713. Article 21 CNDRP 2019, *supra* note 711.
714. Article 19 CNDRP 2019, *supra* note 711.

more than two years after the registration of the domain name,[715] as shown in the domain name WHOIS information.

In 2015, in *Leister Brands AG v. Chen Qiuheng*, Hong Kong International Arbitration Centre (HKIAC)[716] ruled that the transfer of a ".cn" domain name from one party to another constitutes a new registration under the Policy and "resets" the two-year time limit for bringing a domain name complaint.[717] In 2017, HKIAC applied the same logic in *Airbnb Inc. v. Guo Lanzhi*.[718] CNNIC issued an amended CNDRP for consultation, which ended on 9 June 2019. The amended CNDRP, which was implemented on 18 June 2019, extends this time bar from two to three years.[719]

While Section 4(a) UDRP requires the domain name to be identical or confusingly similar to "a trade mark or service mark" and to have a right in this, Article 8 CDNRP requires the domain name to be identical or confusingly similar to a "name or mark", and have a civil right or interest in it.[720] In particular, Article 6 Anti-Unfair Competition Law is referred to by CDNRP panels. The British subsidiary of the Canadian company Entertainment One did not register the mark Peppa Pig for toys; it was protected by Article 5(2) of the 1993 PRC Anti-Unfair Competition Law, which later became Article 6(1) Anti-Unfair Competition Law of 2017 and 2019.[721]

Civil rights include not only trade marks but also copyrights and rights protected by other laws. "Name" used in the CDNRP, should be interpreted in the sense of the Anti-Unfair Competition Law, so that it includes personal names with a certain influence and trade names as a right that can be claimed against domain name registration.[722]

As of Article 6(3) Anti-Unfair Competition Law of 2017 and 2019, a claim can be based on another domain name.

According to CIETAC panels a respondent does not have any legitimate interests in respect of his first name, which is the major part of the domain name. An example

715. Article 2 CNDRP, implemented on 21 November 2014. Available at: https://cnnic.com.cn/PublicS/fwzxxgzcfg/201208/t20120830_35737.htm.
716. *Leister Brands AG v. Chen Qiuheng*, HKIAC DCN- 1500641, 10 October 2015. Available at : www.hkiac.org/sites/default/files/ck_filebrowser/IP/cn/decision/DCN-1500641_Decision.pdf.
717. James Godefroy, 'China: Domain Name Dispute Resolution Policy: Breaking the Two-Year Time Limit', 71 *INTA Bulletin* (15 November 2016), 20. Available at: https://www.inta.org/INTABulletin/Pages/China_2_7120.aspx.
718. *Airbnb Inc. v. Guo Lanzhi*, HKIAC DCN-1700742, 3 July 2017. Available at: http://www.hkiac.org/sites/default/files/ck_filebrowser/IP/cn/decision//DCN-1700742_Decision.pdf.
719. Article 2 CNDRP 2019, *supra* note 707.
720. Jyh-An Lee, 'Domain Name Dispute Resolution in Mainland China and Hong Kong', in Irene Calboli and Jane Ginsburg (eds.), *The Cambridge Handbook of International and Comparative Trademark Law* (CUP, 2020), 399. Article 8 CCNIC, Rules for CNNIC ccTLD Domain Name Dispute Resolution Policy, 30 Aug. 2012, https://cnnic.com.cn/PublicS/fwzxxgzcfg/201208/t20120830_35737.htm.
721. Lee, *supra* note 720, 400. *Entertainment One UK Limited v. Dongguan Huotu Garment Co. Ltd.*, 26 May 2015, HKIAC DCN-1500617, at 6–7. Available at: http://staging.hkiac.org/sites/default/files/ck_filebrowser/IP/cn/decision//DCN-1500617_Decision.pdf.
722. Lee, *supra* note 720, 399.

is *Hugo Boss Trade Mark Management GmbH & Co. KG v. Yuguo Li*,[723] where the disputed domain name was "雨果.中国." "雨果" (Yǔ Guǒ) is the acknowledged transliteration of "Hugo". The respondent, Yuguo Li failed to prove that he had built sufficient reputation on the basis of his given name so that the relevant public would associate the name with him.[724]

(2) Procedure

If the complaint is directed against one domain and the decision is rendered by a one-member Panel, the fee amounts to RMB 8,000; if the decision is rendered by a three-member Panel, the fee amounts to RMB 14,000.[725] The Panel decides on a written award, in accordance with the Policy, the relevant procedural rules, and the principles of independence, impartiality and convenience, between four and 14 days from the date of the appointment of the Panel. The Domain Name Dispute Resolution Body publishes an online roster of experts to be selected by the complainant and respondent. If the complainant or respondent believes that the members of the Panel have a stake in the other party and may influence the fairness of the case, they may request, with facts and reasons, the Domain Name Dispute Resolution Body to ask these experts to withdraw from the Panel. This is decided by the Domain Name Dispute Resolution Body. CNNIC and the domain name registrar do not participate in the dispute resolution procedure in any capacity.

The language of the domain name dispute resolution proceedings shall be Chinese, unless otherwise agreed by the parties or determined by the Panel. The complainant or the respondent may request the Domain Name Dispute Resolution Body to merge multiple disputes into one dispute handed by the same expert(s). Whether or not to merge or not is decided by the expert group.

During the dispute resolution proceedings and before the enforcement of arbitral awards, the domain name holder shall not apply for the transfer or cancellation of the disputed domain name, nor change the registrar, unless the transferee agrees in writing to accept the decision of the Domain Name Dispute Resolution Body. The Domain Name Dispute Resolution Body publishes the complaints and disputes on its website, unless it may damage the interests of one of the parties.

The complainant and the respondent shall bear the burden of proof for their own claims. According to Article 8 CNDRP, a complaint is supported in case of a domain name that is identical or confusingly similar to the complainant's name or mark; the domain name holder has no right or legitimate interest in respect of the domain name or major part of the domain name; or the domain name holder has registered or has been using the domain name in bad faith.

Article 9 CNDRP provides a non-exhaustive list of indications for bad faith registration or use of a domain name: when the purpose of registering or assigning a

---

723. *HUGO BOSS Trade Mark Management GmbH & Co. KG v. Yuguo Li*, CIETAC Case No. CND-2018000007, at 3–5, 18 Apr. 2018. Available at: http://dndrc.cietac.org/web/kindsDecs.action?mz15.CNEN = 1&mz15.textType = 5&mz07.infoType = 1#.

724. Lee, *supra* note 720, 404.

725. Schedule Fees (RMB), HKIAC. Available at: https://www.hkiac.org/ip-and-domain-name/domain-dispute-resolution/domain-name-dispute-resolution-services/cndrp.

domain name is to sell, rent or otherwise transfer the domain name to the complainant or its competitor as the owner of the civil right to obtain an undue advantage;[726] registering the name or logo of the legitimate rights and interests of others as their own domain name to prevent others from using the name or logo of their legitimate rights and interests on the internet in the form of a domain name; when registering or assigning a domain name is to damage the complainant's reputation, to damage the complainant's normal business activities, or to confuse the difference with the complainant and mislead the public, or other malicious situations.[727]

In the case of the confusingly similar *supremeita.cn v. Supreme NY*, the registrant of supremeita.cn was displaying and selling both counterfeit "Supreme NY" products and counterfeit "The North Face" products. Therefore, the panel concluded that the registration was in bad faith.[728]

Article 10 CNDRP provides circumstances that indicate legitimate interests in the domain name: when the respondent has used the domain name or the name corresponding to the domain name in good faith in the process of providing goods or services; although the respondent has not obtained the trade mark, the domain name held by it has gained certain popularity; the respondent uses the domain name reasonably or non-commercially, and there is no intention to mislead the consumer in order to obtain commercial benefits.[729]

(3) Requirements for Transfer or Cancellation of Infringing Domain Names

Any entity or person that considers that a registered domain name conflicts with its legitimate rights or interests may file a complaint with any of the Dispute Resolution Service Providers.[730] A complainant can request to transfer a domain name or cancel the registration of a domain name.[731]

If the domain name dispute resolution agency decides to cancel the domain name or transfer the domain name to the complainant, this will be done after ten days from the announcement. This cancellation or transfer will be suspended if the respondent proves that the judicial body or arbitration institution that has jurisdiction has accepted the relevant dispute within ten days from the date of publication of the ruling.[732] If there is a settlement between the parties, the registrar will enforce the settlement agreement; if the application for litigation or arbitration was rejected, the register will enforce the decision.[733]

726. Panels have frequently held that bad faith can be inferred if a famous trade mark proprietor can prove that the registrant attempted to sell the domain name to him. Paul Godfread and Kristine Dorrain, 'Developments in Domain Names', 66 *Bus. Law.* (2010), 221, 227
727. Article 9 CNDRP 2019, *supra* note 711.
728. HKIAC case DCN-1900891 *supremeita.cn v. Supreme NY*, 12 June 2019, 3. Available at: https://www.hkiac.org/sites/default/files/ck_filebrowser/IP/cn/decision/DCN-1900891_Decision.pdf.
729. Article 10 CNDRP 2019, *supra* note 711.
730. Article 5 CNDRP 2019, *supra* note 711.
731. Article 14 CNDRP 2019, *supra* note 711.
732. Article 16 CNDRP 2019, *supra* note 711.
733. Article 16 CNDRP 2019, *supra* note 711.

(g) Domain Name Litigation

Before, during or after a dispute resolution decision by a panel at CIETAC or HKIAC, either party can institute an action with the court according to Article 15 China ccTLD Dispute Resolution Policy. Although litigation is much more expensive and time-consuming, it extends the courses of action. The complainant can demand not only cancellation or transfer of the domain name, but also all other remedies under TML or Unfair Competition Law.

Lee pointed out that domain name cases adjudicated by the Chinese courts are not limited to those associated with .cn domain names, as long as there is a connecting factor relevant to Chinese law.[734] For example, the Xiamen District Court provided a decision on the domain name thinkstockphoto.com, registered by a Chinese citizen via a Xiamen domain name registration service company.[735]

A trade mark holder that litigates against a domain name holder has to prove a likelihood of confusion between the trade mark and the domain name. In *Tianjin Bradi Security Equipment Co., Ltd. et al. v. Brady Corporation*, the SPC held that the plaintiff's use of the domain name registration did not result in any likelihood of confusion among the public, because the defendant's trade mark BRADY, did not have any reputation in China.[736]

In 2017, the General Rules on Civil Law became effective.[737] These will not replace the General Principles of Civil Law 1986, but in case of a conflict between the two codes, the General Rules of Civil Law prevails. Thus, Article 188 General Rules on Civil Law extends the statute of limitation regarding applications to a court to three years, which is in line with CNDRP of 18 June 2019.

If a rights holder uses the civil litigation route, it can not only retrieve the domain name, but can hold the defendant liable and demand compensation for losses, elimination of adverse effects and making an apology, etc. At any time before a complaint was filed, during the dispute resolution procedure or after a ruling of the panel of experts at a dispute resolution agency, the complainant or respondent may file a lawsuit or submit for arbitration for the same dispute.[738]

A lawsuit based on a conflicting private right must be brought before an Intermediate People's Court where the infringement was committed or where the defendant resides. If either of those locations are hard to find, the location of the computer terminal where the domain name is hosted will be considered as the place of infringement.[739]

734. Lee, *supra* note 720, 409.
735. *Duan Xiang v. Getty Images*, Xiamen District Court, 4747 *Si Min Chu Zi* (2015).
736. *Tianjin Bradi Security Equipment Co., Ltd. et al. v. Brady Corporation*, SPC, 1286 *Min Shen Zhi Di* (2013).
737. General Rules of the Civil Law 2017, *supra* note 420.
738. Article 15 CNDRP 2019, *supra* note 711.
739. Article 1 Interpretation of Several Issues Concerning the Application of Law in the Trial of Civil Disputes in Computer Network Domain Names, Judicial Interpretation [2001] No. 24 (SPC Interpretation 2001), promulgated by the Judicial Committee of the SPC on 26 June 2001, effective on 24 July 2001. Available at: https://bit.ly/3btcBZ6. Amended on 23 December 2020, No. 16. Available at: https://bit.ly/2LBY3eE.

In case of a dispute between domain names and trade marks, it is relevant to distinguish between normal registered trade marks and well-known marks, since the latter have a less onerous burden of proof when taking action against domain name squatters. Article 4(2) SPC Interpretation 2001 extends the protection of any well-known trade mark to all acts of copying, imitation, translation or transliteration. In case of a dispute between a prior well-known mark and a domain name, it is important that the acknowledgment of the well-known mark can be proven.

In *Michelin Group Co., Ltd. v. Li Daowei and others*,[740] the SPC held that Michelin was already well-known before the incorporation of the defendants, and that the registered domain name contained "cenchelyn" as its main component, which highly resembled the well-known mark Michelin, and that engaging in an e-business involving goods in connection with those of the Michelin Group would lead to a likelihood of confusion to the relevant public. In addition, one of the defendants had previously worked as a distributor of the Michelin Group and should have known well how its trade marks were used.

In 2014, in *Macy's West Stores, Inc. v. Beijing Guowang Information Ltd.*, the Beijing Intellectual Property Court ruled that the defendant did not use the domain name macys.com.cn after registration, but intentionally prevented the plaintiff from registering or using it. According to Article 5(3) Interpretation of the SPC on Several Issues Concerning the Application of the Law to the Trial of Civil Disputes Cases Involving Computer Network Domain Names, the defendant's domain name was registered in bad faith.[741]

DreamWorks Animations LLC started using the trade mark DreamWorks in China in 1995. One day after the announcement of the intended formation of the Shanghai-based "Oriental DreamWorks", a joint-venture of DreamWorks and a Chinese company, Zeng Hongyun registered "orientaldreamworks.com"[742] and "shanghaidreamworks.com" with eName Technology in 2011. DreamWorks filed a complaint against the registrant for pre-emptive domain name registration in bad faith before the WIPO Arbitration and Mediation Center in Geneva.[743] After the sole panellist at the WIPO Arbitration and Mediation Center ordered Zeng to transfer the domain names, Zeng appealed to the Xiamen People's Court. The Court held that Zeng had made the registration for a calculated profit, rather than for regular commercial operations. In addition, the defendant had registered another 200 domain

740. *Michelin Group Co., Ltd. v. Li Daowei, Qingtao Senqilin Tire Co., Ltd. and Sentaida Group Co., Ltd.* over Trademark Infringement Dispute, 37 *Min Ti Zi* (2015).

741. *Macy's West Stores, Inc. v. Beijing Guowang Information Ltd.*, Beijing Intellectual Property Court, 9 Jing Zhi Min Chu Zi (2014).

742. The combination of "oriental" and "dreamworks" in the disputed domain name "will actually strengthen the connection between the disputed domain name [...] and the Complainant's registered DREAMWORKS mark, it is likely to cause confusion by the relevant public because China is 'oriental' by itself." *DreamWorks Animation L.L.C v. Su*, HKIAC Case No. DCN-1300561 (7 January 2014).

743. *Dreamworks Animation LLC v. Hongyun Zeng*, WIPO Arbitration and Mediation Center, Administrative Panel Decision, Case No. D2014-0171, 18 April 2014. Available at: https://www.wipo.int/amc/en/domains/search/text.jsp?case=D2014-0171.

names of well-known marks which also contributed to the determination of Zeng's bad faith registrations.[744]

gTLD are not excluded from bad faith registrations. In *Jinbo Liu v. Alibaba Group Holding Ltd.*, the Fujian High People's Court held that the plaintiff, who registered the domain name tmall.company was identical to Alibaba's trade mark tmall and its domain name tmall.com.[745] The gTLD company was not a distinguishing factor and the main part of the disputed domain name, "tmall", was identical to Alibaba's trade mark "tmall" and domain name "tmall.com." The gTLDs Dian Shang Biao (点商标), which means dot trade mark, is run by a company that verifies that only the trade mark holder can register under this gTLD.[746]

In case of a dispute between a prior registered trade mark (without being well-known) and a domain name, the domain name registration and use is considered an act of unfair competition if the proprietor of the registered trade mark can prove that it owns the trade mark and that it is valid, that the defendant's domain name is identical or similar to the plaintiff's registered trade mark, sufficient to cause misunderstanding of the relevant public, that the defendant does not have any lawful interest in the domain name or its main part, nor does it have a valid reason for registering or using the domain name, and the defendant has a bad faith registration and use of the domain name. If a claim is based on unfair competition law, there is a need to show a similarity of goods.

Trade mark infringement of a domain name is generally determined by assessing the similarity of domain name to a registered trade mark, the similarity of the goods, and the likelihood of confusion to the relevant public, as specified in Articles 57(1) and (2) TML 2019. Moreover, Article 1(3) SPC Interpretation 2002 provides that if a person registers a domain name using a text identical or similar to a registered trade mark of another person, and uses such domain name to develop e-commerce involving goods in connection with those of such other person, thereby easily causing confusion to the relevant public, these acts shall be deemed as damaging the exclusive user rights of such other person to the registered trade mark.

In contrast to general trade mark law doctrine, the first sentence of Article 5(2) SPC Interpretation 2001 provides that registering and using domain names that are the same or similar to the plaintiff's registered trade marks, domain names, etc. for commercial purposes, is in principle sufficient to characterize the defendant's behaviour as malicious, without taking the similarity of the goods or services on display at the website into account. This protects the trade mark proprietor against pre-sale confusion. The rationale is to prevent any diversion of traffic, which would constitute unfair competition.[747] In addition, Article 5(2) SPC Interpretation 2001 states that intentionally causing confusion with the plaintiff's products, services,

744. Yuan Shenggao, 'DreamWorks wins cybersquatting case', *China Daily*, 29 March 2019. Available at: http://www.chinadaily.com.cn/cndy/2018-03/29/content_35937827.htm.
745. *Jinbo Liu v. Alibab Group Holding Ltd*, (2016) Fujian High Court, 662 *Min Min Chung* (2016).
746. Lee, *supra* note 720, 415–416.
747. Bai Fan and Hu Ping, 'On Rules for Determination of Trademark Infringement by Domain Names, with Comments on Jiayou Shop Group Co. v. Guizhou Jiayo', *China Intellectual Property*, April 2019. Available at: http://www.chinaipmagazine.com/en/journal-show.asp?id = 1641.

or plaintiff's website, and misleading network users to visit their websites or other online sites is behaviour that can be characterized as malicious. Indications for bad faith include the following:

- having offered to sell, lease or otherwise transfer the domain name at a high price to obtain illegitimate interests;
- after registering the domain name, it does not use or prepare to use it, but intends to prevent the rights holder from registering the domain name;
- other malicious situations.

In case of acts of unfair competition, the court will order the defendant to cease its infringement, cancel the domain name registration, or order the plaintiff to register and use the domain name. The defendant can be ordered to compensate the plaintiff's losses.[748] While Article 6 Several Guiding Opinions of the BHPC on the Trial of IP Disputes Arising From the Registration and Use of Domain Names[749] grants damages only in case of unfair competition disputes, Article 8 SPC Interpretation 2001 grants damages for both infringement and unfair competition disputes.

If the defendant proves that the domain name has gained a certain popularity before the dispute occurred and can be distinguished from the registered trade mark of the plaintiff, or has other circumstances sufficient to prove that it is not malicious, the court may deny bad faith.[750]

748. Article 8 SPC Interpretation 2001, *supra* note 739.
749. Several Guiding Opinions of the BHPC on the Trial of IP Disputes Arising From the Registration and Use of Domain Name, Regulatory Document [2000] No. 276, 15 August 2000. Available at: http://210.73.66.144:4601/law?fn=lar120s021.txt.
750. Article 5(2) SPC Interpretation 2001, *supra* note 739.

CHAPTER 4
Copyright

Peter Ganea

I. HISTORICAL OVERVIEW

1. Ancient China: A Cultural Propensity Towards Copying?

In the 1990s, inadequate Chinese copyright protection was a major issue in Sino-US trade relations. Repeatedly, both countries found themselves on the verge of a trade war, and each time the conflict was resolved last minute, shortly before the US was set to impose trade sanctions.[1] Western commentators back then tended to explain China's alleged disregard of intellectual property by its particular cultural heritage, which would hold the perfect imitation of ancient arts and styles in high regard

1. In order to evade US trade sanctions, China obliged itself in a Memorandum of Understanding (MoU) of 16 January 1992 (25 *Gazette of the State Council* (1994), 1028) to accede to the essential copyright conventions and to introduce criminal sanctions against industrial-scale copyright piracy. Soon afterwards, the US accused China of protecting intellectual property only on paper while failing to enforce it in practice, and urged China to sign a second MOU on 26 February 1995 (Agreement Regarding Intellectual Property Rights, Feb. 26, 1995, U.S.-P.R.C., 34 I.L.M. 881); see also Frank V. Prohaska, '1995 Agreement regarding Intellectual Property Rights between China and the United States: Promises for International Law or Continuing Problems with Chinese Piracy', 4 *Tulsa J. Comp. & Int'l L.* (1996), 169, in which China promised to further improve protection and to strengthen administrative enforcement by task forces. On 17 June 1996, a third round of severe trade disputes on intellectual property protection was resolved by an agreement, in which China, *inter alia*, promised to permanently close a number of illegal CD factories; a comprehensive overview of the trade tensions between China and the US in the 1990s is given by Peter K. Yu, 'From Pirates to Partners: Protecting Intellectual Property in China in the Twenty-First Century', 50 *Am. U.L. Rev.* (2000), 131, available at: https://scholarship.law.tamu.edu/facscholar/381.

and attached little importance to individual originality.[2] Chinese experts countered with reference to historical sources, which, in their opinion, proved that copyright consciousness existed in China at a time when Europe was still deep in the middle ages. They alluded to ancient copyright markings, for example an indication on copies of the classical work *Dongdu Shilüe* (East City Annotations), which prohibited anyone other than the printer *Cheng* to reprint the work.[3] And indeed, today it is common knowledge that printing was not first invented by the German *Johannes Gutenberg* but in China, at a time when the only form of reproduction known in Europe was time-consuming transcription. The first reliable historical record of the existence of printing by means of engraved wooden plates can be traced to the ninth century. During the *Song* dynasty (960–1279), the circulation of one original manuscript among a group of scholars was replaced by the distribution of reprints. Even printing with movable type invented by a certain *Bi Sheng* in 1042 was known, but due to the thousands of characters existing in Chinese script, printing by engraved plates prevailed for about two centuries as the better alternative. Due to the spread of the printing technique, it was only natural that those who bore the initial costs of engraving plates would demand an exclusive reproduction right.

Based on this historical evidence, supporters of the idea of an early copyright consciousness in Imperial China argue that the invention of printing automatically awakened the need for copyright-alike protection.[4] That occasional privileges to authors and printers did not further develop to a full-fledged copyright may have had to do with the social environment in Imperial China, which, in general, held private rights and obligations in little regard, and provided almost no legal infrastructure for the resolution of disputes between private parties. Also, feudalism left little room for a consciousness that rewarded outstanding creative efforts. In the midst of such an environment, individuals could hardly claim a property right resulting from their personal creation.[5]

In sum, it is doubtful whether a copyright consciousness existed in ancient China. Historical allusions to printing privileges, however, at least evidence that China was not much different from the rest of the world in that the availability of a technology allowing cheap mass reproduction of intellectual creations automatically called for protection of the economic rights of those who made the first investment in their dissemination. That the sporadic protection of commercial publishers and book printers could not evolve into real copyright protection may be traced back to an intellectual tradition that showed reserve towards original creations. However, it

2. See W.P. Alford, *To Steal a Book is an Elegant Offense* (Stanford, 1994). Alford's views were heavily criticised by Zheng Chengsi, 'Further on Copyright in Ancient China', 4 *China Patents & Trademarks* (1996), 61.
3. More historical references in Guo Shoukang, 'China §1 (1)', in P.E.Geller and M.B.Nimmer, *International Copyright Law and Practice*, (looseleaf).
4. See Zheng Chengsi, 'Printing and Publishing in China and Foreign Countries and the Evolution of the Concept of Copyright (I,II)', 4 *China Patents & Trademarks* (1997), 39 and 1 (1998), 44; Zhou Baorong, 'Zhongguo gudai banquan baohu de yuantou' (Sources of ancient copyright protection in China), 4 *Zhuzuoquan* (1993), 40.
5. Wang Fei, 'Zhuantong sixiang yu zhuzuoquan zhidu de chansheng' (Traditional thinking and the emergence of a copyright system), 2 *Zhuzuoquan* (1998), 59; W.P. Alford, note 2, 9–29.

would be simplistic to hold the importance attached to the imitation of old masters responsible for the copyright piracy in modern times. This would be like equating the effort of imitating calligraphic or poetic styles with the almost effortless industrial reproduction of optical disks or the upload of infringing content on the internet.

2. From Imperial Legislation to the Copyright Law of 1990

The first Chinese mention of "copyright" (*Banquan* – lit. printing right) dates back to the nineteenth century. In contrast to neighbouring Japan, which, shortly after the *Meiji* restoration of 1868, voluntarily introduced copyright protection as a welcome instrument of nation building (only to be forced a few decades later to join the Berne Convention), China as a quasi-colony of the western powers had little freedom to decide whether copyright protection was suited to the national interest, but was rather forced into the protection of foreign works even before a domestic copyright law was enacted.[6] However, also domestic authors and publishers claimed protection against increasing printing piracy, an undesired by-product of the flourishing publishing industry. In 1910, at the eve of the turmoil which abolished the Imperial order, the luckless emperor *Guangxu* acquiesced to these demands and enacted the Copyright Law of the Great *Qing* Dynasty (*Da Qing Zhuzuoquan Lü*). That *Zhuzuoquan* in the meaning of the Continental European author's right rather than *Banquan*, which would correspond to the Anglo-American copyright, was used in the title, may have to do with the fact that the law has been inspired by the previously enacted Japanese Copyright Law[7] (*Chosakuken-hō*, the same characters in Chinese being pronounced *Zhuzuoquan-fa*, *hō* and *fa* both meaning "law), rather than with a conscious turn towards the Continental European *droit d'auteur* tradition.

The *Qing* law protected only registered works. Copyright exploitation rights were granted for a duration of 30 years *post mortem* if the author was a natural person and 30 years from publication if the work belonged to a legal person. Protection of the moral rights to be named as author and to preserve the work's integrity continued even after the expiration of the protection term. The law defined infringing acts as unauthorised reproduction, impairment of the work's integrity, false accreditation of the author, and finally, though having little relation to copyright protection, the distribution of a work under another person's name and the distribution of answers to textbook questions. The law survived the fall of Imperial China in 1911, and with no major changes was transformed into the Copyright Law of the warlord regime in 1915. In 1928, it was reinstated virtually intact as the Copyright Law of

6. At the turn of the century, some foreign powers, including Japan, urged China to sign trade agreements which contained provisions on the protection of foreign works and to join the Berne Convention. Contemporary Chinese authors especially criticized Japan, referring, *inter alia*, to the problems the Japanese themselves encountered a few years back when being forced to join the Berne – see Li Minshang, 'Cong "Riren meng wo banquan" kan Cai Yuanpei de banquanguan' (Cai Yuanpei's view on copyright, from his essay "The Japanese asking us to join copyright"), 1 *Zhuzuoquan* (1998), 62.
7. Wei Zhi, *Der Urheberrechtsschutz in China* (Copyright Protection in China) (Munich, 1994), 4.

the *Guomindang* government, and finally, after 1949, became the Copyright Law of Taiwan that lasted until 1985.[8]

In 1949, leading up to the proclamation of the People's Republic, all previous laws, including the Copyright Law of 1928, were abolished by the Central Committee of the Communist Party. However, even though copyright represented immaterial "property", the new leadership proved willing to continue rewarding creative effort. This is evidenced by the Decision on the Improvement and Development of Publication Activities,[9] enacted by the newly established General Publication Office on 28 October 1950. It obliged publishers to respect the economic interests of authors by prohibiting them from unauthorized reprint and plagiarism, but also their interest in the work integrity, by prohibiting mutilations of the work. Moreover, and here it became obvious that the Decision was influenced by the Soviet Union's Copyright Law of 1928,[10] the "sale", i.e., the assignment of copyright was prohibited. Despite such legal protection, the following years saw increasing numbers of unauthorised reprints, which called for a strengthening of protection. In 1953, the National Publication Office issued another Decision which strictly prohibited unauthorised copies of printed matter and pictures. In addition, a nationwide system of publishing contracts was established in 1952.[11] In order to counter the rampant print piracy, in November 1957 the National Publication Office issued a draft on the revision of the above-mentioned Decision,[12] which, however, was never enacted. Instead, Legislative efforts instead centred on author's remuneration schemes, as authors were increasingly regarded as employees of the state. On 14 July 1958, the Ministry of Culture enacted the Preliminary Provisions on the Manuscript Remuneration for Literary Books and Books on Social Sciences. The manner of remuneration reflected the disregard for creative effort, as it simply depended on the length of the manuscript and the number of copies rather than on the actual sales revenue.[13]

Disrespect for men of letters and the arts continued until 1978, when the new leadership under *Deng Xiaoping* heralded the reform policy. That same year, the National Publication Office presented a first draft Copyright Law. This early engagement in copyright legislation can be explained in part by the demand to respect intellectual creations expressed by Chinese intellectuals in the course of the Third Plenary Session of the Eleventh Central Committee in 1978, and in part by two bilateral agreements with the US - one on High Energy Physics concluded in January 1979, which contained a clause on mutual copyright protection,[14] the other the mentioned trade agreement signed on 7 July 1979[15] with a similar clause

8. Wei Zhi, note 7, 4 et seq.
9. Cited by Wei Zhi, note 7, 7.
10. Wei Zhi, note 7, 7 (footnote 29).
11. Detailed information about the publication practice of the early fifties contained in Zheng Chengsi, 'The Future Chinese Copyright System and Its Context', 15 *IIC* [1984], 141.
12. Zheng Chengsi, note 4.
13. Wei Zhi, note 7, 8 (footnote 35).
14. NCAC summary, 'Establishment and Development of the Copyright Legal System of Our Country' (Chinese), http://www.ncac.gov.cn/chinacopyright/contents/555/385476.html.
15. See chapter 2, Patents, Utility Models and Designs.

on mutual protection as one prerequisite for China to obtain MFN status.[16] Despite these early initiatives, the drafting of a comprehensive copyright law would last until 1990. In the meantime, the administration enacted a number of copyright-related rules as stop-gap measures, which, however, were only related to certain aspects of copyright protection (e.g. the rules on sound and video recordings enacted by the Ministry for Radio and TV on 23 December 1982,[17] the Preliminary Provisions on the Protection of Copyright in Books and Periodicals enacted by the Ministry of Culture on 15 June 1984[18] or the Preliminary Provisions on the Protection of the Copyright in Audio and Video Publications, enacted by the Ministry for Radio, Film and TV on 15 September 1986.[19]

The establishment of the National Copyright Administration of China (NCAC) on 25 July 1985 laid the foundation for an effective copyright legislation and administration. The NCAC was henceforth competent to prepare copyright legislation, to advise copyright owners, to administer compulsory licences for the reprint and the translation of foreign works and for other international matters, as well as for supervising the local copyright administrations throughout the country, which are in charge of prosecuting copyright infringements in similar manner as the intellectual property administrations mentioned in the chapter on Patents, Utility Models and Designs.

Until the mid-1980s, copyright infringement was mainly a matter of prosecution by various administrative authorities. A first basis for judicial enforcement was the General Principles of Civil Law, adopted by the Fourth Session of the Sixth National People's Congress of 12 April 1986 and in force since 1 January 1987.[20] Article 94 guarantees authors the right to be named in connection with their works, to issue and to publish their works and to be remunerated for their exploitation. Based on this provision and on Article 118 which grants the infringed party the right to claim cessation, elimination of effects and compensation for damages, a number of copyright-related cases were decided by the People's Courts.[21]

16. More about the problematic wording of the corresponding Article 6 of the Agreement, which allegedly contradicted US trade law, in Stephanie L. Sgambati, 'China's Accession to the Berne Convention: Bandaging the Wounds of Intellectual Property Piracy in China', 3 *Fordham Intell. Prop. Media & Ent. L.J.* (1992), 139. Available at: https://ir.lawnet.fordham.edu/iplj/vol3/iss1/10, 139 (150 et seq.).
17. 'Preliminary Provisions on the Administration of Sound and Video Recordings', *Gazette of the State Council* (1983), 15; the provisions related not only to the control of the dissemination of audiovisual products, but also granted the producers a right to exclusively exploit their audiovisual products and obliged them to respect the rights of the authors and artists whose works and performances were incorporated therein.
18. More information on the legislative efforts in the 1980s in Ma Xiaogang, 'Xin Zhongguo zhuzuoquan baohu gailan' (Outline of copyright protection in the New China), 1 *Zhishi Chanquan* (1991), 31.
19. *Zhonghua Renmin Gongheguo falü fagui quanshu* (Collection of laws and provisions of the People's Republic of China), Vol. II (Beijing, 1994–1996), 424.
20. 12 *Gazette of the State Council* (1986), 371.
21. From 1986 to 1991, the year in which the present Copyright Law became effective, 789 copyright-related cases were brought before the People's Courts: reported in Wei Zhi, note 7, 12. Some of these cases gained public attention, especially the case concerning the autobiography of the last emperor of the *Qing* dynasty, Pu Yi, which served as an

On 7 September 1990, the Copyright Law was finally enacted by the Fifteenth Session of the Standing Committee of the National People's Congress.[22] On 30 May 1991, the State Council enacted the Copyright Law Implementing Regulations[23] (hereinafter "Implementing Regulations"), which supplement the Copyright Law provisions and contain guidelines for administrative enforcement. On 4 June 1991, the State Council enacted another important administrative copyright-related provision, namely the Regulations on the Protection of Computer Software (hereinafter "Software Regulations").[24]

On 10 July 1992, China joined the Berne Convention and shortly afterwards, on 30 July 1992, the Universal Copyright Convention. Especially in order to accommodate US demands concerning the increasing phonogram piracy, China also joined the Convention for the Protection of Phonogram Producers against Unauthorized Reproduction of their Phonograms on 5 January 1993. Contrary to the predominantly Continental European orientation of the Copyright Law, which acknowledges independent neighbouring rights of the disseminators of works and other contents, China is not a member to the Rome Convention for the Protection of Performers, Producers of Phonograms and Broadcasting Organizations. However, as a WTO member since 11 December 2001, China has committed itself to grant international protection to performers and phonogram producers. To fill numerous gaps between the protection standard of the Copyright Law of 1990 and the back then effective international treaties and conventions, on 25 September 1992 the State Council enacted the Provisions on the Implementation of International Copyright Conventions (hereinafter International Implementation Rules),[25] which contain a number of preferential treatment clauses for foreign right owners but have become mostly, albeit not entirely meaningless after the overhaul of the Copyright Law of 2001. On 9 March 2007, China joined both the World Copyright Treaty and the

important literary basis for the famous movie *The Last Emperor*. In 1985, the NCAC decided that the autobiography was a joint work in which both Pu Yi and the employee of the Renmin Publishing House who rendered the material provided by Pu Yi in publishable form jointly enjoyed copyright. On the basis of the General Principles of Civil Law, Pu Yi's widow made another attempt to claim sole authorship of her husband before a People's Court. In the last instance, the Supreme People's Court regarded Pu Yi as the sole author of the work and awarded his widow full copyright as legal heir of the last emperor.

22. 4 *Gazette of the Standing Committee of the NPC* (1990), 940; English translation in 1 *China Patents & Trademarks* (1991), 61; the current version after the amendments of 2001 and 2010 can be found in English and in Chinese in the WIPOlex database: https://wipolex.wipo.int/en/legislation/details/6062.
23. *Gazette of the State Council* (1991), 737; English translation in *China Law & Practice* (July 1991), 28; current version of 2013 in Chinese and English on WIPOLex https://wipolex.wipo.int/en/legislation/details/13428.
24. *Gazette of the State Council* (1991), 792; English translation in 4 *China Current Laws* (1991), 13; amended version of 2001 in 3 *Gazette of the State Council* (2002), 14; 2 *China Patents & Trademarks* (2002), 67; last amended on 30 January 2013 to increase administrative fines for software copyright infringement, amendment decision of the State Council at: http://www.gov.cn/zwgk/2013-02/08/content_2330130.htm.
25. *Gazette of the State Council* (1992), 988; English translation in 1 *China Patents & Trademarks* (1993), 98; in Chinese and English also available from the WIPOLex database https://wipolex.wipo.int/en/legislation/details/6326.

World Performances and Phonograms Treaty after having implemented most of the internet-relevant provisions of both treaties in the course of the Copyright Law amendment of 2001.[26] Finally, on 9 July 2014, China ratified the Beijing Treaty on Audiovisual Performances, committing itself to improve the bargaining position of actors and other audiovisual performers (entry into force: 28 April 2020).

II. OVERVIEW OF THE CURRENT COPYRIGHT SYSTEM

1. Basic Features of the Law

The present Copyright Law of 1990 qualifies as a rather modern law which, as mentioned, leans towards Continental European copyright thinking.[27] It distinguishes between the four moral rights of first publication, of indication of authorship, of revising the own work[28] and of preserving the work's integrity, and economic exploitation rights. The catalogue of rights in Article 10 Copyright Law is not confined to an enumeration of specific rights but mentions "any other rights to be enjoyed by the copyright owner". Even before the Copyright Law amendment of 2001 when a right to transmit a work via the Internet was introduced, this non-exhaustive enumeration of rights formed an effective legal basis on which copyright owners could successfully proceed against having their works made available for individual network access.[29] Another Continental European element is the clear separation between copyright and neighbouring rights. Chapter IV of the Copyright Law on "publication, performance, sound recording, video recording and broadcast" is a bit peculiar, however, because it mixes the neighbouring rights with copyright-specific contract law and legal licences.[30] Another Continental European feature are copyright-specific contract provisions, which are rather rudimentary in international comparison, however.[31] Finally, a further feature that sets China's copyright regime apart from the US copyright tradition is the regulation of collective management.[32]

2. The Administrative and Judicial Infrastructure

Copyright is administered by the mentioned NCAC, which, *inter alia*, serves as registry for those who wish to register their rights, as well as for the mandatory

26. More details in III. 1. *infra*.
27. According to Adolf Dietz, 'Chinese Copyright System: Anglo-American or Continental European Model?', 1 *China Patents & Trademarks* (2011), 84 et seq., the Copyright Law comprises the "five pillars" of a modern Continental European copyright law, namely substantive copyright law (objects, owners, content, duration and limitations of protection), neighbouring rights, copyright-specific contract law, regulation of collecting societies and enforcement.
28. This unique right will be explained in VI. 1. (c) *infra*.
29. Decision of the Intermediate People's Court No. 1 of the City of Beijing, 17 December 1999, 1 *Gazette of the SPC* (2000), 28.
30. More details in X. *infra*.
31. More details in VIII. *infra*.
32. More details in IX. *infra*.

registration of copyright assignment and pledge contracts. It furthermore controls the growing collective management business and plays a central role in the preparation of copyright legislation, promotes copyright throughout the country and supervises the copyright administration authorities in charge of administrative enforcement. The NCAC has remained largely unaffected by the institutional reforms of 2019, whereas the bureaucracy in charge of industrial property has undergone a major overhaul and is now largely in the hand of the China National Intellectual Property Administration CNIPA, the former State Intellectual Property Office (SIPO).[33] And, of course, since copyright is granted without examination or any other formality (otherwise China would violate its obligations under Article 5.2 of the Berne Convention and Article 9.1 of the TRIPS Agreement), the NCAC is a bit less present in public perception than the CNIPA, not least because it has no examination guidelines through which it could perform as by-legislator. In spite of not being required to do so, copyright owners are nevertheless well-advised to register their works with NCAC because later on, in an infringement suit, the defendant may cast doubts about the plaintiff's copyright ownership. In such case, previous registration in the name of the plaintiff suffices as evidence of ownership, and also the registration date may serve as proof that the defendant afterwards has had the opportunity to obtain knowledge about the plaintiff's pre-existent work,[34] whereas cases in which the work is merely circulated or published under the name of the plaintiff and the defendant raises plausible doubts about the plaintiff's copyright ownership it would be up to the plaintiff to distract them.[35]

The recent reorganization of the judicial framework for the protection of IP, which has been explained in the Part on Patents, Utility Models and Designs, also impacted on copyright litigation. Whereas disputes pertaining to "conventional" copyright in literary and artistic works continue to be treated in the ordinary courts, software cases, which, even though not expressly stated, should mostly refer to software *copyright* cases, do now belong to the technically difficult subject matter which is exclusively dealt with by the IP Courts in Beijing, Shanghai and Guangdong if filed within their local jurisdiction,[36] whereas in other regions, software cases are still accepted by the ordinary courts in the first instance. Also, according to the SPC Provisions on Several Questions regarding the IP Division of 27 December 2018 (in force since 1 January 2019),[37] software disputes belong to the sort of disputes which

33. Explained in detail in chapter 2, Patents, Utility Models and Designs.
34. See, e.g., the Foshan Intermediate People's Court's decision 219 *Fo Nan Fa Min Si Chu Zi* (2015) of 25 July 2016, https://mp.weixin.qq.com/s/r9OYzmG2wM6T5eAikIN_2Q; People's Court of Keqiao District of Shaoxing City decision 8618 *Zhe 0603 Min Chu* (2019) of 28 February 2020, https://mp.weixin.qq.com/s/9zznZBH8tPLVFfq_l9R-oQ.
35. Wuhan Intermediate People's Court decision 2166 *E 01 Min Chu* (2017) of 24 July 2017; https://mp.weixin.qq.com/s/tEWM7mdtSnJa66EZRcjWLg.
36. SPC Provisions on the Jurisdiction of the Intellectual Property Courts of Beijing, Shanghai and Guangzhou of 31 October 2014, http://shfy.chinacourt.gov.cn/article/detail/2014/11/id/1478799.shtml.
37. https://www.chinacourt.org/law/detail/2018/12/id/149825.shtml, based on the Decision of the NPC's Standing Committee on Several Problems pertaining to Court Procedures in Patent and other Intellectual Property Cases of 26 October 2018 http://www.sohu.com/a/271595713_169411.

can be appealed in the SPC's new IP Division, irrespective of whether the previous-instance court has been an Intermediate People's Court, Intellectual Property Court or Higher People's Court, so that the Higher People's Courts, thus far the next higher instance in all copyright and other intellectual property cases after the Intermediate People's Courts, will sooner or later lose much of their relevance in software-related copyright litigation, just like in invention and utility model patent litigation.[38]

Quite important for copyright litigation are also the new Internet Courts that have been established in several cities, albeit on a rather low level in the court hierarchy, beneath that of the Intermediate Courts.[39] The Internet Courts deal with all kinds of internet-related disputes, not exclusively with copyright, but copyright disputes can be expected to account for a great part of their case load. The Hangzhou Internet Court already rendered a remarkable decision regarding the liability of network service providers for copyright infringing contents uploaded and operated by clients, which will be discussed later.[40]

3. Secondary Law: Administrative Provisions, Judicial Interpretations and Copyright-Relevant General Laws

The main body of China's copyright regime consists of a statute, the Copyright Law, and a set of regulations the enactment of which the Copyright Law explicitly delegates to the State Council. These are the mentioned *Implementing Regulations*, the mentioned *Software Regulations* as delegated by Article 59 of the current Copyright Law (Article 64 after the third Copyright Law amendment's entry into force on 1 June 2021, see below),[41] the *Regulations on Collective Copyright Administration* of 28 December 2004 (amended on January 8, 2011 and on December 12, 2013)[42] as delegated by Article 8(2) of the current Copyright Law (Article 8(4) after the third amendment's entry into force), and the *Regulations on the Protection of the Internet Transmission Right* of 18 May 2006 (hereinafter "Internet Regulations"; last amended on 30 January 2013)[43] as delegated by Article 59 Copyright Law (Article 64 after the third amendment's entry into force), which deal with internet-relevant subject-matter such as the circumvention of technical protection measures and service provider liability. Article 6 Copyright Law also delegates the regulations of folklore protection[44] to the State Council, but thus far, the State Council has not become active in this field.

38. See chapter 2, Patents, Utility Models and Designs.
39. These courts are also quite remarkable in that suits can be filed online, according to the Hangzhou Internet Court's website non-bureaucratically within five minutes, and that later on trials can be followed online in real time; https://www.netcourt.gov.cn/portal/main/domain/index.htm.
40. Decision of 27 February 2019, more details in XI. 2 (note 327).
41. III. 3. *infra*.
42. Current version in Chinese available here: http://www.gov.cn/gongbao/content/2011/content_1860740.htm; an English translation of the first version of 2004 can be obtained from the WIPOLex database at https://wipolex.wipo.int/en/legislation/details/6340; more details in IX. *infra*.
43. In Chinese: http://www.pkulaw.cn/fulltext_form.aspx?Db = chl&Gid = 194533.
44. More details in IV. 2. (f).

Apart from these main statutes, the State Council, the NCAC and the Supreme People's Court have enacted a whole thicket of further regulations and judicial interpretations (this China-specific judge-made law has been explained in the Part on Patents, Utility Models and Designs) on specific aspects of copyright, e.g., on collecting societies and on prosecution of internet-related infringements. The current main secondary law apart from the above main statutes comprises the following:

(a) Secondary Administrative Provisions

On 25 September 1992, the State Council enacted the mentioned *International Implementation Provisions*, which elevated the protection standard for foreigners to the levels required by international treaties, above all the Berne Convention. The *Measures for the Execution of Copyright Administrative Penalties* of July 24, 2003 (amended on April 21, 2009)[45] provide details of administrative protection of Copyright by the local copyright administrations. Quite importantly, they regulate that copyright administrations in all locations where the effects of the infringement have become apparent and not only at the place of initial manufacturing, distribution or dissemination of infringing material shall be competent to prosecute such infringement. The amendment of 2009 aligned the measures with new administrative regulations on internet infringement[46] and on collective management,[47] as well as with new SPC provisions on internet infringement[48] and on criminal IP infringement,[49] and added new administrative penalties such as warning and confiscation of infringing products and (computer) equipment in which infringing fixations are stored. It furthermore clarified that in case of infringing online transmission, the local copyright administration not only at the domicile of the infringer, but also at the place where the server on which the infringing contents are uploaded is located or the place where the infringing website is registered shall be competent to deal with the infringement.[50] The *Regulations of the People's Republic of China on the Customs Protection of Intellectual Property Rights* of December 2, 2003 (last amended on 24 March 2010)[51] deal with border protection of all kinds of intellectual property and will be treated in detail in this book's part on enforcement. One of the main features

45. Official text: 2 *Gazette of the State Council* (2004), 3; English in 1 *China Patents & Trademarks* (2004), 91.
46. Note 43; more details in XI. 2. *infra*.
47. Note 42.
48. Note 52 *infra*; more details in XI. 2 *infra*.
49. More details in XI. 4. *infra*.
50. https://wipolex.wipo.int/en/legislation/details/6342 (Chinese version only); Explanations given by Chang Qing, 'Guojiabanquanju faguisi guanyu "Zhuzuoquan xingzheng chufa shishi banfa" xiuding de wenda' (Q&A on the revision of the "Measures for the Execution of Copyright Administrative Penalties), *Zhongguo Banquan* (China Copyright) (2009), 23 et seq., online available at https://www.ixueshu.com/document/8730561b67e4dc92318947a18e7f9386.html.
51. Amended version officially available only in Chinese, https://wipolex.wipo.int/en/legislation/details/6081; State Council's amendment decision at https://wipolex.wipo.int/en/legislation/details/7765.

of China's border measures is that they are applied not only to the import but also to the export of infringing goods.

(b) Court Interpretations

As discussed in the part on Patents, Utility Models and Designs, the SPC has the authority to enact "interpretations", which form an important and binding guidance for courts throughout China on how to apply the law to specific problems. The *Supreme People's Court Interpretations of Several Questions with Regard to the Application of Law to the Treatment of Civil Copyright Cases* of 12 October 2002 (hereinafter: Copyright Interpretations; amended on 23 December 2020) provide such guidance with regard to a variety of problems encountered in copyright litigation, such as regional jurisdiction, the meaning and scope of certain limitations, attribution of copyright in special cases or damage calculation. On 26 November 2012, the SPC enacted the *Provisions on Several Problems Related to the Application of Law to Civil Cases Relating to the Handling of Infringements of the Dissemination Right through Information Networks* (hereinafter: Network Interpretations; amended on 23 December 2020),[52] which replaced a set of older internet-related interpretations. They provide important guidance with regard to the liability of service providers for infringement committed by their clients.[53] Quite debated are the *Interpretations of the Supreme People's Court and the Supreme People's Procuratorate of Several Issues Relating to the Application of Law to the Treatment of Criminal Cases of Intellectual Property Infringement* of 8 December 2004[54] and of 5 April 2007,[55] which, *inter alia*, regulate the thresholds an infringement has to exceed to be criminally prosecutable, for instance, a fixed amount of illegal income or a certain number of infringing copies. The 2007 Interpretation lowered some of the initial thresholds established in 2004 to appease US concerns that too much non-punishable infringement was possible beneath them. On 11 January 2011, an *Opinion on Several Questions regarding the Application of Law to the Handling of Criminal Intellectual Property Infringement*[56] issued by the SPC, the Supreme People's Procuratorate and the Ministry of Public Security, added further, internet-specific thresholds, e.g., a certain number of accesses to uploaded infringing content.[57] The US have unsuccessfully tried to challenge China's threshold system in a WTO dispute settlement procedure (WTO WT/DS362/R), which will be discussed later.[58]

52. Original version of the Copyright Interpretation at https://wipolex.wipo.int/en/legislation/details/6343 and of the Network Interpretation at http://www.cac.gov.cn/2014-10/11/c_1112781468.htm; 2020 amendments to both at http://www.court.gov.cn/fabu-xiangqing-282671.html.
53. More information in XI. 2 *infra*.
54. http://www.law-lib.com/law/law_view.asp?id=87670 (Chinese).
55. Available from the website of the SPC Gazette: http://gongbao.court.gov.cn/Details/e19129889e7045d07493acac8b6fbb.html (Chinese).
56. Accessible from the website of the SPC Gazette: http://gongbao.court.gov.cn/Details/55559be21508044l5cf7add7b4f0c8.html (Chinese).
57. More details in XI. 4.
58. III. 2. *infra*.

(c) Non-copyright Specific General Laws

Another source of law for copyright disputes is the general, non-copyright specific laws. Article 217 and Article 218 of the *Criminal Code*, for instance, provide criminal sanctions against industrial-scale infringements. They form the basis for the above SPC and People's Procuratorate's interpretations on criminal infringement. Also important is the *Civil Procedures Code*, which has been overhauled in 2012 (latest amendment in 2017).[59] Its new provisions on evidence preservation (Article 81) and measures to preserve property and to order the respondent to act or to cede from an act (Articles 100–109) are much more right owner-friendly than the older copyright-specific ones in Article 50 (cessation, property preservation) and Article 51 (evidence preservation) Copyright Law, in that, for instance, requests for such measures may now also be filed during the trial and not only as a pre-trial measure, or in that the requesting party who filed a pre-trial request enjoys a more generous deadline of 30 days to file suit, which, unlike the deadline of 15 days regulated in Articles 50 and 51 of the Copyright Law, is also largely in compliance with Article 50(b) No. 6 TRIPS. The older copyright-specific provisions have not been officially repealed but in judicial practice, judges do no longer apply them but exclusively resort to the Civil Procedures Code.[60] Substantive Civil Law may also become relevant in copyright litigation, specifically when it comes to interpreting copyright contracts or where general tort liability is at issue. Over the past decades, several standalone laws on various subject matter, such as the *Contract Law* of 1999, the *Tort Liability Law* of 2009 were enacted. Article 36 of the latter contained a general "notice and take down" liability of internet providers for all kinds of infringing acts carried out by users of their services whereas a corresponding Copyright Law provision is absent. As mentioned in the Introduction, these laws have been merged into a Civil Code on 5 June 2020 (in force since 1 January 2021), and were simultaneously reformed, for instance said Article 36 of the Tort Liability Law.[61] The Civil Code entered into force on 1 January 2021. Also relevant is the *Law on Foreign Related Civil Disputes* of 2010, Article 50 of which applies the *lex loci protectionis* principle to determine the applicable law in intellectual property infringement cases.

III. THE THREE COPYRIGHT LAW REFORMS

1. The First Amendment of 2001

The Copyright Law of 1990 soon proved to be insufficient in quite a number of aspects. In summer 2001, when China was on the brink of WTO accession, the time

59. Which is supplemented by the SPC Interpretation of the "Civil Procedures Code of the People's Republic of China" of 18 December 2014, in Chinese available from the website of the SPC's Gazette http://gongbao.court.gov.cn/Details/63ff48da6a9792f8ad1cb65a8b99d1.html.
60. More details in Peter Ganea, 'Zur Reform des einstweiligen Rechtsschutzes im geistigen Eigentum der Volksrepublik China' (On the reform of the P.R.C's preliminary measures system), 4 *Zeitschrift für chinesisches Recht* (Journal of Chinese Law) (2017), 288.
61. More in XI. 2. *infra*.

was ripe for a general overhaul. At its Twenty-fourth Session on 27 October 2001, the Ninth National People's Congress promulgated the Decision on the Amendment of the Copyright Law of the People's Republic of China,[62] which entered into force the same day. Despite numerous significant amendments to the individual rules, the general structure of the Copyright Law remained basically unchanged. New Implementing Regulations were promulgated on 2 August 2002 and entered into force on 15 September 2002.[63] Finally, software protection was significantly improved by the new Software Regulations of 20 December 2001.[64] The above-mentioned International Implementation Rules remained in force, even though the enhancement of the protection standard by the amendments rendered most of their provisions meaningless.

One fundamental clarification entailed by the 2001 amendment concerned copyright contract law. The previous Copyright Law was silent on the *assignability of copyright*. In order to eliminate the legal uncertainty in this respect, the Copyright Law now clearly states that the economic rights can be assigned.

Further important amendments relate to the *scope of protection*. These amendments mainly aimed at harmonizing the Copyright Law with international conventions. Apart from the introduction of the new rights of Internet transmission and rental required to adhere to the World Copyright Treaty (WCT) and the World Performances and Phonograms Treaty (WPPT), the amendment entailed a number of improvements to the existing exploitation rights.

One of the most criticized aspects of the previous *copyright limitations* regime, namely the complete freedom of non-commercial radio to broadcast copyrighted phonograms, was abolished and replaced by a legal licence regime.

The amendment also *abolished or curtailed several legal licences*, which, in violation of the Berne Convention, unduly limited the exclusivity of copyright. One of these legal licences entitled only owners of the copyright in unpublished works to permit their performance, whereas published works could be freely performed under payment of an adequate remuneration (Article 35(2) of the old Copyright Law), another one declared the performance of adaptations, translations, annotations or arrangements of pre-existing works permission-free (Article 35(3) of the old Copyright Law). Both legal licences violated Article 11(1) Berne Convention. The amendment furthermore abolished the legal licence in Article 37 of the old Copyright Law, which permitted phonogram producers to exploit any kinds of published works as well as adaptations, etc., of pre-existing works for the purpose of sound recording, because it exceeded the scope of Article 13(1) Berne Convention on the permission-freedom of sounds recording of certain works only, namely musical works and works composed of words, which have already been authorized by the author to be recorded together with a musical work. The abolished provision was replaced by Article 40(3) Copyright Law, which stipulates that only musical works that have already been lawfully

62. 33 *Gazette of the State Council* (2001), 10; English translation of the amended law in 1 *China Patents & Trademarks* (2002), 83.
63. The Implementing Regulations can be found in Chinese and in English on WIPO's Wipolex database https://wipolex.wipo.int/en/legislation/details/13428; the 2002 version appears upon clicking on "supersedes".
64. More details about software copyright protection in IV. 2. (b).

recorded in sound may be used by a phonogram producer to record them in sound without the copyright owner's permission.

To harmonize copyright with international requirements, the amendment also broadened the scope of *subject matter eligible for copyright protection*, for instance by extending the protection of compilations of works to compilations of mere data. Moreover, in order to protect subject matter prescribed by Article 2 Berne Convention, the amendment included architectural works and three-dimensional models in the catalogue of protected works. Another important reform concerned the protection of computer software, above all that software registration is no longer a prerequisite for protection.

On the other hand, the amendment left the *neighbouring rights* regime basically untouched, in spite of plenty of criticism in the past.[65] Chapter IV of the Copyright Law on "Publication, Performance, Sound Recording, Video Recording and Broadcasting" still forms a rag bag of copyright contract law, legal licences and neighbouring rights. The few amendments made in 2001 were rather specific. Performers were henceforth granted a comprehensive right to communicate their stage performance to the public, to reproduce the sound and video recording of their broadcasts, to distribute such recordings, and to transmit their performance, whether live or recorded, by way of sound or images via the Internet. Moreover, not only producers of sound recordings but also producers of video recordings were granted the new rights of rental and of transmission via the Internet, thus going beyond WTTP standards. Finally, with regard to the special neighbouring right of publishers, the Copyright Law reform finally clarified the actual subject matter of protection, namely the right to exploit the typographical design of the publication for ten years from first publication.

Whereas the previous Copyright Law remained silent on *collective management* and only the Implementing Regulations mentioned the possibility of entrusting works to a collective society, the amended Copyright Law, as mentioned, obliges the State Council to enact special provisions on the supervision and administration of collective societies. In 2004, the State Council enacted corresponding provisions, which since then have undergone two amendments.[66]

Finally, the 2001 reform led to a stricter *enforcement* regime. The circumvention of technical protection mechanisms and the removal or alteration of copyright management information were added to the list of infringing acts. Further improvements pertain to clearer rules on damage calculation and to pre-litigation measures to halt ongoing or imminent infringement, to preserve property and to preserve evidence. But as mentioned, these provisions have become obsolete since the 2012 overhaul of the Civil Procedures Code. Another important amendment was the introduction of the reversal of burden of proof in copyright piracy cases. Accordingly, the publisher of allegedly infringing work copies must prove that he obtained the publication right, and the distributor of an infringing reproduction or the renter of the infringing reproduction of an audiovisual work, a software work or an audio or video recording must prove that they obtained the rented copies from a legal source.

---

65. See, for example, Xu Chao, 'Guanyu xiugai xianxing zhuzuoquanfa de chubu xiangfa – zhi wu' (First thoughts on an amendment to the present Copyright Law), 3 *Zhuzuoquan* (1995), 29 (32).
66. More details in IX. *infra*.

2. The Second Amendment of 2010

This rather small amendment became necessary due to the WTO panel report WT/DS362/R ("China – Measures Affecting the Protection and Enforcement of Intellectual Property Rights") of 26 January 2009, which adopted the view of the US according to which Article 4 Copyright Law on the exclusion of "forbidden works" from copyright protection ("Works the publication or distribution of which is prohibited by law shall not be protected by this Law") violated the Berne Convention, respectively TRIPS, which, with regard to certain subject matter, refers to the Convention. In particular, the panel found that the provision was not in conformity with Article 5(1) Berne Convention (to which Article 9.1 TRIPS refers) on the obligation of member states to ensure that authors enjoy the rights especially granted by the Convention, and Article 41.1 TRIPS, according to which the enforcement procedures as specified by TRIPS shall be available under national law of the members so as to permit effective action against any act of infringement. The latter finding rejected, *inter alia*, China's assertion that from the right owner's perspective, banning the publication and distribution of works under censorship rules would have the same effect as copyright enforcement.

The subsequently amended Article 4 Copyright Law does no longer exclude forbidden works from protection but simply obliges copyright owners to abide by the laws ("Copyright owners shall not violate the Constitution or laws or jeopardize public interests when exercising their copyright. The State shall supervise and administer the publication and dissemination of works in accordance with the law."). Interestingly, Rule 3 of the mentioned Network Regulations, which have been last amended in 2013 and therefore three years after this Copyright Law amendment, still stipulates that it does not protect forbidden works.

In the course of the 2010 amendment, the legislature also inserted a new Article 26 into the Copyright Law that obliges the parties to a pledge over copyright to register their contract with the National Copyright Administration NCAC. On 19 October 2010, the NCAC supplemented this provision by detailed Measures for the Registration of Pledges.[67]

3. The Third Amendment of 2020

A major overhaul of the Copyright Law after 2001 has been debated for almost a decade. After the publication of a draft proposal in June 2014,[68] the further drafting process remained a matter of internal discussion for almost six years. According to a report published on the NCAC website,[69] a new draft was issued by the State Council's Legislative Affairs Office by the end of 2017, but not to the general public. Expectations that the Copyright Law would finally be amended by the end of 2019

67. https://wipolex.wipo.int/en/legislation/details/14327.
68. It seems that the draft has been deleted from all web sources on which it was previously available. A word file without indication of year but obviously containing the 2014 draft can still be downloaded from this site: http://www.gov.cn/foot/2014-06/06/content_2695611.htm or can be accessed here http://www.law-lib.com/fzdt/newshtml/20/20140609090547.htm.
69. http://www.ncac.gov.cn/chinacopyright/contents/555/359813.html.

were not fulfilled. Instead, another draft proposal was issued in April 2020,[70] this time to solicit opinions from the public.[71] With only 65 articles (four more than the current Copyright Law), it was much more conservative than the previous draft of 2014, which contained 90 articles and proposed several changes to the Copyright Law's structure and orientation, amongst others, the introduction of a fair use provision, which would have drawn the Chinese copyright system nearer to the US copyright tradition, and an overhaul of the regime on neighbouring rights. A few months later, on 17 August 2020, the National People's Congress published another discussion draft[72] with several significant changes compared to the April draft version.

The final third Copyright Law amendment of 11 November 2020, which will enter into force on 1 June 2021, has implemented this last draft with only a few changes.[73] The amended law consists of 67 Articles. As the current 2010 version of the Copyright Law will still be in force when this book is published and the accompanying Implementing Regulations and other secondary law still have to be adapted to the amended provisions, the following explanations will be based on the provisions which are currently in force. Of course, they will adequately refer to all changes entailed by the third amendment.

The 2014 draft still proposed the addition of a fair use clause to the list of copyright limitations, allowing permission and remuneration-free use "under other circumstances" than those defined in the preceding list of specific limitations, provided that such use did not interfere with the normal work exploitation or unduly damaged the copyright owner's legitimate interests. The deletion of this exception in the draft of April 2020 came quite as a surprise. By doing so, the drafters positioned themselves against a recent trend in the judiciary to permit acts not explicitly stipulated in the list of single copyright limitations in deviation from the wording of the Copyright Law.[74] The latest draft of August 2020 obviously accommodated public concerns voiced against a complete abolishment and re-introduced a "fair use light", which would allow permission and remuneration free use under "other circumstances", provided, however, that such circumstances are regulated by law or administrative provisions. The final Copyright law amendment adopted this fair use light, which will henceforth be contained in Article 24(1) No.13.

The third Copyright Law amendment as well as the preceding two drafts of 2020 also refrained from the long-awaited overhaul of Chapter IV on "publication,

70. The draft, including a synopsis of current and amended provisions, is available on the NCAC's website at http://www.ncac.gov.cn/chinacopyright/contents/11973/416082.html; further information in English, including an initial translation of the draft provisions in English by Liu Jiarui can be found on Mark Cohen's blog chinaipr.com (entries of 5 and of 11 May 2020).

71. Comments on law proposals can be submitted through this website of the National People's Congress: http://www.npc.gov.cn/flcaw/.

72. The draft, including a synopsis of its provisions and the provisions of the April draft, can be found on this site: https://www.sohu.com/a/413579668_221481.

73. Decision of the NPC's Standing Committee to amend the Copyright Law on the NPC's website: http://www.npc.gov.cn/npc/c30834/202011/272b72cdb759458d94c9b875350b1ab5.shtml; synopsis of new and old provision on this non-official site: https://www.sohu.com/a/431300459_195414.

74. Further explanations in VII. 1. (a) *infra*.

performance, audio and video recording broadcast", a quite unique mix of specific contract law, legal licences and neighbouring rights, maybe out of the consideration that the present provisions have caused less practical problems than expected by some commentators in the past, so that the drafters considered a reorganization unnecessary. The earlier draft of 2014 instead envisaged limiting said Chapter IV to the regulation of neighbouring rights, and to abolish some of the contract provisions and legal licences and to transfer the others to other parts of the law.

The third amendment, furthermore, addresses collective management in greater detail than the current Copyright Law, but the drafters refrained from regulating so-called extended collective licensing, a concept that in the light of internet mass use of works is increasingly popular throughout the world.

With regard to audiovisual subject matter, the draft of April 2020 proposed to replace "cinematographic works and works created by a process analogous to cinematography" by the broader term "audiovisual works", which would also have included interactive video games, etc., as equivalent to traditional cinema movies, etc. The latest draft of August 2020 proposed a different term, namely, "cinematographic works, television works and other audiovisual works", obviously to facilitate the formulation of a privileged copyright attribution to the producers of traditional film works and TV productions in another provision, which will be explained later.[75] The final third amendment, however, readopted the April draft's proposal and stuck with "audiovisual works", even though it still differentiates between traditional cinematographic works and other non-conventional audiovisual works with regard to copyright attribution. Moreover, in contrast to the earlier draft of 2014, the two drafts of 2020 no longer proposed abolishing the neighbouring right in non-creative audiovisual recordings, and also the third amendment retained it.

The third amendment, just as the preceding drafts of 2020, also refrained from readopting the 2014 draft's provisions on orphan works, which stipulated that users who could prove that they had failed to reach the right owner after a diligent search were entitled to request a licence to use the work in digital form against a fee to be paid in advance from an organization to be acknowledged by the NCAC. Some commentators back then found the limitation of uses covered by the legal licence to "use in digital form" too narrow, referring to other legislations where such limitation does not exist.[76]

Even older drafts published before 2014 proposed the introduction of a *droit de suite*, but the 2014 draft already abandoned this idea, maybe out of concern that such a right may render China a less attractive arts market and auction spot.[77]

Finally, the third amendment significantly improved enforcement, especially with regard to damages. It introduced, inter alia, a facilitation of proof of the damage

75. V. 5. *infra*.
76. See, e.g., Jiang Run and An Lina, 'Gu'er zuopin baohu yanjiu – yi "Zhuzuoquanfa" di san ci xiugai wei beijing' (Study on the protection of orphan works – against the background of the "Copyright Law's" third revision), 5 *Juanzong* (2015), 472 et seq.; He Ying, 'Gu'er zuopin shiyong yu falü jiuji tanxi – yi "zhuzuoquanfa" di san ci xiugai wei zhongxin' (Use of orphan works and legal remedies – with a focus on the third revision of the "Copyright Law"), 8 *Chuban faxing yanjiu* (Publication research) (2017), 72 et seq.
77. See Sun Guorui and Bo Liang, 'Questioning Rationality of and Necessity for Incorporating *Droit de Suite* in Copyright Law', 2 *China Patents & Trademarks* (2014), 74 et seq.

amount by obliging the defendant to cooperate in the calculation thereof, a dramatic increase of the highest possible amount of so-called statutory damages, i.e., damages determined by the court based on the available information if calculation of the actual damage, the infringer's profit, etc. is not possible, from presently RMB 500,000 to RMB 5 million and the introduction of punitive damages up to five times the actual damage amount to sanction serious intentional infringement.

IV. PROTECTED WORKS

1. Protected Works in General

Article 3 of the current Copyright Law contains a definition of works as "works of literature, art, natural sciences, social sciences, engineering, technology and the like, which are created in the following manner..." and a non-exhaustive list of work categories, which are further defined in Rule 4 of the Implementing Regulations. Rule 2 Implementing Regulations also defines works as intellectual creations in the literary, artistic and scientific domain that must be reproducible in tangible form. The draft amendment of April 2020 proposed to transfer this definition to Article 3 Copyright Law and to add the requirement that works shall be "original", so that the whole provision would henceforth require protected works to be original intellectual creations in the literary, artistic or scientific domain which are reproducible in a specific tangible form. This definition would then replace the overly detailed enumeration of fields to which a work may pertain ("literature, art, natural sciences, social sciences, engineering, technology...") in the present Article 3. The third Copyright Law amendment, however, adopted the even broader definition proposed by the later August draft, defining the work as "intellectual achievements" to be "expressed in a certain form" (instead of prescribing "tangible reproducibility"), and rendering the catalogue of fields to which a protected work must belong non-exhaustive, in that henceforth subject matter pertaining to literature, arts, science "and the like" domains would be protected.

Finally, the draft of April 2020 proposed the addition of a second paragraph to Article 3 stipulating that works can be registered with registration authority to be determined by NCAC. The August draft and ultimately the third amendment transferred this provision to the second paragraph of a new Article 12, under the stipulation that in absence of proof to the contrary, the person named on the work shall be treated as author. As mentioned, registration of works is already possible under the present provisions, so that the proposed addition can be understood as a clarification to encourage more right owners to register their rights.

Article 3 Copyright Law lists the following work categories:

(a) Literary works, such as novels, poems, essays and theses;
(b) Oral works, which in contrast to literary works do not have to be fixated, but can be in the form of improvisations, lectures or court debates;
(c) Works intended for performance, including:
  (i) Musical works, whether accompanied by vocals or not;
  (ii) Dramatic works, including dramas, opera and local art forms;

(iii) The traditional Chinese "quyi" art form, consisting of funny dialogues, clapper ballads, ballads accompanied by drums, storytelling in the form of recitation or singing or both;
(iv) Choreographic works, which are expressed by successive movements of body and face;
(v) Acrobatic works, which are defined as acrobatic, magic and circus works; and
(vi) works expressed by body movement and artistry.[78]

(d) Works of fine art and architectural works;[79]
(e) Photographic works, which must be original, i.e., the photographer's own creation and, in contrast to most other work categories, fixated. Rule 4 No. 10 Implementing Regulations allows the fixation on light-sensitive material and on "other media", including computer-readable data carriers. Courts require from such photographic works a very modest level of originality. It is sufficient that they express the photographer's intellectual labour in terms of selection of angles, timing, shadows, etc., but a certain level of "artistry" is not required.[80] The third Copyright Law amendment adopted the proposal of the two preceding drafts of 2020 to abolish the special treatment of photographic works with regard to the protection term of the economic rights of 50 years, which, according to Article 21(3) of the present Copyright Law is counted from the publication date, and to henceforth protect them for a term of 50 years from the author's death just as most other kinds of works (except cinematographic works). A new Article 65 simultaneously prevents the revival of already expired protection terms after the amendment's entry into force on 1 June 2021.
(f) Cinematographic works, including works created by a process analogous to cinematography;[81]
(g) Graphic works, consisting of engineering design and product design drawings which are required to be transformable into a three-dimensional product, maps which show geographic phenomena, and sketches which demonstrate the basic characteristics or the structure of an object. It is unclear whether the transformation of engineering and product designs into a three-dimensional object is a copyright-relevant reproduction. Due to the abolishment of the previous Article 52 Copyright Law that clearly precluded this possibility, it

78. By adding this category of works, the legislator took into account China's tradition of artistry. Essential for protection, however, is not the degree of difficulty or danger of an acrobatic presentation, but its aesthetic value: see Li Shunde and Zhou Yang, *Zhonghua Renmin Gongheguo zhuzuoquanfa xiugai daodu* (Guide to the amendments of the Copyright Law of the People's Republic of China) (Beijing, 2002), 44.
79. Further information in 2. (c) *infra*.
80. Decision 35 *Hu Gao Min San (Zhi) Zhong Zi* (2006) of the Shanghai Higher People's Court with regard to an endoscopic image; further case law quoted by Wei Liu and Jiarui Liu, 'Copyright Protection of Sports Programs in China', 64 *J. Copyright Soc'y U.S.A.* (2017), 235 (footnotes 56–58), *inter alia* the Guangdong Higher People's Court's 122 *Yue Gao Fa Min San Zhong Zhi* (2005) decision regarding the work character of product advertising photographs.
81. Further information in 2. (a) *infra*.

can now be assumed that the unauthorised manufacture of three-dimensional products based on copyrighted drawings indeed infringes the reproduction right. The originality that can be expressed by technical plans is often limited by functional aspects. In a decision of 26 December 2019, the Shanghai Pudong People's Court ruled that the plan of an electronic heat tracing system for ships expressed sufficient individuality to be copyright protected because another designer would have had enough leeway to express the same object differently in terms of choice of views, thickness of lines, spaces, etc.[82] From other work categories, such as cinematographic works or works of applied art, a higher degree of originality is required, due to the existence of additional protection under neighbouring rights or design law for less artistic subject matter.[83]

(h) Model works, meaning three-dimensional models of the shape or structure of an object for the purpose of showing, experimentation, or observation (Rule 4 No. 13 Implementing Regulations). The intellectual labour expressed by such works lies in highlighting, omitting, enlarging or minimizing parts of an original object for the purposes of "showing, experimentation or observation". Otherwise, if the model is no more than for instance, an enlarged version of the original object, it would not go beyond a mere reproduction. It nevertheless seems that the Shandong Higher People's Court in a decision of 2012[84] acknowledged the work character of a mere enlarged model of a *Foraminifera* unicellular organism, stating that it expressed "artistic abstraction and aesthetic adornment".[85] The 2014 Copyright Law draft amendment aimed to replace "model works" by "three-dimensional works", i.e., "works created for the purposes of product manufacturing, showing geography or topography or explaining the principles or structures of objects". According to some commentators, such introduction of a new category of protected subject matter would have enhanced confusion, especially because three-dimensional works "for explaining the principles and structure of a manufactured work" would be hardly distinguishable from works of applied art that the draft wanted to re-introduce as a work category on its own.[86] The third Copyright Law amendment, just as the preceding two drafts of 2020, probably considered these concerns, as it refrained from specifically regulating three-dimensional works and works of applied art.

(i) Computer software;[87]

---

82. Decision 4906 *Hu 0115 Min Chu* (2018) of 26 December 2019, https://mp.weixin.qq.com/s/k7GGqXcqge8__j1en3pyWQ.
83. See 2. (a) and (c) *infra*.
84. 33 *Lu Min San Zhong Zi* (2012), original text of the decision could not be found.
85. Quoted from He Huaiwen, 'Copyright Protection for Scientific Models', 3 *China Patents & Trademarks* (2015), 98 et sq., who criticizes the court's reasoning, as the model was purely scientific and not made for artistic purposes, and it would have been sufficient to refer to the modeler's scientific thoughts when selecting the object to be modelled, etc.
86. He Huaiwen, note 85, who finds that model works may be better protected as an unspecified kind of work in the open catalogue of protected subject matter.
87. More details in 2. (b) *infra*.

(j) Other works as provided for in laws and regulations. This provision in Article 3 No. 9 Copyright Law is capable of absorbing future types of creative works which are not yet known. However, it is required that they are typified as works by other laws and regulations. A music fountain installation, for instance, which is nowhere mentioned as a work category, cannot be protected as "other work" but a court decision subsumed it under the definition of "works of fine art" in Rule 4 No. 8 Implementing Regulations.[88] The 2014 Copyright Law draft amendment abolished the requirement in Article 3(9) that these "other works" had to be regulated by laws or regulations, the draft of April 2020 re-adopted it and the third amendment abolished it again, now merely listing "other intellectual achievements that comply with the characteristics of a work" as protected subject matter.

As mentioned, Rule 2 of the Implementing Regulations requires a protected work to be the result of intellectual creation in the fields of literature, art and science, to express originality and to be reproducible in tangible form. That is, there is no general requirement that a work must be fixated for protection. It suffices that it is expressed in a manner that renders fixation possible. This may apply, for instance, to stage performed works, which can be audio or video recorded. The latest draft of August 2020, as mentioned, even proposes to abolish this reproducibility requirement. Photographic works and cinematographic works are treated differently, however. They must be fixated for protection but as will be explained later, recent case law treats this fixation requirement very flexibly at least with regard to cinematographic works respectively works created by a process analogous to cinematography, to also subsume live broadcasts under them.[89]

Mere ideas which are not expressed by any means are excluded from protection.

Excluded from protection is, furthermore, material available in the public domain, e.g., the historical accounts on which a work is based. Protection shall be limited to the concrete expression by the author, which is manifested in the manner in which he individually processed the available information to create his own work, whereas thirds shall be free to resort to the same information to express themselves differently to create another work that can be enjoyed independently from other works that are based on the same situation. Essential is that each author has made use of a leeway to express himself individually and differently from the others when creating the work.

In a decision of 28 November 2014,[90] the SPC stated that the historical events, historical expressions, etc. on which the plaintiff's screenplay was based shall belong to the public domain and that others shall be free to resort to them as basis for their

88. Beijing Intellectual Property Court, 1404 *Jing 73 Min Zhong* (2017) decision of 26 June 2018, more in 2. (c) *infra*.

89. 2. (a) *infra*.

90. SPC decision 1049 *Min Shen Zi* (2013) of 28 November 2014 with regard to a case in which the plaintiff's and the defendant's screenplay for a TV drama relied on the same historical setting, summarized in the WIPO Collection of Leading Judgments on Intellectual Property Rights – People's Republic of China (2011–2018), 77 et seq. in the English version; both the English and Chinese versions of the collection can be downloaded from https://www.wipo.int/publications/en/details.jsp?id=4477.

own independent works. Copyright protection shall be limited to what is individually expressed in the concrete work. A decision of the Shanghai Pudong New Territory People's Court of 24 April 2019[91] found that similarities between the plaintiff's literary work and the defendant's script and subsequent audiovisual work with regard to plot and setting were not sufficient to identify infringement by adopting the pre-existing work's expression because structure and sequence of events of the defendant's work were different from that of the plaintiff.

In another decision, the Beijing Higher People's Court[92] dealt with the idea-expression dichotomy in connection with an infringement of the adaptation right in a screenplay in a case in which the storyline was not predetermined by history or other material but largely created by the plaintiff himself. The court stated that if "the setting of and relation among characters, and the plots, which consist of the occurrence, development and sequence of specific events ... reach such a level of distinctiveness that the author's unique choices, judgments and trade-offs are reflected in the selection of scenes, their structural arrangement and the design of plot progression in a literary work", they are no longer mere ideas but "can become expressions protected by copyright law". Due to substantial similarities in the defendant's work with the plaintiff's plot, character interaction, etc., the court found infringement of the adaptation right. In its decision of 26 November 2018,[93] the Beijing Intellectual Property Court stressed the necessity to keep the non-protected idea, here the subject matter of a historical compilation, apart from those elements that constituted the protected expression, which would consist in the author's selection, the thread of ideas, the overall structure of the work and the expression of critical thoughts.

As will be further outlined below with regard to certain work categories, there is no clear threshold delineating the minimum degree of creativity that a work must provide to be copyright protected. The judiciary has developed a rule according to which subject matter for which alternative protection is available, such as design protection for applied art or neighbouring rights protection for audiovisual recordings, must express a comparably high level of originality, whereas other kind of works, such as photographs, are acknowledged as copyright protected works if the author had a minimum leeway for individual expression in terms of selection, arrangement, etc. At least with regard to audiovisual works, however, this rule is contested by recent case law.

Finally, Rule 3 of the Implementing Regulations stipulates that a "creation" can only be an intellectual activity which directly generates a literary, artistic or scientific work, and that organizational efforts, advisory contributions or comments, the supply with material facilities, etc., are not creative. The logical consequence is that a work can only be created by an individual author and that organizations, for example, the employing enterprise of an author, cannot qualify as authors. However, in the following we will see that under certain circumstances, the organization under which a work came into existence can attain a status close to that of an author.

91. 84551 *Hu 0115 Min Chu* (2017); https://mp.weixin.qq.com/s/gXNwaqem4Hu202JP-mvWMg.
92. 1039 Gao Min (Zhi) Zhong Zi (2015); summarized in English in WIPO Collection of Leading Judgments on Intellectual Property Rights, note 90, 104 et seq.
93. 232 *Jing 73 Min Zhong* (2018), https://mp.weixin.qq.com/s/Kez_unWklB4V5xn3p5O7GQ.

2. Special Work Categories

(a) Cinematographic Works

The previous Copyright Law referred to cinematographic works as "cinematographic, TV and video works", a broad term which was justified by concerns that a more comprehensive term would have been difficult to understand by a public not yet accustomed to copyright terminology.[94] Such concerns seem to have abated by 2001, because the amended Copyright Law uses the internationally accepted term "cinematographic works and works created by a process analogous to cinematography". According to the definition in Rule 4(11) Implementing Regulations, a cinematographic work constitutes "a work fixated on a certain medium[95] and comprised of a sequence of pictures accompanied by sound or without sound, which are projected or transmitted by any other means[96] with the help of the appropriate apparatus". That is, in contrast to other work categories, cinematographic works must be fixated to be protected. Another difference from other work categories (except currently photographic works, see above) is that according to the current Article 21(3) Copyright Law (Article 23(3) after the third amendment's entry into force), the publication right and the economic rights in a cinematographic work are protected for 50 years after the publication, not *post mortem*, considering that copyright in the dependent contributions to a cinematographic work belongs to the producer and therefore not to a natural person.[97]

Numerous court decision also subsumed online video games under this definition. In its decision of 15 March 2017[98] the Shanghai IP Court stated that even if online video games were fundamentally different from conventional cinematographic works in that their sequence of images were not be fixed but interactively manipulated by the player, the variety of possible sequences would nevertheless be predetermined by the creators of the game. Also, the above Copyright Law definition would emphasize the "creation" aspect in that works "created" in a manner analogous to cinematography shall be protected, not only works that were made with help of technical means similar to conventional cinematography. In its more recent decision of 13 November 2019, the lower-ranking Shanghai Pudong People's Court also subsumed video games under cinematographic works,[99] with reference to Article 2(1) Berne Convention, according to which works "expressed", and therefore not necessarily "created" by a

94. Gao Linghan, 'Zhongguo zhuzuoquanfa zhong shiting zuopin de quanli de baohu yu xingshi' (Protection and exercise of the rights comprised in audiovidual works according to the Copyright Law), 3 *Zhuzuoquan* (1993), 18.
95. By using the term "medium" it becomes clear that cinematographic works stored in computer-readable form are covered by the definition, whereas the term "material" used in the previous Implementing Regulations could be understood as restricted to traditional film stripes.
96. The term "transmitted by any other means" replaces the previous term "broadcast", because in the meantime, the network transmission of moving pictures has developed into a possible exploitation form.
97. See V. 5. *infra*.
98. 190 *Hu 73 Min Zhong* (2016), http://data.110.com/a706834.html.
99. 77945 *Hu 0115 Min Chu* (2017), https://mp.weixin.qq.com/s/jNII8t3woP34J2KekeFx8Q.

process analogous to cinematography (i.e. sequences of images), shall be protected like cinematographic works. As mentioned, if the current draft amendment becomes law, the term "cinematographic works and works created by a process analogous to cinematography" will be replaced by "audiovisual works", under which video games and other non-conventional audiovisual content will be easier subsumable.

Another category of audiovisual content that can be protected as a cinematographic work are TV shows[100] such as dating shows or talent competitions, provided that they express originality in terms of arrangement, selection of content, etc., and that they are recorded, due to the fixation requirement in Rule 4 No. 11 Implementing Regulations. Courts do only protect the show's concrete recording as audiovisual work, but categorically exclude the underlying show formats from copyright protection, which are regarded as non-protectible thoughts and ideas.[101]

Finally, also protectible as works created in a manner similar to cinematography are time lapse videos created by arranging thousands of still scenic images.[102]

Apart from copyright protection for cinematographic *works*, the Copyright Law provides neighbouring rights protection for audiovisual *recordings*. Rule 5(3) of the Implementing Regulations defines a "video recording" as an "original recording of a sequence of any interrelated images accompanied by sound or without sound other than cinematographic works or works created by a process analogous to cinematography", whereby "original recording" is to be understood as "first recording", not in the meaning of "originality". The neighbouring right of the producer of a video recording is not as comprehensive as the copyright of the producer of a cinematographic work.[103]

As already indicated, the Copyright Law draft amendment of 2014 proposed abolishing the neighbouring right in video recordings, whereas cinematographic works should continue to be protected under the broader notion of "audiovisual work". If this proposal had become law, it may have motivated courts to subsume more subject matter of very low originality, for instance TV sports broadcasts, under audiovisual works, as it would no longer be necessary to distinguish them from mere "recordings" by requiring a particularly high degree of originality.[104] As also

100. Beijing Intellectual Property Court decision 1535 *Jing 73 Min Zhong* (2018), https://mp.weixin.qq.com/s/DJBhYtGe0Vcc0LtCLf7_eA.

101. Item 10 of the Beijing Higher People's Court's Answers to Several Questions with regard to the Handling of Copyright Disputes pertaining to Variety Shows (announcement 62/2015), available on Baidu upon entering the Chinese title "北京市高级人民法院关于审理涉及综艺节目著作权纠纷案件若干问题的解答"; for subscribers downloadable from http://www.cnki.com.cn/Article/CJFDTotal-ZGBQ201503003.htm; see also summary of a related decision of the Beijing Haidian District People's Court of 2005 at https://www.chinacourt.org/article/detail/2006/01/id/192117.shtml (exact date, filing number and original text not available).

102. Beijing Internet Court Decision 8606 *Jing 0491 Min Chu* (2019) of 12 August 2019, https://mp.weixin.qq.com/s/xK2SdOvh5nIGC9LCbLnH8g.

103. More in X. 3. *infra*.

104. There is an abundance of court decisions that partly contradict each other on this subject, see Seagull Haiyan Song, 'China's Copyright Protection for Audio-Visual Works – A Comparison with Europe and the U.S.', *IIC* (2015), 410, 426.

mentioned, the third Copyright Law amendment thwarted such hopes and retained the neighbouring rights protection for audiovisual recordings.

Therefore, until recently it seemed rather likely that sports broadcasts would also in future hardly qualify as "works" under Copyright Law. Most recent case law speaks a different language, however, as will be further outlined below. Since the Beijing Olympics of 2008, during which unauthorized streaming of live sports broadcasts has been rampant, full-fledged copyright protection for broadcasts of sports events is one of the most vividly debated copyright issues in China. Given the fact that sports events generate the highest value when they are live broadcast, streamed or otherwise transmitted, the strong interest of event organizers and broadcasters in a full-fledged copyright becomes understandable. One great obstacle to such protection is that the leeway to express originality while filming, for instance, a soccer game is conceivably low. Supporters of copyright protection, however, counterargue that the cameramen and other contributors would have about the same leeway for individually selecting angles, distances, camera foci, etc., as the authors of a vast majority of copyright protected photographs, so why should the filming of sports events be treated differently?[105] Neither protection as producers of audiovisual recordings according to Article 42 of the current Copyright Law (Article 44 after the third amendment's entry into force) nor the re-broadcasting right of broadcasting organizations according to Article 45(1) of the current Copyright Law (Article 47(1) after the third amendment's entry into force) would provide sufficient protection against the real-time online re-transmission, because at the very time of the live broadcast a recording as a prerequisite for protection as "producer of a recording" does not yet exist, the re-broadcasting right of broadcasting organizations does not cover the realtime re-transmission through the internet, and under the present Copyright Law, broadcasting organizations also do not enjoy the right to transmit their broadcasts through the internet.[106] The third Copyright Law amendment endowed broadcasting organizations with an internet transmission right in Article 47(1) No.3,[107] but it remains doubtful whether this right also extends to the real-time internet re-transmission, as Article 10(12) of the amended Copyright Law continues to define the internet transmission right as communicating the work to the public in a manner that members of the public have access to it from a place and *at a time individually chosen by them*. Under certain circumstances, unauthorized internet streaming of sports events can be dealt with under Article 2(1) of the Unfair Competition Law of 1993, a provision that is widely understood as a general clause that extends to acts not specified in the Unfair Competition Law itself. It remained largely unchanged in

105. Wei Liu and Jiarui Liu, note 80; see also Yan Bo, 'Beyond the Signal: a View from China on the Copyright Protection of Live Sports Programming', 2 *WIPO Magazine* (2019), https://www.wipo.int/wipo_magazine/en/2019/02/article_0002.html; Huang Liang, 'Tiyi saishi banquan baohu de kunjing ji pojie' (Difficulties of copyright protection of sports events and their analysis), 2 *Zhongguo Banquan* (China Copyright) (2019), 21 et seq.

106. Beijing Intermediate People's Court decision 3199 *Yi Zhong Min Zhong Zi* (2014) of 26 May 2014, https://v1.iphouse.cn/cases/detail/21378.html; German courts instead which subsume the live internet streaming, for instance of Pay TV programs, under the rebroadcasting right, see, e.g., Hamburg District Court decision of 23 February 2017, 310 O 221/14.

107. See VI. 2 (b) (4) *infra*.

the course of the 2017 reform, prescribing that business operators shall observe the principles of voluntariness, equality, fairness and good faith, and respect the laws and market ethics. Absent an adequate copyright provision, the Beijing Intermediate People's Court already applied this provision to protect a broadcasting enterprise against unauthorized re-transmission of its sports broadcasts through the internet.[108] Critical commentators, however, refer to the uncertainties arising from non-specific principles like fairness, good faith, etc., and to the applicability of unfair competition provisions to "business operators" only, which would exclude most individuals streaming sports broadcasts through peer-to-peer networks.[109]

Until very recently, the judiciary has been reluctant to subsume sports programs under "audiovisual works". On 30 June 2015, the Beijing Chaoyang District People's Court rendered the first decision[110] (*Sina Hulian v. Beijing Tianying Jiuzhou*, hereinafter: *Sina* decision) that acknowledged the work character of a live sports broadcast, finding sufficient individuality in the choice of camera position, focusing, cutting, etc. The court also stated that anything that was individually created and not a copy of another work shall be regarded as original and worthy of copyright protection. The second-instance decision of the Beijing Intellectual Property Court of 30 March 2018,[111] just as a few later decisions pertaining to broadcast sports events,[112] did not adopt this view, however, finding that the sports event broadcast at issue did not express sufficient originality. In its parallel "FIFA Brazil" decision of 30 March 2018,[113] which overruled the preceding Beijing Shijingshan District People's Court decision (but not with regard to the work quality of sports broadcasts, which was also denied by the lower court),[114] the Beijing Intellectual Property Court, again, stated that the soccer game broadcast at issue did not express a sufficient creativity in terms of selection, etc., to be treated as a cinematographic work.[115] The court identified parts of the broadcast that expressed originality, but these parts would not suffice for copyright protection, as a cinematographic work had to express originality in its entirety. In this case, however, the soccer broadcast at issue could at least be awarded neighbouring rights protection as an "audiovisual recording" because the infringing transmission was made with a delay, after the end of the live broadcast when the

108. The mentioned Beijing Intermediate People's Court decision of 26 May 2014, note 106.
109. Wei Liu and Jiarui Liu, note 78; the Shanghai Pudong New Territory People's Court's decision 88829 *Hu 0115 Min Chu* (2017) of 8 April 2020 (https://mp.weixin.qq.com/s/M_B27gMCstzhIFWZwJ3zTA) also pointed to the weaknesses of alternative Unfair Competition Law protection and chose to protect a live soccer TV broadcast under copyright instead.
110. 40334 *Chao Min (Zhi) Chu Zi* (2014).
111. 1818 *Jing Zhi Min Zhong Zi* (2015), http://www.jintiankansha.me/t/uFHjVrPibT.
112. Decision of the Beijing Shijingshan District People's Court 752 *Shi Min (Zhi) Chu Zi* (2015), (overruled by the Beijing Intellectual Property Court, see *infra*); decision 174 *Shen Fu Fa Zhi Min Chu Zi* (2015) of the Shenzhen Futian District People's Court.
113. 1055 *Jing Zhi Min Zhong Zi* (2015), http://www.iprdaily.cn/article_19189.html.
114. Beijing Shijingshan District People's Court decision, note 112.
115. Similarly, the decision 12496 *Jing 0105 Min Chu* (2019) of the Beijing Chaoyang District People's Court of 20 November 2019 (https://mp.weixin.qq.com/s/Ze-hXlmQ-QEazZ-2SAILcvg) denied the makers of a non-fictional video that showed the rescue of a young wolf protection as an audiovisual work due to lack of originality, but qualified for protection under the neighbouring right of producers of audiovisual recordings.

whole series of broadcast images had been stably fixed, so that a "recording" as a prerequisite for such neighbouring right existed, whereas in the parallel *Sina* case, the streaming was carried out in real time, when the broadcast signals were not yet fixated. That is, in the *Sina* case, the mere lack of durable fixation precluded both protection as cinematographic work, which, according to Rule 4 No. 11 Implementing Regulations, must also be "recorded on a medium"[116] and as "audiovisual recording", whereas in the FIFA case the plaintiff could at least resort to the neighbouring right in audiovisual recordings, which includes the right to communicate the recording through the internet (Article 42(1) of the current Copyright Law, Article 44(1) after the third amendment's entry into force), obviously also by way of real-time transmission.

In its appeal decision of 23 September 2020,[117] however, the Beijing Higher People's Court, overturned the Beijing Intellectual Property Court's *Sina* decision, especially with regard to the work character of live sports broadcasts and the fixation requirement. It found that live broadcasting a sports event provided the plaintiff with enough leeway for individual choice of camera perspectives, etc., to accomplish a "work created in a manner analogous to cinematography". Decisive for copyright protection would be whether originality was expressed at all, not the degree of originality. The court, furthermore, introduced a quite idiosyncratic interpretation of the requirement that cinematographic works must be fixated on a medium pursuant to Rule 4(11) Implementing Regulations, stating that such medium does not necessarily have to be a carrier in which the work is stably fixated, but that putting the sports event in a state that it can be perceived and appreciated by viewers and transmitted through the internet shall be sufficient for meeting this requirement. If this interpretation were to prevail in future case law, the fixation requirement, thus far an almost insurmountable bar for the protection of live broadcasts, would be virtually abolished. It should be noted that the Higher People's Court's decision is very similar to the earlier decision of the Shanghai Pudong New Territory People's Court of 8 April 2020[118] dealing with another soccer broadcast-related dispute. It directly refuted the view that different categories of works would justify different minimum degrees of originality as expressed in the Fifa Brazil decision and also found that decisive for copyright protection would be whether the work expressed originality at all or not. With respect to the sports broadcast at issue, the court found originality, *inter alia*, in the selection of camera perspectives and in the dramaturgic creation of an antagonistic atmosphere by aligning the camera work with the narration, by slow motion replays of exciting scenes, etc. Thus, it would deserve copyright protection as a "work created in a manner analogous to cinematography". The court also regarded the fixation requirement according to Rule 4(11) Implementing Regulations as fulfilled because the content caught on camera would be immediately recorded, otherwise the slow-motion replays would not have been possible. Therefore, streaming of the live broadcast formed infringement of the plaintiff's copyright, albeit not of a specific right like the broadcasting right or the internet transmission right, but of the unspecific "other rights copyright owners are entitled to enjoy" pursuant to Article 10(1) No. 17 Copyright Law.

116. Which is not required by the Berne Convention.
117. 128 *Jing Min Zai* (2020), https://mp.weixin.qq.com/s/QQwXNLPuO7HLH_OYmiy2bg.
118. 88829 *Hu 0115 Min Chu* (2017), note 109.

It remains to be seen whether these most recent court decisions will entail a general reorientation of case law towards a more generous protection of live sports event broadcasts. Such reorientation may have farther-reaching consequences, for instance, with regard to the mentioned, thus far prevailing view that the availability of alternative protection instruments within specific work categories, here the neighbouring right in audiovisual recordings as an alternative to copyright protection in cinematographic works, would preclude copyright protection of content of low originality.

The attribution of copyright ownership in cinematographic works will be explained below.[119]

(b) Computer Software

Mass software piracy during the past decades has not only been a constant issue of Sino-US disputes but also caused great harm to domestic software developers,[120] some of whom invented drastic technical measures to protect themselves against pirates.[121] In spite of these setbacks, China has generated a capable software industry, which is on par with the world's top innovators in the areas of Internet of Things (IoT), Blockchain technology or Financial Technologies (Fintech). It is beyond the scope of this paper to elaborate on the extent to which this is also a result of a government-guided austerity that motivated Chinese industries to build a purely Chinese environment of social media, messenger services, electronic commerce and so on, and whether the present US government's policy of blocking "foreign adversaries"[122] (i.e. first and foremost China) from the supply with – presently – most advanced US semiconductors and other technologies is likely to further invigorate China's strive for technological independence.

Copyright protection is increasingly regarded as insufficient to ascertain further growth of the domestic software industry, and patent protection is likely to play a greater role in future. As detailed in the Part on Patents, Utility Models and Designs, several amendments to CNIPA's Examination Guidelines of the past years have rendered patent protection better accessible for developers of software, which, however, must still be part of an invention that has at least a loose connection

119. V. 5.

120. During the 1990s and the early 2000s mostly in form of sale of infringing physical copies; case law from back then reported by Xiu Qianfeng, 'Xiaoshou daoban guangban anjian chuli sunzai wenti de sikao' (Considering remaining problems of disputes related to the sale of pirated CDs), 1 *Zhongguo Banquan* (2002), 49.

121. In 1998, the Public Security Office of Beijing Municipality fined a producer of an anti-virus software, arguing that attaching a so-called "logic bomb" to his software that activated itself once an unauthorized copy was made to block the hard disc of the user, was disproportionate and contravened administrative rules on computer safety; case without decision date reported and commented by Li Caoying, 'Legal Issues of Intellectual Property Involving the Case of KV300', 4 *China Patents & Trademarks* (1998), 65.

122. According to President Trump's Executive Order on Securing the Information and Communications Technology and Services Supply Chain of 15 May 2019, https://www.whitehouse.gov/presidential-actions/executive-order-securing-information-communications-technology-services-supply-chain/.

with the physical world to be regarded as "technical" enough to fulfil the patent prerequisites. Software *per se* such as office software, which, apart from its interaction with the hardware on which it is run, has no impact on the physical world, can only be copyright protected.

Article 3(8) Copyright Law mentions computer software as a work category of its own. Article 59 (Article 64 after the third amendment's entry into force) delegates the detailed regulation to the State Council, which enacted the first the Software Regulations on 4 June 1991 and overhauled them on 20 December 2001 in connection with the first Copyright Law reform. On 30 January 2013, they were again amended to increase the administrative fines for infringement.[123]

The special character of software works as an intellectual creation of mainly commercial character became evident by a clear stipulation in the previous Regulations of 1991 that permitted software copyright transactions in the form of assignment, whereas the previous Copyright Law of 1990 remained silent on this issue with regard to other works. Since 2001, however, assignability is no longer a special feature of software, as all kinds of works have become assignable. Also other, meanwhile abolished provisions of the previous Regulations hinted at a certain reluctance to regard software as just another category of works. Unregistered software, for instance, was virtually denied protection, as Rule 24 required registration as a precondition for filing an infringement suit. In 1993, however, the Supreme People's Court issued an Interpretation, which contradicted Rule 24 by ordering the lower courts to also accept cases related to unregistered software.[124] Also in contrast to other kinds of works, the protection term for software was confined to merely 25 years from the first issuance, with the possibility of extension for another 25 years.

In particular the US was anything but satisfied with this low protection standard. In a Memorandum of Understanding of 1992, which obliged China to accede to the Berne Convention, the US wrested a promise from China to introduce legislation protecting at least foreign software as literary works.[125] As a result, Rule 7 of the International Implementation Provisions of 1992 provides that foreign computer software be protected as a literary work for a term of 50 years. As a starting point for this protection term, however, Rule 7 only mentioned the date of publication, even though treatment as a literary work would have required a protection of 50 years *post mortem* if the software copyright owner was a natural person. Article 7(3) of the Berne Convention allows a shorter protection term of 50 years from publication only in the case of anonymous works, e.g., for software published under the name of the enterprise which supervised its creation. As will be outlined below, this discrimination of nationals has been terminated by the overhaul of the Software Regulations in 2001, which elevated software copyright protection to internationally acceptable standards.

Accordingly, registration, rather than being a prerequisite for court action, is now optional. The certificates issued by the registration authority serve as *prima facie* evidence of the indications made in the registered documents (Rule 7(1)),

123. In Chinese at http://www.gov.cn/gongbao/content/2013/content_2339471.htm.
124. 1 *Zhuzuoquan* (1994), 64.
125. Text available at the website of the U.S. Trade Compliance Center, www.tcc.mac.doc.gov/cgi-bin/doit.cgi?226:64:634243457:1:191.htm.

but this is also the case with regard to other kinds of works. The modalities of the voluntary registration not only of software but also of software licensing contracts and software assignment contracts are regulated by the Methods of Registration of the Copyright in Computer Software, enacted by the NCAC on 20 February 2002.[126] Taking the copyright owner's interest in confidentiality into account, Rule 12 of the Methods allows, *inter alia*, blacking out relevant passages and according to Rule 13, the submitted material may be sealed.

Software licensing contracts are governed by the Third Book of the new Civil Code on contracts and by specific Copyright Law provisions. Formal requirements are absent, a software licensing contract may also be concluded by Email exchange if the will of both parties to enter in a contractual relationship becomes clear.[127] A recent matter that has become relevant in copyright litigation are so-called "copyleft" licences, under which the licensee can freely use the software, provided that he allows further licence-seekers to also freely use the improvements he made to that software. In its decision of 12 April 2018, the Beijing Intellectual Property Court stated that it would acknowledge a GNU Public Licence (GPL), the most popular copyleft scheme, but found that in the present case the plaintiff's software was not distributed under a GPL as asserted by the defendant, so that the defendant who used the software without the plaintiff's permission committed old-fashioned copyright infringement.[128]

Protection of a software work starts with its completion (Rule 14(1) Software Regulations) and lasts 50 years from the creator's death respectively 50 years from the last surviving creator if the software was jointly developed (Rule 14(2)). If copyright is owned by a legal person or other organization, the protection term of 50 years begins with the date of release, provided that the software is not released after the expiration of 50 years from development (Rule 14(3)). In all these cases, the protection term ends on 31 December of the 50th year.

In contrast to other work categories, the moral rights of first publication, indication of authorship and preservation of the software work's integrity (i.e. to make additions to or deletions from the software or to modify the instruction or statement sequence of the software) are not perpetually protected, so that their duration is confined to 50 years either from the death of the author or from the date of publication. Also, the name of the software creator does not have to be indicated

126. Original version in English in 2 *China Patents & Trademarks* (2002), 74.

127. Beijing Higher People's Court decision of 3 July 2019, 441 *Jing Min Zhong* (2018), https://mp.weixin.qq.com/s/u-SKPytGB-NlFOO77mdvbQ

128. 631 *Jing Zhi Min Chu Zi* (2015); in a similar fashion, also the Ningbo Higher People's Court in its decision of 12 February 2018 (3852 *Zhe 02 Min Zhong* (2017)) rejected the defendant's argument that he used the plaintiff's software freely under a GPL, because of the defendant's failure to produce evidence of the existence of such licence, signalling that it would have acknowledged the legitimateness and validity of copyleft licence terms if they actually existed; see also Jyh-An Lee, 'Tripartite Perspective on the Copyright-sharing Economy in China', 35:4 *Computer Law & Security Review* (August 2019), 434 et seq.; available at https://www.sciencedirect.com/science/article/pii/S0267364919301803#cit_226.

if its omission belongs to established business practice, e.g., if the software is part of a larger product unit and performs a specific function.[129]

With regard to occupational works, Rule 13 of the Regulations facilitates the availability of software copyright to the industrial software producers by stating that the copyright shall belong to the employer if only one of the following covering the relationship between the employer and the software developer applies:

(a) The software is the result of a task explicitly assigned in the course of employment;
(b) The software is a foreseeable or natural result of the normal occupational duties;
(c) The software has been developed mainly with help of the fund, equipment, not publicly available documentation or other material or technical facilities provided by that legal entity or other organization.

That is, even if the software is not the result of an assigned task and also not a foreseeable or natural result of normal duties, but has only been developed with help of the employer's material or technical facilities, copyright still belongs to the employer.[130] Rule 13 complies with Article 16(2) Copyright Law (Article 18(2) after the third amendment's entry into force), which classifies software works among other types of works of predominantly commercial character (e.g. drawings of engineering or product designs), the copyright of which belongs to the employer, provided that it was created by mainly using the employer's facilities and under his guidance.

That Article 3(8) Copyright Law does not refer to "software works" but to "computer software" should not lead to the conclusion that all types of computer software can be protected under the Copyright Law and the related regulations. As computer programs necessarily form a subcategory of "works" under Article 3 Copyright Law, they must comply with the requirements set forth in Rules 2, 3 Implementing Regulations, according to which a protected work can only be an intellectual creation. At least one minimum requirement with special regard to software is expressively mentioned in Rule 4 of the Software Regulations, namely that it must be individually created by its developer and materially fixated. As protected subject matter, the Regulations mention not only the software as such which is ready to be run on the computer (source and object code of the same program are regarded as the same work – Rule 3), but also the related documentation (Rule 2), namely "text material and charts used to describe the contents, composition, design function, state of development, test results and modes of use, e.g., explanations of the program design, flow charts and user manuals" (Rule 3(2)). That is, not only the completed program but also intermediate information, for example, information on the state of development, come into question as an object of software copyright protection. However, to marginal cases in which software development is at a very initial stage, Rule 6 on the exclusion of ideas, operating methods or mathematical conceptions from protection should be applicable.

129. Beijing Higher People's Court decision 442 *Jing Min Zhong* (2018) of 3 July 2019, https://mp.weixin.qq.com/s/u-SKPytGB-NlFOO77mdvbQ.
130. Xue Hong, 'The Latest Development in Chinese Software Protection', 6:2 *The Journal of World Intellectual Property Review* (March 2003), 359.

End users of software respectively legal owners of a software copy bear a stricter liability for infringement than end users of other kinds of works, which until 2001, when the Software Regulations were overhauled, may have been justified by the wide gap between the significant costs of software creation and the minimal costs of infringement by making digital copies.[131] According to Rule 16 Software Regulations, owners of legal software copies are only allowed to reproduce software by means of installing it on the computer for their own personal use, to make a backup copy that is to be deleted once the ownership in the purchased copy has ceased to exist, and to amend the software to enable its operation within a certain computer application environment or to improve its function. Another exception is contained in Rule 17, which allows unsanctioned and unremunerated use of software in the form of installation, display, transmission or storage for purposes of studying the underlying programming principles. This limitation is much more restrictive than the one contained in the previous Software Regulations, which stated that the use of a limited number of copies for school instruction, scientific research and governmental use was permissible and remuneration free.[132] As the Software Regulations do not expressly address reverse engineering, it remains unclear whether this form of use is permitted under Rule 17.[133] Chinese experts advised the courts to decide according to the circumstances of a particular case. If reverse engineering serves a legitimate purpose, namely securing the interoperability of the program with other programs, it should not be regarded as infringing, provided the legitimate interest of the copyright owner remains unprejudiced.[134]

Article 50 No. 5 of the recently amended Copyright Law allows the circumvention of technical protection measures for the purposes of encryption research or of research on software reverse engineering. The limitation of allowable circumventions to the purposes of "research" on reverse engineering implies, however, that not all kinds of reverse engineering, e.g., for commercial purposes, will be permissible. It might be advisable to further define "reverse engineering research" in the coming Implementing Regulations.

The 2014 Copyright Law draft amendment proposed to transplant the software-specific limitations of the Software Regulation to the Copyright Law (Articles 45–46), while it extended the notion of the privileged party from the "legitimate owner" of the software copy to the "legitimately authorized user". Furthermore, the draft added a new limitation that allows the reproduction and translation of those parts of the software that were necessary to obtain the information to ensure the interoperability necessary for normal use, provided that the information obtained in

131. Xu Chao, 'Is Software Overprotected in China?', 3 *China Patents & Trademarks* (2002), 24.

132. Especially the permissibility of governmental use soon turned out to be too generous in an environment in which a huge part of economic life was still governed by official or quasi-official authorities. Therefore, since 1995 the NCAC and the State Council issued several announcements on the prohibition of governmental use of illegal software copies: detailed information in Tang Zhengyu, 'China's Rocky Road to Computer Software Protection', *China Law & Practice* (Nov. 2002), 25.

133. Xue Hong, note 130.

134. Xue Hong and Zheng Chengsi, *Intellectual Property Law in the 21st Century* (Hong Kong 2002), 124 et seq. (with reference to the old provisions).

such a way is not used in a manner that exceeds the purpose of ensuring interoperability, is not offered to other parties, is not used for the development, making or sale of essentially similar software or used for any other copyright infringing purposes. These extensions of software-specific limitations were no longer proposed by the two drafts of 2020 and also the finally amended Copyright Law is void of them, which does not necessarily mean, however, that they have been completely abandoned. They may instead become part of future Software Regulations.

The amendment to the Software Regulations of 2013 substantively increased the fines for certain software copyright infringements if they, in addition to infringing civil rights, also violate the public interest (Rule 24). In case of unauthorized reproduction, distribution, rental, or internet transmission, the fine shall be RMB 100 per copy or one to five times the total value.[135] If technical protection measures are circumvented or removed, rights management information is altered and, quite peculiar, software of another party is transferred or licensed, a fine of not more than RMB 200,000 shall be imposed. Pursuant to Rule 28 and 29, software publishers or producers who fail to prove that they have obtained a permission to publish or to distribute or distributors or renters of software who fail to prove that they have obtained the software from a legitimate source shall also be held liable for infringement. The local copyright administrations may furthermore order cessation, confiscate illegal revenues and confiscate and destroy infringing copies. In serious cases, they can confiscate the material, tools, equipment, etc., used for infringing reproduction and transfer the administrative case to the criminal authorities for further prosecution. Rule 23 stipulates civil remedies in case of publishing or registering software without authorization, publishing or registering the software of another party as one's own, publishing or registering co-developed software as software developed by oneself without permission of the co-developers, attaching one's name to another party's software or altering the name attached to the software or amending or translating software without authorization. An innocent user who possesses an infringing software copy is not liable for damages but must cease from further use and destroy the infringing copy (Rule 30). Only if he suffers unreasonable damage from such treatment will he be allowed to further use the infringing copy but is obliged to adequately remunerate the copyright owner.

Finally, it should be noted that software as "technology" may fall under the Regulations on the Administration of Technology Import and Export enacted by the State Council on 10 December 2001.[136] Amongst others, the Regulations require official approval should certain software intended for licensing abroad pertain to so-called "restricted technology".

135. Likely the price/licence fee for the original software.

136. 2 *Gazette of the State Council* (2002), 17; *China Law & Practice* (February 2002), 56; last amended on 2 March 2019, abolishing some of its most criticized provisions that imposed heavy burdens on licensors, mostly in response to US demands http://www.gov.cn/zhengce/content/2019-03/18/content_5374723.htm (amendments to the Technology Import and Export Regulations in Item 38).

(c) Works of Fine Art, Architectural Works and Works of Applied Art

Article 3 No. 4 Copyright Law lists works of fine art and architectural works as one category of works. Rule 4 Implementing Regulations defines works of fine art form "two- or three-dimensional works of aesthetic quality, comprised of lines, colours and other elements, such as paintings, calligraphy, sculptures, buildings, etc." (No. 8). A Beijing Intellectual Property Court decision of 26 June 2018[137] understood the term "other elements" as opening the catalogue of works of fine arts for new kinds of artistic works, in this case a musical fountain, i.e., light effects synchronized with played music, which, however, in contrast to classical artistic works, are dynamic and only temporarily appreciable.[138]

Rule 4 No. 9 Implementing Regulations defines architectural works as "works of aesthetic quality expressed in the form of architectural buildings or constructions". The latter term "constructions" is a general term which includes subject matter other than what is commonly perceived as "architectural", e.g., a canal. Certain works of fine art, e.g., calligraphic works, do not have to meet too high prerequisites as to originality to be protected. It is sufficient that they are the author's own creation and not the copy of another work.[139] Another subcategory of works of fine art, namely works of applied art, has to meet stricter originality requirements, as will be explained below.

The Copyright Law does not specifically address works of applied art. With regard to domestic works, Article 7 of the pre-2001 Copyright Law instead contained a general stipulation that seemed to prohibit protection of works of applied art. According to this provision, works of science and technology that could be protected under the Patent Law provisions on design protection were not simultaneously protectable under the Copyright Law. This provision was interpreted as excluding works of applied art for which design patents under the Patent Law were available. In order to comply at least with international standards set forth in Article 7(4) Berne Convention, Rule 6(1) of the International Implementation Rules provided that foreign works of applied art shall be protected for a minimum term of 25 years from completion. Moreover, an interpretation rule issued by the NCAC stated that only where the artistic part of an item was separable from the functional part, could the aesthetic part (apparently mere decorations) be copyright protected. Accordingly, aesthetic forms in the meaning of the actual "design" of a product which could not

137. 1404 *Jing 73 Min Zhong* (2017); criticized by Yuan Feng, 'Lun yinyue penquan de zhuzuoquan fadingxing – jianping woguo "yinyue penquan zhuzuoquan diyi an"' (About the copyright character of musical fountains – also a first comment on "China's first musical fountain copyright case"), 7 *Dianzi Chishi chanquan* (Electronics Intellectual Property) (2019), 11 et seq., not only for this categorization but for protecting a mainly computer-generated content under Copyright (more in V. 1. *infra*).

138. Which as such should not give reason to exclude the fountain from protection as a work of fine art, however. Otherwise, also Jean Tinguely's famous *Homage to New York* installation of a machine that destroyed itself (1960), which is widely perceived as a highlight of modern art history, would have to be regarded as non-copyrightable.

139. Decision 139 *Yu Fa Zhi Min Zhong Zi* (2014) of the Henan Higher People's Court, without date, summarized at: https://www.chinacourt.org/article/detail/2015/04/id/1602086.shtml.

be appreciated separately from the use of the respective item were excluded from copyright protection.[140] Article 7 was abolished in the course of the 2001 Copyright Law reform, so that copyright protection for works of applied art, albeit not explicitly mentioned, is available since then. This, in turn, should have rendered Rule 6(1) of the International Implementation Rules meaningless. Otherwise, its perpetuation would rather discriminate against foreigners, as full copyright protection pursuant to the amended Copyright Law would now be granted for 50 years *post mortem*, whereas special protection for foreign right owners would remain limited to 25 years from the completion of the work.[141] As mentioned, the 2014 Copyright Law draft amendment envisaged a reintroduction of the explicit protection of works of applied art, for the shortened protection term of 25 years previously reserved to foreigners. The finally amended Copyright Law, however, does not feature such a provision.

The Beijing Higher People's Court's still applied Rule 6(1) of the International Implementation Rules in its *Interlego* decision of 18 December 2002, which found that the design of the majority of the industrially manufactured *Lego* toy blocks at issue were artistic enough to be eligible for copyright protection as works of applied art.[142] In another decision of 29 November 2013,[143] again with *Lego* as plaintiff, the SPC denied the toy blocks at issue copyright protection, stating that their shapes were too functional to express enough originality for protection as works of fine art. In its decision of 12 August 2006, the Beijing Intermediate People's Court No. 2 recognized the famous *Gaultier* perfume flacons shaped in a male and in a female torso as works of fine art, with reference to their high degree of originality.[144] The S-shape of a toothbrush[145] and the outer appearance of an adhesive tape cutter[146] were instead denied copyright protection, the former because such shape was dictated by a specific function to release pressure while brushing teeth, the latter because the form at issue did not express enough artistry to be eligible for copyright protection. Two cases regarding children's accessories highlight the difference between product shapes that express a sufficient degree of creativity to be eligible for copyright protection and product shapes that at best come into question as subject matter of design protection. Whereas a night stool and related utensils which are shaped

140. According to the interpretation, aesthetic decorations etc. which existed independently of the practical use of the decorated item could be copyright protected, so that the protection exclusively granted to foreigners according to the International Implementation Rules had to be understood in a broader sense, namely as including creative forms which cannot be separated from the function of the product: reported by Zhang Xiaodu, 'Shiyong mishu zuopin falü baohu yantaohui de shengyin' (Comments made at the conference on the legal protection of works of applied art), 2 *Zhongguo Banquan* (2002), 18.

141. Zhang Xiaodu, note 140.

142. 279 *Gao Min Zhong Zi* (2002), summarized and commented by Zhong Ming at http://chncase.cn/case/viewer/web/viewer?nid=1031271; English case report by Zhang Guangliang, 'Comments on and Analysis of the Case Interlego AG v. Kegao Company and Fuxing Business Centre Arising from Dispute over Copyright in Work of Applied Art', 2 *China Patents & Trademarks* (2003), 77.

143. 1269 *Min Shen Zi* (2013), https://www.chinacourt.org/article/detail/2014/01/id/1209663.shtml.

144. 7070 *Er Zhong Min Chu Zi* (2006).

145. Beijing Intermediate People's Court No. 1, 3515 *Yi Zhong Min Chu Zi* (2002).

146. Shenzhen Intermediate People's Court, 402 *Shen Zhong Fa Min San Chu Zi* (2005).

in form of funny animals express enough originality to be protected as works of fine art, even though they were simultaneously registered for design protection,[147] a chair for children that has even won a design prize but nonetheless looks like nothing more than a chair is not eligible for copyright protection.[148] In its decision of 30 August 2016, the Jiangsu Higher People's Court found that furniture can be aesthetic enough to be subsumed under works of applied art.[149] The decision also clarified that if the defendant asserts that he created the allegedly infringing furniture independently, the burden of proof shall be on him. Again with regard to furniture, the Higher People's Court of Sichuan Province's decision of 29 November 2019[150] elaborated on how to determine originality in case of works of applied art and on the required degree of such originality. Accordingly, copyright relevant originality shall be established where the aesthetic components of the product can be separated from its functional components, so that alterations to the former would not result in the loss of functionality. Also, the court stuck to the opinion that only such objects of applied art that expressed an especially high degree of originality shall be protected, whereas protection of less original objects of applied art shall be reserved to design protection. Otherwise, too much subject matter would fall under the longer and broader copyright protection.

In sum, China's judiciary, in the absence of clear legal provisions, adheres to a concept that comes close to the former German "step theory" (*Stufentheorie*), which requires a relatively high degree of originality from subject matter of applied art to be protected not only under design law but also under copyright law. Decisive for Chinese courts is that the artistic elements of the product of applied art can be clearly separated from its function, so that a form that is mainly dictated by the product's function, however appealing to the eye it is, is not eligible for copyright protection but should be reserved to design protection. This treatment of works of applied art until recently complied with the mentioned previous case law on cinematographic works, in that also here, courts set the originality bar that a work eligible for protection has to pass relatively high because another protection instrument, here the neighbouring right in non-creative audiovisual recordings, is available for subject matter of lower originality. This may change, however, as has been explained in detail above.[151]

(d) Adaptation, Translation, Annotation and Arrangement

Pursuant to Article 12 of the current Copyright Law (Article 13 after the third amendment's entry into force), the copyright in a work created by adaptation, translation, annotation or arrangement of an existing work belongs to the person who actually made the adaptation, etc., provided that such copyright is not exercised in a manner prejudicial to the copyright in the original work. "Adaptation" and "translation" are

147. Beijing Intermediate People's Court No. 2, 12293 Er Zhong Min Chu Zi (2008).
148. Decision of the Shanghai Intermediate People's Court No. 2, 187 Hu Er Zhong Min Wu (Zhi) Chu Zi (2008).
149. 00085 *Su Zhi Min Zhong Zi* (2015), https://mp.weixin.qq.com/s/KBc9UQbPanXcVKgSU8otnQ.
150. 176 *Chuan Zhi Min Zhong* (2019), https://mp.weixin.qq.com/s/NhlKO8q74C-FIaiKw2Uw7w.
151. 2. (a) *supra*.

defined in Article 10 Copyright Law,[152] not as protected works, however, but as uses which require the original author's or copyright owner's permission, whereas "annotation" and "arrangement" are not further defined by the law and the administrative rules. Rule 5 No. 10 and No. 12 of the previous Implementing Regulations contained definitions of both "annotation" as "explanation of characters, words of sentences of a written work" and "arrangement" as "organization and systemization of existing written works or materials the contents of which are diffuse and incoherent, for example, the punctuation or the completion of ancient works". Itemizing "arrangement" as a form of creative intellectual activity may appear doubtful, as it is a mainly reconstructive activity, which admittedly requires a high degree of sophistication, but which some may still find difficult to subsume under "creative" works.[153] The German Copyright Act, for instance, does not grant a copyright but a neighbouring right to the editor of so-called scientific editions (Article 70), i.e. the reconstructions of no longer available or incomplete ancient texts, which comes close to what is protected as "arrangement" under the Chinese Copyright Law.[154]

In 2018, the SPC confirmed full-fledged copyright in the arrangement of a historical work by adding punctuation, dividing the ancient text in paragraphs, etc., stating that the arranger had enough leeway to choose between various forms of arrangement, that another arranger would have arranged the same text differently, depending on his own educational background and experience, so that the presently chosen arrangement expressed sufficient originality and individuality.[155] [156] In 2019, the Chaoyang District Court of Beijing arrived at a similar decision with regard to the unauthorized publication of a version of an ancient literary work that had been added annotations and interpunctuations as well as been divided into paragraphs by a deceased author.[157]

Finally, where a work is created by adaptation, translation, annotation or arrangement, the exercise of the copyright in it by the adapter, etc., shall not

152. Article 10(1) No. 14 Copyright Law defines the adaptation right as the right of the author to create a new and creative work by adapting his pre-existing work. No. 15 of the same provision stipulates that the translation right is the right to translate the work from one language into another.
153. Bai Yuhua, 'Lun dui zhuantong xiju minjian wenxue yishu de zhengli, gaibian zuopin zhuzuoquan de queren ji xingshi' (Discussion of the determination and exercise of the copyright in works of arrangement and adaptation of traditional opera and folklore), 2 *Zhuzuoquan* (1998), 28.
154. "Scientific editions" according to German law are reconstructive or critical editions distinctive from previous editions of the same work: see Dorothee Thum, in Artur-Axel Wandtke and Winfried Bullinger (eds.), *Praxiskommentar Urheberrecht* (5th ed. 2019), § 70 para. 1.
155. Decision of 21 May 2018, 175 *Zui Gao Fa Min Zai* (2016), https://mp.weixin.qq.com/s/saIfRAn63Y7yCeITGCtvxw.
156. Wang Dengping, 'Shilun zuopin de duchuangxing' (Tentative discussion on the originality of works), 3 *Zhuzuoquan* (1993), 26 added another reason for such protection, namely inequity that would arise if historians who strictly stick to the facts when using historical sources would remain without protection, whereas those who enhance their arrangements with fiction would be regarded as creative authors deserving copyright protection.
157. Decision of 30 December 2019, 10975 *Jing 0105 Min Chu* (2019), https://mp.weixin.qq.com/s/oSZ1BuONSmnlcH_y0gVmrw

prejudice the rights of the owner of the copyright in the original work (Article 12 of the current Copyright Law, which will become Article 13 after the third amendment's entry into force), and where a publisher, performer or producer of sound or video recordings seeks to publish, perform or record the adaptation, translation, annotation or arrangement, he shall also ask the owner of the copyright in the original work for permission and remunerate him (Articles 35, 37(2), 40(2) of the current Copyright Law). The Copyright Law draft amendment of April 2020 proposed to merge these separate provisions into a single rule and to expand their scope by providing that those who want to use a work created by adaptation, translation, annotation or arrangement in any form (i.e., no longer only in form of publication, performance and sound or video recording) shall ask both the owner of the copyright in the adaptation, etc., and the owner of the copyright in the original work for permission. The latest draft of August 2020 retained the proposal to merge the separate provisions into one article but cut the uses for which permission must be sought back to the current scope, i.e., publication, performance and sound and video recording. It further-more added "compilations" to the derivative works encompassed by the provision and clarified that also remuneration must be paid to the owners of the copyright in both the original work and the derivative work. The third Copyright Law amendment adopted this latest draft stipulation without any changes. It will be accommodated in a new Article 16 after the amendment's entry into force.

(e) Compilations and Databases

In accordance with Article 10(2) TRIPS Agreement, Article 14 of the current Copyright Law (Article 15 after the third amendment's entry into force) stipulates that a protected compilation may not only consist of works or fragments of works but also of unprotected data, provided that it reflects originality by reason of selection or arrangement. Rule 5 No. 11 of the pre-2002 Implementing Regulations instead denied mere data collections copyright protection in providing that to be protected they had to be compilations of works or fragments of works. To comply with international requirements, only foreign compilations of mere data were protected by Rule 8 of the International Implementation Provisions, another provision that discriminated against Chinese nationals and has become obsolete after the 2001 amendment.

Despite sporadic calls[158] for a right of the compilers of non-original databases such as telephone books or address lists, which may nevertheless form a significant investment, to forbid large-scale excerpting and use, no such protection is available under China's Copyright Law. However, in the past courts have shown a willingness to protect non-creative data collections under Article 4 of the General Principles of Civil Law, inter alia, on fairness and good faith[159] (today they would resort to Articles

158. Wei Zhi, 'Lun shujuku zhuzuoquan' (On copyright in databases), 3 *Zhuzuoquan* (1996), 21, calling for a neighbouring right in databases similar to the German model; see also Zheng Yichuan, 'Huibian zuopin he shujuku de falü baohu wenti' (Problems of legal protection for collections and databases), 2 *Zhuzuoquan* (1999), 29.

159. Intermediate People's Court of Liuzhou District, decision of 25 November 1994, 1 *Gazette of the SPC* (1996), 25: the court held that even though the weekly TV program published by the plaintiff, a TV program publisher, did not constitute a work in the sense of the

4–8 of the General Part of the Civil Code, which regulate these general principles in greater detail) or under Article 2(1) of the Unfair Competition Law on the principles of equality, fairness, honesty and credibility and on the obligation to observe the business ethics.[160] The latter is apparently understood as a general clause that can be applied to such unfair acts which are not explicitly stipulated by the Unfair Competition Law.[161] It should be noted that said Article 2 has not significantly changed after the overhaul of the Unfair Competition Law of 2017, and that its character as a general clause is still debated.[162]

Calls for an even farther-reaching immaterial property in data to be granted to the party which has been responsible for their collection to create incentives for the formation of Big Data markets are rare. A potential starting point for such immaterial property could be Article 127 of the General Part to the Civil Code (*"Where the protection of data and virtual network property is regulated by law, such regulations shall be applied."*)[163]

(f) Expressions of Folklore

Article 6 Copyright Law contains a provision according to which "measures for the protection of copyright in works of folk literature and art shall be enacted by the State Council separately." So far, however, the State Council has made very little use of this power. On 20 May 1997, it enacted the "Provisions on the Protection of Traditional Crafts and Arts",[164] a set of rules related only to a segment of traditional

CA, the defendant who reprinted the program in his own newspaper offended the general rules on fair business practices set forth in Article 4 of the General Principles of Civil Law.

160. Higher People's Court of the City of Beijing, 17 July 1998 (case reported in Shao Jiandong (ed.), *Jingzhengfa jiaochang* (Competition Law Course) (Beijing, 2003), 41 et seq.). In applying Article 2(1) of the Unfair Competition Law to the case, the Higher People's Court substantially corrected the first instance decision which held that the commercial transmission of business data originally submitted to the defendant for the purpose of enabling him to develop his own analytic software constituted a breach of a technology contract and an unauthorized communication of a business secret: reported and commented by Sun Jian and Liu Yong, 'Judicial Protection of Information Resources as Viewed from the Litigation by Sunlight Company Against Bacai Company', 4 *China Patents & Trademarks* (1997), 84.
161. That also the Supreme People's Court understands Article 2(1) Unfair Competition Law as a general clause is evidenced by the Interpretations concerning Several Questions of the Application of Law to Civil Procedures related to Internet Domain Names of 26 June 2001 (4 *Gazette of the SPC* (2001), 133), Rule 7 of which stipulates that to cases of unauthorized domain name registration which do not conform with acts specified by law but are "unfair" in a general sense, either Article 4 of the General Principles of Civil Law or Article 2(1) of the old Unfair Competition Law shall be applied.
162. Yaotian Chai, 'The New Anti-Unfair Competition Law of the People's Republic of China 2018', *GRUR Int.* (2018), 636.
163. Discussed in detail by Lei Yi, 'Daten als eigentumsrechtlicher oder immaterialgüterrechtlicher Gegenstand in China' (Data as subject matter of property or of intellectual property in China), *GRUR Int.* (2019), 238 et seq.
164. An official source could not be found but the provisions are traceable e.g., on Baidu, by searching for the Chinese title "传统工艺美术保护条例".

arts, namely traditional handicraft, which is defined as pieces or techniques of handicraft manufactured or applied for more than 100 years and clearly perceivable as elements of folklore of a certain nationality. Arts and crafts deserving such special protection must be approved by a special committee established by the responsible department of the State Council. Arts and crafts of outstanding quality are excluded from export. Preferential treatment with regard to the establishment of workshops, education of apprentices, etc., is granted to masters of traditional craftsmanship. Apart from their limited applicability, these old provisions seem to be partly dedicated to protecting the national cultural heritage and not so specifically to a regulating a folklore "right" to be vested in communities as a reward for efforts dedicated to preserving traditional arts and crafts, and it is unclear, anyway, whether they have ever been applied in practice. Judges who are confronted with folklore cases in which local communities or even individuals request protection against the usurpation of the specific form of art they and their ancestors helped to preserve do not resort to these rules but rather tend to interpret the Copyright Law in a manner that allows them to protect the interests of the claimants in spite of the lack of clear legal or administrative rules.

In its *Ethnic Hezhe Sipai Village* decision of 17 December 2003,[165] the Higher People's Court of the City of Beijing found that a traditional folk song melody of an ethnic minority that had been usurped by a singer and a TV station does not belong into the public domain. The delegation of the formulation of folklore-specific provisions to the State Council in Article 6 Copyright Law expressed the legislature's intention to protect folklore as a kind of property, which, in this case, the local People's Government shall be entitled to claim on behalf of the minority. The court, obviously well aware of the unchartered territory in which it had to render a decision, rejected the plaintiff's compensation claim and ruled that the defendants henceforth had to indicate the that song was an adaptation of the *Hezhe* folk song when using it in future, to publish a corresponding statement in the Legal Daily and to bear the litigation costs.[166]

In the *Bai Guancheng v. Beijing Daoxiangcun Foodstuff* case decided by the Beijing Dongcheng District's People's Court in 2010,[167] the plaintiff, one of two remaining artists capable of handcrafting traditional *Beijing Zongren* bristle dolls, sued a food company for attaching to its food packages two-dimensional pictures of scenes of bristle dolls that he had arranged and exhibited. Also here, the court referred to the legislative intention of Article 6 Copyright Law, but this time directly applied the Copyright Law when ordering the defendant to refrain from further attaching pictures of scenes with *Zongren* dolls on the packages of his products, to publish a public apology and to compensate the plaintiff. Unlike the preceding *Hezhe* folk song

165. 37 *IIC* (2006), 482, commented by Bryan Bachner.

166. See Bryan Bachner, 'Back to the Future: Intellectual Property and the Modernization of Traditional Chinese Medicine', in Christopher Heath and Anselm Kamperman Sanders (eds.), *New Frontiers of Intellectual Property Law: IP and Cultural Heritage – Geographical Indications – Enforcement – Overprotection* (IIC Studies, Hart Publishing 2005), 1 et seq. (34).

167. 02764 *Dong Min Chu Zi* (2010), discussed by Judge Qi Lei in http://www.chinaipmagazine.com/journal-show.asp?1018.html (Chinese) and http://www.chinaipmagazine.com/en/journal-show.asp?id=752 (English)

case, however, subject matter of the present case were dolls that expressed sufficient individuality to be regarded as the plaintiff's own works, not exactly items of folklore that could not be assigned to a specific author or copyright owner. The decision even expressly referred to the non-existence of identical prior works.

In a dispute decided by the Guiyang Intermediate People's Court on 19 December 2015,[168] the plaintiff's work was inspired by a traditional batik style, which prompted the defendant to object that his use of the plaintiff's work on as an object of folklore could not be copyright infringing. The court, however, found sufficient originality in the plaintiff's pattern to protect it as an artistic work. Moreover, it valued the fact that the pattern's creator was an important representative of the regional folk art at issue as an aggravating circumstance when calculating the amount of damage compensation.

(g) Unprotected Subject Matter

Another category of works excluded from copyright protection are works which in the widest sense belong into the public domain. Article 5 Copyright Law enumerates (a) laws and regulations, resolutions, decisions and orders of state authorities and other legislative, administrative or judicial documents and their official translations, (b) news on current affairs and (c) calendars, numerical tables and forms of general use such as formulas as subject matter excluded from copyright protection. The provision also helps to undermine abusive copyright exercise in order to deny public access to official information. With regard to the exclusion of reporting on current events, ideally pure factual information without individual analysis and judgement involved, Rule 16 of SPC's Copyright Interpretation stipulates that if they are made publicly available by mass media but prepared by others, the source must be indicated. The third Copyright Law amendment followed the proposal of the two drafts of 2020 and replaced the "news on current affairs" by "mere factual news", probably to reduce the likelihood of excluding news reports and the like, which express a relatively high degree of originality, from copyright protection. Simultaneously, a broader limitation in Article 24(3) of the amended Copyright Law will facilitate the use of works for the purpose of news reporting, by no longer limiting the purpose of permission-free use to reporting on "current events" as Article 22(3) of the current Copyright Law, so that works can henceforth be used without permission for any kind of news reporting.[169] Also, due to the amendment to the provision on occupational works which has simultaneously been transferred from Article 16 to Article 18, authors employed by any kind of news disseminators will henceforth have to accept severe restrictions to the individual exercise of their copyright.[170] All these amendments significantly enhanced the status of news reporting agencies and facilitate their business.

Finally, the exclusion of calendars, numerical tables, forms of general use and formulas in Article 5 No. 3 Copyright Law can be understood as substantiation of

168. 17 *Zhu Zhi Min Chu Zi* (2015), summarized in English in WIPO Collection of Leading Judgments on Intellectual Property Rights, note 89, 83 et seq.
169. More in VII. 1. (b) (3) *infra*.
170. More in V. 3.

the general principle that information, ideas, operation modes, etc., as such are not copyright protected.[171]

V. COPYRIGHT OWNERSHIP

1. General

As mentioned above, the Chinese Copyright Law largely adheres to the Continental European view, which emphasizes the natural relationship between the human author and the result of his intellectual creation. According to Rule 2 Implementing Regulations, a work must be an "intellectual creation", and therefore a creation made by humans, which excludes, *inter alia*, works generated by computer software, including artificial intelligence (AI).[172] With regard to future legislation, academic circles are divided over the question whether future legislation should render copyright accessible to machine-generated works. Some commentators see sufficient leeway for copyright-relevant originality expressed by machines at least where the machine-generated content is not predetermined in a manner that the same input can only produce exactly the same result,[173] others insist that copyright protection remain reserved to human creations.[174] The mentioned Beijing Intellectual Property Court decision of 26 June 2018 in the musical fountain case,[175] which qualified a music fountain as a new kind of artistic work, was partly criticized as ignoring the fact that the fountain at issue was operated autonomously by intelligent software, whereas the human input was limited to non-creative preparatory acts, so that the publicly visible and appreciable "work" was actually machine-generated.[176] In another decision of 25 April 2019, the Beijing Internet Court found sufficient human involvement in the creation of an analysis report that was to a large extent generated

171. Guo Shoukang, in Geller and Nimmer, note 3, §2(1) (b).
172. See the article by Yu Wenwen, 'Rengong zhineng shengcheng neirong de zhuzuoquan' (Copyright in AI-generated content) of 21 August 2019 on the website of the Cyberspace Administration of China, http://www.cac.gov.cn/2019-08/21/c_1124902661.htm.
173. Yan Xinlong, 'Lun rengong zhineng shengchengwu de zhuzuoquan baohu' (About copyright protection for AI-generated content), 11 *Fazhi yu Jingji* (Legal Economy) (2019), 27 et seq., who would like to see copyright in such content vested in the person who has made the necessary arrangements for its generation (in a manner similar to Sec. 9(3) of the UK Copyright, Designs and Patent Act of 1988) but is undecided about who that actually should be (the programmer, the user of the programme?); Lu Haijun, 'Zhuzuoquanfa yiyi shang de "zuopin" – yi rengong zhineng shengchengwu wei qierudian' ("Works" in the meaning of copyright – from the perspective of AI-generated content), 6 *Qiusuo* (2019), 74 et seq.
174. For instance Cao Xinming and Xian Chenxu, 'Rengong zhineng zuowei zhishichanquan zhuti de lunli tantao' (Ethical discussion on AI as the subject of intellectual property), 1 *Xibei Daxue Xuebao* (Journal of Northwest University) (2020), 94 et seq.; Cao Bo, 'Rengong zhineng shengchengwu de zhili caichan shuxing bianxi' (Analysis of the attribution of intellectual property to AI-generated content), 4 *Bijiaofa Yanjiu* (Comparative Law Studies) (2019), 138 et seq.
175. 1404 *Jing 73 Min Zhong* (2017).
176. Yuan Feng, note 137.

by a query tool developed by *Wolters Kluwer* to grant copyright protection. The court, furthermore, rendered a general statement that denied copyright protection in content generated solely by AI but argued that even such works deserved some kind of investment protection.[177] A newer decision of the Shenzhen Nanshan District People's Court of 24 December 2019[178] also found sufficient human intervention in the selection and arrangement of the input inserted into Tencent's *Dreamwriter* that automatically generated the final article to qualify such article as a work expressing human creativity. That is, also this latter decision denied solely computer-generated content the character of a copyright protectable work. It seems that courts are willing to protect computer generated works as long as they express at least a minimum of human intervention.

At least for the time being, another concern seems more pressing than the copyright protection of machine-generated works, namely that verifying the authenticity of content will become more difficult as the use of intelligent software in publishing, etc., increases, in that humans claim to have created a content by themselves while they have in fact instructed AI to generate it.[179] A proposal of "Data Security Administration Methods" released for public discussion by the Cyberspace Administration of China on 28 May 2019,[180] for instance, wants to oblige internet operators to mark news, blogs, comments, etc., that have been automatically composed with help of Big Data or artificial intelligence with a corresponding note (Rule 24).

Whatever future legislation will bring, current law only allows results of human intellectual labour to be copyright protected. And also in another respect, Chinese copyright appears to be rather strongly author-oriented and not so much perceived as an instrument of generating economic incentives to create, notwithstanding the stipulation in Article 1, which emphasizes the social usefulness of copyright as a means for advancing society. This becomes most evident from the existence of the above-mentioned moral rights to decide on the first publication of the work, to be named in context with the work, the peculiar right to revise the own work and the right to maintain the work's integrity (Article 10(1) Nos. 1–4).[181] The orientation towards Continental Europe is also evidenced by the designation of "copyright" as "zhuzuoquan" which literally means the "right in a work creation" and comes close to the European notion of "author's right". However, the term "banquan", which is the Chinese translation of "copyright" in the Anglo-American sense, can be synonymously used, and Article 57 of the current Copyright Law (Article 62 after the third amendment's entry into force) explicitly points out that both notions have the same meaning.[182] The official Chinese name of the NCAC, for instance, is

177. 239 *Jing 0491 Min Chu* (2018), https://www.bjinternetcourt.gov.cn/cac/zw/1556272978673.html; see also Kan He's comments on IPKat http://ipkitten.blogspot.com/2019/11/feilin-v-baidu-beijing-internet-court.html.
178. 14010 *Yue 0305 Min Chu* (2019), https://mp.weixin.qq.com/s/jjv7aYT5wDBIdTVWXV6rdQ, see also Kan He's comment on IPKat http://ipkitten.blogspot.com/2020/01/another-decision-on-ai-generated-work.html.
179. Voiced, for instance, by Cao Bo, note 174.
180. Published on http://www.gov.cn/xinwen/2019-05/28/content_5395524.htm.
181. More details on moral rights in VI. 1. *infra*.
182. More details on the debates about an appropriate designation in the run-up to the Copyright Law enactment are presented by Guo Shoukang in Geller and Nimmer, note 3, §1(3)(b).

Banquan-ju" ("ju" can be translated into "administration"), not "Zhuzuoquan-ju". Also, in 2002, the copyright journal "Zhuzuoquan" was renamed into "Zhongguo Banquan" (China Copyright), which may be interpreted as a shift towards the Anglo-American work-orientation. And indeed, the following explanations will show that Articles 11–19 of the current Copyright Law on "copyright ownership" (Articles 11-21 after the third amendment's entry into force) contain some severe deviations from the Continental European author-friendliness.

Finally, it should be noted that the third Copyright Law amendment renamed the addressees of copyright attribution throughout the Copyright Law, thus far "citizens, legal persons and other organizations", into the more accurate "natural persons, legal persons and organizations without legal personality".

2. Authorship of Legal Persons and Other Organisations

As a general rule, Article 11(1) Copyright Law provides that copyright shall belong to the author of the work, except, however, "where otherwise stipulated in this law", and para. (2) of the same provision in the current Copyright Law defines the author as the immediate (human) "citizen" who created the work. The third Copyright Law amendment replaced "citizen", which implied that only Chinese nationals could become authors, by the more accurate term "natural person". An exception according to para. (1) is contained in the subsequent paragraph (3) of Article 11, which stipulates that in the case of works accomplished under the supervision of and representing the will of a "legal person or other organization" ("legal person or organization without legal personality" after the third amendment's entry into force) which bears responsibility for the work, that legal person or organization shall be deemed to be the author. To "be deemed to be the author" means that not only the exploitation rights but also the moral rights are attributed to that entity. Such mutilations of the pure Continental European doctrine are not peculiar to China, however. A similar provision, which is said to have served as a legislative model for China,[183] is contained in Article 15 of the Japanese Copyright Law, which assigns full authorship, including the moral rights, to the legal person under whose name the work has been published. However, whereas the Japanese provision is limited to works created in employment relationships, Article 11(3) of the Chinese Copyright Law goes a step further, requiring only that the work must be created under the supervision of that legal person and represents its will, and that the legal person or other organization bears the responsibility for it. In most cases, works of this kind are created in the course of employment, but it is also imaginable that works created on request or on the basis of any other principal-agent relationships fall under the authorship of the legal entity or organization. The legislative motive behind Article 11(3) may have been to prevent individual authors from usurping works they accomplished at the initiative of a state authority, e.g. official reports or opinions, by employing their individual copyright.

As will be subsequently explained in greater detail, Articles 16 and 17 of the Chinese Copyright Law (Articles 18 and 19 after the third amendment's entry into

183. Zheng Chengsi, 'Special Features, Merits and Shortcomings of China's Laws for Intellectual Property Protection (Part II)', 2 *China Patents & Trademarks* (1994), 12.

force) regulate the attribution of copyright in occupational works and commissioned works, which can also be assumed to be in most cases generated under the supervision and in accordance with the intention of an employer or a principal, and it is well imaginable that quite a number of employers and principals would feel tempted to pose off as quasi-authors according Article 11(3). Unfortunately, clarifying case law that would help to grasp the difference between occupational works and commissioned works on the one hand and works created under the supervision of an entity or other organization on the other hand does not seem to be available. The existing case law on occupational and on commissioned works, however, rather implies that they are mostly dealt with under the corresponding provisions in Article 16 and Article 17 of the current Copyright Law, so that only a minor part of employers and principals to commissioned works seem to want to "be deemed to be authors" according to Article 11(3). None of the published draft amendments to the Copyright Law proposed the abolishment of Article 11(3) and also the final third amendment retained it, which may also be a sign that it has not caused too much confusion in legal practice.

3. Occupational Works

Article 16 Copyright Law (Article 18 after the third amendment's entry into force) specifically regulates the copyright in works created in the course of employment is. Its paragraph (1) provides that the copyright in works "created in the fulfilment of assigned tasks" (which refers to the obligations the employee is required to perform in the course of employment) shall belong to the employed author, but that the employing "legal person or other organization" ("legal person or organization without legal personality" after the third amendment's entry into force) shall enjoy a preferential, and for two years from the date of completion, i.e. the date of delivery to the employer (Rule 12 Implementing Regulations), exclusive right to exploit the work within the scope of its business activities. During these two years the author may license the work to others to exploit it in the same manner as the employer only with the employer's consent and share the licence revenues as agreed upon. The 2014 Copyright Law draft amendment proposed to give stronger priority to contractual freedom, stating that the attribution of copyright in occupational works shall be regulated by contract, and that only the in absence of an agreement the employer shall have a right to exclusively use the work for two years (Article 20(1) and (3) of the draft). The final third amendment did not adopt these stipulations, however.

The term "assigned tasks" mentioned in Article 16(1) of the current Copyright Law (Article 18(1) after the third amendment's entry into force) is further defined by Rule 11(1) of the current Implementing Regulations, namely as "duties which citizens are required to perform by a legal person or other organization".

Pursuant to the current Article 16(2) No. 1, however, the rather author-friendly provision of Article 16(1) does not apply to occupational works that consist in the drawing of an engineering or product design, a map, a software[184] or other work (the third amendment added "sketch map" to this enumeration, which will henceforth be contained in Article 18(1) No. 1 Copyright Law) created mainly by using the employer's material and technical facilities and "under the employer's responsibility"

184. For software copyright attribution see IV. 2. (b) *supra*.

(note that such "responsibility" is also a prerequisite for the vesting of copyright in the supervising institution according to Article 11(3)), which, according to Rule 11(2) Implementing Regulations, refers to capital, equipment and material provided for the purpose of completing the work. In such case, a mere right to be named remains with the author, whereas all other rights are enjoyed by the employer. Moreover, according to Article 16(2), the employer may, but does not have to remunerate the author. Also, drawings, maps and software are only examples of works for which Article 16(2) No. 1 of the current Copyright Law attributes copyright to the employer.

As mentioned, the third Copyright Law amendment expanded this employer-friendly provision, adding works created in the context of employment within newspapers, magazines, news reporting services and broadcasting organizations to the catalogue of works in which the employing legal person or organization without legal personality enjoys all copyright apart from the right to be named (Article 18(2) No. 2).

According to Article 16(2) No. 2 (Article 18(2) No. 3 after the third amendment's entry into force), also in case of occupational works in general, i.e., not necessarily drawings, maps, software, etc., created by using the employer's material and technical resources and under his responsibility, copyright shall belong to the employer if so prescribed by law or by contract. Rule 12 of the pre-2001 Implementing Regulations contained an example of an administrative regulation that assigned copyright to the employer, stating that entities that funded and organized the compilation of encyclopedia, dictionaries, teaching material, large photographic illustration books, etc., enjoyed the entire copyright in such compilations. Under which circumstances copyright in occupational works can be vested in the employer "by contract" is not clear, maybe a stipulation in the employment contract that the copyright in any future work of the employee created in the course of employment shall belong to the employer is sufficient.

4. Commissioned Works

Article 17 Copyright Law (Article 19 after the third amendment's entry into force) provides that in the case of a commissioned work, the copyright ownership shall be established by contractual agreement. However, in the absence of an agreement, copyright shall belong to the commissioned party, i.e., the creator of the work. Rule 12 of the SPC's Copyright Interpretation clarifies that where the copyright in the commissioned work is enjoyed by the principal, he shall be entitled to use the work within the scope agreed upon. In the absence of an agreement, the permitted free-of-charge use by the principal shall be determined by the purpose of the commissioning contract.[185]

185. A court decision of the early 1990s first adopted this rule, holding that in the absence of a contractual agreement on the allowed scope of use, the requesting party was not allowed to license the production and distribution of sound recordings of a musical work without the authorization of the plaintiff who originally created it for specific use as a theme song in a cinematographic work: case summarized by Zhang Xiaomei and Xiao Li, 'Zang Tianshuo yu guoji jianzai shinian yishu xilie zuweihui zhuzuoquan ji biaoyanzhequan jiufen'an sheji de jige falü wenti' (Several legal issues involved in the copyright and

Where one author requests another author to jointly create a work, Article 17 (henceforth: Article 19) on commissioned works prevails over other provisions on joint authorship, so that also in this case the requesting party is entitled to remuneration-free use of the work within the agreed scope.[186] The submission of a work upon a proposal solicitation is not regarded as a mere invitation to offer but as sufficient ground for the formation of a commissioning contract.[187] In judicial practice, courts frequently deal with disputes pertaining to deadlines[188] or the quality of the submitted interim material[189] in connection with larger commissioned works such as scripts for TV series, which have thus far been resolved under the Contract Law of 1999 (now the Third Book of the new Civil Code on contracts).

5. Copyright Ownership in Cinematographic Works

Just what exactly constitutes a cinematographic work and to whom the copyright in it shall be attributed are difficult questions to answer, as is reflected in the diverse copyright legislation of various countries. The German Copyright Law, for instance, has opted for a dual-track solution of special limitations to the copyright of the authors of dependent film contributions in order to secure a smooth film exploitation, whereas a neighbouring right in the "film strip" protects the commercial investment of the film producer. Other legislation, for example, Japan's, directly endow the film producer with the film copyright in the form of a *cessio legis*.

China has opted for a solution that is remotely similar to the German model. According to Article 15 of the current Copyright Law (Article 17 after the third amendment's entry into force), the film producer enjoys the right ownership in the dependent creative contributions. Only the authorship right remains with the director, cutter or cameraman. However, authors of the scenario or the film music and similarly *independently* exploitable contributions shall be entitled to independently exercise their respective copyright. In addition to the protection of cinematographic works, the Copyright Law provides for the mentioned neighbouring right of the producers of non-original video *recordings* (Article 42 of the current Copyright Law, Article 44 after the third amendment's entry into force). Whereas the producer of

performer's right dispute between *Zang Tianshuo* and the Organising Committee for the Artistic Series in Honour of the International Decade for Fighting Natural Disasters), 3 *Zhuzuoquan* (1995), 25; See also the decision of the Higher People's Court of Sichuan Province of 15 December 2006, 330 *Chuan Min Zhong Zi* (2006), https://xin.baidu.com/wenshu?wenshuId=cd286610cb75d5d9cf9a7ecd88aa19468c3cfd7d&fl=1&castk=LTE%3D.

186. Decision of the Shanghai Intermediate People's Court No. 1 of 22 December 2004, 134 *Hu Yi Min (Wu) Zhi Chu Zi* (2004), summarized and commented at http://lawyers.66law.cn/s290336c6a803d_i169777.aspx
187. Decision of the Higher People's Court of Guangxi Zhuang Autonomous Region of 18 May 2005, (2005) Gui Min San Zhong Zi No. 3, summarized and commented at: http://www.chncase.cn/case/viewer/web/viewer?nid=1045324.
188. As in the Beijing Intellectual Property Court decision of 20 January 2020, 3415 *Jing 73 Min Zhong* (2019), https://mp.weixin.qq.com/s/o4i2rkmqy9teayrvu0vFDw.
189. Beijing Intellectual Property Court decision of 8 July 2019, 2067 Jing 73 Min Zhong (2018), https://mp.weixin.qq.com/s/02FYHWIxV2oLZnqMz1j23w.

a cinematographic work enjoys copyright in the dependent film contribution, a mere recording pursuant to the current Article 42 cannot possibly incorporate any dependent creative contents that would justify such protection. With regard to video recorded works or performances, Article 42(2) of the current Copyright Law provides that a reproduction, distribution or network transmission of such a recording by a licensee requires not only the permission of its producer but also that of the authors or performers.[190] After the third amendment's entry into force, the provision, which has been moved to Article 44(2) Copyright Law, will also explicitly entitle performers to permit the rental of sound and video recordings incorporating their performance and to claim remuneration for such use by the producer's licensees.

The 2014 Copyright Law draft amendment contained much more detailed provisions on the attribution of rights in cinematographic works, but the third Copyright Law deleted them all.

The draft of August 2020, which, as mentioned renamed the preceding draft's "audiovisual work" to "cinematographic works, television works and other audiovisual works" proposed to reserve the above privileges of producers to the producers of traditional cinematographic and television works and to add a new second paragraph to specifically deal with the "other audiovisual works", e.g., video games. Accordingly, copyright in audiovisual works that constitute jointly created works (see 3. below) or occupational works (see b) above) shall be attributed in accordance with the respective provisions. Where the audiovisual work was neither jointly created nor accomplished in fulfilment of occupational duties, copyright attribution should be agreed upon by the parties. In absence of a clear agreement, copyright should, according to the latest draft proposal, be attributed to the producer but the actual authors shall retain their moral right to be named and be entitled to remuneration. Also, where the producer exploits the work beyond the agreed scope or "established industry practice", he shall ask the author for permission.

The third Copyright Law amendment retained this bifurcation of initial copyright attribution to the producer in case of traditional cinematographic and TV works on the one hand and priority of contractual agreement in case of non-conventional audiovisual works on the other. However, it significantly curtailed the draft's mentioned provision on copyright attribution in non-conventional audiovisual works. Article 17(2) of the amended Copyright Law now simply stipulates that copyright attribution in such works shall be governed by contract and that in absence of a clear agreement, copyright shall be attributed to the producer whereas the contributing authors shall retain their right to be named and the remuneration right. A right of the authors to permit uses that go beyond the agreed scope or difficult to determine "established industry practices" is no longer mentioned.

Finally, the amendment did not change the stipulation in Article 15 of the current Copyright Law that authors of independent contributions shall be entitled to independently exercise their respective copyright, which has been moved to a new paragraph (3) of Article 17.

190. Not included in this enumeration is the rental right. This is because apart from the producers mentioned in that provision, only the owners of the rights in cinematographic works and software producers enjoy a rental right.

6. Joint Authorship

Article 13 of the current Copyright Law (Article 14 after the third amendment's entry into force) distinguishes between joint authorship in separately exploitable contributions, where each author is permitted to independently exploit his part provided that such exploitation does not prejudice the rights of the other authors, and joint authorship in works which cannot be separately exploited. Contributions of mere auxiliary character, e.g. advisory assistance in the course of work creation, are not regarded as worthy of protection under joint copyright.[191] In order to prevent individual co-authors from exercising their rights to the detriment of the others, Rule 9 of the current Implementing Regulations provides that in the case of inseparable joint works, the co-authors must agree upon a work exploitation mode. If they fail to agree, no one may prevent the others from exercising their rights, except the right to transfer the work, without justifiable reason.[192] Rule 9 further clarifies that even if a joint work is exploited without the authorization of all co-authors, the revenues from exploitation shall be fairly distributed among them. The third amendment transferred the content of Rule 9 to Article 14(2) Copyright Law, with the addition that not only the transfer but also the grant of exclusive licences and the pledge of copyright shall be exempt from the exercise by individual authors.

Another frequently disputed topic, namely the name order in case of co-authored works, was resolved by Rule 11 of the above-mentioned SPC Copyright Interpretation. Accordingly, the People's Courts may determine the name order in accordance with the contribution of each author, the arrangement of the contributions within the work, the order of the characters or according to other factors.

7. Exceptional Cases of Copyright Attribution

The Copyright Law and its accompanying rules provide for further special cases of copyright ownership and authorship attribution. The Copyright Law mentions one instance in which copyright may be assigned to the state, namely where the state becomes the successor of a legal person or other organization in the absence of any

191. Higher People's Court of Sichuan Province, decision of 1 December 1990 (1 *Gazette of the SPC* (1990), 43), which was still based on the General Principles of Civil Law, since the Copyright Law was not yet enacted.

192. The simpler wording of Rule 11 of the pre-2001 Implementing Regulations implied that individual co-authors could exploit the work without first asking the others for their consent if they subjectively found no justifiable reason to disagree to the exploitation, see Luo Dongchuan, 'Zhuzuoquan sifa shenpan zhong de jige falü wenti' (Several legal questions encountered in judicial copyright cases), 4 *Zhuzuoquan* (1998), 42; Luo, at that time judge at the No. 1 Intermediate People's Court of the City of Beijing, referred to a case which was an example of unauthorized copyright exercise by a co-author. In the first instance, the Beijing People's Court of the Sicheng district of the City of Beijing ruled that no justified reason existed for prohibiting such exercise. The second instance overruled this decision, thereby referring to the fact that the alleged infringer could not prove that he had asked his co-author for permission before exploiting the work on his own.

other successor (Article19(2) of the current Copyright Law, Article 21(2) after the third amendment's entry into force).

Further special provisions on copyright attribution are contained in the SPC Copyright Interpretation. Rule 13 provides that in cases where a report or a speech is drafted by a person other than the one who proofread the manuscript and under the name of whom the report or speech is publicly presented, the copyright shall belong to the reporter and speaker, who is advised but not obliged to remunerate the drafter. The problem of copyright attribution in this particular case was resolved to the advantage of the person who publicly presents the contents, provided that he bears the final responsibility for them, which is to be evidenced by the fact that he has made the final corrections and issued the work under his own name. Another matter regulated by the SPC Copyright Interpretation is the attribution of copyright in biographies. According to Rule 14, the biographer and the portrayed person may agree upon copyright attribution. In the absence of such an agreement, the copyright shall belong to the latter.

VI. MORAL RIGHTS AND ECONOMIC RIGHTS

The Copyright Law enumerates the moral and the economic rights without distinction in one and the same non-exhaustive catalogue of rights (Article 10(1)), the moral rights in Nos. 1–4, the economic rights in Nos. 5–17. The 2014 Copyright Law draft amendment placed stronger emphasis on the differences between these two sets of rights, by regulating them separately in two paragraphs but the more recent drafts of 2020 as well as the final third amendment abandoned this idea and left the structure of Article 10 untouched.

1. Moral Rights

The Copyright Law protects the moral rights of first publication, to be named in context with the work, to amend the own work and to preserve the work integrity (Article 10(1) Nos. 1–4 Copyright Law). Pursuant to Article 20 of the current Copyright Law (Article 22 after the third amendment's entry into force), the right to be named, the right to amend the work and the integrity right are not limited in time, a provision which reflects the dualistic character of the Chinese Copyright Law. According to Rule 15(1) Implementing Regulations, the right of authorship attribution, the right to revise the own work and the integrity right shall be "protected", i.e., not "enjoyed" by the author's successor or trustee. That is, the successor or trustee does not inherit the moral rights but he is entitled to protect them so as to safeguard the moral interests that the author would have claimed if he were still alive, which, as will be explained below, limits the remedies that can be obtained in case of *post mortem* moral rights infringement. In the absence of successors, the NCAC is responsible for the *post mortem* protection of moral rights (Rule 15(2) Implementing Regulations). Moral rights are not only available to individual authors. As explained above, in the case of works created under the aegis of a legal entity or other organization, dependent contributions to a cinematographic work and certain occupational works, the moral rights thereto are entirely or partly waived to the responsible entity, film producer or employer.[193] In order not to impede the exploitation of computer software, the moral rights in such works are restricted to the publication right and to the right to be indicated as author (Rule 8, No. 1, 2 Software Regulations). In addition, Rule 8 No. 3 Software Regulations mentions a right to "amend" the software work, meaning the right to make additions to or deletions from the software or to amend the instruction or sentence sequence. The moral rights quality of this right remains questionable, however.

Moral rights are, in general, inalienable and cannot be disposed of by contract. This becomes obvious from paragraphs (2) and (3) of Article 10 Copyright Law, pursuant to which only the economic rights enumerated in the preceding para. (1) can become subject matter of an assignment or a licensing contract. On the other hand, Rule 19(1) Implementing Regulations allows the omission of the indication of the author's name not only in cases in which specific manner of exploiting the work renders the indication impossible, but also where the parties have agreed upon the omission.[194]

As far as the enforcement of moral rights is concerned, moral rights infringements give rise to a China-specific remedy, the "apology", previously according to Article 134 (1) No. 10 of the General Principles of Civil Law of 1986, later on according to Article 15 (1) No. 7 of the Tort Liability Law of 2009. The apology has originally been intended as a tortfeasor's personal apology to the infringed party who suffered a personal, emotional rather than monetary damage from the tort. "Apology" is therefore different from the "elimination of effects", which has previously been regulated by Article 134 (1) No. 9 of the General Principles of Civil Law and subsequently by Article 15 (1) No. 8 of the Tort Liability Law. It includes the restoration of the damaged parties' reputation and can be done publicly, *inter alia*, by way of publishing an apology in a newspaper. This kind of remedy also aims at healing economic damages, for instance, due to an impairment of the reputation not only of natural but also of legal person, whereas a mere "apology" can only be ordered to be made to a living natural person capable of appreciating the apology as a remedy to heal emotional wounds directly incurred to him or her. The heir of a deceased author can therefore not claim apology from the infringer of his moral rights because, as noted above, he does not enjoy these rights and therefore cannot personally suffer from their infringement, but only protects them on behalf of the deceased.[195] Also, courts normally deny an apology if the moral rights infringement was not on purpose, e.g., if an author's name was misspelt or omitted out of negligence.[196] The difference between apology and elimination of effects was not always clearly recognized in past judicial practice, in that, for instance, an order to apologize in a newspaper has been wrongly subsumed under the remedy "apology" and not under "elimination of

193. V. 2., 3., 5.
194. Adolf Dietz, note 27.
195. Decisions of the Shanghai Intermediate People's Court No. 1, 51 *Hu Yi Zhong Min Wu (Zhi) Zhing Zi* (2013) and of the Hangzhou Intermediate People's Court, 967 *Zhe Hang Zhi Chu Zi* (2011), quoted by Chen Ruwen and He Huaiwen, 'Apology as Remedy under Chinese Copyright Law', 2 *China Patents & Trademarks* (2015), 79 et seq.
196. Numerous case examples given by Chen Ruwen and He Huaiwen, note 195.

effects".[197] More recent court decisions deny apology as a remedy if infringement of economic rights is at issue, stating correctly that such remedy shall only be available to those who have suffered a personal damage.[198] This is now also clarified by the new Civil Code, which still lists the apology in the catalogue of remedies in Article 179 of its General Part, but later on only mentions it as a specific remedy to those who suffered personality right infringements (Articles 995 and 1000).

(a) Right of First Publication

According to Article 10(1) No. 1 Copyright Law, authors enjoy the right to decide on the publication of their work. Pursuant to Rule 9 of the SPC Copyright Interpretation, "publication" means that the work is made available to an undefined public and does not require that the public is in fact aware of its existence. The publication right of authors is different from other moral rights in that it is not perpetually protected but confined to a duration of 50 years *post mortem* (expiring on 31 December of the 50th year) in order to avoid a perpetual exclusion of the public from access to the work (Article 21(1) of the current Copyright Law).[199]

According to the current Article 21(2) and (3), also entities, which enjoy copyright as employers according to the current Article 16(2) (henceforth: Article 18(2)) or as producers of cinematographic works according to the current Article 15 (henceforth: Article 17), enjoy the right of publication, along with the exploitation rights, for a term of 50 years from the first publication (ending on 31 December of the 50th year), unless the work has not been published within this term. After the third amendment's entry into force, paragraphs (2) and (3) of Article 23 Copyright Law, to which the protection term provisions have been transferred, will stipulate that the 50-years-term of the publication right in works of legal persons and persons without legal personality as well as in audiovisual works shall be counted from the completion of the work. whereas the protection term of the economic rights will continue to be counted from the date of first publication.

In the past, the very essence of the right to decide on the first publication, which is to allow the author to determine when his creation is ready to go public, has not been commonly understood in China. This is evidenced by the *Li Jiancheng v. Chen Ming* decision of the Chongqing Intermediate People's Court of 24 December 1992,[200] which obviously understood the publication right as a "right to be published", holding that a publisher infringed the plaintiff's moral right because he failed to publish his work, allegedly due to loss of the manuscript. Apparently in order to avoid such

197. Case examples in Chen Ruwen and He Huaiwen, note 195; the authors are fundamentally opposed to "apology", which, if not made voluntarily but ordered by court, would mean nothing but an empty ritual.
198. Beijing Chaoyang District Court decision of 30 December 2019, 10975 *Jing 0105 Min Chu* (2019); Chaoyang District People's Court of 20 November 2019, 12496 *Jing 0105 Min Chu* (2019), https://mp.weixin.qq.com/s/Ze-hXlmQ-QEazZ2SAILcvg; Nanjing Railway Transportation Court decision of 27 July 2017, 669 *Su 8602 Min Chu* (2016), https://mp.weixin.qq.com/s/4lFY6bh4LIiWDbaUh2VicQ.
199. Li Shunde and Zhou Yang, note 78, 69 et seq.
200. 273 *Min Shang Zi* (1992), text of the decision can be downloaded from this site http://www.chncase.cn/case/judge/2083930.

misinterpretations in future, Rule 23 the SPC Copyright Interpretation stipulates that if a publisher cannot publish the entrusted work due to the loss of the manuscript, only the Civil Code's contractual rules and rules concerning the damage to another party's property shall apply.

In a decision that is somewhat similar to the Tokyo High Court's *Mishima Yukio* decision of 2000,[201] the Beijing Intermediate People's Court No. 2[202] ordered a preliminary injunction to stop the auctioning of private letters of a deceased writer at the request of his widow, acknowledging the work character of private letters, the entitlement of the widow as successor of the author to protect his moral right on his behalf and the urgency of the claim that gave raise to preliminary measures to avert irreparable damage to the plaintiff.

(b) Authorship Right

Article 10(1) No. 2 Copyright Law regulates the authorship right, which is defined as the right to claim authorship in respect of and to have the author's name mentioned in connection with the work. Even though not explicitly mentioned, the right to be indicated as author includes the right to determine the manner of indication, for instance, under a pseudonym, and to decide whether or not to be indicated.[203] Article 11 Copyright Law contains an assumption rule, according to which in the absence of proof to the contrary, the citizen, legal entity or other organisation whose name is indicated on the work shall be deemed to be the author. Rule 13 of the Implementing Regulations stipulates quite uniquely that where the identity of the author is not clear, the owner of the work original shall be entitled to exercise copyright except for the authorship right, and that once the author has become known, copyright shall revert to the author or his successors. The provision may be understood as a rudimentary regulation of orphan works, ascertaining that at least where a meaningful exploitation of the work original is possible, which would mostly be the case in the area of fine arts, the owner of the original shall temporarily exercise copyright in lieu of the unknown author. Rule 18 Implementing Regulations further provides that the exploitation rights in anonymous works shall be protected for 50 years from the first publication, which, however, will be extended to 50 years *post mortem* if the author becomes known, both terms expiring on 31 December of the 50th year.

In comparison with the other moral rights, the authorship right is the one which is most closely connected to the author, since it remains with him also in cases where all other rights are attributed to the film producer or the employing entity (Articles 15, 16(2) of the current Copyright Law, Articles 17, 18(2) after the third amendment's entry into force).

The Copyright Law also addresses an aspect of authorship attribution that, strictly speaking, has little to do with copyright in the meaning of protecting the author and his relation to the work he created, namely false attribution of authorship to a person who is not the actual author of the work. Remedies against

201. Decision of 23 May 2000, 1725 *Hanrei Jihō*, 165.
202. 09727 *Er Zhong Bao Zi*, summarized in English in WIPO Collection of Leading Judgments on Intellectual Property Rights, note 90, pp.89 et seq.
203. Li Shunde and Zhou Yang, note 78, 71.

such misrepresentation[204] are regulated in Chapter V Copyright Law on copyright enforcement. Pursuant to Article 48 No. 8 of the current Copyright Law (Article 53 No. 8 after the third amendment's entry into force) "producing or selling a work with the counterfeit signature of another person" calls for civil liability, in severe cases even for administrative or criminal consequences, which are further regulated in Article 217 of the Criminal Law of 1997. The Shanghai Higher People's Court had applied this provision, which was formerly contained in Article 46 No. 7 of the pre-2001 Copyright Law in its "Portrait of *Mao Zedong*" decision, which held that attributing the portrait to the plaintiff, a famous painter, whereby it was actually created by another person, violated the Copyright Law.[205] The 2001 amendment to the Copyright Law extended this provision, which was previously restricted to works of the fine arts, to all work categories. But even before the amendment, Article 99 of the General Provisions of Civil Law, which prohibited the misappropriation of a person's name could be applied to cases in which authorship was falsely attributed to other kinds of works, for example, to literary works.[206]

(c) Right to Amend the Own Work

Article 10(1) No. 3 Copyright Law provides for a quite unique moral right, namely the right of the author to amend his own work and to authorize others to do so. Even though at first glance this appears as a right to preserve the work's integrity, it means something different, namely a right of the author to amend his work at his own initiative, for instance if he is no longer satisfied with its content.[207] In this sense, it is sometimes interpreted as a partial compensation for the absence of a right to recall the work, which was not incorporated into the Copyright Law out of concerns that a total work recall may cause huge losses to the exploiter.[208] The right to amend one's own work therefore appears to be a halfway solution. The author may invoke it, for instance, if he has already submitted a manuscript to a publisher and thereby given his consent to have it published but then finds a mistake or wants to have it altered for other reasons, but not after the publication. The right to amend the work may furthermore be invoked against a publisher who reprinted or republished a work without having notified the author as prescribed in Article 32(3) of the current Copyright Law (Article 34(3) after the third amendment's entry into

204. This provision is not a Chinese particularity, however. Article 84 of the British Copyright, Designs and Patent Act, for example, contains a similar provision. Also, pursuant to Article 121 of the Japanese Copyright Act, false attribution of authorship forms a punishable act.

205. Decision of 11 March 1996, 2 *Gazette of the SPC* (1996), 67; commented by Adolf Dietz in *GRUR Int.* (1997), 850.

206. Decision of the People's Court of the Lianhu District of the City of Xi'an, reported by Shen Rengan, 'A Brief Discussion on the Rights of Authorship', 4 *China Patents & Trademarks* (1997), 64.

207. Wang Guang, 'Lun xiugaiquan he baohu zuopin wanzheng quan' (Discussion on the revision right and the right to preserve the work's integrity), 2 *Zhuzuoquan* (1993), 21; the distinction between these two moral rights is also difficult in judicial practice, see Anhui Higher People's Court decision of 14 March 2003, 3 *Wan Min San Zhing Zi* (2003), https://www.66law.cn/topic2010/zpfbqjf/65892.shtml.

208. Wei Zhi, note 7, 67 et seq.

force) and thereby deprived him of the opportunity to update the work or to make other amendments.[209] Pursuant to the current Article 20 Copyright Law (Article 22 after the third amendment's entry into force), also the right to amend the own work is unlimited in time, and Rule 15 Implementing Regulations stipulates that it shall be protected by the deceased author's successors or legatee, which, for instance, would mean that they are entitled to amend the deceased author's literary work in a manner that would have corresponded to his will if he were still alive if a new edition of his literary work is due.

The 2014 Copyright Law draft amendment suggested the abolishment of this peculiar moral right, respective to subsume it under an enlarged right to preserve the work integrity, which, apart from the right to prohibit distortions and mutilations of the work, would then also have included a right to allow others to amend the work. The final amendment however, did not adopt this stipulation which would have been even more confusing than the present provisions, as it implied that the author could dispose of his integrity right by licensing others to amend his work.

(d) Right of Integrity

The integrity right granted in Article 10(1) No. 4 Copyright Law goes beyond the standards set by the Berne Convention, since it allows authors to proceed against any distortions or mutilations of their works and not only against acts which are prejudicial to honour and reputation. An integrity right infringement that simultaneously damages the reputation or honour of the author can, however, add to the gravity of infringement.[210] Reportedly, the main motive behind this rather strong right is to facilitate the judicial handling of disputes, as courts only need to determine whether the work integrity as such has been impaired in that the altered version no longer represents what the author originally wanted to express, without having to investigate whether the distortion is simultaneously prejudicial to the author's honour or reputation.[211] Some authors nevertheless prefer to interpret the law as requiring a damage to the author's reputation as prerequisite for an integrity right infringement,[212] but the landmark "Nine-level monster tower" decision of the

209. Zheng Chengsi and Michael Pendleton, *Copyright Law in China* (North Ryde et al., 1991), 91.

210. So stipulated by the Higher People's Court of Anhui province in its decision of 14 March 2003, note 207.

211. Zhang Dongmei, 'Tongshi qinfan baohu zuopin wanzheng quan yu mingyuquan, ruhe rending yu chuli' (On the question of how to determine and how to treat the simultaneous infringement of the right to preserve the integrity of the work and of the reputation right), 6 *Zhongguo Banquan* (2002), 25: the author quotes a decision of Higher People's Court of the City of Beijing, which held a publisher who placed a photographic work in a context not desired by the author liable for infringement of the integrity right.

212. Wang Qing, 'Baohu zuopin wanzhengquan de yousun shengyu yaojian: shiran yu yingran "Jiuceng Yaota" an er shen panjue yinfa de sikao' (The requirement of reputation damage as prerequisite for the protection of the integrity right – thoughts inspired by the second-instance decision in the "nine level monster tower" case), 1 *Dianzi zhishi chanquan* (Electronics Intellectual Property) (2020), 70 et seq.

Beijing Intellectual Property Court[213] thwarted such ideas, explicitly stating that the infringement of the integrity right, here by modifying a literary work when adapting it to a cinematographic work, did not depend on a simultaneous prejudice to the author's reputation.

Whereas the Copyright Law is silent on possible limitations to this quite comprehensive integrity right, Rule 10 of the current Implementing Regulations contains one special limitation with regard to works incorporated in cinematographic works in order to secure their smooth exploitation. Accordingly, the permission of the "copyright owner" (i.e., not necessarily the immediate author) to use his work for the production of a cinematographic work implies the consent to make the necessary modifications. However, these may not distort or mutilate the work. The borderline between a permissible modification and a prohibited distortion or mutilation may be drawn by the term "necessary", in the sense that only modifications which are indispensable to enable the film production and exploitation are permitted. Case law that would allow modifications also with regard to other work categories if, for instance, deemed necessary to achieve the aim of the assignment or licencing contract, could not be found.

Marginal alterations to the work that do not change its main content, e.g., the removal of ink spots between the characters of a calligraphic work, are not regarded as infringement of the integrity right.[214]

As an exemption from the integrity right rather than from the above right to amend one's own work, newspaper or periodical publishers are permitted to correct or to abridge contributions without the author's consent. For modifications of the content, however, they need to obtain the author's permission (Article 34(2) Copyright Law). Revisions of works published in books are only permissible with the author's consent (Article 34(1) Copyright Law). The third Copyright Law amendment moved the content of the current Article 34 to Article 36 but left it otherwise unchanged.

2. Economic Rights

As mentioned, the catalogue of copyright exploitation rights in Article 10(1) No. 5 to 17 Copyright Law is non-exhaustive, covering any other, not yet itemized form of exploitation. Copyright exploitation rights of authors are granted for a term of 50 years *post mortem* (Article 21(1) of the current Copyright Law, Article 23(1) after the third amendment's entry into force). An exception are cinematographic works and photographic works, which according to the current Article 21(3) are only protected for 50 years after publication, provided that they are published within 50 years from creation. As mentioned, after the third amendment's entry into force, the provision, which has been moved to Article 23(3), will no longer cover photographic works, so that only the economic rights in cinematographic works (henceforth: "audiovisual works") will be protected from the publication date, whereas the term of protection for photographic works will be counted from the author's dead. If the copyright is owned by a legal person or another organization, the protection term is counted from

213. 587 *Jing 73 Min Zhong* (2016).

214. Beijing Intermediate People's Court decision of 16 December 2003, 10610 *Er Zhong Min Zhong Zi* (2003), https://www.66law.cn/topic2010/zpfbqjf/65894.shtml.

the first publication of the work, provided that such publication does not take place later than 50 years from the creation (Article 21(2) of the current Copyright Law).

As also mentioned, Article 23(2) of the amended Copyright Law, which will henceforth accommodate this provision, stipulates that the publication right enjoyed by the legal person or organization without legal personality shall be protected for a term of 50 years from the completion of the work, whereas the protection term of the economic rights shall continue to be counted from the date of publication. According to the new Article 23(3), the same applies to the 50-years protection term of the publication right and the economic rights in audiovisual works. In all these cases, the protection term expires on 31 December of the 50th year.

Although copyright exploitation rights are simply enumerated, the order of their enumeration implies three categories of exploitation, namely exploitation in material form (reproduction, distribution, rental, exhibition), exploitation by communication to the public (performance, visual presentation, broadcasting, internet transmission), exploitation in the form of adaptation (cinematography, adaptation, translation),[215] and, unique to China, a right to authorize the compilation of the own work or parts of it into a new work.

(a) Rights to Exploit the Work in Material Form

(1) Reproduction Right

According to the legal definition in Article 10(1) No. 5 Copyright Law, a reproduction means one or more copies of a work by printing, photocopying, lithographing, making a sound recording or video recording, duplicating a recording, or duplicating a photographic work or by any other means. The number of copies is of no relevance - a single copy can be considered a reproduction the sense of copyright, which is relevant especially for the protection of architectural works.[216] As already mentioned in connection with graphic works, the copyright relevant reproduction was extended to reproduction in the form of modelling a three-dimensional item out of a two-dimensional plan.[217] Moreover, as seen in connection with the *Zongren* bristle dolls case,[218] the judiciary also regards the two-dimensional graphic or photographic representations of three-dimensional objects as copyright-relevant reproductions.

Since the Copyright Law amendment of 2001, one form of copying, namely *linmo* in the meaning of imitating works of the fine arts and calligraphic works by hand, is no longer specified as a copyright-relevant, maybe due to criticism that this form of copying represented a traditional art form that required a high degree of sophistication and personal skill and went far beyond a mere mechanical reproduction in the copyright sense. However, as the possible forms of reproduction are not exhaustively enumerated, *linmo* transcriptions which have the same effect as a

215. Adopted for example by Wei Zhi, note 7, 69 et seq.
216. Wei Zhi, note 7, 69.
217. IV. 1. *supra*.
218. IV. 2. (f) *supra*.

mechanical infringement in that they clearly prejudice the interests of the author of the original, should not be categorically excluded from prosecution as infringing acts.[219]

Interestingly, Article 47 No. 5 Copyright Law (Article 52 No. 5 after the third amendment's entry into force) lists "plagiarizing another person's work" as an act that gives rise to civil liability. "Plagiarism" is a common term and hard to grasp under copyright exploitation rights. It may best be categorised under the authorship right because it normally involves the misrepresentation of another person's work as one's own work. In Chinese copyright terms, "plagiarism" seems to mean something different, however, namely an infringement of the reproduction right or of the adaptation right. In a decision of 5 June 2017, the Beijing Intellectual Property Court found not enough substantial similarity between the plaintiff's cartoon characters and the defendant's allegedly infringing characters to establish infringement in the form of "plagiarism", in the same manner as it would have examined the cartoons of both parties to find out whether the reproduction right or the adaptation right of the plaintiff had been infringed.[220] This becomes obvious from a decision of the Jiangsu Higher People's Court of 30 August 2016 pertaining to infringement of copyright in furniture as works of applied art, in which the court carried out a very similar comparison as to "substantial similarity" to find infringement of the reproduction right and, subsequently, of the distribution right according to Article 10(1) No. 5 and No. 6 Copyright Law, not infringement in form of plagiarism.[221]

One important issue is not addressed by the present copyright provisions, namely whether the transient storage of digital contents in the course of internet transmission, etc., forms a copyright relevant reproduction. Concerning search engines, two older decisions of the People's Court of the Haidian District of Beijing found that such transient reproductions were no reproductions in the sense of copyright.[222] In the absence of any specific limitation rules exempting from the reproduction right forms of reproduction which are part of a technical process, enable the normal use, have no significant economic meaning, etc., this restrictive interpretation seems to be the only plausible one, otherwise the reproduction right may be abused to prevent legitimate uses. On the other hand, a more generous definition of copyright-relevant

219. In an administrative copyright case, the Shanxi Province Copyight Administration Authority regarded the production of calligraphic *linmo* without authorisation of the original calligraphers as an infringing reproduction: reported by Wang Zhongqiu, 'Falü ying jiyu linmo shufa beike zuozhe fuzhiquan' (The law must acknowledge a reproduction right of the author of imitations of Ccalligraphic works), 3 *Zhuzuoquan* (1993), 49; see also Zheng Chengsi, 'Linmo, duchuangxing yu banquan baohu' (Linmo, originality and copyright orotection), 2 *Faxue yanjiu* (1996), 77 (an English version of the same article can be found in 1 *China Patent & Trademarks* (1997), 44); Zheng Chengsi, '"Linmo" yu "fuzhi" shifo ying dengtong?' (Are "linmo" and "reproduction" the same?), 4 *Zhuzuoquan* (1996), 3.

220. 1078 *Jing 73 Min Zhong* (2016), https://mp.weixin.qq.com/s/OMD26sS6-PGe6vG7066xLA; see also https://www.sohu.com/a/158059081_196394.

221. 00085 *Su Zhi Min Zhong Zi* (2015), https://mp.weixin.qq.com/s/KBc9UQbPanXcVKg SU8otnQ.

222. Decisions 21 and 22 June 2001, reported by Feng Gang, 'Sheji sousuo yinqing de qinfan zhuzuoquan jiufen yanjiu' (studies on copyright infringement cases related to search engines), 3 *Zhongguo Banquan* (2002), 26.

reproductions also covering transient copies in certain cases, accompanied by adequate limitations, may help to protect live sports broadcasts against unauthorized real-time streaming.[223]

The question of how to deal with the defendant's counterclaim that he has not copied the plaintiff's work but created a very similar or identical work on his own has been answered in a decision that dealt with the cinematography right, but its findings should also be applicable to the reproduction right. Accordingly, such counterclaim shall be rejected if it can be proven the alleged infringer has had the opportunity to get in touch with the plaintiff's work, which is normally given if the latter has been publicly accessible before the defendant reproduced it or, as in the present case, adapted it by way of cinematography. Firm proof that the defendant actually had accessed the work is not required.[224]

(2) Distribution Right

Article 10(1) No. 6 Copyright Law defines the distribution right as the right to offer the original or reproductions of the work to the public by way of sale or donation. The rental right is regulated separately.[225] An importation right is not explicitly mentioned, but border protection of intellectual property, which will be treated in more detail in this book's part on enforcement, extends to the prevention not only of the import but also of the export of copyright infringing items. Also, at least with regard to works created by foreigners, the International Implementation Regulations stipulate that foreign authors shall be protected not only against the import of infringing reproductions of their works but also against the import of reproductions from countries in which their copyright is not protected (Rule 15). That foreigners enjoy an importation right in these two specific cases implies that a third kind of import, namely parallel imports of reproduction first sold abroad with the foreign copyright owner's consent, is permitted. Consequently, as the Implementation Regulations lean towards the international exhaustion doctrine with regard to works of foreigners, Chinese nationals, who are protected on an even lower level, should *a fortiori* be deprived of a right to control parallel imports of copies of their works. Whereas the Patent Law contains a clear provision on international patent exhaustion, corresponding provisions were neither introduced in the course of the second Copyright Law amendment of 2010 nor in the course of the two Trade Mark Law amendments to the Trade Mark Law of 2014 and 2019, and neither has the third Copyright Law amendment clarified this matter.

Also case law is silent on another exhaustion issue, namely whether the copyright in books, videos, etc., sold online exhausts upon first sale, which would be a question of the scope of the internet transmission right rather than of the right

223. See IV. 2. (a) *supra*.
224. Beijing Haidian District People's Court decision of 14 June 2019, 17683 *Jing 0108 Min Chu* (2018), https://mp.weixin.qq.com/s/PXGHEzfikK4JMzGaDflY6A; Hangzhou Internet Court decision of 13 June 2019, 6851 *Zhe 0192 Min Chu* (2018), https://mp.weixin.qq.com/s/-n2w6L7gYi0mlqr3oL2iQQ.
225. More detailed explanations in (3) *infra*.

to distribute physical copies anyway. It is debated in academic circles,[226] but mostly with reference to foreign law, in particular the diverging decisions reached by the United States District Court for the Southern District of New York in the *ReDigi* case[227] and by the European Court of Justice in the *UsedSoft* case.[228]

(3) Rental Right

The separate mention of the rental right as a right to authorize others to temporarily use the work clarifies its special character as an exemption to the exhaustion principle. In contrast to the pre-2001 Copyright Law which granted the rental right as a subcategory of the distribution right in all kinds of works, the present Article 10(1) No. 7 restricts the rental right to cinematographic works and computer software, so that it only meets the minimum standards set by TRIPS and the WCT. With regard to computer software, the same provision clarifies that the software must be the essential subject matter of rental. The Copyright law draft amendments of 2020 propose a clarification that the rental right shall be granted in reproductions of the cinematographic work or the software work, i.e., the original and copies of it.

A rental right is also granted to producers of phonograms and audiovisual recordings (Article 42(1) of the current Copyright Law. After the third amendment's entry into force, Article 39(1) No.5 will also grant a rental right to performers, not only in performances fixed in phonograms as required by the WPPT but also in video recorded performances. An addition to the amended Article 44(2) (Article 42(2) of the current Copyright Law), furthermore, stipulates that parties who received a licence from the producer to rent the audio or video recording of a performance shall also seek the performer's permission and remunerate him.[229]

(4) Exhibition Right

Article 10(1) No. 8 Copyright Law defines the exhibition right as the right to publicly display the original or copies of a work of the fine arts or a photographic work. One distinctive feature of the exhibition right in the case of works of fine arts is that

226. *See*, e.g., Gui Shuang, 'Shuzi wangluo huanjing xia faxingquan yongjin yuanze tantao dui "ReDigi" an he "usedsoft" an de sikao' (Thoughts about *ReDigi* and *UsedSoft* with regard to the doctrine of distribution right exhaustion within the digital network environment), 3 *Dianzi zhishi chanquan* (Electronics Intellectual Property) (2015), 55 et seq.; Chen Qiaoqiao, 'Dianzi chubanwu ershou shichang cunzai de helixing yu kexingxing' (On the appropriateness and practicabilty of a second-hand market for digital publications), 2 *Lingnan Shifan Xueyuan Xuebao* (Lingnan Normal University Journal) (2016), 33 et seq.; see also Deng Xinxin, 'Shuzi zuopin zhuanshou xingwei de zhuzuoquanfa guizhi – jianlun shuzi faxingquan youxian yongjin yuanze de queli' (Copyright provisions on the transfer of digital works – also on the establishment of a limited exhaustion doctrine with regard to the electronic distribution right), 5 *Fashang Yanjiu* (Studies in Law and Business) (2014), 22 et seq., proposing, *inter alia*, a broader definition of the distribution right so as to include distribution online.

227. *Capitol Records, LLC v. ReDigi Inc.*, 934 F. Supp. 2d 640 (S.D.N.Y. 2013).

228. *UsedSoft v. Oracle* decision of 3 July 2012 (case C-128/11).

229. See X. 2. *infra*.

once the ownership right in the work piece has changed, the new owner shall enjoy the right to exhibit his property. Hereby, Article 18 of the current Copyright Law speaks in a quite undetermined manner of "works of fine art and the like". After the third amendment's entry into force, the provision, which has been transferred to Article 20, will stipulate that the transfer of ownership in the original of any kind of work, no longer of "works of fine art and the like", shall not entail any changes to copyright ownership but that the owner of the original of a work of fine art as well as of a photographic work (which is probably meant by "and the like" under the current Article 18) shall enjoy the right of exhibition. The amendment furthermore introduced a clarifying second paragraph to Article 20, stipulating that where the author has transferred ownership in the original of an unpublished work of fine art or photographic work, the owner may exhibit it without infringing upon the publication right.

Article 22(1) No. 10 of the current Copyright Law stipulates that if the owner decides to exhibit the work at an outdoor public place, the public may freely copy the work, make *linmo* drawings of it, photograph or make video recordings of it. After the third amendment's entry into force, the prerequisite that the work must be exhibited "outdoors" will fall away (Article 24(1) No. 10 of the amended Copyright Law) so that *linmo* drawings, etc., can also be made of works exhibited in publicly accessible indoor locations.

(b) Rights in Communication to the Public

(1) Right of Public Performance, Including Mechanical Performance

Article 10(1) No. 9 Copyright Law defines the performance right as the right to authorize the live performance of the work and the right to transmit the performance to the public by any means. "Means" are not restricted to the communication of the live performance to a broader public, for example, with help of loudspeakers, but also covers the playing of sound recordings in discotheques and the like.

(2) Right of Showing

The right of showing mentioned in Article 10(1) No. 10 refers to the right to play images of works, especially of works of fine arts, photographic works, cinematographic works and works created analogous to cinematography, not only by motion pictures but also by projection of still images, or by any other technical means.

In a recent case, a screenwriter asserted in addition to the cinematography right in Article 10(1) No. 13 the right of showing his screenplay that had been incorporated in a cinematographic work without his authorization. The court did not find infringement at all, however, and left the question whether the author of the literary work adapted into a cinematographic work without his authorization could not only proceed against the cinematography but also against the subsequent exploitation of such film work unanswered.[230] As will be explained below with regard to the various rights of adaptation, the Copyright Law does not provide the authors of or the owners of the copyright in adapted, translated, etc., works with a general right to join in the exploitation of the adaptations.

(3) *Broadcasting Right*

The current Copyright Law regulates a quite comprehensive concept of "broadcasting", which includes broadcast or otherwise dissemination to the public by wireless means, the public communication of the broadcast work by wire or by wireless rebroadcast, and the public communication of the broadcast work by loudspeaker or similar facilities of transmitting signals, sounds or images (Article 10(1) No.11). The third Copyright Law amendment introduced a simpler definition. "Broadcast" shall henceforth be the transmission or retransmission of a work by wire or by wireless means (and its communication to the public by loudspeaker or similar means of transmitting signals, sounds or images). That is, the transmission by wire will be treated equal to wireless transmission and no longer be regarded as a means of re-transmitting a wirelessly broadcast work. An online service that enables TV viewers to replay and to repeatedly watch received broadcast content goes beyond the scope of the broadcasting right. It instead interferes with the network transmission right as defined by Article 10 No. 12 Copyright Law (see below).[231] Also, the simultaneous online streaming of a broadcast work is not tantamount to a rebroadcast, even though it has the same effect on the recipient, as has been explained in connection with cinematographic works.[232]

In the past, the broadcasting right, especially of music authors, was severely limited by Article 43 of the previous Copyright Law, which left the radio broadcast of already published phonograms completely copyright free. In the course of the 2001 reform, however, this limitation was changed into a legal licence, so that authors now at least enjoy a remuneration right.[233]

(4) *Network Transmission Right*

Since 2001, the Copyright Law provides an "network transmission right", which is defined as the right to make the work available to the public through information networks, so that the members of the public have access to it from a location and at a time individually chosen by them (Article 10(1) No. 12 Copyright Law). Even though at first glance the act of "transmitting" the work appears to be the act relevant to that right, the definition clarifies that it refers to the "making available to the public", that is, holding a work uploaded on a server ready for individual access. This is also clarified by Rule 3 of the SPC Network Interpretation, according to which

230. Bejing Intellectual Property Court decision of 22 September 2019, 1117 *Jing 73 Min Zhong* (2017), https://mp.weixin.qq.com/s/VTTbYoCpONbLAPYVpuVESQ.

231. Beijing Intellectual Property Court decision of 20 January 2020, 3778 *Jing 73 Min Zhong* (2019), https://mp.weixin.qq.com/s/Cg6W0aBq-sAqiWWUwFbf2g.

232. IV. 2. (a) *supra*.

233. See VII. 2. (d) *infra*.

the network transmission right is infringed if the work or other protected content is made available on the web, *inter alia*, by uploading it on a server, by setting up shared files or by using filesharing software so as to enable individual members of the public to obtain these works by downloading, browsing or other means at a time and place chosen by themselves.

According to a decision of the Beijing Intellectual Property Court of 21 October 2016,[234] providing links to content that has been legally uploaded on the plaintiff's website does not constitute infringing internet transmission. Hereby the court referred to the above Rule 3 of the SPC Network Interpretation, according to which a transmission to the public can only be made by uploading or otherwise connecting a work with the internet so as to put it in a state that it can be publicly accessed, but not by providing links to content that is already online available. This applies only to links provided to legally uploaded works, however. Providing links to infringingly uploaded content can give rise to civil, even criminal liability.[235] The decision overturned the preceding Beijing Haidian District People's Court's decision which held the defendant liable for infringement due to his efforts to organize and classify on his own site the content to which he provided the links (allegedly, he even circumvented the plaintiff's technical protection measures to obtain access to the linked content), the enlargement of the circle of users having access to the work and the independent economic importance of the linking with the potential to cause damage to the plaintiff's economic interests. The Beijing Intellectual Property Court's decision, however, rejected all these concerns as irrelevant quite similar to the *Svensson* decision of the European Court of Justice,[236] which even denied frame linking (i.e., embedding the linked content in the own website) the character of communication to the public.

The Copyright Law is, moreover, void of any specific provisions on the liability of internet service providers for hosting contents uploaded by their clients, even after its third amendment. A legal basis for establishing liability of service providers for any kind of tort committed by their clients is contained in the mentioned Articles 1194-1197 of the Civil Code, which replaced the . much more generally worded single Article 36 of the former Tort Liability Law. Two provisions on a lower level in the norm hierarchy, the administrative Internet Regulations and the judicial Network Interpretations, provide further details specifically with regard to service provider liability for copyright infringement.[237]

Finally, it seems that infringements of the internet transmission right, which can easily result in huge economic losses, enhanced the popularity of interim injunctions, an instrument which is otherwise rarely applied, most likely due to high procedural hurdles.[238] Recently, however, the SPC demonstrated a certain eagerness to include

234. 143 *Jing 73 Min Zhong* (2016) (http://blog.sina.com.cn/s/blog_6e3ff8d00102xrf5.html), comparatively commented by Szu-Ting Chen, 'Providing Hyperlinks to Watch Illegal Videos on YouTube Does not Communicate Works to the Public in Taiwan', in Kung-Chung Liu (ed.), *Annotated Leading Copyright Cases in Major Asian Jurisdictions* (City University of Hong Kong Press, 2019), 54 et seq.
235. See XI. 4. *infra*.
236. C-466/12.
237. Explained in detail in XI. 2. *infra*.
238. An overview is given by Peter Ganea, note 60.

cases in which interim injunctions play a central role in its various collections of landmark intellectual property cases. For instance, three out of six copyright cases published in the *Collection of Leading Judgments on Intellectual Property Rights – People's Republic of China (2011–2018)* that the SPC co-edited with WIPO in 2019[239] deal with interim injunctions. One such injunction had been issued by the Wuhan Intermediate People's Court[240] against a cloud music platform which disseminated allegedly pirated music through its services. The court justified the issuance of a desist order mostly with the likelihood of substantial damage to the requesting party due to the rapidly growing web coverage of the respondent's service. Quite instructive with regard to the factors to be considered before issuing an interim injunction was the Guanghzou Intellectual Property Court's *Blizzard* decision of 9 March 2015[241] pertaining to the web dissemination of a plagiarized version of the famous computer game *World of Warcraft*, stating that, *inter alia*, the likelihood that the requesting party will win the case and the danger of irreparable harm shall be considered. In this case, the court considered the potential harm as especially high because the respondent had used obscenities in the advertisement of his game version, which bore the danger of additional damage to the requesting parties' reputation.

It should also be noted in this context that the Copyright Law draft amendment of April 2020 deleted all provisions on pre-trial injunctions and evidence preservation measures, which are currently regulated in Articles 50 and 51 of the Copyright Law with reference to an older version of the Code of Civil Procedure that is no longer in force and regulating an outdated period of 15 days from the date of evidence preservation measure in which the requesting party has to file suit (current Civil Procedures Law: 30 days). The latest draft of August 2020 and finally also the third amendment, however, readopted the two provisions on pre-trial measures and pre-trial evidence preservation in Articles 56 and 57, but in a more general wording without determining time limits, etc., which would henceforth be governed by the Code of Civil Procedure and judicial interpretations.

(c) Adaptation Right, Cinematography Right and Translation Right

A third bundle of rights are "adaptation rights" to exploit a work by way of changing its mode of expression, which, in China, apart from a general adaptation right, also include the cinematography right and the translation right.

(1) General Adaptation Right

According to Article 10(1) No. 14 Copyright Law, adaptation means the creation of a new and creative work by adapting a pre-existing work. A general right of the owner of the copyright in the original work that is subject to adaptation to participate in the

239. Available in hardcopy or downloadable from https://www.wipo.int/publications/en/details.jsp?id=4477.

240. 00005 *E Wu Han Zhing Zhi Jin Zi* (2014), summarized in English in WIPO Collection of Leading Judgments on Intellectual Property Rights, note 90, 93 et seq.

241. 2-1 *Yue Zhi Fa Zhu Min Chu Zi* (2015), summarized in English in WIPO Collection of Leading Judgments on Intellectual Property Rights, note 90, 98 et seq.

exploitation of the adaptation is not mentioned, Article 12 relates the owner of the copyright in the original work to the exploitation of the adaptation only insofar as it prohibits exploitations that are prejudicial to his copyright. However, as mentioned, in three more specific instances the owner of the copyright in the original work has a say in the exploitation of the adaptation, in that publishers, performers or producers of sound or video recordings have to seek his permission and remunerate him before they can publish, perform or record the adaptation (Articles 35, 37(2), 40(2) Copyright Law). As also mentioned, these rights of the original owner have been bundled and expanded in a new Article 16.

The holder of an exclusive licence to adapt the work, e.g., by transforming a literary work into an online mobile phone game displaying the characters, scenery and other features of the original work, is entitled to sue in his own name against the unauthorized adaptation of the same literary work by transforming it into another online game, whereby the infringed rights are the adaptation right exclusively licensed to him and the right to transmit online the content that is covered by the exclusive licence.[242]

Subject matter of a copyright relevant adaptation can only be that part of the original work that expresses the author's originality. In its decision of 13 June 2019,[243] the Hangzhou Internet Court clarified with regard to the adaptation of a novel series that the original author's writing style, the general story theme and the macro context, e.g., the historical context of the story, pertained to non-protected subject matter and their imitation alone would not infringe upon the adaptation right. Copyright protected would be the expression, meaning a specific plot, characters and their relationship as well as the personal features of the characters, and the language used to express them would be the protected "expression". In a similar manner, albeit not expressly with regard to the adaptation right, the SPC in its judgment of 28 November 2014[244] stated that the historical events, etc. on which the plaintiff's literary work was based shall belong into the public domain and that others shall be free to resort to them as basis for their own independent works. Copyright protection shall be limited to what has been individually expressed by the author.

(2) Cinematography Right

Article 10(1) No. 13 Copyright Law defines the right of cinematography quite technically, namely as "right to fixate a work on a medium with help of cinematography or any other means analogous to cinematography", a wording that rather hints at a right to reproduce the work by audiovisual fixation. Such wording may have prompted some courts to treat, e.g., the alleged transformation of a screenplay into an audiovisual work, as an undetermined form of work exploitation ("any other rights copyright owners are entitled to enjoy" according to Article 10(1) No. 17)

242. Beijing IP Court decision of 14 January 2020, 1410 *Jing 73 Min Zhong* (2019), https://mp.weixin.qq.com/s/nvHjU46MFAVHdhfS-jPHTw.
243. 6851 *Zhe 0192 Min Chu* (2018), https://mp.weixin.qq.com/s/-n2w6L7gYi0mlqr3oL2iQQ.
244. 1049 *Min Shen Zi* (2013), summarized in the WIPO Collection of Leading Judgments on Intellectual Property Rights, note 90, p.77 et seq. in the English version.

rather than to subsume it under the cinematography right.[245] As mentioned, Rule 10 Implementing Regulations facilitates exploitation by way of cinematography, stipulating that once the owner of the copyright in the pre-existing work has permitted adaptation by cinematography, he shall be deemed to have also consented in the necessary alterations, which, however, shall not go so far to distort or mutilate the original work. The term "owner of the copyright" is broader than "author", so that theoretically also economic entities to whom copyright in the pre-existing work has been assigned by contract or by law come into question as parties who have to accept necessary alterations while being entitled to object to distortions and mutilations.

In separately regulating cinematography as a special form of adaptation, China followed the Berne Convention, which in Article 12 regulates the general adaptation right and in Article 14 the special right of adaptation by cinematography. However, in contrast to the Berne Convention, the Chinese provisions do not clarify that the cinematography right does not only include the right to adapt the work by cinematography, but also the right to permit the exploitation of the cinematographic adaptation, especially in form of distribution, performance, public communication and further adaptation.

An adaptation by cinematography is at least given if the cinematographic work expresses both the storyline and the characters of the original work.[246] Due to its specific audiovisual expression form that allows for a broader variety of means to render a work perceivable than just by words, a cinematographic adaptation necessarily contains elements that are not part of the original literary work.[247]

(3) Translation Right

Article 10(1) No. 15 Copyright Law defines the translation right as right to translate the original language of the work into another language. Article 12 Copyright Law grants the translator a dependent copyright in his translation, but simultaneously obliges him to respect the copyright in the translated work. With regard to computer programs, Rule 8(1) No. 8 Software Regulations defines the translation right as translating the original software from one natural language or code system into another.

According to the current Copyright Law, the owner of the copyright in a translated work enjoys the right to permit the publication, the performance and the sound or video recording of the translation and to obtain a remuneration for such uses, in case of performances also directly from the performer, just as the owner of the copyright in an adapted work (Articles 35, 37(2), 40(2) of the current Copyright Law). As mentioned, the third Copyright Law amendment has abolished these separate provisions and bundled and expanded the rights of the original author to permit the use of adaptations of his work and to get remunerated in a new Article 16.

245. Bejing Intellectual Property Court decision of 22 September 2019, 1117 *Jing 73 Min Zhong* (2017); on the other hand, the Beijing Haidian District People's Court decision 17683 *Jing 0108 Min Chu* (2018) of 14 June 2019 (https://mp.weixin.qq.com/s/PXGHEzfikK4JMzGaDflY6A) found that the transformation of an autobiographic work into a film work violated the original author's cinematography right.

246. Beijing Haidian District People's Court decision of 14 June 2019, note 245.

247. Stressed by the above Beijing Haidian District People's Court's decision, note 245.

(d) Compilation Right

Article 10(1) No. 16 Copyright Law provides authors with the specific right to authorize the incorporation of the works or parts of it into a creative compilation by selection or arrangement. Article 14 Copyright Law further rules that the copyright in such a creative compilation shall belong to the compiler, provided that its exercise does not prejudice the copyright of the authors of pre-existing works. Also, the original author of a work incorporated in a compilation enjoys the right to permit publishers and performers to publish/perform the compilation and to be remunerated for such use (Articles 35 and 37(2) Copyright Law).

VII. LIMITATIONS AND LEGAL LICENCES

1. Limitations

(a) A China-Specific Fair Use Doctrine?

Article 22(1) of the current Copyright Law lists twelve instances in which a work can be used without permission and without paying remuneration, provided that the author's name and work title are indicated and the other rights enjoyed by the copyright owner according to the Copyright Law are not prejudiced. In addition, Rule 21 of the amended Implementing Regulations stipulates that a use permitted under Copyright Law shall not affect the normal work exploitation and unreasonably prejudice the legitimate interests of the copyright owner, the so-called "three step test" as prescribed by Article 9(2) Berne Convention and later on implemented in Article 13 TRIPS Agreement and Article 10 of the WCT. The third Copyright Law amendments has transferred this stipulation to Article 24(1) Copyright Law, according to which single uses as defined in the subsequent No. 1-13 shall only be allowed if the author's name is indicated, if the normal exploitation of the work is not affected and if the legitimate interests of the right owners are not unreasonably prejudiced, i.e., the three-step-test is now accommodated in Article 24(1) Copyright Law. The stipulation in Article 22(1) of the current Copyright Law that "the other rights enjoyed by the copyright owner according to this law" shall not be prejudiced by otherwise permitted uses has been abolished.

As explained, the 2014 Copyright Law draft amendment proposed the addition of an open clause to the exhaustive list of permitted uses, stipulating "other circumstances" under which a work can be freely used, the latest draft of 2020 withdrew these "other circumstances" and the latest draft of August 2020 re-introduced them but limited them to circumstances explicitly regulated by law or administrative provisions. This last proposal has been adopted by the third Copyright Law amendment. A new No. 13 to the list of special circumstances giving reason to permission and remuneration-free uses, which will henceforth be contained in Article 24(1) Copyright Law, stipulates "other circumstances as defined by law and administrative decree".

A full-fledged fair use clause as envisaged by the 2014 draft would inevitably have alienated the Copyright Law from its Continental European roots and brought it closer to the US copyright tradition. Due to the absence of established, coherent case law on fair use,[248] it would also very likely have entailed legal uncertainty with regard to the scope of permitted uses. On the other hand, courts have already reinterpreted China's limitations regime as allowing a fair use interpretation under consideration of several or all of the factors which are also listed in the fair use-provision in 17 US Code §107.[249] The propensity towards a more flexible limitations regime may have been sparked by newly emerging digital work uses, in particular the transformation of pre-existing works to new creative works by netizens (so-called user generated content).

The decision of the Beijing Intermediary People's Court No. 1 of 10 November 2004 is reported to be one of the first to have applied fair use,[250] stating that the defendant's projection of a painting, its reproduction and the distribution of the copies to specified clients for the purpose of auctioning, were non-infringing uses, which neither affected the normal use of the work nor prejudiced the plaintiff's legitimate interests. Also, in a decision related to the Google Book Project,[251] the Beijing Higher People's Court applied the fair use principles instead of the exhaustive list of permitted uses to assess whether Google's act of reproducing the plaintiff's work and making excerpts of it online available formed copyright infringement. The court finally affirmed infringement but also stated that in principle, fair use would be a valid defence if accompanied by proof that such use is acceptable in the light of its purpose and character and the amount and substantiality of the portion used. The decision may have been influenced by a previous Supreme People's Court's Opinion of 16 December 2011 on Several Issues Related to Fully Enfolding the Effect of Intellectual Property Litigation for a Great Development and Prosperity of the Socialist Culture and for Fostering the Autonomous and Coordinated Economic Development,[252] according to which in the "special case" (obviously meaning the first step of the three-step test) of uses that promote technical innovation and business development, a more flexible limitations regime shall be admissible, provided that the use is appropriate in light of its character and purpose, the kind of the work, the amount and substantiality of the portion used in relation to the work, the effect of the use on the market for the work or on the value of the work and other factors. Furthermore, such use shall not exceed the scope permitted by the steps two and

248. A few courts have already applied a flexible fair use-like interpretation of copyright limitations, but in a rather incoherent manner, see *infra*.

249. Cases until 2011 quoted and explained by Seagull Haiyan Song, 'Reevaluating Fair Use in China – A Comparative Copyright Analysis of Chinese Fair Use Legislation, the U.S. Fair Use Doctrine, and the European Fair Dealing Model', 51 *IDEA* (2011), 453, 453, 480, article online available at https://papers.ssrn.com/sol3/papers.cfm?abstract_id=2118957.

250. 12064 *Yi Zhong Min Chu Zi* (2003), https://www.weibo.com/p/1001603715302755013297; however, the defendant was found liable for the infringement of the author's right to be named.

251. 1221 *Gao Min Zhong Zi* (2013), commented in detail by Sampsung Xiaoxiang Shi and Qian Wang, 'The Google Book Search Project Could Have Qualified as Fair Use in China', in Kung-Chung Liu, note 234, 244 et seq.

252. http://zzzy.chinacourt.gov.cn/article/detail/2013/01/id/1626944.shtml.

three of the three-step test, i.e., it shall not interfere with the normal use of the work and not unreasonably prejudice the right owner's legitimate interests.[253]

Rule 5(2) of the SPC's Network Interpretations is also interpreted as breathing the spirit of fair use. According to this provision, internet service providers who make legally uploaded works publicly available by screenshots as, for instance, Google in its "cached page" service, in form of thumbnails or by other methods, shall not be held liable for infringement if such making available does not interfere with the normal exploitation of the work or unreasonably prejudice the legitimate interest of the right owner.[254] The provision may have been inspired by the Ninth Circuit US Court of Appeals' *Kelly v. Arriba* decision,[255] which found that the display of thumbnail images of copyright protected photographs by a search engine formed fair use, respectively "transformative" use, as the thumbnail images served the purpose of providing information and facilitating searching, which would be different from the purpose of the original work, which is to be aesthetically appreciated by viewers.

On 10 December 2013, the Beijing Intermediate People's Court No. 1 decided that a search engine's continuous caching of a website on which a literary work had been infringingly uploaded even after it had been taken down from that site formed fair use.[256] Hereby, the court did not resort to the above Rule 5(2) of the Network Interpretations but interpreted Rule 21 of the Implementing Regulations on the three-step test in a manner that suited the fair use doctrine, opining that the prerequisites for a permissible use under step two and three (no interference with normal exploitation, no unreasonable damage to the right owner's legitimate interests) were met if such use did not compete with the exploitation of the work in the market place and if the user did not directly earn a profit from it. In the present case, the cached web information in form of still images would not compete with the normal use of the work, and due to the absence of advertisement on the caching site, the defendant did not earn any direct profits. The decision, furthermore, emphasized the public interest, referring to the benefits that caching services brought to the information-seeking general public, which would be jeopardized if its providers were overly burdened with the duty to search their caching inventories for possibly infringing content. Such reference to the public interest is largely compliant with Rule 8 of above-mentioned SPC's Opinion, according to which copyright limitations shall be more generously applied to uses that are beneficial to the advancement of technology and new businesses.

In sum, many courts, above all the SPC, are eager to limit copyright much more generously than arranged for by the present Copyright Law. As explained, however, the drafters the third Copyright Law amendment have turned reluctant towards a

253. Further explanations by Jyh-An Lee, 'Tripartite Perspective on the Copyright-sharing Economy in China', 35:4 *Computer Law & Security Review* (August 2019), 434 et seq.; can be downloaded from https://www.sciencedirect.com/science/article/pii/S0267364919301803#cit_226; translation of the provisions by Sampsung Xiaoxiang Shi and Qian Wang, note 251, 254.
254. Sampsung Xiaoxiang Shi and Qian Wang, note 251, 253.
255. F. 3d 811 (9th Cir. 2003).
256. 12533 *Yi Zhong Min Zhong Zi* (2013), summarized and discussed in detail by Haochen Sun and Johnny Xuyang Han, 'Requirements for Recognizing a New Type of Fair Use under PRC Copyright Law', in Kung-Chung Liu (ed.), note 234, 257 et seq.

full-fledged fair use provision. The "other circumstances" under which a work can be used without permission and without having to pay remuneration according to Article 24(1) No. 13 of the amended Copyright Law can at best be regarded as "fair use light", as they must still be regulated by law, albeit not necessarily by Copyright Law. Their addition obviously aims at facilitating the introduction of new limitations especially by administrative decree whenever deemed necessary. It would also somewhat confirm existing legislation practice. As will be outlined below, Rules 6 and 7 of the Internet Regulations already expanded the scope of certain permission and remuneration free uses from Article 22 Copyright Law (henceforth Article 24 if the present draft becomes law) to facilitate the online use of works. By and large, however, the coming amendment is likely to retain an exhaustive enumeration of single, well-defined limitations and to refrain from a full-fledged US-style fair use provision.

(b) The Catalogue of Permission- and Remuneration-Free Uses

(1) Use for Personal Study

Article 22(1) No. 1 of the current Copyright Law (Article 24(1) No. 1 after the third amendment's entry into force), stipulates that a published work may be used for individual study, research or appreciation. At least according to the wording of this provision, this right seems to be confined to the immediate user. "Private use" would imply a broader application, allowing, for example, more than one work reproduction for distribution among relatives or friends.

(2) Quotations

Article 22(1) No. 2 of the current Copyright Law (Article 24(1) No. 2 after the third amendment's entry into force) allows quotations as a verbatim extract from another person's published work in one's own work for the specific purpose of introducing or commenting on a certain work or explaining a certain topic. Rule 6 No. 1 Internet Regulations clarifies that quotations shall also be possible by internet transmission, i.e., appropriately quoting another person's published work in the own work that has been made available on the internet shall be permissible.

(3) Reporting News on Current Events

Article 22(1) No. 3 of the current Copyright Law allows newspapers, periodicals, broadcasting organizations and "other media", the latter including Internet content providers (which is confirmed by Rule 6 No. 2 of the Internet Regulations), to quote or include a published work in their coverage for the purpose of reporting news on current events, provided that such use is "unavoidable", apparently in the light of the purpose to inform. As mentioned, the third amendment abolished the term "current events" from the provision, which will henceforth be contained in Article 24(1) No. 3, so that henceforth the use of works for the reporting of all kinds of news will be permissible.

(4) *Republishing and Re-broadcasting of Articles*

Article 22(1) No. 4 of the current Copyright Law allows newspapers, periodicals, broadcasters and other media to reprint or rebroadcast material already published in a newspaper or magazine or already broadcast by a broadcasting organization. The amendment of 2001 reduced the scope of what can be freely used in this manner from "editorials or articles" in general to "articles concerning politics, economic and religious questions", to harmonize the limitation with the corresponding provision in Article 10*bis* Berne Convention. The limitation cannot be applied if the author has declared that such use is not permitted. Rule 6 No. 7 of the Internet Regulations allows, in addition, the making available of articles concerning political and economic (but not religious) questions that were already made public on the internet. Rule 10(1) clarifies that the author may object to such use in advance. The third amendment replaced "author" by "copyright owner" in the provision, which will henceforth be contained in Article 24(1) No. 4.

(5) *Publication or Broadcast of Public Speeches*

Article 22(1) No. 5 of the current Copyright Law (Article 22(1) No. 5 after the third amendment's entry into force) permits newspapers, periodicals, broadcasters and other media to reprint or rebroadcast a speech held at a public gathering, except where the author declares that such use is not permitted. Rule 6 No. 8 of the Internet Regulations also permits the making available of speeches delivered to the public but the author may object to the making available (Rule 10(1)).

(6) *Translation and Reproduction for Educational Purposes*

According to Article 22(1) No. 6 of the current Copyright Law, the translation or reproduction of a published work in a limited number of copies by teachers or researchers for the purpose of use in the classroom or for scientific research is permissible, provided that the copies are not published or distributed. Rule 6 No. 3 Internet Regulations adds to this permitted use the permissibility of the internet transmission of small amounts of published works to a limited number of students or scientific researchers for the purpose of classroom teaching or research. It would appear logical to permit such use only in connection with effective technical protection measures to ascertain that the number of work recipients remains controllable. However, Rule 10 No. 4 of the Internet Regulations, which actually prescribes the application of technical protection with regard to other permitted uses, remains silent on this particular limitation. On the contrary, Rule 12 No. 1 Internet Regulations even declares the circumvention of technical protection measures permissible if necessary to enable the making available of works to small number of students or researchers.

The third Copyright Law amendment further enlarged the scope of permitted uses under this limitation, which will henceforth be contained in Article 24(1) No. 6, by "amendment", "compilation" and "transmission".

(7) Use by State Organs for the Fulfilment of Official Tasks

Article 22(1) No. 7 of the current Copyright Law (Article 24(1) No. 7 after the third amendment's entry into force) allows state organs to use published works to fulfil their official duties. Since the 2001 amendment, such use may not go beyond a reasonable scope. State organs include judicial organs, public security organs and other administrations, but not state-run enterprises or education facilities.[257] According to Rule 6 No. 4 of the Internet Regulations, organs may also make works available on the internet to communicate them to the public for the purpose of fulfilling their official tasks. Furthermore, Rule 11 No. 3 permits the circumvention of technical protection measures if necessary to enable such use.

(8) Reproduction and Other Uses by Libraries, etc.

Article 22(1) No. 8 of the current Copyright Law allows libraries, archives, memorial halls, museums, art galleries, etc., to reproduce works that are part of their collections for the purpose of display or preservation. This privileged use has been significantly enhanced by Rule 7 of the Internet Regulations, which allows libraries, etc., to make available to visitors inside their premises legally published digital works that belong to their collection and to digitize works for the purpose of displaying or preserving them. The permission to digitize applies to works the hardcopies of which are damaged or about to be damaged, or which are lost or stolen, or which are stored in an outdated format and are hard to retrieve on the market at a reasonable price, but such use shall not generate direct or indirect profits. Also, the libraries or other institutions may agree otherwise with the authors (or the collecting societies representing them, albeit not explicitly mentioned). Authors cannot object to such uses in advance, but Rule 10 No. 4 of the Internet Regulation prescribes that libraries, etc., shall apply technical protection measures to prevent outsiders from accessing the protected contents and to prevent the recipients of the contents from reproducing them in a manner that jeopardizes the legitimate interests of copyright owners.

The third Copyright Law amendment of August 2020 added "cultural centres" to the institutions privileged by this limitation, which will henceforth be regulated in Article 24(1) No. 8.

(9) Free Live Performances

According to Article 22(1) No. 9 of the current Copyright Law, work performances for which no fees are charged and for which no remuneration is paid to the performers can be conducted without permission and remuneration to the author. Chinese commentators justify this quite broad copyright freedom with the special situation in China's rural areas and the legislator's motive to encourage local performances by artistic troupes, a cultural activity which should counter "unhealthy" leisure time activities of the rural poor, such as gambling.[258] Permission-free is only the

257. Zheng Chengsi and Michael Pendleton, note 209, 159 et seq.
258. Zheng Chengsi and Michael Pendleton, note 209,160.

live performance, but not its further exploitations, e.g., its broadcast.[259] The third Copyright Law amendment has slightly narrowed this limitation, which will henceforth be regulated in Article 24(1) No. 9, by adding another restriction to the above requirements that no fees shall be charged and no remuneration be paid to the performers, namely that the performance shall be for no profit at all.

(10) Copying of Publicly Accessible Objects

Article 22(1) No. 10 of the current Copyright Law allows the copying of exhibited works of fine arts by means of *linmo* copying, drawing, photography or video-recording. As only the above-mentioned forms of reproduction are cited, the three-dimensional modelling of a building from a plan and other forms of reproduction should not fall under this limitation.[260] It has already been mentioned that the third Copyright Law amendment expanded this limitation, which will henceforth be contained in Article 24(1) No. 10, in that it rendered *linmo* copying, etc., of fine art displayed anywhere publicly, not necessarily in outdoor places, permissible.

(11) Translation into Minority Languages

Article 22(1) No. 11 of the current Copyright Law allows domestic publication and distribution of translations of works which are published in *Han* Chinese into China's minority languages. To avoid complaints from abroad, the amended provision confines the subject matter of this limitation to printed matter which is first published by "Chinese nationals, legal persons or other organizations". Moreover, the clarification according to which only works "created" in Chinese and therefore not first created in another language and then translated into and published in Chinese fall under this limitation, was transferred from the Implementing Regulations into the law during the 2001 amendment. Rule 6 No. 5 of the Internet Regulations clarifies that making a work translated in a minority language can be made available to the respective minorities through the internet.

The third Copyright Law amendment has modified this limitation, which will henceforth be contained in Article 24(1) No. 11, insofar as it no longer refers to the translation of published works created in *Han* Chinese but in "standard spoken and written language", which should correspond to the standard language regulated by the Law of the People's Republic of China on Standard Spoken and Written Language" of 31 October 2000.[261] The amendment should have narrowed the previous limitation, as it no longer allows the translation of everything created and published in Chinese, but only of content expressed in standard Chinese and standard characters.

259. Suzhou Intermediate People's Court decision of 1 April 2016, 673 *Su 05 Min Zhong* (2016).
260. Wei Zhi, note 7, 82.
261. http://www.gov.cn/ziliao/flfg/2005-08/31/content_27920.htm.

(12) Making Perceivable for the Visually Disabled

Article 22(1) No. 12 of the current Copyright Law allows the transliteration of published works into Braille and the publication of the Braille version. Rule 6 No. 6 Internet Regulations significantly extends this limitation, by permitting the transformation of published literary works into any format perceivable by blind people, not only Braille, and to make them available on the internet for non-profit purposes. Rule 12 No. 2 even allows the circumvention of technical protection measures to the extent necessary to enable the making available of works to blind people. The extension of the limitation accommodates most but not all requirements of the WIPO Marrakesh Treaty to Facilitate Access to Published Works for Persons Who Are Blind, Visually Impaired, or Otherwise Print Disabled of 2013, which China has signed on 28 June 2013 but not yet ratified, in that, for instance, the circle of beneficiaries is still limited to actually blind people. The third Copyright Law amendment largely adapted this this limitation to the Marrakesh Treaty. The expanded limitation, which has been moved to Article 24(1) No. 12 Copyright Law, stipulates the permission-freedom of the "making available of a published work to visually disabled persons in a format so that they can perceive it".

(13) Circumvention of Technical Protection Measures for Testing Purposes

Rule 12 No. 4 Internet Regulations contains a further limitation that is different from the conventional copyright limitations insofar as it does not permit a specific work use but merely regards an actually unlawful act as permissible under certain circumstances, stipulating that the circumvention of technical protection measures shall be permitted for the purposes of testing the safety function of a computer and its system or network. Not covered by this limitation is offering the circumvention technology or corresponding equipment or parts to third parties.

2. Legal Licences

The main part of the legal licence provisions is contained in the specific provisions on publishing, performance, sound and video recording and broadcasting contracts. The Internet Regulations broadened the scope of permitted uses by extending the ones regulated by the Copyright Law to the internet environment and by adding a new legal licence that allows the internet transmission of certain protected content to the rural poor. Rule 10 clarifies that in any of these cases of permission-free use, the work title and the author's name shall be indicated (No. 2) and that the right holder's other legitimate interests shall not be jeopardized (No. 5).

The 2014 Copyright Law draft amendment proposed a more coherent regime of legal licences, which would also involve collecting societies, *inter alia*, to facilitate the collection of remuneration payments but the two later drafts of 2020 and finally also the third amendment refrained from any changes to the current structure of the Copyright Law.

The present Copyright Law and the Internet Regulations provide for the following six legal licences:

(a) Reprinting of Articles

Article 33(2) of the current Copyright Law (Article 35(2) after the third amendment's entry into force) permits newspaper and periodical publishers to reprint a published newspaper or magazine article, to print an abstract of it or to print it as reference material, provided that the copyright owner is remunerated according to official standards and has not declared in advance that such reprints are not permitted. Rule 30 Implementing Regulations requires such declaration to be made simultaneously with the first publication. Pursuant to Rule 22 Implementing Regulations, the remuneration for such use has to be paid according to official standards, which were first regulated by the Provisional Rules on the Remuneration Standard for the Legal Licence to Reprint or Excerpt from Periodicals enacted by the NCA on 1 August 1993.[262] These seem to have been supplemented by the NCAC's Provisions on the Remuneration for the Publication of Literary Works of 5 April 1999,[263] which regulated the remuneration for reprinting (Rule 18), and were later on fully replaced by a new Method on the Remuneration for the Use of Literary Works of 21 August 2014 jointly enacted by the NCAC and the National Development and Reform Commission (Rule 13 on the remuneration for reprinting).[264] Both the abolished Regulation of 1999 and the Method of 2014 are not limited to remunerations for the legal licence to reprint but regulate further standard fees for uses of literary works that actually require the permission of copyright owners for cases in which the parties have failed to clarify the fees by contract. Rule 13 of the Method stipulates that those who reprint a published literary work under the legal licence shall pay RMB 100 per 1,000 characters (half of that if the number of reprinted characters is lower than 500). The remuneration may alternatively be paid to the China Written Works Copyright Society (CWWCS)[265] along with information on postage and the reprinted work, and the CWWCS will then transfer the remuneration to the respective copyright owner and record its receipt and transfer. Afterwards, the publisher is cleared of any obligation to directly remunerate the copyright owner. Interestingly, the provision is worded as if publishers who want to reprint an article can resort to the CWWCS in any case, irrespective of whether the respective copyright owner is a member of it or not, which would factually entitle the collecting society to represent non-members, albeit extended copyright licensing is nowhere regulated.

When reprinting a contribution to a periodical, the publisher shall also indicate the name of the author and the original source, otherwise the court may order him to eliminate the harmful effects and to issue a public apology (Rule 17 of the SPC Copyright Interpretation).

Rule 3 of the SPC's old Network Interpretations of 2000 interpreted this legal licence very generously, as also allowing the web reprint of articles published in paper form as well as made available on the internet, provided that the copyright owner or the internet service provider who had been entrusted by the copyright owner did not object to such use and that remuneration according to the legal standards was

262. 4 *Zhuzuoquan* (1993), 57.
263. http://project.mofcom.gov.cn/1800000121_23_68561_0_7.html.
264. http://www.ncac.gov.cn/chinacopyright/contents/481/255835.html.
265. More in IX. *infra* on collective copyright management.

paid. In the course of the 2006 amendment to these Interpretations, however, the SPC deleted said Rule 3. Since then, the legal licence remained confined to the analogous world, so that online service providers who want to make an already published article available online must seek the copyright owner's permission and it is no longer up to the copyright owner to take the initiative and to object to such use.

Finally, it should be noted that with regard to the reprint of published articles from abroad, Rule 13 of the International Implementation Rules remains effective. It limits the subject matter of what can be freely reprinted to current articles concerning economic, political or social topics, obviously to not exceed the scope of permitted uses allowed by Article 10*bis* Berne Convention.[266] That is, articles of Chinese nationals can be reprinted irrespective of their content, whereas foreign articles can only be reprinted if they are specifically on current economic, political or social issues.

(b) Sound Recordings of Already Recorded Musical Works

Article 40(3) of the current Copyright Law (Article 42(2) after the third amendment's entry into force) regulates in conformity with Article 13 Berne Convention that a musical work that has already been lawfully recorded in sound may be used by a phonogram producer to record it in sound without the copyright owner's permission but under payment of a remuneration, unless the author declared in advance that he does not want to grant such permission. Rule 31 Implementing Regulations stipulates that such statement shall be made at the date of the initial recording. The Model Contract on Sound Recording issued by the NCA on 11 August 1997 contains a corresponding reservation clause.[267] According to Rule 22 Implementing Regulations, the remuneration standards shall be determined by the NCAC and the administration in charge of pricing. The only available remuneration standards are regulated in the very old Preliminary Method on the Remuneration Standard for the Legal Licence to Record in Sound of 1993, still with reference to the far-reaching legal licence in Article 37 of the 1991 Copyright Law.[268] The Method still seems to be effective, however, because it is listed among the regulatory materials on the NCAC's website.[269]

(c) Broadcasts of Published Works

According to Article 43(2) of the current Copyright Law (Article 46(2) after the third amendment's entry into force), a radio or television broadcasting organization that broadcasts a published work (except cinematographic works) created by another person does not need a permission from the copyright owner but shall remunerate him ("remunerate him according to the provisions" after the third amendment's entry into force). The legislature regarded this provision as compliant with Article 11*bis* (2) Berne Convention, which entrusts member states with the actual implementation of the broadcasting right and other public communication rights, provided that

266. Which actually speaks of articles on "current economic, political or *religious* topics".
267. 4 *Zhuzuoquan* (1997), 57; see also Sun Qiuning, 'Dui Zhuzuoquanfa di 39 tiao de sikao' (Thoughts on Article 39 Copyright Law), 3 *Zhongguo Banquan* (2002), 16.
268. See III. 1. *supra*.
269. http://www.ncac.gov.cn/chinacopyright/contents/481/17562.html.

under no circumstances the moral rights of authors and their right to be equitably remunerated will be prejudiced. Oddly, thus far neither the current Copyright Law nor the Implementing Regulations provided that the State Council or the NCAC shall issue a remuneration standard for this rather severe limitation to copyright exclusivity, and also a stipulation that copyright owners may announce in advance that they do not want to have their works broadcast without permission is absent. Reportedly, due to the absence of such provisions, works were usually broadcast without any remuneration to authors and copyright owners. The situation is different in case of the legal licence to broadcast published sound recordings of musical works in Article 44 of the current Copyright Law, which, however, has been abolished by the third Copyright Law amendment.[270] Here, remuneration standards have been in place[271] and the copyright owners can rely on the enforcement of their remuneration claims by the Music Copyright Society of China (MCSC).[272] Due to the lax payment attitude of broadcasting organizations, previous drafts of a third Copyright Law amendment proposed the abolishment of the legal licence to broadcast published works.[273] The third amendment retained it in Article 46(2), albeit with the mentioned addition that remuneration shall be paid "according to the provisions", i.e., remuneration standards will have to be established in the near future,

As already indicated, the legal licence to broadcast published works does not extend to cinematographic works. Article 46 of the current Copyright Law (Article 48 after the third amendment's entry into force) also exempts non-creative audiovisual recordings from its application. For the TV broadcast of both, a permission must be sought from the respective producer, not from the authors or performers of the incorporated works or the incorporated or recorded performances. However, where a TV station intends to broadcast an audiovisual *recording*, it must also seek the permission of the owner of the copyright in the recorded work.

(d) Broadcast of Published Sound Recordings

An important amendment of 2001 related to the permission-free broadcast of published sound recordings in Article 44 of the current Copyright Law, which has been quite debated in the past. The old provision allowed radio stations to broadcast published sound recordings without permission of and even without remuneration to the authors, performers and phonogram producers for non-commercial purposes. The objective behind this limitation was to promote China's broadcasting industry. On the one hand, the amended provision substantively weakened this severe limitation at least with regard to copyright owners, stipulating that published sound recordings

270. Explained in (d) *infra*.
271. See (b) *supra*.
272. More about collecting societies IX. *infra*.
273. A thorough overview of the practice of this legal licence is given by Hu Kaizhong, 'Guangbo diantai dianshitai bofang zuopin fading xuke wenti yanjiu – jianlun woguo "zhuzuoquanfa" de xiugai' (Study about problems associated with the legal licence for radio and TV broadcasting organizations to broadcast works – also debating the "Copyright Law" reform), 3 *Zhishi Chanquan* (Intellectual Property) (2013), 3 et seq., online accessible at http://www.doc88.com/p-5844101717790.html.

can still be broadcast without permission, but that remuneration[274] shall be paid to the copyright owners (but not to the phonogram producers or performers). On the other hand, it is no longer limited to broadcasts for non-commercial purposes. As mentioned, Article 11*bis* (2) of the Berne Convention allows its members to determine the conditions for exercising the broadcasting right, provided that these conditions apply only in the countries which have prescribed them. As a minimum standard, Article 11*bis* (2) further provides that under no circumstances shall the moral rights of authors and the right to obtain equitable remuneration be prejudiced. The Chinese legislature regards this prerequisite as fulfilled by Article 44.[275] Some commentators think that the use of published works incorporated in sound recordings may also be subsumed under the legal licence to broadcast published works, and that remuneration standards should be evenly available for the broadcast of both published works in general and for works incorporated in sound recordings.[276] The two Copyright Law draft amendments of 2020 propose to abolish this legal licence.

The removal of the limitation of this legal license to non-commercial broadcasts gave rise to another problem, namely the complete lack of a broadcasting right of phonogram producers and of performers in phonograms respectively in performances fixated in phonograms. Article 43 of the previous Copyright Law, which banned copyright owners such as performers and phonogram producers from exercising their respective rights against *non-commercial* broadcasting of phonograms, at least allowed a reverse interpretation, namely that not only authors but also performers and phonogram producers were in the position to authorise *commercial* broadcasts of their phonograms. This lack of protection, however, complies with TRIPS, Article 14(1)–(2) which provides for no broadcasting right of neighbouring rights owners in sound fixations, but for a mere right of the performer to broadcast his live performance. As China is not a member to the Rome Convention, it is not obliged to adhere to Article 12 of that treaty which grants performers and/or phonogram producers the right to claim a single remuneration for the broadcast of phonograms incorporating the result of their respective efforts.

The third Copyright Law amendment followed the proposals of the two drafts of 2020 and completely abolished this legal licence. Moreover, as will be further outlined below,[277] it created a new legal licence that allows phonogram producers to obtain at least a remuneration for the broadcast of their phonograms by wire or wireless means or their public communication by mechanical sound transmission devices.

274. The standards, which depend mainly on the proportion of the sound recording in the whole broadcast, are regulated in the Preliminary Measures on the Remuneration Standards for the Broadcasting of Sound Recordings by Broadcasting Organizations of 11 December 2009, in Chinese at http://www.ncac.gov.cn/chinacopyright/contents/479/17541.html.

275. This becomes obvious from the statement concerning the draft on amending the Copyright Law, made by Shi Chongyuan, President of the Press and Publication Administration, in the course of the 19th Session of the Standing Committee of National People's Congress on 22 December 2000 (7 *Gazette of the Standing Committee of the NPC* (2001), 518 (521)).

276. Hu Kaizhong, note 273.

277. See X. 3. *infra*.

(e) *Use of Work Fragments or Works in Textbooks for Compulsory School Education*

Article 23 of the current Copyright Law stipulates that passages of works or whole literary or musical works of shorter extent, single works of fine art or photographic works can be incorporated into textbooks intended for compulsory nine-year school education or the implementation of the educational state plan without copyright owner's authorisation and under payment of remuneration, provided that the respective work is published, the work title is indicated and the actual author (not the "copyright owner") has not declared that such use is not permitted. The same legal licence applies to the neighbouring rights of publishers, performers, phonogram producers and broadcasters. Rule 8 Internet Regulations extends this to the internet, stipulating that the above works or work excerpts may also be used as course material to implement the compulsory education and the state plan for education via the internet, in that distance learning institutions can make such course material produced by themselves or legally obtained from thirds available through the internet to registered students without the copyright owner's permission but under payment of a remuneration. Rule 10 No. 4 of the same Regulations obliges the beneficiaries of such legal licence to employ technical protection measures to prevent other parties from accessing the protected content.

The third Copyright Law amendment extended this legal licence, which will henceforth be accommodated in Article 25, in several respects. First, the author will no longer be entitled to prohibit such use in advance and second, the legal licence shall henceforth be applicable to graphical works. Also, the purpose of permitted use shall be compulsory education in general and no longer be limited to the compulsory "nine-year" education, whatever the practical implications of this amendment will be.

The remuneration standards for this legal licence, which, according to Rule 22 Implementing Regulations have to be determined by an administrative decree, are regulated in the NCAC's and the National Development and Reform Commission's Method on Remuneration for the Use of Works under the Legal Licence for Schoolbooks of 29 October 2013,[278] mostly as a fixed fee per amount of used work, e.g., RMB 300 per 1,000 characters if literary works are used or RMB 300 per piece of music in case of musical works. The Method stipulates as its legal bases the Copyright Law, the Implementing Regulations, and the Collecting Societies Regulation, not the Internet Regulations, so that it is unclear whether these remuneration standards are also applicable to the internet use, e.g., whether a user also has to pay RMB 300 per 1,000 characters of a literary work if he makes it available for distance learning. It is well conceivable that this legal licence has gained considerable importance during the Corona epidemic, which forced school and universities to switch to online teaching.

(f) *Making Available to the Rural Poor*

Rule 9 of the Internet Regulations provides for an entirely new legal licence, which permits the free-of charge and non-for-profit internet transmission of published works of Chinese (i.e., not foreign) citizens, legal persons or other organizations that deal

278. http://www.ncac.gov.cn/chinacopyright/contents/481/159551.html.

with planting, breeding, disease prevention, disaster prevention, poverty reduction, etc., or works that satisfy the basic cultural demands to the public in rural areas.

Copyright owners are entitled to object to this use in accordance with a procedure that is different from that of other legal licences, however, in that service providers who intend to make a work available to the rural poor shall announce the respective work titles, copyright owners and remuneration in advance. Copyright owners then have 30 days to object, but they may think twice before doing so because the provider's announcement has already gone public and alleviation of rural poverty is a sensitive topic, so that they may quickly find themselves in the eye of a public outrage labelling them as greedy and heartless. If the copyright owner does not object, the service provider can make the respective work publicly available and shall pay remuneration according to the announced mode, which obviously is to be freely determined by the service provider because no official standards are in place. If an author objects to such use afterwards, the work must be taken down and remuneration be paid for the period of use. Also, according to Rule 10(4), the service provider shall employ technical protection measures to prevent others than the target recipients from accessing the protected content.

The Internet Regulations specifically mention violations of the prerequisites for this legal licence as acts that give rise to civil, administrative and criminal liability. Who, according to Rule 18(1) No. 4, exceeds the permitted scope of use, does not pay remuneration according to the announced standards or does not take the copyrighted material down after the right owner has denied his consent in the transmission shall bear civil liabilities such as cessation, elimination of effects, apology, compensation. If the infringement also violates the public interest, the competent administration may order cessation, confiscate the illegal profits and impose a fine of up to five times the illegal business revenue if such revenue exceeds RMB 50,000. If the illegal revenue is beneath that threshold or if there is no revenue at all, a fine of up to RMB 250,000 can be imposed. The same fines apply to the making available without prior announcement of the title of protected content, the name of the right owner and the mode of remuneration. In serious cases, also the equipment used for the infringing transmission can be confiscated, and where a crime has been committed, the case shall be transferred to the criminal prosecution authorities.

VIII. COPYRIGHT TRANSACTIONS

1. General Rules

The Chinese copyright contract provisions can be divided into a general part, which is contained in Chapter III on Copyright Licensing and Assignment Contracts (Articles 24–29 of the current Copyright Law, Articles 26-31 after the third amendment's entry into force), and a specific part (Chapter IV), which regulates the publishing contract (Articles 30–36 of the current Copyright Law, Articles 32-37 after the third amendment's entry into force), the performance contract (Articles 37–39 of the current Copyright Law, Articles 38-41 after the third amendment's entry into force), the sound recording and video recording contract (Articles 40–42 of the current Copyright Law, Articles 42-45 after the third amendment's entry into force)) and the broadcasting contract (Articles 43–46 of the current Copyright Law, Articles 46-48 after the third amendment's entry into force).[279]

As already outlined, the 2001 amendment clarified in Article 10(2) that the assignment of copyright exploitation rights constitutes a permissible copyright transaction, the details of such contracts being regulated in Article 25 of the current Copyright Law (Article 27 after the third amendment's entry into force). The silence about copyright assignment in the previous rules caused legal uncertainties. To some commentators, the non-committal attitude of the law reflected the intention of the legislature to not categorically exclude the change in copyright ownership by contract, while avoiding a clear invitation to effect such transactions.[280]

Assignment contracts must be in written form and indicate the work title, the kind of the assigned right, the territory covered by the contract, the assignment fee and mode of payment, liability clauses in case of breach of contract and other matters the parties deem necessary (Article 25(2) of the current Copyright Law, Article 27(2) after the third amendment's entry into force). The obligation to indicate the kind of rights subject to the contract and the territory covered by the contract implies a protective attitude towards authors in the Continental European tradition, who should be prevented from an unintentionally far-reaching disposal of their economic rights.[281] The same is true with regard to Article 27 (Article 29 after the third amendment's entry into force), according to which the 'other party" (not only assignees but also licensees and, since 2010 also pledgees according to the amended Article 26 of the current Copyright Law (Article 28 after the third amendment's entry into force)[282] shall not exercise any right not explicitly assigned or licensed by the copyright owner in the contract unless the copyright owner has given his permission.[283] If, for example, a publishing contract only refers to the "publication" in the meaning of reproduction and distribution (Article 58; Article 63 after the third amendment's entry into force), the publisher is not permitted to make the work available on the internet on the basis of this contract.[284]

Assignment contracts can be submitted to a copyright administration agency for registration.

Apart from assignment as the most absolute form of copyright disposal, the law regulates the permission to use as another form of copyright transaction. The

279. The subdivision into a general and a specific part is suggested by A. Dietz, 'China – Einführung', in *Quellen des Urheberrechts* (Luchterhand Publishing House, looseleaf), 22 et seq.

280. Shen Rengan, 'Zhuzuoquanfa de zhiding he lifa jingshen' (Establishment of the Copyright Law and legislative intention), in Copyright Course of the Supreme People's Court, *Zhuzuoquanfa jiangzuo* (Lectures on the Copyright Law) (Beijing, 1991), 15 (30).

281. See Adolf Dietz, note 27.

282. With regard to pledge agreements, the Copyright Law draft amendment of August 2020 proposes a clarification that not copyright as a whole but only the economic part of it can be subject to such agreement.

283. A corresponding provision is contained in Rule 18(2) of the Software Regulations, which, however, only mentions software licensing contracts, but not software assignment contracts.

284. Xue Hong, '"Digitized Publication" and Its Copyright-Related Legal Issues', 2 *China Patents & Trademarks* (2003), 72.

Copyright Law does not require licence contracts to be concluded in writing, but according to the current Article 24 (Article 26 after the third amendment's entry into force), they shall at least regulate the category of the licensed right, the exclusive or non-exclusive character of the licence, the territory and duration of the licence, the remuneration and the mode of payment, the liabilities in case of breach of contract and other matters the parties deem necessary. Email exchanges that reveal an expression of intent of both parties to enter into a contractual relationship are regarded as valid contracts.[285] Moreover, Rule 23 of the current Implementing Regulations provides that at least exclusive licensing contracts shall be concluded in writing, except where the work is intended for publication in a periodical. According to Rule 25 Implementing Regulations, licence contracts can be registered at a local copyright administration authority.

Copyright licensors are advised to clearly determine the degree of exclusivity because otherwise the licence will be interpreted to their disadvantage, as exclusive and therefore as banning the licensor from exploiting the work in the same manner (Rule 24 Implementing Regulations). Rule 33 of the pre-2001 Implementing Regulations was much more licensor-friendly, because it stipulated the opposite, namely that a licence contract which remained silent on exclusivity would be interpreted as non-exclusive and therefore as allowing continued exploitation and licensing to third parties by the licensor. With regard to software licensing contracts, however, the previous system remains in force. Accordingly, in the absence of a written contract or a clear stipulation on exclusivity, the software licence shall be regarded as non-exclusive (Rule 19(2) Software Regulations). The parties to a licence contract should therefore be aware that in absence of clear agreement about exclusivity, software licensing contracts and licensing contracts with regard to other types of works will be interpreted differently, namely in favour of the licensor in the case of software and in favour of the licensee in the case of other work categories. Apparently, the favoured treatment of software licensors can be traced back to the official policy of promoting the software industry. In connection with the different licence types, it should be noted that whatever licence is chosen, in the absence of an agreement to the contrary, it does not include the permission to grant sublicences to third parties (Rule 24 Implementing Regulations).[286]

As another step back in terms of author-friendliness can be interpreted the abolishment of the extendable validity term of licensing contracts to 10 years (Article 26 of the pre-2001 Copyright Law; Rule 18 of the previous Software Regulations), which enabled the licensor to re-enter consultations on adequate licence terms after a foreseeable period, e.g. if a work proved to be exceptionally successful on the market, and therefore displayed the function of a claim to adjust the licensing terms.[287] The abolishment is explained by non-conformity with international practice.[288]

With regard to remuneration for use, Article 28 of the current Copyright Law (Article 30 after the third amendment's entry into force) gives priority to contractual

285. Beijing Higher People's Court decision of 3 July 2019, 441 *Jing Min Zhong* (2018), https://mp.weixin.qq.com/s/u-SKPytGB-NlFOO77mdvbQ.
286. The Software Regulations contain no corresponding rule.
287. Xue Hong and Zheng Chengsi, note 134, 90.
288. Xue Hong and Zheng Chengsi, note 134, 90.

autonomy in stipulating that, in general, the licence fee shall be determined by the parties, and that only in the absence of a contractual agreement shall official standards to be enacted by the NCAC apply. With regard to literary works, these would be the mentioned Method on the Remuneration for the Use of Literary Works of 21 August 2014 jointly enacted by the NCAC and the National Development and Reform Commission.[289]

Finally, Article 29 of the current Copyright Law (Article 31 after the third amendment's entry into force) contains the self-evident obligation of publishers, performers, producers of sound and video recordings and broadcasters to respect the moral rights of authors and their right to be remunerated.

2. Specific Rules

The specific rules on copyright contracts are summarized in Chapter IV Copyright Law, currently on "Publication, Performance, Sound and Video Recording, Broadcasting", henceforth on "Rights Related to Copyright" after the third amendment's entry into force, but continuously not being exclusively about these related "rights" but also addressing specific contract law and the already discussed legal licences.

(a) Publishing Contracts

Article 30 of the current Copyright Law (Article 32 after the third amendment's entry into force) emphasizes that the publication of a book requires a publishing contract with and the payment of remuneration to the author. Moreover, the current Article 35 clarifies that if an adaptation, translation, etc., is published, both the author of the adaptation and the author of the original work must be asked for permission and remunerated. As mentioned, the third amendment has deleted this provision respectively integrated it in a comprehensive Article 16, which obliges those who wish to publish, perform or record in sound or video derivative works to ask the owners of the copyright in both the original and the derivative work for permission and to remunerate them.

In accordance with the general contractual rules, written contract form is only required if the authorization to publish the work is exclusive and does not refer to publication in periodicals (Rule 23 Implementing Regulations). The pre-2001 provision, which restricted the contract term to 10 years, was abolished in the course of the first reform of the Copyright Law and the Implementing Regulations. Article 30 of the current Copyright Law (henceforth: Article 32) instead emphasizes that it shall be left to the parties to determine the conditions of the contract.

Upon conclusion of a publishing contract, the publisher enjoys an exclusive publishing right within the scope determined by the contract. In the absence of other contractual stipulations, it shall be interpreted as entitling the publisher to exclusively publish the original or revised edition of the work in the same language within the term of validity of the contract and within the regional scope determined by contract (Rule 28 Implementing Regulations). In addition to this exclusive position, which,

289. http://www.ncac.gov.cn/chinacopyright/contents/481/255835.html.

however, is completely dependent on the contractual relationship with the author, publishers enjoy an independent neighbouring right in the particular layout of their publication, which will be discussed in a later chapter.

Further details on the rights and obligations of the parties to a publishing contract are regulated in Articles 32 to 35 of the current Copyright Law (Articles 34-36 after the third amendment's entry into force). Article 32(1) (henceforth: Article 34(1)) obliges the copyright owner to deliver the work and the publisher to publish the work within the agreed terms. If the publisher fails to publish the work in a timely fashion, he will be held liable for breach of contractual obligations according to civil law and contract law provisions. Before reprinting or republishing a work, the publisher must notify the copyright owner and remunerate him. If the book is out of print but the publisher refuses a reprint or republication, the copyright owner can terminate the contract (Article 32(3) of the current Copyright Law, Article 34(3) after the third amendment's entry into force). In order to prove that the books are in fact not available on the market, the copyright owner shall present two book orders which could not be fulfilled within six months (Rule 29 Implementing Regulations).

Article 33(1) of the current Copyright Law (henceforth: Article 35(1)) aims at balancing the interests of authors who deliver articles to newspapers or magazines at their own initiative and periodical publishers who are often confronted with the practice of one author submitting his manuscript to several periodicals. Accordingly, an author may offer his contribution to another publisher if he has not heard from the newspaper publisher within 15 days or from the magazine publisher within 30 days from the date of the manuscript submission, provided that the parties have not agreed otherwise.

According to Article 34 of the current Copyright Law (henceforth: Article 36), a book publisher may amend a work if the author permits him to do so. A publisher of periodicals is allowed to make editorial modifications or abridgements without asking the author for permission. Amendments to the content, however, require the author's permission.[290]

Authors may also assign their copyright to publishers, who would then become copyright owners. Publishers warmly welcomed the introduction of copyright assignability in 2001.[291]

(b) Performance Contracts

Article 37(1) of the current Copyright Law (Article 38 after the third amendment's entry into force) contains a self-evident provision that obliges individual performers to obtain permission from and to pay remuneration to the author of the performed work. The second sentence of the provision has a certain independent meaning, however, obliging the organizer of organized performances to obtain permission from and to pay remuneration to the author. Rule 45 of the old Implementing Regulations instead provided an unclear stipulation that the performer had to obtain the permission and pay remuneration "through" the organizer. The amended wording helps authors

290. See VI. 1. (d) *supra*.

291. Lu Changqi, 'Zuozhe he chubanshe quanli xin de falü pinghengdian' (A New balance between the rights of authors and publishers), 6 *Zhongguo Banquan* (2002).

to identify the contract partner, especially in case of mass events in the course of which numerous works are performed by different artists and troupes.[292] Article 37(2) of the current Copyright Law clarifies that also the owner of the copyright in the original work shall be asked for permission and remunerated if the work intended for performance is an adaptation. As mentioned, the third amendment integrated this provision in a new Article 16, according to which those who wish to publish a derivative work, perform it or record it in sound or video shall seek the permission of the owners of the copyright in both the original work and the adaptation, etc., and to remunerate them.

(c) Sound and Video Recording Contracts

Article 40(1) of the current Copyright Law (Article 42 after the third amendment's entry into force) stipulates that the producers of sound and video recordings shall obtain the permission of and pay remuneration to the author before producing a sound or video recording of his work, again a rather self-evident stipulation the content of which can also be concluded from the reproduction right and from the general contractual rules. Moreover, Article 40(2) of the current Copyright Law provides that if the work to be sound recorded or audiovisually recorded forms an adaptation, translation, annotation or arrangement, the producer shall ask both the owner of the copyright in the adaptation, etc., and the owner of the copyright in the original work for permission and remunerate them As mentioned, the third Copyright Law amendment integrated also this provision in a new Article 16 on the obligation of those who wish to publish perform or record in sound or video an adaptation or other derivative work to ask the owners of the copyright in both the adaptation, etc., and in the pre-existing work for permission and to remunerate them.

Furthermore, Article 41 of the current Copyright Law (Article 43 after the third amendment's entry into force) reminds producers of sound and video recordings that they are also obliged to conclude a contract with and to pay remuneration to the performers of the recorded works.

The legal licence which allows phonogram producers to record already legally recorded musical works has been discussed above.

(d) Broadcasting Contracts

Article 43 Copyright Law (which will become Article 46 after the third amendment's entry into force) on broadcasting contracts remained basically unchanged since the enactment of the Copyright Law in 1991. Accordingly, only in cases of broadcasts of unpublished works shall the radio or TV station seek the permission of the copyright owners, whereas broadcasters who broadcast a published work only have to remunerate the author but are not required to ask his permission under the above-discussed legal licence.[293] As discussed above, the third amendment added the stipulation that the remuneration to be paid for such broadcast shall comply with

292. Li Shunde and Zhou Yang, note 78, 142.
293. See VII. 2. (c) *supra*.

yet to be established regulations, which can be regarded as a statutory obligation of the copyright administration to finally establish a remuneration standard.

IX. COLLECTIVE MANAGEMENT

Article 8(1) of the current Copyright Law stipulates that copyright owners and owners of neighbouring rights shall be entitled to authorize a collecting society to administer their rights, and that the collecting society shall, upon authorization, be entitled to assert the entrusted rights in its own name and to become a party in court or in an arbitration procedure (and, after the third amendment's entry into force, also in a mediation procedure). This includes foreign right owners who are members of a foreign collecting society with which the corresponding Chinese society has a mutual representation agreement.[294] Article 8(2) (Article 8(4) after the third amendment's entry into force) delegates the enactment of provisions regulating the mode of the establishment of a collecting society, its rights and obligations, the collection and distribution of the royalties and the supervision and administration of collective management to the State Council. On 28 December 2004, the State Council enacted the mentioned *Regulations on Collective Copyright Administration*, which have been last amended on 12 December 2013.[295]

The third Copyright Law amendment added two paragraphs to Article 8. The new paragraph (2) stipulates that collecting societies may negotiate with user representatives about fee standards, and that, if the negotiations fail, the NCAC may be asked to arbitrate. If a party is not satisfied with result of the arbitration it may further proceed in court but it may also directly file suit in a People's Court without first going through arbitration. The new paragraph (3) commits collecting societies to regularly report to the public about the collection and distribution of fees, deductions and other circumstances as well as to provide rights information for right owners and users, and obliges the NCAC to lawfully conduct control and administration of collecting societies. The amended text corresponds to the last draft proposal of August 2020. The preceding discussion draft of April 2020 instead proposed to oblige the NCAC to "strengthen" control and administration, but obviously many commentators bemoaned that such rather declaratory provision would hardly be translatable into a firm legal obligation.

294. Court decisions that confirmed this mostly with regard to the relationship between the Music Copyright Society of China (MCSC) and Hong Kong's music copyright society CASH are quoted by Yahong Li, 'Music Copyright Society of China has Legal Right and Standing to Bring Lawsuit in its Own Name', in Kung-Chung Liu (ed.), note 234, 98 et seq.

295. Current version in Chinese available at http://www.gov.cn/gongbao/content/2011/content_1860740.htm; an English translation of the first version of 2004 can be obtained from the WIPOLex database at https://wipolex.wipo.int/en/legislation/details/6340, which, as both amendments of 2011 and 2013 have been rather minor (the amendment of 8 January 2011 changed the references to the Copyright Law, as the sequence of articles has changed after the 2010 Copyright Law reform, the amendment of 7 December 2013 amended Rule 15 on the procedure of official approval of amendments to a collecting societies' statute) is mostly up to date.

As delegated by Article 8(2) of the current Copyright Law, which will become Article 8(4) after the third amendment's entry into force, the details of collective management are to be regulated by State Council's provisions, the mentioned *Regulations on Collective Copyright Administration* of 28 December 2004, which have been amended twice, on 8 January 2011 and on 12 December 2013.[296] According to Rules 5, 15 and Chapter V on supervision and chapter VI on enforcement, collecting societies are approved, supervised and, in case of misconduct, sanctioned by the NCAC. According to Rule 7, a collecting society can be founded by no less than 50 right owners (individuals, organizations) in a specific area of copyright exploitation that is hard to control by individual right owners, provided that its activities do not overlap or coincide with that of an already registered society, that the society can handle nationwide copyright management and has a statute that meets the requirements in Rule 8 with regard to assembly, board of directors, internal organization cost structure, etc.). That is, normally only one collecting society per field of copyright exploitation is allowed but where exceptionally two or more societies turn out to be in charge of the same type of use (which may, for instance, occur if the playing of Karaoke videos falls under the competencies of a society in charge of music and another society in charge of audiovisual recordings), the societies shall consult with each other to determine one society in charge of fee collection and to agree on a mode of distributing the revenues between each other (Rule 26).

Pursuant to Rule 13, the fee setting shall take into account the duration, form and regional scope of use of works, etc., the kind of right managed, the difficulty of concluding licensing contracts and collection of fees shall be considered.

Collecting societies are, furthermore, under the obligation to contract, i.e., a society may neither deny membership to authors and right owners who fall within its field of activity (Rule 19) nor may it deny a licence-seeking party a licence at a reasonable fee (Rule 23). Refusals to contract can be reported to the NCAC (Rules 33, 34).

According to Rule 20, once the author has entrusted a collecting society to exercise his rights, he can no longer exercise the same rights on his own or allow another party to exercise them. This provision contradicts the rather old SPC Reply on Several Legal Problems in the Relationship between the Music Copyright Society of China and Music Copyright Owners of 14 September 1993, which stated that a copyright owner may very well continue to exercise his rights on his own by suing infringers if the respective collecting society does not proceed in court or if he otherwise sees the necessity to sue on his own.[297]

Copyright owners may at any time withdraw their membership but already granted licences will continue to be in force until their expiry and the right owner will remain entitled to obtain the revenues from the licence and to inspect the corresponding business documents (Rule 21). Foreign or stateless right owners may, on the grounds of a reciprocal agreement that with a foreign collecting society in

296. Current version in Chinese available here: http://www.gov.cn/gongbao/content/2011/content_1860740.htm; an English translation of the first version of 2004 can be obtained from the WIPOLex database at https://wipolex.wipo.int/en/legislation/details/6340; more details in IX. *infra*.

297. 35 *Fa Min* (1993), quoted by Yahong Li, note 294.

the same area of copyright exercise, authorize a Chinese society to administer their rights (Rule 22).

As far as the relationship between collecting societies and work users is concerned, Rule 23 obliges the collecting societies, as mentioned, to offer a licence at reasonable conditions to any user. The same provision also prescribes that such licences shall not be exclusive and not exceed a duration of two years, but they may be renewed after expiry. According to Rule 25, the exact amount of fees may be negotiated in accordance with standards set by the NCAC, if any, but there is no room for such negotiations where an exact standard for uses under the legal licences in Articles 23 (use in textbooks for school education), 33(2) (reprinting in newspapers or periodicals), 40(3) (making of sound recordings of musical works), 43(2) (broadcasting of published works) or 44 (broadcasting of sound recordings) Copyright Law has been determined. As illustrated above,[298] there is no such standard for the legal licence to broadcast a published work. Pursuant to Rule 27, users are obliged to inform the collecting society truthfully about the works they intend to use, the names of the right owners and the scope, duration and other circumstances of use, otherwise the NCAC may order them to correct their behaviour and the collecting society may terminate the licence agreement with them (Rule 43). Users may, however, request that such data be kept confidential if they form a business secret.

Collecting societies may deduct administrative fees but the deduction must be moderate, i.e., the proportion of administrative fees shall gradually decrease as the revenues increase (Rule 28). Chapter V of the Regulations on "supervision" subdues collecting societies under a regime of documentation obligations and of examination and inspection by the NCAC, which appears to be quite strict, at least on paper. As mentioned, right owners and users may report misconduct, but reports from the general public about possible violations of the Regulations are also welcome (Rule 35). Chapter VI of the Regulations contains a catalogue of misconduct and corresponding sanctions, which range from correction over the dismissal of the general assembly or the board of directors to confiscation of illegal gains or even criminal prosecution of individuals in serious cases.

Collective management is a growing business in China. The Music Copyright Society of China (MCSC), which has been founded in 1992 and therefore long before the enactment of the above Regulations, has more than 7000 members and managed to collect RMB 216.5 million (EUR 28.6 million) in licensing fees in 2017, about one third accounting for internet use.[299] The MCSC is also very active in prosecuting copyright infringement, especially by unauthorized internet use. Its enforcement-related activity gained momentum in the early 2000s, when it successfully proceeded against the unremunerated MP3 reproduction of published sound recordings.[300] The enactment of the Regulations on Collective Management in 2004 has also laid the foundation for several other societies administrating different kind of works: the China Audio

298. See VII. 2. (c) *supra*.

299. The MCSC report of 2017 with annual statistics can be downloaded at http://www.mcsc.com.cn/pdf/phpmEB0Ez.pdf.

300. On 14 April 2003, the SCMS won a lawsuit against a music publisher which reproduced published musical works without remunerating the authors: decision of the Intermediate People's Court No. 2 of the City of Beijing, reported in *IP News* of 17 April 2003, 2.

Video Copyright Association (CAVCA) in 2005, the China Written Works Copyright Society (CWWCS) in 2008, the Image Copyright Society of China (ICSC) in 2008 and the China Film Copyright Association (CFCA) in 2009, i.e., one society per work category as prescribed by the Regulations. Especially the MCSC's membership and annual revenue has dramatically increased over the years but in comparison with collecting societies in much less populous countries, e.g., the German GEMA (members: 72,518; revenue: roughly EUR 1 billion)[301] it still performs on a rather small scale, and it can be assumed that the vast majority of authors in China are not yet represented by a collecting society. CAVCA is also reported to enforce the copyright of its members quite aggressively. Interestingly, it seems to supplement copyright enforcement by the MCSC in that it specializes in the prosecution of unauthorized Karaoke video playing.[302]

Many Chinese commentators showed sympathy towards extended collective licensing in general,[303] while only rather specific details such as the scope of rights subject to it or the necessity of a stronger state control of collecting societies that administer the rights of non-members[304] seemed to be under debate. The latest Copyright Law draft amendments of 2020 as well as the final amendment remained nevertheless silent on extended collective licensing.

Occasionally, collecting societies, especially the MCSC, which has become quite dominant, are criticized for abusing their market power (and courts for supporting this). In a decision of 1 April 2016,[305] the Suzhou Intermediate People's Court held that the broadcast of a non-for-profit performance of musical works formed copyright infringement and that the MCSC, who had been entrusted to exercise the respective author's rights, was entitled to claim damage compensation. According to commentators, the court should have found delayed payment of royalty for the legal licence in Article 43(2) Copyright Law, which allows the permission-free broadcast of published works, rather than copyright infringement.[306]

X. NEIGHBOURING RIGHTS

ical design of their publications, the rights enjoyed by performers in their performances, the rights enjoyed by the producers of sound and video recordings in their respective recordings and the rights enjoyed by radio and TV broadcasters in their broadcast programs.

As mentioned, the neighbouring rights are regulated together with specific contract law and legal licences in Chapter IV on "Publication, Performance, Sound

301. The GEMA business and transparency report 2017: https://www.gema.de/fileadmin/user_upload/Gema/geschaeftsberichte/GEMA_Geschaeftsbericht2017.pdf
302. Ye Jiang, 'Changing Tides of Collective Licensing in China', 21:23 *Michigan State International Law Review* (2013), 729 et seq.
303. E.g. Ye Jiang, note 302.
304. See, e.g., Han Wenqi, 'Dui "zhuzuoquanfa" di san ci xiugai zhong yanshenxing jitiguanli zhidu de sikao' (Thoughts about the Extended Licensing System in the third amendment to the "Copyright Law", 6 *Fazhi Yuandi* (2017), 232.
305. 673 *Su 05 Min Zhong* (2016).
306. Yahong Li, note 294, who comments on the case.

Recording, Video Recording and Broadcast" of the current Copyright Law (which, as mentioned, has been renamed into "Rights Related to Copyright" by the third amendment). At first glance, their amalgamation with the contractual rules implies that neighbouring rights are accessory to copyright, that they come into existence as result of an author's permission to publish, to perform, to record or to broadcast a certain work and that as a consequence, performances, recordings of unprotected subject matter cannot be protected under the neighbouring rights provisions. This would be a false conclusion, however. Neither the law nor its accompanying regulations require that the publisher's right shall be confined to publications of protected works, or that a performer's right can only be granted in performances of works which are still copyright protected. That publications, performances, recordings or broadcasts are protected irrespective of a contract with the author becomes especially evident from Rule 5 No. 5 of the Implementing Regulations which defines phonograms as "recording of the sounds of a performance and other sounds" so that a neighbouring rights protected phonogram is not even required to be a sound recording of a work performance, but can be a fixation of anything that can be recorded in sound.

As also mentioned, the Copyright Law draft amendment of 2014 gave rise to the expectation that the coming overhaul of the Copyright Law will put an end to this mishmash of rights, contract law and legal licences, but the final third amendment left the current structure of Chapter IV untouched. Insofar, the chapter's renamed title "Rights related to Copyright" seems to be less accurate than the previous title "Publication, Performance, Sound Recording, Video Recording and Broadcast" in that it obscures the fact that Chapter IV continues to be not just about "rights" but also about contracts and legal licenses.

With regard to foreign and stateless neighbouring rights owners, the old Implementing Regulations stated that only performances in China and sound and video recordings produced and distributed in China were protected. In order to comply with the international obligations imposed by TRIPS, Rules 33 to 35 of the current Implementing Regulations now provide that foreign performances, sound recordings and broadcasts are protected according to the international treaties to which China is a member.

Finally, it should be noted that the limitations to copyright are applied *mutatis mutandis* to neighbouring right owners (Article 22(2) of the current Copyright Law, Article 24(2) after the third amendment's entry into force).

1. Publishers

Article 36 of the current Copyright Law (Article 37 after the third amendment's entry into force) regulates the right of the publisher to permit others to exploit the "typographical design" of any book or periodical he publishes and confines this protection to a term of ten years from the first publication (expiration on 31 December of the tenth year) of the book or periodical in which the typographical design is used. That only the typographical design but no longer the outside appearance of the books or periodicals is protected may be explained by the simultaneous availability of copyright protection for the latter, so that a conflict between the copyright of an individual creator and a publisher's neighbouring right in the same design can be avoided.[307]

2. Performers

Performers enjoy a quite comprehensive set of rights, including moral rights and exploitation rights. Pursuant to the definition in Rule 5 No. 6 of Implementing Regulations, the protected subject matter is confined to "performances of literary and artistic works". However, as Article 3 No. 3 Copyright Law includes acrobatic works as a work category, circus artists should be considered "performers" in the copyright sense. The 2014 Copyright Law draft amendment proposed a clarification that "performers" shall include those who perform expressions of folklore, which, as explained above, do not have to be works, also to comply with the definition in Article 2(a) of the Beijing Treaty on Audiovisual Performances. The later two drafts of 2020, however, no longer contained such clarification and also the finally amended Copyright Law is silent on it.

Article 38 of the current Copyright Law (Article 39 after the third amendment's entry into force) regulates the moral rights and the exploitation rights of performers, the former being perpetually protected, the latter confined to a protection term of 50 years, not *post mortem*, however, but from the date the performance took place (Article 39(2) of the current Copyright Law, Article 41(2) after the third amendment's entry into force) and lasting until 31 December of the 50th year.

Performers enjoy the right to be identified with their performance and the right to prevent distortions of the image inherent in their performance (Article 38(1) No. 1 and 2 of the current Copyright Law, Article 39(1) No. 1 and 2 after the third amendment's entry into force)). These two moral rights are not limited in time (Article 39(1) of the current Copyright Law, Article 41(1) after the third amendment's entry into force).

Despite criticism in the past, the past three Copyright Law amendments left the moral rights of performers unchanged. As the performer's right to prevent distortions of the image inherent in his performance is not confined to distortions prejudicial to his reputation, it goes beyond the standards set by the majority of foreign laws as well as by Article 5(1) WPPT and, with regard to audiovisual performances, by Article 5(1) (ii) of the Beijing Treaty. With regard to audiovisual works, film actors are at least theoretically in the position to exercise their integrity right against modifications, even those inevitable to enable a smooth exploitation. As seen, the moral rights of authors who contribute to a cinematographic work are severely restricted, and even authors of independent pre-existing works have to accept inevitable modifications in order to ensure smooth exploitation (Rule 10 Implementing Regulations).

The 2014 Copyright Law draft amendment contained provisions on employed performers and, specifically, on actors employed by film producers. The latter provision in Article 37 of the draft also sought to balance the relationship between performing actors and film producers, but in a rather confusing manner, differentiating, *inter alia*, between "main actors" and others. Commentators suggested

307. See Yao Boyue, 'Shilun chubanzhe de banshi, zhuangzheng shejiquan' (On the publisher's right in the typographical and layout design), 4 *Zhuzuoquan* (1995), 22.

abolishing this distinction.[308] The finally amended Copyright Law no longer contains film actor-specific provisions at all but retained the largest part of the 2014 draft's provision on employed performers in general in a newly added Article 40. Accordingly, in the absence of a clear agreement to the contrary, all rights in the performance except the right to be named as performer and the right to prevent distortions of the image inherent in their performance shall be enjoyed by the employing "performing entity" (which may also cover producers of audiovisual works, provided that they actually employ the respective actors), but even if the performer has retained his economic rights by contract, the entity shall be entitled to use his performance free of charge within the scope of its business.

According to Article 38(1) of the present Copyright Law, performers enjoy the following exploitation rights:

(a) The right to broadcast and to communicate to the public their live performance and to obtain remuneration;
(b) The right to permit others to record the sounds or images of their performance and to obtain remuneration;
(c) The right to permit others to reproduce and to distribute sound recordings and audiovisual recordings of their performance and to obtain remuneration;
(d) The right to permit others to transmit their broadcast via the Internet and to obtain remuneration.

The above catalogue goes beyond the standards of the relevant international conventions in that the rights in recorded performances are granted for both sound and audiovisual recordings, whereas TRIPS and the WPPT confine protection to sound recordings of live performances. A rental right is not yet available under the current Copyright Law, not even to performers whose performances are fixed in phonograms as prescribed by Article 9 WPPT, but the third Copyright Law amendment finally added the right to permit the rental of both performances fixed in phonograms as well as performances fixed in audiovisual recordings and to claim remuneration for such use, which will henceforth be accommodated in Article 39(1) No. 5. Due the extension of the rental right and other rights to audiovisually fixated performances, the Chinese performer's rights regime now complies with Article 9 of the Beijing Treaty on Audiovisual Performances.[309]

On the other hand, under the present Copyright Law, performers have no right to obtain remuneration for the broadcast of their recorded performance, not to mention a right to control such broadcast,[310] and also the third Copyright Law did not entail

308. See also Zuo Juan, '"Zhuzuoquanfa" songshengao beijingxia de biaoyanzhequan' (Performer's rights against the background of the draft "Copyright Law"), 13 *Shang* (Business) (2016), 220 (available at http://www.wanfangdata.com.cn/details/detail.do?_type=perio&id=shang201613191) who suggested to abolish the special treatment of main actors.

309. Zuo Juan, note 308, with regard to the 2014 draft amendment, which proposed the same.

310. China ratified the Beijing Treaty on Audiovisual Performances of 2012 on 9 July 2014 (treaty notification No. 5, at https://www.wipo.int/treaties/en/notifications/beijing/treaty_beijing_5.html) under the proviso that it will not apply Article 11(1) and (2) on the exclusive broadcasting and public communication right and, alternatively, on a right of performers to be remunerated for broadcasting and public communication.

any changes to this. As far as the TV broadcast of video recordings of performances is concerned, Article 46 of the current Copyright Law (Article 48 after the third amendment's entry into force) explicitly assigns the right to control such broadcast to the video producer. To maintain this rather limited protection standard, China has made a corresponding reservation that it will not be bound by Article 15(1) of the WPPT on a single equitable remuneration to performers and phonogram producers for the broadcasting or other communication to the public of their phonograms published for commercial purposes,[311] and by Article 11(1) and (2) of the Beijing Treaty, which prescribe an exclusive right of the performer in the broadcast and the communication to the public of their performances fixed in audiovisual recordings or, alternatively, a right to be remunerated for such use.[312] Interestingly, the Intellectual Property Chapter of the Regional Comprehensive Economic Partnership Agreement that China signed together with numerous Asian-Pacific countries shortly after the third amendment, on 15 November 2020[313] prescribes the opposite at least with regard to performances fixed in phonograms, namely that performers shall be entitled to a single equitable remuneration or, alternatively, to royalties for the direct or indirect use of commercial phonograms for the purpose of broadcasting (Article 11.11.).

3. Phonogram and Video Producers

Even though not prescribed by international treaties, the Copyright Law since 1990 granted a neighbouring right not only to phonogram producers, but also to producers of video recordings which do not constitute cinematographic works. Both neighbouring rights are regulated in Article 42(1) of the current Copyright Law, which will become Article 44(1) after the third amendment's entry into force.

Accordingly. producers of sound and video recordings are entitled to permit others to reproduce, distribute, rent and to transmit their recordings via the Internet and to obtain remuneration. The rights of rental and transmission via the Internet, which are required by the WPPT with regard to phonogram producers (the rental right also by Article 14(4) TRIPS, with regard to phonogram producers and other right holders in phonograms), were added in 2001. The duration of protection for phonograms and video recordings is 50 years, counted from the first production and lasting until 31 December of the 50th year.

The current Copyright Law does not include a broadcasting right in the enumeration of neighbouring rights. From the explanations above we have learned that under the present provisions phonogram producers do not even enjoy a mere remuneration right for the broadcast of their phonograms (Article 44 of the current Copyright Law). In this regard, the producers of video recordings are in a privileged position, because Article 46 of the current Copyright Law (Article 48 after the third amendment's entry into force) stipulates that not only producers of cinematographic works but also producers of mere unoriginal video recordings shall be asked for permission and remunerated by the broadcasting enterprise.

311. https://www.wipo.int/treaties/en/notifications/wppt/treaty_wppt_66.html.
312. https://www.wipo.int/treaties/en/notifications/beijing/treaty_beijing_5.html.
313. The chapters of the agreement can be downloaded from this newly established website https://rcepsec.org/legal-text/

The third Copyright Law amendment has significantly improved the status of phonogram producers, in that it created a new legal license in Article 45, according to which phonogram producers shall at least be remunerated for the dissemination of their phonograms by wire or wireless means or the communication of their phonograms to the public by mechanical sound transmission devices.

As repeatedly mentioned, the earlier 2014 Copyright Law draft amendment proposed the abolishment of the video producer's neighbouring right, but the later drafts withdrew from this plan.

4. Broadcasting Organizations

The current Copyright Law entitles radio and TV broadcasters to prevent others from rebroadcasting their radio or TV broadcasts and from recording in sound or video and making further copies of such recordings without authorization (Article 45). The third Copyright Law amendment transferred the neighbouring rights of broadcasting organizations to Article 47 and expanded them. It no longer limits the reproduction right of the broadcasting organizations to "making sound or video recordings", but replaced it by a technologically more neutral right to prohibit the "fixation" of the broadcast and the fixation's further reproduction (Article 47(1) No. 2). The amendment furthermore added the right to prohibit the communication of the broadcast through the internet (Article 47(1) No.3). As discussed above, it is quite questionable if such a right could also be invoked against the re-al-time internet transmission because the definition of the internet communication right in Article 10(12) Copyright Law presupposes that it is made available in a manner that the members of the public can access the work from a place and *at a time individually chosen by them*. TV broadcasters, anyway, seem to prefer a copyright in their broadcasts as "audiovisual works" over an extension of their neighbouring right to the internet environment, and recent case law has, as discussed, become more accommodating towards their demands.[314] On the other hand, a new paragraph (2) to Article 47 stipulates that broadcasting organizations, while exercising their expanded rights, shall not affect, limit or violate the rights of other parties to exercise their respective copyright or neighbouring rights.

Rule 26 Implementing Regulations specifies that the subject matter of the neighbouring right of broadcasting organizations shall be the broadcast radio and TV "program", which implies that the content rather than the actual broadcast is subject matter of protection, and also Article 45 of the present Copyright Law refers to the "broadcast program" as protected subject matter.[315] The Copyright Law draft amendment of April 2020 actually proposed to rename the protected subject matter into "program-carrying signal" but obviously many commentators found this term too technical, so that the draft of August 2020 and ultimately also the third Copyright Law amendment renamed it again, into "radio and TV broadcast".

314. See IV. 2. (a) *supra*.

315. More about the term program in Huang Wei, 'Jianlun dianshitai zhizuo de dianshi jiemu goucheng zuopin' (Short discussion whether TV programs produced by TV broadcasters constitute works), 3 *Zhongguo Banquan* (2002), 38.

According to Article 45(2) of the current Copyright Law, which will become Article 47(3) after the third amendment's entry into force, the neighbouring right of broadcasting organizations lasts 50 years from the first broadcast and expires on 31 December of the 50th year. Not included is the TV broadcaster's right of communication to the public, as prescribed by Article 14(3) of the TRIPS agreement. In this context, Chinese commentators refer to the last sentence of this TRIPS provision, which allows its members not to protect broadcasting organisations, as long as they protect the copyright owners in the broadcast works in compliance with the corresponding Berne provisions.[316]

XI. SPECIAL ASPECTS OF COPYRIGHT ENFORCEMENT

Just like the enforcement of other intellectual property, enforcement of copyright is bifurcated in that right owners can choose between judicial and administrative proceedings. In charge of the latter are the local copyright administrations under the supervision of the NCAC, which proceed primarily according to the enforcement provisions in the various above-mentioned statutes enacted by the State Council, for instance, the Implementing Regulations, the Internet Regulations or the Software Regulations. The latest available administrative copyright enforcement report on the NCAC website is of 2015[317] and therefore no longer representative. Quite interestingly, it shows that in 2015 there were significantly fewer administrative proceedings than in 2014, and the 2014 report shows a similar decrease in comparison with 2012 (a report for 2013 was not published).[318] Newer data on whether this trend continued or whether administrative enforcement has been reinvigorated in the years after 2015 are not available. The data on judicial enforcement are more up to date. According to the 2018 and 2019 White Books on Judicial Intellectual Property Enforcement published by the SPC,[319] courts throughout China accepted 195.405 new copyright cases in 2018, which represents an increase of 42.36 percent over 2017, and 293.066 cases in 2019, an increase of almost 50 percent over 2018.

As mentioned, a major part of the third Copyright Law amendment has been focused on enforcement. Apart from easier access to damages, higher compensation amounts and more detailed regulations on the legal protection of technical protection measures and digital rights information, which will be treated below, Chapter V of the Copyright Law, currently on "Legal liability and enforcement measures", henceforth on "Protection of Copyright and of Rights related to Copyright", also clarifies the competencies of the local copyright administrations and regulates the sanctions they may impose on infringers in more detail.

Administrative enforcement as a peculiarity of Chinese intellectual property protection has already been explained in the part on Patents, Utility Models and Designs and will be further treated in the part on enforcement. Distinct about administrative

316. Li Shunde and Zhou Yang, note 78, 158.
317. http://www.ncac.gov.cn/chinacopyright/contents/506/314694.html.
318. All annual reports from 2000–2015 can be accessed here http://www.ncac.gov.cn/chinacopyright/channels/506.html.
319. White Book for 2018: http://www.iprdaily.cn/news_21514.html; white book for 2019: https://www.chinacourt.org/article/detail/2020/04/id/5049570.shtml.

copyright enforcement is that it is carried out by special local copyright bureaus, not by the intellectual property agencies mentioned in the other parts of this book, which are in charge of industrial property. The third Copyright Law amendment introduced a new Article 55 that entitles the local administrations to question the parties, to conduct on-the-spot inspections of locations and items, to inspect and to copy documents such as contracts and to seal and detain premises and items, whereby the parties are under the obligation to cooperate and to refrain from obstruction. The amendment furthermore details the administrative sanctions against specific infringing acts that violate the public interests in a reworded Article 53 (thus far: Article 48). They will henceforth include a "warning" apart from cessation orders, confiscation of illegal gains, confiscation or destruction of illegal copies, confiscation of material, tools, devices, etc., used for the infringing production and fines. The amendment furthermore added the destruction not only of the illegal copies but also of the material, tools, devices, etc., used for the production of the infringing copies to the list of administrative sanctions, emphasizing that such destruction shall be carried out "in a non-hazardous manner".[320] The fines shall henceforth be up to five times the illegal turnover if such turnover exceeds RMB 50,000, or up to RMB 250,000 in the absence of an illegal turnover if the illegal turnover is less than RMB 50,000 or cannot be determined. The latest draft amendment of August 2020 proposed to also add the infringement of the new rental right of performers in phonograms or video recordings incorporating their performance, of the rental right of the producers of audio and video recordings and of the new right to transmit the broadcast through the internet to the list of administratively punishable acts but for whatever reason, the final amendment added only the unauthorized internet transmission of broadcasts to the list of administratively punishable acts. Also administratively punishable will henceforth be violations of the below-discussed new bans on the making, etc., of devices or components that enable the circumvention or deletion of technical protection measures or on offering corresponding services and on publicly offering works and other protected contents the rights management information of which has been altered or moved.

Finally, the third amendment followed the latest draft of August 2020 and did not readopt the provisions proposed by the discussion draft of April 2020 on the protection of the public against the abuse of copyright and related rights. For this, the April draft first proposed an addition to Article 4 Copyright Law, which would have obliged right owners to refrain from abusing their rights in a manner that affects the normal dissemination of works. A new Article 50 in Chapter V would then, quite contrary to the chapter's new title "Protection of Copyright and of Rights related to Copyright", have regulated the sanctions against such abuse by right owners, ranging from correction orders over warnings to confiscation of unlawful revenues and fines of up to five times the illegal turnover if it exceeds RMB 50,000 or, where the turnover is lower than RMB 50,000, difficult to determine or absent, a fine of up

320. Article 54(5) of the amended Copyright Law clarifies that People's Courts shall have similar competencies to destroy not only infringing copies but also materials, tools and devices without compensation to the infringer, but only upon the right owner's request. If special circumstances speak against such destruction, the court may instead prohibit the materials, tools and devices from flowing back into channels of commerce.

to RMB 250,000. Obviously, these provisions on punishing rather than protecting authors and right owners, accommodated in the Copyright Law's Chapter V of the on "Protection of Copyright and Rights Related to Copyright" of all places, were heavily criticized by those who followed the invitation to comment on the draft.

1. Circumvention of Technical Protection Measures and Alteration of Copyright Management Information

Article 47 No. 6 of the current Copyright Law provides that the intentional circumvention or deletion of technological measures adopted by copyright owners or neighbouring rights owners in order to protect their rights is an infringement that calls for civil liability and, if the public interest is simultaneously harmed, also for administrative sanctions. Rule 24 No. 3 Software Regulations contains a similar regulation with regard to the circumvention or deletion of software protection measures. However, the wording of these provisions appears to be quite superficial because they neither require the protection mechanisms to be technically "effective" nor do they include important preparatory acts such as the commercial sale or internet transmission of circumvention of deletion devices or programs. It was up to the Internet Regulations to provide more details. Rule 19(1) of the Internet Regulations includes the intentional (i.e., not negligent) making, importing and offering devices or parts for the circumvention or destruction of technical protection measures, as well as providing technical services to help others to circumvent or to destroy protection measures into the catalogue of acts that are administratively punished with confiscation of the devices etc., and a fine of up to five times the illegal business revenue if such revenue exceeds RMB 50,000 and up to RMB 250,000 if the revenue is below RMB 50,000. The third Copyright Law amendment transferred this enumeration of acts to a new Article 49(1) Copyright Law. Article 49(2) of the amended Copyright Law furthermore defines technical protection measures as effective technologies, devices or parts that prevent or limit the unauthorized browsing or appreciation or the making available on the internet of works and neighbouring rights protected content.

Another deficiency of the current Copyright Law is that its relevant provisions are not aligned with the limitations and other forms of permitted uses (legal licences). Therefore, even circumventions that aim at enabling uses privileged by the limitations in its Article 22 (Article 24 after the third amendment's entry into force) or uses of subject matter that is not even copyright protected at all appear to be unlawful. Also here, the Internet Regulations in Rule 12 thus far provided some relief to legitimate users, stipulating that the circumvention of technical protection measures per se but not the circulation, etc., of devices enabling a circumvention are permitted for the following purposes:

(a) classroom teaching or distribution among researchers for scientific purposes, provided that the works are already published, the number of teachers or researchers which are given access is small, and the works can only be obtained through the internet;
(b) making the works accessible on the web for blind people in a format that is readable to them, provided that the works are only obtainable through the internet;

(c) pursuing official duties by administrative and judicial organs;
(d) for testing the security functions of a computer and its system or network through the internet.

Whereas the limitations (a)–(c) may be subsumed under numbers 1, 6 and 12 of the mentioned catalogue of limitations in Article 22(1) (henceforth: Article 24(1)) Copyright Law on the permissibility of use for private research and study, for school education and for making literary works accessible to the blind, the permissibility of the circumvention for the purpose of computer system and network testing (d) is a new one that could thus far not be deduced from the higher-ranking Copyright Law.

This state of uncertainty came to an end with the third Copyright Law amendment, which transferred this list of exceptions in amended form to a new Article 50, rewording, for instance, the limitation that privileges the blind to bring it in conformity with the Marrakesh Agreement. Article 50 of the amended Copyright Law is also more generous towards legitimate users than Rule 12 of the Internet Regulations, which are focused on the internet environment, in that not only non-availability outside the internet justifies circumvention for teaching and research purposes and for the sake of the visually disabled, but non-availability "though ordinary channels" is sufficient, be it through the internet or within the analogous world. Also, with specific regard to the permissibility of the circumvention for teaching purposes, the prerequisite that the number of persons to whom the content obtained by way of circumvention is made accessible does no longer have to be "small" as required by Rule 12 of the Internet Regulations. The amendment furthermore added another, already mentioned limitation according to which technical protection measures may be circumvented to enable encryption research and research on software reverse engineering.

The growing popularity of paywalls and other barriers to content, protected or not, raises concerns about the structural imbalance between powerful content providers and individual users, to the extent that the latter are even deprived of their informational self-determination rights if they want to access information.[321] The few available court decisions demonstrate that courts are trying to strike a fair balance of the interests of authors and of the general public.

A decision of the Beijing Intermediate People's Court No. 1 of 30 January 2007[322] dealt with the question whether the circumvention of technical protection measures formed an infringing act if it enabled access to a non-copyright protected online service. In this particular case, in which the defendant circulated software that enabled users to circumvent a subscription mechanism and therefore caused harm to the plaintiff's economic interests, the court found a violation of general provision in Article 2 Unfair Competition Law (prior to the amendment of 2017), according to which business operators shall adhere to the principles of voluntariness, equality, fairness and good faith. The court also imposed a relatively high burden of proof on the plaintiff, who had to evidence that his technical arrangement actually formed a technical protection measure and that the defendant's acts actually resulted in its

321. Wang Qing and Chen Xuanbo, 'Shuzi shidai banquan jishu baohu cuoshi yu yinsiquan de chongtu yu xietiao' (Technical copyright protection measures, their conflict as well as balance with privacy rights in the digital age), 5 *Xuexi yu Tansuo* (Study and Exploration) (2019), 63 et seq.

322. 8569 *Yi Zhong Min Chu Zi* (2006), http://www.cnipr.net/article_show.asp?article_id=4454.

circumvention. In another case pertaining to the circumvention of software encryption that aimed at securing that the licensed software was used within the licensed scope, the Wuhan Higher People's imposed a lower burden of proof on the plaintiff, finding that initial physical evidence that the number of computers on which the same software was used in spite of the purchase of licence for use on far fewer devices, along with evidence that the network cards in the defendant's computers all had the same serial number, formed sufficient proof of the defendant's manipulation of his own devices to match the encryption files of the software.[323] Another decision of the Shanghai Higher People's Court[324] found that the technical measures circumvented by the defendant did not protect the plaintiff's computer program but only the data files generated by the program, which were not copyright protected subject matter. Obviously, the court in this case did not find the data files worthy of alternative Unfair Competition law protection.

The current Copyright Law provisions on the civil and administrative liability for intentional removal or alteration of rights management information are as rudimentary as the provisions on legal protection of technical protection measures. In contrast to the corresponding WIPO treaty provisions,[325] Article 48(7) of the current Copyright Law only sanctions the intentional removal or alteration of rights management information *per se* but remains silent on the further exploitation of the works or work copies with manipulated rights management information. It was, again, up to the Internet Regulations to clarify in Rule 5(2) the infringing character of the most relevant of these subsequent acts, namely making available such works on the internet, provided that the offender uploaded such works in spite of having knowledge or reason to know about the manipulation of the rights management information. The current Copyright Law instead only requires that the offender who altered or removed the rights management information acted "intentionally", which is probably not enough to meet the requirements of the WIPO treaties according to which also those offenders shall be held liable who had "reasonable grounds to know" that the removal or alteration helped to induce, enable, facilitate or conceal an infringement.[326]

The third Copyright Law amendment finally removed the deficiencies of the current provisions. A new Article 51 will henceforth prohibit not only the intentional removal or alteration of rights management information unless such removal or alteration is unavoidable for technical reasons, but also the offer of works and other

323. Decision of the Wuhan Intermediate People's Court 59 *Wu Zhi Chu Zi* (2007), upheld by the Higher People's Court of Hubei Province, 23 *E Min San Zhong Zi* (2008); unfortunately the full texts of the decisions was not traceable but the Intermediate People's Court's decision is summarized and commented in the master's thesis of Liu Guicen, *Case Studies of Technological Protection Measures for Computer Software*, submitted to Shanghai Jiaotong University on 25 April 2011, accessible upon subscription on the database www.cnki.net, at http://kreader.cnki.net/Kreader/CatalogViewPage.aspx?dbCode = cdmd& filename = 1011299489.nh&tablename = CMFD2012&compose = &first = 1&uid = .

324. 110 *Hu Gao Min San (Zhi) Zhong Zi* (2006), http://www.law-lib.com/cpws/cpws_view.asp?id = 200401177969.

325. Article 12 WCT; Article 19 WPPT.

326. Article 12 WCT; Article 19 WPPT.

protected content to the public while knowing or having reasonable grounds to know that the rights management information therein have been manipulated or removed.

Article 48 of the current Copyright Law (which will become Article 53 after the third amendment's entry into force) also mentions the possibility of criminal sanctions against various offences, including the deletion or circumvention of protection measures and the manipulation of rights management information, but the Criminal Code of 1997 does not specify these acts as criminally punishable.[327]

Finally, it should be noted that at least in one respect, the Chinese provisions go beyond the standard of the WIPO Treaties and other international copyright conventions in that they do not only protect copyright owners, performers and phonogram producers against circumvention of technical protection measures and against removal or alteration of neighbouring rights information, but also broadcasting organizations.

2. Liability of Internet Service Providers

The Copyright Law is silent on internet service provider liability. The only legal basis for holding providers liable for infringement committed by the clients has previously been the mentioned Article 36 of the Tort Liability Law of 2009, according to which internet service providers of any kind could avoid joint and several liability for compensation if they expeditiously react to the tort victim's notification by taking the necessary measures to delete, block or disconnect the infringing content. Also, according to this provision, service providers had a certain duty of care insofar as they could be held jointly and severally liable if they knew about the tortuous act of a user but they did not have to proactively take measures to prevent it. As mentioned, the content of Article 36 Tort Liability Law has been expanded and transferred to Articles 1194–1197 of the new Civil Code. Article 1195 now regulates in greater detail that the notification shall contain initial evidence of infringement and the infringed party's real personal information, that the service provider shall notify the client alleged of infringement and take the necessary blocking measures according to the initial evidence, both in a timely manner because otherwise the provider will bear joint and several liability for the grown damage, and also that the right owner shall be held liable if he wrongly notifies a provider of infringement and this resulted in a damage to the provider or the client. Article 1196 Civil Code takes into account the possibility of wrong infringement accusations, clarifying that the alleged user shall be allowed to deny infringement it in a substantiated manner, by providing the provider with initial evidence of non-infringement. The provider shall then forward the counterstatement to the right owner with a request to file a complaint with a competent authority or to file infringement suit in court, and, if the provider does not receive a notification about such complaint or lawsuit within a reasonable period of time, it shall lift the blocking measures in a timely manner. Article 1197, finally, provides that not only service providers who actually knew (as regulated by the previous Article 36 Tort Liability Law) but also those who had reason to know that

327. There are examples, however, in which courts criminally prosecuted copyright infringers for acts not expressly specified as punishable by the Criminal Code, see 4. *infra*.

a client uses their services for infringement and did not take measures to prevent such infringement shall bear joint and several liability.

The above provisions are not specific to copyright but read on any infringement of civil rights committed by using the services of online providers. A plethora of copyright-specific provisions on provider liability can be found on a lower level in the norm hierarchy:

The Internet Regulations contain provisions on the liability of internet service providers, which resemble Articles 12–15 of the EU E-Commerce Directive 2000/31/EC insofar as the degree of liability depends of the kind of service provided.

The lowest degree of liability bear services which provide access to works, performances or audio or visual recordings (hereinafter: protected content) at a user's request or automatically transmit content at a user's request (Rule 20) and caching services that automatically store protected content received from other web services to make it available at request in order to improve the transmission efficiency (Rule 21). They are neither liable for compensation if they enable access to infringing contents nor do they have to take contents down or block further access upon a right owner's notification. To be completely released from liability, however, transmission and access providers shall not engage in selecting or altering the transmitted content or content they provide access to and must ensure that the content transmitted or provided access to is only made available to the specific requesting user and not to other parties. A caching service provider who wants to be freed of any liability shall not engage in altering the cached content and must ensure that its service does not impact on the interaction between the original web service and the user and that it automatically modifies, deletes or screens protected content if such content is modified, deleted or screened by the original web service.

Services that provide users with storage space, which would largely correspond to the "online content-sharing service providers" regulated by the EU DSM Directive 2019/790, bear a higher liability risk, in that they can only escape liability if they (a) have openly indicated that their service aims at storing content of their clients, together with name, contact person and website address, (b) do not alter the hosted content, (c) do not know and have no reason to know about infringing content uploaded by their clients, (d) do not reap a direct profit from the uploaded content (e.g. pay per view) and (e) have reacted expeditiously to a right owner notification of infringement in accordance with the notice and take down procedure, which is detailed in Rules 14–17. According to Rule 23, the same duty of care applies to providers of search and linking services, who have to delete the link to infringing contents upon a right owner' notification, and who are only released from liability for damages if they had no knowledge and no reason to know about the infringing character of the linked content. It is unclear whether and to which extent host providers are obliged to employ technical measures, respectively "content recognition technologies" in the language of the EU DSM Directive 2019/790, to browse their platforms for possibly infringing contents in order to avoid liability as parties who "had reason to know" of infringement.

No reason to know about the infringement and thus not liable for damages is a service provider who has been authorized to transmit the work through the internet by the holder of an original licence to broadcast whom the original right owners have not also authorized to sublicense their work. In such a case, it may occur that the licensing party will be held immediately liable for the internet transmission made by the innocent provider.[328]

A right owner who believes that his network transmission right has been infringed or that his rights management information has been altered in connection with the use of a hosting or search/link provider, may notify the provider thereof in writing and request the deletion of content or the removal of the link to the content. The request must contain the right owner's name, contact information and address, title and web address of the infringing content and initial proof of infringement (Rule 14). Also, the requesting party bears responsibility for the truthfulness of the request. According to Rule 15, the hosting or link provider shall then react by expeditiously deleting or blocking the allegedly infringing content and by forwarding the right owner's request to the user responsible for the upload or link. If the user has not left his contact information so that the request cannot be forwarded, it shall instead be made public online. Rule 16 provides the alleged user with the opportunity to object by filing a written counter-request, which must contain the user's name, address and contact information, the title and internet address of the content to be restored or deblocked and initial evidence of non-infringement. The service provider shall then expeditiously restore or deblock the content and forward the counter-request to the respective right owner. The right owner shall then not again request the deletion or blocking of the same content (Rule 17).

On 26 November 2012, the SPC enacted the parallel Network Interpretations[329] with even more detailed provisions on internet service provider liability, which replaced the Interpretation of Several Issues Relating to the Adjudication of and Application of Law to Copyright Disputes Related to Computer Networks of 22 November 2000 (last amendment on 22 December 2006).[330] As a general rule, the first sentence of Rule 4 Network Interpretations stipulates that internet service providers and third parties who collaborated to offer a work or other protected content to the public shall bear joint liability for infringement. The second sentence, however, exempts those providers from joint liability *who can* prove that they merely offered technical services such as automatic access provision or transmission, storage space,[331] browsing, linking and text sharing. That is, in contrast to the Internet Regulations, the Network Interpretation does not predefine categories of non-liable transmission or caching providers, but a service provider which wants to escape liability due to the technical character of its service must prove its innocence in each individual case. Rule 6 Network Interpretations somewhat repeats this, stipulating that if the plaintiff has initial evidence that the provider has offered his work or other protected content, but the provider can counterprove that he offered a mere network service

328. Beijing Chaoyang District People's Court of 20 November 2019, 12496 *Jing 0105 Min Chu* (2019), https://mp.weixin.qq.com/s/Ze-hXlmQ-QEazZ2SAILcvg.

329. In Chinese: https://www.chinacourt.org/law/detail/2012/12/id/146033.shtml.

330. https://wipolex.wipo.int/en/legislation/details/6485.

331. Obviously meaning cloud services, but without any further definition like in Article 2(6) of the DSM Directive (EU) 2019/790, which clarifies that only business-to-business cloud services and services that allow users to upload content for their own use, shall not pertain to the "online content-sharing service providers", which are liable for infringing content uploaded by their users pursuant to Article 17 of the Directive.

(obviously one of the above technical services) and is therefore without fault, the courts shall not establish infringement.

One important question on which the administrative Internet Regulations are silent is addressed in Rules 7–9 of the Network Interpretations, namely of the impact of the provider's involvement in a third parties' infringement on the provider's liability. Of central importance is the extent to which the provider committed "aiding and abetting". According to Rule 7, such aiding and abetting shall be established if the provider by word, by recommending technical assistance, awarding scores or other inducements encourages users to infringe a copyright owner's online transmission right. Liability shall also be found if the provider does not take down, block, etc., content while knowing or having reason to know about the infringement, or if he offers technical assistance to commit infringement. If, in turn, the provider does not expeditiously take down or block the content or takes other measures upon being notified about the infringement, he shall be regarded as having known about the infringement (Rule 13). Whether the provider has acted "expeditiously" shall be assessed under comprehensive consideration of factors such as the manner and the accuracy of the notification, the difficulty of taking measures, the character of the service and the nature of the work, its fame, the number of works, etc. (Rule 14).

According to Rule 8 Network Interpretations, establishment of provider liability shall also depend on whether the provider knew about the infringement or should have known about it. Whether the provider should have known about the infringement shall, according to Rule 9, be determined along the following factors: (a) the information management abilities that the provider has had in light of the nature and method of his services and their potential of generating infringement, (b) the popularity of the disseminated content and the corresponding apparentness of infringement, (c) the degree of active involvement of the provider in selecting, editing, modifying or recommending, etc., the content uploaded on his platform (which is central to Japanese courts when determining the liability of intermediaries),[332] (d) whether the provider has actively taken measures to prevent infringement, (e) whether the provider has put in place a convenient procedure of receiving complaints about infringement and of timely and reasonably responding to them, (f) whether the provider has taken appropriate measures against users who repeatedly used his services to commit infringement and (g) other factors.

Rule 8 also clarifies that there is no general obligation on providers to browse their platforms for each and every infringement. If a provider can prove that it was impossible for him to detect an infringement in spite of having taken appropriate and effective measures, it shall be released from liability. Rule 11 stipulates that if the provider reaps a direct profit from the works and other protected content made available on its site (e.g., through pay-per-view), from which, however, advertisement revenues, service fees, etc., that are not related to specific content shall be excluded, its duty of care shall be significantly higher. With regard to the special case of hosting popular film and TV works, Rule 10 clarifies that courts shall determine that the

332. Peter Ganea and Masahiro Motoyama, '§21 Urheberrecht' (Copyright), in Harald Baum and Moritz Bälz, *Handbuch des japanischen Handels- und Wirtschaftsrechts* (Handbook on Japanese Commercial and Economic Law) (2nd ed., Wolters Kluwer, forthcoming 2021).

provider has known about infringement if he actively listed, catalogued, indexed the uploaded works or provided short descriptions or content summaries of them and rendered them easily downloadable, browsable or otherwise obtainable through its site. Where a popular film or TV work is placed on the provider's main site or another location where it can be easily found or where the provider has actively engaged in its selection, editing, etc., or where all kind of protected content is made available in a manner that it becomes obvious that the content is used without authorization and that no appropriate measures have been taken to prevent such use, court shall assume that the provider should have known about the infringement (Rule 12).

Finally, Rule 15 assigns regional jurisdiction to deal with internet infringement cases to the court at the domicile of the infringer or at the location where the infringement has been committed (i.e., where the server or terminal computer used for the infringement is located). Where the location cannot be determined or is abroad, the court at the location in which the plaintiff detected the infringement shall have jurisdiction.

In judicial practice, it seems that courts do rather freely choose the set of secondary provisions that they want to apply when determining ISP liability for infringement, either the rather technical administrative Internet Regulations, according to which liability largely depends on the technical character of the services offered by the service provider with little room for interpretation, or the SPC Network Interpretation, which place more emphasis on the provider's concrete acts, the degree to which it involved in the infringement and the measures for its prevention it should have taken, and oblige courts to comprehensively consider the circumstances of each individual case.

In its decision of 27 February 2019,[333] which was entirely based on the Internet Regulations as administrative copyright-specific interpretation of the former Article 36 Tort Liability Law, the Hangzhou Internet Court freed *Tencent*, the corporation behind China's famous instant messaging and multiple-purpose service *WeChat*, from any liability for incorporating in its environment so-called mini programs, i.e., apps that are not downloaded on the mobile phone but can be accessed through the internet, which hosted infringing contents. The court found that *Tencent* formed a mere "provider of automatic access or transmission services" according to Rule 20 of the Internet Regulations, without control over the suppliers of the mini programs. Also, the only way of blocking the infringing content would be to cut the connection to the mini program, which, according to the court, would have gone beyond the "necessary" measures required by the old Article 36 Tort Liability Law (as well as by Article 1195 of the new Civil Code). The decision is quite remarkable, considering that these mini programs are developed and operated within an environment that is entirely under the defendant's control.

In its decision of 13 January 2016,[334] the Shanghai Intellectual Property Court found that deep linking an infringingly uploaded content formed accessory infringement, especially because it enticed viewers to remain on the defendant's video website instead of switching to the site on which the infringing content was originally

333. Excerpts of the decision published on the Pkulaw site: http://www.pkulaw.cn/Case/pal_a3ecfd5d734f711d853207585d4cbb24c71f77d095387105bdfb.html?match=Exact.
334. 213 *Hu Zhi Min Zhong Zi* (2015).

uploaded and thus generated a significant economic benefit to the defendant. The decision, in contrast to the above Hangzhou Internet Court's findings, rather adhered to the standards of the SPC Network Interpretation, which puts more emphasis on considering the circumstances of each individual case. A decision rendered by the Beijing Intellectual Property Court on 25 November 2019[335] held the defendant liable for hosting the plaintiff's font software that had been uploaded on the defendant's site by a client without authorization. According to the court, the defendant had "selected and arranged" the infringing software uploaded by the client in the meaning of Rule 9(3) of the Network Interpretations, which would also be proof that he had knowledge about the infringement and therefore aided and abetted according to Rule 7 of the same Interpretations. As will be further outlined below, linking infringing content may even be qualified as criminal unauthorized "distribution", due to a rather unique interpretation of the available criminal provisions on criminal copyright piracy.[336]

In sum, however, the Chinese legislature, in parts also the judiciary, is comparably lenient towards service providers that host or otherwise render accessible content uploaded by their clients, giving them ample leeway to head for safe harbours that shelter them from infringement liability. This is in stark contrast to the stance taken by the EU in its DSM Directive 2019/790, which holds large and well-established online content sharing providers directly liable for infringing content uploaded on their premises, without hardly any possibility of escaping liability. In connection with a broadened extended collective licensing regime, they are instead expected to seek the permission of right owners and to develop standards of remunerating them for the use of their works. The different approaches may be explained by the fact that in China, all noteworthy internet companies are domestic. YouTube, Instagram, Google, Facebook and many other services that dominate the internet outside the Great Firewall are censored and only accessible through Virtual Private Networks (the use of which is prohibited, and which are likely to be barred by effective technical means in the near future), so that an EU-style liability regime would exclusively hit China's domestic internet companies. The EU, in contrast, has almost nothing to offer in terms of innovative internet services but is entirely dominated by powerful US players (with the exception of the Chinese social media service TikTok, which has gained some popularity among Europe's youth), so that there is no danger that a too strict liability regime would put European companies at a competitive disadvantage.

3. Copyright-Specific Aspects of Damage Calculation

According to Article 49(1) of the current Copyright Law, damages shall be calculated according to the plaintiff's losses and, if this is not possible, according to the infringer's profit (Article 49(2)). If both calculation methods cannot be applied, the court can determine a statutory damage of up to RMB 500,000 depending on the circumstances of infringement. The third Copyright Law amendment, which moved the provisions on the determination of damages to Article 54, drastically increased the upper limit of statutory damages to RMB 5 million, following the trend towards higher damages that has been described in other chapters of this book.

335. 494 *Jing 73 Min Chu* (2018), https://mp.weixin.qq.com/s/ivewkjfqpREBc1xQGoAViQ.
336. See 4. *infra*.

The current Copyright Law does not explicitly mention damage calculation in licence analogy as a third alternative before the court may resort to statutory damages, but according to Rule 25 of the SPC's Copyright Interpretation, the court may consider the licence fee that the copyright owner may have obtained in the absence of infringement, among other aspects such as the kind of the infringed work, the nature of infringement and its consequences that have to be comprehensively considered, when determining a statutory damage. For this, courts may consider the fees agreed upon in previously concluded licence agreements,[337] provided that the previous agreement is related to a comparable work use.[338] Analogy can also be drawn to standard licence fee terms fixed by the party that exclusively licensed the infringed work to the plaintiff, for instance the fees the visual content company *Getty Images* determines for uses of images in different resolutions, and the defendant be ordered to pay damages in accordance with the fee standard that corresponds to his mode of use.[339] In the absence of reference licence fees, courts shall consider the gravity and/or the magnitude of infringement and its consequences. A decision that dealt with the unauthorized adaptation of a literary work found such gravity to be especially high because the adaptation incorporated the content, storyline, etc., expressed by the original work and has been uploaded on internet portals that give access to a large number of visitors.[340] Also, if works of fine art are attached to product packages without authorization, the total revenue from the product sales may serve as a starting point for statutory damage calculation.[341]

Article 54(1) of the amended Copyright Law, furthermore, explicitly lists the licence analogy as third alternative of damage calculation if the damage cannot be calculated by the other two methods. It also clarifies that the plaintiff can choose between calculation according to the actual damage and calculation according to the infringer's profit, whereas the wording of Article 49(1) of the current Copyright Law implies that the plaintiff can only resort to the infringer's profit if the actual damage cannot not be determined. Finally, Article 54(1) of the amended Copyright Law also regulates China's first copyright-specific punitive damages, which can amount to up to five times the damage actually suffered by the plaintiff, calculated as infringer's profit or determined in licence analogy (but not estimated as statutory damage) if the circumstances of infringement are serious.

337. Foshan Intermediate People's Court's decision of 25 July 2016, 219 *Fo Nan Fa Min Si Chu Zi* (2015), https://mp.weixin.qq.com/s/r9OYzmG2wM6T5eAikIN_2Q.

338. Beijing Internet Court decision of 12 August 2019, 8606 *Jing 0491 Min Chu* (2019), https://mp.weixin.qq.com/s/xK2SdOvh5nIGC9LCbLnH8g.

339. Tianjin Intermediate People's Court decision of 10 July 2019, 1865 *Jin 01 Min Zhong* (2019), https://mp.weixin.qq.com/s/fG9uVVgWDtg9_ON1o_hw4g.

340. Beijing Haidian District People?s Court decision of 14 June 2019, 17683 *Jing 0108 Min Chu* (2018), https://mp.weixin.qq.com/s/PXGHEzfikK4JMzGaDflY6A; see also Hangzhou Internet Court decision of 13 June 2019, 6851 *Zhe 0192 Min Chu* (2018), https://mp.weixin.qq.com/s/-n2w6L7gYi0mlqr3oL2iQQ; in this decision the court found the amount of the infringingly adapted content of a literary work to produce another literary work decisive when determining a statutory damage.

341. Decision of the Nanjing Railway Transportation Court of 27 July 2017, 669 *Su 8602 Min Chu* (2016), https://mp.weixin.qq.com/s/4lFY6bh4LIiWDbaUh2VicQ.

As already mentioned in the part on Patents, Utility Models and Designs, courts in intellectual property litigation frequently lean towards statutory damages due to the difficulty of calculating more realistic damage amounts based on the other three methods, which resulted in notoriously low compensation amounts. To facilitate calculation by the other three methods, Article 54(4) of the amended Copyright Law, just as the recently amended Patent Law,[342] shifts the burden of proof of the damage amount to the defendant in cases in which the plaintiff has done everything to comply with the duty to prove the claimed damage amount, but where conclusive proof can only be found in account books, material and other resources under the control of the defendant. In such cases, the court may order the defendant to hand over the relevant documents. If the defendant refuses to do so or provides false documents, the court may determine the damage amount on grounds of the claims and the evidence provided by the plaintiff.

The parties may alternatively settle the damage question among themselves, which shall then be acknowledged by the court. Also, just as in case of other intellectual property infringement, only the "reasonable" expenses for the prosecution of rights, lawyer's fees, collection of evidence, etc. shall be included in the damage calculation. In the past decades the "reasonable expenses" determined by courts have been notoriously lower than the actual expenses incurred to the plaintiff but, as already outlined in the Part on Patents, Utility Models and Designs, courts now seem to be more willing to consider the actual expenses, lawyer's fees, etc., also in copyright litigation.[343]

4. Criminal Copyright Enforcement

To comply with Article 61 of the TRIPS Agreement according to which at least wilful trademark counterfeiting and copyright piracy "on a commercial scale" shall be punishable, the Criminal Code of 1997 introduced two articles on criminal copyright infringements. According to Article 217, the "reproduction and/or distribution" (more about this term later) of works without permission of the copyright owners and specifically the reproduction and/or distribution of audiovisual works without their producer's permission, furthermore the publication of books the copyright in which is exclusively owned by another party, and the making and selling of artistic works that bear the false signature of others (false attribution of authorship) shall be punished by prison of up to three years, criminal detention and/or a fine, provided that such acts were committed for profit, generated a relatively high illegal revenue or other serious circumstances are given. In case of an especially high illegal revenue or other especially serious circumstances, the term of imprisonment may be raised from at least three to at longest seven years, and also the fine may be correspondingly raised. According to Article 218 Criminal Code, also those who knowingly sold illegally made work copies for the purpose of reaping a profit and gained a huge illegal revenue shall be imprisoned for up to three years and/or fined.

342. See XIV. 8. in this book's Part on Patents, Utility Models and Designs.
343. Foshan Intermediate People's Court's decision of 25 July 2016, note 337; see also the mentioned decisions of the Tianjin Intermediate People's Court of 10 July 2019, note 339, and of the Nanjing Railway Transportation Court of 27 July 2017, note 341.

The question of what a "relatively high illegal revenue" or "serious circumstances" actually mean has been first answered by the Supreme People's Court and the Supreme People's Procuratorate in their Interpretation on Several Questions pertaining to the Concrete Application of Law to Handling Criminal Cases of Intellectual Property Infringement of 8 December 2004.[344] Rule 5 states that a relatively high revenue shall be at least RMB 30,000, and also the "other serious circumstances" were translated into thresholds, namely an illegal business turnover of not less than RMB 50,000 or a number of not less than 1,000 illegal copies, and, again "other serious circumstances" to keep the catalogue of serious circumstances open. An "especially high illegal revenue" according to the second sentence of Article 217 shall be not less than RMB 150,000 and especially serious circumstances are existent if the illegal business turnover exceeds RMB 250,000, the number of illegal copies exceeds 5,000 illegal or where "other especially serious circumstances" are found.

The US were highly dissatisfied with both the criminal threshold system *per se* and the fixed minimum amounts, arguing against the latter that it was easily possible to profitably engage in copyright piracy beneath them. In a follow-up Interpretation of 4 April 2007,[345] the SPC and the Supreme People's Procuratorate attempted to appease this criticism by lowering the minimum number of infringing copies to 500 (2500 to establish a "especially serious" circumstance), but to no avail. China's threshold system became one of three items raised by the US in the mentioned WTO WT/DS362/R dispute. The US challenged the thresholds as a) *per se* not in compliance with WTO rules because the "industrial scale" requirement for criminal prosecution regulated by TRIPS shall be understood qualitatively, not quantitatively, and b) as being too high, anyway, excepting too much infringing activity beneath them from criminal prosecution. With regard to both, however, the US failed to convince the WTO Panel, so that China could maintain its threshold system. Also the Economic and Trade Agreement Between the United States of America and the People's Republic of China – Phase 1 (hereinafter: "Sino-US ETA") on 15 January 2020[346] obliges China only to abolish its thresholds specifically with regard to trade secret infringement, so that also the theft of trade secrets that have not yet amounted to a huge loss can be criminally prosecuted (Article 1.7), but leaves the present system with regard to copyright (and trademark) piracy untouched.

A fourth criminal-law related issue raised earlier by the US was the confusing formulation "reproduction-distribution" in Article 217 of the Criminal Law, which is also applied in the 2004 Criminal Infringement Interpretations and can be either read as "reproduction and distribution", i.e., as combining both the reproduction and the distribution to one infringing act that can only be prosecuted if the infringer committed both the reproduction and the distribution but not, for instance, the reproduction alone, or as "reproduction *or* distribution". The latter translation appeared less convincing both linguistically as well as in terms of legislative technique. From a

344. http://www.law-lib.com/law/law_view.asp?id=87670 (Chinese).
345. Available from the website of the SPC Gazette: http://gongbao.court.gov.cn/Details/e19129889e7045d07493acac8b6fbb.html (Chinese).
346. Available on the USTR's website: https://ustr.gov/sites/default/files/files/agreements/phase%20one%20agreement/Economic_And_Trade_Agreement_Between_The_United_States_And_China_Text.pdf.

legislative perspective, if "distribution" alone could be prosecuted, one would have to ask why Article 218 separately regulated the "sale" of infringing copies because such act would then be subsumable under "distribution".[347] Nevertheless, the mentioned second Interpretation of the SPC and the Supreme People's Procuratorate of 2007 finally opted for the latter translation and clarified in Rule 2 that both reproduction and distribution could be separately prosecuted, so that this issue has been removed from the list of US complaints submitted to the WTO.

The Criminal Code provisions of 1997 soon turned out to be insufficient to prosecute another, back then not yet rampant form of infringement, namely the unauthorized making available of works on the internet. Rule 11(3) of the Criminal Infringement Interpretations of 2004 arguably solved this problem by subsuming "network transmission" under "reproduction or distribution". According to Article 104 of China's Legislation Law (last amended in 2015), the SPC's interpretations are binding law for the lower courts, but their *raison d'etre* is still to interpret higher-ranking statutes that passed the National People's Congress and not to enhance their content. Insofar, the solution presented by the 2004 Criminal Interpretations appears quite daring, as it subsumes the act of network transmission that is regulated as a separate right in the Copyright Law, under two other acts in which the Copyright Law also grants separate exclusive rights, namely the reproduction/distribution, here obviously to be understood as immaterial "online distribution". Also, the Interpretation deals with aspects of criminal law, a legal area in special need of legal certainty, which is the reason why most modern criminal codes are governed by a ban on creating crimes by analogy. Commentators therefore suggest to amend the Criminal Code to regulate internet-related criminal copyright infringement directly there.[348] In spite of such concerns, the Opinion on Several Questions regarding the Application of Law to the Handling of Criminal Intellectual Property Infringement of 11 January 2011[349] issued by the SPC, the Supreme People's Procuratorate and the Ministry of Public Security, further affirmed the notion of criminal internet "distribution" of works and other protected subject matter, by determining new thresholds from which on internet copyright infringement shall be punishable, namely an illegal sales volume of RMB 50,000 or more, 500 or more transmitted work copies, 50,000 or more clicks on the illegally transmitted content or transmission to 1,000 or more members of an environment that requires subscription. If none of the above thresholds is fully met but more than half of at least two of them, criminal liability may nevertheless be established. Also, the catalogue is not closed, so that other, unspecified serious circumstances can also give rise to criminal liability (Rule 13).

In judicial practice, the SPC's and the criminal authorities' interpretation of the unauthorized internet transmission as criminal distribution seems to have encouraged

347. Guobin Cui, 'Distribution of Copyrighted Works by Framed Links and Peer-to-Peer Service Constitutes a Crime of Copyright Infringement under Chinese Criminal Law', in Kung-Chung Liu (ed.), note 234, 227 et seq.

348. Guobin Cui, note 347, refers to nine amendments to the Criminal Law since 1997 which would have provided plenty of opportunities to introduce a clear criminal provision on unauthorized internet transmission.

349. Accessible on the website of the SPC Gazette: http://gongbao.court.gov.cn/Details/55559be2150804415cf7add7b4f0c8.html (Chinese); also mentioned by Guobin Cui, note 347.

some lower courts to criminally sanction acts that did not even infringe upon a right specified by the Copyright Law, be it frame linking to infringing content[350] or transferring certification numbers of legally purchased software to thirds under violation of the software licence agreement.[351]

5. No Cumulative Protection under Copyright and Unfair Competition Law

As seen above, in certain cases in which the subject matter of litigation, for instance a live broadcast, cannot be categorized under works or neighbouring rights protected subject matter, it is possible to seek alternative protection under the Unfair Competition Law, mostly under the general obligation of business operators to adhere to business ethics, etc., in Article 2. Where infringement can be found under copyright law, however, courts will deny additional protection under Unfair Competition Law.[352]

350. The Shanghai Putuo District People's Court's decision 11 *Pu Xing (Zhi) Chu Zi* (2013) of 23 May 2014 sentenced the accused infringer to 15 months of imprisonment and a fine of RMB 30,000 for criminal "distribution" by providing framed links to torrent files on his website that led users to infringingly uploaded content within a peer-to-peer network (http://www.law-lib.com/cpws/cpws_view.asp?id = 200402394322); commented by Guobin Cui, note 347, 227 et seq.

351. Shanghai Pudong New Area District People's Court decision of 11 July 2008, 990 *Pu Xing Chu Zi* (2008), http://www.chinalawedu.com/new/17800a179a2011/2011716caoxin9528.shtml.

352. As clarified by a decision of the Beijing Internet Court of 11 November 2019, with regard to the unauthorized upload of a lawyer's article on another law firm's website, 14533 *Jing 0491 Min Chu* (2019), https://mp.weixin.qq.com/s/Cc4QGWKhDiddDga0MfA1Fw.

CHAPTER 5

Unfair Competition and Antitrust Law

Jyh-An Lee

Unfair competition law and antitrust law are the cornerstones of competition law, which aims to enhance economic efficiency, protect consumers and promote private competitive markets. In China, the Anti-Unfair Competition Law and Anti-Monopoly Law accordingly constitute the country's main regulatory structure of competition policy. China began to adopt antitrust rules only after its transition to the market economy in the late 1970s and early 1980s. With the purpose of fostering a market economy, the Chinese government started its legislation on fair and free market competition in the 1990s. The promulgation and implementation of the first Anti-Unfair Competition Law in 1993 was considered a swift success and a milestone from this perspective. On the other hand, although legislators since 1994 had been making endeavours to enact the country's Anti-Monopoly Law, the first codified version was not adopted until 2007.

This chapter introduces the regulatory framework of Anti-Unfair Competition Law and Anti-Monopoly Law. In addition to the anti-competitive, monopolistic, and abusive conducts prohibited by the law, the chapter also focusses on the interface and relationship between IP and these two laws.

I. ANTI-UNFAIR COMPETITION LAW

1. Legal History and Current Legislation

(a) The Evolution of the Anti-Unfair Competition Law

The Anti-Unfair Competition Law of the People's Republic of China ("AUCL") was enacted in 1993 with the purpose of maintaining the sound development of the socialist market economy, encouraging and protecting fair competition, preventing acts of unfair competition, and safeguarding the lawful rights and interests of businesses and consumers.[1] In the absence of a clear and well-functioned regulatory structure at that time, the 1993 AUCL opted for a broad yet rough way of regulation and had partly taken up the role of other departmental laws such as the Advertising Law, the Anti-Monopoly Law, the Bidding Law and the Price Law, as none of these regulations were available at the time.[2]

It was not until 24 years later that the first amendment of the AUCL came into force. The 2017 Amendment was based on two major considerations: first, in view of the enactment of relevant legislations and the sophistication of the regulatory framework, the provisions of the 1993 AUCL had overlapped with other legislative instruments. Therefore, the temporary role assigned to the AUCL in 1993 was assumed by other laws and regulations. This is why the provisions of predatory pricing, tying, and abuse of administrative powers were all deleted in the 2017 Amendment, given their more detailed regulation in the Anti-Monopoly Law and relevant regulations.[3] Second, market conditions of the country had significantly changed over time and the provisions of the 1993 law had become obsolete and thus unable to cover emerging areas such as, for example, unfair practices in the online environment. A new order had to be established for the new economy in China.[4]

In April 2019, the Standing Committee of the National People's Congress (NPCSC) released their decision on launching the second amendment of the AUCL.[5] Unlike the 2017 amendment which had come after more than two decades since the law's enactment, the second amendment was initiated within two years of the 2017 AUCL coming into force. Notably, all revisions were made to the provisions regarding trade secrets. It is thus an educated guess that the 2019 Amendment of the AUCL was a product of the intense trade war and rounds of negotiations between China and the United States starting from 2018, as a response to the US' accusation of China's theft of US companies' technology, know-how and trade secrets.[6] In particular, the 2019 AUCL explicitly listed electronic intrusion as a form of misappropriation,[7] broadened the scope of "trade secret" to cover other commercial information in

1. Anti-Unfair Competition Law of the People's Republic of China 1993 ("AUCL 1993") [Zhonghua Renmin Gongheguo Fan Buzhengdang Jingzheng Fa], Art. 1.
2. The first Advertising Law of the People's Republic of China was launched in 1994; the Price Law was first introduced in 1997; the Bidding Law first came into effect in 2000; and the Anti-Monopoly Law was not available until 2007.
3. See e.g. Anti-Monopoly Law of the People's Republic of China 2008 ("AML 2008") [Zhonghua Renmin Gongheguo Fan Longduan Fa] Arts. 17.2, 17.5, 32, 33.
4. See e.g. Anti-Unfair Competition Law of the People's Republic of China 2017 ("AUCL 2017") [Zhonghua Renmin Gongheguo Fan Buzhengdang Jingzheng Fa], Art. 22, which regulated the conduct of entrepreneurs engaging in production or distribution activities online.
5. See Decision of the Standing Committee of the National People's Congress to Amend Eight Laws Including the Construction Law of the People's Republic of China [Quanguo Remin Daibiao Dahui Changwu Weiyuanhui Guanyu Xiugai Zhonghua Renmin Gongheguo Jianzhu Fa Deng Babu Falv De Jueding], Art. 7.
6. Office of the United States Trade Representative, 'Findings of the Investigation into China's Acts, Policies and Practices Related to Technology Transfer, Intellectual Property, and Innovation Under Section 301 of the Trade Act of 1974' 22 March 2018, Section V, https://ustr.gov/sites/default/files/Section%20301%20FINAL.PDF accessed 25 May 2020.
7. Anti-Unfair Competition Law of the People's Republic of China 2019 Amendment ("AUCL 2019") [Zhonghua Renmin Gongheguo Fan Buzhengdang Jingzheng Fa], Art. 9.1(i).

addition to technological or operational information,[8] and expanded the scope of potential wrongdoers from entrepreneurs to other individuals or entities.[9] Moreover, for information not acquired by illicit means, the circumstances that give rise to a misappropriation were restricted in the 2017 AUCL to those where an "agreement" or the owner's manifest intention ("agreement") existed to keep the information in confidence.[10] The 2019 AUCL has replaced the term "agreement" with "duty of confidence".[11] Meanwhile, the 2019 AUCL further prohibits third-parties' inducements to breach of confidence[12] and increases the cap of compensatory damages, statutory damages and administrative fines.[13] Last but not least, the 2019 AUCL adds a new rule of burden of proof in the trade secret litigation, which is that as long as *prima facie* evidence could be adduced by the trade secret owner, it is the alleged infringer's onus to prove it has not misappropriated the subject information.[14] This new rule was in line with the US' concern of the high evidentiary threshold in trade secret litigation in China. Most of the revisions in the 2019 Amendment were reflected in the subsequent Economic and Trade Agreement ("US-China Phase One Deal") entered into by the two countries on 15 January 2020.[15]

(b) The Role of International Treaties

International treaties had played an indispensable role in the establishment of the anti-unfair competition system in China in 1993. As a member country of the Paris Convention and the World Trade Organization ("WTO"), China needed to incorporate the unfair competition provisions of international treaties into its national laws to fulfil its obligations. There are three types of unfair competition conducts explicitly mentioned by the Paris Convention:

(1) all acts of such a nature as to create confusion by any means whatever with the establishment, the goods, or the industrial or commercial activities, of a competitor;
(2) false allegations in the course of trade of such a nature as to discredit the establishment, the goods, or the industrial or commercial activities, of a competitor; and
(3) indications or allegations the use of which in the course of trade is liable to mislead the public as to the nature, the manufacturing process, the characteristics, the suitability for their purpose, or the quantity, of the goods.

---

8. *Ibid.*, Art. 9.4.
9. *Ibid.*, Art. 9.2.
10. AUCL 2017, note 4, Art. 9.1(iii).
11. AUCL 2019, note 7, Art. 9.1(iii).
12. *Ibid.*, Art. 9.1(iv).
13. *Ibid.*, Arts. 17.3, 17.4, 21.
14. *Ibid.*, Art. 32.
15. 'Economic and Trade Agreement between the Government of the United States of America and the Government of the People's Republic of China' 15 January 2020 ("US-China Phase One Deal 2020") https://ustr.gov/sites/default/files/files/agreements/phase%20one%20agreement/Economic_And_Trade_Agreement_Between_The_United_States_And_China_Text.pdf accessed 25 May 2020, Arts. 1.3, 1.4, 1.5.

On the basis of the Paris Convention, the Agreement on Trade-Related Aspects of Intellectual Property Rights ("TRIPS") further added the misappropriation of trade secrets as a type of unfair competition. However, the 1993 AUCL failed to comprehensively cover these four categories of unfair competition. For example, while Article 10bis (3)(iii) of the Paris Convention regulates all indications or allegations which may mislead the public as to the nature, the manufacturing process, the characteristics, the suitability for their purpose, or the quantity, of the goods, the scope of application of the same article in the 1993 AUCL only mentioned false indications or allegations that were misleading.[16] This loophole has been fixed in the 2019 AUCL.[17]

(c) SPC Interpretation

The SPC promulgated an Interpretation on Some Issues Concerning the Application of Law in the Trial of Civil Cases Involving Unfair Competition ("SPC Interpretation")[18] in 2007 to guide the judicial application of the AUCL. Notably, this SPC Interpretation was issued prior to the first amendment of the AUCL 2017 and there was no subsequent revision or replacement of the same. Consequently, some provisions in the SPC Interpretation are outdated under the latest 2019 AUCL. For instance, the SPC Interpretation provides that the party making the infringement claim shall bear the burden to prove that the subject information has met the statutory requirements of a trade secret, including the format, contents, and commercial value of the information as well as the specific precautionary measures adopted by the owner to maintain its secrecy.[19] In contrast, in the 2019 AUCL, the burden is shifted to the alleged infringer to demonstrate that the subject information falls short of a trade secret, as long as *prima facie* evidence has been adduced by the owner showing that preventive measures have been taken and the subject information has been misappropriated.[20] While the 2019 AUCL shall certainly prevail where discrepancy exists,[21] to the extent that the SPC Interpretation does not contradict the amended AUCL, it is still in full force.

(d) Relationship between the AUCL and Other Laws

Both business operators and consumers have the standing to sue a wrongdoer under the AUCL. It happens occasionally that these business operators and consumers in

16. AUCL 1993, note 1, Art. 9.1 ("A business shall not, by advertisement or other means, conduct any misleading false publicity in respect of the quality, ingredients, functions, usage, producer, shelf life, and place of production of commodities.")
17. AUCL 2019, note 7, Art. 8.1.
18. Interpretation of the Supreme People's Court on Some Issues Concerning the Application of Law in the Trial of Civil Cases Involving Unfair Competition 2007 ("SPC Interpretation 2007") [Zuigao Renmin Fayuan Guanyu Shenli Buzhengdang Jingzheng Minshi Anjian Yingyong Falv Ruogan Wenti De Jieshi]
19. *Ibid.*, Art. 14.
20. AUCL 2019, note 7, Art. 32.1.
21. See Legislation Law of the People's Republic of China 2015 Amendment ("Legislation Law 2015") [Zhonghua Renmin Gongheguo Lifa Fa], Arts. 88.1, 92.

the unfair competition cases can simultaneously resort to other laws, such as the Anti-Monopoly Law, the Consumer Protection Law, the Advertising Law and IP laws.

(1) The Anti-Monopoly Law

Although unfair competition and antitrust are both closely related to market competition, they are different legal concepts. Unfair competition law regulates the conducts of market participants in business competition, whereas antitrust law governs the market structure. While unfair competition law aims to maintain the *fairness* in competition, antitrust law is designed to ensure the *freedom* of competition. Accordingly, unfair competition law forbids unfair competitive conduct, and antitrust law prohibits monopolistic conduct lessening market competition.

While antitrust and anti-monopoly are different legal concepts, their distinction was blurred when China enacted the AUCL in 1993. At that time, China had an urgent need for a comprehensive competition law system to ensure both free and fair competition. Therefore, the 1993 AUCL includes certain antitrust provisions, such as those associated with predatory pricing, tying, and abuse of administrative powers. Since its promulgation in 2007, the AML has overlapped with the AUCL in regulating these monopolistic conducts. In order to distinguish unfair competition law from antitrust law, the 2017 AUCL deleted all provisions regarding these monopolistic conducts which were already regulated by the AML.

(2) The Advertising Law and Consumer Protection Law

The AUCL, the Advertising Law and the Consumer Protection Law all regulate false or misleading allegations or indications in commerce. While all these three laws aim to protect consumer interests to a different extent, the AUCL focuses more on maintaining a healthy market order. Article 8 of the AUCL provides that:

> A business shall not conduct any false or misleading commercial publicity in respect of the performance, functions, quality, sales, user reviews, and honours received by its commodities, in order to defraud or mislead consumers. A business shall not help another business conduct any false or misleading commercial promotion by organizing false transactions or by any other means.[22]

Similar provisions also appear in the Consumer Protection Law and Advertising Law. Article 20.1 of the Consumer Protection Law reads:

> Businesses shall provide consumers with true and complete information on the quality, performance, use, and useful life, among others, of commodities or services; and shall not conduct any false or misleading promotion.[23]

Article 4 of the Advertising Law likewise stipulates that:

---

22. AUCL 2019, note 7, Art. 8.
23. Law of the People's Republic of China on the Protection of Consumer Rights and Interests 2013 Amendment ("Consumer Protection Law 2013") [Zhonghua Renmin Gongheguo Xiaofeizhe Quanyi Baohu Fa], Art. 20.1.

> Advertisements shall not have any false or misleading content or defraud or mislead consumers.[24]

The overlap of the three laws inevitably leads to the controversy over which one should be applied to allegedly false or misleading indications. First of all, all three laws can be used as a vehicle for both public and private enforcement. The law-enforcement body or the court first needs to determine whether the false indication is an advertisement. Commercial advertising activities in China are described in the Advertising Law as the activities in which "commodity dealers or service providers directly or indirectly introduce, via certain media and in certain forms, goods or services marketed by them within the territory of the People's Republic of China."[25] If the false indication is regarded as an advertisement by the law-enforcement agency or the court, the Advertising Law will prevail over the AUCL. As specified by Article 20.2 of the AUCL, a business publishing any false advertisements in violation of Article 8 of this Law shall be punished in accordance with the Advertising Law of the People's Republic of China.[26]

In *Hangzhou Namei Science and Technology Co. Ltd. v. Administration for Market Supervision of Fengquan District, Xinxiang City*,[27] the local Administration for Market Supervision ("AMR"), *inter alia*, fined a toothpaste manufacturer RMB 500,000 based on Article 20 of the AUCL for the unverified descriptions on its toothpaste box regarding the functions of its product as well as its collaborative relationship with the Chinese Academy of Sciences. The plaintiff argued before the local AMR that the Advertising Law rather than the AUCL should be applied. The first-instance court eventually ruled for the local AMR by holding that the packaging of the toothpaste was not a form of media promotion but a necessary process before the products enter the market. This opinion was further upheld by the appellate court.[28]

The Consumer Protection Law has little effect in this regard, because although there is a prescribed form and amount of administrative penalties, the provision is only applicable "in the absence of other provisions in laws or regulations". [29] Therefore, as specific provisions are applicable in the Advertising Law and the AUCL,

---

24. Advertising Law of the People's Republic of China 2018 Amendment ("Advertising Law 2018") [Zhonghua Renmin Gongheguo Guanggao Fa], Art. 4.
25. *Ibid.*, Art. 2.1.
26. AUCL 2019, note 7, Art. 20.2.
27. *Hangzhou Namei Science and Technology Co. Ltd. v. Administration for Market Supervision of Fengquan District, Xinxiang City*, Xinxiang Intermediate People's Court's decision of 26 March 2020, 08 *Yu Xing Zhong* (2020).
28. *Ibid.*
29. Consumer Protection Law 2018, note 23, Art. 56.1 ("Under any of the following circumstances, business operators shall, in addition to corresponding civil liabilities, be governed by other applicable laws and regulations which provide for the punishing authorities and forms of punishment; or in the absence of such provisions in laws or regulations, the administrative departments for industry and commerce or other relevant administrative departments shall order them to make correction, and may, according to the circumstances, warn the business operators, confiscate their illegal income, impose a fine of not less than the illegal income but not more than ten times the illegal income or, if there is no illegal income, a fine of not more than RMB 500,000, or impose a combination of the above penalties on them; and if the circumstances are serious, order them to suspend business for

the enforcement authority will generally not apply the Consumer Protection Law to regulate such false advertising conduct. This principle was reflected in *Shandong Dao Tian Cun Food Co., Ltd. v. Administration for Market Supervision of Donggang District, Rizhao City*,[30] where the plaintiff operated an online store through which various snacks were sold targeting babies and young children. Having received multiple complaints by consumers, the Donggang AMR investigated and decided that the indication made on the plaintiff's online store, which labelled the products as 'baby food supplement' and listed the recommended age completely in accordance with the age range stated in the relevant national standards would mislead the relevant public into believing that the plaintiff's products were standardized baby food supplements. With respect to the application of law, the Donggang District Court ruled that:

> Dao Tian Cun Company's behaviour had violated Article 20(1) of the Law of the People's Republic of China on the Protections of Consumer Rights and Interests, which stated that "business operators shall provide consumers with true and complete information on the quality, performance, use, and useful life, among others, of commodities or services; and shall not conduct any false or misleading promotion", and thus should be sanctioned in accordance with Article 55(1)(vi) thereof. However, said article stipulates that "where it is provided in other laws or regulations regarding the enforcement authority or the form of penalties, the provisions of such other laws or regulations should be followed", while Article 8 of the Anti-Unfair Competition Law of the People's Republic of China had indeed regulated the misleading publicity conduct of Dao Tian Cun Company. Therefore, whoever violates said article [in the Consumer Protection Law] should be subject to the relevant provisions regarding the applicable penalties in the Anti-Unfair Competition Law of the People's Republic of China.[31]

This decision was later upheld by the Rizhao Intermediate Court in a second trial.[32]

While the AUCL and the Advertising Law are applied much more often than the Consumer Protection Law by the law enforcement authorities, the Consumer Protection Law still has its unique function in civil litigation. Compared to the AUCL providing an actionable ground to "any other person" whose interests have been injured,[33] the Consumer Protection Law as well as the Advertising Law only aims to

---

rectification or revoke their business licences: ... (vi) Promoting commodities or services in a false or misleading manner ...")

30. *Shandong Dao Tian Cun Food Co., Ltd. v. Administration for Market Supervision of Donggang District, Rizhao City*, Rizhao District Court's decision of 15 July 2019, 59 *Lu 11 Xing Zhong* (2019).
31. *Shandong Dao Tian Cun Food Co., Ltd. v. Administration for Market Supervision of Donggang District, Rizhao City*, Donggang District People's Court, 88 *Lu 1102 Xing Chu* (2018).
32. *Ibid.*
33. AUCL 2019, note 7, Art. 17.1 ("A business causing any damage to another person in violation of this Law shall assume civil liability according to the law."); Advertising Law 2018, note 21, Art. 56(1) ("Where a false advertisement is published in violation of this Law to defraud or mislead consumers, causing any damage to the lawful rights and interests of consumers who purchase goods or receive services, the advertiser shall assume civil liability in accordance with the law. If the advertising agent or advertisement publisher is unable

protect consumers.[34] Therefore, the plaintiff needs to be a consumer so that he can claim under the Consumer Protection Law or the Advertising Law. Further, while both the AUCL and the Advertising Law require there to be an actual loss caused by the false or misleading indication, no similar requirement is found in the Consumer Protection Law.[35]

(3) IP Laws

Anti-unfair competition regulations and IP laws are closely related. The Paris Convention for the Protection of Industrial Property ("Paris Convention") has explicitly included the repression of unfair competition as one of its objects.[36] On the one hand, AUCL is overlapping with IP laws with the mutual goal of discouraging unfair competition behaviour. For instance, a rightful owner may opt to assert its trade mark, design patent, or copyright against a unique pattern used on the packaging of its counterfeit, or simply rely on the AUCL's prohibition on acts of confusion. On the other hand, the AUCL supplements IP laws' inadequacy by protecting trade secrets, trade names, domain names and unregistered trade marks, etc.

Specifically, the 2019 AUCL correlates with IP laws in two aspects: its regulation against acts of confusion, and its protection of trade secrets. In practice, claiming trade mark infringement and AUCL violation simultaneously is a common strategy adopted by brand owners to combat counterfeits. Technically speaking, however, where registered trade marks are involved, it is the Trade Mark Law rather than the AUCL that is applicable. This is evidenced by the 2017 Amendment's removal of "the unauthorized use of another's registered trade mark" and "the use of fake quality marks" as express examples of confusion.[37] Instead, the trade mark owner should claim infringement based on Article 57 of the Trade Mark Law.[38] The unfair competition claim has an arguably wider application scope than the Trade Mark Law since it does not require a prior registration with a competent authority. As a successful trade mark infringement claim depends heavily on, for example, the registration period and the classification of goods or services on which the trade mark is registered, the AUCL may step in as an alternative if the owner's registration is flawed or if the infringement cannot be established.

---

to provide the advertiser's true name and address or valid contact information, consumers may require the advertising agent or advertisement publisher to make compensation in advance.")

34. Advertising Law 2018, note 24, Art. 1; Consumer Protection Law 2013, note 23, Art. 1. See also, *Yingkuan Zhang v. China Education Network Television*, Beijing No. 2 Intermediate People's Court's decision of 29 May 2020, 2378 *Jing 02 Min Zhong* (2020).
35. AUCL 2019, note 7, Art. 17.1.
36. Paris Convention for the Protection of Industrial Property 1967 (as amended 28 September 1979) ("Paris Convention 1967"), Art. 1(2) ("The protection of industrial property has as its object patents, utility models, industrial designs, trademarks, service marks, trade names, indications of source or appellations of origin, and the repression of unfair competition.")
37. The two conducts were listed in the 1993 AUCL as examples of acts of confusion while subsequently deleted in the 2017 AUCL. See AUCL 1993, note 1, Art. 5(ii)(iv).
38. Trade Mark Law of the People's Republic of China 2019 Amendment ("Trade Mark Law 2019") [Zhonghua Renmin Gongheguo Shangbiao Fa], Art. 57.

Moreover, the AUCL is the sole weapon for trade secret owners in most cases. There is no separate Trade Secret Act despite pressure to enact one.[39] The existing protection is fragmented and mirrored in the Criminal Law, the Labour Contract Law and the AUCL of the PRC. As criminal accountability requires a high threshold[40] and the Labour Contract Law is binding exclusively in the employment context,[41] the AUCL remains the most important law protecting confidential information. This is a typical example where the AUCL has filled the gap where IP law is silent.

(4) The Criminal Law

Article 31 of the AUCL provides that "[w]here a violation of this Law is criminally punishable, the offender shall be held criminally liable according to the law".[42] The various conducts prohibited under the AUCL can result in criminal liability, provided that the threshold imposed by the Criminal Law could be met. For example, an act of commercial bribery prohibited by the AUCL, which discourages the operators' solicitation of business by bribing the employees or agents of the other transacting party, or any other person who may unduly influence the transaction,[43] may trigger criminal liability if the conduct simultaneously constitutes a bribery in violation of Article 164 of the Criminal Law.[44] Moreover, where such other party is a governmental

39. See e.g. Liang Li, 'Zhongguo Shangye Mimi Lifa De Wuqu Yu Jinlu – Lun Queli Caichanquan Lilun He Wuguocuo Zeren De Biyaoxing' (The Misunderstanding and Improvement of Trade Secret Legislation in China – A Discussion on the Significance of the Establishment of Property Theory and Non-Fault Liability), 30 *Market Modernization* (2006), 257 et seq.
40. Criminal Law of the People's Republic of China 2017 Amendment ("Criminal Law 2017") [Zhonghua Renmin Gongheguo Xingfa], Art. 219.1 ("Whoever engages in one of the following activities which encroaches upon commercial secrets and brings significant losses to persons having the rights to the commercial secrets is to be sentenced to not more than three years of fixed-term imprisonment, criminal detention, and may in addition or exclusively be sentenced to a fine; or is to be sentenced to not less than three years and not more than seven years of fixed-term imprisonment and a fine, if he causes particularly serious consequences: (1) acquire a rightful owner's commercial secrets via theft, lure by promise of gain, threat, or other improper means; (2) disclose, use, or allow others to use a rightful owner's commercial secrets which are acquired through the aforementioned means; (3) disclose, use, or allow others to use, in violation of the agreement with the rightful owner or the rightful owner's request of keeping the commercial secrets, the commercial secrets he is holding.")
41. Labor Contract Law of the People's Republic of China 2013 [Zhonghua Renmin Gongheguo Laodong Hetong Fa], Art. 23 ("An employer may enter an agreement with his employees in the labor contract to require his employees to keep the business secrets and intellectual property of the employer confidential. For an employee who has the obligation of keeping confidential, the employer and the employee may stipulate non-competition clauses in the labor contract or in the confidentiality agreement and come to an agreement that, when the labor contract is dissolved or terminated, the employee shall be given economic compensations within the non-competition period. If the employee violates the stipulation of non-competition, it shall pay the employer a penalty for breaching the contract.")
42. AUCL 2019, note 7, Art. 31.
43. *Ibid.*, Art. 7.
44. Criminal Law 2017, note 40, Art. 164. ("Whoever gives any property to a staff member of a company, an enterprise or any other entity for any illicit benefit shall be sentenced to

body, public institution or state-owned enterprise, the instigator will be held liable under Article 389 of the Criminal Law.[45] Notably, the criminal threshold for bribing officials of a non-governmental enterprise is set at RMB 10,000 for individuals and RMB 200,000 for entities,[46] while for state-affiliated institutions, the mutual threshold is RMB 10,000.[47]

Additionally, trade secret misappropriation regulated by the AUCL is subject to criminal liability as well.[48] This criminal liability is established if "(1) losses of more than RMB 500,000 are caused to the owner of the trade secret; (2) the amount of illegal gains from infringing upon the trade secret is more than RMB 500,000; (3) as a result, the owner of the trade secret goes bankrupt; or (4) great losses are caused to the owner of the trade secret in other ways".[49] However, this criminal liability has not sufficiently addressed foreign investors' concerns over the risk of trade secret infringement in China. Therefore, the US persuaded China into agreeing that "China's criminal procedures and penalties shall at least encompass cases of trade secret misappropriation through theft, fraud, physical or electronic intrusion for an unlawful purpose, and the unauthorized or improper use of a computer system in the scope of prohibited acts" in the US-China Phase One Deal.[50] China's promise is expected to be included in the next amendment of the Criminal Law.

Some other acts prohibited by the AUCL such as false advertising and defamation against another's reputation may constitute crimes subject to the scale of illegal

---

imprisonment of not more than three years or criminal detention in addition to a fine if the amount of property is relatively large; or be sentenced to imprisonment of not less than three years but not more than ten years in addition to a fine if the amount of property is huge. Whoever gives any property to a functionary of a foreign country or an official of an international public organization for any improper commercial benefit shall be punished according to the provision of the preceding paragraph.")

45. *Ibid.*, Art. 389 ("An act of giving state functionaries articles of property in order to seek illegitimate gain shall be considered a crime of offering bribes. In economic activities, whoever gives articles of property to state functionaries in violation of state provisions, when the amount is fairly large, or gives a kickback or service charges of various types to state functionaries in violation of state provisions is to be dealt with as committing the crime of offering bribes. Whoever gives articles of property to state functionaries due to extortion but receives no illegitimate gain shall not be considered as committing the crime of offering bribes.")
46. Provisions (II) of the Supreme People's Procuratorate and the Ministry of Public Security on the Standards for Filing Criminal Cases under the Jurisdiction of the Public Security Organs for Investigation and Prosecution 2010 ("SPP and MPS Provisions II 2010") [Zuigao Renmin Jianchayuan Gongan Bu Guanyu Gongan Jiguan Guanxia De Xingshi Anjian Lian Zhusui Biaozhun De Guiding (II)], Art. 11.
47. Interpretation of the Supreme People's Court and the Supreme People's Procuratorate on Several Issues concerning the Specific Application of Law in the Handling of Criminal Cases of Offering Bribes 2012 ("SPC and SPP Interpretation 2012") [Zuigao Renmin Fayuan Zuigao Renmin Jianchayuan Guanyu Banli Xinghui Xingshi Anjian Juti Yingyong Falv Ruogan Wenti De Jieshi], Art. 1 ("Whoever offers bribes in the amount of RMB 10,000 or more to a state functionary for any illegal benefit shall be subject to criminal liability under Article 390 of the Criminal Law.")
48. Criminal Law 2017, note 40, Art. 219.
49. SPP and MPS Provisions II 2010, note 46, Art. 73.
50. US-China Phase One Deal 2020, note 15, Art. 1.8.

operation, amount of illicit gains or other factual circumstances. The crime of false advertising is stipulated in Article 222 of the Criminal Law[51] and is triggered by the amount of illegal gains being more than RMB 100,000.

The monetary threshold for the crime of commercial disparagement[52] is set much higher at "direct economic losses of more than RMB 500,000", or if the alleged defamation was conducted publicly on the internet or using any other media, has caused the victim to cease business or production for more than six months or to go bankrupt, or if the circumstance is exceptionally severe.[53] In addition, the unfair competition act utilizing computing and technical means[54] is also criminally accountable if regarded as an offence under Article 286 of the Criminal Law.[55]

2. Competitive Relationship

Article 1 of the AUCL declares that the law aims to protect rights and legitimate interests of business operators and consumers for the purposes of promoting the sound development of the socialist market economy, encouraging and protecting fair competition, and preventing acts of unfair competition.[56] If a business entity claims against another one under the AUCL, a common defence raised by the latter is that there is no competitive relationship between these two parties. However, Article 17.2 of the AUCL stipulates that "a business operator whose lawful rights and interests are impaired by any act of unfair competition can bring a lawsuit to a people's court".[57] This Article does not require a competitive relationship to exist as a prerequisite for an unfair competition claim. Still, whether a competitive relationship is required in an AUCL claim has been an important legal issue.

Currently the majority viewpoint taken by the Chinese courts is that while a competitive relationship is required in an AUCL claim, this relationship should be construed broadly to include indirect competition where two parties are not in the same industry. The Shanghai Second Intermediate Court once recognized an "intangible competitive relationship" between Louis Vuitton Malletier ("LV"), whose main business interests were in luxury retail, and two real estate companies in Shanghai. The two real estate firms published an outdoor billboard advertisement with the image of a model carrying a LV handbag (containing LV's registered trade mark) taking up almost one third of the poster. Despite the remote business scope of the parties, the Court held that if a business entity has any influence over another's operational costs, operation modes or transaction opportunity, the former then affects

51. Criminal Law 2017, note 40, Art. 222.
52. *Ibid.*, Art. 221.
53. SPP and MPS Provisions II 2010, note 46, Art. 74.
54. AUCL 2019, note 7, Art. 12.
55. Criminal Law 2017, note 40, Art. 286(1) ("Whoever violates states regulations and deletes, alters, adds, and interferes in computer information systems, causing abnormal operations of the systems and grave consequences, is to be sentenced to not more than five years of fixed-term imprisonment or criminal detention; when the consequences are particularly serious, the sentence is to be not less than five years of fixed-term imprisonment.")
56. AUCL 2019, note 7, Art. 1.
57. *Ibid.*, Art. 17.2.

the latter's overall competitiveness. Consequently, a competitive relationship can be found between these two parties and the AUCL can be possibly applied therein.[58]

In *Zhejiang Ant Financial Services Group Co., Ltd. et al. v. Suzhou Langdong Network Technology Co., Ltd.*,[59] while the plaintiffs operate a mobile app "Alipay", providing the most popular payment service in China, the defendant's main product "Qichacha" is a different mobile app, delivering data and analytics of China-based private and public companies. The plaintiffs sued the defendant for commercial defamation on the basis that the latter distributing misleading information concerning the plaintiff. The court ruled for the plaintiff and held that "a competitive relationship in the context of the AUCL includes both direct and indirect ones. The AUCL protects both the fair competition between competitors among which a direct competitive relationship exists, and the order of the overall market competition. In the Internet economy... competition is mainly reflected in...securing competitive advantages through attracting consumers' attention. Even if there is no direct competition, a business entity will form a competitive relationship with another one through jeopardizing the latter's competitive advantage."[60]

The SPC even ruled once in *Wuhan Huaqi Film and Television Co., Ltd. v. Beijing Enlight Media Co., Ltd. et al.*[61] that a competitive relationship is not required in an unfair competition claim:

> an unfair competition act can impair either certain competitors or the legitimate interests of consumers or the general public, and consequently affect the social and economic order. Neither the harm to certain competitors nor the existence of a competitive relationship is necessary [in the establishment of an unfair competition claim]. The defence that the defendants Mr. Zheng Xu and Enlight Media are not market 'competitors' who have a competitive relationship under the AUCL with Huaqi Company ... is ungrounded and thus not supported by the Court.[62]

In summary, the Chinese courts have either defined the competitive relationship broadly or justified the application of the AUCL where the competitive relationship is not established. In more and more cases, the courts do not view a strict competitive relationship as an indispensable factor in the application of the AUCL.

3. Legal Subjects

Business operators are the main legal subjects regulated by the AUCL. In the 2019 AUCL, a business operator is defined as "a natural person, a legal person,

58. *Louis Vuitton Malletier v. Shanghai Xingui Real Estate Development Co., Ltd. et al.*, Shanghai Second Intermediate People's Court, 242 *Hu Er Zhong Min Wu (Zhi) Chu Zi* 242 (2004).
59. *Zhejiang Ant Financial Services Group Co., Ltd. et al. v. Suzhou Langdong Network Technology Co., Ltd.*, Hangzhou Railway Transportation Court's decision of 26 April 2020, 1594 *Zhe 8601 Min Chu* (2019).
60. *Ibid.*
61. *Wuhan Huaqi Film and Television Co., Ltd. v. Beijing Enlight Media Co., Ltd. et al.*, SPC's decision of 31 December 2017, 4 *Min San Zhong Zi* (2015).
62. *Ibid.*

or a non-legal person organization that engages in the production or distribution of commodities or the provision of services".[63] Most provisions in the AUCL are targeted at business operators and their employees, agents, representatives, or the administrative authorities that take up a supervisory role. However, the legal subject of trade secret misappropriation includes other natural persons and entities as well. According to Article 9.2 of the AUCL, in addition to business operators, any other natural person, legal person or unincorporated organization can be the legal subject of trade secret infringement.[64]

4. Acts of Unfair Competition

The AUCL defines the "act of unfair competition" as the conduct which disrupts the order of market competition and causes damages to the lawful rights and interests of other businesses or consumers in their production or distribution activities in violation of the law.[65] The AUCL lists seven types of unfair competition, including acts of confusion, commercial bribery, false or misleading indications, trade secret misappropriation, fraudulent or excessive premium campaign, libel and slander to damage another's reputation, and disruption or sabotage against another's online operation through technical means. Among these seven types of conducts, the acts of confusion, false or misleading allegations or indications, commercial defamation to damage another's reputation or goodwill and trade secret misappropriation are manifested in the Paris Convention and the TRIPS Agreement. These seven categories of unfair competition are not exhaustive. Article 2.2 of the AUCL is a general catch-all provision to include other types of unlisted acts of unfair competition.

(a) Misappropriation of Commercial Achievements by Acts of Confusion

Article 6 of the AUCL prohibits:

> (1) using without permission a label identical or similar to the name, packaging or decoration, among others, of another person's commodity with a certain recognition;
>
> (2) using without permission another person's name with certain recognition, such as the name (including abbreviations and trade names) of an enterprise, the name (including abbreviations) of a social organization, or the name (including pseudonyms, stage names and name translations) of an individual;
>
> (3) using without permission the principal part of a domain name, the name of a website, or a web page with certain recognition, among others, of another person; and
>
> (4) other acts of confusion sufficient to mislead a person into believing that a commodity originates from another person or has a particular connection with another person.[66]

63. AUCL 2019, note 7, Art. 2.3.
64. *Ibid.*, Art. 9.2.
65. AUCL 2019, note 7, Art. 2.2.
66. *Ibid.*, Art. 6.

According to the SPC Interpretation, generic names, graphics and models, descriptive names that merely indicate the quality, raw materials, functions, uses, weight, quantity or other features of the product, the natural shape of the product or the artificial shape that is formed only to obtain technical effects or give economic value, and any other name, package or decoration that lack distinctiveness are generally excluded from the scope of protection, unless distinctiveness has been acquired through the owner's exclusive use.[67]

(1) Unregistered Trade Marks

Since the trade mark system aims at retaining fair market competition, some scholars construe trade mark infringement as "a type of unfair competition".[68] However, as mentioned above, the 2017 AUCL removed "using another's registered trade mark" from acts giving rise to confusion; therefore, the AUCL has been inapplicable to registered trade mark infringement since then. Put differently, while the AUCL intends to protect symbols identifying the source of a product or service, such as trade names, domain names, or special packaging arrangement associated with a product, these symbols do not include registered trade marks. Nonetheless, because the language of Article 6 includes certain trade mark concepts, such as certain recognition, confusion, and misleading character, Chinese courts have employed trade mark concepts when applying this provision.[69] For example, in *FERRERO SpA v. Montresor Food (Zhangjiagang) Co Ltd and Zhengyuan Marketing Co Ltd in Tianjin Economic and Technological Development Zone,* the defendant's packaging for Tresor Dore chocolate was quite similar to that of the plaintiff's signature product, Ferrero Rocher chocolate.[70] The defendant argued that confusion did not exist among consumers because these two products were fairly different in price, quality, taste, targeted market, and trade mark.[71] Nevertheless, the Supreme People's Court eventually ruled that the defendant's package had violated the AUCL because it was very similar to that of the plaintiff in terms of overall visual impact and the likelihood of confusion among consumers did exist.[72] In finding the similarity between the packages of both parties, the SPC explained that the gold, spherical shape package of Ferrero Rocher chocolates was highly distinctive, and held that the defendant's was a blatant imitation of Ferrero Rocher chocolate's packages, which functioned as a source identifier and was therefore an act of unfair competition.[73] Although the subject matter here was a get up (product packaging) instead of a trade mark, the court's approach to determining likelihood of confusion and infringement was the same as that used in

67. SPC Interpretation 2007, note 18, Art. 2.1(2).
68. J. Thomas McCarthy, *1 McCarthy on Trademarks and Unfair Competition* (5th edn, Clark Boardman Callaghan, 2019), §2:7.
69. Jyh-An Lee and Yangzi Li, 'The Obscure Consumer in the Chinese Intellectual Property Law', 42 *EIPR* (2020), 55, 63.
70. SPC, *FERRERO SpA v. Montresor Food (Zhangjiagang) Co. Ltd. and Zhengyuan Marketing Co. Ltd. in Tianjin Economic and Technological Development Zone,* Case No. 3 (2008).
71. *Ibid.*
72. *Ibid.*
73. *Ibid.*

trade mark cases. This case also exemplifies how existing trade mark doctrines and concepts are employed in the application of the AUCL.

The SPC Interpretation has adopted the trade mark concept of likelihood of confusion in the application of the AUCL by noting that "where it is sufficient to cause the misunderstanding of the relevant public with respect to the source of a commodity, including that such commodity comes from the licensee or affiliated company of the entrepreneur who owns a well-known commodity".[74] A likelihood of confusion in the AUCL is established where an identical or substantially indistinguishable name, package or decoration is used on an identical product.[75] The SPC Interpretation also makes clear that the determination of similarity among names, packages or decorations under the AUCL could make reference to the standard of similarity under the Trade Mark Law.[76]

A certain market recognition is another element in Article 6 of the ACUL, which is relevant to Trade Mark Law. The ACUL and the Trade Mark Law are concurrently applicable if symbols are used as unregistered trade marks. The Trade Mark Law provides three types of protection for unregistered marks: well-known marks (Article 13.2), prior rights (Article 32), and prior use defences (Article 59.3). While Articles 13.2 and 32 provide owners of unregistered, well-known trade marks and prior rights a legal basis for invalidating a conflicting registration, Article 59.3 only provides a defence for prior users against the subsequent registrant's infringement claim.[77] Moreover, Articles 13.2, 32 and 59.3 all require a certain reputation of unregistered marks. While Article 13.2 requires marks to be "widely known" among the relevant public, Articles 32 and 59.3 use the term "certain recognition" (a verbatim translation would be: "certain influence") in their respective requirements.

The AUCL likewise requires that all names, marks, symbols, labels or packages must have attained "certain recognition" or reputation among consumers to be protected under Article 6. Controversy arises with respect to whether the "certain recognition" in the AUCL should be referred to the criterion in Articles 13.2, 32 or 59.3 of the Trade Mark Law. The majority viewpoint taken by the Chinese courts is that the standard of determining "certain recognition" in Article 6 of the AUCL is the same as that of Article 32 and 59.3 of the Trade Mark Law.[78]

---

74. SPC Interpretation 2007, note 18, Art. 4(1).
75. *Ibid.*, Art. 4.2.
76. *Ibid.*, Art. 4.3. According to the Standards for Determination of Trademark Infringement issued by the National Intellectual Property Administration ("CNIPA Standards 2020") in June 2020, when determining whether there is a likelihood of confusion under the Trade Mark Law, the following factors should be taken into consideration: (1) the similarity between the trademarks; (2) the similarity between the designated goods or services; (3) the distinctiveness and reputation enjoyed by the registered mark; (4) the characters of the designated goods or services and the method of use of the trademark; (5) the attention and degree of recognition of the relevant public; and (6) other relevant factors.
77. For detail analysis of these three articles, see Jyh-An Lee and Jingwen Liu, 'Prior-Use Defence in the Chinese Trade Mark Law', 42 *EIPR* (2020), 751, 757–760.
78. The CNIPA Standards interpreted "trademark with certain recognition" in Article 59.3 of the Trade Mark Law as being known to the relevant public within a certain area, the factors to be considered include the duration of the use, sales volume, turnover and advertising activities. See CNIPA Standards 2020, note 77, Art. 33(1)(2).

Notably, the AUCL since its 2017 amendment has abandoned the concept of "well-known products" according to which only packaging and decorations that were "uniquely associated with a well-known product" were protectable against blatant imitations. The threshold of "well-known products" and being "uniquely associated with a well-known product" in the 1993 AUCL is a relatively high standard to establish unfair competition. In *Liu Jun et al. v. FILA Sports Co. Ltd.*, the alleged infringement happened in 2016, one year before the promulgation of the AUCL 2017 Amendment. FILA Sports therefore invoked, *inter alia*, the relevant article in the 1993 AUCL and contended that the defendants had infringed upon its unique shoe box design which incorporated the stylized letters "FILA" in red and blue colours for its footwear products.[79] Although the Beijing Xicheng District Court upheld the plaintiff's claim for trade mark infringement, it denied the plaintiff's unfair competition claim, holding that although the evidence adduced by FILA Sports could show a certain reputation enjoyed by the FILA footwear products, it was insufficient to prove that the packaging was exclusively associated with the FILA sneakers.[80] The District Court's decision was later upheld by the Beijing Intellectual Property Court ("Beijing IP Court").[81]

The revised AUCL has lowered the threshold for claiming unfair competition. In *Beijing Niu Lan Villa Beverage Co., Ltd. et al. v. Beijing Red Star Co., Ltd.*,[82] the Beijing IP Court acknowledged that the plaintiff's packaging and decoration of its liquor product Red Star Erguotou had "certain influence" among the relevant public based on its audit reports, the awarded prices, and relevant promotional materials. Therefore, this packaging and decoration was held protected by Article 6 of the 2019 AUCL.[83] The court further explained that "the prerequisite for the packaging or decoration of a product with certain recognition to be protected under the AUCL is that the packaging or decoration is highly distinctive when being compared with similar products."[84]

The comparison of *FILA* and *Red Star* reveals that the threshold of AUCL protection for acts of confusion has been substantially lowered since 2017. Additionally, in *New Balance Trading (China) Co., Ltd. and Niu Ba Lun (China) Co., Ltd.*, the Shanghai Pudong New District Court held that the stylized "N" letters on both sides of the New Balance sneakers had achieved the status of a "decoration of products with certain recognition", in a way that the relevant consumers can easily associate the "N" letter decoration with a New Balance product. Despite the defendant having secured a trade mark registration for the stylized "N" letter under its own name, the court ruled that since the reputation associated with the "N" letters on the New Balance shoes had been obtained prior to the defendant's trade mark registration, the defendant, as a competitor in the same industry, should have had knowledge of the

79. *Liu Jun et al. v. FILA*, Beijing Xicheng District People's Court's decision of 7 July 2017, 2431 *Jing 0102 Min Chu* (2017).
80. *Ibid.*
81. *Liu Jun et al. v. FILA*, Beijing IP Court's decision of 5 March 2018, 1991 *Jing 73 Min Zhong* (2017).
82. *Beijing Niu Lan Villa Beverage Co., Ltd. et al. v. Beijing Red Star Co., Ltd.*, Beijing IP Court's decision of 26 April 2020, 38 *Jing 73 Min Zhong* (2020).
83. *Ibid.*
84. *Ibid.*

plaintiff's reputation and should have acted in good faith to avoid market confusion.[85] The takeaway of this decision resulting in a damage of RMB 10.8 million is that Article 6 of the AUCL can be used to curtail trade mark registrations in bad faith.

(2) Trade Mark and Company Name

Sometimes a plaintiff's claims based on the Trade Mark Law and the AUCL for a registered trade mark would both prevail in a single lawsuit. This is because the subject trade mark happens to the plaintiff's company name, while the claim for the protection of the company name can be substantiated under the AUCL.[86] In *Nikon Corp v. Shaanxi Xi'an Taihua Electric Bicycle Wholesale Market Co Ltd*, the plaintiff, Nikon, was a Japanese multinational enterprise renowned for its optics and imaging products. The plaintiff registered its English name "Nikon" in 1979 and its Chinese name (Ni Kang) in 1986, both of which were recognized as well-known marks by the State Administration for Industry and Commerce ("SAIC") in 2009. The defendant was a manufacturer of electric bicycles, changing its company name from Wuxing (Five Star) to Zhejiang Ni Kang in 2006. The company's trade mark (Ni Kang) on "electronic vehicles and electronic bicycles" was granted in 2002, and this trade mark and its English translation "NICOM" had been widely used on the defendant's products and website. Xi'an Intermediate Court held that the defendant had infringed the plaintiff's well-known trade mark.

The court explained that the plaintiff's trade marks were well-known marks primarily because they enjoyed a high degree of reputation among consumers. It is obvious that the defendant planned to piggyback on the plaintiff's reputation associated with the trade mark and misled consumers by changing its company name in 2006 and later using Ni Kang on its products. In this case, the plaintiff's marks were so well known that consumers would always associate the marks with the plaintiff's products. Although the plaintiff's English trade mark "Nikon" was different from the defendant's one "NICOM", the pronunciations and spellings of two marks were similar enough to mislead and confuse consumers. Therefore, the court held that the defendant infringed the plaintiff's trade mark according to the Trade Mark Law. Furthermore, because Ni Kang was also the plaintiff's company name, the defendant's behaviour had violated the Anti-Unfair Competition Law by free-riding on the plaintiff's company name.

(b) Commercial Bribery

Unfair competition conducts also include seeking transaction opportunities or competitive edges by bribing the employee or consignee of the other party to a transaction, or other powerful entities or individuals that are capable of unduly affecting

85. Aaron Wininger, 'New Balance Scores Chinese Unfair Competition Victory against New Barlun' (*China IP Law Update*, 16 April 2020) http://www.chinaiplawupdate.com/2020/04/new-balance-scores-chinese-unfair-competition-victory-against-new-barlun/ accessed 25 May 2020.
86. Lee and Li, note 69, 62.

a transaction.[87] While the AUCL allows a business to "explicitly pay a discount to the other party to the transaction, or pay a commission to an intermediary,"[88] such explicit discount or commission is permitted only when it is faithfully recorded in the account book of both the giving and receiving party.[89] It should be noted that the term "bribing " or "bribery" in the AUCL is not completely the same as under Criminal Law. A bribery in commercial activities under the AUCL will only trigger criminal liabilities should it meet the threshold set by the relevant provisions of the Criminal Law. [90]

(c) False or Misleading Indications

Business operators are prohibited from making any false or misleading indications in their promotions concerning the performance, functions, quality, sales, users' comments, and honours received by its products with a purpose to defraud or mislead consumers.[91] Further, a business shall not help another business to conduct any false or misleading commercial promotion by fabricating a transaction or any other means.[92] The SPC Interpretation exemplifies several typical false indications which would cause a misunderstanding of the relevant public, including (1) conducting lopsided promotion or comparison of products; (2) promoting products by advancing unsupported scientific viewpoints or phenomena as uncontroversial facts; and (3) promoting products with discriminatory language or through other misleading means.[93] However, promoting the products with an obviously exaggerated rhetoric which will not lead to any misunderstanding among the relevant public will not be deemed to be a false advertisement.[94] When determining whether an advertisement is false or would mislead the relevant public, the court should consider factors such as normal people's daily experiences, the general attention of the relevant public, what actually causes the misunderstanding, and the target group of the advertisement, etc.[95]

A claim of false or misleading indication is frequently made in trade mark infringement cases. Typically, the plaintiff would claim that by making an unauthorized use of others' trade marks, the alleged infringing party intends to mislead consumers into believing that the product bearing the infringing mark is provided by or associated with the actual brand owner, which constitutes a false indication prohibited by the AUCL. More importantly, if the trade mark infringement claim fails due to the lack of proper trade mark registration, the plaintiff can still claim that the defendant's false indication violated the AUCL. For example, in *The University of Shanghai for Science and Technology v. Hujiang Educational Technology Co., Ltd.*, the Shanghai Intellectual Property Court ("Shanghai IP Court") dismissed the plaintiff's claim

87. AUCL 2019, note 7, Art. 7.1.
88. *Ibid.*, Art. 7.2.
89. *Ibid.*
90. See text accompanying notes 42–47.
91. AUCL 2019, note 7, Art. 7.1.
92. *Ibid.*, Art. 7.2.
93. SPC Interpretation 2007, note 18, Art. 8.1.
94. *Ibid.*, Art. 8.2.
95. *Ibid.*, Art. 8.3.

that the distinctive part of its former name "沪江 (Hu Jiang in Chinese characters)" qualified as an unregistered well-known trade mark protected under Trade Mark Law. However, the Shanghai IP Court ruled for the plaintiff that the defendant's promotional materials had constituted a false and misleading indication in that the online educational services it provided were related to the former Hujiang University.[96]

In *Beijing Golden Holiday Travel Agency Co., Ltd. v. Ctrip Computer Technology (Shanghai) Co., Ltd.*, the SPC ruled that if a business claims damage against its competitors under false indications provision in the AUCL, three elements must be fulfilled: (1) a competitive relationship between the businesses; (2) defendant's indication is likely to mislead the relevant public; and (3) plaintiff's direct damage.[97] This viewpoint has been followed by some lower courts.[98] Nevertheless, it is always challenging for a business to prove damage resulting from its competitor's false or misleading indications. In *Shenzhen Sunyield Technologies Co., Ltd. v. Shanghai EM-Testing Co., Ltd.*, the Shanghai IP Court ruled for the defendant because the defendant's false statements on its official website did not refer to the plaintiff[99] and the latter did not suffer any damage from the defendant's false statement.[100] Due to the difficulties of proving direct economic loss and the causal link between the loss and a competitor's false indication, many businesses usually lack the incentive to sue a competitor under the AUCL. Quite a few disputes of this kind are therefore resolved through administrative methods, i.e., filing a complaint with the local Administration for Market Supervision ("AMR") and requesting its intervention.

However, the three elements set up in *Ctrip* have been loosened in recent years. In *Guangzhou Pharmaceutical Holdings Limited et al. v. Jiaduobao (China) Beverages Co., Ltd. et al.*, the SPC explicitly ruled that "considering the legislative intent of the AUCL's regulation on false indications, the direct loss of the infringed is not a component of a false indication claim".[101] The SPC further explained that by prohibiting false indications, the AUCL aimed to secure fair and orderly market competition.[102] Legitimate business interests could certainly be affected in two possible ways: first, wrongdoers could gain a competitive advantage and transaction opportunities through making false indications; second, consumers were easily misled by such false indications, which in turn hampered the interests of other businesses.[103] This viewpoint broadens the definition of "damage" in the AUCL to include not only

96. *USST v. Hujiang*, Shanghai IP Court's decision of 30 August 2017, 368 *Hu 73 Min Chu* (2016).
97. *Beijing Golden Holiday Travel Agency Co., Ltd. v. Ctrip Computer Technology (Shanghai) Co., Ltd.* SPC, 2 *Min San Zhong Zi* (2007).
98. See e.g., *Shenzhen Fangjinsuo Financial Services Co., Ltd. et al. v. Shanghai Xinju Financial Information Services Co., Ltd.*, Shanghai IP Court's decision of 29 August 2016, 107 *Hu 73 Min Zhong* (2016).
99. *Shenzhen Sunyield Technologies Co., Ltd. v. Shanghai EM-Testing Co., Ltd.*, Shanghai IP Court's decision of 12 February 2018, 330 *Hu 73 Min Zhong* (2017).
100. *Ibid.*
101. *Guangzhou Pharmaceutical Holdings Limited et al. v. Jiaduobao (China) Beverages Co., Ltd. et al.*, SPC's decision of 30 March 2016, 2802 *Min Shen Zi* (2015).
102. *Ibid.*
103. *Ibid.*

direct losses but also indirect ones. This approach is consistent with the trend of interpreting "competitive relationship" broadly in recent judicial practices.

(d) Misappropriation of Trade Secrets and Know-How, Restrictive Covenants[104]

According to Article 9.4 of the AUCL, "trade secret" refers to "technical, operational or other commercial information unknown to the public and is of commercial value for which the right holder has taken corresponding confidentiality measures." [105] In Regulations on Some Issues Concerning the Application of Law in the Trial of Cases Involving Trade Secret Infringement recently promulgated by the SPC ("the SPC Regulations"),[106] "technical information" was defined as "information on the structure, raw materials, ingredients, formulations, materials, samples, patterns, propagation materials of new plant varieties, processes, methods or steps, algorithms, data, computer programs and related documentation, etc. related to technologies",[107] whereas "operational information" was defined as "information relevant to business activities, creativity, management, sales, finance, planning, samples, bidding materials, customer information, data, etc. ".[108] Customer information refers to "customer's name, address, contact information, transaction habits, intentions, and other information".[109]

Notably, there are three elements so as to qualify for a trade secret according to the AUCL:

(1) secrecy requirement;
(2) utility requirement; and
(3) confidentiality requirement or the protective measure: the owner has taken measures to maintain the secrecy of the information.

In terms of the secrecy requirement, the SPC Interpretation explains that trade secrets should be unknown to and difficult to be obtained by persons in the relevant sector.[110] The SPC Regulations further explain that secrecy should be determined at the time when the alleged infringement takes place.[111] The SPC Regulations provide a negative list of information which fails to meet the secrecy requirement:

(1) common sense or industrial practice for persons in the relevant technical or economic field;

104. Shin Hailing, *The Protection of Trade Secrets in China* (2nd ed., Kluwer Law, 2012).
105. AUCL 2019, note 7, Art. 9.4.
106. Regulations of the Supreme People's Court on Some Issues Concerning the Application of Law in the Trial of Civil Cases Involving Trade Secret Infringement 2020 ("SPC Regulations 2020") [Zuigao Renmin Fayuan Guanyu Shenli Shangye Mimi Qinquan Minshi Anjian Yingyong Falv Ruogan Wenti De Guiding].
107. *Ibid.*, Art. 1.1.
108. *Ibid.*, Art. 1.2.
109. *Ibid.*, Art. 1.3.
110. SPC Interpretation 2007, note 18, Art. 9.1.
111. SPC Regulations 2020, note 106, Art. 3.

(2) information only relates to the size, structure, and the simple combination of materials and components that can be directly obtained by relevant personnel in the field by observing the products at issue;
(3) information which has been publicly disclosed on any publication or other media;
(4) information which has been disclosed through public reports or exhibits; or
(5) information can be obtained by the relevant personnel in the field from other public channels.[112]

Although public information listed above does not constitute trade secret, the arrangement, improvement, and value-added processing of existing public information can possibly generate new information unknown to the public and therefore protected as trade secrets.[113] Moreover, easily accessible information is not eligible for trade secret protection. While customer information is viewed as a protectable trade secret in many cases, public information such as customers' websites, email addresses, and contact information cannot be protected as trade secrets.[114] The SPC Regulations explain that maintaining a stable long-term business relationship with the customer does not directly lead to any trade secret.[115] Similarly, business and operating rules or applications that can be easily understood through a public website are not subject to any trade secret protection either.[116] It should be noted that if a trade secret becomes known to the public as a result of an infringing act, the court may take into account the commercial value of the trade secret when determining the amount of damage.[117] When determining the commercial value of a trade secret for this purpose, the court shall consider the cost of research and development, the revenue and other interests from the trade secret, and the time of which the competitive advantage can be maintained.[118]

As to the utility requirement, the SPC Interpretation provides that trade secrets must "have an actual or potential commercial value and be capable of bringing competitive advantage for the owner".[119] Progressive achievements made in business operations are capable of being "commercially valuable" as long as the preceding condition could be met.[120]

112. *Ibid.*, Art. 4.1.
113. *Ibid.*, Art. 4.2.
114. *Apex Recruiter (Beijing) Co., Ltd. (Qingdao Branch) v. Liu Lu et al.*, Qingdao Intermediate People's Court's decision of 9 August 2019, 3468 *Lu 02 Min Zhong* (2019).
115. SPC Regulations 2020, note 106, Art. 5.
116. *Hangzhou Dihuo Science and Technology Co. Ltd. v. Beijing Sankuai Technology Co. Ltd.*, Hangzhou Intermediate People's Court's decision of 22 July 2019, 3166 *Zhe 01 Min Chu* (2018).
117. SPC Regulations 2020, note 106, Art. 19.1.
118. *Ibid.*, Art. 19.2.
119. SPC Interpretation 2007, note 18, Art. 10. It should be mentioned that the SPC Interpretation was launched in 2007 as a supporting document of the 1993 AUCL, which had defined the utility requirement in a trade secret as "being capable of bringing benefits to the owner, and having practical applicability", and thus Article 10 of the SPC Interpretation was actually an illustration of the 1993 AUCL.
120. SPC Regulations 2020, note 106, Art. 7.2.

Thirdly, the SPC Interpretation defines "confidentiality measures" as "the proper protection measures suitable for the commercial value or other specific situation in order to prevent information leakage".[121] The SPC Regulations specify that such measures should have been placed prior to the alleged infringement takes place.[122] Further, the SPC Interpretation exemplifies several confidentiality measures, such as limiting the access of the classified information and only notifying the contents to relevant persons that should have access to the information; locking the carrier of the classified information up or adopting any other preventive measure; indicating a confidentiality mark on the carrier of classified information; adopting passwords or codes on the classified information; concluding a confidentiality agreement; limiting visitors to the classified machinery, factory, workshop or any other place or putting forward any confidentiality request; or adopting any other proper measure for guaranteeing the confidentiality of information.[123] The SPC Regulations provide several other examples of appropriate confidentiality measures, including contractual arrangements through a non-disclosure agreement (NDA) or a confidentiality clause in an agreement; imposing confidentiality requirements on employees, former employees, suppliers, customers, visitors through articles of association, trainings, rules and regulations, and written communication; restricting visitors to or providing segregated management to confidential production and business premises such as factories and workshops; distinguishing and managing the trade secret and its carrier by marking, classifying, isolating, encrypting, sealing, limiting the persons by whom it can be accessed or obtained; taking measures such as prohibiting or restricting the use, access, storage and reproduction for computer equipment, electronic devices, network equipment, storage devices, software through which trade secrets can be accessed and obtained; and requiring departing employees to register, return, remove or destroy the trade secret and its carrier that he or she has accessed or obtained and to continue to undertake the duty of confidence.[124]

A misappropriation would be found if a person commits any of the following acts:

(1) acquiring a trade secret from the owner by theft, bribery, fraud, coercion, electronic intrusion, or any other illicit means;
(2) disclosing, using, or allowing another person to use a trade secret acquired from the owner by any means as specified in the preceding subparagraph;
(3) disclosing, using, or allowing another person to use a trade secret in its possession in violation of its duty of confidence or the requirements of the owner to keep the trade secret confidential; and
(4) abetting a person, or tempting, or aiding a person in acquiring, disclosing, using, or allowing another person to use the trade secret of the owner in violation of his or her duty of confidence or the requirements of the owner to keep the trade secret confidential.[125]

121. SPC Interpretation 2007, note 18, Art. 11.1.
122. SPC Regulations 2020, note 106, Art. 5.1.
123. SPC Interpretation 2007, note 18, Art. 11.3.
124. SPC Regulations 2020, note 106, Art. 6.
125. AUCL 2019, note 7, Art. 9.1.

The SPC Interpretation provides two exceptions to trade secret misappropriation. First, obtaining others' trade secret through independent research and development or reverse engineering does not constitute trade secret misappropriation.[126] However, reverse engineering is not a legitimate defense if the infringer had infringed the trade secret by other unfair means before conducting the reverse engineering.[127] Second, if a company's customer voluntarily chooses to do business with the company's ex-employee or his new employer only because of the customer's trust in that ex-employee, the ex-employee should not be deemed as an infringer of trade secret.[128] These two exceptions also appear in the SPC Regulations.[129]

"Reverse engineering" in this context refers to acquiring relevant technical information of a product through technical means by dismantling, mapping or analysing the product obtained from a public source.[130] In *Kunshan Yamada Press Co., Ltd. v. Ningbo Vanda Press Technology Co., Ltd. et al.*,[131] the trial court ruled that a reverse engineering defence can be established on two conditions: (1) the product being reversely engineered must be obtained through an open and public source; and (2) the persons conducting the reverse engineering must not be the ones who have a duty to keep in confidence the trade secret in issue. In this case, the court dismissed the reverse engineering defence of the individual defendants, who were ex-employees of the plaintiff. The decision was upheld by the Zhejiang High Court in a second trial.[132] It remains unclear whether the court would consider the defendant's cost of conducting reverse engineering in evaluating a reverse engineering. In judicial practice, very few reverse engineering defences have succeeded since the promulgation of the SPC's 2007 Interpretation.

The second exception of the SPC Interpretation concerns relations between customers and ex-employees. Indeed, employee mobility poses an unneglectable threat to a company's trade secrets and employers normally incorporate a non-compete clause in either an employee's employment agreement or a separate non-disclosure agreement, with a view to govern an ex-employee's post-employment behaviour.[133] However, such a restrictive covenant should be reasonable and necessary to protect

---

126. SPC Interpretation 2007, note 18, Art. 12.1. "Reverse engineering" refers to the relevant technical information on the products as obtained through dismantling, mapping or analysing the products gotten from technical means or other public channels. In case any party knows the business secrets of someone else by unjustifiable means and then claims its acquisition as lawful for the reason of reverse engineering, it shall not be supported.
127. SPC Regulations 2020, note 106, Art. 14.3.
128. SPC Interpretation 2007, note 18, Art. 13.2. See also SPC Regulations 2020, note 106, Art. 2.2: "... if it can be proved that the customer voluntarily chose to trade with the employee or the employee's new company after the employee left the former employer, the people's court shall determine that the employee did not use unfair means to obtain the trade secrets of the right holder [.i.e. the former employer]".
129. SPC Regulations 2020, note 106, Arts. 2.2, 14.2.
130. SPC Interpretation 2007, note 18, Art. 12.2; SPC Regulations 2020, note 106, Art. 14.2.
131. *Kunshan Yamada Press Co., Ltd. v. Ningbo Vanda Press Technology Co., Ltd. et al*, Zhejiang Higher People's Court's decision of 27 April 2015, 60 *Zhe Zhi Zhong Zi* (2014).
132. *Ibid.*
133. Kung-Chung Liu and Xiuqin Lin, 'Employees, Trade Secrets and Restrictive Covenant in Greater China', in Christopher Heath and Anselm Kamperman Sanders (eds.), *Employees, Trade Secrets and Restrictive Covenants* (Kluwer, 2016).

the legitimate interests of the employer, being the trade secrets or other intellectual properties in China. Article 23 of the Labour Contract Law provides that:

> An employer may enter into an agreement with an employee in the employment contract, requiring the employee to keep confidential the trade secrets and intellectual property of the employer. For employees who bear a duty of confidence, the employer and the employee may, in the employment contract or in a confidentiality agreement, include a non-compete clause, and agree that when the employment contract is dissolved or terminated, the employee shall be remunerated within the duration of the restriction. If the employee violates the non-compete covenant, it shall pay the employer a penalty for the breach.[134]

Article 24 of the Labour Contract Law further defines the reasonable scope of a non-compete clause:

> The persons bound by a non-compete clause shall be limited to senior managers, senior technicians, and other employees, who owe a duty of confidence to the employer. The scope, geographical range and duration of the restraint shall be agreed upon by the employer and the employee. The content of the restrictive covenant must not contravene any laws or regulations. After the employment contract is terminated, the duration for restricting any of the persons mentioned in the preceding paragraph to be employed by another employer, who produces or distributes products of the same kind or conducts business of the same kind, or to be self-employed to produce or distribute products of the same kind or conduct business of the same kind as with the ex-employer shall not exceed two years.[135]

In summary, according to Articles 23 and 24 of the Labour Contract Law, a non-compete covenant is valid unless (1) there is no protectable trade secret; (2) the employee is neither a senior or technical manager of the company, nor is he in possession of any trade secret of the employer and thus obliged to keep the same in confidence; (3) the employer does not provide adequate remuneration to the employee; (4) the duration of post-employment restraint exceeds two years; or (5) it in any other forms contravenes the statutory laws or regulations of the PRC.

While the parties can agree on the amount of remuneration resulting from a non-compete clause, the SPC provides in its *Interpretation (IV) on Several Issues on the Application of Law in the Trial of Labour Dispute Cases* an approach to determine the remuneration in the absence of contractual arrangements.[136] If there is no agreement on the amount of remuneration, the employee is entitled to claim compensation at a rate of 30 percent of his average monthly salary within the last 12 months prior to the termination of the employment.[137] If the calculated amount is lower than the local minimum wage standard, the local minimum wage standard shall prevail.[138] If the employer fails to pay the overdue remuneration for three consecutive months,

134. Labour Contract Law 2012, note 41, Art. 23.
135. *Ibid.*, Art. 24.
136. Interpretation (IV) of the Supreme People's Court on Several Issues on the Application of Law in the Trial of Labour Dispute Cases 2013 [Zuigao Renmin Fayuan Guanyu Shenli Laodong Zhengyi Anjian Shiyong Falv Ruogan Wenti De Jieshi].
137. *Ibid.*, Art. 6(1).
138. *Ibid.*, Art. 6(2).

the employee could request to terminate the restrictive covenant.[139] If the employer applies to a people's court to terminate a restrictive covenant at any time within the duration of the restriction, the employee will be entitled to an extra three-month remuneration.[140]

Because trade secrets are typically utilized and infringed in a secret way, it is always challenging for the trade secret proprietors to prove trade secret infringement in court proceedings. Therefore, the AUCL and the SPC Regulations have provided special rules of burden of proof for trade secret infringement in civil proceedings. Once the plaintiff provides prima facie evidence that it has taken confidentiality measures for the claimed trade secret and reasonably indicates that the trade secret has been infringed upon, the burden of proof shifts to the defendant to prove that the claimed trade secret is not actually a trade secret.[141] If the plaintiff provides prima facie evidence to reasonably indicate that the trade secret has been infringed upon, and provide any of the following evidence, the burden of proof is on the defendant to prove its non-infringement: (1) evidence that the defendant has a channel or an opportunity to access the trade secret and that the information it uses is substantially the same as the trade secret; (2) evidence that the trade secret has been disclosed or used, or is at risk of disclosure or use, by the defendant; or (3) evidence that the trade secret is otherwise infringed upon by the defendant.[142] Where the plaintiff provides prima facie evidences of the gains of the infringer from the infringement, and the account books and materials related to the act infringing on the trade secret are in the possession of the infringer, the court may order the infringer to provide such account books and materials in accordance with the plaintiff's application.[143] Where the infringer refuses to provide or fails to truthfully provide them without justification, the court may determine the gains of the infringer from the infringement based on the claims of the plaintiff and the evidences on record.

(e) *Fraudulent or Excessive Premium Campaign*

Article 10 of the AUCL stipulates that a business' premium campaign is unlawful if it falls under any of the following circumstances:

(1) the information on the types of prizes, conditions for claiming the prizes, the amount of the prizes or premiums, etc., is ambiguous in a way that it will affect the claim for the premium;
(2) the prize does not actually exist or the winners have been internally decided beforehand; or
(3) in the case of a lottery-based premium campaign, the amount of the top prize exceeds RMB 50,000.[144]

139. *Ibid.*, Art. 8.
140. *Ibid.*, Art. 9.
141. AUCL 2019, note 7, Art. 32.1
142. *Ibid.*, Art. 32.2.
143. SPC Regulations 2020, note 106, Art. 24.
144. AUCL 2019, note 7, Art. 10.

Additionally, the SAIC issued Certain Regulations on Prohibiting Unfair Competition in Prize-Attached Sales[145] in 1993 to facilitate the implementation of above Article 10 in the AUCL. However, as the Regulations were enacted in accordance with the 1993 AUCL, some of the provisions thereof have become obsolete, although the document *per se* is still effective. For example, the Regulations set the cap of the prize in a lottery at RMB 5,000,[146] which is significantly lower than that in the amended AUCL.

In January 2019, SAMR published a consultation paper on the proposed amendment of the SAIC Regulations.[147] In the consultation paper, the SAMR listed more unlawful acts in relation to the information disclosure process, the amount, quantity and quality of the prizes or awards, or the methods for determining the winners, etc.[148] Moreover, given the growth of Internet commerce, the proposed amendment also includes provisions governing online businesses that offered physical assets, monetary awards or any other economic benefits for promotion or solicitation.[149] According to the SAMR's proposed amendment, "relevant parties who have been injured by the unfair competition acts in a premium campaign can bring a lawsuit to a people's court and claim for compensation in accordance with Article 17 of the Anti-Unfair Competition Law".[150] The "relevant parties" here include both competitors and consumers. Market supervision authorities can also apply Article 22 of the AUCL and impose a fine of RMB 50,000 to RMB 500,000 for any breach of the Regulations.[151]

(f) ***Libel and Slander***

Fabricating or disseminating false or misleading information to damage the goodwill of a competitor or the reputation of a competitor's product is regarded as an act of unfair competition.[152] Sometimes, also the distribution of true but misleading information may trigger AUCL liability.[153] In *Tencent Technology (Shenzhen) Co., Ltd. et al. v. Beijing Qihoo 360 Technology Co. Ltd. et al.*, the SPC held that "the core element in determining a commercial defamation is whether the act of the relevant business has caused damage to a competitor's commercial goodwill or the reputation of a

145. Certain Regulations of the State Administration for Industry and Commerce on Prohibiting Unfair Competition in Prize-Attached Sales 1993 [Guojia Gongshang Guanli Zongju Guanyu Jinzhi Youjiang Xiaoshou Huodong Zhong Buzhengdang Jingzheng Xingwei De Ruogan Guiding].
146. *Ibid.*, Art. 4.1.
147. Certain Regulations of the State Administration for Market Supervision on Prohibiting Unfair Prize-Attached Sales Conducts (Consultation Paper) 2019 [Shichang Jiandu Zongju Guanyu Jinzhi Buzhengdang Youjiang Xiaoshou Xingwei De Ruogan Guiding (Zhengqiu Yijian Gao)].
148. *Ibid.*, Arts. 3, 4, 5, 6, 7.
149. *Ibid.*, Art. 9.
150. *Ibid.*, Art. 11.
151. *Ibid.*, Art. 10. See also AUCL 2019, note 7, Art. 22.
152. AUCL 2019, note 7, Art. 11.
153. John Wolff, 'Unfair Competition by Truthful Disparagement', 47 *Yale L.J.* (1938), 1304, 1332.

competitor's product in a misleading manner" and that "even if a piece of information is true ... it can still be regulated by Article 14 of the [1993] AUCL".[154]

An unjustified or groundless threat of IP infringement may constitute libel or slander under the AUCL. In *Foshan Shunde Fangchuang Electronics Co., Ltd. et al. v. Guangzhou Daidaijia Trading Co., Ltd.*, the defendant was held liable for libel and slander associated with its groundless patent infringement allegations against the plaintiff.[155] In *Yu Jifeng v. Lan Xia*,[156] the defendant filed a complaint to the Alibaba e-commerce platform, alleging the plaintiff had infringed her registered trade mark by forging a registration certificate in Class 25. This allegation caused Alibaba to take down the plaintiff's allegedly infringing products. However, the court found that the defendant's trade mark was actually registered in Class 35, not Class 25, and therefore held that the defendant's complaint to Alibaba had damaged the plaintiff's commercial goodwill. A damage of RMB 50,000 was then awarded to the plaintiff under the AUCL.[157]

While IP owners may use Article 2 of the AUCL to further protect their IP (see below), they themselves may be subject to unfair competition liability under the same Article for wrongfully claiming IP infringement. In *Shijiazhuang Shuanghuan Automobile Co., Ltd. v. Honda Motor Co., Ltd.*, the SPC ruled that Honda violated Article 2 of the AUCL by sending cease-and-desist ("C&D") letters to Shuanghuan's distributors during the parties' design patent dispute.[158] The SPC explained that patent owners bear different levels of duty of care when sending C&D letters to different parties.[159] Honda's C&D letters to Shuanghuan were reasonable because Honda expected Shuanghuan to stop production and to seek a licence after receiving the C&D letters. However, Honda violated Article 2 of the AUCL by sending C&D letters to Shuanghuan's distributors without sufficiently explaining the comparison and similarities of those two designs and the pending litigation.[160] The distributors would thus tend to stop transacting with Shuanghuan. Therefore, sending C&D letters to parties, such as a competitor's distributors, importers, or customers may interfere in the market competition for relevant products.[161]

Comparative advertising is not *per se* illegal in China, but it may trigger unfair competition liabilities under certain circumstances. Article 9 of the Advertising Law

154. *Tencent Technology (Shenzhen) Co., Ltd. et al. v. Beijing Qihoo 360 Technology Co. Ltd. et al.*, SPC's decision of 18 February 2014, 5 *Min San Zhong Zi* (2013). Notably, the decision was made in accordance with the 1993 AUCL, which regulated only "false" indications made by an entrepreneur. The prohibition on "misleading" indications was added by the 2017 Amendment.
155. *Foshan Shunde Fangchuang Electronics Co., Ltd. et al. v. Guangzhou Daidaijia Trading Co., Ltd.*, Foshan Intermediate People's Court's decision of 27 April 2015, 4 *Fo Zhong Fa Zhi Min Zhong Zi* (2015).
156. *Yu Jifeng v. Lan Xia*, Sichuan Higher Court's decision of 31 March 2020, 134 *Chuan Zhi Min Zhong* (2019).
157. *Ibid.*
158. *Shijiazhuang Shuanghuan Automobile Co., Ltd. v. Honda Motor Co., Ltd.*, SPC's decision of 8 December 2015, 7 *Min San Zhong Zi* (2014).
159. *Ibid.*
160. *Ibid.*
161. *Ibid.*

prohibits the use of "national", "highest", "best" or connotations of the same kind in an advertisement,[162] which implies the subject product or service is better than all other ones. However, Articles 8 and 11 are more frequently applied in cases concerning comparative advertising. In *Guangzhou Carslan Enterprise Management Co., Ltd. v. Liu Zetian et al.*, the defendant was held liable by stating online that its makeup kit was "better than Carslan". The court found that the defendant's statement was a false or misleading indication and thus violated Article 8 of the AUCL.[163] In *Cixi Bull Electric Co., Ltd. v. Guangdong Pisen Electric Co., Ltd. et al.*, the defendant displayed product components of its "smart power strip" and traditional power strips together with a written comparison of these two types of product.[164] While the defendant did not identify any specific manufacturer of traditional power strips, the components of traditional power strips it displayed were marked with a character "Bull", which was the distinctive part of the plaintiff's trade mark and trade name.[165] The court ruled that the defendant's act constituted libel and slander, which was a violation of Article 11 of the AUCL.[166]

(g) Acts of Unfair Competition Committed Online

Since the 2017 Amendment, the AUCL has incorporated a provision specifically regulating online business.[167] According to Article 12.2 of the AUCL:

> No business may, by technical means to affect users' options, among others, commit the following acts of interfering with or sabotaging the normal operation of online products or services legally provided by another business:
>
> (1) inserting a link or forcing a URL redirection in an online product or service legally provided by another business without its consent;
> (2) misleading, defrauding, or forcing users into altering, shutting down, or uninstalling an online product or service legally provided by another business;
> (3) causing in bad faith incompatibility with an online product or service legally provided by another business; or
> (4) other acts of interfering with or sabotaging the normal operation of online products or services legally provided by another business.

As this is a non-exhaustive list, online business may still be subject to legal liabilities for their unfair competition conducts according to other articles of the AUCL.

162. Advertising Law, note 24, Art. 9.3.
163. *Guangzhou Carslan Enterprise Management Co., Ltd. v. Liu Zetian et al.*, Shanghai Xuhui District People's Court's decision of 31 July 2019, 29255 *Hu 0104 Min Chu* (2018).
164. *Cixi Bull Electric Co., Ltd. v. Guangdong Pisen Electric Co., Ltd. et al.*, Shanghai Yangpu District People's Court's decision of 30 October 2017, 3376 *Hu 0110 Min Chu* (2017).
165. *Ibid.*
166. *Ibid.*
167. AUCL 2019, note 7, Art. 12.2.

(h) Other Acts of Unfair Competition

In addition to the acts of unfair competition conducts enumerated above, Article 2.2 of the AUCL has been frequently applied by the Chinese courts as a catch-all provision for other acts of unfair competition:

> For the purpose of this Law, unfair competition refers to any business operator's act of participating in the production and operation activities in violation of the provisions herein to disrupt the competition order in the market and infringe the legitimate rights and interests of other business operators or consumers.[168]

This catch-all provision is occasionally applied to unfair competition cases concerning IP, particularly copyright. For example, in *Cha v. Young*, a famous *wuxia* novelist, Jin Yong, claimed that the young writer Jiang Nan, whose fiction borrowed characters from Jin Young's novels, had engaged in copyright infringement.[169] The Guangzhou District Court held that Jiang Nan did not infringe Jin Young's copyright because the former only used the latter's ideas, instead of expressions. Furthermore, the defendant Jiang Nan's expression of storyline was completely different from the plaintiff Jin Young's novels. However, the court held that the defendant's use of the characters in the plaintiff's books violated Article 2.2 of the AUCL because the defendant obtained economic advantage from his publication and consequently diminished the plaintiff's market share.[170] Moreover, the defendant's competitive behaviour was not justified because it violated the doctrine of good faith and publicly-recognized business ethics.[171] Consequently, the court ruled that the defendant had to pay Jing Young damages in the amount of RMB 1,680,000.[172]

In *Youku Information Technology (Beijing) Co Ltd v. Hangzhou SEVEN Co Ltd*, the plaintiff Youku was one of the major platforms of online episodes or movies in China. Consumers used the software AdClear developed by the defendant, SEVEN, to bypass the advertisements on the plaintiff's video platform.[173] In other words, consumers could freely watch commercial-free videos on the plaintiff's platform with the AdClear software. Both the Hangzhou District Court and the Intermediate People's Court of Hangzhou City ruled for the plaintiff and opined that the defendant's behaviour had constituted unfair competition according to Art. 2 of the AUCL.[174]

What is noteworthy in the *Youku* case is that both courts explained that anti-competitive behaviour need not necessarily be targeted against competitors.[175] Although the plaintiff and defendant did not compete against each other in the market, the defendant had infringed the plaintiff's legitimate interests by selling its AdClear

168. AUCL 2019, note 7, Art. 2.2.
169. *Cha v. Young*, Guangzhou Tianhe District People's Court's decision of 16 August 2018, 12068 *Yue 0106 Min Chu* (2016).
170. *Ibid.*
171. *Ibid.*
172. *Ibid.* See also Jyh-An Lee, 'Tripartite Perspective on the Copyright-Sharing Economy in China', 35 *Com L. & Security Rev.* (2019), 434, 438.
173. *Youku Information Technology (Beijing) Co Ltd v. Hangzhou SEVEN Co Ltd*, Hangzhou Intermediate People's Court's decision of 5 May 2018, 231 *Zhe 01 Min Zhong* (2018).
174. *Ibid.*
175. *Ibid.*

software to consumers. Youku's revenue from advertisements would likely decrease if consumers used AdClear to block advertisements. Therefore, the defendant's profit from AdClear was not justified because the profit was made at the expense of the plaintiff's legitimate interest. The courts recognized that Youku's revenue from online advertisements did not violate any law and was thus legitimate.[176] Instead, Youku had invested an enormous amount of resources in acquiring or producing high-quality copyrighted works.[177] While the defendant argued that the AUCL did not protect specific business models, the courts held that it was the legitimate business interest underlying the plaintiff's business model rather than the business model itself that should be protected by the law.[178]

The implication of the above cases is that the potentially wide application of Article 2.2 in the AUCL may effectively supplement the inadequacy not only of other provisions of the AUCL, but also IP laws. However, courts should be cautious about the possible overreaching of the AUCL when applying this Article 2.2.

5. Remedies and Enforcement

(a) Liability

For each of the examples of unfair competition conduct listed above, the AUCL imposes civil and administrative remedies against wrongdoers under its supervision in addition to a possible criminal liability.[179] Competitors whose legitimate interests have been injured by unfair competition are entitled to bring a private lawsuit to court and claim compensation.[180] The damages are to be calculated based on the actual loss to the victim caused by the unfair competition plus costs, or an account of profits if the actual loss is hard to calculate.[181] For acts of confusion and trade secret misappropriation, if either the actual loss of the injured or the illegal gain of the wrongdoer is quantifiable, the discretionary compensation should be determined by a court with a statutory cap of RMB 5 million.[182] Trade secret owners are also entitled to exemplary damages ranging from one to five times of the actual loss or account of profit, where the misappropriation is conducted in bad faith and the circumstances are so severe that exemplary damages should be applied to show the court's discouragement.[183]

In addition to assuming civil liabilities when being sued, the wrongdoer is also subject to administrative penalties prescribed by the AUCL. The most frequent form of penalty is an order to cease the unlawful act together with an imposition of a fine on the disobedient entity. The amount of fine for the seven categories of unfair competition are as follows:

---

176. *Ibid.*
177. *Ibid.*
178. *Ibid.* See also Lee and Li, note 69, 60–61.
179. See text accompanying note 32.
180. AUCL 2019, note 7, Art. 17.2.
181. *Ibid.*, Art. 17.3.
182. *Ibid.*, Art. 17.4.
183. *Ibid.*, Art. 17.3.

(1) For acts of confusion, the amount is within five times of the value of the infringing products, if the latter has exceeded RMB 50,000. Otherwise, a fine of no more than RMB 250,000 could be imposed;[184]
(2) For commercial briberies, in addition to an account of profit, a fine ranging from RMB 100,000 to RMB 3 million could be imposed;[185]
(3) For false or misleading indications, the range of penalty is from RMB 200,000 to RMB 1 million, or RMB 1 to 2 million if there is an aggravated circumstance. If the act constitutes a false advertisement, however, the amount should be determined in accordance with the Advertising Law of the PRC;[186]
(4) For trade secret misappropriation, the administrative fine ranges from RMB 100,000 to RMB 1 million, or RMB 500,000 to RMB 5 million if there are aggravated circumstances;[187]
(5) For fraudulent or excessive premium campaigns, the fine could range from RMB 50,000 to RMB 500,000;[188]
(6) For slander and libel, the wrongdoer could be fined from RMB 10,000 to RMB 500,000, or RMB 500,000 to RMB 3 million if the circumstance is severe;
(7) For technical sabotage against another's online operation, the fine is set at RMB 100,000 to RMB 500,000, or RMB 500,000 to RMB 3 million if the circumstance is severe.

Revocation of business certificate is also a form of penalty imposed for acts of confusion, commercial briberies and false or misleading indications under an aggravated circumstance.[189] On the other hand, the AUCL also provides an mitigating factor in that if the wrongdoer voluntarily eliminates or mitigates the adverse effect of its wrongdoing, a mitigated penalty should be adopted accordingly. If there is only a minor breach of the law, which has been modified in a timely manner and no adverse influence is generated therefrom, the wrongdoer could be exempted from any administrative penalty.[190]

The AUCL simultaneously stipulates civil, criminal and administrative remedies against wrongdoers. Where the assets of the entity are insufficient to cover all liabilities incurred, civil liabilities enjoy the top priority to be compensated.[191]

(b) Private Enforcement

Market players hampered by any act of unfair competition can enforce their rights through a private lawsuit or a complaint filed with the local administrations. Injunctive relief is frequently sought by parties initiating litigation based on the AUCL. If the defendant refuses to follow the court-granted injunction, the plaintiff may report this disobedience to the relevant authorities or the court, which may facilitate the

184. *Ibid.*, Art. 18.1.
185. *Ibid.*, Art. 19.
186. *Ibid.*, Art. 20.
187. *Ibid.*, Art. 21.
188. *Ibid.*, Art. 22.
189. *Ibid.*, Arts.18, 19, 20.
190. *Ibid.*, Art. 25.
191. *Ibid.*, Art. 27.

enforcement by confiscating the infringing products or imposing a further fine on the defendant. If the defendant has been repeatedly or extremely uncooperative, it may be sanctioned under criminal law as well.[192] In the dispute between New Balance in China and Shenzhen Xin Ping Heng Sports Equipment Co., Ltd. and others in 2017, New Balance had applied for an interlocutory injunction before trial based on the established status of its "N" logo as a decoration with certain influence. The application was approved by the Suzhou Intermediate Court, which required the defendants to immediately cease production and sales of the sneakers with the "N" logo and remove all misleading indications on their official websites and social media accounts.[193] However, all defendants refused to comply with the injunction order. The Suzhou Court therefore imposed a fine of RMB 1 million, RMB 500,000, RMB 100,000 and RMB 100,000 on the four defendants respectively, regardless of the final result in the substantive examination.[194] The decision was upheld by the Jiangsu High Court in appeal.[195]

(c) Public Enforcement

Most unfair competition cases are enforced though administrative approaches because public enforcement of the AUCL is more cost-efficient to most aggrieved parties. Moreover, market supervision authorities are obliged to monitor the behaviour of businesses. Therefore, competent authorities may initiate administrative raids on the premises of suspected market players. According to the 2019 Annual Report of the SAMR, unfair competition cases handled by market supervision administrations had reached a total number of 10,300 in 2019, with the total value of confiscation and fine amounting to RMB 402 million.[196] In terms of unfair competition cases handled by the judiciary, a random search at China Judgments Online for a claim of unfair competition led to 1,391 cases in the same year.[197]

---

192. Criminal Law 2017, note 40, Art. 331 ("Whoever refuses to execute a judgment or ruling rendered by a people's court while he or she is able to do so shall be sentenced to imprisonment of not more than three years or criminal detention or a fine if the circumstances are serious; or be sentenced to imprisonment of not less than three years but not more than seven years in addition to a fine if the circumstances are especially serious. Where an entity commits the crime as provided for in the preceding paragraph, a fine shall be imposed on it, and its directly responsible person in charge and other directly liable persons shall be punished in accordance with the provisions of the preceding paragraph.")
193. *New Balance Trading (China) Co., Ltd. v. Shenzhen Xin Ping Heng Sports Equipment Co., Ltd. et al.*, Suzhou Intermediate People's Court's decision of 13 September 2016, 537 *Su 05 Min Chu* (2016).
194. *New Balance Trading (China) Co., Ltd. v. Shenzhen Xin Ping Heng Sports Equipment Co., Ltd. et al.*, Suzhou Intermediate People's Court, 001 *Su 05 Si Cheng* (2017).
195. *New Balance Trading (China) Co., Ltd. v. Shenzhen Xin Ping Heng Sports Equipment Co., Ltd. et al.*, Jiangsu Higher People's Court's decision of 1 February 2018, 4 *Su Si Cheng Fu* (2018).
196. SAMR, 'Annual Report of 2019 of the State Administration of Market Supervision on the Construction of a Law-Based Government', 31 March 2020, http://gkml.samr.gov.cn/nsjg/fgs/202003/t20200331_313722.html accessed 11 July 2020.
197. The database is updated from time to time. Omission or repetition of cases do occur. The number 1,391 was reached using the search criteria (1) claim: unfair competition claims;

Article 4 of the AUCL provides that "[t]he departments performing the functions of industry and commerce administration of the people's governments at and above the county level shall investigate and dispose of acts of unfair competition, unless a law or administrative regulation requires any other department to do so".[198] Accordingly, the law enforcement body in unfair competition cases is generally the local AMR. One exception is that, according to Telecommunication Regulation, unfair competition in the telecom industry shall be regulated by the Ministry of Information Industry ("MII") or telecommunications authorities at provincial level.[199]

II. ANTITRUST LAW

1. Introduction

China promulgated the current Anti-Monopoly Law ("AML") in August 2007, which came into effect on 1 August 2008. The AML aims at preventing and curbing monopolistic conducts, protecting the fairness of market competition, enhancing economic efficiency, maintaining both consumer and public interests, and promoting the healthy development of the socialist market economy.[200] While a major part of the AML was transplanted from the Western capitalist states to sustain the market economy, the AML also includes certain socialist characteristics.[201] In China, the state is not only the market regulator but also a major market player via state-owned enterprises (SOEs). Therefore, the AML is designed to supervise both market actors and the administrative regulatory power.[202] Therefore, the AML adopts a whole chapter, Chapter 5, to regulate administrative monopolies.[203] Moreover, the AML is sometimes used by the government as an instrument of price supervision.[204] Last but not least, some foreign investors have had the impression that there is an industrial policy goal underlying the enforcement of the AML, which is to protect domestic businesses.[205] Such a policy goal is sometimes extended to protect the national and economic security of the country.[206]

---

(2) document type: judgments; and (3) year: 2019.

198. AUCL 2019, note 7, Art. 4.
199. Telecommunication Regulation of the People's Republic of China 2016 Amendment ("Telecommunication Regulation 2016") [Zhonghua Renmin Gongheguo Dianxin Tiaoli], Art. 71.
200. AML 2008, note 3, Art. 1.
201. Wendy Ng, 'The Influence of Socialist Principles on the Legal Regulation of Markets in China: The Anti-Monopoly Law' in Hualing Fu et al. (eds.), *Socialist Law in Socialist East Asia* (CUP, 2018), 357–358.
202. *Ibid.*, 252–253.
203. See, generally, Zhanjiang Zhang and Baiding Wu, 'Governing China's Administrative Monopolies under the Anti-Monopoly Law – A Ten-Year Review (2008–2018) and Beyond', 15 *J. Competition & Econ.* (2019), 718.
204. *Ibid.*, 373.
205. Thomas J. Horton, 'Antitrust or Industrial Protectionism? Emerging International Issues in China's Anti-Monopoly Law Enforcement Efforts', 14 *Santa Clara J. Int'l L.* (2016), 109, 115, 128–131.
206. *Ibid.*, 123–128.

The AML regulates (1) the monopolistic conducts in economic activities within the territory of the People's Republic of China ("PRC") and (2) the monopolistic conducts outside the territory of the PRC that eliminate or restrict competition on the domestic market.[207] There are three types of monopolistic conducts regulated by the AML: (1) the monopoly agreements reached among business operators; (2) the abuse of a dominant market position by business operators; and (3) the concentration of business operators that may have the effect of eliminating or restricting competition.[208] These three monopolistic conducts will be analysed in sections 3–5 below. In order to implement the AML in a more predictable way, the State Administration for Market Regulation ("SAMR") on 26 June 2019 issued three interim regulations on, respectively, anti-monopoly agreements,[209] abuse of dominant market position,[210] and abuse of administrative power to eliminate or restrict competition[211]. All three interim regulations came into effect on 1 September 2019.

There used to be three government authorities in charge of the AML enforcement: the Ministry of Commerce ("MofCom"), the National Development and Reform Commission (NDRC), and the State Administration for Industry and Commerce ("SAIC"). While the MofCom was in charge of merger review (or review of business concentration), the NDRC and SAIC shared enforcement responsibility for monopoly agreements and abuse of a dominant marketing position. The NDRC was in charge of pricing-related violations, whereas the SAIC was responsible for non-price-related conducts. These three anti-monopoly agencies were restructured and consolidated in 2018. While the MofCom and NDRC no longer have any AML enforcement power, the SAIC was integrated into the newly established SAMR, which is directly supervised by the State Council. There is no longer an organizational differentiation between price-related investigations and non-price-related ones. Nevertheless, the MofCom is still in charge of merger review or review of business concentration.

2. IP and Antitrust

The relationship between IP and antitrust is always complicated. On the one hand, while IP confers legitimate monopoly rights for a certain period of time,[212] antitrust

207. AML 2008, note 3, Art. 2.

208. *Ibid.*, Art. 3.

209. Provisions of the State Administration for Market Regulation on Prohibiting Monopoly Agreements 2019 ("Interim Provisions on Prohibiting Monopoly Agreements 2019") [Guojia Shichang Jiandu Guanli Zongju Jinzhi Longduan Xieyi Zanxing Guiding].

210. Provisions of the State Administration for Market Regulation on Prohibiting Abuse of Dominant Market Position 2019 ("Interim Provisions on Prohibiting Abuse of Dominant Market Position 2019") [Guojia Shichang Jiandu Guanli Zongju Jinzhi Lanyong Shichang Zhipei Diwei Xingwei Zanxing Guiding].

211. Provisions of the State Administration for Market Regulation on Prohibiting the Acts of Eliminating or Restricting Competition by Abuse of Administrative Power 2019 ("Interim Provisions on Prohibiting the Acts of Eliminating or Restricting Competition by Abuse of Administrative Power 2019") [Guojia Shichang Jiandu Guanli Zongju Zhizhi Lanyong Xingzheng Quanli Paichu Xianzhi Jingzheng Xingwei Zanxing Guiding].

212. Daniel C.K. Chow, 'A Comparison of EU and China Competition Laws That Apply to Technology Transfer Agreements', 9 I/S *J.L. & Pol'y for Info. Soc'y* (2014), 497, 520.

laws are designed to prevent the loss of public welfare caused by monopolistic conduct of individual market players.[213] On the other hand, the two share the mutual goals of promoting competition and innovation, improving economic operation efficiency, and protecting the interests of consumers.[214] To maintain the balance between fair competition and innovation, it is crucial to construct a balanced interface between IP and antitrust laws.[215]

Article 55 of the AML provides a regulatory foundation for the relationship between IP and antitrust:

> This law shall not apply to the conduct of business operators to exercise their intellectual property rights according to the laws and relevant administrative regulations on intellectual property rights; however, this Law shall apply to the conduct of business operators to eliminate or restrict market competition by abusing their intellectual property rights.[216]

Article 20.2 of the Patent Law also establishes the interface between Patent Law and the AML:

> Any misuse of patent rights, elimination or restriction of competition, which constitutes monopolistic conduct, shall be governed by the Anti-Monopoly Law of the People's Republic of China.[217]

The State Administration for Industry and Commerce ("SAIC"), which has been restructured as SAMR, in August 2015 released the *Provisions on Prohibiting the Abuse of Intellectual Property Rights to Preclude or Restrict Competition*.[218] The Provisions for the first time specifically clarified the AML's potential application to business operators' abuse of IP to preclude or restrict competition, and further defined the IP-relevant non-compliant conducts prohibited by the AML. The Provisions were further updated by the SAMR on 23 October 2020 ("the SAMR Provisions").[219]

213. Liyang Hou, 'Antitrust Regulation of Intellectual Property Rights in China' [2015] https://ssrn.com/abstract=2648736 accessed 25 May 2020.
214. Provisions of the State Administration for Industry and Commerce on Prohibiting the Abuse of Intellectual Property Rights to Preclude or Restrict Competition 2015 ("SAIC Provisions") [Guojia Gongshang Guanli Zongju Guanyu Jinzhi Lanyong Zhishi Chanquan Xianzhi Jingzheng Xingwei De Guiding], Art. 2.
215. Giuseppe Colangelo and Roberto Pardolesi, 'Intellectual Property, Standards, and Antitrust: A New Life for the Essential Facilities Doctrine? Some Insights from the Chinese Regulation', in Peter Drahos, Gustavo Ghidini and Hanns Ullrich (eds.), *Kritika: Essays on Intellectual Property* (Edward Elgar, 2017), 70.
216. AML 2008, note 3, Art. 55.
217. Patent Law of the People's Republic of China 2020 [Zhonghua Renmin Gongheguo Zhuanli Fa], Art. 20.2.
218. SAIC Provisions, note 214.
219. Provisions of the State Administration for Market Regulation on Prohibiting the Abuse of Intellectual Property Rights to Preclude or Restrict Competition 2020 ("SAMR Provisions") [Guojia Shichang Jiandu Guanli Zongju Guanyu Jinzhi Lanyong Zhishi Chanquan Xianzhi Jingzheng Xingwei De Guiding].

3. Monopoly Agreements

Article 13.2 of the AML defines "monopoly agreements" as "agreements, decisions or other concerted behaviour that may eliminate or restrict competition".[220]The AML prohibits monopoly agreements reached by competitors in the same market (horizontal monopoly agreements), and by upstream suppliers and downstream retailers (vertical monopoly agreements).

(a) *Horizontal Monopoly Agreements*

Article 13.1 of the AML specifies five types of horizontal monopoly agreements together with a catch-all provision, which include agreements involving (1) fixing or changing commodity prices, (2) restricting the amount of commodities manufactured or marketed output restriction, (3) splitting the sales market or the purchasing market for raw and semi-finished materials, (4) restricting the purchase of new technologies or equipment, or the development of new technologies or product markets, (5) joint boycotting of transactions, and (6) other monopolistic agreements as specified by the authority for the enforcement of the AML under the State Council. [221]

The Interim Provisions of September 2019 define five types of horizontal monopoly agreements as below:

(1) price fixing is the conduct of fixing or changing the price level, range of price changes, profit level or discount, commission fees and other expenses; agreeing to adopt a standard formula for calculating prices; restricting the self-determined pricing power of operators participating in an agreement; or fixing or changing the price by other means;[222]
(2) an output restriction may be achieved by ways of restricting the production volume, fixing the production volume, ceasing production, or restricting the production volume of goods of specific varieties and models; restricting the volume of launch of goods, restricting the sales volume of specific goods; or by other means;[223]
(3) a market division occurs when horizontal competitors divide the sales area, market share, sales target, sales income, and sales profit or the category, volume and time of goods sold; divide the procurement area, category, volume, time or suppliers of raw materials, semi-finished products, components and parts and related equipment; or divide the sales market or raw materials procurement market by other means;[224]
(4) a technology restriction includes operators' agreements restricting the purchase or use of new technologies and new techniques; restricting the purchase, lease or use of new equipment and new products; restricting the investment in, research and development of new technologies, new

220. AML 2008, note 3, Art. 13.
221. *Ibid.*, Art 13.1.
222. Interim Provisions on Prohibiting Monopoly Agreements 2019, note 209, Art. 7.
223. *Ibid.*, Art. 8.
224. *Ibid.*, Art. 9.

techniques or new products; refusing to use new technologies, new techniques, new equipment and new products; and restricting the purchase of new technologies and new equipment, or restricting the development of new technologies and new products by other means;[225] and

(5) a joint boycott refers to competitors jointly refusing to supply or sell goods to specific operators; jointly refusing to purchase or sell goods of specific operators; jointly restricting specific operators from trading with operators that are competitors; and jointly boycotting trade by other means.[226]

(b) Vertical Monopoly Agreement

Article 14 of the AML bans vertical monopoly agreements involving (1) fixing the prices of commodities resold to a third party; (2) restricting the lowest prices for commodities resold to a third party; and (3) other monopoly agreements confirmed as such by the authority for enforcement of the AML under the State Council.[227] To be specific, the AML only prohibits producers and retailers agreeing on a fixed retail price or an agreed minimum price. However, it does not restrict producers from imposing a maximum resale price to the retailers. One possible explanation is that unlike a fixed resale price or a stipulated minimum resale price, which will have an instant and profound impact on market competition, the pro-competitive effect of fixing a maximum resale price may outweigh its anti-competitive harm.

(c) Safe Harbour

Article 15.1 of the AML provides a safe harbour to exempt liabilities associated with monopoly agreements.[228] Under this Article, business operators will not be subject to legal liabilities associated with Articles 13 and 14 if the monopoly agreement is entered into for any of the purposes below:

(1) improving technologies, or engaging in research and development of new products;
(2) improving product quality, reducing cost, and enhancing efficiency, unifying specifications and standards of products, or implementing specialized division of production;
(3) increasing the efficiency and competitiveness of small and medium-sized undertakings;
(4) serving public interest in energy conservation, environmental protection and disaster relief;
(5) mitigating a sharp decrease in sales volumes or obvious overproduction caused by economic depression;
(6) safeguarding legitimate interests in foreign trade and in economic cooperation with foreign counterparties; or

225. *Ibid.*, Art. 10.
226. *Ibid.*, Art. 11.
227. AML 2008, note 3, Art. 14.
228. *Ibid.*, Art. 15.1.

(7) other purposes as prescribed by law or the State Council.

Business operators will bear the burden of proof to show that their conduct falls under any of the circumstances listed above. For monopoly agreements made for the purposes of (1)-(5), business operators are further required to prove that the agreement will not substantially restrict competition in the relevant market and can enable consumers to share the benefits from the agreement.[229]

(d) IP and Monopoly Agreement

Articles 13 to 15 of the AML set up the fundamental framework regulating monopoly agreements in the PRC. This framework can be applied to the abuse of IP to restrict or eliminate competition as well. Article 4 of the SAMR Provisions explicitly prohibit businesses from violating Articles 13 and 14 of the AML by exercising IP, unless evidence could be adduced to prove that they fall under the exceptional circumstances stipulated under Article 15.[230]

In addition to Article 15 of the AML, Article 5 of the SAMR Provisions further provides two exemptions to antitrust liability associated with exercising IP:

(1) in the context of a horizontal agreement, the aggregate market share of competing businesses in the relevant market affected by the conduct shall not exceed 20 percent, or, at a minimum, four other substitutable technologies subject to independent control may be obtained at reasonable costs in the relevant market;[231] or

(2) neither the business nor the transaction counterparty has a market share exceeding 30 percent in the relevant market, or, at a minimum, two other substitutable technologies subject to independent control can be obtained at reasonable costs in the relevant market.[232] However, if there is any evidence to the contrary, i.e., the agreement has any effect of precluding or restricting competition, the exemption will not apply.[233]

These exemptions make economic sense because a relatively low market share implies that the business operator is not able to cause a significant impact on market competition. Furthermore, the existence of alternative technologies will considerably mitigate the market power enjoyed by the IP owner.

4. Abuse of Dominant Market Position

(a) The Relevant Market

The determination of a relevant market is normally an initial step in antitrust enforcement. The AML defines relevant market as:

229. *Ibid.*, Art. 15.2.
230. SAMR Provisions, note 219, Art. 4.
231. *Ibid.*, Art. 5(1).
232. *Ibid.*, Art. 5(2).
233. *Ibid.*, Art. 5.

> the range of the products for which, and the regions where, business operators compete with each other during a given period of time for specific products or services.[234]

Therefore, the determination of a relevant market involves the determination of both the relevant product market and the relevant geographical market as a requirement to decide whether there is an abuse of the dominant market position. In 2009, the Anti-Monopoly Committee of the State Council promulgated the Guide of the Anti-Monopoly Committee of the State Council for the Definition of the Relevant Market ("Committee Guide 2009") to further define the relevant product market and the relevant geographical market.[235] According to the Committee Guide 2009, the relevant product market refers to

> a market comprised of a group or a category of products that are considered by consumers to have a relatively strong substitution relationship based on the characteristics, uses and prices of the commodities. These products have a relatively intense competitive relationship, and it may be considered as the product scope within which business operators compete with each other in the anti-monopoly law enforcement.[236]

And the relevant geographic market refers to

> a scope of geographic areas within which consumers can acquire products that have a relatively strong substitution relationship. Such areas have a relatively intense competitive relationship with each other, and it may be considered as the geographic scope within which business operators compete with each other in the anti-monopoly law enforcement.[237]

The Committee Guide 2009 particularly points out the role of IP in the determination of relevant market:

> Where such factors as production cycle, life time, seasonal features, fashion style or protection period of intellectual property rights have become the commodity characteristics that cannot be ignored, the factor of time shall be considered in the definition of the relevant market.
>
> In the anti-monopoly enforcement of technology trade, licence agreements or any other issue involving intellectual property rights, the relevant technology market may need to be defined with the influence of factors such as intellectual property and innovation being taken into account.[238]

Based on the AML and the Committee Guide 2009, the SAMR Provisions further stipulate that:

234. AML 2008, note 3, Art. 12.
235. Guide of the Anti-Monopoly Committee of the State Council for the Definition of the Relevant Market 2009 ("Committee Guide 2009") [Guowuyuan Fanlongduan Weiyuanhui Guanyu Xiangguan Shichang Jieding De Zhinan].
236. *Ibid.*, Art. 3.2.
237. *Ibid.*, Art. 3.3.
238. *Ibid.*, Art. 3.4–3.5.

> [i]n the law enforcement against monopolies involving intellectual property licensing, among others, the relevant product market may be the technology market or the product market containing particular intellectual property rights. The relevant technology market is the market formed by competition between the technologies involved in the exercise of intellectual property rights and the existing interchangeable technologies of the same kind.[239]

Both the Committee Guide and the SAMR Provisions reveal that the definition of a relevant market concerns the indispensability of the subject product or service market, i.e., whether the subject product or service can be replaced by any competing product or service of the same kind. Similar logic is applied to the technology market, and the decisive factor would be whether there exists any technically and financially feasible alternative.

In *Huawei v. IDC*, the plaintiff Huawei, as a standard implementer, defined the relevant product market as the combination of the licensing market of *each* patent which was essential to the implementation of several 3G standards in China and the US owned by the defendant IDC, a standard-essential patents (SEPs) owner.[240] This viewpoint was accepted by the Shenzhen Intermediate People's Court, ruling that there was no available alternative to any of IDC's SEPs in issue.[241] IDC then appealed to the Guangdong Higher People's Court, arguing that the licensing market should be considered as the combination of *all* patents essential to the implementation of the subject standards. IDC further argued that as different SEPs were owned by different companies, owning one or some of such patented technologies did not grant IDC the monopoly power in the end product market. Hence, the court should not oversimplify the market definition by solely relying on the substitution analysis. However, IDC's arguments were not accepted by the Guangdong Higher People's Court, which, on the contrary, applied a substitution analysis from both the demand and supply sides.[242]

(b) Dominant Market Position

According to the AML, a "dominant market position" refers to a market position held by a business operator that has the ability to control the price or quantity of commodities or other transaction conditions in the relevant market or block or affect the entry of other business operators into the relevant market.[243] The term "other transaction conditions" here refers to other factors that can have a substantial impact on transactions on the market other than the price and quantity of goods, such as variety and quality of goods, terms of payment, mode of delivery, after-sales services,

239. SAMR Provisions, note 219, Art. 3(2).
240. *Huawei Technology Co., Ltd. v. InterDigital Technology Corp. et al.*, Shenzhen Intermediate People's Court, 857 *Shen Zhong Fa Zhi Min Chu Zi* (2011).
241. *Ibid.*
242. *Huawei Technology Co., Ltd. v. InterDigital Technology Corp. et al.*, Guangdong Higher People's Court's decision of 21 October 2013, 306 *Yue Gao Fa Min San Zhong Zi* (2013) ("*Huawei v. IDC*").
243. AML 2008, note 3, Art. 17.2.

transaction selection, technical constraints, etc.[244] The ways in which a dominant player can obstruct or affect other operators from entering into the relevant markets under the AML includes excluding other operators from entering into the relevant markets, delaying other operators' entering into the relevant markets within a reasonable period of time, or forcing other operators to enter into the relevant market at substantially increased costs and leading to their inability to conduct effective competition with the existing operators, etc.[245]

Notably, the AML provides an analytical framework for defining a dominant player in a relevant market: Article 19 of the AML creates a presumption of dominance where one or more market players are presumed to have a dominant position if (1) the market share of one business operator accounts for one half or more in the relevant market; (2) the joint market share of two business operators accounts for two-thirds or more in the relevant market; or (3) the joint market share of three business operators accounts for three-quarters or more in the relevant market. [246] Under the circumstances prescribed in (2) or (3), if any of the business operators has a market share of less than 10 percent, that business operator shall not be considered to have a dominant position.[247] In other words, in an alleged abuse of dominance case, if a plaintiff is capable of adducing *prima facie* evidence to show that there is an alleged abusive conduct and the market share of the defendant(s) has satisfied any of the above conditions, the dominance of the defendant(s) will be presumed in the absence of contrary evidence.

Nevertheless, the presumption of dominance is rebuttable.[248] That is, the defendant is allowed to adduce contrary evidence to prove either its market share has not met the presumed-dominance threshold, or its market power is rather limited considering other decisive factors. These factors include (1) the market share of the business operator and its competitive status in the relevant market;[249] (2) the ability of the business operator to control the sales market or the raw material supply

244. Interim Provisions on Prohibiting Abuse of Dominant Market Position 2019, note 210, Art. 5.2.
245. *Ibid.*, Art. 5.3.
246. AML 2008, note 3, Art. 19.
247. *Ibid.*
248. *Ibid.*
249. Interim Provisions on Prohibiting Abuse of Dominant Market Position 2019, note 210, Art. 6: "According to Article 18.1 of the Anti-Monopoly Law, in the determination of the market share of an operator in a relevant market, the proportion of the sales amount, sales volume or other indicators of the operator's specific goods in the relevant market within a certain period of time. In the analysis of the competition situation in a relevant market, the development status of the relevant market, number and market shares of the existing competitors, degree of diversity of goods, innovation and technical changes, sales and procurement models, situation of potential competitors, and other factors may be considered."

market;[250] (3) the financial and technological capability of the business operator;[251] (4) the extent of reliance on the business operator by other business operators in transactions;[252] (5) the level of difficulty for other business operators to enter the relevant market;[253] and (6) other factors relevant for the determination of a dominant market position of the business operator.[254]

Where the defendant is not presumed to be dominant, a court may still initially apply the dominance test taking into consideration the abovementioned factors to find whether a dominant market position exists. The determination process involves the consideration of various factors which are infused with subjective judgments.[255] One could conclude from the AML's considerations that a market player's control over other competitors and over the relevant market are the core of the establishment of a market dominance.

Ownership and use of IP are often relevant in a dominant market position. Given the exclusive nature of IP, it is frequently used by business to control market entrance and restrict competition. In *Huawei v. IDC*, both the first- and second-instance courts recognized IDC's dominant position in the relevant SEP licensing market on the basis that IDC was the sole supplier of the patents which were essential to implementing the relevant 3G standards, and thus its market share in each independent licensing market was 100 percent.[256] The court then ruled that IDC had control over the terms

250. *Ibid.*, Art. 7: "According to Article 18.2 of the Anti-monopoly Law, in the determination of an operator's capacity of controlling the sales market or the raw material procurement market, the operator's capacity of controlling the upstream and downstream markets of the industrial chain, controlling the sales or procurement channels, affecting or deciding the price, volume, contract term or other transaction conditions, and obtaining the raw materials, semi-finished products, spare parts, relevant equipment, and other resources that need to be input required for the production and business operation of enterprises in priority may be considered."
251. *Ibid.*, Art. 8: "According to Article 18.3 of the Anti-monopoly Law, in the determination of an operator's financial strength and technical conditions, the operator's asset size, profitability, financing capability, research and development capability, technical equipment, capacity of technology innovation and application, intellectual property rights owned and so on, as well as the way and degree by which the financial strength and technical conditions can promote the operator's business expansion or consolidation and maintaining of the market status, and other factors may be considered."
252. *Ibid.*, Art. 9: "According Article 18.4 of the Anti-monopoly Law, in the determination of the degree of other operators' dependence on an operator in transaction, the transaction relationship, volume of transaction, and duration of transaction between other operators and the operator, the degree of difficulty in turning to other transaction counterparts within a reasonable period of time, and other factors may be considered."
253. *Ibid.*, Art. 10: "According to Article 18.5 of the Anti-monopoly Law, in the determination of the degree of difficulty for other operators to enter into a relevant market, the difficulty in market access and obtaining necessary resources, status of control over the procurement and sales channels, scale of capital investment, technical barriers, brand dependence, costs for transformation of users, consumption habits, and other factors may be considered."
254. AML 2008, note 3, Art. 18.
255. Owen Nee, *Competition Law in China*, (Sweet & Maxwell, 2014), §6:4.
256. *Huawei v. IDC*, note 242.

of the licence as well as Huawei's entrance to the relevant market, which made it a dominant player in each independent relevant market.[257]

Although IP owners are occasionally charged with having excessive market power, the SAMR Provisions clearly point out that ownership of IP is only one of the factors to be considered in the determination of the dominant position; this factor alone should not directly lead to the conclusion of a dominant position.[258] Put differently, owning IP does not necessarily result in a dominant position. To determine whether an IP owner is a dominant market player, the court or the antitrust authorities should consider the substitutability of the IP, degree of dependence of the downstream markets on the goods involving IP, counterparties' bargaining power in the transaction, etc.[259]

(c) Abuse of a Dominant Market Position

Once a market player's dominant position is established, its conduct may be deemed an abuse of its market dominance. The AML lists several abusive conducts, including excessive pricing, predatory pricing, refusal to deal, exclusive dealing, tying, unfair trading conditions, discrimination, and other anti-competitive conducts.[260] Additionally, the SAMR Provisions[261] elaborate on two scenarios: patent pools and SEP-related monopolies.[262] This part will illustrate the role of IP in the abuse of the dominant market position.

(1) Refusal to Deal

The AML prohibits a business operator with a dominant market position from refusing to trade with a trading party without any legitimate reason.[263] Notably, an operator's refusal to deal could be either explicit or implicit by substantively reducing the volume of existing transactions with the counterparty, delaying or interrupting existing transactions with the third parties, refusing new transactions with the third parties, setting restrictive conditions to make it difficult for third parties to transact with them, or refusing to allow third parties to use their essential facilities in production and business operations under reasonable conditions.[264] The SAMR's Interim Provisions on Prohibiting Abuse of a Dominant Market Position further lists several factors to be considered when third parties are refused use of the essential

257. *Ibid.*
258. SAMR Provisions, note 219, Art. 6.2.
259. Interim Provisions on Prohibiting Abuse of Dominant Market Position 2019, note 210, Art. 12.
260. AML 2008, note 3, Art. 17.
261. The SAIC Provisions addressed the abuse of IP in four of the six situations specified by the AML, namely refusal to deal, exclusive dealing, tying or unfair conditions, and discrimination, but did not touch upon the issues of excessive and predatory pricing, for reasons which will be explained later.
262. SAMR Provisions, note 219, Arts. 12, 13.
263. AML 2008, note 3, Art. 17.3.
264. Interim Provisions on Prohibiting Abuse of Dominant Market Position 2019, note 210, Art. 16.1.

facilities, such as the feasibility of separately building the facilities with reasonable investment, the degree of dependence of the third parties on said facilities for effectively carrying out production and business operation activities, the possibility of the business operator for providing said facilities, the impact on its production and business operation activities, etc.[265] The Interim Provisions on Prohibiting Abuse of a Dominant Market Position also provide some exemption of antitrust liability regarding refusal to deal under circumstances such as (1) the transactions are unable to be conducted due to *force majeure* or other objective reasons, (2) the soundness of the transactions is affected by poor credit records or deteriorated business operation of the counterparties, (3) the transactions will lead to inappropriate impairment of the interests of the business operator, or (4) other justified conduct.[266]

IP in some circumstances can also be viewed as an essential facility. Article 7 of the SAMR Provisions stipulate that "a business that has a dominant market position shall not, without any justification, refuse to license other businesses to use its intellectual property rights under reasonable conditions to preclude or restrict competition if the IPR is part of the necessary facilities for production and trading".[267] According to the SAMR Provisions, an IP constitutes an "essential facility" if (1) the IP cannot be substituted reasonably in the relevant market, and the IP is necessary for other business to participate in competition in the relevant market; (2) refusing to license the IP will have an adverse effect on competition or innovation in the relevant market, and damage the interests of consumers or the public interest; and (3) licensing the IP will not cause any unreasonable damage to the business.[268] Accordingly, once an IP is defined as an essential facility, its holder's refusal to license with the purpose of precluding or restricting competition would constitute an abuse, which may consequently trigger antitrust liability.

(2) Exclusive Dealing

The AML prohibits dominant market players from restricting their trading party to deal exclusively with themselves or with their designated business operators without any justified reason.[269] According to the SAMR Provisions, the prohibited exclusive dealing under the AML also includes transactions involving IP.[270]

According to the Interim Provisions, a dominant market player is not allowed to restrict its counterparty from transacting with certain other parties on a negative list.[271] Moreover, the Interim Provisions on Prohibiting Abuse of Dominant Market Position also provide exemptions for permitted exclusive dealing, including the scenarios in which (1) transactions are unable to be conducted due to *force majeure* and other objective reasons; (2) the safety of transactions is affected by adverse credit records

265. *Ibid.*, Art. 16.2.
266. *Ibid.*, Art. 16.3.
267. SAMR Provisions, note 219, Art. 7.1.
268. *Ibid.*, Art. 7.2.
269. AML 2008, note 3, Art. 17.4.
270. SAMR Provisions, note 219, Art. 8.
271. Interim Provisions on Prohibiting Abuse of Dominant Market Position 2019, note 210, Art. 17.1 (iii).

or deteriorated business operation situations of the transaction counterparty; (3) transactions with the transaction counterparties will lead to inappropriate impairment of the interests of the operator; or (4) other reasons that can justify the acts. [272]

(3) *Tying and Imposing Unfair Conditions*

Tie-in sale is an abusive conduct under the AML.[273] A tying arrangement refers to a transaction in which the availability of one product (the "tying" product) is conditioned upon the purchase, lease or license of another product (the "tied" product), or at least upon agreeing not to purchase, lease or license the tied item from other suppliers.[274] While tie-in sale is one of the most common antitrust claims,[275] not all tying arrangements are illegal.[276]

The AML thus only treats tying arrangements without "justified reasons" as illegal.[277] In addition to tying arrangements, the AML also regulates other unfair trading conditions imposed by the dominant party on the contract term, means of payment, means of transport and delivery, means of service provision, sales region, target consumers, after-sale services, unreasonable charges and other irrelevant conditions.[278] Collectively, a dominant market player's imposing of tying provisions or other unfair trading conditions may be justified if it complies with the appropriate commercial norms, or is necessary for product safety or specific technological considerations.[279]

According to the SAMR Provisions, tie-in arrangements concerning IP are prohibited if

(1) the tie-in sale or package sale of different products is conducted in violation of the trading practices or consumption habits or in disregard of the products' functions; or
(2) the tie-in sale extends the business's dominant position in the tying product market to the tied product market, precluding or restricting the competition of other businesses in the tying product or tied product market.[280]

In *Huawei v. IDC* case, the Guangdong Higher People's Court found IDC's tying of SEPs with non-SEPs abusive and thus illegal according to the AML.[281]

The SAMR Provisions also regulate other unfair trading conditions concerning IP. According to the SAMR Provisions, a dominant market player is forbidden from:

272. *Ibid.*, Art. 17.3.
273. AML 2008, note 3, Art. 17.1(v).
274. *Northern Pac. Ry. Co. v. U.S.*, 356 U.S. 1, 5–6, 78 S. Ct. 514, 2 L. Ed. 2d 545 (1958).
275. William M. Hannay, 'Tying', 34(2) *Corp. Couns. Quarterly* (2018), Art. 4
276. James L. Petersen and Angela M. Fifelski, 'State Tying Claims: Do You Know What May Be Lurking?', 21 *Franchise L.J.* (2002), 118.
277. AML 2008, note 3, Art. 17.5.
278. Interim Provisions on Prohibiting Abuse of Dominant Market Position 2019, note 210, Art. 18.1 (ii)-(v).
279. *Ibid.*, Art. 18.2.
280. SAMR Provisions, note 219, Art. 9.
281. *Huawei v. IDC*, note 242.

(1) requiring the counterparty to exclusively grant back the technologies improved by the latter;
(2) prohibiting the counterparty from challenging the validity of its intellectual property rights;
(3) restricting the counterparty from using competing products or technologies without infringing upon any intellectual property rights after the licensing agreement expires;
(4) continuing to exercise any intellectual property rights with an expired term of protection or determined as invalid;
(5) prohibiting the counterparty from trading with any third party; or
(6) requiring the counterparty to attach any other unreasonable restriction.[282]

(4) Discriminatory Treatment

Discriminatory treatment is an abusive conduct under the AML. A dominant market player is forbidden from applying differential prices and other transaction terms without justified reasons among their trading counterparties with the same standing.[283] Apart from the pricing of the product, the differential treatments could also be found in the volumes, varieties and quality grades, volume-based discount or other preferential conditions, terms of payment and means of delivery, warranty, maintenance, supply of spare parts, technical guidance, and other after-sales service conditions, etc.[284] Justified reasons for discriminatory treatment include (1) implementing different terms of transaction on the basis of the actual needs of transaction counterparts and in compliance with the justified transaction habits and industry practices; (2) preferential promotion offers for the first transactions of new users within a reasonable period of time; and (3) other reasons that can justify the acts.[285]

(5) Excessive Pricing

Dominant market players are susceptible to antitrust liability should they sell any product at an unfairly high price or buy any product at an unfairly low price.[286] According to the Interim Provisions on Prohibiting Abuse of Dominant Market Position, in determining an "unfairly high price" or "unfairly low price," the court or the antitrust authorities should consider:

(1) whether the selling price or purchasing price is significantly higher or lower than the price of a same or comparable goods sold or bought by other operators under the same or similar market conditions;

282. SAMR Provisions, note 219, Art. 10.
283. AML 2008, note 3, Art. 17.6.
284. Interim Provisions on Prohibiting Abuse of Dominant Market Position 2019, note 210, Art. 19.1.
285. *Ibid.*, Art. 19.2.
286. AML 2008, note 3, Art. 17.1.

(2) whether the selling or purchasing price is significantly higher or lower than the price of the goods sold or bought by a same operator in other regions with the same or similar market conditions;
(3) whether the selling price is raised or the purchasing price is lowered beyond the normal range when costs are basically stable;
(4) whether the price of goods sold is raised significantly faster than the cost growth rate, or the price of goods bought is lowered significantly faster than transaction counterparts' cost reduction rate; and
(5) other relevant factors that need to be considered.[287]

Overpricing royalties are not uncommon in the IP licensing market. For instance, in *Huawei v. IDC*, the court found IDC's offer to Huawei was evidently higher than the royalty rate or one-off payment that IDC had offered to other manufacturers including Apple and Samsung, which had not only violated its fair, reasonable and non-discriminatory (FRAND) commitment made to the standard-setting organization (SSO) European Telecommunications Standards Institute (ETSI), but also constituted an unfair excessive pricing as prohibited under the AML.[288]

(6) Patent Pools

In addition to the conducts of abuse listed in the AML, the SAMR Provisions stipulate two other abusive conducts, both of which concern the exploitation of IP: namely using patent pools and taking advantage of standard setting to preclude or restrict competition. A patent pool is an aggregation of multiple owners' patent rights for the purposes of cross-licensing among each other, or joint package licensing to third parties,[289] which is a common practice in the IP market. A patent pool can have both procompetitive and anti-competitive effect. The formation of a patent pool *per se* does not create a monopoly. It only attracts antitrust concerns when a patent pool becomes a vehicle to facilitate other monopolistic conducts such as price fixing, exclusive dealing, tying, discrimination, etc.

The SAMR Provisions explicitly view the following as an abuse of a dominant position:

(1) restricting a patent pool member from licensing any patent as an independent licensor outside the patent pool;
(2) restricting a patent pool member or a licensee from, independently or in conjunction with a third party, developing any technology competing with a patent in the pool;
(3) compelling a licensee to exclusively grant back any technology improved or developed by the latter to the patent pool management organization or a patent pool member;

287. Interim Provisions on Prohibiting Abuse of Dominant Market Position 2019, note 210, Art. 14.2.
288. *Huawei v. IDC*, note 242.
289. Geertrui Van Overwalle, Esther van Zimmeren, Birgit Verbeure and Gert Matthijs, 'Models for facilitating access to patents on genetic inventions', 7 *Nat. Rev. Genet.* (2006), 143, 144

(4) prohibiting a licensee from questioning the validity of a patent in the pool;
(5) applying differential treatment to patent pool members meeting the same conditions or to licensees in the same relevant market in trading conditions; or
(6) any other conduct of abusing its dominant market position as determined by the State Administration for Market Supervision.[290]

A patent pool can be viewed as anti-competitive not only because of its abuse of market dominance. The SAMR Provisions also banned individual patent owners from entering into unlawful monopoly agreements in the disguise of a patent pool. In other words, a patent pool member is prohibited from entering into a monopolistic agreement as prohibited by Article 13 or 14 of the AML by using any sensitive information on competition such as patent pool exchange yield and market division. Individual patent pool members may be subject to this liability even if the patent pool does not have a dominant market position.

(7) Exploitation of SEPs

Competition law issues regarding SEPs have drawn attention from academia, the courts, and competition authorities in China. These issues are generally categorized into two genres: the SEP holder's abuse of market dominance, and the excessive merger of large SEP holders.[291] While this part will focus on the former, SEP-related merger control will be discussed in section 5, Excessive Concentration.

The SAMR Provisions define an SEP as a "patent which is essential to the implementation of the standard",[292] and stipulate that "undertakings with a dominant market position shall not, without justification, engage in the acts below to exclude or restrict competition in the process of setting and implementing standards:

(1) In the course of participating in the standard setting, the undertaking intentionally fails to disclose information on its rights to the standard setting organization, or, though having expressly abandoned its rights, claims its patent rights against the party that implements the standard after its patent has become part of a certain standard.
(2) After its patent becomes a standard-essential patent, the undertaking, in violation of the principles of fairness, reasonableness and non-discrimination, rejects licensing, conducts tie-in sale of products, attaches any other unreasonable trading conditions in trading, or otherwise precludes or restricts competition. [293]

290. SAMR Provisions, note 219, Art. 12.3.
291. Liyang Hou and Mengchi Tian, 'IPR Protection and Antitrust Regulation of SEPs in China', in Kung-Chung Liu and Reto M. Hilty (eds.), *SEPs, SSOs and FRAND: Asian and Global Perspectives on Fostering Innovation in Interconnectivity* (Routledge, 2019).
292. SAMR Provisions, note 219, Art. 13.3.
293. *Ibid.*, Art. 13.1.

Put differently, two types of abuse could be inferred from the SAMR Provisions: an SEP holder's violation of its disclosure obligation *ex ante*, and violation of the FRAND principle *ex post*.

i. Disclosure Obligation

Most SSOs require their members to disclose their potential proprietary rights in a proposed technology before it is considered to be included in a standard.[294] Failure to timely disclose the proprietary rights to an SSO or an intentional misrepresentation may result in the inability to afterwards enforce these rights, in particular patents.[295] More importantly, not only has the deceptive SEP owner lost its grounds in claiming compensation for infringement, it may also be subject to certain antitrust liabilities.

According to Article 13.1 of the SAMR Provisions, three elements must be established to find a non-disclosure conduct abusive under Article 17.7 of the AML: (1) the participating patent owner is a dominant market player; (2) the participant intentionally concealed or misrepresented the potential patent rights it owns or is aware of in the proposed technology; (3) the failure to disclose has anti-competitive impact, i.e., there are other alternatives in the competing market and the proposed technology may not have been selected had the incorporated patent rights been known to the standardization committee.

According to the Interim Provisions on the Administration of National Standards Involving Patents jointly issued by the Standardization Administration of China (SAC) and the State Intellectual Property Office (SIPO, which has been renamed as the National Intellectual Property Administration), if the standard is a national standard, participants of the standard setting or standard revision are obliged to disclose the SEPs to the relevant national standardization technical committee or the entity in charge of standardization.[296]

ii. FRAND Obligations

Most SSOs require their members to declare that they agree to license their SEPs under FRAND terms.[297] FRAND is designed to balance the interests of SEP holders

294. See e.g., European Telecommunications Standards Institute, 'RULES OF PROCEDURE ANNEX 6: ETSI Intellectual Property Policy' Art. 4.1: "Subject to Clause 4.2 below, each MEMBER shall use its reasonable endeavours, in particular during the development of a STANDARD or TECHNICAL SPECIFICATION where it participates, to inform ETSI of ESSENTIAL IPRs in a timely fashion. In particular, a MEMBER submitting a technical proposal for a STANDARD or TECHNICAL SPECIFICATION shall, on a bona fide basis, draw the attention of ETSI to any of that MEMBER's IPR which might be ESSENTIAL if that proposal is adopted."

295. See, e.g., *Hynix Semiconductor Inc. v. Rambus Inc.*, 645 F.3d 1336, 1347–1348, 98 U.S.P.Q.2d 1711 (Fed. Cir. 2011).

296. Interim Provisions of Standardization Administration of China and State Intellectual Property Office on the Administration of National Standards Involving Patents 2013 [Guojia Biaozhun Sheji Zhuanli De Guanli Guiding (Zanxing)], Art. 5.

297. Jorge L. Contreras, 'Fixing FRAND: a pseudo-pool approach to standards-based patent licensing', 79 *Antitrust L.J.* (2013), 47, 51; Thomas F. Cotter, 'Comparative law and

and standard implementers by ensuring the former's fair compensation and the latter's access to the standard. Standard implementers normally claim FRAND obligation against SEP holders who previously made FRAND commitments.[298] The legal effect of a FRAND declaration also extends to the way in which SEP holders and implementers negotiate with each other.[299] In *Iwncomm v. Sony*, the Beijing High People's Court ruled that SEP holders were obliged to negotiate in good faith with the implementer based on their FRAND declaration.[300] If the implementer seeks a FRAND-compliant license from the patentee, it likewise needs to negotiate with the patentee in good faith.[301] The obligation of good-faith negotiation on both SEP holders and implementers has been again confirmed by recent FRAND litigations between Huawei and Samsung.[302] However, whether the SEP holder has made a FRAND commitment may not be a deciding factor under the AML. As the nature of SEPs typically leads their holders to a dominant market position, SEP holders' refusal to license, tying SEPs and non-SEPs, and other inappropriate leverage of SEPs naturally trigger antitrust liability.[303]

Huawei v. IDC and NDRC's investigation against Qualcomm are the most high-profile antitrust cases concerning SEP in China. In *Huawei v. IDC*, the Guangdong Higher People's Court held that the SEP holder IDC had violated its FRAND declaration and abused its dominant market position by seeking injunctive relief against the standard implementer Huawei during their licence negotiation.[304] The court explained that while Huawei negotiated with IDC in good faith, the latter did not likewise do so. Instead, IDC forced Huawei to agree on excessive licensing terms via threats of injunction and litigation. As a result, IDC had violated the AML.[305] It should be noted that the decision has not yet been enforced because the Supreme People's Court in December 2018 decided to hear this case.

---

economics of standard-essential patents and FRAND royalties', 22 *Texas Intellectual Property L.J.* (2014), 311, 312; Jay P. Kesan and Carol M. Hayes, 'FRAND's forever: standards, patent transfers, and licensing commitments', 89 *Indiana L.J.* (2014), 231, 233; Jyh-An Lee, 'Implementing the FRAND Standard in China', 19 *Vand J. Ent. & Tech. L.* (2016), 37, 44; Mark A. Lemley and Carl Shapiro, 'A simple approach to setting reasonable royalties for standard-essential patents', 28 *Berkeley Tech L.J.* (2013), 1135, 1136–1137

298. Lee, note 297, 52–63.
299. Jyh-An Lee and Sang Jo Jong, 'Beneficiaries and Enforcement of FRAND Declaration/ Commitment: Asian Perspectives', in Kung-Chung Liu and Reto M. Hilty (eds.), *SEPs, SSOs and FRAND: Asian and Global Perspectives on Fostering Innovation in Interconnectivity* (Routledge, 2019).
300. Xian Xidian Jietong Wuxian Wanglao Tongxin Gufen Youxian Gongsi Su Suoni Yidong Tongxin Chanpin (Zhongguo) Youxian Gongsi [Iwncomm v. Sony], 2017 Jing Min Zhong No. 45 (Beijing High People's Ct. 2018).
301. *Ibid.*
302. Huawei Jishu Youxian Gongsi Su Sanxing (Zhongguo) Touzi Youxian Gongsi Deng, 2016 Yue 03 Min Chu No. 816 (Shenzhen Intermediate People's Ct. 2018); Huawei Jishu Youxian Gongsi Su Sanxing (Zhongguo) Touzi Youxian Gongsi Deng, 2016 Yue 03 Min Chu No. 840 (Shenzhen Intermediate People's Ct. 2018).
303. King Fung Tsang and Jyh-An Lee, 'Unfriendly Choice of Law in FRAND', 59 *Va. J. Int'l L.* (2019), 220, 232-235.
304. *Huawei v. IDC*, note 242.
305. *Ibid.*

On 10 February 2015, the NDRC, which had been one of the three competition law authorities in China until 21 March 2018, fined Qualcomm RMB 6.08 billion for abuse of its dominant market position by charging royalties for expired patents, demanding free grant-back licences, charging excessive royalty rates based on the net wholesale prices of devices, and bundling SEPs with non-SEPs.[306] While NDRC did not consider whether Qualcomm had made any FRAND declaration, it held that Qualcomm violated the AML by conducting unfair licensing practices associated with SEPs against the standard implementers or potential implementers.

5. Excessive Concentration

The AML defines "concentration of business operators" as

(1) merger of business operators;
(2) a business operator acquiring control over other business operators by acquiring their equities or assets; or
(3) a business operator acquiring control over other business operators or is able to exert a decisive influence on other business operators by contract or any other means.[307]

Business operators shall declare in advance the concentration reaching the threshold of declaration prescribed by the State Council to the AML enforcement agency. According to the Provisions of the State Council on the Standard for Declaration of Concentration of Business Operators (2018 Amendment), if the concentration of business operators meets any of the following thresholds, the business operators concerned shall declare their planned concentration to the AML authority beforehand:

(1) the worldwide business volume of all the business operators involved in the concentration exceeds RMB 10 billion in the last accounting year, and the business volume in China of at least two business operators among them exceeds RMB 400 million separately in the last accounting year; or
(2) the business volume in China of all the business operators involved in the concentration exceeds RMB 2 billion in the last accounting year, and the business volume in China of at least two business operators among them exceeds RMB 400 million separately in the last accounting year.[308]

Where a proposed concentration does not reach the above-mentioned threshold, but the facts and evidence collected show that this concentration has or may have the effect of eliminating or restricting competition, the authority may investigate according to the AML.[309] Additionally, the AML provides exceptions for a parent

306. NDRC, Administrative Sanction Decision No. 1 (2015) (NDRC Decision 2015), 9 February 2015.
307. AML 2008, note 3, Art. 20.
308. Provisions of the State Council on the Standard for Declaration of Concentration of Business Operators ("2018 Amendment") [Guowuyuan Guanyu Jingyingzhe Jizhong Shenbao Biaozhun De Guiding (2018 Xiuzheng)], Art. 3.1.
309. *Ibid.*, Art. 4.

company taking over its subsidiaries, as well as the merger of sibling companies, which may not need the authorities' approval *ex ante*.[310]

It is quite common for the MofCom to attach certain conditions to its merger approval. These conditions are normally categorized into structural conditions and behavioural conditions. The structural conditions are one-off with a view to preserve competitive market conditions, whereas behavioural conditions are designed to constrain ongoing behaviours.[311] While antitrust authorities in most countries prefer to impose structural conditions, the MofCom often imposes behavioural conditions to supervise business concentrations on an ongoing basis.[312] This preference for the behavioural conditions reflects China's administrative culture of supervising and monitoring the private sector.

IP has become an increasingly important issue in the antitrust review of business concentration. For example, the MofCom expressed concerns regarding Google's acquisition of Motorola:

> Motorola possesses large quantity of patents in the mobile communication area, a large proportion of which are essential patents. Google's primary goal of acquiring Motorola is to acquire these mobile phone patents...Upon acquiring Motorola as well as its SEPs, Google will have the motivation and ability to impose unfair licensing conditions to other end-product manufacturers and impair market competition.[313]

The MofCom indicated that since Google's Android system enjoyed high market share in the mobile operating system market, it may favour Motorola by stopping licensing the most updated version to mobile manufacturers other than Motorola and therefore extending its dominance in the operating system market to the end product market. In order to obtain the antitrust authority's approval for business concentration, Google agreed to make four commitments: (1) continuing to license the Android system free and open-source, (2) not imposing any discriminatory treatments to any of the mobile manufacturers, (3) sticking to Motorola's FRAND declaration in the licensing of Motorola's SEPs, and (4) employing an independent supervisor to oversee the fulfilment of these commitments. This case illustrates how IP has become an important factor to be considered by the antitrust authorities in the review of business concentration.

---

310. AML 2008, note 3, Art. 22. "Under any of the following circumstances, business operators may not need to file a concentration declaration to the Anti-monopoly Law Enforcement Agency under the State Council: (1). Among all business operators involved in the concentration, one business operator possesses 50 percent or more of the voting shares or assets of every other business operator; or (2). A business operator not involved in the concentration possesses 50 percent or more of the voting shares or assets of every business operator that is involved in the concentration."
311. Ng, note 201, 375.
312. *Ibid.*
313. Notification of the Ministry of Commerce No. 25 of 2012 – The Notification of the Anti-Monopoly Investigation Decision of Concertation of Business Operators on the Conditional Approval of Google's acquisition of Motorola Mobile [Shangwubu Gonggao 2012 Nian Di 25 Hao Guanyu Fujia Xianzhixing Tiaojian Pizhun Guge Shougou Motuo Luola Jingyingzhe Jizhong Fanlongduan Shencha Jueding De Gonggao].

Chapter 6
Technology Transfer

Jyh-An Lee

I. INTRODUCTION

Technology transfer is the process by which knowledge and technologies are diffused throughout various human activities,[1] such as international trade, foreign direct investment, research and development collaboration, education, and the movement of personnel. Technology transfer typically takes place in the form of intellectual property (IP) assignment or, more commonly, in the form of an IP licence.[2] Nonetheless, technology transfer is not the transfer of IP alone; it also usually involves the building of institutional capacity for knowledge management.

Technology transfer has played a critical role in economic and technological development in many countries.[3] Some even view technology transfer as one of the main objectives of the international IP regime. Article 7 of the Trade-Related Aspects of Intellectual Property Rights ("TRIPS Agreement") states that "The protection and enforcement of IP rights should contribute to the promotion of technological innovation and to the transfer and dissemination of technology, to the mutual advantage of producers and users of technological knowledge and in a manner conducive to social and economic welfare, and to a balance of rights and obligations."[4] Some

1. David M. Haug, 'The International Transfer of Technology: Lessons that East Europe Can Learn from the Failed Third World Experience', 5 *Harv. J.L. & Tech.* (1992), 209, 211.
2. Daniel C.K. Chow, 'A Comparison of EU and China's Competition Laws that Apply to Technology Transfer Agreements', 9 *I/S: J. L. & Pol'y for Info. Soc'y* (2014), 497, 503.
3. See, e.g., Thomas K. Cheng, 'A Developmental Approach to the Patent-Antitrust Interface', 33 *Nw. J. Int'l L. & Bus.* (2012), 1, 47; Keith E. Maskus, 'The Role of Intellectual Property Rights in Encouraging Foreign Direct Investment and Technology Transfer', 9 *Duke J. Comp. & Int'l Law* (1998), 109, 135, 136, 147; Van Smith, 'Enabling Environments or Enabling Discord: Intellectual Property Rights, Public-Private Partnerships, and the Quest for Green Technology Transfer', 42 *Geo. J. Int'l L.* (2011), 817, 824.
4. Trade-Related Aspects of Intellectual Property Rights (1994), Art. 7.

commentators therefore view Article 7 of the TRIPS Agreement as a legal basis to use technology transfer as a policy tool to foster productivity and economic growth.[5]

In China, technology transfer, especially in the form of IP licensing, has become and will continue to be an important part of industrialisation, economic growth and technological development. The current legal structure governing technology has three sets of laws and regulations: (1) Civil Code, (2) foreign investment regulations, and (3) regulations on the import and export of technologies. While the Civil Code provides general principles for technology transfer, the last two sets of regulations have played important roles in the governance of transnational technology transfer.

II. CIVIL CODE

Technology transfer in China is subject to numerous laws, regulations, and judicial interpretations. Under China's current legal framework, technology transfer includes both the assignment and the licensing of IP.[6] The Chinese Contract Law used to set out the basic principles governing technology transfer in the country. However, while the Contract Law was abolished by the Chinese Civil Code in January 2021, most of the former's provisions have survived and been incorporated in the Civil Code.[7] Specifically, five types of technology contract are regulated by the Civil Code, namely technology development, transfer, licensing, consulting and service contracts.[8] Moreover, in 2004, the Supreme People's Court issued the Interpretation of Some Issues on Application of Law for the Trial of Cases on Disputes over Technology Contracts ("the Interpretation"), which supplements technology transfer regulations in the Civil Code.[9] Article 863(3) of the Civil Code stipulates that a technology transfer or licensing contract shall be in writing.[10] Article 864 stipulates that, while the parties to a technology transfer or licensing agreement can agree on the scope of patent practice and the utilisation of technical secrets, the agreement cannot be used to restrict competition and development of technologies;[11] otherwise, the contract will be deemed invalid.[12] The "scope of patent practice and the utilisation of technical secrets" here includes the duration, area and methods of exploitation as well as the persons

5. See, e.g., Sunil Kanwar, 'Intellectual Property Protection and Technology Licensing: The Case of Developing Countries', 55 *J.L. & Econ.* (2012), 539, 539–540.
6. Contract Law of People's Republic of China 1999 ("Contract Law 1999") [Zhonghua Renmin Gongheguo Hetong Fa], Art. 342.1.
7. Civil Code of the People's Republic of China 2020 ("Civil Code 2020") [Zhonghua Renmin Gongheguo Minfa Dian].
8. As defined by the Regulations of the People's Republic of China on the Administration of Import and Export of Technologies (2019 Revision) (TIER), technology transfer in this context includes the licensing and/or assignment of patents, rights to apply for patents, technical know-hows, and technical service. See TIER, Art. 2(2).
9. Interpretation of the Supreme People's Court Concerning Some Issues on Application of Law for the Trial of Cases on Disputes over Technology Contracts 2004 ("The Interpretation 2004") [Zuigao Renmin Fayuan Guanyu Shenli Jishu Hetong Jiufen Anjian Shiyong Falv Ruogan Wenti De Jieshi].
10. Civil Code 2020, note 7, Art. 863.3.
11. *Ibid.*, Art. 864.
12. *Ibid.*, Art. 850.

with access to the technical secret.[13] If there is no agreement or if the agreement is unclear about the duration mentioned above, the transferee should be free for any duration for patent practice and the utilisation of technical secrets.[14] Nevertheless, Article 877 of the Civil Code specifically points out that, where the relevant laws or administrative regulations provide otherwise with respect to technology import or export contracts or with respect to patent contracts or contracts for patent application, such provisions shall prevail.[15] Numerous special regulations have been tailored for technology import and export contracts, which however are not always consistent with that of the Civil Code. These special regulations prevail over the Civil Code in their own domains. The following section introduces the general framework regulating technology transfers in China specified by the Chinese Civil Code.

1. Obligations of the Transferor and the Transferee

Articles 870 and 871 set out the general obligations of the transferor and transferee in all types of technology transfer agreements. While the transferor's general obligation is to guarantee the ownership and quality of the technology,[16] the transferee should keep confidential the undisclosed secret underlying the transferred technology according to the agreed scope and duration.[17] The Civil Code further stipulates the obligations of the transferor and transferee in the patent licence agreement and technical secret transfer agreement, respectively.

(a) Patent Licence Agreement

A patent licence agreement is valid only during the term of the patent.[18] Once the term of the patent expires or the patent is declared invalid, the patentee is not allowed to enter into any patent licence agreement with any party in respect thereof.[19] The Interpretation, however, provides the possibility of maintaining the effectiveness of the agreement even if the subject patent expires. According to the Interpretation, if the subject patent has entered into the public domain before or during the term of the agreement, the licence agreement would possibly turn into a technology service contract if the provider has fulfilled its obligation in accordance with the licence agreement by offering guidance, knowledge, or solutions to the recipient's technical problems, and the agreed transfer fee could be deemed as a commission for the services provided.[20] Nevertheless, if it is evidently unreasonable to treat such payment as a service fee, either party can request the court to decide a reasonable

13. The Interpretation 2004, note 9, Art. 28.
14. *Ibid.*
15. Contract Law 1999, note 6, Art. 355
16. *Ibid.*, Art. 870.
17. *Ibid.*, Art. 871. See also Art. 501 of the Civil Code, which stipulates in general the parties' obligation to keep in confidence all trade secrets obtained during the conclusion of a contract, regardless of the whether the contract is ultimately concluded.
18. Contract Law 1999, note 6, Art. 865.
19. *Ibid.*
20. The Interpretation 2004, note 9, Art. 34.1.

amount of service.[21] The Interpretation provides the following three types of patent licence agreement. (1) *Exclusive licence*: licensed patents can only be practised by the transferee or licensee. Even the transferor or licensor is not allowed to practise the patents during the contract period. (2) *Sole licence*: Only the transferor or licensor and the transferee or licensee can exploit the patents. (3) *Non-exclusive licence* (or "normal patent licence"): The transferor or licensor has the discretion to license the same patent to any third party.[22] If the agreement does not define or is ambiguous on the type of licence for the exploitation of the patent, the licence should be deemed non-exclusive.[23] If the agreement stipulates that the transferee or licensee may sub-license others to exploit the patent, such sub-licence is deemed non-exclusive unless the parties agreed otherwise.[24]

The Civil Code and the Interpretation provide the principal obligations of the transferor and transferee in the patent licence agreement. According to Article 866 of the Civil Code, the transferor or licensor is obliged to enable the transferee or licensee to practise the patent, handing over the technical materials related to the exploitation of the patent and providing the essential technical guidance.[25] The transferor or licensor is obliged to cooperate with the transferee or licensee in carrying out the patent and to restrain from interfering or even impeding the latter's enjoyment of the patent in accordance with the agreement.[26] In *Zhongshan Dongfeng County Ming Fa Electronics Factory v. Zhongshan Na Bao Electronics Technology Co., Ltd.*, the licensor claimed patent infringement against the distributors of the licensee, who was entitled to implement but by no means sub-license the subject patent. The court viewed the licensor's suits against the licensee's distributors as an impediment to the licensee's right to exploit the patent and therefore the suits were a breach of the licensing agreement.[27] The Interpretation further requires that the transferor or licensor maintain the validity of the patent within the duration of the contract.[28] This obligation includes paying the annual patent fee according to the law and actively responding to any invalidity claims made by a third party.[29]

On the other hand, Article 867 of the Civil Code states that the transferee or licensee should pay the licence fee and exploit the patent in the way that the licence agreement stipulates.[30] The transferee or licensee should not sub-license the patent to any third party without a stipulation to that effect in the licence agreement.[31] In the dispute between Ming Fa Factory and Na Bao Company,[32] the Court tended to

21. *Ibid.*, Art. 34.
22. *Ibid.*, Art. 25.
23. *Ibid.*
24. *Ibid.*
25. Civil Code 2020, note 7, Art. 866.
26. *Zhongshan Dongfeng County Ming Fa Electronics Factory v. Zhongshan Na Bao Electronics Technology Co., Ltd.*, Guangdong Higher People's Court's decision of 25 December 2018, (2017) Yue Min Zhong No. 1335.
27. *Ibid.*
28. The Interpretation 2004, note 9, Art. 26.
29. *Ibid.*
30. Civil Code 2020, note 7, Art. 867.
31. *Ibid.*
32. *Ming Fa Factory v. Na Bao Company*, note 26.

support the contention that OEM production was not a sub-licence as prohibited by the principal licensing agreement, yet still found the licensor was not in breach of the agreement by initiating court proceedings against the second batch of distributors. Taking into account the scholarly ambiguity in categorising OEM production as "manufacturing conduct" in the Patent Law context, it reasoned that the law should not overburden the licensor to see through the nature of OEM production when seeking to enforce its patent right.[33] In other words, the Court was trying to strike a balance between the enforcement of the patent and the contractual right of working the patent by the licensee. When the licensor was not sure of whether the alleged infringement was a sub-licence, its attempt to enforce the subject patent was reasonable and justifiable, and thus did not contravene its contractual and statutory obligations.[34]

(b) Technical Secret Transfer or Licensing Agreement

A technical secret or know-how is normally protected as a trade secret, which is a major component in the technology transfer. According to Article 868 of the Civil Code, the transferor or licensor is obliged to provide technical materials according to the agreement, offer technical guidance, guarantee the practicability and reliability of the technology, and keep such information confidential. [35] Nevertheless, the transferor's confidentiality obligation in Article 868 should not prevent him or her from filing patent applications unless otherwise agreed by the parties. [36] The transferee, on the other hand, is obliged to exploit the technology in a way compliant with the agreement, pay the licence fee, and keep the technical secret confidential.[37]

2. Liabilities

Both the transferor and the transferee assume liabilities for their own breaches of contract in accordance with the general principles of the Civil Code. The law also sets out the fundamental obligations for the transferor and the transferee in a technology transfer agreement. Where the transferor or licensor fails to transfer the technology in accordance with the contract, he or she shall refund or partially refund the licensing fee and assume liability for breach.[38] Where the transferor or licensor exploits the patent, uses the technical secret beyond the agreed scope, or unilaterally allows the

33. In a related case of *Zhongshan Na Bao Electronics Technology Co., Ltd. v. Beijing Zuo Ming You Qi Trading Co., Ltd.*, where the licensor sued one of the distributors of the licensee, the Guangdong High Court precluded OEM consignment from the scope of "manufacture" as stipulated in the Patent Law. The Court identified the alleged infringing product was sold by the licensee to the distributor, during which the patent had been exhausted. See *Zhongshan Na Bao Electronics Technology Co., Ltd. v. Beijing Zuo Ming You Qi Trading Co., Ltd.* Guangdong Higher People's Court's decision of 26 December 2018, (2017) Yue Min Zhong No. 1392.
34. *Ming Fa Factory v. Na Bao Company*, note 26.
35. Civil Code 2020, note 7, Art. 868.1.
36. *Ibid.*, Art. 868(2). See also the Interpretation 2004, note 9, Art. 29.
37. Civil Code 2020, note 7, Art. 869.
38. *Ibid.*, Art. 872.

patent to be exploited or the technical secret to be used by a third party in breach of the contract, he or she shall cease the breach and be held liable for it.[39] Where the transferor or licensor breaches any agreed confidentiality obligation, he or she shall also be liable for breach of contract.[40]

Patent Law stipulates that only the patentee and "any interested party" may initiate an infringement lawsuit and apply for a preliminary injunction against a third party infringer.[41] According to the interpretation of the SPC, only exclusive licensees can act independently in filing an infringement lawsuit or applying for a preliminary injunction against a third party infringer.[42] The licensee in a non-exclusive licensing agreement can do the same only if the patentee himself refrains from acting.[43] In other words, the licensee in other types of agreement does not enjoy the same standing.

On the other hand, the transferee or licensee is obliged to pay the overdue licensing fee and liquidated damage should he or she fail to pay the agreed licensing fee; otherwise, he or she should cease the exploitation of the patent and the use of the know-how, return the technical information, and assume all liabilities for breach of contract.[44] As the timely payment of the licensing fee is usually regarded as the principal obligation of the licensee, failure to fulfil the duty is deemed a substantive breach and enables the licensor to unilaterally terminate the agreement.[45] Furthermore, the transferee or licensee should cease the breach and bear liabilities when he or she exploits the patent, utilises the know-how beyond the agreed scope, or unilaterally allows a third party to exploit the patent or use the know-how without the transferor's permission.[46] Scope of use clauses are frequently used in technology transfer agreements in China, and their lawfulness has been recognised by the Chinese Ministry of Commerce ("MofCom") in the Sino-German Model Contract for Know-How and Patent Licence signed by it and The Federal Ministry for Economic Affairs

39. *Ibid.*
40. *Ibid.*
41. See Patent Law of the People's Republic of China 2008 ("Patent Law 2008") [Zhonghua Renmin Gongheguo Zhuanli Fa], Arts. 60, 66.
42. Several Provisions of the Supreme People's Court on the Application of Law on Preliminary Injunctions against Patent Infringement 2001 [Zuigao Renmin Fayuan Guanyu Dui Suqian Tingzhi Qinfan Zhuanliquan Xingwei Shiyong Falv Wenti De Ruogan Guiding], Art. 1.2.
43. *Ibid.*
44. Civil Code 2020, note 7, Art. 873.
45. Art. 94 of the Contract Law stipulates statutory circumstances under which one party may unilaterally terminate a contract, as opposed to a conditional termination mutually agreed by the parties: (1) Where it is rendered impossible to achieve the purpose of contract due to an event of *force majeure*; (2) Where, prior to the expiration of the period of performance, the other party expressly states, or indicates through its conduct, that it will not perform its main obligation; (3) Where the other party delayed performance of its main obligation after such performance has been demand, and fails to perform within a reasonable period; (4) Where the other party delays performance of its obligations, or breaches the contract in some other manner, rendering it impossible to achieve the purpose of the contract; (5) other circumstances as provided by law. See Contract Law 1999, Art. 94. See also *Fuchao Li v. Jun Liang*, Beijing IP Court's decision of 20 July 2016, (2015) Jing Zhi Min Chu Zi No. 1326.
46. Civil Code 2020, note 7, Art. 873.

and Energy of Germany ("BMWi").[47] However, an over-restrictive field of use clause could easily be interpreted as an abuse of market dominance and consequently trigger antitrust liabilities according to the Anti-Monopoly Law of the People's Republic of China, should the licensor be a dominant player in the relevant market.[48] Lastly, the transferee or licensee is liable for breaching any agreed confidentiality obligation.[49]

As a practical issue, although the Civil Code has set out the obligations of both parties in a technology transfer or licensing agreement, parties deviate from those principles from time to time. Pecuniary and non-pecuniary liabilities such as damages, specific performance or remedial measures against a breach are provided under the general provisions of the Civil Code.[50] The parties may also stipulate a liquidated damage or deposit clause in the agreement.[51] However, the prescribed liabilities for breach only have limited effect of deterrence. For example, the law provides that the sum deposited should not exceed 20 percent of the subject matter, otherwise the amount beyond the cap will not be regarded as a deposit.[52] While parties may agree *ex-ante* either on a fixed sum or the method of calculation of liquidated damages, a court or arbitrator may discretionarily adjust that amount, if so required by a party, where the agreed sum is significantly higher or lower that the actual loss.[53] Moreover, the defaulting party will be exempted from assuming liabilities where such breach arises from *force majeure*.[54] He or she is also exempt from compensating the additional loss incurred due to the other party's failure to take appropriate measures to prevent the enlargement of the injury.[55]

Apart from liabilities for breach, the Civil Code also regulates third party infringement claims resulting from the performance of the technology transfer agreement. Article 874 provides that "Where the exploitation of the patent or the use of the technical secret by the transferee or licensee in accordance with the contract infringes on the lawful interests of any other person, the liability shall be borne by the transferor or licensor, except as otherwise agreed upon by the parties."[56] In other words, contracting parties can contract around the general principle set forth in Article 874 and agree that the transferee assume the infringement liability claimed by the third party.

47. Ministry of Commerce of the People's Republic of China and Federal Ministry for Economic Affairs and Energy of Germany, Sino-German Model Contract for Know-How and Patent Licence, 11 December 2002, Art. 2.
48. Anti-Monopoly Law of the People's Republic of China 2008 ("Anti-Monopoly Law 2008") [Zhonghua Renmin Gongheguo Fan Longduan Fa], ch. 3.
49. Civil Code 2020, note 7, Art. 873
50. *Ibid.*, Art. 577.
51. *Ibid.*, Arts. 585, 586.
52. *Ibid.*, Art. 586.2.
53. *Ibid.*, Art. 585.2.
54. *Ibid.*, Art. 590.
55. *Ibid.*, Art. 591.
56. *Ibid.*, Art. 874.

3. Grant-Back Clauses

A grant-back clause refers to the provision in the licence agreement which requires that a licensee convey or license to the licensor improvements, patents, or other technology subsequently developed or obtained by the licensee. The purpose of the grant-back provision is to prevent the originally licensed technology from becoming obsolete because of the licensee's improvements of it.[57] Without the grant-back arrangement, a licensee may easily compete with the licensor based on the improvement of the latter's licensed technology.[58] From a policy perspective, the advantage of the grant-back arrangement is that it rewards the licensor for enabling further innovation based on or informed by the licensed technology. Nevertheless, the grant-back arrangement also leads to competition law concerns in that it potentially hinders the licensee's incentive to innovate.

The Civil Code recognises the lawfulness of the grant-back provision in the licence agreement. Article 875 stipulates that parties can agree on the way to share subsequent improvements resulting from the exploitation of the patent or use of the technical secret based on reciprocity.[59] If there is no mutual agreement or if it is not made clear in the contract and cannot be determined by relevant provisions of the contract or business norms, such a grant-back arrangement is not presumed and neither party is entitled to share any subsequent improvement created by the other.[60]

Nevertheless, grant-back clauses in international technology transfer agreements had been explicitly prohibited in the Regulations of the People's Republic of China on the Administration of Import and Export of Technologies ("the TIER") until the TIER were amended in 2019.[61] Before the 2019 amendment, the TIER mandated any improvements on the transferred technology to be vested in the party making the improvement[62] and prohibited transferors from restricting transferees' making or using the subsequent improvements.[63]

III. FOREIGN INVESTMENT REGULATIONS

While the Civil Code provides a general legal structure regulating technology transfers in China, certain special regulations prevail if the technology transfer is associated with foreign investment.[64] Currently, the most important regulations are

---

57. Timothy J. Engling, 'Improvements in Patent Licensing', 78 *J. Pat. & Trademark Off. Soc'y* (1996), 739, 741.
58. *Ibid.*
59. Civil Code 2020, note 7, Art. 875.
60. *Ibid.*
61. TIER, note 8.
62. Regulations of the People's Republic of China on the Administration of Import and Export of Technologies (2011 Revision) ("TIER 2011") [Zhonghua Renmin Gongheguo Jishu Jinchukou Guanli Tiaoli], Art. 24.3. Art. 27.
63. *Ibid.*, Art. 29.3.
64. *Ibid.*, Art. 355: "Where the relevant laws or administrative regulations provide otherwise in respect of technology import/export contracts or in respect of patent contracts or contracts for patent application, such provisions prevail."

the Foreign Investment Law[65] and its implementing regulations ("the Implementing Regulations").[66] Foreign investment is therein defined as the direct or indirect investment activities conducted by foreign natural persons, enterprises, or other organisations in China, including but not limited to establishing foreign-funded enterprises independently or jointly with other investors, acquiring shares, equities, share of property, or other titles of such kind in an enterprise, and investing in any new construction project independently or jointly with other investors in China.[67] The promulgation of the Foreign Investment Law and the Implementing Regulations, which both came into effect on 1 January 2020, had taken over the function of the three main foreign investment laws – the Law on Sino-Foreign Equity Joint Ventures, the Law on Sino-Foreign Contractual Joint Ventures, and the Law on Foreign-Capital Enterprises – which were enacted between 1979 and 1990, as well as the Regulation on the Implementation of the Law of the People's Republic of China on Chinese-Foreign Equity Joint Ventures ("the JV Regulation"),[68] which was last amended in 2019 and functioned temporarily in governing foreign investors' activities when forming a Sino-foreign joint venture.

1. Forced Technology Transfer

Forced technology transfer refers to an informal government practice which requires the transfer of technology from foreign investors as a condition of market access or investment.[69] Because forced technology transfer policies are usually implemented without formal written laws or rules,[70] it is difficult to detect, prove, or combat the practice.[71] While forced technology transfer is not rare internationally, China

65. Foreign Investment Law of the People's Republic of China 2019 ("Foreign Investment Law 2019") [Zhonghua Renmin Gongheguo Waishang Touzi Fa].
66. Regulation for Implementing the Foreign Investment Law of the People's Republic of China 2019 ("Implementing Regulations") [Zhonghua Renmin Gongheguo Waishang Touzi Fa Shishi Tiaoli].
67. Foreign Investment Law 2019, note 65, Art. 2(2).
68. Regulation on the Implementation of the Law of the People Republic of China on Chinese-Foreign Equity Joint Ventures (2019 Revision) ("JV Regulation") [Zhonghua Renmin Gongheguo Zhongwai Hezi Qiye Fa Shishi Tiaoli].
69. Jyh-An Lee, 'Forced Technology Transfer in the Case of China', 26 *B.U. J. Sci. & Tech. L.* (2020), 324, 328-329.
70. Greg Mastel, *American Trade Laws After the Uruguay Round* (Routledge, 1996), 64.
71. See Mark Wu, 'Export Policies, Technology Transfer Policies, and Investment Reviews: How States Compete in the Era of Global High-Tech Value Chains', in Shin-yi Peng et al. (eds), *Governing Science and Technology under the International Economic Order: Regulatory Divergence and Convergence in the Age of Megaregionals* (EE, 2018), 90, 100–101; Office of the United States Trade Representative (USTR), 'Findings of the Investigation into China's Acts, Policies and Practices Related to Technology Transfer, Intellectual Property, and Innovation Under Section 301 of the Trade Act of 1974' 22 March 2018 ("2018 Section 301 Report"). https://ustr.gov/sites/default/files/Section%20301%20FINAL.PDF accessed 20 June, 2020. ("The fact that China systematically implements its technology transfer regime in informal and indirect ways makes it 'just as effective [as written requirements], but almost impossible to prosecute.'").

in particular is known for this practice[72] as part of its industrial policy.[73] China's investment regulations once included "market for technology" rules that granted foreign investors limited market access if they were able to transfer advanced technologies to the country.[74] China abolished these regulations with its accession to the World Trade Organization ("WTO").[75] Nevertheless, the practice of requiring foreign investors to transfer technology to local parties allegedly continues through equity restrictions and administrative approvals.[76]

(a) Foreign Ownership Restrictions

The very nature of Chinese–foreign joint ventures has created certain IP risks for the foreign party because it inevitably needs to share its confidential information with the partnering Chinese company.[77] This is one type of the so-called "forced technology transfer". Although foreign businesses normally prefer to invest in China through the structure of a wholly owned foreign enterprise ("WFOE"),[78] China's Catalogue of Industries for Guiding Foreign Investment ("Foreign Investment Catalogue 2017") and other regulations, such as the Special Administrative Measures (Negative List) for the Access of Foreign Investment, require foreign companies that seek to invest in certain industries to enter into cooperative agreements, especially joint venture agreements, with Chinese partners. According to the Foreign Investment Catalogue 2017, in the exploration and development of both oil and natural gas and medical institutions, foreign enterprise investors are required to form contractual joint ventures ("CJVs") or equity joint ventures ("EJVs") with Chinese firms.[79] The Chinese party must be the controlling shareholder in joint ventures that involve the following: (1) the selection and cultivation of new varieties of crops and production of seeds; (2) the manufacturing of commercial aircraft; (3) the construction and operation of nuclear power plants; and (4) basic telecommunications services.[80] Moreover, the Chinese party's investment cannot be lower than fifty percent in the automobile

72. Mastel, note 70, 64.
73. Mastel, note 70, 202.
74. See, e.g., Julia Ya Qin, 'Forced Technology Transfer and the US-China Trade War: Implications for International Economic Law', 22 *J. Int'l Econ. L.* (2019), 743, 749.
75. *Ibid.*, 750.
76. *Ibid.*
77. See, e.g., Office of the United States Trade Representative, 'Update Concerning China's Act, Policies and Practices Related to Technology Transfer, Intellectual Property, and Innovation' 20 November 2018 ("Update Concerning China's Act, Policies and Practices") https://ustr.gov/sites/default/files/enforcement/301Investigations/301%20Report%20Update.pdf accessed 20 January 2020, 23–27; White House Office of Trade and Manufacturing Policy, 'How China's Economic Aggression Threatens the Technologies and Intellectual Property of the United States and the World' 1 (2018) https://www.whitehouse.gov/wp-content/uploads/2018/06/FINAL-China-Technology-Report-6.18.18-PDF.pdf accessed 2 December 2019, 6.
78. USTR, 2018 Section 301 Report, note 71.
79. *Ibid.*
80. *Ibid.*

manufacturing business, whereas foreign investment cannot exceed fifty percent in the business of value-added telecommunications services.[81]

Once a foreign company forms a joint venture with a Chinese enterprise, it has no choice but to provide the partnering Chinese company with trade secrets and confidential information.[82] Moreover, because government approvals are required for JV operation, the government may compel the foreign party to transfer its proprietary technology and information to its Chinese partners, which the foreign party might otherwise be unwilling to do.[83] Further, the partnering Chinese company might become a potential competitor of the foreign company in the future.[84] Some foreign businesses, such as DuPont, claim that the Chinese government enables forced technology transfer by using regulatory powers, such as antitrust investigations, to threaten foreign businesses during IP disputes with local partners.[85] Many experts believe that the mandatory JV arrangement has successfully facilitated technology transfer from abroad and upgraded China's technological standard to the international level[86] in sectors such as automotive, aviation, and high-speed rail.

On 30 June 2019, the State Development and Reform Commission and the Ministry of Commerce jointly issued the Special Administrative Measures (Negative List) for the Access of Foreign Investment (2019) ("2019 Negative List"), which came into effect on 30 July 2019.[87] In this new 2019 Negative List, the Chinese government maintained the previous structure of foreign investment restrictions, but announced a plan to loosen up its ownership restrictions in certain sectors, as outlined below:

(1) Under the current scheme, "[f]or the manufacturing of automobiles other than special-purpose vehicles and new energy vehicles, the Chinese party shall have a stake of not less than 50%, and the same foreign investor may establish not more than two equity joint ventures manufacturing the same line of automobiles in China", but "[f]or the manufacturing of commercial vehicles, the restriction on foreign stake will be cancelled in 2020. In 2022, the restriction on foreign stake for the manufacturing of passenger vehicles and the restriction that the same foreign investor may establish not more

81. *Ibid.*

82. See, e.g., USTR, 2018 Section 301 Report, note 71, 26–27; Jyh-An Lee, 'Shifting IP Battlegrounds in the U.S.–China Trade War', 43 *Colum. J. L. & Arts*, (2020), 147, 153.

83. See USTR, 2018 Section 301 Report, note 71, 38.

84. See, e.g., Qin, note 74, 747.

85. See, e.g., Kevin Hamlin, 'Forced or Not? Why U.S. Says China Steals Technology', *Washington Post* (17 June 2019), www.washingtonpost.com/business/forced-or-not-why-us-says-china-steals-technology/2019/06/15/1f83e73c-8fb9-11e9-b6f4-033356502dce_story.html https://perma.cc/MNV5-L67Z accessed 9 August 2020.

86. See Thomas J. Holmes, Ellen R. McGrattan, & Edward C. Prescott, 'Quid Pro Quo: Technology Capital Transfers for Market Access in China', Rev. Econ. Stud. (2015), 1154, 1162 (citing the work of John Van Reenen and Linda Yueh, which "shows that these forced technology transfer deals actually work as intended, namely they upgrade the domestic partner").

87. Special Administrative Measures (Negative List) for the Access of Foreign Investment (2019) ("2019 Negative List") [Waishang Touzi Zhunru Tebie Guanli Cuoshi (Fumian Qingdan) (2019 Nian Ban)], Order No. 25 of the National Development and Reform Commission and the Ministry of Commerce of the People's Republic of China (30 June 2019) (China).

than two equity joint ventures manufacturing the same line of automobiles in China will be cancelled."[88]

(2) Under the current scheme, "[t]he foreign stake in a securities company shall not exceed 51%, and the foreign stake in a securities investment fund management company shall not exceed 51%", but "[t]he restriction on foreign stake [in this sector] will be cancelled in 2021."[89]

(3) Under the current scheme, "[t]he foreign stake in a securities company shall not exceed 51%", but "[t]he restriction on foreign stake will be cancelled in 2021".[90] The same restriction and deregulation plans are also applied to companies providing futures investment advice or broker services as well as to life insurance companies.[91]

What is the Chinese government signalling with the 2019 Negative List? First, its relaxation increases market access for foreign businesses. Second, the lifting of ownership restrictions reduces the risk of IP theft by Chinese partners of foreign investors. For example, the 2019 Negative List and the Special Administrative Measures (Negative List) for the Access of Foreign Investment in Pilot Free Trade Zones (2019) (自由贸易试验区外商投资准入特别管理措施[负面清单][2019年版]) ("Negative List for Free Trade Zones") completely scrap the limit on foreign ownership of new energy vehicle ("NEV") ventures.[92] This relaxation has clearly been welcomed by Tesla's founder and chief executive officer, Elon Musk, who once argued that foreign ownership rules created an uneven playing field for his company in China.[93] Based on the new *Negative List for Free Trade Zones*, Tesla has been able to establish a wholly owned company and production line in Shanghai.[94] More importantly, Tesla can better protect its IP and technology in its own plant.[95]

(b) Trade Secret Divulgation in Exchange for Administrative Approval

Another type of "forced technology transfer" in China is that government officials are allegedly endowed with considerable discretion to impose an oral or informal

88. *Ibid.*
89. *Ibid.*
90. *Ibid.*
91. *Ibid.*
92. Special Administrative Measures (Negative List) for the Access of Foreign Investment in Pilot Free Trade Zones (2019) [Ziyou Maoyi Shiyanqu Waishang Touzi Zhunru Tebie Guanli Cuoshi (Fumian Qingdan) (2019 Nian Ban)] (promulgated by the Nat'l Dev. & Reform Comm'n and the Ministry of Commerce, 30 June 2019) (Chinalawinfo).
93. See, e.g., Adam Jourdan and Norihiko Shirouzu, 'Tesla Registers Shanghai Electric Car Firm Ahead of Ownership Rule Change', *Reuters* (24 May 2018), https://perma.cc/2FQT-SMZP accessed 9 August 2020.
94. *Ibid.*; Daniel Ren and Maggie Zhang, 'Tesla Sets up Shanghai Beach Head with Wholly-Owned Plant in World's Largest Electric Car Market', *South China Morning Post* (10 July 2018), https://perma.cc/G23B-42A7 accessed 9 August 2020; *Xinhua News*, 'Tesla Breaks Ground on Gigafactory in Shanghai', *China Daily* (8 January 2019), https://perma.cc/TSB9-BL7V accessed 9 August 2020.
95. Jourdan and Shirouzu, note 93.

technology transfer requirement for JV investment applications.[96] Foreign investors are therefore pressured to share confidential information relevant to their proprietary technologies with government officers in the administrative approval process. [97] Foreign investors indicate that such forced technology transfer, which exists at various levels of government, has significantly increased the risk of trade secret leakage.

China has denied any forced technology transfer in the country. According to a statement issued by the State Council in China, all technology transfers in the country have been based on voluntariness and freedom of contract.[98] Furthermore, to alleviate "forced technology transfer" and other concerns raised by foreign investors and the Office of the United States Trade Representative, China promulgated the Foreign Investment Law as well as its Implementing Regulations in March and December 2019 respectively.[99] Many believe that the message of the new law is that Beijing aims to level the playing field for foreign investors and to address issues raised by Washington in the US–China trade frictions that took place from 2017 to 2020.[100] This is also the first time Chinese law has touched upon the problem of forced technology transfer. Article 22 of the Foreign Investment Law stipulates that:

> The State protects the intellectual property rights of foreign investors and foreign-invested enterprises, protects the legitimate rights and interests of intellectual property right holders and related right holders, and holds intellectual property rights infringers legally accountable in strict accordance with the law.
>
> The State encourages technical cooperation based on the voluntariness principle and commercial rules in the process of foreign investment. The conditions for technical cooperation are determined by equal negotiation between the parties to the investment in accordance with the principle of fairness. Administrative agencies and their staff are prohibited from using administrative means to force any technology transfer.[101]

96. USTR, 2018 Section 301 Report, note 71, 36.
97. *Ibid.*, 48.
98. Information Office of the State Council, The People's Republic of China, 'The Facts and China's Position on China-US Trade Friction' September 2018 http://english.www.gov.cn/archive/white_paper/2018/09/26/content_281476319220196.htm accessed 2 December 2019.
99. Foreign Investment Law 2019, note 65.
100. See, e.g., Zhou Xin, 'China Approves New Foreign Investment Law Designed to Level Domestic Playing Field for Overseas Investors', *South China Morning Post* (Hong Kong, 15 March 2019) www.scmp.com/economy/china-economy/article/3001780/china-approves-new-foreign-investment-law-designed-level accessed 2 December 2019; Kinling Lo, Kimmy Chung and Tony Cheung, 'China's Foreign Investment Law Will Apply to Hong Kong, Macau and Taiwan', *South China Morning Post* (Hong Kong, 3 March 2019) www.scmp.com/news/china/diplomacy/article/2188608/chinas-foreign-investment-law-will-apply-hong-kong-macau-and accessed 2 December 2019 ("[t]he draft law … comes against the backdrop of the China–US trade war, with Beijing under pressure to address Washington's allegations of unfair competition between foreign and domestic firms, intellectual property theft, and forced technology transfers.)
101. Foreign Investment Law 2019, note 65, Art. 22.

Article 23 protects the trade secrets of foreign investors from being disclosed by government officers:

> The administrative organs and their staff shall keep confidential the trade secrets of foreign investors and foreign-invested enterprises that they are aware of during the performance of their duties, and shall not disclose or illegally provide them to others.[102]

The Implementing Regulations restate these obligations by forbidding administrative agencies (including any organisation empowered by any law or regulation to administer public affairs) and their staff from forcing, whether explicitly or in a disguised form, foreign investors and foreign-funded enterprises to transfer technologies by administrative means such as the grant of administrative licences, administrative inspection, administrative punishment, and administrative compulsion.[103] Where an administrative agency's performance of duties in accordance with the law requires a foreign investor or a foreign-funded enterprise to provide any materials and information relating to a trade secret, it shall be limited to the extent necessary for the performance of duties. Access to the trade secret shall be strictly controlled, and persons unrelated to the performance of duties shall have no access to the relevant materials and information. Meanwhile, administrative agencies shall establish and improve internal management rules, and take effective measures to protect the trade secrets of foreign investors and foreign-funded enterprises to which they have access during the performance of their duties. [104] If it is necessary for the administrative agency to share the information with any other administrative agency in accordance with the law, the former shall take confidentiality measures to protect the trade secrets from leakage.[105]

Further, the legal liability for violating Articles 22 and 23 of the Foreign Investment Law can be found in Article 39:

> If a staff member of an administrative organ abuses his/her power, neglects his/her duties or engages in malpractice in the promotion, protection and management of foreign investment, or leaks or illegally provides others with trade secrets that he/she knows in the course of performing his/her duties, he/she shall be punished according to law; if he commits a crime, he/she shall be held criminally responsible.[106]

Article 43 of the Implementing Regulations similarly provides that:

> Where an administrative agency or any of its staff forces, whether explicitly or in a disguised form, any foreign investor or foreign-funded enterprise to transfer technology by administrative means, the directly liable official in charge and other directly liable persons shall be punished according to the law.

102. *Ibid.*, art 23.
103. Implementing Regulations, note 66, Art. 24.
104. *Ibid.*, Art. 25.
105. *Ibid.*
106. *Ibid.*, Art. 39.

The first paragraph of Article 22 of the Foreign Investment Law is nothing more than an official declaration that foreign investors' IP will be protected seriously, whereas its second paragraph spells out the principles of voluntariness and fairness and explicitly prohibits forced technology transfer. Article 23 forbids government officials from disclosing the trade secrets of foreign investors. While it is clear that both Articles 22 and 23 deal with alleged "forced technology transfer", what is more important is the legal liability and enforcement mechanism of these two articles. According to Article 39 and Article 43 of the Implementing Regulations, government officials who force technology transfer or disclose trade secrets of a foreign investor will be subject to administrative liability (penalty) and possible criminal liability.

Although some foreign investors have been hopeful about these provisions strengthening IP protection in China, especially the possibility of criminal liability,[107] Article 39 actually leaves some uncertainties in terms of enforcement. First, the administrative liability or penalty is not defined in the law; therefore, the government has broad discretion in imposing such liability, which might constitute an action as light as giving the breaching official a warning. Hence, more detailed administrative regulations would be helpful for enforcing the administrative liability stipulated in Article 39. Second, while Article 39 mentions criminal liability, it does not actually impose any criminal liability on the breaching officials – whether the involved government official has committed a crime depends on the application of criminal law and other relevant laws. In other words, although Article 39 indicates the possibility of establishing criminal liability, it has not actually changed or established any criminal liability.

An additional relevant reform is the newly added trade secret provision, Article 5, of the Administrative Licence Law:

> Without the consent of the applicant, an administrative agency, its functionaries, or an expert on a panel shall not disclose any trade secret, undisclosed information, or confidential business information submitted by the applicant, unless the law provides otherwise, or national security or the material social and public interest is involved; and if the administrative agency discloses such information of the applicant to the public according to the law, the applicant shall be allowed to file an objection within a reasonable period of time.[108]

Similar to Article 22 of the Foreign Investment Law, Article 31 of the Administrative Licence Law prohibits forced technology transfer:

> The administrative organ may not ask the applicant to submit technical materials and other materials that have nothing to do with the matters under the administrative licence.

107. Zhou, note 100, (quoting the comment of Jake Parker at the US–China Business Council that "the business community has collectively advocated for years for the Chinese government to impose criminal penalties for [intellectual property] infringement, we need to recognize this positive progress to that end.").

108. See Administrative Licence Law of People's Republic of China, [Zhonghua Renmin Gongheguo Xingzheng Xuke Fa] (promulgated by the Standing Comm. Nat'l People's Cong., 23 April 2019, effective 23 April 2019), Art. 5(2) (Chinalawinfo).

> An administrative agency and its functionaries shall neither grant an administrative licence conditional on transfer of technology nor directly or indirectly require transfer of technology in the process of implementation of an administrative licence.[109]

Article 72 of the Administrative Licence Law provides the administrative liability for the violation of Article 5:

> Where an administrative agency or any of its functionaries violates the provisions of this Law and has any of the following circumstances, its superior administrative agency or the supervisory agency shall order corrective action to be taken; and if the circumstances are serious, administrative action shall be taken against the directly responsible person in charge and other directly liable persons in accordance with the law:
>
> ...
>
> (5) Illegally disclosing any trade secret, undisclosed information or confidential business information submitted by an applicant.[110]

In terms of the similarity and dissimilarity of forced technology transfer provisions between the Foreign Investment Law and the Administrative Licence Law, both address trade secret protection during the administrative process, which is a key issue of forced technology transfer. However, there are some important differences between the trade secret provisions in these two laws. First, the Administrative Licence Law is a general law governing administrative applications, including those by Chinese nationals,[111] whereas the Foreign Investment Law is a special law regulating foreign investment activities in China.[112] Second, while the subject of Administrative Licence Law includes both administrative staff and external experts on a panel, the Foreign Investment Law regulates only the confidential duty of the administrative staff. The inclusion of external experts in the Administrative Licence Law stems from the belief of foreign businesses and the Office of the United States Trade Representative that external experts coming from the government, academia, or industry are possible sources of trade secret leaks.[113] Lastly, the legal liability for the violation of the Administrative Licence Law is administrative, whereas the Foreign Investment Law mentions both administrative and criminal liabilities.

China and the United States agreed upon terms for the so-called Phase One trade deal in December 2019 and signed the agreement on 15 January 2020.[114] Among other things, the two countries agreed that any transfer or licensing of technology

109. *Ibid.*, Art. 31.
110. *Ibid.*, Art. 72.
111. *Ibid.*, Arts. 1–2.
112. Foreign Investment Law, note 65, Art. 2.
113. See, e.g., USTR, 2018 Section 301 Report, note 71, 42.
114. Economic and Trade Agreement Between the Government of the United States of America and the Government of the People's Republic of China ("US–China Economic & Trade Agreement"), 15 January 2020, https://ustr.gov/sites/default/files/files/agreements/phase%20one%20agreement/Economic_And_Trade_Agreement_Between_The_United_States_And_China_Text.pdf accessed 9 August 2020.

should be based on market terms and voluntariness.[115] Technology transfer should not be required or pressured by the government in acquisitions, joint ventures or other investment transactions,[116] nor should the government require or pressure technology transfer as a condition for approving any administrative or licensing requirements.[117] While China has already addressed these issues in its Foreign Investment Law as mentioned previously, this is the first time the country has agreed to prohibit forced technology transfer as a condition for market access in an international agreement. China's justification for these compromises was that the agreement is of mutual benefit and consistent with its current reform.[118]

2. Profit Repatriation

Profit repatriation is another concern for foreign investors entering into technology transfer agreements in China. The strict foreign exchange control in China has been a concern for foreign investors planning to transfer their profits to their overseas parent company. [119] Profit repatriation by allocating dividends was subject to various prerequisites such as full capital injection, tax clearance, accumulated loss offset, and where applicable, the fulfilment of a mandatory amount of surplus reserve fund.[120] Additionally, large-sum foreign exchange remittance was subject to strict

115. *Ibid.*, Art. 2.1.
116. *Ibid.*, Art. 2.2.
117. *Ibid.*, Art. 2.3.
118. 'China, US Agree on Text of Phase One Trade Deal', *Xinhua News* (13 December 2019), https://perma.cc/U5FK-2EWB. ("The agreement is generally in line with the main direction of China's deepening reform and opening-up as well as the internal needs for advancing high-quality economic development. Implementation of the agreement will help enhance intellectual property rights protection, improve the business environment, expand market access, better safeguard the legitimate rights and interests of all companies including foreign firms in China, and protect the legitimate rights and interests of Chinese firms in their economic and trade activities with the United States."); see also Donna Barak, 'Trump Signs First Stage of Trade Deal with China', *CNN News* (15 January 2020), https://edition.cnn.com/2020/01/15/politics/us-china-trade-deal-phase-one-signed/index.html (reporting that China's President Xi Jinping wrote to US President Donald Trump that the trade deal was "good for China, the U.S. and the whole world") accessed 8 August 2020.
119. *China Briefing*, 'Profit Repatriation from China' (31 July 2019) http://www.china-briefing.com/news/profit-repatriation-from-china/ accessed 10 June 2020.
120. See e.g. JV Regulation Art. 76: "The principles for distribution of profits after payment of income taxes in accordance with the Enterprise Income Tax Law of the People's Republic of China shall be as follows: (1) Certain percentages of the profits as determined by the board of directors shall be set aside as reserve funds, reward and welfare funds for employees, and enterprise development funds. (2) In addition to cover the losses of the equity joint venture, reserve funds may be used with the approval of the approving authority to increase the equity joint venture's capital for expansion of production capacity. (3) If the board of directors determines to distribute the profits available for distribution after deduction of the three types of funds as mentioned in item (1) of this article, the profits shall be distributed according to the capital contribution proportion of all the parties to the equity joint venture"; Art. 77: "Profits may not be distributed before losses in previous years have been covered. Undistributed profits from previous years may be

scrutiny regarding the remitter's genuine intention and legal compliance, which required documentary proof including a resolution of the board of directors (or a resolution of partners) on the distribution of profits, original tax recordation form, and audited financial statements to be filed and recorded with the commercial bank handling the remittance, which was obliged to conduct due diligence investigations.[121] Consequently, the difficulty facing foreign investors in claiming dividends had shaped alternative ways of profit repatriation, such as through intercompany payments (for services, human resources or royalties for intangible assets, etc.) and transnational loans.[122] While transnational loans were strictly restricted to related companies with shareholding relationships, profit repatriation through intercompany payment could possibly attract even stricter scrutiny from tax authorities, as the conduct could easily be interpreted as a signal of profit shifting and tax avoidance.[123]

Article 22 of the Implementing Regulations specifically addresses this issue by stipulating that:

> A foreign investor may, in accordance with the law, freely remit into or out of China, in RMB or foreign exchange, its contributions made, profits, capital gains, proceeds from disposition of assets, royalties derived from IP licences, indemnity or damages lawfully acquired, and income from liquidation, among others, within China. No entity or individual may illegally restrict the currency type, amount, and frequency of inward and outward remittances, among other things.
>
> The wages and other lawful income of the foreign employees and the employees from Hong Kong, Macao and Taiwan of foreign-funded enterprises may be freely remitted out of China in accordance with the law.[124]

---

included in the profits of the current year available for distribution"; Detailed Rules for the Implementation of the Law of the People's Republic of China on Wholly Foreign-owned Enterprises (2014 Revision) [Zhonghua Renmin Gongheguo Waizi Qiye Fa Shishi Xize], Art. 56: "A foreign-funded enterprise shall retain certain amount from its profits after the income tax has been paid in accordance with Chinese tax law as reserve funds, bonus and welfare funds for workers and staff members. The amount retained for the reserve funds shall not be less than 10 percent of the profits (profits after the income tax has been paid), the withdrawal may stop when the accumulated amount withdrawn has been up to 50 percent of the registered capital of the enterprise. The amount retained for bonus and welfare funds for workers and staff members shall be determined by the foreign-funded enterprise itself. No foreign-funded enterprise may distribute its profits unless and until its deficits of previous fiscal years have been made up; undistributed profits of the previous fiscal years may be distributed together with the distributable profits of the current fiscal year." Both regulations have been superseded by the Foreign Investment Law and/or its Implementing Regulations.

121. See, e.g., Notice of the State Administration of Foreign Exchange on Further Promoting the Reform of Foreign Exchange Administration and Improving the Examination of Authenticity and Compliance 2017 [Guojia Waihui Guanli Ju Guanyu Jinyibu Tuijin Waihui Guanli Gaige Wanshan Zhenshi Hegui Xing Shenhe De Tongzhi], points VII, VIII.

122. *China Briefing*, 'Profit Repatriation from China', note 119.

123. *Ibid.*

124. Implementing Regulations, Art. 22.

The Implementing Regulations also makes clear that government officials who illegally restrict the inward or outward remittance of funds by foreign investors will be held liable in accordance with laws and regulations.[125] In summary, the Implementing Regulations indicate China's willingness to relax the foreign exchange control, which is of great importance to facilitate more transnational technology transfer agreements.

IV. REGULATIONS OF THE IMPORT AND EXPORT OF TECHNOLOGIES

Transnational technology transfer is also subject to the regulations of the TIER, which were initially issued in 2001 and subsequently revised in 2011 and 2019.[126] The TIER define the "import and export of technology" as "the technology transfer from outside of the People's Republic of China ("PRC") into the PRC or from inside of the PRC to outside of the PRC by means of trade, investment or economic-technological collaboration."[127] The TIER further explain that technology transfer includes the transfer of patents, the right to file patents, the licensing of rights to implement patents, the assignment of technical know-how, technical service, etc.[128] Unless otherwise forbidden by laws and administrative regulations, the free import and export of technologies is generally permitted.[129] As the TIER were enacted according to the Foreign Trade Law,[130] they re-elaborate the limitations on technology import and export set forth in the latter.[131] Article 16 of the Foreign Trade Law stipulates that

The state may restrict or forbid the import or export of relevant goods or technology if:

1. it is necessary to restrict or forbid the import or export for the purpose of maintaining state security, social public good or public morality;
2. it is necessary to restrict or forbid the import or export for the purpose of protecting human health or security, protecting the life or health of any animal or plant, or protecting the environment;
3. it is necessary to restrict the import or export for the purpose of implementing the measures relating to the import or export of gold or silver;
4. it is necessary to restrict or forbid the export of any of the exhaustible natural resources that are in short supply or subject to effective protection;
5. it is necessary to restrict the export due to the limited market capacity of the destination country or region;
6. it is necessary to restrict the export due to the serious disorder of the export business management;
7. it is necessary to restrict the import for the purpose of establishing or accelerating the establishment of a particular domestic industry;
8. it is necessary to restrict the import of any form of product in the agriculture, animal husbandry, or fishing industry;

---

125. Implementing Regulations, Art. 41(3).
126. TIER, Art. 1.
127. *Ibid.*, Art. 2.1.
128. *Ibid.*, Art. 2.2.
129. *Ibid.*, Art. 5.
130. *Ibid.*, Art. 1.
131. *Ibid.*, Art. 8.1, Art. 29.1.

9. it is necessary to restrict the import for the purpose of safeguarding the international financial status of the state or of the international balance of payments;
10. it is necessary to restrict or forbid the import or export under any other circumstance as provided for in any other law or administrative regulation; or
11. it is necessary to restrict or forbid the import or export under any other circumstance as provided for in any international treaty or agreement that China has concluded or acceded to.[132]

1. Type of Technology

The TIER stipulate that the State Council and its relevant authorities should formulate and adjust the Catalogue of Prohibited or Restricted Import Technologies and the Catalogue of Prohibited or Restricted Export Technologies[133] and, more importantly, they classify technology into three categories: (1) prohibited technology, (2) restricted technology and (3) unrestricted technology.

(a) Prohibited Technologies

According to the draft revisions of the Catalogues which have been published for public consultation in July 2018, technologies (1) the import of which will endanger the national security or social morality; (2) the import of which will significantly affect the health or safety of humans, the life or health of animals or plants, or sabotage the ecosystem of the country; (3) the import of which will cause significant impact on public welfare; (4) that are processing techniques which have become obsolete according to national laws or administrative regulations; (5) that should be prohibited for importation according to the law or administrative regulations; and (6) that should be prohibited for importation according to the international treaties or international agreements to which China is a party will be prohibited for importation.[134] Technologies that are prohibited from export are mainly included for the purpose of (1) maintaining the national security, public social welfare or morality; (2) protecting the health or safety of humans, the life or health of animals or plants, or the environment; (3) complying with the law or administrative regulations; (4) complying with international treaties or international agreements to which China is a party.[135] Prohibited technologies are not allowed to be imported or exported at all.[136]

132. Foreign Trade Law of the People's Republic of China (2016 Revision) ("Foreign Trade Law 2016") [Zhonghua Renmin Gongheguo Duiwai Maoyi Fa], Art. 16.
133. TIER, Art. 8.2, Art. 29.2.
134. Catalogue of Prohibited or Restricted Import Technologies ("2018 Draft for Consultation") [Zhongguo Jinzhi Jinkou Xianzhi Jinkou Jishu Mulu].
135. *Ibid.*
136. TIER, Art. 9, Art. 30.

(b) Restricted Technologies

Restricted technologies can only be imported or exported with licences.[137] Applicants are required to apply for preliminary licences and official licences from the relevant authorities under the State Council.[138] No party is allowed to enter into an agreement to import a restricted technology without the preliminary licence issued by relevant authorities.[139] Upon signing the technology import contract, the importer shall submit copies to the contract, together with other supporting documents, to the relevant authorities to apply for the official licence.[140]

For technology export, the TIER set out that the exporter is not allowed to embark on substantive negotiation and conclusion of an export contract before obtaining a preliminary licence from the government.[141] After concluding the export contract, the technology exporter shall submit the following documents to apply for an official licence: (1) the preliminary licence, (2) a copy of the technology export contract, (3) a list of the exported technologies and their technological information, and (4) documents proving the legal status of both parties.[142] In practice, however, the approval procedures are much more complicated. The approval of export of restricted technology is co-administered by the division of commerce and division of science and technology at provincial level.[143] Prior to applying for a preliminary licence as required by the TIER, the exporter shall complete an Application Form for the Export of Technologies Restricted from Export by China, which can be downloaded from the website of the MofCom, and submit it to the local administration for commerce to proceed. Where the exported technology also includes state secret technology, the exporter shall go through the confidentiality review according to the Provisions on the Review of Export of Confidential Technologies of the State[144] and obtain a Confidentiality Review Approval for the Export of State Secret Technology issued by the authority in charge.[145] The application for a licence should be filed with the provincial administration of commerce, which shall transfer the materials received from the applicant to the provincial administration of science and technology.[146] The administration will conduct, respectively, a commercial[147] and technical

137. *Ibid.*, Art. 10, Art. 31.
138. *Ibid.*, Art. 11, Art. 32.
139. *Ibid.*, Art. 13.2.
140. *Ibid.*, Art. 14.1.
141. *Ibid.*, Art. 34.2.
142. *Ibid.*, Art. 35.
143. Measures for the Administration of Technologies Prohibited or Restricted from Export 2009 [Jinzhi Chukou Xianzhi Chukou Jishu Guanli Banfa], Art. 4.
144. Provisions on the Review of Export of Confidential Technologies of the State 1998 [Guojia Mimi Jishu Chukou Shencha Guiding].
145. Measures for the Administration of Technologies Prohibited or Restricted from Export, note 143, Art. 5.
146. *Ibid.*, Art. 7.
147. The commercial review will look into (1) whether the export of such a technology conforms to the foreign trade policies of China and contributes to promoting export in foreign trade; (2) whether the export of such a technology conforms to the industrial export policies of China and contributes to promoting the development of national economy; and (3)

examination[148] and reach a decision as to whether a preliminary licence shall be granted within 30 days upon receipt of the application.[149] A preliminary licence issued is only valid for three years.[150] Where no substantive contract was entered into within the term of the preliminary licence, the exporter shall re-file another application for a preliminary licence before concluding a contract for export.[151] In practice, the procedures vary in different localities and more detailed documentation may be required by the administrative organs. Take the example of Beijing: to apply for a preliminary licence, enterprises are required to submit, where applicable, the Business Certificate and Import and Export Qualification Certificate of the exporter, Application Form for Export of Restricted Technology, agreement for commissioned or cooperative technology development, detailed implementing instructions of the exported technology, documentary proof of IP ownership, a diagram showing the main technical specifications, Confidentiality Review Approval for the Export of State Secret Technology (which is to be applied with the Beijing Municipal Science and Technology Commission, the local administration for science and technology), a licence for export of resources (where the technology export also involves export of resources), information of the technology proposed to be exported, other necessary materials and a list of all materials submitted.[152] In addition to the materials listed in the TIER, the Department of Commerce of Beijing also requires an Application Form for Technology Export Contract, a Datasheet of Technology Export Contract, documentary proof of IP ownership, approval from company management (resolution of board of directors or office of the general manager), other necessary materials and a list of the materials provided at this stage.[153] Another example is that in Yunnan Province, approvals from the local IP department, science and technology department, agriculture and forestry department, etc. are also necessary if the exported technology involves patents, integrated circuit layout designs, new plant varieties, or copyright of computer software.[154] After the technology export contract has been concluded,

---

whether the export of such a technology conforms to the commitments made by China. See *ibid.*, Art. 8.

148. The technical review shall cover (1) whether the export of such a technology jeopardises national security; (2) whether the export of such a technology conforms to the scientific and technological development policies of China and contributes to the scientific and technological advancement; and (3) whether the export of such a technology conforms to the industrial technology policies of China and promotes the production of large-scale and complete plants, equipment and high-tech products, and the economic and technological cooperation. See *ibid.*, Art. 9.
149. *Ibid.*, Art. 6.1.
150. *Ibid.*, Art. 10.1.
151. *Ibid.*, Art. 12.
152. Public Service Platform for Small and Medium-Sized Enterprise of Beijing, Licence for Restricted Import and Export of Technology – Licence for Restricted Technology Export, 26 June 2016, https://policy.smebj.cn/cms/show.action?code=publish_4028806d-5b8abeda015b8e2b89ba0004&siteid=100000&newsid=61e213ba1e7c4c23ab1158cc54f-37cb0&channelid=0000000001 accessed 10 June 2020.
153. *Ibid.*
154. Department of Commerce of Yunnan Province, Guide to Licence for Restricted Import and Export of Technology 10 February 2020, http://swt.yn.gov.cn/wszwfwdt/202002/t20200210_920750.html accessed 10 June 2020.

the exporter is also obliged to record the contents of the contract online through the MofCom's Technology Import and Export Contract Information Management System before collecting the official licence at the local Department of Commerce.[155] The technology export agreement will come into effect upon the issuance of the official licence by the authorities.[156] The export of some special technologies, including nuclear technologies, dual-use nuclear technologies, technologies concerning the production of controlled chemicals, and controlled military technologies, are specifically addressed by other relevant administrative regulations.[157]

(c) Unrestricted Technologies

Only contract registration, rather than approval by the authorities, is required for the import or export of unrestricted technologies.[158] In other words, obtaining ex-ante approval from the authorities is not necessary; ex-post registration suffices.[159] In contrast to restricted technologies, the transfer agreement of free-import technology comes into effect immediately upon its conclusion, which is not subject to the fulfilment of the registration requirement.[160] The parties are, however, obliged to register the contract with the local Department of Commerce within 60 days after the contract comes into effect, unless the payment is to be calculated based on the percentage of sales.[161] In the latter case, the registration procedures should be completed within 60 days after base figure is finalised for the first time, and a registration for amendment should be fulfilled every time when an updated payment base is formulated.[162] To fulfil the registration requirement, the parties will also have to record the contents of the contract through the MofCom's online Information Management System for Technology Import and Export Contracts beforehand,[163] and then provide the authorities with three sets of document in person: (1) the application document, (2) copies of the technology import or export contract and (3) documents proving the legal status of the contracting parties.[164] The contents required to be recorded include the contract number,[165] the contract name, the supplier, recipient and actual implementer

155. Measures for the Administration of Technologies Prohibited or Restricted from Export, note 143, Art. 16.
156. *Ibid.*, Art. 37.
157. *Ibid.*, Art. 43.
158. *Ibid.*, Art. 17.1, Art. 37.1.
159. *Ibid.*, Art. 37.
160. *Ibid.*, Art. 17.2.
161. Administrative Measures for the Registration of Technology Import and Export Contracts 2009 [Jishu Jinchukou Hetong Dengji Guanli Banfa], Art. 6.
162. *Ibid.*, Art. 7.
163. *Ibid.*, Art. 8.
164. TIER, Art. 18, Art. 38; See also Administrative Measures for the Registration of Technology Import and Export Contracts, note 161, Art. 8.
165. Each contract will be allocated a standardised code consisting of 17 digital numerals, the first nine of which are fixed: The first two numbers indicate the year when the contract is signed (last two digits of the year), the second two digits indicate the importing or exporting country (two-digit GB code), the third two digits indicate the region of location of the import or export enterprise (two-digit GB code), the seventh digit indicates whether

of the subject technology, a brief introduction of the contract, value of the subject matter, payment method, and the contract term.[166] The Departments of Commerce at provincial level have the authority not only to conduct such registration for free import and export of technologies, but also to delegate the power to its lower branches at municipal or even county level.[167] Upon receipt of the requisite materials, the authority in charge shall notify the enterprise in case inconsistencies occur and request an amendment, or issue the Technology Import Contract Registration Certificate or Technology Export Contract Registration Certificate in due course.[168] Like the procedures for obtaining approval for the import of export of restricted technologies, the practice associated with unrestricted technologies in different regions are not always consistent. For example, the Department of Commerce of Yunnan Province has not yet released the authority for handling such registrations to its lower branches, and requires substantially more documents than the three sets mentioned in the TIER.[169] Additionally, although the TIER explicitly state that the effectiveness of an import or export contract for unrestricted technologies is not subject to the fulfilment of registration procedures, local administrations have, as a practical matter, indicated their power to disapprove a registration during examination.[170] When faced with an unfavourable decision, enterprises are allowed to bring an administrative review or litigation proceedings according to the relevant laws and regulations.[171] Lastly, every time the contract is amended, the parties will need to record the amendment with the authorities accordingly.[172]

2. Obligations

Similar to the Civil Code framework, the TIER also prescribe the respective obligations of the parties to the technology transfer agreement. The TIER, however, focus more on the transferor's obligations. The transferor shall guarantee that he or she is the lawful owner of the subject technologies and therefore has the right to assign or

it is for export of import (Y for import and E for export), and the eighth and the ninth digits indicate the industry category of the imported or exported technology (two-digit GB code). The last 8 digits shall be defined by the enterprise. See Administrative Measures for the Registration of Technology Import and Export Contracts, note 161, Art. 11.

166. *Ibid.*, Art. 10.
167. *Ibid.*, Art. 5.
168. *Ibid.*, Art. 9.
169. Department of Commerce of Yunnan Province, Guide to Register a Freely Import or Export Technology Contract, 10 February 2020 http://swt.yn.gov.cn/wszwfwdt/202002/t20200210_920789.html accessed 10 June 2020.
170. See e.g. Bureau of Commerce of Tianjin Municipality, Flow Chart of Registering a Freely-Import or Export Technology Contract, http://qzqd.tjbb.gov.cn/flowChart/1092134 accessed 10 June 2020.
171. See generally, Administrative Reconsideration Law of the People's Republic of China 2017 [Zhonghua Renmin Gongheguo Xingzheng Fuyi Fa]; Administrative Litigation Law of the People's Republic of China 2017 [Zhonghua Renmin Gongheguo Xingzheng Susong Fa].
172. Administrative Measures for the Registration of Technology Import and Export Contracts, note 161, Art. 12.

license them.[173] He or she shall further guarantee that the technologies provided are complete, correct and effective and meet the target agreed upon in the contract.[174] In the meantime, the transferee is required to use the technologies pursuant to the contract. Upon being charged for infringement against third parties' rights, the transferee shall immediately notify the transferor, who shall, upon being notified, assist the former to remove the obstruction.[175] Additionally, both parties are obliged to maintain the confidentiality of the undisclosed information regarding the transferred technologies during the period stipulated in the contract.[176] However, the party's confidentiality obligation shall immediately terminate if the confidential information is disclosed to the public for reasons other than the party's behaviour.[177] Upon the expiration of the contract, the transferor and transferee shall negotiate and make an agreement on the continuous use of the technology based on the principles of fairness and reasonability.[178] If there is any change in the technology import or export contract, the technology importer or exporter is obliged to apply for a new licence or a new registration certificate.[179] The termination of such a contract should also be recorded with the relevant authorities.[180]

3. Liabilities

The TIER provide detailed liabilities for the violation of the above provisions as well. First, persons or organisations that import or export technologies which fall within the Catalogues of Prohibited Import and Export Technologies or that import or export restricted technologies without a licence face criminal charges, such as for smuggling, illegal business activities, divulgence of state secrets, etc.[181] In case the illegal conduct is not serious enough to constitute a crime, the person or organisation shall be sanctioned according to the customs laws and regulations or receive a warning from the authorities, and the illegal profits shall be confiscated.[182] A fine of one to five times greater than the illegal profits is imposed as well.[183] Furthermore, the government authorities may revoke the breaching party's business licence to conduct foreign trade.[184]

Second, persons or organisations that import or export technologies that are restricted from import or export out of their licensed scope face criminal charges, such as illegal business activities.[185] In case the illegal conduct is not serious enough to constitute a crime, the person or organisation shall be sanctioned according to

173. TIER., Art. 24.1.
174. *Ibid.*, Art. 25.
175. *Ibid.*, Art. 24.2.
176. *Ibid.*, Art. 26.
177. *Ibid.*
178. *Ibid.*, Art. 27.
179. *Ibid.*, Art. 41.1.
180. *Ibid.*
181. *Ibid.*, Art. 44.
182. *Ibid.*
183. *Ibid.*
184. *Ibid.*
185. *Ibid.*, Art. 45.

the customs laws and regulations or receive a warning from the authorities, and the illegal profits shall be confiscated.[186] A fine of one to three times greater than the illegal profits is imposed as well.[187] Furthermore, the government authorities may revoke the breaching party's business licence to conduct foreign trade.[188]

Third, persons or organisations that forge, alter, buy or sell licences for import or export of technologies or registration certificates face criminal charges of illegal business activities or forgery, alteration or buying and selling of official documents, certificates, seals and stamps of state organs.[189] In case the illegal conduct does not meet the threshold of the aforementioned crimes, the persons or organisations are sanctioned according to the customs laws and regulations.[190] Meanwhile, the right of the persons or the organisations to engage in foreign trade activities may be suspended or even revoked.[191]

Fourth, where licences for import or export of technologies were obtained by fraud or by other illegal means, the persons or organisations shall have their licences revoked, and their rights to engage in foreign trade activities may be suspended or even revoked.[192]

Notably, the TIER do not touch upon the liabilities for not duly completing the registration procedures for the import or export of unrestricted technologies. However, failing to record a technology import or export contract with the authorities could have a substantive impact on whether the transacting party can remit royalties from China because a registration certificate is always required when buying or selling foreign exchange at any designated commercial bank.[193] Further, if an enterprise fails to register the contract within the prescribed deadline (i.e. usually 60 days after the conclusion of the contract), the authorities would generally refuse to issue a certificate.

4. Government Officers' Duties of Confidentiality

Under the TIER, relevant authorities under the State Council and their employees should maintain the confidentiality of state secrets and trade secrets obtained when handling technology export cases.[194] State employees who violate these regulations may face criminal charges for divulging state secrets or encroaching upon trade secrets,[195] abusing or neglecting power, bribery or other crimes. [196] If such behaviour

186. *Ibid.*
187. *Ibid.*
188. *Ibid.*
189. *Ibid.*, Art. 46.
190. *Ibid.*, Art. 44, Art. 45, Art. 46.
191. *Ibid.*
192. *Ibid.*, Art. 47.
193. Circular of the Ministry of Foreign Trade and Economic Cooperation (MOFTEC) and the State Administration of Foreign Exchange (SAFE) on Strengthening the Administration of Foreign Exchange Sale and Payment Related to Technology Import Contracts 2002 ("MOFTEC and SAFE Circular") [Duiwai Jingji Maoyi Hezuo Bu Guojia Waihui Guanli Ju Guan Yu Jiaqiang Jishu Jinchukou Hetong Shoufuhui Guanli De Tongzhi], Art. 2.
194. *Ibid.*, Art. 42.
195. *Ibid.*, Art. 49.
196. *Ibid.*, Art. 50.

does not meet criminal thresholds, the employees should be subject to administrative disciplinary actions.[197]

5. Discriminatory Licensing Restrictions

In 2019, the Chinese government deleted three contestable articles which were regarded as discriminatory against foreign investors: the previous Article 24(3), Article 27 and Article 29 of the 2011 TIER.[198] Article 24(3) of the 2011 TIER previously mandated all indemnity risks to be borne by the transferor, which was a mandatory provision around which parties could not negotiate.[199] However, the general rules set by the Chinese Civil Code allocate third party infringement risks to the transferor as a default unless "otherwise agreed upon by the parties".[200] Because this mandatory provision in the TIER did not apply to technology transfer agreements between two domestic companies, the provision was believed to be discriminatory against foreign licensors. Furthermore, the previous Article 27 mandated that, between the licensor and licensee, all improvements belong to the party making the improvement; while the parties cannot negotiate shared ownership or the licensor owning improvements made by the licensee,[201] neither can the licensor stop the licensee from making improvements to the technology according to Article 29(3) of the previous provision.[202] This mandatory provision enabled the Chinese licensee to own severable improvements without a licence from the foreign licensor.[203] However, where the technology transfer agreement was entered into by two domestic parties, the parties have the freedom to

197. *Ibid.*
198. TIER 2011, Art. 24.3: "The assignee or licensee shall make use of the technologies of the licensor according to the stipulations of a technology import contract. Where any of the lawful interests of any other person is infringed upon, the liabilities shall be borne by the licensor". Art. 27: "During the term of validity of a contract of import of technologies, the right over any improvement on the technologies shall be vested with the party which has made the improvement". Art. 29: "The following restrictive clauses shall not be included in a contract of import of technologies: (1) Clauses requiring the assignee or licensee to accept such conditions which are not indispensable for the import of the technologies as purchasing unnecessary technologies, raw materials, products, equipment or services; (2) Clauses requiring the assignee or licensee to pay fees or assume certain obligations for using technologies the patented period of which has expired and the patent of which has been declared as void; (3) Clauses restricting the assignee or licensee to make improvement on the technologies or to use such improved technologies; (4) Clauses restricting the assignee or licensee to obtain from sources other than the assignor or licensor technologies similar to or competitive with those provided by the assignor or licensor; (5) Clauses unreasonably restricting the channels or sources for the assignee or licensee to purchase raw materials, spare parts, products or equipment; (6) Clauses unreasonably restricting the quantity, type and price of the products of the assignee or licensee; (7) Clauses unreasonably restricting the export of the products produced by the assignee or licensee by using the imported technologies."
199. USTR, 2018 Section 301 Report, note 71, 49.
200. Contract Law 1999, note 6, Art. 353.
201. TIER 2011, Art. 27.
202. *Ibid.*, Art. 29.3.
203. USTR, 2018 Section 301 Report, note 71, 49–50.

negotiate the licensing terms with one another. According to Article 875 of the Civil Code, "[T]he parties to a technological transfer contract may, in accordance with the principle of mutual benefit, stipulate the method for sharing any subsequently improved technological result obtained from the patent exploitation or utilisation of the technical know-how."[204]

In March 2018, the US filed a request for consultations with China in the WTO alleging that China's TIER and JV Regulations caused discriminatory technology licensing, and the dispute advanced to the panel stage in January 2019. The US indicated that these restrictions violated Article 3(1) (national treatment) and Article 28 (exclusive rights conferred) of the TRIPS Agreement. On 3 June 2019, the US requested the panel to suspend its proceedings until 31 December 2019. On 12 June 2019, the panel informed the Dispute Settlement Body of its decision to grant the request made by the US and suspend its work. The 2019 amendment of the TIER abolishing all three provisions which allegedly facilitated discriminatory licensing practices should be regarded as a major breakthrough in the two countries' negotiations to resolve the issue.

While China has lifted the absolute ban on grant-back clauses in the TIER, it remains unclear under which circumstance grant-back clauses can be adopted in a licensing agreement. Licensors imposing such a clause as a trading condition are exposed to a certain degree of risk of antitrust violation. Specifically Article 10 of the Provisions of the State Administration for Market Regulation on Prohibiting the Abuse of Intellectual Property Rights to Preclude or Restrict Competition ("the SAMR Provisions") prohibits IP right holders with a dominant market position from, without justification, attaching unreasonable restrictions to preclude or restrict competition, including demanding the counterparty to grant back an exclusive licence for any improvement made by the latter on the licensed technology.[205] Such will constitute an abuse of market dominance as prohibited by the Anti-Monopoly Law and be subject to a fine of 1 to 10 percent of the sales volume of the last fiscal year, in addition to confiscation of all illegal profits.[206]

Apart from individual IP owners, patent pools with market dominance are prohibited from demanding an exclusive grant-back of the improved technology as well.[207] Although market dominance should not be inferred from the possession of IP

---

204. Civil Code 2020, note 7, Art. 875. See also USTR, 2018 Section 301 Report, note 71, 53 ("[t]he PRC Contract Law also provides a default position for parties to domestic technology transfer agreements such that, should the parties fail to agree on how to determine ownership of any improvements, or if the contractual language regarding improvements is vague, then the default is that neither party owns any improvement made by the other party to the contract. This default provision only provides a non-mandatory backstop position for technology transfer contracts, as well as a position from which to negotiate such contracts, yet such flexibility is only available to companies transferring technology domestically.").

205. Provisions of the State Administration for Market Regulation on Prohibiting the Abuse of Intellectual Property Rights to Preclude or Restrict Competition 2020 ("SAMR Provisions") [Guojia Shichang Jiandu Guanli Zongju Guanyu Jinzhi Lanyong Zhishi Chanquan Paichu Xianzhi Jingzheng Xingwei De Guiding], Art. 10.1.

206. Anti-Monopoly Law 2008, note 48, Arts. 17, 47.

207. SAMR Provisions, note 205, Art. 12.3(iii).

per se,[208] owners of valuable IP potentially have stronger market power, and thereby possibly a dominant market position.[209] Even if the licensor is not a dominant market player, the licensor is still subject to an antitrust violation risk if the technology transfer agreement with a grant-back clause would be viewed as a monopoly agreement prohibited by the Anti-Monopoly Law, which will lead to a fine of 1 to 10 percent of the sales volume of the last fiscal year, or a fine of no more than RMB 500,000 if the monopoly agreement has not yet been implemented, in addition to confiscation of illegal profits.[210]

V. CONCLUSION

From an international perspective, technology transfer can stimulate strong economic side effects by enhancing the economic development and global competitiveness of both the donor and recipient countries.[211] Technology transfer from overseas has also played a vital role in China's economic growth and modernisation.[212]

Chapter 20, Book 3 of the Civil Code sets a series of basic rules governing various technology contracting activities, including technology transfers. However, where foreign technologies are involved, the Civil Code has referred to foreign investment regulations and technology import and export regulations. China has used these special regulations as policy tools for its industrial development. Nevertheless, with China's growing global competitiveness, the country has faced increasing pressure from its trading partners and foreign investors to reform its technology transfer regime. Recent reform reveals that IP has become a main concern for foreign investors in the country. Moreover, China's technology transfer regime has moved in the direction of more party autonomy and less governmental intervention.

208. *Ibid.*, Art. 6.2.
209. Anti-Monopoly Law 2008, note 48, Art. 18: "The dominant market position of a business operator shall be determined according to the following factors: ... (3) The financial and technological conditions of the business operator."
210. Anti-Monopoly Law 2008, note 48, Arts. 13, 14, 46.
211. Smith, note 3, 824.
212. The 7th Five-Year Plan of the People's Republic of China for Economic and Social Development, 28 April 1986, 16–17; Zhang Yuqing and James S. McLean, 'China's Foreign Economic Contract Law: Its Significance and Analysis', 8 *Nw. J. Int'l L. & Bus.* (1987), 120, 144.

CHAPTER 7

Enforcement

Douglas Clark

I. INTRODUCTION

Since foreign companies began actively enforcing IP rights in China in the 1990s the system has improved markedly. In the early years, counterfeiting was rampant. The only partially effective remedy was administrative action. It was almost impossible to bring effective civil or criminal actions.

The situation in the 2020s has changed dramatically. While there is still substantial infringement of IP rights in China, outright counterfeiting has dropped substantially (at least in relative terms). Rights owners now face problems with look-alike products or the use of similar trade marks. Patent infringement cases have increased substantially. The biggest challenge for many right holders these days is how to enforce rights against online infringers. Reflecting this latter point, one of the main focusses of the first stage US-China trade deal in late 2019 was improved enforcement against online platforms.

Civil actions are now a very common method for enforcement of IP rights with substantial damages being awarded by the courts. Administrative enforcement remains an option, particularly against low level infringers but can also be a useful tool to gather evidence to support civil cases. Criminal prosecutions, while less common than in many other countries, are brought and can act as a deterrent to infringement.

1. Dual System for Civil Enforcement

In order to bring a civil enforcement action in China, right holders may bring a civil action in court, or can make a complaint to administrative bodies who will investigate (or "raid") the premises of the alleged infringer.

In the early years of IP enforcement, almost all foreign companies relied solely upon administrative enforcement. Raids could be arranged quickly and efficiently. The administrative bodies would impose fines on the respondents and in some cases could order compensation. It was only in the early 2000s that foreign – and, indeed, Chinese – right holders started to bring civil actions in the courts. This was partly due to amendments of the IP laws as part of the accession process of China to the World Trade Organization in 2001. Some fundamental changes were made at that time, in particular, the courts were given the sole power to award damages and rules for the grant of preliminary injunctions were introduced. Appeals from administrative decisions relating to IP rights to the courts were also introduced.

For court cases it is also possible to "forum shop" and avoid the local jurisdiction of the defendant,[1] whereas administrative actions almost invariably have to be brought in the hometown of the defendant. Administrative bodies also only handle relatively simple cases and as cases became more complex it became necessary to file actions in court.

To this day, administrative actions are more common in trade mark and unfair competition cases where most cases are clear-cut and infringement is easily proven. In more complex patent and copyright matters, it is more difficult to prove either the existence of a right (copyright) or the infringement (patents).

2. TRIPS Compliance

China's accession to the World Trade Organization ("WTO") brought enormous pressure on China to change and improve its IP legislation. In theory, the Trade Related agreement on Intellectual Property rightS ("TRIPS") that is part of the WTO is directly applicable.[2] In reality, it is not necessary to rely on TRIPS to assert a right because China's written IP laws are TRIPS compliant. As in any other country, TRIPs can be referred to when dealing with courts and officials to remind them that certain provisions are designed to implement treaty obligations.[3]

II. CIVIL ENFORCEMENT THROUGH THE COURTS

1. General Remarks

The number of IP cases dealt with in Chinese courts has risen exponentially over the years. In 2019, the local courts accepted 399,031 and concluded 394,521 first instance civil intellectual property cases with respective year-on-year increases of 40.79 percent and 44.02 percent. Among the newly accepted cases, 22,272 were patent cases (2.64 percent year-on-year increase); 65,209 trade mark cases (25.41 percent year-on-year increase); 293,066 copyright cases (49.98 percent year-on-year increase). There were also 3,135 cases on technology contract disputes, (16.98 percent year-on-year increase) and 4,128 unfair competition cases, including 70 monopoly cases, (49.71

1. Choice of jurisdiction is discussed further *infra*.
2. In civil law jurisprudence, treaties are generally considered to be "self-executing". Thomas Pattloch, *Das IPR des Geistigen Eigentums in der VR China* (Tübingen, 2003), 80, 81. See also the introductory chapter for a detailed discussion on direct applicability of international agreements in China.
3. While rare, the current author has twice relied on TRIPS obligations to assist in discussion with administrative bodies about their interpretation of laws.

percent year-on-year increase). Other civil intellectual property disputes constituted 11,221 cases, or 49.71 percent more than last year. For second instance appellate cases, 49,704 were accepted and 48,710 concluded, giving a year-on-year increase of 79.95 percent and 85.29 percent respectively. The Supreme People's Court accepted 2,504 new civil intellectual property cases and concluded 1,976 cases, respectively 174.26 percent and 260.97 percent higher than the previous year.[4]

Almost all large cities have established specialist IP chambers. In 2014, specialist IP Courts were established in Beijing, Shanghai and Guangdong and in 2019 a specialist tribunal of the Supreme People's Court was established to directly hear second instance appeals in patent and other complex IP matters. Three internet courts have also been established in Hangzhou, Beijing and Guangzhou to try IP cases relating to infringement on the internet online.

Court decisions in China unlike those in Anglo-Saxon jurisdictions are, in general, not binding on other courts (that is, there is no *stare decisis*). However, to ensure consistency in judicial practice, the Supreme People's Court issues judicial interpretations of the law and a number of "Guiding Cases".[5] These interpretations of law and Guiding Cases of the Supreme Court should be followed by all lower courts in the PRC. The SPC has issued a number of judicial interpretations directly in relation to IP cases as well as a number of interpretations applicable to civil procedure. The SPC has to date issued over 100 "Guiding Cases" some of which deal with intellectual property issues. These are discussed more detail below.

Higher People's Court in each province, autonomous region or city directly under the central government[6] can also issue local judicial interpretations which the lower courts in that province are required to follow. Decisions of courts in other cases can be used as reference material by courts in making decisions, particularly if they have dealt with a novel point of law.

The costs of bringing civil proceedings in comparison to other jurisdictions are relatively low although nowhere near cheap. Patent litigation, especially, can require substantial financial resources. Some Chinese law firms will act on a partial contingency. Recently, some local and international litigation funders have also started funding litigation in China.

This chapter deals with the enforcement of intellectual property rights through the courts focussing on patents, trade marks and copyright. The courts do not, at first instance, deal with question of validity of patent and trade marks. Validity is challenged in the Re-examination and Invalidation Department (formerly Patent Re-examination Board) and Trademark Review and Adjudication Department of the China National Intellectual Property Administration ("CNIPA") (which was formerly

4. Intellectual Property Protection by the Chinese Courts in 2019, People's Court Publishing House, 2020 (available in Chinese and English at: https://www.chinacourt.org/article/detail/2020/04/id/5049570.shtml).
5. Both authorized by Article 18 of the People's Court Organization Law.
6. The Mainland of China has 23 provinces, 5 autonomous regions (Tibet, Guangxi, Ningxia Inner Mongolia and Xingjiang) and municipalities under direct control of the central government (Beijing, Shanghai, Tianjin and Chongqing). For convenience these will be referred to as provinces below. There are also two Special Administrative Regions (Hong Kong and Macau) with different legal systems. Taiwan is also claimed by the Mainland to be a province. It has a different legal system as well.

in English the State Intellectual Property Office ("SIPO")). These procedures are not dealt with in this chapter.

2. Competent Courts

In the PRC, there exist four levels of courts with a two instance trial system. First instance judgments are automatically stayed if an appeal is filed. Decisions of appellate courts are immediately binding and enforceable.[7]

The lowest level of courts are the Basic People's Courts. One tier above are the Intermediate People's Courts. Each major city has an Intermediate People's Court and larger cities can have two or more. The Intellectual Property Courts established in Beijing, Shanghai and Guangzhou in 2014 are equivalent in status to Intermediate People's Court. In each province the highest court is the Higher People's Courts. Higher People's Courts generally act as appellate courts from Intermediate People's Courts but can also hear large first instance cases.

Finally, the highest court for civil, administrative and criminal cases is the Supreme People's Court located in Beijing. In relation to IP cases, since 2019, the SPC has established an IP Tribunal that acts as a direct appellate court from first instance decisions of intermediate or higher people's Courts in patent and complex IP cases. The SPC IP Tribunal is discussed in more detail below. The SPC also has first instance jurisdiction for cases with "a significant impact on the whole country".[8]

Each level of court is discussed below with some discussion of the jurisdiction of the courts. There is more detailed discussion of jurisdiction in IP cases later in this chapter.

(a) Basic People's Courts

Basic people's courts are established at county and city level with more than 3,000 such courts throughout the country. They have jurisdiction to hear civil cases except as otherwise provided by law.[9] IP matters previously were only heard at this level in domestic copyright and trade mark matters, but not if a foreign party was involved. Nowadays some basic people's courts, particularly in large cities, handle trade or copyright mark matters even when they involve foreign parties. For example in the cities where IP Courts have been established (Beijing, Shanghai and Guangzhou), basic people courts have jurisdiction to try all trade mark, copyright and unfair competition cases without reference to the amount in dispute.[10] Some basic people's courts have also been given jurisdiction to handle design patent cases (but not invention patent or utility model cases).

The Hangzhou Internet Court, established in 2017, has jurisdiction to handle online copyright infringement cases within the jurisdiction of basic people's courts in Hangzhou. Special procedures are adopted so that the entire process of filing the

7. Article 155, Code of Civil Procedure.
8. Article 20, Code of Civil Procedure.
9. Article 17, Code of Civil Procedure.
10. Supreme People's Court Notice of Jurisdiction of IP Courts, 24 December 2018.

case, dealing with evidence and the hearing are handled online.[11] The Beijing and Guangzhou Internet Courts, both founded in 2018, will handle cases relating to the ownership of copyright, infringement of copyright and domain name disputes within the jurisdiction of basic people's courts in Beijing and Guangzhou respectively.[12]

(b) Intermediate People's Courts

Intermediate People's Courts, presently numbering close to 400, are established at a regional level in each province. In some areas and large cities such as Beijing and Shanghai there are two or more Intermediate People's Courts. Actions can be brought in any Intermediate People's Court with territorial jurisdiction.

Article 18 of the Code of Civil Procedure provides that major cases involving foreigners should be heard by Intermediate People's Courts, however, as noted above in cities where IP Courts have been established, first instance jurisdiction has been given to basic people's courts for trade mark, copyright and unfair competition cases. Some other cities have also given jurisdiction to basic people's court to hear foreign related cases.

Patent infringement cases may, however, only be heard in courts that have been specially designated by the Supreme People's Court with jurisdiction to hear patent cases.[13] Designated courts, which number about 80, are Intermediate People's Courts in the capitals of the provinces and certain other large cities. Their territorial jurisdiction for patent cases is broader than the city in which they are located and will cover other cities in their region where intermediate courts have not been granted jurisdiction to try patent cases.

Intellectual Property Courts and Tribunals

Since 2014, specialised intellectual property courts have been established in Beijing, Shanghai and Guangzhou. The Beijing and Shanghai courts have jurisdiction over all IP cases in those cities. The Guangzhou court has jurisdiction over cases in Guangdong Province other than Shenzhen.[14] Shenzhen is a special economic zone next to Hong Kong and has its own well-regarded IP Tribunal.

The Intellectual Property Courts (IP Courts) generally have first instance jurisdiction over civil and administrative cases involving invention patents, utility models, new plant varieties, IC layout design, technical secret and computer software

11. The Hangzhou Internet Court website is at: https://www.netcourt.gov.cn
12. The Beijing Internet Court website is at: https://www.bjinternetcourt.gov.cn (also with an English site) and the Guangzhou Internet Court website is at: https://www.gzinternetcourt.gov.cn/index.html
13. Article 2 of the 2015 Judicial Interpretation of the Code of Civil Procedure; Article 2 of the 2001 Patent Trial Guidelines. Certain Basic People's Courts have been given jurisdiction in design cases.
14. Decision of the Standing Committee of the National People's Congress on the Establishment of Intellectual Property Courts in Beijing, Shanghai and Guangzhou, 31 August 2014. Rules of the Supreme People's Court on Issues Related to the Jurisdiction of Intellectual Property Courts, 2014

and civil cases involving the recognition of well-known marks. They also have first instance jurisdiction over anti-monopoly cases.

The IP Courts also act as the appellate court for IP cases from basic people's courts in their cities.[15] This means in Beijing and Shanghai all IP appeals go to the IP Courts. In Guangdong Province, appeals from basic people's courts in Guangzhou are heard by the Guangzhou IP Court, but appeals from decisions of basic people's courts in other cities will be heard by the Intermediate People's Court in that city.

The Beijing IP Court also has jurisdiction over appeals from decisions of the Trademark Review and Adjudication Department and Re-examination and Invalidation Department (formerly Patent Re-examination Board) concerning the registrability of patents and trade marks.

There are also 18 specialized regional IP tribunals in important cities in 15 provinces which are established as part of local Intermediate People's Courts but are given special jurisdiction to try IP cases. These include major regional cities such Shenzhen, Nanjing and Hangzhou.

(c) Higher People's Courts

There are 32 Higher People's Courts, one in each province, autonomous regions and municipalities directly under the central government. IP cases are usually heard by Higher People's Courts at second instance on appeal.

Higher People's Courts may also hear cases at first instance.[16] Until 2019 the financial thresholds for filing a claim in a Higher People's Court varied from province to province. In more economically developed cities and provinces (Beijing, Shanghai, Jiangsu, Zhejiang and Guangdong) the threshold was set at RMB 500 million (USD 85 million) ranging down to RMB 100 million (USD 17 million) in less developed areas. [17] However in 2019, the financial threshold for all Higher People's Courts nationwide was increased massively to RMB 5 billion[18] (USD 850 million) in effect, turning Higher People's Courts into appellate courts for all but the biggest cases.

Cases may also be transferred to a Higher People's Court where the matters are complex or deal with novel and general points of law. A Higher People's Court may also transfer a case to a lower court for trial and lower courts may request a higher court to try a case in its place if it considers it necessary.[19]

Traditionally, one reason for bringing an action in a Higher People's Court has been to allow for a direct appeal to the Supreme People's Court to avoid local protectionism. However, this is now less important because in patent and high technology cases there is now a direct appeal to the SPC IP Tribunal (discussed below). The consideration is still be relevant for cases where appeals as of right still

15. Article 6.
16. Article 38(1) Code of Civil Procedure.
17. Supreme People's Court Notice on First Instance Jurisdiction of Intermediate People's Courts issued on 3 March 2015.
18. Notice of the Supreme People's Court on Adjusting the Standards First Instance Cases for Civil and Commercial Cases Some Higher People's Courts and Intermediate People's Courts, 2019.
19. Article 38(2) Code of Civil Procedure.

go to the local Higher People's Courts but given the very high financial threshold of RMB 5 billion (USD 850 million) very few, if any, first instance cases will be able to be filed in a Higher People's Court.

(d) Supreme People's Court

The Supreme People's Court, based in Beijing, is a much larger court and has a wider power than supreme courts in most other countries. The total number of judges in the SPC is over 300.

The Supreme People's Court acts, with leave, as the appellate court from appellate decisions of Higher People's Courts. It also acts as an appellate court as of right from first instance decisions of Higher People's Courts. However, as already noted, in 2019, the minimum financial threshold for a Higher People's Court to accept a first instance case was increased nationwide to RMB 5 billion (USD 850 million) meaning that first instance cases will be very rare in Higher People's Courts and appeals as of right to the Supreme People's Court are equally rare.

Since 2019 there has also been established an IP appellate tribunal for appeals as of right in complex IP cases from Intermediate People's Courts. The jurisdiction of this tribunal is discussed in detail below.

The Supreme People's Court also has first instance jurisdiction in any case "the Supreme People's Court deems it should try itself." This means, that if it wishes, the court may *ex officio* designate itself to hear a particular case no matter at which level according to the law the case should originally be heard. The SPC may review cases not only in respect of legal questions, but also supervise and correct mistakes made by the lower courts as to finding of facts and evaluation of those findings.[20]

Judicial Interpretations and Guiding Cases

The Supreme People's Court also has the power to interpret application of the law in Judicial Interpretations, Notices, Opinions or Circulars. [21] It may also publish "Guiding Cases".[22] The basic effect of judicial interpretations and Guiding Cases is to provide guidance to judicial authorities when they handle cases. This has been necessary in relation to business law because the Chinese economy in the past 20 years has developed rapidly and legislation often fails to keep up with the pace of

20. See *Heilongjiangsheng Jianshe Shejiyuan v. Hubeisheng Mianhua Gongsi, Hubeisheng Mianhua Gongsi Rangfan Zhongchuan Chubeiku und Wuhanshi Gongye Daxue Shejiyuan*, decided by the Supreme People's Court, case number 37 *Zhijianzi* (1998), in the case study Jiang Zhipei (ed.), *Zuigao Renmin Fayuan zhishi chanquan panli pingjie* (Commentary on IP Decisions Made by the SPC) (Beijing Zhishi Chanquan Chubanshe, 2001), 523, and the case "ZL-9 Multifunction Metal Treatment Fluid" ("ZL-9 Duogongneng Jinshu Chuliye") 5 *Jingzhi Zi*, *ibid.*, 527.
21. Article 18, People's Court Organization Law; Resolution of the NPC Standing Committee Providing an Improved Interpretation of Law, issued 10 June 1981; Regulations of the Supreme People's Court Concerning Judicial Explanation Work, Article 6.
22. See Stanford Law School's China Guiding Case Project at: https://cgc.law.stanford.edu. See also, Susan Finder, 'China's Evolving Case Law System In Practice', 9 *Tsinghua China L. Rev.* (2017), 245, for a discussion of the use of case law by Chinese courts.

change. These interpretations go well beyond just interpretation of provisions of a law and are often very long and include detailed provisions, such as in patent law, for claim interpretation. The interpretations are to this extent more akin to legislation and are generally interpreted by the courts as such. The Guiding Cases effectively act as case law principles to be applied by the courts below. In 2020, the Supreme Court expanded the use of case law by issuing the Guiding Opinions on Strengthening Searches for Similar Cases to Unify the Application of Law which require courts to search for similar cases and to allow parties to submit similar cases for reference.[23]

3. The System of Trial

(a) No Separation of Powers

Courts in China are not as independent as they are in other jurisdictions although, in theory, Article 126 of the PRC Constitution stipulates so.[24] Fundamentally, the PRC court system is not based on the theory of separation of powers.[25]

The hierarchy in Chinese courts consists of altogether 12 ranks with the roles of President, Vice-President, Members of an Adjudication Committee as well as (Chief) Judges and Associate (Chief) Judges of Divisions within the various courts.[26] The President of the Supreme People's Court at the highest rank is officially elected for a term equal to that of the National People's Congress and subject to dismissal by the National People's Congress at any time with or without reason. In fact, it is the Communist Party of China that first discusses personnel, decides on who serves as President and Vice-President and then formally forwards the names to Congress for confirmation.

Usually a court president is also the Communist Party Secretary of the court.[27] The Members of the Adjudication Committee, Chief Judges and Associate Chief Judges of Divisions and the judges are officially appointed and dismissed by the Standing Committee of the National People's Congress upon recommendation of the President of the Supreme People's Court.[28] The same method applies for the President and other judges at the various state levels with the People's Congress at the same level electing the president and approving other appointments.

---

23. See: Susan Finder, 'Supreme People's Court's new guidance on similar case search', https://supremepeoplescourtmonitor.com/2020/07/27/supreme-peoples-courts-new-guidance-on-similar-case-search/
24. Article 126 of the Chinese Constitution provides "The people's courts exercise judicial power independently, in accordance with the provisions of law, and not subject to interference by any administrative organ, public organization or individual."
25. This has been explicitly stated by senior PRC leaders on a number of occasions in recent years. See for example: 'Xi: China Must Never Adopt Constitutionalism, Separation of Powers, or Judicial Independence', *The Diplomat*, 19 February 2019.
26. See Chapter 4 of the People's Court Organization Law.
27. This is to guarantee dual leadership, meaning the local Communist Party Committee and government is in charge in matters of organization and personnel, the hierarchical central organ and superiors lead in substantive questions.
28. Article 42, People's Court Organization Law.

This power of People's Congresses to remove a judge if needs be means, effectively, that an appointed judge has no independence. According to Articles 67, 104 and 128 of the PRC Constitution, the Supreme People's Court is responsible to the National People's Congress and the Standing Committee that created it. Additionally, for their financial funding the courts depend on their respective People's Congress. For example, the Intermediate People's Courts are funded by the local governments.

It is also normal for Chinese judges in a lower court to consult the court above it about a pending case to ensure that the higher instance court does not have to overrule the decision of the lower court. Strong personal relationships between judges, party cadres and congress members may result in obscure decision-making procedures and an apparent lack of transparency.

(b) Expertise of Judges

IP judges in the Chinese system today, especially those in IP chambers of the various courts or in the newly established IP Courts, have a high level of proficiency and often also have a technical background.[29] In addition, the CNIPA sometimes dispatches its experts to assist in tackling technical questions at the court.

The Chinese system has assistant judges and fully qualified judges hearing a case. In the procedure and the hearing, three judges will usually be involved; however, even at the level of the Supreme People's Court, due to the high caseload there is a tendency to handle and try cases, including even re-trial hearings by one single judge (which as of now is not the rule).

The role of the judges is divided into the presiding judge guiding the procedure and giving directions during the trial, a reporting judge (usually the key judge preparing the case and decision) and a more junior judge. During the preparation of the trial, the court clerk also plays an important role, handling issues such as communication and preparation of the hearing.

(c) Lawyers and Other Litigation Representatives

Parties can represent themselves or be represented in court by PRC qualified lawyers.[30] Patent attorneys on the other hand are generally authorized to represent a client in front of the CNIPA (including the Re-examination and Invalidation Department (formerly Patent Re-examination Board)) and trade mark agents may generally only appear before the Trademark Review and Adjudication Department. Patent and trade

29. Previously, the poor legal training of judges was an issue. However, at least in IP cases, this has generally been remedied and IP Courts and tribunals are staffed by well trained and educated judges.
30. Article 263, Code of Civil Procedure. Previously, parties could also be represented by "citizen representatives", that is, non-lawyers who appeared on behalf of a party. Foreign lawyers could also appear to represent foreign clients. The rules allowing for this type of representation have been repealed.

mark agents who have been given permission to appear in patent or trade mark related court cases may also act for a party.[31]

Chinese lawyers are required to pass the bar exam which is principally a test of rote memory skills. Patent attorneys are required to pass an exam by CNIPA which in the past has been very strict. As a result, quality in patent matters is very high in China especially when compared to many other Asian countries. Only Chinese nationals may qualify as a lawyer or patent attorney in China. If a Chinese lawyer or patent attorney takes another nationality, they lose their right to practise.

Chinese lawyers may represent clients in patent lawsuits without any additional qualification beyond passing the bar exam. In practice, a smaller group of patent litigators has emerged. Of the total of about 200,000 lawyers or so registered in China today, only a small percentage is actually involved in patent litigation, making access and time for proper preparation of an action a difficult issue at times.

Lawyers in general have a relatively weak and much more passive role in the Chinese judicial system than compared to the US or other jurisdictions, and are dependent on a judge allowing them, for example, to conduct cross-examination of witnesses. Usually, judges will keep a tight leash on attorneys in the hearing, while at the same time following a quite rigid formal process of questions and answers put forward in order to guarantee impartiality and the possibility of each party to present its case.

In court hearings, a maximum of two attorneys may represent a client. The power of attorney from a foreign entity needs to be notarized and legalized. A change of attorney is possible, but can be very complicated and in principle will also require leave by the court.

(d) First Instance Decisions, Appeals and Re-trials

First instance cases usually are heard by a panel composed of three judges or in simple cases by one judge only. In complex cases a panel of up to seven judges may sit.

Appellate cases are heard by a panel consisting of three to five judges. The presiding judge of the panel is appointed by the president of the court or the chief judge of a court division. Decisions are made by majority with, very rarely, the scope for a public dissenting opinion. In some cases, judges will place a non-public dissenting opinion on the court file.[32]

A unique feature of Chinese civil litigation is the "adjudication committee". The duties of adjudication committees are "to bring together adjudication experience, discuss serious or difficult cases as well as other problems that arise in adjudication work."[33] An adjudication committee oversees the decisions made by judges and has the power to overrule decisions made by judges either before a decision is made or, if a decision has become effective, after a reference by the chief judge of the court. The adjudication committee is made up of senior judges who are generally, if not invariably, Communist party members. The committees can serve a useful oversight

31. Supreme People Court Notice No. Fa 317 of 2012 concerning the handling of cases under the new Code of Civil Procedure.
32. Called in Chinese a "保留意见" or "reservation of opinion".
33. Article 10(1) of the People's Court Organization Law

role and ensure that decisions are being made correctly by the panel of judges on a court. The other role is to provide political oversight to cases and ensure that decisions are made in line with party policy or objectives. The adjudication committee is the highest authority in the internal court organization. Litigants cannot know or challenge this mode of deciding a case because it officially only concerns internal affairs of the court and no files are accessible to lawyers of the parties.

China also has a system of "re-trial" which is not found in most other countries.[34] The Supreme People's Court or the court that gave the final judgment (or the appellate court above it) may *ex officio* through its adjudication committee review a case and order a re-trial at the original level if the case has been decided wrongly. The People's Procuratorate may also initiate such a review. Concerned parties may also apply for re-trial within six months although chances that such an application will be successful are very slim. The system of re-trial is very rarely used in IP cases.

4. Court Jurisdiction in IP Cases

Jurisdiction matters generally are regulated in Articles 18 *et seq.* of the Code of Civil Procedure. Special rules for foreign related cases are found in Articles 265 *et seq.* of the Code of Civil Procedure. Administrative appeals from administrative decisions relating to patents, trade marks and customs-related matters are governed by Articles 13 *et seq.* of the Administrative Procedure Law. There are also a number of interpretations issued by the Supreme People's Court and local Higher People's Court setting out jurisdiction in relation to certain cases.

The basic jurisdiction of the IP Courts in Beijing, Shanghai and Guangzhou is governed by the Decision of the Standing Committee of the National People's Congress on the Establishment of Intellectual Property Courts in Beijing, Shanghai and Guangzhou dated 31 August 2014 ("IP Court Establishment Decision"). Subsequently, other rules have been issued to supplement this decision.

(a) Subject Matter Jurisdiction

(1) Patents

According to Article 2 of the 2001 SPC Interpretation Relating to Patent Cases, patent disputes, other than those relating to validity, should in the first instance be brought before Intermediate People's Courts designated to handle cases by the Supreme People's Court. There are about 80 such courts plus the three IP Courts. The types of claims that can be brought include disputes over ownership, assignment, infringement, service inventions, pre-litigation, compulsory licences and dissatisfaction with administrative decisions.[35]

Challenges to the validity of patents must, in the first instance, be brought before the Re-examination and Invalidation Department (formerly Patent Re-examination

34. Chapter XVI, Code of Civil Procedure, Articles 198 *et seq* set out the rules discussed in this paragraph.
35. Article 1 2001 SPC Interpretation Relating to Patent Cases.

Board) of the CNIPA. Appeals from the Re-examination and Invalidation Department are now required to be brought before the Beijing IP Court.[36] Previously appeals went to the Beijing No. 1 Intermediate Court.

In the case of a challenge to a seizure by Customs, the Intermediate People's Court with jurisdiction in the place of the seizure will have jurisdiction.[37] If the court in that city does not have jurisdiction to hear patent cases, the intermediate court with jurisdiction to hear patent cases in that city will hear the case.

The SPC IP Tribunal may also hear first instance trials over disputes over which it has appellate jurisdiction (discussed below) if they involve highly important and complicated nationwide matters. Such cases should be extremely rare.

(2) Trade Marks

Trade mark infringement and other trade mark related cases can be filed in any court with subject matter jurisdiction. For foreign parties this is usually in the intermediate court where the defendant is located or where the infringement has occurred. For local parties (and in some cities now, foreign parties) smaller cases are heard in basic people's courts. In Beijing, Shanghai and Guangdong Province where IP Courts have been established, in general, trade mark cases will be heard in basic people's courts.

The types of trade mark cases that can be heard include:[38]

- disputes over the ownership of right;
- infringement cases;
- disputes over contractual assignment or licences;
- cases of application for pre-trial interim injunctions and property and evidence preservation measures.

Appeals from decisions of the Trade Mark Review and Adjudication Department (formerly Board) are heard by the Beijing IP Court.[39]

(3) Copyright

In copyright cases, Article 2(1) SPC Interpretation Relating to Copyright Cases grants jurisdiction to the Intermediate People's Courts in first instance involving cases of infringement, disputes over copyright or copyright-related rights and interests; and attribution of rights and contractual disputes.

As with trade mark related cases, depending on the locality, basic people's courts may hear copyright cases involving local parties and some foreign parties.

36. Article 2, Decision of the Standing Committee of the National People's Congress on the Establishment of Intellectual Property Courts in Beijing, Shanghai and Guangzhou, 2014
37. Article 15, Administrative Litigation Law.
38. Article 1 SPC Trade Mark Jurisdiction Rules
39. Article 2, Decision of the Standing Committee of the National People's Congress on the Establishment of Intellectual Property Courts in Beijing, Shanghai and Guangzhou, 2014.

(4) *Domain Names*

The same basic jurisdiction rules apply for domain names. However the place of infringement may include the location where the alleged network servers or computer terminals are located.

It is also possible to seek to resolve domain name disputes involving .cn domain names by way of administrative dispute resolution methods. There are three providers for such services: China International Economic and Trade Arbitration Commission (CIETAC), the Hong Kong International Arbitration Centre and World Intellectual Property Organization. All claims must be brought within three years of the registration of the domain name.[40] In general, complaints should be in Chinese, but panels do have jurisdiction to apply a different language.[41]

(b) *Territorial Jurisdiction*

The general principle for jurisdiction in tort actions in the PRC is that action may be commenced in either the place where the infringer is domiciled or the place where the infringing act took place (i.e., the place where the acts were undertaken as well as where the infringing results took place).[42] Where there are multiple defendants with different domiciles, action can be brought in any of the places the defendants are domiciled. It is, therefore, quite common in the PRC to join a retailer or wholesaler as a defendant to an action to obtain jurisdiction away from the home court of the manufacturer.

Care should be taken in sending any warning letters to alleged infringing parties, because this can trigger the right to bring a declaratory action for non-infringement in the recipient's home court. Article 18 of the SPC 2010 Interpretation Relating to Patent Cases provides that if a party sends a warning letter and does not within one month of receipt (or two months of dispatch) bring an action or withdraw the claim, the recipient may bring an action seeking a declaration that they did not infringe. In a 2019 decision of the SPC IP Tribunal, bringing an administrative action was also found to be an act for which a party could seek a declaration of non-infringement.[43]

With regard to patents, Article 5 of the 2001 SPC Interpretation Relating to Patent Cases defines places where infringement has occurred as places where acts such as manufacture, use, offer for sale, selling or importing of allegedly infringing products or of a patented process take place, including the places where consequences of the preceding infringing acts are evident.

40. Article 2, CNNIC ccTLD Dispute Resolution Policy. There is a question if the date of registration is the original date of registration or the date of a subsequent transfer. ADNDRC has advised parties that it cannot accept a case if the date of registration is earlier than three years before. However, WIPO has accepted such cases and panellists have ordered transfers. See, e.g.: *Rhythm & Blue Inc. Limited v. Xu Zhenlin*, WIPO case no. DCN2019-0009.
41. Article 6, CNNIC ccTLD Dispute Resolution Policy.
42. Article 28, Code of Civil Procedure.
43. *VMI Holland Besloten Vennootschap & Anor v. Safe-Run (Suzhou) Co., Ltd*, 5 *Zui Gao Fa Zhi Min Zhong* (2019).

Article 4(1) SPC Interpretation Relating to Copyright Cases gives jurisdiction to the court of the place where the infringing goods are kept, seized or detained. Article 4(2) defines these places as sites where infringing reproductions are stored or hidden away in large quantities on a regular basis. The places where infringing products are seized are deemed to be those where the customs, copyright administrative department or SAMR have seized or detained infringing products.

Article 7 of the SPC Interpretation Relating to Trade Mark Cases makes similar provision in relation to places where infringing goods are stored or seized by the SAMR.

(c) Financial Thresholds

Since 2019, Intermediate People's Courts have jurisdiction to hear cases valued up to RMB 5 billion (USD 850 million). The three intellectual property courts are subject to the same upper limit for trade mark, copyright, design patent cases but not for high technology cases. The lower threshold for jurisdiction varies from province to province depending on the level of economic development. In Jiangsu and Zhejiang Provinces and Shenzhen, the value of the claim where one party is not from the province should be over RMB 50 million, in Tianjin over RMB 20 million, in Jilin, over RMB 10 million and in Tibet, over RMB 5 million. Cases below these thresholds should be brought in basic people's courts unless they do not have subject matter jurisdiction.[44] For Beijing, Shanghai and Guangdong where IP Courts are established, the basic people's courts have financial jurisdiction up to RMB 50 billion for cases that are not within the subject matter jurisdiction of the IP Courts.

(d) Jurisdiction in Respect to Preliminary or Interim Injunctions

The same rules for jurisdiction are applied in application for preliminary or interim injunctions. The rules and procedures for applying for a preliminary or interim injunction are discussed further below.

(e) Review of Administrative Decisions

For appeals from decisions of local administrative agencies, the courts where the agency is located have jurisdiction.[45]

(f) Appellate Jurisdiction

In general, the next court in the hierarchy above a court has appellate jurisdiction. That is, appeals from basic people's courts are to Intermediate People's Courts (or

44. Notice of the Supreme People's Court on Adjusting the Standards First Instance Cases for Civil and Commercial Cases Some Higher People's Courts and Intermediate People's Courts, 2019.
45. Article 18, Administrative Litigation Law.

where there are IP Courts, to the IP Courts); appeals from Intermediate People's Courts or IP Courts will go to the Higher People's Court in the province or city it is located.

However, with the establishment of the Supreme People's Court IP Tribunal, cases involving patents and high technology cases from IP Courts, intermediate courts or Higher People's Courts are now appealed to the Supreme People's Court IP Tribunal. The specific cases are:

(i) appeals against first instance decisions and rulings issued by Higher People's Courts, IP Courts and Intermediate People's Courts in relation to infringement and ownership disputes for invention patents, utility models, new plant varieties, IC layout design, technical secret and computer software as well as anti-monopoly disputes;
(ii) appeals against first instance decisions of the Beijing IP Court in relation to re-examination and invalidation decisions regarding invention patents, utility models, design patents, new plant varieties and IC layout designs; and
(iii) appeals against first instance administrative review decisions and rulings of local Higher People's Courts, IP Courts and Intermediate People's Courts in relation to administrative rulings made by administrative bodies relating to invention patents, utility models, new plant variety, IC layout design, technical secrets, computer software and anti-monopoly disputes.

In 2019, the SPC IP Tribunal accepted a total of 1,945 technology-related IP cases and concluded 1,433 cases, with a closing rate of 73.7 percent. Among the newly accepted cases, 962 were civil appeals, of which 586 were concluded; 241 were administrative appeals, of which 142 were concluded; 481 appeals on jurisdiction challenges, of which 446 were concluded; and 261 were other types of cases, of which 259 were concluded.[46]

Notably, in one case the SPC IP Tribunal heard appeals on both the validity and infringement of a patent in the same hearing so as ensure the same standard for claim construction was applied.[47]

As the SPC IP Tribunal issues more decisions, parties expect to see more certainty and transparency in patent and high technology cases.

(g) *Table Summarizing Jurisdiction*

The table below summarizes the jurisdiction of the courts in civil IP cases.

46. *Annual Report of the Intellectual Property Tribunal of the Supreme People's Court* (2019).
47. *Xiamen Shizheng Electronic Technology Co., Ltd vs. Tianjin Lejin Electronic Appliance Co., Ltd*, 142 *Zuigao Fazhi Xingzhong* (2019) and 366 *Zuigao fazhi Minzhong* (2019).

Court	Subject Matter	Territorial	Financial thresholds
Supreme People's Court	All IP matters on re-trial from SPC IP Tribunal First instance in very important cases (which will be very rare with establishment of SPC IP Tribunal)	All of China	None
SPC IP Tribunal	First instance in very important cases Second Instance appeal court for civil and administrative cases relating to patent infringement and validity cases, high technology cases (not including design patents) and anti-monopoly cases from Higher People's Courts or Intermediate People's Courts Second Instance appeal on all other IP matters from Higher People's Courts "Re-trial court" for final IP decisions	All of China	None
Higher People's Courts	First instance in high value cases Appeals from Intermediate People's Courts in TM, copyright, unfair competition cases and design cases NOT appeals in high technology cases and anti-monopoly cases which go to SPC IPC Tribunal	Whole province D in province Infringing act in province On appeal: from a court in province	Over RMB 5 billion (USD 850 million) Important cases not subject to this limit if Higher People's Court accepts case
Beijing IP Court	First instance patent and high technology cases Anti-monopoly cases Appeals in IP cases from Basic People's Courts in Beijing Appeals from Trademark Review and Adjudication Department and Re-examination and Invalidation Department	Beijing D in Beijing Infringing act in Beijing On appeal: Basic People's court in Beijing	Up to RMB 5 billion in TM, copyright, unfair competition cases and design patent infringement cases. No limit in patent (not including design patent) infringement cases, high technology matters and anti-monopoly cases
Shanghai IP Court	First instance patent and high tech cases Anti-Monopoly cases Appeals in IP cases from Basic People's Courts in Shanghai Review of city level administrative decision relating to IP	Shanghai D in Shanghai Infringing act in Shanghai On appeal: Basic people's court in Shanghai	As for Beijing IP Court

Court	Subject Matter	Territorial	Financial thresholds
Guangzhou IP Court	First instance patent and high technology cases Anti-Monopoly cases Appeals in IP cases from Basic People's Courts within its territorial jurisdiction	Guangdong Province except Shenzhen D in Guangdong (except Shenzhen) Infringing act in Guangdong (except Shenzhen) On Appeal: basic people' court in Guangzhou City.	As for Beijing IP Court
Inter-mediate People's Courts (except where IP Courts have been established)	Patent cases (not all IPCs have jurisdiction) Major cases involving foreigners Appeals from decisions of Customs Cases above financial threshold for basic people's court	Area/Region/City in which they are based Cross region jurisdiction for patent cases	Up to RMB 5 billion Minimum where one party not from same province Jiangsu Zhejiang, Shenzhen: Over RMB 50 Million Tianjin etc: Over RMB 20 million Jilin etc: Over RMB 10 million Tibet etc: Over RMB 5 million
Basic People's Courts where IP Courts established	IP Cases not in jurisdiction of IP Courts	Guangzhou: within own area In Beijing 6 of 16 and in Shanghai, 4 of 16 BPC's have been given cross district jurisdiction to hear IP cases	Less than RMB 5 billion
Basic People's Courts (Except where IP Courts established)	IP Cases not otherwise reserved to intermediate courts Some basic people's courts have jurisdiction to hear design patent cases	Within own area	Below minimum threshold for Intermediate People's Court
Beijing, Hangzhou and Guangzhou Internet Courts	Online copyright cases	Within jurisdiction of basic people's courts within their cities	Within the jurisdiction of basic people's court for that city

5. Introduction to Court Procedure

(a) Relevant Legal Provisions

The most important legal sources governing court procedure in China are the Code of Civil Procedure, which was amended in 2012 and 2017, the SPC Interpretation of the Code of Civil Procedure issued in 2015 and the Supreme People's Court's Several Provisions Regarding Evidence in Civil Proceedings, which were amended in 2019 with the amendments coming into effect on 1 May 2020 ("2020 Evidence Provisions").

The Code of Civil Procedure provides basic rules for civil procedure. Chapter VI (Articles 63 to 81) deal specifically with evidence. The SPC Interpretation of the Code of Civil Procedure and the 2020 Evidence Provisions provide more detailed rules for the actual procedure to be used during preparations for and at trial.

(b) Length of Proceedings

The length of the procedure from filing a case to a decision as a whole is roughly six to nine months for a first instance case and three to six months for an appeal if no foreign parties are involved and the case is not too complex. In more complex cases, the total length of the procedure up to an appellate decision may take between 18 months to two years. Nevertheless, Chinese procedures, in spite of the high case load, are very fast,[48] and deadlines for notifications of hearings are short.[49] This can put severe pressure on the parties in case additional or new evidence and arguments are introduced.

(c) Bifurcation of Issues

Liability and damages are usually decided at the same trial. Although, in one recent case the Intellectual Property Tribunal of the Supreme People's Court upheld a decision of the Shanghai IP Court to issue a partial judgment on liability leaving damages to be assessed later.[50]

For patent and trade mark cases, the questions of infringement and validity are bifurcated with the courts handling infringement at first instance and the Department of Re-examination and Invalidation (until March 2019 referred to as the Patent Re-examination Board) or Trademark Review and Adjudication Department of CNIPA deciding validity at first instance.[51] There are appeals to the Beijing IP Court for validity with a subsequent appeal in patent cases to the Supreme People's Court IP Tribunal and in trade mark cases to the Beijing Higher People's Court. In 2019, the Supreme Court IP Tribunal heard appeals in relation to infringement and validity

48. Article 149 Code of Civil Procedure with a deadline of six months for domestic cases; foreign-related cases are not subject to this deadline.
49. A minimum of three days. Article 136 Code of Civil Procedure.
50. *Valeo Systèmes d'Essuyage v. Xiamen Fu Ke Auto Parts Co., Ltd, 2 Zuigao fa zhi minzhong* (2019).
51. See Chapter 2, on Patents, Utility Models and Designs for details of invalidation proceedings.

of a patent at the same time reducing the risk of inconsistent decision regarding infringement and validity.

(d) Standing to Bring an Action

The right holder has the right to bring an action before the courts.

The Patent Law (Article 65) and Trade Mark Law (Article 60) further provide that a "related injured party" may also bring action. The Copyright Law (Article 57) provides that "a person with a right related to the copyright right" may bring action. These terms are not defined in any of the laws. However, Article 2 of the Supreme People's Court Interpretation on Interim Measures in IP Cases, which came into effect on 1 January 2019, provides that an exclusive licensee may apply for interim measures itself; a sole licensee may apply if the right holder does not apply itself; and, a licensee may if the right holder gives consent. As the applicant for interim measures is required to bring a main action, these provisions provide guidance as to the standing to sue for different types of licensees.

(e) Limitation Periods

Until 2018, the general limitation period for bringing a civil claim in China was two years from the date the right holder has known or has reason to know about the infringement. (Article 135, General Principles of Civil Law).

Under Article 188 of the General Provisions of Civil Law which came into effect in 2018 (and have now been incorporated as Part (or Book) One of the Civil Code[52]), the general limitation period is now three years from the date the right holder is or ought to be aware of infringement, unless the law provides otherwise. This will apply to trade mark, copyright, unfair competition and trade secrets cases.

With regard to patents, from 1 June 2021, the limitation period under new Article 74 of the Patent Law is also three years. Prior to that, the former Article 68 of the PRC Patent Law provides a limitation period of two years. However, a number of courts have held that the three-year limitation period under the General Provisions of Civil Law applies, in any event.

In repeat or continuous infringement cases, which consist of more than one independent action (e.g., the manufacture of infringing goods), the limitation period runs from each act of infringement and claims may be made for any acts within the three-year limitation period. In such cases, the damages will be calculated, at the earliest, from the date three years before the filing of the infringement action.[53]

52. In 2017, a new General Provisions of Civil Law was enacted coming into effect from 1 October 2018. In June 2020, the PRC Civil Code was enacted whereby the General Provisions of Civil Law form Part One (or Book One) of the Civil Code. The General Provisions have many provisions similar to the 1986 General Principles of Civil Law but when first enacted did not repeal the 1986 General Principles. In the case of inconsistency, the General Provisions applied. With effect from 1 January 2021, the General Principles of Civil Law have been repealed (Article 1260 Civil Code).

53. 2001 Patent Trial Guidelines, Article 23.

Article 196 of the General Provisions further provides that the limitation period shall not apply to a claim for cessation of infringement, meaning that actions solely for injunctive relief can be brought outside the limitation period.

6. Pre-trial and Interim Measures

(a) Introduction

Article 100 of the Code of Civil Procedure provides that the courts may order preliminary or interim measures in civil cases. Additionally, all of the PRC laws governing IP contain special provisions allowing for preliminary or interim injunctions to be applied.

The application for preliminary or interim measures in IP cases is now principally governed by the Provisions of the SPC Governing Preliminary Preservation Measures in Intellectual Property Disputes which came into force on 1 January 2019 ("SPC Interim Measures Provisions").

(b) Right to Apply

In IP cases, the right holder or his successor in title may apply for a preliminary or interim injunction. In addition, an exclusive or sole licensee generally may apply for an interim injunction on his own if the right holder takes no action against infringing activities. Simple licensees cannot apply for such measures without the written consent of the right holder (Article 2, SPC Interim Measures Provisions).

(c) Procedure

The application for pre-trial measures should be submitted to the court with jurisdiction over a main action. An application for interim measures should be made to the court seized of the case. According to Article 4 of the SPC Interim Measures Provisions, the application should contain the following:

(a) the identity, address, and contact information of the applicant and the respondent;
(b) the content and time limit of the applied act preservation measures;
(c) the facts and reasons on which the application is based, including the specific description of, for example, the irreparable loss in the lawful rights and interests to be suffered by the applicant and the potential difficulty in enforcement of the judgment of the case due to the respondent's actions;
(d) the property information or credit certificates as guarantee for the act preservation, or the reasons for not providing the guarantee;
(e) other matters that need to be stated.

(d) Supporting Evidence

The applicant must submit documentary evidence proving the authenticity and validity of his right(s), including valid certificates, claims, description, receipt of payment of the annual patent fee and in case of utility models a search report by CNIPA. An interested party also must submit the patent licensing contract and the proof of filing the contract with CNIPA. If he does not have this proof, he must submit the certificate of the patentee or other evidence that proves that he enjoys the right. Sole licensees must submit proof that the patentee does not want to file himself for the injunction. Heirs must also prove their legal status.

Most notably, the applicant must submit evidence that proves that the respondent is committing or about to commit an act of infringement, including, in patent cases, the allegedly infringing product and technical features of the patented technology as well as of the allegedly infringing product.

(e) Pre-action Preservation of Evidence

A party may apply for preservation of evidence prior to starting the action "where it is likely that evidence may be destroyed, lost or become difficult to obtain later on",[54] for example, to obtain samples of alleged infringing products or to show usage of infringing software on computers. The general rules on evidence preservation discussed below apply to such an application. Such pre-action evidence preservation can be very useful if the proposed defendant cooperates. However, defendants will often claim not to have evidence and the judges executing the order will not (and usually do not have the power to) force a defendant to hand over evidence.

(f) Security

According to Article 11 SPC Interpretation Measures Provision, security must be provided when applying. The necessary amount of security is determined by the court based on the possible loss to be suffered by the respondent due to the preservation measures, including the reasonable loss of sale proceeds and custody expenses of the products involved in order to stop the infringement. Even if an injunction is granted and then executed, wherein the process of execution the opponent suffers even greater losses than originally assumed by the court due to the adoption of the measure, the court may order additional security and cancel or partially cancel the measure the amount not paid in due time.

(g) Cross Security will not Lift Measures

As the most important difference to injunctions granted only on the basis of the Civil Procedure Code, Article 12 of SPC Interim Measures Provisions stipulates that any measure taken to execute the ruling of the court to stop the act of infringement will not be stopped because the party against which the application has been filed provides a cross security, unless the other party consents.

54. Article 81, Code of Civil Procedure. See also Patent Law Article 73.

(h) Institution of the Main Action

Where the court has granted pre-trial relief, the applicant must initiate legal proceedings within 30 days after the court takes measures to stop the relevant act. If no lawsuit is filed, the measure will be removed (Article 16, SPC Interim Measures Provisions). Otherwise the ruling of the court generally remains effective until the date set for the measures to remain in place or judgment (Article 13, SPC Interim Measures Provisions).

(i) Review of Decision to Grant Preliminary or Interim Measures

If the parties are not satisfied with the decision of the court, they may apply for reconsideration within ten days from the date of receipt of the ruling (Article 14, SPC Interim Measures Provisions). They may also apply to cancel the measures (Article 17, SPC Interim Measures Provisions).

The party against which the application is filed may, if the right holder does not start legal proceedings as stipulated or if the measures should not have been granted, initiate legal proceedings with the competent court requesting compensation (Article 105, Code of Civil Procedure and Article 18, SPC Interim Measure Provisions).

(j) Pre-action Disclosure from Third Parties to Lawyers

Outside the procedures for preliminary or interim measures, it is also possible to apply for pre-action disclosure of information from third parties where this is necessary to bring an action. This is particularly important in relation to online infringement with sellers on platforms whose identity cannot be ascertained. The lawyer of the right holder may apply to the court for an Investigation Order providing the details of the infringement and requested information, such as the name, address and bank account information. If the court accepts the request, the court will issue an Investigation Order that will be sent to the platform who will then within two to four weeks provide the information to the lawyers requesting the information.[55]

7. Main Trial Proceedings

(a) Filing of Complaint

A lawsuit is initiated by filing a complaint with a court with subject matter, territorial and financial jurisdiction. The complaint will often be a relatively general allegation of infringement with the plaintiff leaving it to later stages to plead a full case before the court after all evidence has been filed. The plaintiff is required to pay a filing fee which depends on the damages claimed according to a sliding scale of 4 percent for cases claiming RMB 50,000 (USD 8,000) or less than 0.5 percent for claims over RMB

55. The jurisdiction for making such lawyer investigation orders is given by Article 35 of the Lawyers Law.

100 million (USD 14 million).[56] The court fees for an appeal are calculated on the same basis as for the first instance trials. If a party is a foreigner, the power of attorney and evidence obtained or originating from abroad must be notarized and legalized.[57] The plaintiff may submit evidence in support of the case with the complaint.

The court will conduct a formality check and then usually accept the case. In the past, the acceptance chamber of a court would review a case substantively which could delay the bringing of an action. However, in general, now this is no longer done. As part of the acceptance process, the judge in charge of the case will determine one or more deadlines until which all evidence relevant for the case will have to be presented. In some rare instances, the court does not set a specific deadline for providing evidence which has the effect that evidence submitted at a later stage may not be precluded as late-filed.

Within five days of acceptance, the court should serve the complaint on the defendant.

(b) Defence

Depending on whether it is a domestic or foreign party, the defendant is allowed 15 or 30 days to file a defence which is then served by the court on the other party within another five days.[58] A defendant may also file a counterclaim.

Very often defendants do not file a defence preferring to see what evidence the plaintiff has to support its case. Article 125 of the Code of Civil Procedure provides that a defendant shall file a defence but does not require any substantive defence to be set out.[59] Article 125 also provides that if a defence is not filed, this does not affect the handling of the case by the court, meaning that the case will proceed in the absence of defence. There are no default judgement procedures.

(c) Challenge to Jurisdiction

Under Article 127 of the Code of Civil Procedure, a defendant may challenge the jurisdiction of the court to hear a case and request that the matter be transferred to another court. If a defendant files a defence they are treated as having accepted the territorial jurisdiction of the court. Filing a defence does not constitute acceptance

---

56. People's Courts Measures for the Collection of Procedural Fee issued with effect from 1 April 2007.
57. A very cumbersome process: Usually the local notary confirms the signature of the person signing the POA, the signature of the notary then has to be authenticated by his or her supervising government authority whose authentication in turn must be authenticated by its supervising body. This is then legalized with the Chinese consulate or embassy to confirm that bodies power to authenticate. Such a process can take several weeks and may require substantial amounts of time and money.
58. Chapter XII of the Code of Civil Procedure, Article. 125 *et seq.*
59. The SPC Evidence Rules (formerly Article 32, now Article 49) requires a defence of at least some substance be filed. The rules provide that a defendant should file a defence stating its opinion on the plaintiff's claim and the facts and reasons on which such opinion is based. However, courts have not strictly enforced this rule.

of subject matter jurisdiction. A court may also transfer a case that is not within its jurisdiction to another court.

Jurisdiction challenges are quite common, even if they have a limited chance of success. Defendants will often use a challenge to jurisdiction as a way to buy more time in a case, while the court has to rule on its jurisdiction and an appeal is dealt with.[60]

(d) Stay of Proceedings in Patent Cases

When sued for patent infringement a defendant will usually seek to invalidate the patent by filing an invalidation action with the Department of Re-examination and Invalidation (formerly the Patent Re-examination Board) of CNIPA. Where the defendant seeks a stay of the action due to its invalidation action, the defendant must file its invalidation action within the time limit for submitting evidence (Articles 9 and 11, 2001 SPC Several Provisions Relating to Patent Cases).

The general rule is that the court will not stay an action for an invention patent (which has already been examined) unless there is good evidence it may be invalidated. For utility models and design patents (which are not examined), the courts will generally stay the action if the stay application is made within the prescribed time limit. Under Article 9 of the 2001 SPC Several Provisions Relating to Patent Cases, a stay will normally not be granted in any of the following cases:

(a) where in the search report produced by the plaintiff there is no technical documentation to lead to the loss of novelty or inventiveness of the patent or utility model;[61]
(b) where the evidence submitted by the defendant is sufficient to prove that the technology it uses was already common knowledge;
(c) where the evidence or grounds the defendant has submitted for requesting the invalidation of the patent right in question is obviously insufficient; or
(d) any other circumstances where the people's court considers that the proceedings should not be stayed.

Additionally, a stay will not normally be granted where the Department of Re-examination and Invalidation of CNIPA (formerly the Patent Re-examination Board) has already upheld the validity of the patent right. In the latter case, the court must proceed (Article 11, 2001 SPC Several Provisions Relating to Patent Cases).

Where the court decides to grant a stay, it may at the same time, upon application by the plaintiff, grant an interim injunction (Article 12, 2001 SPC Several Provisions Relating to Patent Cases).

---

60. Article 52 of the 2020 SPC Evidence Provisions provides that evidence collection is stayed pending resolution of a jurisdiction challenge.
61. When filing a utility model or design patent action, a plaintiff is required by Article 66(2) to file an evaluation (or search) report prepared by CNIPA. An alleged infringer or interested party may also file a request. See Chapter 2 on Patents, Utility Models and Designs for more details.

(e) Burden of Proof

Article 64 of the Code of Civil Procedure sets out a general rule which places the burden of proof on the party which asserts a matter. This has traditionally placed a very heavy burden of proof on plaintiffs in IP cases to prove their case.

There are cases where the burden of proof is shifted by statute. These include in IP cases:

(a) In cases involving process patents for manufacture of a new product, the burden of proof is shifted to the defendant to prove that a different process has been used (Article 66, Patent Law).[62]

(b) Article 59 of the Copyright Law, expressly provides that the publisher or producer of a copyright work who cannot prove that its publication or production has been authorized; and, the distributor or renter of a cinematographic (or similar) work, computer software, sound recording or video recording who cannot prove that the copies it has distributed or rented reproduction have been obtained from a lawful source, shall bear legal liability.

Further, in certain circumstances the court may reverse the burden of proof where a party can establish they have no way of gathering evidence or where they can show they have taken all possible steps to obtain the evidence.

A number of rules have been introduced by the 2020 Evidence Provisions that will make it easier for parties to discharge their burden of proof including allowing for adverse inferences to be drawn if evidence is not produced (Articles 48 and 95, 2020 Evidence Provisions). New rules make admissions by lawyers binding on a party, as well as, if a lawyer or party does not deny certain facts, they can be deemed to have admitted them (Article 4, 2020 Evidence Provisions).

Article 47 of the 2020 Evidence Rules introduces rules for making document requests pursuant to Article 113 of the SPC Interpretation of the Code of Civil Procedure (which was promulgated in 2015, but has not been generally used given the lack of implementing rules). Article 113 provides that if a party does not comply, the court can impose a fine pursuant to Article 111 of the Code of Civil Procedure. Article 47, in particular, requires a party to produce documents favourable to the other party and financial books and records.

(f) Evidence

After accepting a case, the court will issue a summons for exchange of evidence between the parties. Evidence is exchanged in the presence of at least one judge assigned to hear the case. The time limit for submitting the evidence must be at least 15 days after service of claim (Article 51, 2020 Evidence Rules). If a party wishes to call witnesses this must be indicated within the time period of producing evidence (Article 117, SPC Interpretation of the Code of Civil Procedure). If evidence is not submitted at all in due time, the party is deemed to have waived its right to

62. This issue is further discussed in Chapter 2 on Patents, Utility Models and Designs.

submit evidence. Evidence submitted after the deadline will not be admitted for cross-examination unless the opposing party agrees.

The procedure for evidence exchange is by no means as extensive, formal or sophisticated as for example in common law jurisdictions. There are no depositions or interrogatories, no discovery and no extensive obligation to produce all files and documents of possible relevance for the case. In general, only evidence on which a party seeks to rely is introduced in the proceedings. A requirement to produce all relevant documents does not exist. However, under the 2020 Evidence Provisions, Article 47(2) has introduced an obligation to produce evidence that helps the other side's case. Further, Articles 48 and 95 of the 2020 Evidence Rules also introduces for the first time the power of a court to draw an adverse inference if a party who controls evidence does not produce it. The combination of these rules may result in parties feeling obliged to produce some evidence that is against their interests, although it is unlikely parties will produce all documents against interest.

At the evidence exchange hearing, each party is required to explain the relevance of evidence when it is produced. In this pre-trial hearing the court determines the admissibility of the evidence exchanged. All evidence will be examined as to relevance, truthfulness and authenticity. Chinese judges tend to have very high standards and are quite demanding in terms of conclusive evidence and an unbroken chain of evidence. In addition, unless admitted to by the other party, evidence which is not notarized (in case it originates from inside China) or notarized and legalized (in case it originates from outside China) will rarely be accepted as a basis for the decision. This makes it necessary to intensively prepare for trial and conduct intensive and costly investigations with the help of notaries in order to secure admissible evidence.

Generally, original documents or samples must be submitted as evidence. Only if originals are difficult to obtain and the court consents a party may submit copies of documents or items be submitted if they are not in dispute (Article 11, 2020 Evidence Provisions).

For purchases from online sellers, it is often important to notarize the entire chain of the transaction from the purchase to the delivery of the goods to establish that the products came from the seller.

Evidence originating from abroad must be notarized and legalized in the country of origin before being submitted as evidence (Article 16, 2020 Evidence Provisions). There are special rules for evidence from Hong Kong, Macau and Taiwan. In the case of Hong Kong and Macau, evidence must be verified by a China Appointed Attesting Officer who is a local Hong Kong or Macau lawyer and who has passed a test to allow them to certify documents for use in Mainland China. For documents from Taiwan, these are certified by the Straits Exchange Foundation.[63]

For public documents from abroad (such as court judgments) that can be accessed over the internet in China (that is, on sites that are not blocked), courts will generally accept a local notary certificate that the document has been downloaded. The 2020 Evidence Provisions also contain a provision that public documents from

63. See: Association of China Appointed Attesting Officers Ltd: http://www.caao.org.hk/eng/; Straits Exchange Foundation: http://www.sef.org.tw/mp.asp?mp = 300.

abroad do not need to be legalized if notarized abroad. It is not clear to what extent courts will apply this provision.

Article 14 of the new 2020 Evidence Rules also provide specific rules for the introduction of electronic evidence, such as webpages, blogs, text messages, emails, and electronic documents. Under Article 15 copies which the author has made or print outs can be considered original. Until 2019, all electronic evidence required notarization. Under the new rules, the courts may be more flexible depending on the way the evidence is produced.

All evidence submitted in a foreign language must be translated into Chinese.[64] It is permissible to provide a partial translation of long documents. If there are challenges to the accuracy of a translation, the translation should be certified by an authorized translation agency. If two authorized translations are produced which are inconsistent, the court may receive expert evidence on the translation.

Any evidence submitted to the court should be obtained by legal means in order to be admitted in court. Article 187 of the SPC Interpretation of the Code of Civil Procedure provides that evidence obtained in a manner seriously prejudicing the legitimate rights and interests of others, prohibited by law or seriously impacting social order should not be used as evidence. This leaves a discretion when dealing with evidence that may have been obtained by some underhand means but not necessarily meeting the threshold of seriously prejudicing rights or interests. For example, evidence obtained by trap purchases is generally admitted taking into account the fact that it is often impossible to obtain evidence without a trap purchase.[65]

Evidence obtained from overseas from procedures not known in China, such as an *Anton Piller* Order (in English common law jurisdictions) or cross-examination at trial can be admitted in China provided it is properly authenticated. Documents disclosed in discovery can also be used provided that the party is not breaching any obligations to keep the documents confidential in the jurisdiction they were disclosed.[66]

At the evidence exchange hearing, the court will also identify the key issues of the case, examine possible counterclaims, determine if any witnesses are needed, and if it has not already done so, fix the date for the trial hearing.

(g) Evidence Preservation

A party may also apply to the court for evidence preservation either from the other side or from third parties. (Article 64(2), Code of Civil Procedure). Evidence preservation is often carried out in IP cases, particularly in patent and software cases where it is difficult to prove infringement. Evidence preservation is a process whereby the court

64. Article 70, Code of Civil Procedure and Article 17 2020 Evidence Provisions.
65. *Beijing Founder Group Corp. v Beijing Gaoshu Tianli Science & Technology Co. Ltd. and Beijing Gaoshu Science and Technology Co. Ltd.*, Beijing Higher People's Court Judgment No. Gaomingzhongzi 194/2002. Rule 8(2) SPC Interpretation Copyright Cases.
66. Generally, there is an obligation not to make use of documents disclosed in discovery for any other purpose. This obligation is usually lifted once documents are disclosed in open court. A party may also apply to the court for permission to make use of the documents.

will attend the premises of a party or third party to preserve and collect evidence. It is quite commonly used in China.

If a party wishes to apply for evidence preservation, it must do so within the evidence submission period (Article 20, 2020 Evidence Rules). As discussed above in urgent cases where evidence may be destroyed the application may be made before the action is commenced. In executing an evidence preservation order, the court may seal up, seize, take notes, audio or video tape, and take copies. It may also ask an expert to give an opinion on what has been found or seen (Article 27, 2020 Evidence Provis Rules ions). The court may ask both parties or the representative of the plaintiff to be present when taking the measures (Article 27, 2020 Evidence Rules). If the evidence preservation may cause damage to the other party, the court may order the applicant to give security and if damage is caused, the court can order the applicant to pay damages (Articles 26 and 28, 2020 Evidence Rules).

(h) Protection of Trade Secrets during Proceedings

A party may wish to produce trade secrets or confidential information in court. How to handle the matter of trade secrets raised as a defence by an alleged infringer remains difficult in Chinese legal proceedings, especially when the defendant claims to use a new process which at the same time is a trade secret warranting protection. The general rule in Article 68 of the Code of Civil Procedure is that evidence shall be presented in court and cross-examined by the parties. However, evidence including state secrets, trade secrets and personal privacy shall be kept confidential.

Some Chinese courts therefore have adopted confidentiality agreements obliging the parties having access to allegedly confidential parts of a process to use it for litigation purposes only and not to disclose it to third parties. This practice has no clear legal basis and is not applied by all courts throughout the country.

(i) Judicial Appraisal/Expert Evidence

Article 76 of the Code of Civil Procedure provides that where the court faces specialist issues the parties may request a judicial appraisal by a judicial appraisal institute. These are bodies which the courts have authorized to conduct examinations and inspect evidence. The parties should seek to agree on an appraisal institute but if agreement cannot be reached the court may appoint the institute. Even if the parties do not make a request, the court may also of its volition appoint a judicial appraisal institute. A judicial appraisal institute representative is permitted to speak to the parties and witnesses to understand the case and to issue a written report.

The court can require a representative of a judicial appraisal institute to attend court or provide further written explanations. If they refuse to appear in court, their evidence will not be admissible (Articles 79 to 81, 2020 Evidence Provisions).

Article 79 of the Code of Civil Procedure provides that a party may apply to the court for permission to call a person with specialist knowledge to provide an appraisal opinion or provide an opinion on a specialist issue. Article 122 SPC Interpretation of the Code of Civil Procedure provides that one or two expert assessors may be called by a party and that the party calling the expert assessor shall bear the costs. Article

83 of the 2020 Evidence Rules provides that the application to call an expert should state the expertise and purpose of calling the witness.

Such witnesses, who are referred to as expert assessors, are being more and more commonly called and courts are quite receptive to the use of an expert assessor and their reports. The court and parties are entitled to ask the expert assessor questions. In practice, the procedure is more like a round table discussion rather than a formal cross-examination. The opposing side may also apply to call an expert assessor to provide counter evidence.

(j) Judging Panel

IP cases are usually heard by a panel of three judges with one presiding judge. The presiding judge is usually responsible for the handling of the case, including evidence exchange hearings, and drafting the judgment. Before and after the hearing the presiding judge must call together the panel to discuss the case and make a decision which is theoretically made by majority vote. However, in practice the other judges tend to follow the opinion of the presiding judge.

(k) Trial

The trial of an action is open to the public unless the case involves trade secrets, personal privacy or state secrets (Article 124, Code of Civil Procedure). Hearing dates for cases open to the public should be announced before holding the trial and citizens are allowed to attend. Foreigners, however, are required to obtain permission in advance to attend any type of hearing. Chinese citizens are required to register with their ID cards when entering a court house.

Article 138 to 141 of the Code of Civil Procedure regulates the hearing procedure in general, including statements, witnesses, documentary evidence, reading of conclusions, debate, and final argument.

Judges in the Chinese procedure take a very strong role in guiding the parties and defining the points of discussion during trial. Trials rarely last longer than three to five hours or, in extreme cases, one or two days. In general, a trial will proceed on a documents-only basis with the court considering the evidence that has been submitted and oral legal arguments. Factual witnesses are rarely called, but if one party relies on expert evidence the experts may be called for questioning by the court and the other side.

The trial in front of Chinese courts follows a rather rigid and formal set of steps where the attorneys on both sides find themselves in a much more limited role than in the US procedure or even some jurisdictions under continental law. Preparation of the hearing is very crucial in order to be able to answer questions quickly and in a concise manner and to take part in discussions put forward by the judge. It is crucial for the representative to properly explain the technical points of the case.

Lawyers have to follow a rigid procedure and will usually try to deliver short and not extensively argued written statements. After the hearing, the attorneys will be provided with transcripts of the procedure which need to be supplemented or signed. Following the hearing, a written submission will usually be prepared and submitted by both parties to the court. This is often the most important document submitted to the court because it summarizes the law and the evidence submitted and, often for the first time, sets out each party's case in full.

After the trial is concluded, it will usually take a couple of months until a written decision is issued. Written decisions always follow the same style and will mention the cause of action, the claims, and the facts and reasons on which the judgment is based. At the end of the judgment, the decision is summarized with the order made, as well as an order as to who should bear costs. Usually, the order is quite short and not very detailed.

(l) Appeal

Either party may appeal to the next higher court within 15 days of receipt of the decision (Articles 165 to 167, Code of Civil Procedure). If the case has been decided by an IP Court or Intermediate People's Court, the appeal will be to the Higher People's Court of the province or city except for patent and high technology cases which are now appealed to the SPC IP Tribunal. The appellate court usually is composed of a bench of three judges and will usually rehear a case in full (Article 168, Code of Civil Procedure). The procedure is identical to the first instance and the judgment of appeal is final.

It is possible to apply for a "re-trial" from a final judgment. An application for re-trial may be filed within six months from the second instance judgment to the Supreme People's Court (or Higher People's Court if the second instance decision was from an Intermediate People's Court). Important reasons are, among others, new evidence which may be sufficient to overrule the original judgment or which may show that the facts were forged, failure to take into account main evidence, an error in the application of law or a violation of legal procedures (Chapter XVI, Code of Civil Procedure).

While re-trials were very rare in the past, the Supreme People's Court has made strong efforts to improve its control over lower level courts and provide guidance to the judicial system. The number of re-trials has meanwhile increased quite significantly to several hundred a year and SPC decisions are rendered more frequently than in the past.

8. Remedies

Article 179(1) of the General Provisions of Civil Law in the Civil Code provides that copyright, patent and trade mark right holders whose rights have been infringed may demand that the infringement be stopped, its ill effects eliminated and damages compensated. The court can also order specific performance, which will generally not be applicable for IP cases. Each of the specific IP laws also provides for certain remedies.

The court may also order confiscation of property used in carrying out illegal activities. This can include infringing goods, fake trade mark labels, materials, and tools and equipment used in infringement. However, except for cases of counterfeiting and passing-off, only in rare circumstances will the court order the destruction of infringing goods or moulds.

(a) Injunctions

The main object of right holders in intellectual property infringement cases is to obtain an injunction. In general, if a court finds a defendant liable it will grant an injunction.

There are exceptions, principally in patent cases. Article 26(1) of the 2016 SPC Judicial Interpretation on Patent Cases provides that: "if to stop the infringer from implementing the patent would harm national or public interests or cause serious imbalance between the parties, the people's court may decide not to order the infringer to stop the acts of working, but instead to pay a reasonable royalty."

Injunctions may also not be granted in the case of patents declared to a standard (Article 24(2), 2016 SPC Judicial Interpretation on Patent Cases).[67]

(b) Confiscation and Destruction

Another highly effective remedy is the confiscation and/or destruction of infringing goods. The costs of destruction usually have to be borne by the infringer. This can be ordered generally under Article 179 of the General Provisions of Civil Law which provides for the elimination of the effects of infringement.

In trade mark cases, Articles 60 and 63 of the Trade Mark Law allows for confiscation and destruction of products and tools by the administration bodies and courts respectively.

In copyright cases, the right holder can demand the infringing party to destroy books, pictures, drawings, etc., or even film visuals, videos and the like made without consent (see Article 53 Copy-right Law) as well as tools and materials used to make infringing products (Article 54 Copyright Law). Illegal income may also be confiscated by the court. Requests for destruction are more easily granted by the courts since the pirated CDs and DVDs have no other legitimate use.

In the case of infringement of trade secrets, the right holder may also petition the courts to order the infringer to destroy products that have been made as a result of the unauthorized use of trade secrets, or which, should they be put on the market, could lead to the disclosure of such secrets if the right holder does not agree to proceed otherwise. In practice, courts will not order such destruction if the injured party is already manufacturing the product.

(c) Damages

Until very recently, except for outlying cases, damage awards in intellectual property cases in China have been low.[68] This has changed in the late 2010s and in 2020 and the courts have made some very substantial awards. For example, in enterprise

67. This issue is discussed further in Chapter 2 on Patents, Utility Models and Designs and Chapter 6 on Technology Transfer.
68. In 2007, French company Schneider was ordered to pay RMB 335 million (USD 55 million) by the Wenzhou Intermediate Court for utility model infringement in a case brought by its Chinese competitor, Chint. The case was settled for about half the sum. This was and remains the largest damages award ever made in an IP case China. 'Schneider settles 3-yr Chint patent suit', *Reuters*, 15 April 2009.

software cases, Dassault Systems has been awarded damages of over RMB 15 million (USD 2.2 million) in two cases and in a decision in 2020, Spin Master, a Canadian toy company was awarded RMB 15 million (USD 2.2 million) in a patent case.

For damages in intellectual property cases, three methods of calculation can be used:[69]

(1) actual losses suffered by the right holder;
(2) the profits directly gained by the infringer during the period of the infringement;
(3) reasonable royalties; or,
(4) statutory compensation.

Actual Losses – Lost Profits

Lost profits can be determined by multiplying the total decrease in the number of the plaintiff's products sold, with the profit for each product that the plaintiff could reasonably expect to make. If the decrease in sales is difficult to determine, the lost profit can be determined by multiplying the total number of items that the infringer sold with the profit for each product that the patentee could reasonably expect to make.

Infringer's Gains

Damages can also be determined from infringer's gains. Usually evidence preservation of the defendant's books will lead to a successful determination of damages based on this method. The infringer's gains can be calculated by multiplying the total number of items that the infringer sold with the reasonable profit for each product sold by the infringer. Generally, the profit obtained by the infringer as a result of the infringement shall be calculated based on the operating profits of the infringer.

For an infringer who totally depends on patent infringement for a living, profits may be calculated based on the sales profits. Where a product which infringes an invention or utility model patent is a part or component of another product, the court will reasonably determine the amount of compensation according to the value of the part or component, its role in the realization of profits from the finished product, and other factors (Article 16, 2010 SPC Patent Infringement Interpretation).

Reasonable Royalty

If neither the plaintiff's loss nor the infringer's gain can be ascertained, damages can be calculated with reference to the reasonable royalty of a licence. The damages awarded can be a multiple of between one and five times the reasonable royalty. If the plaintiff has licensed its intellectual property, reasonable royalties can be proven by producing its licence agreements. If it does not license, the plaintiff can seek to introduce evidence of industry standards for royalties. The major obstacle is that for

69. Article 71, Patent Law, Article 63, Trade Mark Law, Article 54, Copyright Law. Damages in patent and copyright actions are also discussed in Chapter 2 on Patents, Utility Models and Designs and Chapter 4 on Copyright respectively.

this method to apply, reference must be made to comparable licensing fees, which includes a consideration of normal licensing rates and the way in which infringement actually occurred, and differences between timing and scale, but also the idea that infringement damages should be higher than normal licensee fees.

Statutory Damages

If it is difficult to determine based on the above three methods, the court may award damages within a range specified by each IP law.[70] These ranges were between RMB 30,000 and RMB 5 million for patent infringement, between RMB 500 and RMB 5 million for copyright infringement and up to RMB 5 million for trade mark infringement. Such damages are often called "statutory damages". Strictly speaking they are not, as there is no specific statutory amount set out for each infringing act. Courts will often award damages on this basis given the difficulty the plaintiff faces proving losses. Where there is evidence that the loss is significantly more than the maximum statutory damages, greater damages may be awarded.

Punitive Damages

Trade Mark Law, Copyright Law and Patent Law all provide that in case of wilful and serious infringement the courts may award punitive damages of between one and five times the damages awarded.[71] These provisions were all added by amendments made in 2019 and 2020 and are intended to discourage intellectual property infringement

Other Costs

(1) Court fees

Courts usually order court fees to be borne by the losing party. The method of calculation of these fees has been mentioned above.

(2) Lawyers' fees

In China, attorneys' fees are usually not ordered to be paid by the losing side. However, in copyright, trade mark and patent disputes there are provisions that allow a court to order the other side to pay reasonable expenses which include lawyers' fees.[72] Even if such an order is made, it will usually not cover the full costs of instructing lawyers.

(3) Investigation costs

The court may also order the payment of investigation costs. These can include reasonable travel and accommodation costs and expenditures for the purchase of

70. Article 71 Patent Law, Article 63 Trade Mark Law and Article 54 Copyright Law.
71. Article 71 Patent Law, Article 63 Trade Mark Law and Article 54 Copyright Law. The articles also provide that if the defendant does not produce evidence to show its level of infringement or produces false evidence, the court may rely on the allegations of the plaintiff and the evidence it has been able to produce.
72. Article 54 of the Copyright Law, Article 71 Patent Law, Article 63 Trade Mark Law.

the infringing party's product to be used as evidence. The reimbursement of these costs is not subject to the injured party having suffered damage or the infringing party having made a profit.

(d) Public Apology

Courts do from time to time order a defendant to apologize for infringement. This is usually done by public notice published in a local newspaper.

(e) Enforcement of Judgments

Applications for enforcement are made to the enforcement chambers of the court. An award of damages may be enforced by the court making the award or any other court in China of equal status at the place where the defendant's assets are located (Article 224, Code of Civil Procedure). The most common way in which damages are enforced is by freezing bank accounts (Article 243). If money has already been frozen under a pre-trial asset freezing order, this will be transferred to the court. Enforcement may also be done by the seizing and auctioning of assets or by garnisheeing income.

The enforcement on injunctions is not a well-developed area of law in China. Article 111 of the Code of Civil Procedure allow People's Courts to fine individuals and entities as well as detain individuals who breach court orders or refuse to perform a legally effective judgment or ruling. Key personnel of an entity in breach of the order may also be detained up to 15 days. Any fine or imprisonment must be approved by the President of the Court. Article 115 of the Code of Civil Procedure provides that the maximum fine that can be imposed on an individual is RMB 100,000. For an entity, the fine can be between RMB 50,000 and RMB 1,000,000. For detention, the courts are required to hand the individuals to the Public Security Bureau.

III. ARBITRATION

Generally, intellectual property infringement disputes are not arbitrated because in order for an arbitrator to have jurisdiction the parties must have agreed to arbitrate. This is generally not the case where an infringer has simply copied another company's trade mark or technology. It is sometimes possible to reach an arbitration agreement after a dispute has arisen, but usually one party will consider that litigation will give it an advantage, so will not agree.

In recent years, there has, however, been a growth in arbitration under technology transfer contracts or intellectual property licence agreements where the parties have agreed to arbitrate as part of the original agreement.

Arbitration can have advantages for foreign parties. In particular, it is possible to avoid the difficult evidence requirements in Chinese courts and to agree to arbitrate in English (or at least bilingually). Further, because China is member of the New York Convention of the Recognition and Enforcement of International Arbitration Awards, arbitral awards are enforceable in China.

The favoured arbitration bodies for arbitration involving China include the China International Economic and Trade Arbitration Commission (CIETAC) with headquarters in Beijing and branches in Shanghai and Hong Kong, the Hong Kong International Arbitration Centre and Singapore International Arbitration Centre.

There are two issues to be particularly conscious of if agreeing to arbitration IP disputes involving China.

First. Article 16 of the PRC Arbitration Law requires that an arbitral institution be named. It is important that the arbitration clause specifically identify the institution and not just the rules of the arbitration institution to be applied.

Second, Article 3(2) of Arbitration Law provides that parties may not arbitrate issues that are to be determined by administrative bodies. Validity of trade mark and patent rights are determined by Trade Mark Adjudication Department and Re-examination and Invalidation Department (formerly Patent Re-examination Board) of CNIPA – both are administrative bodies. If a case will involve the validity of patents or trade marks this can cause problems, particularly in patent cases because invalidity is usually the major defence. If the arbitrator decides the case on the basis that the patent is valid or invalid, this may raise enforcement issues. One solution is to simply ask an arbitrator to make an award as to what sum of money is owed without specifically deciding validity.

IV. ADMINISTRATIVE ENFORCEMENT

1. Introduction

Administrative enforcement for patent, trade mark, and copyright infringement, as well as unfair competition infringement has been a feature of intellectual property enforcement in China since the 1980s. Until the mid-2000s it was the preferred method of enforcement for most foreign companies.

In 2019, major changes were announced to the administration of intellectual property in China where the State Administration of Industry and Commerce (SAIC) (which was responsible for the registration and enforcement of trade marks), the State Intellectual Property Office (SIPO) (which dealt with patents) and the General Administration of Quality Supervision, Inspection and Quarantine (GAQSIC) (which dealt with some trade mark enforcement) were all merged into a new body the State Administration for Market Regulation. The SAIC and GAQSIC were dismantled. The SIPO was renamed in English as the China National Intellectual Property Administration (CNIPA) – the Chinese name was not changed. The reason for the change to use "China National" at the beginning was to be in line with the IP offices of other major nations where the first initials indicate the country such as USPTO, UKIPO, JIPO.[73]

The SAMR through its Economic Inspection Bureau now handles the administrative enforcement of patents and trade marks. In addition, the National Copyright Administration (NCA) handles copyright registration and enforcement and customs deals with border seizures. The NCA was not merged into the SAMR. It was formerly part of the State Administration of Press, Publication, Radio, Film and Television

73. Discussion by author with a Vice-Commissioner of CNIPA.

of China under the State Council but that organization has been abolished and the NCA is now directly under the publicity department of the Communist Party. The actual enforcement of copyright is carried out by Cultural Enforcement Departments.

2. Basic Procedures

Administrative proceedings have the advantage of being less formal and relatively simple, although the same principles must be followed. For example, if an infringement can be proven, but the infringer cannot be identified, the administration will not accept the case, because it can only decide on clear facts and does not have the power and ability of the police to track down and locate alleged infringers.

The basic procedure for all administrative actions is to first collect evidence of infringement. Unlike in court cases, this does not have to be notarized or necessarily sufficient to fully make out a case. With evidence in hand, a complaint is then made to the appropriate administrative body that will determine if they will accept the case. This may require some negotiation or submission of further evidence. If the case is accepted, the next step is to conduct an on-site inspection (often called a raid) to gather evidence. The administrative body will, in the case of trade mark and copyright, seize infringing products and, in the case of patents, seal on site. The administrative body will then investigate the case further, including interviewing the alleged infringer and, if it finds infringement, issue an administrative penalty decision. The penalty decision will include to stop infringement and usually impose a fine.

In patent cases, there may also be an additional step of a formal hearing to hear arguments in relation to the alleged infringement. The patent enforcement body may also seek to mediate the case between the parties.

3. Trade Marks

There are no detailed procedures for handling administrative enforcement in trade mark cases. Under Article 60 of the Trade Mark Law the trade mark proprietor or other injured party (usually an exclusive licensee) may make a complaint to the administrative body or file a complaint in court. Article 77 of the Trade Mark Law Implementing Regulations provides that any person may file an administrative complaint in relation to trade mark infringement. This means that regardless of whether they have any rights being infringed a complaint may be made.

Under Article 62 of the Trade Mark Law, the administrative body may question the alleged infringer, make photocopies of contracts, invoices, books and other relevant materials, make on the spot inspections of places where infringing activities are carried out or were conducted previously, examine articles that have some connection with the infringement, seal up or seize infringing items.

Under Article 60 of the Trade Mark Law, the administrative body can order an infringer to stop infringement, confiscate and destroy infringing goods, destroy tools especially used to manufacture infringing goods such as moulds, and impose a fine of up to five times the illegal income, with a maximum of RMB 250,000 (USD 40,000).

Fines can be imposed upon the infringer himself, the illegal manufacturer, sellers, those executing transports and storage who cannot prove that the goods concerned were legitimately obtained.

4. Patents

(a) Patent Infringement

The administrative body will not accept a case where the interested party has already instituted proceedings in the People's Courts in respect of the patent dispute (Rule 5, Patent Enforcement Measures).

The patentee or, if the patentee does not take action an exclusive licensee is required to file a request clearly identifying the respondent and the specific issues of the case (Article 5, Patent Enforcement Measures).

The complainant will usually request the authorities to conduct an inspection (or raid) according to Article 27 *et seq.* Patent Enforcement Measures. An inspection can be extremely useful to obtain clear evidence of infringement as well as evidence of the scale of infringement to support a later damages claim in court. When conducting an inspection, the administrative enforcement authorities, may inspect and copy contracts, account books and other relevant documents of the case, question interested parties and witnesses and also measure, take photos and make audio or video records. The authorities may not, however, confiscate all alleged infringing goods and instead are required to seal them on site.

In infringement cases relating to manufacturing processes, the administrative body may ask the respondent to demonstrate how the process works. The administration may also take samples (Article 29, Patent Enforcement Measures) such as part of the products or in the case of process patents, a part of the products directly obtained by the process. The quantity must suffice to verify the facts.

The process of inspection is recorded by taking notes which have to be signed by the parties and sealed by the staff members (Articles 28 and 29, Patent Enforcement Measures). The alleged infringer must co-operate and assist in the investigation (Article 31, Patent Enforcement Measures). In case of obstruction of the investigation, Article 41 of the Patent Enforcement Measures allows imposing penalties or even criminal sanctions may apply.

Usually, the administrative body will hold a hearing after giving a minimum of three days' notice before making a decision, although this is not mandatory (Rule 10, Patent Enforcement Measures). In December 2019, CNIPA issued very detailed guidelines[74] (of over 260 pages) for deciding administrative patent cases dealing with jurisdiction, evidence, hearing procedures, how to apply the patent law and writing a decision. A decision must contain the facts and reasoning on which the decision is based.

Patent administrative authorities may order an infringer to immediately cease the act of manufacture, using, offering for sale, or import of infringing products, and to destroy the equipment or moulds especially used for the manufacture of infringing

74. Available in Chinese at: http://www.sipo.gov.cn/gztz/1144945.htm.

products or exploitation of the patented process, and may order the infringer not to sell and/or use the infringing products that have not been sold nor to market them in any form. If such products are difficult to store, their destruction can be ordered; in the case of import, the relevant customs authority may be notified by the Resolution Decision (Article 33, Patent Enforcement Measures).

(b) *Patent Passing Off*

In patent passing-off cases,[75] false indications of patent numbers will be ordered to be removed or, if this is not possible, the goods so marked are destroyed. Advertising material must be destroyed as well and the ill effects must be eliminated (e.g. by way of public rectification in newspapers). Contracts which contain wrongly "patented" products must be rectified, and forged or falsified documents and patent certificates must be handed in to the administration (Rule 36, Patent Enforcement Measures).

Under Article 68 of the Patent Law the administrative body may confiscate illegal income and impose a fine. Where products are sold, the illicit income is determined by the sales price of the passed off products times the quantity of the products sold; or, where a contract is concluded for passing-off a patent, the income collected according to this contract is considered the illicit income (Article 38, Patent Enforcement Measures). Where only parts of the infringing product are delivered by the infringer, the relevant percentage of the value of these parts compared to the sales price of the goods will be taken as the basis of calculation.

Fines must be paid within 15 days of the date of receipt of the decision of punishment; non-observance leads to imposition of additional 3 percent of the fine per day (Article 40, Patent Enforcement Measures).

(c) *Damages*

Article 65 of the Patent Law provides that the administration may mediate between the patentee and infringer to reach an agreement on liability and compensation. Prior to 2000, the patent administration authorities had the power to award damages. However, this power was removed with China's accession to the WTO. Now under Article 65, legal proceedings can, instead, be instituted in the courts to claim damages. The CNIPA has from time to time proposed amendments to the law to allow it to again award damages. These have not been enacted.

(d) *Appeal to Courts*

If a party is not satisfied with a decision of the administrative body regarding infringement, Article 65 of the Patent Law provides that an appeal may be made within 15 days under the Administrative Litigation Law to the court. If 15 days have passed without legal proceedings being initiated, the administration may apply to the courts for compulsory execution.

---

75. See also Chapter 2 on Patents, Utility Models and Designs for further discussion of patent passing off.

Where the defendant institutes proceedings in the court challenging an infringement decision of an administrative body, the enforcement of the decision is not stayed during the proceedings in court (Article 34(1), Patent Enforcement Measures). The court would have the power to order a stay of enforcement.

5. Copyright

The Measures for the Enforcement of Copyright Administrative Penalties ("Copyright Enforcement Measures") issued by the NCA on 21 April 2009 and in force since 15 June 2009[76] grant copyright administrations the right to order the infringing act to cease, to confiscate illicit benefits and infringing reproductions, to impose fines or other administrative penalties in accordance with the law, as well as to confiscate material, instruments and equipment mainly used for making infringing reproductions (Article 4, Copyright Enforcement Measures). Protection for Computer Software is also provided for under the Computer Software Protection Rules last amended in 2013.

Under Article 37(2) of the Copyright Law Implementing Rules and Article 3 of the Copyright Enforcement Measures, administrative enforcement is only available where the infringement causes "damage to the public interest". Authorities are also generally only willing to take action where the issues are not complex. As such, administrative enforcement is generally not suitable for cases involving single or low-volume infringements; non-identical copying; indirect infringement (e.g. linking or P2P services); or technologically complex cases.

Administrative action requires a formal complaint with the local copyright administration at the place of infringement (Article 5, Copyright Enforcement Measures). After filing, the copyright administration must decide whether to put the complaint on file (Rule 11, Copyright Enforcement Measures). In urgent cases, measures such as an order to cease and desist further infringement, and the recordal and seizure of infringing reproductions, material and equipment may be taken by the authorities before officially putting the case on file. Sealing up in urgent cases may also be done before formally preparing an evidence sample list in the presence of parties concerned (Rule 21(2), Copyright Enforcement Measures).

The complaint must include proof of copyright (such as a copyright registration certificate), evidence of infringement, address of the infringer and, where necessary, a power of attorney. The need to prove ownership has generally meant that a party will register its copyright before applying to the administrative body.

After a review, the copyright administration will decide on whether and how to take action and may require the applicant to file further evidence. The copyright administration can then conduct an inspection of the premises to obtain samples and other evidence such as copies of software or moulds. (Rule 16, Copyright Enforcement Measures). Within seven days after any inspection, the copyright administration is required to make a decision to uphold or dismiss the case, or if necessary to seek expert examination. The copyright administration can also transfer the case to another body, such as the Public Security Bureau. (Rule 22, Copyright Enforcement Measures).

76. These replaced a regulation of the same name issued in 2003. Draft amendments were published in 2015 but have not been promulgated.

According to Article 52 of the Copyright Law and Article 24 Software Protection Rules, the Copyright Administration may order cessation of infringement, confiscate unlawful income from the act, confiscate and destroy infringing reproductions and impose a fine; in serious circumstances it may also confiscate the materials, tools and equipment mainly used for making the infringing reproductions.

According to Article 36 of the Copyright Law Implementing Regulations, the fines in copyright infringement cases may not exceed five times the amount of the illegal business turnover. Where the illegal business turnover is difficult to calculate, the maximum fine is RMB 250,000. In software cases, the fine is calculated according to Article 24(2) of the Software Protection Rules at either RMB 100 apiece or no more than five times the amount of the value of the goods where software is copied, distributed, rented or communicated on a network, or RMB 200,000 in other cases.

Infringers must be given advance notice before fines and administrative penalties are imposed on them. They are permitted to make submissions within seven days (30 days where the notification was by public notice because the infringer could not be located). The punishment referred to in the advance notification may not be increased as a result of statements contained in the infringer's submission (Articles 27 and 28, Copyright Enforcement Measures). Fines may not be imposed for minor unlawful acts. If a fine is to be levied on the infringer, it is to be calculated pursuant to the Copyright Law and rules in Article 29 of the Copyright Enforcement Measures. Additional fines may not be imposed if the acts of infringement have already resulted in a fine being imposed by another administrative authority.

If the circumstances of the infringement are deemed serious, materials, equipment and instruments used mainly for making the infringing reproductions may be confiscated. Serious circumstances are described in Article 31 of the Copyright Enforcement Measures as illegal profit to the amount of RMB 2,500, illegal turnover of RMB 15,000, or 250 or more infringing reproductions, or in cases of repeated infringement or other matters having serious consequences. In the case of fines of RMB 20,000 or more for an individual (RMB 100,000 or for an entity), a hearing must be held prior to imposing the fine (Article 33, Copyright Enforcement Measures).

If an interested party is not satisfied with the decision of the Copyright Administration, it may apply for administrative reconsideration and subsequently appeal to the court. An administrative penalty is not suspended during reconsideration unless the law provides otherwise (Article 38, Copyright Enforcement Measures).

6. Interim Injunctions by Administrative Bodies

Administrative bodies do not have the power to order interim injunctions. However, in some cases as described above, raids and seizure of infringing goods can be conducted without prior notice. If the administrative body seizes or seals infringing products, this acts effectively as an interim injunction in relation to those products.

V. CRIMINAL LAW ENFORCEMENT

In China trade mark and copyright infringement are criminal offences.[77] Patent infringement is not crime in China. However, Article 216 of the Criminal Law makes patent passing off an offence with punishment under serious circumstances of a three-year sentence and/or a fine.

For serious counterfeiters, criminal prosecution is often the only way to stop their activities. Administrative penalties are seen as a cost of doing business and sophisticated counterfeiters are able to structure their businesses to make it very hard for civil action to be effective.

In 2020, the Chinese Supreme People's Procuratorate released a report revealing that over the past 20 years, the number of individuals prosecuted for IP infringement has increased by 56 times, with trade mark crimes accounting for more than 80 percent. Statistics show that in 2019, procuratorial authorities approved the arrest of 7,430 persons in 4,346 cases involving IP infringement, up 31.5 percent and 24.3 percent respectively.

Despite the general deterrence effect of criminal prosecution, criminal cases have been relatively rare when compared to administrative and civil cases. There are four principal reasons for this. First, administrative action is relatively simple and easy for trade mark cases, making it the first choice of action for many trade mark orders. This leads to the second issue that it is often hard to transfer a case from administrative bodies to the Public Security Bureau (PSB). Often the PSB will reject a case because the evidence has not been collected to a high enough standard. Administrative bodies also prefer to keep a case to impose a fine. Third, there are relatively high thresholds for the PSB to take on a case. The PSB will usually only take on very serious cases. This means that the right holder will generally have, through investigators, to gather a large amount of evidence of infringement before the PSB will take the case. Fourth, even if the PSB accept the case prosecutors may reject the case for lack of evidence. In recent years criminal actions have become more prevalent and certain PSB offices are more willing to take on cases. It is, however, necessary for right holders to prepare cases thoroughly.

Under Chinese law, individuals 16 years old or above may be prosecuted. Article 220 of the Criminal Law also provides that an organization can also be punished for the commission of intellectual property infringement and can be fined. The persons responsible for the organization may also be punished individually.

The PSB may become involved with the investigation of trade mark and copyright infringement cases in three ways:

(a) through the transfer of cases initially handled by the said administrative authorities;
(b) by direct filing of a complaint by the right owner; or
(c) through its own investigations.

As already, mentioned, the transfer of cases from administrative bodies is rare, but does happen from time to time.

---

77. Article 67 of the Trade Mark Law; Chapter 7 (Articles 213 to 219) of the Criminal Law. Criminal Copyright enforcement is discussed in more detail in Chapter 4 on Copyright.

Under the Criminal Procedure Law, the PSB is responsible for the investigation, arrest and preliminary examination of criminal cases. Cases may be filed directly with the PSB or they may be transferred to the PSB by administrative bodies.

The PSB will generally only take on serious cases. The criteria to be applied have been set out in Judicial Interpretations issued in 200, 2007 and 2011. The most recent interpretation is the Supreme People's Court, Supreme People's Procuratorate, Ministry of Public Security, and Ministry of Justice Opinion on Several Issues Concerning the Application of Law in Handling Criminal Cases of Infringement of Intellectual Property. The basic principles are that the volume of illegal business operation is more than RMB 50,000 or the amount of illegal proceeds is more than RMB 30,000. Repeat infringers who have infringed within the past two years should also be prosecuted if the accumulated amount reaches the criminal threshold.

A right holder may file a complaint themselves, although representation by a lawyer or other agent is recommended especially for foreigners. When filing, evidence of the infringement, certificates, trade mark samples or copies of works used by the right holder and those used by the counterfeiter should be submitted. Evidence should best include samples of the original and fake trade marks and goods such as photographs, samples, promotional materials, invoices and others, and written and oral statements of witnesses including evidence obtained secretly.

Following investigation, the PSB will either decide to terminate the case or prosecute. If they decide to prosecute the case, the case is then transferred to the People's Procuratorate for prosecution in court. The People's Procuratorate can have very high standards for accepting cases and will often send a file back for further investigation. If the People's Procuratorate decided to prosecute, an indictment is filed in court and there will be a public hearing of the case.

It is also possible to bring a private prosecution. According to Article 210 of the Criminal Procedure Law private criminal prosecutions may be brought in the following cases: (1) the victim has evidence to prove a minor offence (2) or where property rights have been infringed but the PSB or People's Procuratorates have decided not to pursue a case. In the first case, due to the lightness of the crime, right holders tend to bring an administrative or civil case. It is necessary to prove that the PSB or Procuratorate has decided not to proceed with a case. This can be difficult to obtain. However, in some recent cases, foreign parties have successfully brought private prosecutions.[78]

VI. BORDER ENFORCEMENT

Regulations of the PRC regarding Customs Protection of IP Rights were first issued in 1995 and amended in 2004, 2010 and 2018. Importantly, the regulations cover both the export and import of goods.

78. See, for example 'Spin Master Wins Record Damages in China Over Toy Knockoff', *Bloomberg*, 21 April 2020

1. Competent Authorities and Procedures

Chinese Customs has the authority to detain imported or exported goods suspected of infringing IP rights recorded with the General Administration of Customs of China (GACC) either *ex officio*, (Rule 16, Customs Regulations) or upon request of a right holder (Article 13, Customs Regulations). Patents, trade marks and copyright may be recorded (Article 2, Customs Regulations). However, the registration of a right is no precondition for seizure; if the right has been registered, the application for seizure should state so (Article 13(2), Customs Regulations). The period allowed for registration amounts to 30 days from filing the application to issuing a certificate to the proprietor. The period of validity of such registration is ten years from the day of approval of registration with GACC.

The GACC has a computerised network connected to all local customs offices of Mainland China so they may access the database. Either upon registration of the IP right, or *ex officio*, Customs may intercept infringing products being imported into or exported from China.

Procedures to transfer serious cases for investigation to the Chinese police have not yet been formulated although Articles 26 and 30 of the Customs Regulations prescribe an obligation to submit serious cases to the public prosecutor according to the Criminal Code. This has been emphasized again in a notice issued by the SAMR, PSB, Agricultural Ministry, Customs, the NCA and CNIPA in 2019 announcing "Measures to Strengthen Enforcement of IP in relation to Online Purchases and Import Export Areas".

2. Security Bonds

If goods are seized, right holders are required to put up a bond based on the declared value of the goods[79] to cover any damages to the consignor or consignee and customs expenses, such as storage fees. For seizures up to RMB 20,000, the bond shall be the full value of the goods; between RMB 20,000 and RMB 200,000 the bond shall be 50 percent of the value but not less than RMB 20,000; and over RMB 200,000, the maximum bond is RMB 100,000 (Article 14, Customs Regulations). It is possible for a right holder to put up a general bond in relation to trade mark seizures.[80]

The bond will be returned after the subtraction of fees for, e.g. warehousing, storage and disposal of detained goods, once a decision has been made by the customs or judicial authorities. If the consignor or consignee does not consider that the detained goods infringe a patent, he may apply for clearance, providing a counter-bond equal to the value of the goods (Article 19, Customs Regulations), upon which Customs will release the goods (Article 24(3), Customs Regulations). The consignor or consignee can also provide evidence that the invoked rights have not been infringed after receiving the Customs Detention Notification. If the evidence is convincing to Customs, the goods will be released (Article 24(4), Customs Regulations).

79. IP Customs Regulations Article 14.
80. IP Customs Regulations, Implementing Provisions, Article 24.

If the right holder fails to place the bond, or pay storage fees, or fails to file a notice with the court seeking further detainment of goods after 20 or 50 working days (depending on where the detention was upon application or *ex officio*), Customs must release the goods. The bond to be posted by a right holder must be paid within three working days, otherwise goods are to be released. In cases of clear infringement and confiscation *ex officio*, no court order will be required and Customs must decide within 30 working days.

Right holders or consignors/consignees may bring action in court to obtain an order for temporary seizure of goods (Article 23, Customs Regulations) and subsequently to determine if there has been infringement.

If goods are found to be infringing, they will be confiscated and can be donated to a charitable organization or sold to the brand owner. If the right holder is not amenable to this, the goods will be auctioned off after the infringing features have been removed. Only where the infringing labels, etc., cannot be removed will the infringing goods be destroyed (Article 27, Customs Regulations).

VII. CONCLUSION

While the enforcement of IP rights in China has improved markedly over the past three decades, there remain problems, in particular, local protectionism can still be an issue where local authorities will protect important local businesses. The ability to bring civil proceedings in other jurisdictions and, for patent and high technology cases, the creation of the SPC IP Tribunal help to reduce this impact. The main issues that remain are with manpower and resources, particularly with administrative copyright enforcement and Public Security Bureaux. The lack of resources makes copyright and criminal enforcement difficult (particularly in getting the PSB to accept a case transferred from an administrative body).

In practice, it is also increasingly difficult to determine who is actually responsible for manufacturing fakes. Counterfeiters have become increasingly professional and very well organized with sophisticated methods in selling fake products, particularly for online sales. For example, counterfeit goods are sold on the internet and shipped directly to consumers by courier. The only way to successfully battle this process is a strategic approach trying to identify the source combined with take down notices.

Right owners should keep in mind that Chinese parties can also use IP laws against foreign parties. Samsung was sued by Huawei in China as part of their global patent dispute and many foreign parties have been sued by trade mark and patent "trolls". Generally, foreign parties have been able to defend themselves by invalidating the relevant rights, but risks remain.

On the whole, however, the system is becoming more and more transparent and it is generally possible to bring or defend and IP action in China with a predictable outcome.

Index

N

O

P

T

MAX PLANCK SERIES ON ASIAN INTELLECTUAL PROPERTY LAW

1. Christopher Heath & Kung-Chung Liu (eds), *The Protection of Well-Known Marks in Asia*, 2000 (ISBN 90-411-9705-2).
2. Christoph Antons, *Intellectual Property Law in Indonesia*, 2000 (ISBN 90-411-9803-2).
3. Christopher Heath, *The System of Unfair Competition Prevention in Japan*, 2001 (ISBN 90-411-9837-7).
4. Christopher Heath & Kung-Chung Liu (eds), *Legal Rules of Technology Transfer in Asia*, 2002 (ISBN 90-411-9883-0).
5. Christopher Heath (ed.), *Intellectual Property Law in Asia*, 2002 (ISBN 90-411-9894-6).
6. Byung-Il Kim & Christopher Heath (eds), *Intellectual Property Law in Korea*, (2nd Edition), 2015 (ISBN 978-90-411-5831-4).
7. Christopher Heath (ed.), *Intellectual Property Law in Taiwan*, 2003 (ISBN 90-411-9920-9).
8. Christopher Heath & Anselm Kamperman Sanders (eds), *Industrial Property in the Bio-Medical Age*, 2003 (ISBN 90-411-9926-8).
9. Christopher Heath (ed.), *Parallel Imports in Asia*, 2004 (ISBN 90-411-2114-5).
10. Christoph Antons, Michael Blakeney & Christopher Heath (eds), *Intellectual Property Harmonisation within ASEAN and APEC*, 2004 (ISBN 90-411-2292-3).
11. Peter Ganea, Danny Friedmann, Jyh-An Lee & Douglas Clark. Christopher Heath (ed.), *Intellectual Property Law in China*, (2nd Edition), 2021 (ISBN 978-94-035-1952-4).
12. Peter Ganea, Christopher Heath & Hiroshi Saitô (eds), *Japanese Copyright Law: Writings in Honour of Gerhard Schricker*, 2005 (ISBN 90-411-2393-8).
13. Shan Hailing, *The Protection of Trade Secrets in China* (2nd Edition Rev.), 2012 (ISBN 978-90-411-3893-4).
14. Christoph Antons (ed.), *Traditional Knowledge, Traditional Cultural Expressions and Intellectual Property Law in the Asia-Pacific Region*, 2009 (ISBN 978-90-411-2721-1).
15. Christoph Antons (ed.), *The Enforcement of Intellectual Property Rights: Comparative Perspectives from the Asia-Pacific Region*, 2011 (ISBN 978-90-411-3219-2).
16. Kung-Chung Liu & Reto M. Hilty (eds), *The Enforcement of Patents*, 2011 (ISBN 978-90-411-3527-8).
17. Christopher Heath & Atsuhiro Furuta (eds), *Japanese Patent Law – Cases and Comments*, 2019 (ISBN 978-90-411-9419-0)

www.ingramcontent.com/pod-product-compliance
Lightning Source LLC
La Vergne TN
LVHW020003031026
849161LV00023B/859
9789403519524